RESEARCH HANDBOOK ON AUSTRIAN LAW AND ECONOMICS

RESEARCH HANDBOOKS IN LAW AND ECONOMICS

Series Editors: Richard A. Posner, *Judge, United States Court of Appeals for the Seventh Circuit and Senior Lecturer, University of Chicago Law School, USA* and Francesco Parisi, *Oppenheimer Wolff and Donnelly Professor of Law, University of Minnesota, USA and Professor of Economics, University of Bologna, Italy*

Edited by highly distinguished scholars, the landmark reference works in this series offer advanced treatments of specific topics that reflect the state-of-the-art of research in law and economics, while also expanding the law and economics debate. Each volume's accessible yet sophisticated contributions from top international researchers make it an indispensable resource for students and scholars alike.

Titles in this series include:

Research Handbook on Public Choice and Public Law
Edited by Daniel A. Farber and Anne Joseph O'Connell

Research Handbook on the Economics of Property Law
Edited by Kenneth Ayotte and Henry E. Smith

Research Handbook on the Economics of Family Law
Edited by Lloyd R. Cohen and Joshua D. Wright

Research Handbook on the Economics of Antitrust Law
Edited by Einer R. Elhauge

Research Handbook on the Economics of Corporate Law
Edited by Brett McDonnell and Claire A. Hill

Research Handbook on the Economics of European Union Law
Edited by Thomas Eger and Hans-Bernd Schäfer

Research Handbook on the Economics of Criminal Law
Edited by Alon Harel and Keith N. Hylton

Research Handbook on the Economics of Labor and Employment Law
Edited by Michael L. Wachter and Cynthia L. Estlund

Research Handbook on Austrian Law and Economics
Edited by Todd J. Zywicki and Peter J. Boettke

Research Handbook on Austrian Law and Economics

Edited by

Todd J. Zywicki

George Mason University Foundation Professor of Law, Antonin Scalia Law School, George Mason University, USA

Peter J. Boettke

University Professor of Economics and Philosophy, Department of Economics, George Mason University, USA

RESEARCH HANDBOOKS IN LAW AND ECONOMICS

Cheltenham, UK • Northampton, MA, USA

Published by
Edward Elgar Publishing Limited
The Lypiatts
15 Lansdown Road
Cheltenham
Glos GL50 2JA
UK

Edward Elgar Publishing, Inc.
William Pratt House
9 Dewey Court
Northampton
Massachusetts 01060
USA

Paperback edition 2019

A catalogue record for this book
is available from the British Library

Library of Congress Control Number: 2017941915

This book is available electronically in the **Elgar**online
Law subject collection
DOI 10.4337/9781788113106

ISBN 978 1 84980 113 3 (cased)
ISBN 978 1 78811 310 6 (eBook)
ISBN 978 1 78990 524 3 (paperback)

Typeset by Servis Filmsetting Ltd, Stockport, Cheshire
Printed and bound by CPI Group (UK) Ltd, Croydon, CR0 4YY

To Henry G. Manne (1928–2015): Founder of the George Mason School of Law & Economics and master academic entrepreneur

Contents

PART IV   BASIC LAW

PART V   CONCLUSION

Contributors

Bruce L. Benson, Professor Emeritus of Economics, Department of Economics, Florida State University, USA

Peter J. Boettke, University Professor of Economics and Philosophy, Department of Economics, George Mason University, USA

Donald J. Boudreaux, Professor of Economics, Department of Economics, George Mason University, USA

Henry N. Butler, Dean and Professor of Law, Antonin Scalia Law School, George Mason University, USA

Eric R. Claeys, Professor of Law, Antonin Scalia Law School, George Mason University, USA

Christopher J. Coyne, F.A. Harper Professor of Economics, Department of Economics, George Mason University, Fairfax, USA

Michael E. DeBow, Professor of Law, Cumberland School of Law, Samford University, USA

M. Todd Henderson, Michael J. Marks Professor of Law, The University of Chicago Law School, USA

Steven Horwitz, Schnatter Distinguished Professor of Free Enterprise, Department of Economics, Ball State University, USA

Peter G. Klein, W.W. Caruth Chair and Professor of Entrepreneurship, Department of Entrepreneurship, Baylor University, USA.

Martín Krause, Professor of Economics, University of Buenos Aires, Argentina

Thomas A. Lambert, Wall Chair in Corporate Law and Governance and Professor of Law, University of Missouri School of Law, USA.

Peter T. Leeson, Duncan Black Professor of Economics and Law, Department of Economics, George Mason University, USA

Jeffrey S. Parker, Professor of Law, Antonin Scalia Law School, George Mason University, USA

Gerald J. Postema, Cary C. Boshamer Professor of Philosophy and Professor of Law, University of North Carolina, Chapel Hill, USA

Shruti Rajagopalan, Assistant Professor of Economics, Purchase College, State University of New York, USA

The late **Larry E. Ribstein,** former Mildred van Voorhis Chair and Associate Dean for Research, University of Illinois College of Law, USA

David Skarbek, Senior Lecturer, Department of Political Economy, King's College London, UK

Edward P. Stringham, Davis Professor of Economic Organizations and Innovation, Trinity College, and President, American Institute for Economic Research, USA

Richard E. Wagner, Holbert L. Harris Professor of Economics, Department of Economics, George Mason University, USA

Todd J. Zywicki, George Mason University Foundation Professor of Law, Antonin Scalia Law School, George Mason University, USA

PART I

INTRODUCTION

1. Law and economics: the contributions of the Austrian School of Economics
Peter J. Boettke and Todd J. Zywicki

I. INTRODUCTION

> It is regrettable, though not difficult to explain, that in the past much less attention has been given to the positive requirements of a successful working of the competitive system than to these negative points. The functioning of competition not only requires adequate organization of certain institutions like money, markets, and channels of information – some of which can never be adequately provided by private enterprise – but it depends, above all, on the existence of an appropriate legal system, a legal system designed both to preserve competition and to make it operate as beneficially as possible. . . . The systematic study of the forms of legal institutions which will make the competitive system work efficiently has been sadly neglected. (Hayek 1944 [2007]: 87)

Commercial life always exists inside of an *institutional framework*. Whether social life exhibits Adam Smith's human propensity to "truck, barter, exchange" or Thomas Hobbes's human capacity to "rape, pillage, plunder" is a function of the *institutional framework* within which social life is played out. It is the *framework* that determines the marginal benefit/marginal cost calculus that individuals face in pursuing sociability. If the marginal benefits for productive specialization and peaceful cooperation exceed the marginal benefits of predation and confiscation, then that society will tend toward the Smithian expansion of commercial and civil society. But if the calculus tends toward the other way, then Hobbes's depiction of life as being "nasty, brutish and short" comes to dominate. Most of human history, in fact, is best characterized as Hobbesian. But starting with the "Great Enrichment"[1] as Deirdre McCloskey has dubbed it, the history of humanity took a different turn. McCloskey puts great emphasis on the ideas that generated this transformation. We do not disagree with the primacy of ideas, but our focus is on the *framework* that these ideas

---

[1] The Great Enrichment refers here to increase in income per capita by a factor of 40 to 100 that began first in northwestern Europe around 1800. See McCloskey's *The Bourgeois Virtues* (2006), *Bourgeois Dignity* (2010), and *Bourgeois Equality* (2016).

legitimated, and the practices that were engendered by that *framework*. As the great Austrian school economist Ludwig von Mises put it:

> Saving, capital accumulation, is the agency that has transformed step-by-step the awkward search for food on the part of savage cave dwellers into the modern ways of industry. The pacemakers of this evolution were the ideas that created the *institutional framework* within which capital accumulation was rendered safe by the principle of private ownership of the means of production. Every step forward on the way toward prosperity is the effect of saving. The most ingenious technological inventions would be practically useless if the capital goods required for their utilization had not been accumulated by saving. (emphasis added, 1956 [2006]: 24)

This emphasis on the *institutional framework* was lost in the first half of the 20th century due to the rise of formalism in economic reasoning. The classical political economists – say from Smith to Mill – were also philosophers and historians, as well as political and legal theorists. They also sought to produce logically sound arguments, rather than merely logically valid ones. This meant that realism of assumptions mattered greatly in the theoretical systems being constructed. They sought to steer an intellectual course between purely free-floating abstractions and momentary concrete description. Political economy was a theoretical edifice consisting of realistic abstractions that aided and guided empirical investigations. But understanding human society is complex; there are no constants. As a result, there was (and always will be) scope for varied interpretations of events. This was often mistaken in the late 19th century and early 20th century as a sign of the immaturity of the science, and due to the nature of verbal reasoning. Ambiguity resulted because the same words were being used to mean different things, or because different words were being used to mean the same thing. As a result, disputes about fundamental issues seemed to be repeated without resolution. So this could all be cleared up, the thought was, by substituting mathematical models for verbal chains of reason. Now, hidden assumptions would be eliminated, and the ambiguity of words would be replaced by the clarity and precision of mathematical expression. There was some resistance to this transformation of economic science for the first few decades of the 20th century, precisely because it was understood that this transformation moved critical reasoning in the social sciences from a quest for logical soundness to a quest for logical validity. Thus, early 20th century thinkers who resisted formalism continuously stressed the lack of realism of assumptions as a problem. The formalistic turn required simplifying assumptions – that is different than the earlier use of abstract reasoning in the construction of theory. But as advances were made in statistical analysis, the belief was that these statistical techniques could effectively sort between the array of logically valid models those which were empirically meaningful from those that were empirically useless. Thus, modern neoclassical economics was born, and classical political economy was discarded.

One of the key casualties of this transformation was the explicit recognition of the *institutional framework*, let alone its analysis. In fact, a formalistic rendering of the structure of economic reasoning in the 1930–1960s strove to be *institutionally antiseptic*.[2] First, the *framework* was assumed to be given and fixed for the purposes of analysis. Second, its very "givenness" eventually resulted in the *institutional framework* being forgotten.[3] The classic example of this was in the debate in the 1920s–1940s over the possibility of economic calculation under socialism – with one side emphasizing the importance of private property rights and freedom of contract, and the other side insisting that the optimality conditions that defined economic efficiency could be established through judicious economic planning and effective public administration. This debate, we will argue, played an essential role in the re-discovery of the *institutional framework* in the post-WWII era. But before we walk through that argument, let us put in context the contributions of Austrian economics to law and economics, which is the study of endogenous rule formation, or the spontaneous evolution of social institutions, going back to the founder of the Austrian School, Carl Menger.

While Menger's emphasis on spontaneous institutional analysis was born out of the *Methodenstreit,* a methodological battle engaged against the German Historical School, we argue in this introduction that the unique Austrian contribution to law and economics emerged directly from

---

[2] See Francis Bator (1957: 31), where he states that the theorems of welfare economics are "antiseptically independent of institutional context." Furthermore, he argues that the optimality conditions are "technocratic" and that the theorist seeks to avoid any "institutional overtones." Bator is in the intellectual line of economic thinking that developed from Lange-Lerner, to Samuelson-Bergson, and eventually to Arrow-Hahn-Debreu. The flip-side to this evolution was the rebirth of classical political economy and the rise of neoclassical institutionalism between 1950 and 2000 that we are highlighting.

[3] Barry Weingast (2016) recently identified what he dubbed the "neoclassical fallacy." First, the standard economist treats the institutional framework as given and fixed for analysis, and thus eventually forgets the central role in the analysis and assessment of alternative economic systems that institutions must play. Second, upon realizing this intellectual error, the standard economist will acknowledge the importance of institutions, but remain silent on the analysis of the working mechanisms of those institutions for their maintenance, stability and/ or fragility. In our narrative, exposing and correcting the "neoclassical fallacy" is one way to think about the Austrian-inspired law-and-economics revolution in the second half of the 20th century.

the socialist calculation debate against market socialism. This debate, we will argue, played an essential role in the re-discovery of the institutional framework in the post-WWII era. In the aftermath of the socialist calculation debate, the earlier Mengerian emphasis on the spontaneous emergence and evolution of the rules that govern economic and social interaction was reemphasized by F.A. Hayek, who in turn influenced the early pioneers of law and economics, particularly Aaron Director, Ronald Coase and Bruno Leoni.

II.   FROM SMITH TO MENGER TO MISES: THE REFINEMENT OF INVISIBLE HAND THEORIZING

Classical political economy consists of a set of ideas about how to understand the social order that follows from the Scottish Enlightenment moral philosophers, namely David Hume and Adam Smith, and was further developed by the French liberals, namely J.B. Say, and the British utilitarians, namely Jeremy Bentham, David Ricardo, and John Stuart Mill. From Hume, we learn that the foundation of civil society is to be found in property, contract and consent. In order for the human condition to be characterized by productive specialization and peaceful cooperation, that society must have security and stability of possession, the keeping of promises, and the transference of property by consent (see Hume 1739 [2000], Book III, Part 2, Sec. II–IV: 311–31). Where property is insecure, promises are not kept, and violent taking characterizes the social situation; human sociability will be truncated and the Hobbesian propensities will prevail. On the other hand, when the social situation is characterized by property, contract and consent, the Smithian propensities prevail and peace and prosperity prevail. Smith's argument in *An Inquiry into the Nature and Causes of the Wealth of Nations* must be understood in this two-stage manner. Yes, the greatest improvements in the material conditions of mankind are due to the refinement in the division of labor. But, as Smith pointed out, the division of labor is limited by the extent of the market. The division of labor is, to use more modern language, a proximate cause of development. The fundamental cause is what gives rise to the expansion of the market, and thus the refinement of the division of labor. That fundamental cause – as mentioned already by Mises – are the ideas that gave rise to the institutional *framework* that made savings and capital accumulation safe. As Smith (1795 [1982]: 322) stated in his lecture notes that he used to develop *The Wealth of Nations*: "Little else is requisite to carry a state to the highest degree of opulence from the lowest barbarism but peace, easy taxes, and a tolerable administration of justice; all the rest being brought about by the natural course of things." Unpacking precisely the institutional infrastructure that produces those consequences has been one of the central tasks of political economists and social philosophers ever since Smith.

The early neoclassical economists in the wake of the marginal revolution in value theory did not see their tasks as all that radically different than Smith's. They just had a new set of analytical tools to utilize in explaining value, exchange and productive activity within the market economy. The Austrian economist Carl Menger was one of the founders of the marginal revolution – alongside co-discoverers Leon Walras and William Stanley Jevons. Yet, what distinguished Menger from the other founders of the marginal revolution was in applying invisible hand theorizing, as emphasized by his predecessors in classical political economy, to the analysis of social institutions. In distinguishing Menger from his counterparts in the marginal revolution, Bruce Caldwell writes the following: "The marginal concept was only a small part of a much larger contribution, namely, a theoretical demonstration that individuals, acting in their own self-interest, give rise to social institutions that have effects that no one intended and that are in many cases benign" (2004: 73–4).

All the early neoclassical theorists from the founders to Wicksell, Wicksteed, Clark, and Knight possessed a deep appreciation of the *institutional framework* within which economic activity takes place. However, most theorists simply began their analysis by assuming well-defined and strictly enforced property rights. Taking the next step and analyzing the emergence of the rules that govern social interaction, the enforcement of those rules, and the effect of changes in those rules was unique to Menger and his junior colleagues in Vienna – Eugen Bohm-Bawerk and Friedrich Wieser. The label – the Austrian School of Economics – was given to this group of thinkers by their intellectual opponents, the German Historicists. Originally, Menger thought he was contributing to the German language scientific tradition by providing the theoretical grounding for the historical and institutional analysis that the German Historical School claimed they wanted to conduct. Menger's point, for our purposes, was rather a basic one – you can do historical and institutional analysis guided by an articulated and defended theory, or you can do it with an unarticulated and non-defended theory, but what you cannot do is conduct the analysis without any theory. The German School rejected the classical political economists because they found the theory too abstract, based on an unrealistic theory of human nature, and for ignoring the historical and institutional details of the situation. So while the older German Historical School of Roscher would have perhaps met Menger's overture with gratitude, the "younger" German Historical School of Schmoller violently rejected such an effort to provide theoretical foundations. Menger was dismissed as "the Austrian," and thus was born the first school of neoclassical institutional economics – what later became known as New Institutionalism, of which the entire field of law and economics is a part.

Menger responded to Schmoller and the German Historical School's rebuff by engaging in the *Methodenstreit* and followed up his *Principles of Economics* (1871) with *Investigations into the Method of the Social Sciences* (1883). While Menger's work was grounded in economic theory, this book discusses general sociology, politics, and jurisprudence, as well as history. It is important to note that at the University of Vienna, advanced economics education took place within the school of law. So in addition to technical economics, students studied jurisprudence, sociological theory, political theory, and history. Economics was a branch, though the most developed branch, of a more general theory of social interaction. But the Austrian economists argued that the most scientifically productive way forward in this general social theory was to ground the analysis in *methodological individualism*. As Menger put it in *Principles of Economics* (1871 [1981]: 108), man "is himself the point at which human economic life begins and ends." The analytical focus was on the rational actor's arrangement of scarce means to satisfy unlimited wants in the most efficacious manner possible. These actors were acting in an uncertain world and with very limited knowledge, so errors of judgment and errors of execution could plague their efforts, but the basic structure of striving to achieve the most for the least is not deterred by this recognition of man's imperfections. In fact, it is precisely our imperfections and the possibilities for change that motivate acting man, and lead acting man to learn through time how better to pursue his purposes individually and through exchange with others who are similarly trying to improve their lot in life.

The Austrian school of Menger, Bohm-Bawerk, and Wieser divided economic science into three branches: pure or exact theory; applied theory or institutionally contingent theory; and empirical examination (both historical and contemporary public policy). Critics thought incorrectly that the classical political economists and Austrian school economists worked exclusively in the realm of pure theory, but this was mistaken. As Buchanan (2001: 290) notes, "to Adam Smith, the 'laws and institutions,' the political-legal framework within which persons interact, one with another, are important and necessary elements in the inclusive 'constitution' for the political economy." Or consider how Hayek (1978: 124–5) summed up Smith's position: "Adam Smith's decisive contribution was the account of a self-generating order which formed itself spontaneously if the individuals were restrained by appropriate rules of law."

The interaction of pure theory of the logic of choice with the institutional context that defined the logic of the situation simply was missed by critics, and as we have mentioned, by the formalists. This is perhaps because the critics among the German Historicists and the American Old Institutionalists believed there was an ideological commitment to reform, and one of the serious implications of the classical political economists and the early neoclassical Austrians was that reform faced its own set of constraints.[4] Note we did not say reform was impossible. Rather, we just merely said that it faced constraints, but that was enough to invoke the ire of the would-be reformists who like Adam Smith's "man of systems" were very wise in their "own conceit" and thus believed they could "arrange the different members of a great society with as much ease as the hand arranges the different pieces upon a chessboard." (Smith 1759 [1982], VI.ii.2.17: 234) Stressing the play between context and choice, and under-standing intended and unintended consequences – the seen and the unseen; immediate effects and long-run effects – is essential to analyzing the impact of reform measures. Such an analysis was too irksome to the aspirations of the reformers, and too nuanced and subtle in the institutional contingencies for the formalists.

III.   THE SOCIALIST CALCULATION DEBATE: THE CRITICAL JUNCTURE BETWEEN THE EARLY AUSTRIAN SCHOOL AND THE MODERN AUSTRIAN SCHOOL

The Austrian school economists were caught between historicism and formalism as 20th-century economics was evolving throughout Europe and the United States. Between WWI and WWII, a new generation of theorists emerged to carry the banner, namely Ludwig von Mises and F.A. Hayek. They would be involved as primary actors in three intellectual dramas during those years: the debate over socialist calculation; the debate over business cycles; and the debate over the methodology of economics. For our purposes, what matters most is how each of these debates were interconnected and resulted ultimately in Hayek's turn in the post-WWII era to an explicit focus on the institutional *framework* as seen in *The Constitution of Liberty* (1960) and *Law, Legislation and Liberty* (1973–79). In both the socialist calculation debate and the business cycle debates, the unique "Austrian" contribution related to the guiding role of

---

[4]   On the reform mentality of the Old Institutionalist thinkers see Thomas Leonard's *Illiberal Reformers* (2016).

relative prices in the processes of exchange and production. The coordination of economic plans – whether the production plans meshing with consumption demands, or the savings of some with the investment plans of others – was guided by relative prices in those respective markets. And, the very existence of those relative prices is based on private property rights. Prices without property is a grand illusion, since property, as we saw from Hume, is the basis of exchange and contract. Without private property in the means of production, Mises argued, there would be no market for the means of production, and without a market there would be no relative prices established in the means of production. And, without those relative prices, there could be no rational economic calculation of the alternative use of scarce resources (Mises 1920 [1975]: 111; Mises 1922 [1951]: 119; see also Boettke 1998: 134). Prices guide production; calculation aids coordination of complex economic arrangements. Advanced material production and wealth creation is only possible within the context of the private property market economy.

But during the interwar years, economic science had taken a turn toward excessive formalism and excessive aggregation, and in the process tended to cloud our understanding of the subtleties of economic coordination. Consider, for example, the problems associated with coordinating the use of capital within a firm, let alone within an entire economy. Capital goods are heterogeneous but possess multi-specific uses; they are not homogeneous and perfectly fungible. Yet, modeling is more tractable if one abstracts from the heterogeneous characteristics and assumes capital is homogeneous and perfectly fungible in production plans. But making this assumption results in two things – first, the coordination of production activities through time appears to be simple, and second, errors in the process of coordination are less costly. This rather trivial step in the assumptions had very significant implications. In the socialist calculation debate, the absence of private ownership in capital goods, and thus a working market-based price system, did not cause concern and instead a planning procedure of trial and error could easily substitute to achieve the optimality conditions of general equilibrium. In the business cycle dispute, the manipulation of money and credit would not be seen as generating a costly malinvestment in the capital structure, and any errors that were induced could easily be corrected within the model; the problem with macroeconomic volatility wasn't seen as a bug, but a feature of a more realistic rendering of the market economy, where agent optimism and pessimism and prices do not play a guiding role in exchange and production activity. In short, the conclusion by the end of the 1930s was that models of market socialism were workable and that the market economy was inherently unstable and could suffer from aggregate demand deficiencies that could only be dealt with through activist government intervention.

The teachings of classical political economy, as well as the early neoclassical school of economics, was overturned not by historicism and institutionalism, but by a formalistic version of neoclassicism that drew attention away from the institutional context, and an excessive aggregation that drew attention away from the active choices of individual actors within the economic system. The logic of choice and the logic of the situation in studying the processes of complex coordination were replaced by the economics of control characterized by macroeconomic demand management and market socialism to address any microeconomic imperfections and inefficiencies. Abba Lerner, in fact entitled his book, *The Economics of Control* (1944). Milton Friedman's review of Lerner is instructive for our narrative because Friedman points out that Lerner's analysis was logically valid, but was impractical because he did not address the administrative costs associated with his proposals (Friedman 1947: 415).

Recall our emphasis from Adam Smith on a "tolerable administration of justice." One simply cannot do political economy without addressing the institutional infrastructure within which economic activity takes place. Yet, during the period of 1940–60 the economics profession turned increasingly away from paying attention to institutions. The pockets of resistance to this trend are seen in particular developments during this period, especially in the 1950–70 period of property-rights economics, public choice economics, and law-and-economics associated with names such as Armen Alchian, James Buchanan, and Ronald Coase, respectively.[5] But Mises and Hayek actually started this intellectual trend during the debate over socialism, the debate over business cycles, and the debate over methodology. They entered into the last debate because of the communicative frustration experienced in the first two. As Mises would often stress, nothing in his proposal for praxeology should be seen as new, but instead as the methodology that was followed by all the leading economists past and present. And besides the emphasis on the pure logic of choice, Mises's praxeological analysis required the economist to take into account the *institutional framework* within which economic activity takes place. This is the basis of his comparative institutional analysis of the unhampered market economy, socialism, and interventionism, as well as his examination of bureaucracy,

---

[5]   For our purposes, Ronald Coase is the critical figure of these three, but as suggested earlier we also would highlight the role that Aaron Director played before in developing the law-and-economics movement, and Bruno Leoni after for his work focusing on the lessons from the socialist calculation debate on how we should approach the study of the evolution of law.

the war economy, and the total state. The pure logic of choice does not change in each of these institutional settings, but the manifestations of that choice, and the consequences of the interactions among choosers, will vary depending on the institutional context.

In one of the most ironic twists of modern intellectual history, and very telling for our purposes, Oskar Lange actually accused Mises of being an old-style institutionalist because of his emphasis on private property in the means of production and a market price system for the rational calculation of alternative uses of scarce resources in investment projects (see Lange and Taylor 1938: 62). The fact that many in the economics profession at the time found Lange persuasive, and even found Hayek and Robbins's respective rebuttals to be wanting, shows that the insidious influence of formalism was already taking hold in the minds of economists by the end of the 1930s. Institutionless economics resulted in purging not only law, politics, history, and sociology, but ultimately also the human decision-maker and the agony of choice the human decision-maker must embrace in trying to sort through the uncertainty of the future.

To Menger, man was caught between alluring hopes and haunting fears, as he attempted to envision a future path in bettering his condition. The institutional environment was thus seen as a useful guide, or a hindrance, in this effort to be better off tomorrow than one is today. In an uncertain future, one characterized by ceaseless change, the *institutional framework* provides the background to give the world some predictability for coordinating our actions.[6] Thus, to the classical political economists and the early neoclassical economists, a constantly shifting *framework* and/or a deteriorating *framework* would simply compound the problem of coordination. Coordination failures, which are not to be ignored, resulted from *framework* issues, and were not inherent in the operation of a private property market economy. This last point is essential to understanding the rise of New Institutional Economics in the 1950–70s. Markets *per se* do not fail, but the *rules* that govern human interaction in the market could be, and often are, imperfect and result in significant deviations from ideal allocations of resources. Unexploited opportunities for mutually beneficial exchange are overlooked, and least cost technologies are not fully employed in production. There was among the classical and early neoclassical economists a general recognition of so-called market failures of

---

[6]   This argument would later become the basis for one of the classic papers in the Austrian approach to law and economics, Mario Rizzo's "Law Amid Flux" (1980), and the even later Richard Epstein's *Simple Rules for a Complex World* (1995).

monopoly power, externalities, the provision of public goods, and macro-economic volatility. There were, in short, problems of poverty, ignorance, and squalor in the world that must be addressed. Mass unemployment and systemic inequality were just as much of a concern for Adam Smith as they were for Alfred Marshall and as they are today for Joseph Stiglitz and Paul Krugman. The differences in opinion among these thinkers is not in the recognition of the problem or even in the normative desire to ameliorate and hopefully eradicate the problem, but in the diagnosis of the cause and the recommendation for the remedy. For classical political economists, such as Hume, Smith, Say, Bentham, and Mill, as well as Austrian econo-mists, such as Menger, Mises and Hayek, the cause was to be found not in the frailty of human beings (which was after all omnipresent), but in the institutional context within which these fallible but capable human actors were interacting. As a result, the solution was to be found not in any trans-formation of the human being, nor in the *deus ex machina* of benevolent and omniscient state action, but in the positive program for *laissez faire* as laid out in the reform proposals for changing the rules found in Smith, in Mill, in Hayek, and in more modern times Friedman and Buchanan.

Reform was to be found neither in policy dictates to mimic what an ideal pattern of economic activity would result as in the market socialist model, where state planners were simply told to price equal to marginal cost and produce at the level of output that minimizes the average cost of production. Nor, as was critical to the emerging field of law and econom-ics, was it to be found in pursuing Pigouvian remedies of either taxing or subsidizing until private marginal benefits/costs were aligned with social marginal benefits/costs. As Hayek pointed out in his paper "Economics and Knowledge" (1937), the optimality conditions of the market were a by-product of the competitive process, and *not* an assumption going into the analysis. Competition is an activity, not a description of a state of affairs where all activity has ceased. Hayek, in particular, tended to blend his institutional turn in research in the 1940s with his *epistemological* turn in research. Institutions did not just structure the incentives that actors faced in making their decisions and thus influencing the manner in which they interact with other, but they also impact the quality of information and the flow of new knowledge that decision-makers have at their disposal in making those decisions. Much of the most important knowledge that must be utilized is contextual in nature. Outside of specific institutional contexts, it isn't just difficult to acquire; it simply ceases to exist. Social scientists are still struggling to catch up to Hayek's fundamental insights in his papers on the utilization of knowledge within an economic system and the role that alternative institutions play in that analysis.

IV.   HAYEK, THE INSTITUTIONAL TURN, AND THE EMERGENCE OF LAW AND ECONOMICS

In the 1940s, Hayek published *The Road to Serfdom* (1944), and in that book – a further elaboration of a monograph entitled *Freedom and the Economic System* (1939). In those works, Hayek turned his attention to the rule of law and democracy, and how the economic system interacts with legal and political institutions. A close reading of these works, and his subsequent works dealing with the interaction of legal, political, and social institutions and the operation of the economic system such as *The Constitution of Liberty* and *Law, Legislation and Liberty* (1973–79), Hayek both examines how alternative institutional arrangements impact the economic forces at work, and how the tools of basic economic reasoning can be deployed to analyze the institutional logic of proposed rule changes in the legal, political and social spheres. For example, in *The Road to Serfdom*, the reader is first introduced to the argument that comprehensive economic planning will be inconsistent with the rule of law and democracy. This is the rationale for the title of the work, which is meant to capture a tragic tale. Remember, Hayek was not addressing his book to the advocates of communism in Soviet Russia, or the advocates of the total state in Nazi Germany, but to his colleagues in Britain who believed they could combine socialist economic planning with liberal democratic institutions such as the rule of law and individual freedom. The suppression of individual freedom and the erosion of democratic institutions that Hayek envisioned as the logical outcome of efforts to substitute comprehensive economic planning for the market economy was a tragic warning to his colleagues. Their vision of a rational economic order would result in a political nightmare from their own point of view as the rule of law and democracy would prove to be incompatible with the organizational logic of economic planning.

The arrow of argumentative direction in Hayek's line of reasoning was directed at the aspirations to remake the economic system via the political order. One of his main points of emphasis was how political control over economic means was not merely a control over material factors, but necessarily a control over the means by which we pursue our most lofty goals. "Economic control," Hayek wrote, "is not merely control of a sector of human life which can be separated from the rest; it is the control of the means for all our ends. And whoever has sole control of the means must also determine which ends are to be served, which values are to be rated higher and which lower, in short, what men should believe and strive for" (1944 [2007]: 127). Freedom of speech, religion, and the press, e.g., is an empty phrase unless we also have the ability to own the means of the press. Human rights are ultimately property rights. Coming from the grand debate in economic theory over rational economic planning under socialism, Hayek moved the conversation from the technical arguments concerning the price system and the allocation of scarce resources to the institutional environment that would need to compliment that planning task. The rule of law and democratic institutions are the means by which individuals are left free to pursue a great variety of purposes. They provide the institutional impediments to the necessary power and discretion of the planners, making it possible for individuals to pursue their individual plans with a fair degree of certainty as to how government officials will exercise their coercive power. The rule of law allows for the mutual adjustment of conflicting plans through voluntary exchange via market prices as guides to production and consumption. However, the rule of law is inconsistent with political discretion, for government planning can only succeed through the suppression of individual plans by political actors willing to exercise force. At this point, Hayek develops a slightly different argument. In his chapter on "Why the Worst Get On Top," Hayek explains how the selection process among leaders of the planning effort will take place. In this, he follows Frank Knight (1932; 1938), and simply uses an argument about the comparative advantage in exercising discretion and power over fellow citizens and the characteristics of such a person. In short, Hayek argues that even if someone of the character of Mother Teresa was to be put in charge of the planning bureau she would either have to change her character to be more ruthless, or she would lose out in the political struggle for leadership. As Knight put it, only a certain type of character can survive to control the whip on a plantation; it is not a job for everyone. It is the same with those placed in charge of executing comprehensive economic plans.

The fields of public choice and law-and-economics from a Hayekian perspective should be seen as intertwined and as two sides of the same effort to refocus economists' attention on the *institutional framework*. The work of various sociologists during this same era – whether Peter Berger, Rodney Stark, or James Coleman – also sought to integrate social institutions such as norms, mores, beliefs, etc. into this focus on the *framework* in a way consistent with the basic economic way of thinking, but the consensus in this research is less solidified than in public choice and law-and-economics so the integration is not as easily envisioned.

Methodologically, the approach to the study of political and legal institutions works initially in a rather straightforward linear fashion – an animating rational actor initiates that inquiry, that actor finds themselves interacting within an institutional filter, defined by the formal and informal rules of social interaction and their enforcement, that institutional filter structures the incentives and provides the information and knowledge that actors need to act on the incentives, and that in turn results in certain equilibrating tendencies which the system exhibits. As Buchanan often stressed, same players, different rules, produce different games. The explanatory thrust in this approach is to be found not in the behavioral attributes we assign to the individual actors, but in the alternative institutional *frameworks* within which they operate.

As Robert Van Horn (2013) has documented with rich archival research, the relationship between Hayek and Aaron Director in the decade prior to *The Road to Serfdom* and the decade after its publication was indeed a deeply committed one. They saw themselves as "comrades in arms" against the collectivist threat to the competitive order. Director was a student at the LSE in the 1930s, and viewed Hayek as his teacher. Director would use his connections to push for the publication of Hayek's *The Road to Serfdom* by the University of Chicago, and he would review the book extremely favorably in the *American Economic Review*. In addition, when private donors wanted to establish a program at the University of Chicago to study in depth the private enterprise system, and though they approached Hayek to lead this effort (even though he was not at Chicago at the time), Hayek recommended that they work with Director instead, and they did. The project – sometimes referred to as the "Hayek project" in internal memos and correspondence between the principals – was housed at the University of Chicago Law School. The focus of the project turned to a theme captured in our headquote to this chapter, namely the forms of legal institutions which aid, or hinder, the operation of the competitive system.

Ronald Coase was another product of the LSE in the 1930s, and as he has described his own work it was to examine the *institutional framework* that made possible the workings of firms, markets, and economies. Coase is sometimes referred to as an advocate of a pragmatic-empirical brand of economics. But Coase was not an old style institutionalist. He was trapped, as Hayek was, between historicism and formalism. Moreover, like Hayek (and Plant and Robbins), Coase in good LSE fashion was trained in basic economic reasoning and price theory. He was a neoclassical institutionalist, and as such focused on exchange and the institutions within which exchange takes place. This is seen not only in his development of the transaction cost theory of the firm, which he developed directly from his reflections on the socialist calculation debate as taught to him by Arnold Plant, but in the development of the "Coase Theorem" as articulated in his paper, "The Federal Communications Commission" (1959), and then more fully developed in "The Problem of Social Cost" (1960). We do not have to repeat here the arguments in those papers about the allocation of resources and the initial distribution of rights under the assumption of zero transaction costs, or in the face of positive transactions costs, but suffice to say Coase pioneered comparative institutional analysis. He argued that in making the comparison one must take into account that in moving the decision arena away from the market sphere one must recognize that they will have to forgo the monetary calculation of benefits and costs, the division of knowledge throughout the economy, and must account for the additional costs of vested interest groups (see 1959: 18).

In setting up the various contributions to this volume, what matters is that from Hayek one can draw not an indirect line of influence, but a direct line of influence to the founding of the law-and-economics movement after WWII and its development in the 1940s–60s by Aaron Director and Ronald Coase. We do not contend that this development was linear, but instead it went in a variety of new and interesting directions. But the influence was direct nevertheless, and it was seen as a corrective to the disregard for the *institutional framework* by mainstream economists in the 1930s–50s that resulted in fundamental confusions about that operation of the competitive order, and the vital role that legal institutions play in its effective operation.

V.   HAYEK, LEONI, AND ENDOGENOUS RULE FORMATION

One final point of emphasis in the Hayekian perspective on the institutional *framework* that has caused confusion among readers is the question of the origin and maintenance of this *framework*. Alexander Hamilton in *Federalist #1* put the puzzle as follows: will we base our constitutions on accident and force, or on reflection and choice? The obvious answer to this question so put is to rely on reflection and choice. One way to think about Hayek's discussion of rational constructivism versus spontaneous order is to see him working through Hamilton's question. Hayek is simply pointing out that we cannot just design institutions out of thin air and place them. We are constrained in our quest for rational institutional design by the historical path we are on. But that does not mean we cannot engage in positive reform of the rules and in efforts at institutional design. The critical rationalist is permitted, and in fact, must, challenge all of society's values, but they cannot challenge all of them at once. This is why Hayek's position cannot be considered "conservative," since he wants to hold nothing as sacred, yet Hayek is not a "constructivist" because he argues we cannot design society from nothing according to our will. It is a subtle and nuanced dance of evolution and design that makes up the spontaneous order of society and the institutional *framework* that shapes that order. Hayek makes this point in *Law, Legislation, and Liberty*:

At the moment our concern must be to make clear that while the rules on which a spontaneous order rests, may also be of spontaneous origin, this need not always be the case. Although undoubtedly an order originally formed itself spontaneously because the individuals followed rules which had not been deliberately made but had arisen spontaneously, people gradually learned to improve those rules; and it is at least conceivable that the formation of a spontaneous order relies entirely on rules that were deliberately made. (Hayek 1973: 45)

The crucial step in Hayekian analysis was to argue that not only the pattern of social interaction within the *framework* was a result of spontaneous order, but that the very *framework* itself was the product of another spontaneous process of ordering. This focus on endogenous rules, rather than processes within exogenous rules, is what separated Hayek from the earlier Austrians (except Menger) and the later New Institutionalists (except Elinor Ostrom).

The Italian classical liberal political economist Bruno Leoni was one of the earliest writers to see the connection between the socialist calculation debate and this focus on the endogenous evolution of law. In his now classic work *Freedom and Law*, Leoni argues that the theoretical impossibility of economic central planning is considered only a part in a more general problem, regarding the possible action of the legislator in society.

[T]his demonstration [that a centralized economy does not work] may be deemed the most important and lasting contribution made by the economists to the cause of individual freedom in our time. However, its conclusion may be considered only a as a special case of a more general realization that no legislator would be able to establish by himself, without some kind of continuous collaboration on the part of all the people concerned, the rules governing the actual behavior of everybody in the endless relationships that each has with everybody else. No public opinion polls, no referenda, no consultations would really put the legislators in a position to determine these rules [. . .]. The actual behavior of people is continuously adapting itself to changing conditions. (Leoni 1961 [1972]: 18–19)

In correspondence with Hayek after the publication of *Freedom and the Law*, Leoni summed up his argument as follows:

I think that the underlying idea of such a theory is that there is a market of the law as well as there is a market of goods. The rules correspond to the prices: they are the expression of the conditions requested for the exchange of actions and behaviours, just as the prices are the expression of certain conditions requested for the exchange of the goods. And the rules, as well as the prices are not imposed, but found out. I said before that the rules are found out by some special kind of people. But even this is true only partially. Everybody can find out a rule under given circumstances: this happens whenever people exchange their actions, their behaviours etc. at certain conditions without being compelled to consult anybody. (quoted in Masala 2003: 228)

If market coordination through the price system requires competition to sort out errors and provide corrective adaptations and adjustments, then so does a working legal system require competition to discover errors in judgment and rulings, to adapt and adjust to changing circumstances, to minimize conflicts, and promote productive specialization and peaceful social cooperation. The law, like the market, to Leoni, is a discovery procedure. Legislation, like centralized planning, curtails learning and thus becomes an impediment to progress in social intercourse and economic well-being.

The contrast is most starkly seen in the contrast in points of emphasis concerning spontaneous order within a framework of law, and spontaneous order of the framework of law itself in the presentations of Hayek and Buchanan. For our purposes, we want to stress that the contrast is overblown. Hayek's emphasis on the spontaneous order of common law versus the constructivist rationalism of legislation led to confusion in the modern discussions in political economy about the role of constitutional construction in Hayek's system. By drawing on the discussion of conservativism and constructivism, we argue that while there is no doubt a tension, this tension need not be a source of confusion, but instead a source of inquiry. Constitutional construction is a constrained intellectual exercise, but a necessary one for the maintenance of the liberal order. Law evolves, but it can also be improved upon when this evolution is derailed in perverse directions in relationship to liberalism. Hayek stresses, in this sense, constitutional construction from the bottom up, but there is nothing in his system that would prevent constitutional design on the margins.

On the other hand, one of the most challenging research questions law and economics scholars have puzzled over in the past quarter of century in the face of the collapse of communism, the continued failure of state-led development planning in Africa and Latin America, and war-torn failed and weak states around the globe, has been how does one "grow" a rule of law. As Rajan (2004) so eloquently put it, you cannot proceed under the assumption of well-defined and enforced property rights in a world that has completely fallen apart institutionally. The reason why these societies are dysfunctional is precisely because they lack the *institutional framework* that more functional systems possess. We must, as Rajan put it, "Assume Anarchy" if we are going to make any progress. That is our starting point of analysis, and the question is how law develops. As Peter Leeson (2014) has stressed repeatedly, one cannot just assume that in such an environment you can impose a working Western-style government. In such a dysfunctional environment the most likely outcome is an abusive dysfunctional government that will be unleashed to predate on the people, rather than be constrained in its predatory propensities. So one possible avenue of research that has been opened by this is the role of *informal* institutions in providing the impetus for development.

To tie this back to Buchanan, consider the conclusion that Buchanan and Tullock are led to in *The Calculus of Consent* (emphasis added, 1962 [1999]: 80–81) concerning social cleavages:

> The evolution of democratic constitutions from the discussion of rational individuals can take place only under certain relatively narrowly defined conditions. The individual participants must approach the constitution-making process as "equals" in a special sense of this term. The requisite "equality" can be insured only if the existing differences in external characteristics among individuals are accepted without rancor and if there are no clearly predictable bases among these differences for the formation of permanent coalitions. On the basic of purely economic motivation, individual members of a dominant and superior group (who consider themselves to be such and who were in the possession of power) would never rationally choose to adopt constitutional rules giving less fortunately situated individuals a position of equal partnership in governmental processes. On noneconomic grounds the dominate classes might choose to do this, but, as experience has so often demonstrated in recent years, the less fortunately situated classes will rarely interpret such action as being advanced in their favor. *Therefore, our analysis of the constitution-making process had little relevance for a society that is characterized by a sharp cleavage of the population into distinguishable social classes or separate racial, religious, or ethnic groupings sufficient to encourage the formation of predictable political coalitions and in which one of these coalitions has a clearly advantageous position at the constitutional stage.*

So if we take them at their word, either Buchanan and Tullock's analysis is irrelevant to the world of dysfunctional institutions, or we have to embrace the challenge of studying endogenous rule formation in the field of law-and-economics and public choice.

VI.   SO WHAT IS "AUSTRIAN" ABOUT "AUSTRIAN" LAW AND ECONOMICS?

The term "Austrian" in the Austrian school of economics can be interpreted in 1 of 2 ways. First, it could be understood as a cultural setting of the founding of a certain approach to economics in *fin-de-siècle* Vienna. This Viennese intellectual and artistic culture was a unique period of human creativity, and the discipline of economics was no different. So the time period is worthy of study for anyone intrigued by intellectual history (see Dekker 2016). On the other hand, the term "Austrian" also designates a certain approach to the study of economics. The interaction of these two is quite fascinating for scholars of law and economics. At the University of Vienna, the economics faculty was located within the School of Law. And, the Austrian economists in their economic analysis always placed great importance on the institutional framework of property and contract.

Boettke (2010: xi–xviii) provides a summary of the ten propositions that are the defining substantive position of the contemporary Austrian school of economics. They are:

1. Only individuals choose.
2. The study of the market order is fundamentally about exchange behavior and the institutions within which exchange takes place.
3. The "facts" of the social sciences are what people believe and think.
4. Utility and costs are subjective.
5. The price system economizes on the information that people need to process in making their decisions.
6. Private property in the means of production is a necessary condition for rational economic calculation.
7. The competitive market is a process of entrepreneurial discovery.
8. Money is non-neutral.
9. The capital structure consists of heterogeneous goods that have multispecific uses that must be aligned.
10. Social institutions are often the result of human action, but not of human design.

These propositions are evident in the various contributions to Austrian law and economics as well. As we have seen, traditional law and economics emerged from taking two fields of study and combining them into one. There was the traditional economic analysis of exchange relationships and competitive behavior within a given set of institutions. And, there is the application of the rational choice tools of analysis developed in economics to study the institutional rules themselves. There are subtle and important differences between an approach that attempts to examine how alternative institutional arrangements impact the operation of an economic system, and the use of economic reasoning to address the efficiency, or possible efficiency, of a set of institutional arrangements. For our purposes, both approaches can be pursued from an "Austrian" perspective, and have been by various scholars as is evident within the pages of this volume.

The Austrian school of economics is identified with methodological individualism, methodological subjectivism, and market process analysis. It is a school of economic thought that focuses on the processes by which individuals coordinate their plans through time. Its first task is to render all human phenomena intelligible in terms of the purposes and plans of individual actors, and then it seeks to trace out the unintended – both desirable and undesirable – consequences of those actions and interactions. It is an approach that takes seriously the subjective evaluations, assessments, and expectations of actors, as well as the decision-making environment within which individuals are pursuing their plans, an environment characterized by uncertainty, ignorance and the passage of time. In short, the Austrian school of economics studies the economy as a complex system.

This approach is to be contrasted with an approach to the study of economic behavior and organization which treats economic phenomena as a simple system. In the extreme, it is a system characterized by mathematical functions that are smooth and continuous and twice differentiable. Such a system is close-ended and exhibits a single exit. These are *equilibrium* theories of market exchange and the social order.

In the process approach, the law provides the institutional framework within which the complex and dynamic processes of exchange and entrepreneurial adaptation and adjustment to constantly changing conditions takes place. Thus, the analysis informs us on how alternative legal regimes impact economic performance. But the Austrian school also developed a process approach to the institutional framework. From Carl Menger to Mises and Hayek, Austrian law and economics studies the evolution of legal rules as a prime example of spontaneous order analysis. "How can it be," Menger (emphasis original, 1883 [1985]: 146) famously asked, "that institutions which serve the common welfare and are extremely significant for its development come into being without a common will directed toward establishing them?" Hayek (1952 [1979]: 69) went further and argued that to the extent that the social institutions are a result of deliberate design, there would be no necessity for theoretical inquiry in the sciences of man and society. It is only because we are dealing with institutions that are the result of human action, but not of human design that we as social scientists have a need for theoretical sophistication and refinement.

In this, as in many other ways, the modern Austrian school was simply updating the political economy and social philosophy of the Scottish Enlightenment philosophers by way of refining economic theory that followed from the marginalist revolution and the development of the subjective theory of value. The equilibrium approach that also emerged in the first half of the 20th century often clouded rather than clarified the fundamental relationship between the institutional framework and economic performance, as well as the study of that institutional framework itself. Hayek famously wrote:

> Nothing is solved when we assume everybody to know everything and that the real problem is rather how it can be brought about that as much of the available knowledge as possible is used. This raises for a competitive society the question, not how we can "find" the people who know best, but rather what institutional arrangements are necessary in order that the unknown persons who have knowledge suited to a particular task are most likely to be attracted to that task. (Hayek 1948: 95)

This argument of Hayek's was deployed to examine the coordinating role played by prices in a competitive economy, and the consequences of distortions to that guiding role that result with interference in the operation of the price system. But the broader point about the evolution of an institutional environment that is conducive to economic growth would be a persistent theme in Hayek's work and was developed in *The Road to Serfdom*, *The Constitution of Liberty* and *Law, Legislation and Liberty*. It is these works that form the classic writings in Austrian law and economics, and as we have stressed they exhibit throughout the emphasis on individual choice not only against constraints, but in an environment of ignorance and uncertainty. The coping function of institutions is to deal with uncertainty by providing predictability and stability in the framework, yet maintain a mix of coherence and flexibility to enable the necessary adaptations and dynamic adjustments to the rules with the passage of time to accommodate the changing circumstances.

VII.   CONCLUSION

So we have individuals *and* institutions; we examine how alternative institutional arrangements impact economic performance *and* how the tools of economic reasoning help us better understand the operation of institutions. We study law as the product of evolutionary processes and thus a quintessential example of a spontaneous order *and* the constitutional structures that are most effective at constraining the predatory capacities of the state so as to preserve a framework that allows human beings to flourish. The Austrian school of economics in its historical and contemporary embodiment, as well as the various thinkers that it influenced along the way, such as Alchian, Buchanan, Coase, Director and Leoni, has contributed significantly to the development of law and economics in the post-WWII era, and continues today into the 21st century with a new generation of scholars.

In the volume that follows, we have contributions from a variety of scholars whose work has contributed to the ongoing development of law-and-economics both from within law schools and within economics departments, business schools and in the social sciences and humanities. The range of topics covered run from methodology of analysis, to the evolution of contemporary legal practice, to the teachings of basic law. We believe this provides a strong overview of the contemporary literature in the Austrian school approach to law and economics, and one that reflects both the examination of how alternative legal arrangements impact economic performance, and how to use the tools of basic economic reasoning to study the operation of legal rules. In our conclusion, we will return to the subject we ended with – the prospects and promises for future research in the field of law and economics that follow from the continued refinement of our understanding of the *institutional framework* and how it impacts economic performance through time.

REFERENCES

Bator, Francis M. 1957. "The Simple Analytics of Welfare Maximization," 47 *The American Economic Review* 22–59.

Boettke, Peter J. 1998. "Economic Calculation: The Austrian Contribution to Political Economy," 5 *Advances in Austrian Economics* 131–58.

Boettke, Peter J. 2010. "Introduction." In Peter J. Boettke, ed., *Handbook on Contemporary Austrian Economics*. Cheltenham, UK and Northampton, MA: Edward Elgar.

Buchanan, James M. 1996 [2001]. "Adam Smith as Inspiration." In *The Collected Works of James M. Buchanan, Volume 19: Ideas, Persons, and Events*. Indianapolis, IN: Liberty Fund.

Buchanan, James M. and Gordon Tullock. 1962 [1999]. *The Collected Works of James M. Buchanan, Volume 3: The Calculus of Consent: Logical Foundations of Constitutional Democracy*. Indianapolis, IN: Liberty Fund.

Caldwell, Bruce. 2004. *Hayek's Challenge: An Intellectual Biography of F.A. Hayek*. Chicago, IL: University of Chicago Press.

Coase, Ronald H. 1959. "The Federal Communications Commission," 2 *Journal of Law and Economics* 1–40.

Coase, Ronald H. 1960. "The Problem of Social Cost," 3 *Journal of Law and Economics* 1–44.

Dekker, Erwin. 2016. *The Viennese Students of Civilization: The Meaning and Context of Austrian Economics Reconsidered*. New York, NY: Cambridge University Press.

Epstein, Richard A. 1995. *Simple Rules for a Complex World*. Cambridge, MA: Harvard University Press.

Friedman, Milton. 1947. "Lerner on the Economics of Control," 55 *Journal of Political Economy* 405–16.

Hayek, F.A. 1937. "Economics and Knowledge," 4 *Economica* 33–54.

Hayek, F.A. 1939. *Freedom and the Economic System*. Chicago, IL: University of Chicago Press.

Hayek, F.A. 1944 [2007]. *The Road to Serfdom*. Chicago, IL: University of Chicago Press.

Hayek, F.A. 1948. *Individualism and Economic Order*. Chicago, IL: University of Chicago Press.

Hayek, F.A. 1952 [1979]. *The Counter-Revolution of Science*. Indianapolis, IN: Liberty Fund.

Hayek, F.A. 1960. *The Constitution of Liberty*. Chicago, IL: University of Chicago Press.

Hayek, F.A. 1973. *Law, Legislation and Liberty Volume 1: Rules and Order*. Chicago, IL: University of Chicago Press.

Hayek, F.A. 1976. *Law, Legislation and Liberty Volume 2: The Mirage of Social Justice.* Chicago, IL: University of Chicago Press.

Hayek, F.A. 1978. *New Studies in Philosophy, Politics, and Economics and the History of Ideas.* London, UK: Routledge & Kegan Paul.

Hayek, F.A. 1979. *Law, Legislation and Liberty Volume 3: The Political Order of a Free People.* Chicago, IL: University of Chicago Press.

Hume, David. 1739 [2000]. *A Treatise of Human Nature.* Oxford: Oxford University Press.

Knight, Frank H. 1932. "The Newer Economics and the Control of Economic Activity," 40 *Journal of Political Economy* 433–76.

Knight, Frank H. 1938. "Lippmann's *The Good Society.*" 46 *Journal of Political Economy* 864–72.

Lange, Oskar and Fred M. Taylor. 1938. *On the Economic Theory of Socialism.* Minneapolis, MN: The University of Minnesota Press.

Leeson, Peter T. 2014. *Anarchy Unbound: Why Self-Governance Works Better Than You Think.* New York, NY: Cambridge University Press.

Leonard, Thomas C. 2016. *Illiberal Reformers: Race, Eugenics, and American Economics in the Progressive Era.* Princeton, NJ: Princeton University Press.

Leoni, Bruno. 1961 [1972]. *Freedom and the Law.* Los Angeles, CA: Nash Publishing Company.

Lerner, Abba P. 1944. *The Economics of Control: Principles of Welfare Economics.* New York, NY: Macmillan.

Masala, Antonio. 2003. *Il Liberalismo di Bruno Leoni.* Milan, IT: Rubbettino.

McCloskey, Deirdre Nansen. 2006. *The Bourgeois Virtues: Ethics for an Age of Commerce.* Chicago: University of Chicago Press.

McCloskey, Deirdre Nansen. 2010. *Bourgeois Dignity: Why Economics Can't Explain the Modern World.* Chicago: University of Chicago Press.

McCloskey, Deirdre Nansen. 2016. *Bourgeois Equality: How Ideas, Not Capital or Institutions, Enriched the World.* Chicago: University of Chicago Press.

Menger, Carl. 1871 [1981]. *Principles of Economics.* New York, NY: New York University Press.

Menger. Carl. 1883 [1985]. *Investigations into the Method of the Social Sciences.* New York, NY: New York University Press.

Mises, Ludwig von. 1920 [1975]. "Economic Calculation in the Socialist Commonwealth." In F.A. Hayek, ed., *Collectivist Economic Planning.* Clifton, NJ: August M. Kelley.

Mises, Ludwig von. 1922 [1951]. Socialism: An Economic and Sociological Analysis. New Haven, CT: Yale University Press.

Mises, Ludwig von. 1956 [2006]. *The Anti-Capitalist Mentality.* Indianapolis, IN: Liberty Fund.

Rajan, Raghuram. 2004. "Assume Anarchy? Why An Unorthodox Economic Model May Not Be The Best Guide For Policy," *Finance & Development* 56–7.

Rizzo, Mario. 1980. "Law Amid Flux: The Economics of Negligence and Strict Liability in Tort," 9 *Journal of Legal Studies* 291–318.

Smith, Adam. 1759 [1982]. *The Theory of Moral Sentiments.* Indianapolis, IN: Liberty Fund.

Smith, Adam. 1795 [1982]. *Essays on Philosophical Subjects with Dugald Stewart's Account of Adam Smith.* Indianapolis, IN: Liberty Fund.

Van Horn, Robert. 2013. "Hayek's Unacknowledged Disciple: An Exploration of the Political and Intellectual Relationship of F.A. Hayek and Aaron Director (1945–1950)," 35 *Journal of the History of Economic Thought* 271–90.

Weingast, Barry. 2016. "Exposing the Neoclassical Fallacy: McCloskey on Ideas and the Great Enrichment," *Scandinavian Economic History Review*, forthcoming.

PART II

METHODOLOGY OF LAW AND ECONOMICS

2. Property rights, the Coase Theorem and informality*
Martín Krause

Austrian economists have had a bivalent view of the foundational contributions of Ronald Coase to modern law and economics, particularly on what was later called the 'Coase Theorem' (Coase 1960), and a much more critical view on the following 'efficiency' view of law.

A benign interpretation would stress his critique of general equilibrium theorizing, the need to consider the institutional framework when transactions costs are sufficiently high to prevent bilateral negotiations and his rejection of Pigou's policy proposals of subsidies and taxes to solve problems of positive and negative externalities (Boettke 1997). In this view, Coase is a pioneer and a main contributor to the now flourishing concern on the role of institutions and, with that, joining a long Austrian involvement on the subject, already present in Menger's work. This view also stresses the importance of voluntary solutions to problems of negative externalities, not considered in Pigou's view.

A second interpretation, which may not exclude the first, rejects a view on the 'reciprocal nature of harm' and, most of all, his proposal that under the presence of transaction costs 'what has to be decided is whether the gain from preventing the harm is greater than the loss which would be suffered as a result of stopping the action which produces the harm' (Coase 1960, p.27),[1] with the corresponding advice to judges, probably coming from some of Coase's followers rather than from Coase himself, to apportion rights following a cost and benefit analysis in a way to maximize the positive aggregate result. The subjective nature of value and the impossibility of interpersonal comparisons of utility would turn such an attempt fruitless if not dangerous.

A long debate on normative considerations ensued, essentially fielding two positions: on one side those supporting a Lockean natural rights

*   The author would like to thank Nicolas Maloberti, Nicolas Cachanosky and Max Stearns for some helpful comments on earlier drafts. Responsibility for errors remains with the author only.
[1]   See Block (1977; 1995), Cordato (1992 [2007]), Rizzo (1980) as examples of a larger literature.

view based on the property over one's own body as a determinant of rights and considerations of justice (Block 1977, 1995) and an efficiency view supporting Coase's, even with a Hayekian evolutionary perspective (Demsetz 1979).[2] According to this last view, 'survival is what will identify what is efficient and what is not' (Demsetz 1979, p. 115). Many Austrians would agree with that although they would not go as far as granting the power to identify efficiency to a judge and would argue that efficiency is a dependent variable to property rights, not the other way around.

Also, on the first issue, most economists just assumed that the mere presence of transaction costs discarded voluntary solutions and concentrated on public policies or institutional reforms.

This chapter is not aimed at solving this debate between efficiency and natural rights and focuses on positive analysis. It will just try to bring into consideration a case study on property rights and the solution to problems of externalities within an environment where the formal system of administration of justice and the solution of disputes is not present, as in the informal neighbourhoods or shanty towns found in most poor and not developed countries. The whole discussion over the Coase Theorem assumed a problem with the clear definition of property rights but also the existence of a formal judicial system and judges to which a certain normative advice was addressed, either to judge according to efficiency or justice criteria.

The 'positive' question, though, is: What do judges actually do? In the case of formal, governmental judicial systems the answer is not easy since, as a part of the political system, we must bring in Public Choice considerations (Stearns and Zywicki 2009). What about informal settings? Is there any informal solution of disputes and in that case, who gives it? And whoever does it, what kind of criteria do we find in place? Does the solution of negative externalities problems follow efficiency, value maximizing, or justice criteria?

2

'Life-styles that promote survival come to be viewed as ethical, and those that fail in this respect come to be viewed as in poor taste, if not as unethical. Our present preferences and tastes must reflect in large part their survival-promoting capabilities.'

'In a loose and general way our life-styles, preferences, and ethical beliefs are not arbitrary but are the product of thousands of centuries of biological and cultural evolution.'

'We are bound to view the proper resolution of legal problems from the perspective of what presently seems efficient, whether or not efficiency is explicitly applied. Our genetic and cultural endowment contains elements of ethical preference that have survived dramatically different environments. It undoubtedly contains some ethical preferences not well suited to present conditions, but then the present is not long with us.' (Demsetz, 1979, pp. 114–15)

Also, do bilateral or multilateral negotiations take place to reduce the effects of negative externalities or are transactions costs a fixed and high enough constraint that prevents them?

Our conclusion will be that both are found in informal slums: voluntary solutions to problems of externalities are widespread even in the absence of formal rules, transaction costs are unobservable for third parties but in many cases must have been low enough to allow them, subjective benefits must be higher than subjective costs, and informal solutions of disputes among neighbours follow a 'rights' approach and do not intentionally look for efficiency, although this may be an unintended or secondary result of allocating rights. Informal mediation services are also present, insinuating the value of their services are less than their cost.

Although focused on informal slums in poor and developing countries, the conclusions extend also to informal neighbourhoods and activities in developed countries as well (Venkatesh 2006).[3]

SLUMS AND SQUATTERS

There are no reliable statistics on the amount of people living in housing without a formal property title but whatever it is, it is not small. Neuwirth (2006) estimates it at one billion, one of every six humans on the planet (p. 9), and on the rise. According to this author, 200,000 people leave the rural regions and move to the cities every day, 73 million a year. By 2030 there would be two billion, one in four people. UN-Habitat estimates the number at 928 million by 2003, 32 per cent of the world's urban population and 43 per cent of the population in not developed countries. The report projects the population in slums will increase by 37 million a year to reach 1.5 billion by 2020. Latin America, which has 9 per cent of the world's population, accounts for 14 per cent of the people living in slums. Estimates include 39.5 per cent of those dwelling in Rio de Janeiro, 50 per

---

[3] For example, Venkatesh (2006, p. xv.) comments on Maquis Park, Chicago, Ill.:

'Quite literally I saw a world open in front of me that I had never before paid any mind, a world whose significance I couldn't have imagined. The innumerable economic exchanges that took place every hour, every day, no longer seemed random or happenstance. There was a vast structure in place, a set of rules that defined who traded with whom, who could work on a street corner or park bench, and what prices could be set and what revenue could be earned. There were codes in place for settling disputes and adjudicating conflicts, unwritten standards that tried to ensure that haggling did not get out of hand.'

cent in El Salvador, 39 per cent in Caracas (Smolka and De Cesare 2010). Cravino (2006) quotes different sources showing informal housing of 63 per cent in Lima, 73 per cent in Managua, between 50 and 65 per cent in México DF, 59 per cent in Bogotá, 22 per cent in Sao Paulo and 50 per cent in Quito.

Life in informal towns was the realm of sociological studies until the work of Hernando de Soto and partners at the Instituto Libertad y Desarrollo in Lima, Perú, brought a completely different perspective. In their book *El Otro Sendero* (1987), '*The Other Path*,' they showed informality in general and in housing in particular as a failure of governments, not markets, and as a reaction of the poor with entrepreneurial spirit to make a living and get housing. The ironic reference to the guerrilla group 'The Shining Path' showed poor Peruvians did not want a socialist revolution, they just wanted property rights and freedom of contracts in trade and production. They estimated by 1982, 42.6 per cent of the housing in Lima was informal and by 1984 the average price of an informal house was US$ 22,038, meaning that the total value of informal housing in Lima was US$ 8,319 million, equivalent to 69 per cent of the foreign debt of Perú at that time. Also, government spending in housing for the poor amounted to US$ 173.6 million, or 2.1 per cent of the informal investment. Finally, De Soto stressed the importance of informal rules of conduct and reported on the takings, the assignment of parcels and informal titles of property.

This view completely challenged the prevailing paradigm based on exploitation theory and purporting a different, and altruistic, logic among the poor. De Soto showed them as individuals pursuing their interests as anybody else, left out of the markets through a heavy layer of regulations, to which they reacted by going around them.

Takings took place in two ways: gradual or violent. The first took place in already existing slums or the surroundings of farms or mining camps where they were tolerated by their employers. The other mainly took place in government property and were led by a group of people from a neighbourhood or family or native group, which built a number high enough to take the land minimizing the risk of immediate expulsion. They would parcel the lots and adjudicate them, hire engineers or engineering students to draw a plan considering future areas for schools and parks and lawyers to submit formal requests for adjudication just to show they had started a formal process when facing the threat of eviction.

Informal negotiations among the squatters amounted to an unwritten 'takings contract' basically setting the limits of the settlement and the responsibilities of the informal organization charged with enforcing it. These are not the only informal organizations, though: clubs, parents' associations, informal schools (Tooley 1999) and churches are also present, among others. A similar pattern is found in most slums in Latin America.

VOLUNTARY SOLUTIONS

In the presence of transaction costs, negotiations over the effects of negative externalities are costly and voluntary solutions may fail. This has led many economists to disregard these kinds of solutions as well as view them as a third-party observer evaluating how high those costs are.

Nevertheless, for Austrian economists costs are subjective as well and inimical to the acting individual. Valuation becomes evident only as 'revealed preference' in action. Therefore, there is not much that an independent observer can say except that if the transaction was made it must be assumed that the parts thought 'it would lead to an increase in the value of production' and if not, that the subjective costs were higher than the subjective benefits.

In a field research experiment in a shanty town in the suburbs of Buenos Aires where there is no formal definition of property rights in housing, we found voluntary solutions widespread (Hidding, Ohlson and Krause 2010).

San Isidro is located some 20 miles north of the place where Buenos Aires was founded in 1580, a border zone between the areas occupied, or rather transited, by the Guaraní and Querandí tribes. Juan de Garay, the founder, distributed parcels in the northern coast of the River Plate among his men, somewhere beyond San Isidro. Only two centuries later a small town to be called San Isidro, Madrid's patron saint, started to grow and completed its development thanks to the migration of people produced by the economic boom of Argentina in the second half of the 19th century.

The large estates were parcelled and became the urban downtown, on the one hand, and a residential neighbourhood of large parcels and houses called Lomas de San Isidro. La Cava is an informal settlement, created mainly over government land, right beside the upscale Lomas. In 1946 the state water company, *Obras Sanitarias*, requested this plot of land from the federal government in order to use the red soil to filter water and manufacture bricks, generating a sink or 'cava,'[4] giving its name to the estate. The digging soon reached groundwater and the project was set aside. The sink was partially refilled and started to be settled by squatters to the 50 acres of its present area. Different censuses estimate between 1,700 to

---

[4] In Spanish, the word cava comes from to dig or to excavate.

2,100 houses and between 8,000 to 11,000 people, though it housed a larger number in the past.

In La Cava only 16 per cent of those polled say they have property title on their houses. Others even asked what that was. Among the rest, 17 per cent said they have an informal document, usually consisting of an informal sale/purchase invoice. Altogether, 84 per cent say they do not have formal documentation. On average, they lived 15 years at the same house, which shows low rotation. Those who say they have a property title also have lived at the same house 15 years on average. When asked how they got the house, 37 per cent bought it, while 26 per cent built it. In many cases they grew as annexes of a family house; 6 per cent say they got their house from the government.

We asked La Cava dwellers how they solved problems with neighbours when there was any conflict related to continued coexistence such as negative externalities. As an example, what happens if a neighbour plays high volume music or emits smoke or nasty odours? What if there are problems with the dividing walls or unclear borders between one property and the next, or someone builds a second floor blocking sunlight or damaging the other? Houses are quite precarious, small and contiguous, and these are real possibilities.

Confirming conclusions from a subjective cost interpretation of the Coase Theorem, 76 per cent said they solve these problems talking with the other side. They prefer not having intermediaries, nor from the same neighbourhood or outside and they avoid violence at any cost. Only in extreme cases do they resort to it. They know they cannot go to justice and that starting violence is a dangerous game. Besides, in a place where people live very close to each other, having good relations with your neighbours is an important asset. Those unresolved have to do with the nature of the neighbour, they must evaluate his/her reaction and sometimes it is better to bear the cost of the externality than the cost of attempting a solution.

In some cases informal organizations administer justice, basically on property and crime issues. In this second case, De Soto (1987: 30) reports on the procedure as allowing the presence of both the victim and the defendant, witnesses and a jury, contrasting with the formal Peruvian judicial system where there is no jury. Penalties include beating, undressing, burying or expulsion which comes with the loss of property. If there is resistance or the expulsion fails a new dweller is allowed to occupy the empty space in the criminal's lot, thereby reducing the informal property right. For homicides the criminal is turned in to the formal police or may get 'lynched,' particularly for child rape.

Regarding property issues, the Peruvian judicial system never got much involved in the solution of disputes. Even the administrative authorities, who were overburdened, turned to the informational organizations, and eventually accepted their decisions. 'Peace judges'[5] are usually called to mediate but they solve the disputes following not formal law but extra-legal norms.

Leaders of informal organizations act as first instance judges and the assemblies as a second instance dealing with issues of property delimitation and sale or rent contracts.

It is important to note that informal organizations administering justice on property issues face a competitive environment: its leaders are removed if they do not succeed in fulfilling the expectations of squatters either with regard to relations with formal authorities, the provision of public goods, or the administration of justice. De Soto also reports they have no remorse whatsoever in changing leadership without taking ideology or political alignment into consideration (p. 28); a view shared by Cravino (2009, p. 163)[6] on shanty towns in Buenos Aires, who finds 'delegates' take decisions and even impose measures of control in cases of 'daily life such as how they build, if they are noisy or have conflicts with other neighbors.' Such a competitive environment would reduce agency problems and align the decisions of judges closer to the values of squatters.

Zarazaga (2010a) has researched on the role of what is called 'punteros' in Argentina, political bosses in poor and informal neighbourhoods who prosper finding and assuring votes to certain political leaders in exchange for many different services. The 'puntero' is a long-time resident who is able to get social plans, food, or building materials in exchange for votes at the time of election. Mayors in these districts build hierarchical networks with these 'punteros' in order to keep political control and get reelected. Most of the mayors in the suburbs of Buenos Aires, where Zarazaga's research is focused, have been reelected several times. But while the vote is the reward for the politician, the 'puntero' may get a fraction of the salary of dwellers or even sexual favours. What is important to our consideration is that it is an exchange based on convenience and devoid of any real political content. The role of 'puntero' is based on a reputation to deliver the goods, he/she knows each dweller and what his/her specific needs are and will keep that position as long as he/she can continue delivering and

---

[5]   Administrative judges dealing mainly with the violation of local regulations.

[6]   'A look at internal conflictiveness, representational disputes, the existence of multiple base organizations taking up particular problems – kindergartens, community restaurants, etc. – or competition to get followers – parishioners for churches or voters for political parties –, shows us there is no pure and undisputed representation,' p. 72.

is available at any time of the day.[7] Otherwise they will be remorselessly abandoned and removed.

As part of his research Zarazaga (2010b), interviewed 120 'punteros' in different Buenos Aires slums, 92 per cent of which had an average of 24 years of political and social activities there, 94 per cent knew the composition and specific needs of each family to which she would deliver goods and services, and 92 per cent knew also the political preferences of the group. Reputation comes from 'problem solving,' including the resolution of disputes.

In Maquis Park, Chicago, Illinois, Venkatesh (2006, p. 4) reports similar services: 'Big Cat (leader of the local gang) not only helped Marlene to police younger gang members; he also gave money to her block club for kids' parties, and members of his gang patrolled the neighborhood late at night because police presence was a rarity.' And regarding the role of churches:

> Pastor Wilkins belongs to this small group of six to ten preachers (the number changes over time) who are the first point of contact for breaches of contract and social disputes between shady dealers –street gangs, prostitutes and burglars among them. These pastors and ministers will retrieve stolen property, mend a broken relationship between pimp and prostitute, and prevent a street gang battle from escalating into a war. One minister estimated that, between 1989 and 1995, he earned approximately $10,000 a year for such services. (p. 258)

JUSTICE

De Soto assigns the informal settlement management organizations a 'value maximizing' goal:

> According to ILD research, the main goal of informal organizations arising from a 'takings contract' consists in protecting and increasing the value of property accessed. In this regard, they perform a number of functions such as negotiations with authorities, protecting public order, attempting the provision of public services, registration of property in the settlement and administration of justice. (1987, p. 27)

Does this mean they follow a Coasean efficiency principle? The reference, though, relates to negotiations with formal authorities, not among

---

[7]   Also Cravino (2009, p. 163): 'The political identity of delegates is diverse, and many times fluctuating, and it does not seem to be the main element of their reputation. Politics, more than an ideological question seems to be constructed as a way to channel monetary resources, goods and services to the neighborhood.'

dwellers. They are forced to negotiate with authorities because informal rights are also weak and vulnerable and dwellers will value any step to consolidate them. Negotiations include different problems ranging from the recognition of the possession to the provision of basic services and infrastructure. De Soto or Zarazaga, though, do not go into what criteria these organizations or social leaders follow in these cases. We will try to deduce them from other sources.

Squatters show a 'Lockean' view on the origin of property rights, possession through occupation. Cravino (2006) reports the following ways to get an informal house:

1. Occupation of a parcel and self-construction of a house; this is 'original possession' and mixing labour with it.
2. Accessing to a portion of a relative's parcel, building a house beside or on top of it. In this case the original possession was the relative who 'donates' part of the possession.
3. 'Allegamiento': when a house is shared by a relative or friend, particularly for a short period of time to allow the newcomer to find a place.
4. Houses lent by relatives, neighbours or friends. Cravino (2009, p. 106) reports an ambiguity between 'taking care' and 'keeping' a house. Even if lent, with time those in the custody of the house will consider they acquired a right over it, particularly if they made improvements or maintenance work.
5. Occupation of a deserted house (the former owner was an immigrant and returned to his/her original place of residence). Usually this requires the approval of a community organization, a delegate or a church.
6. In only a few cases, they get housing from the local government.

Chávez Molina (2010) finds the same principle with the allocation of stands at the informal trade fair of Francisco Solano. A southern suburb of Buenos Aires, it is the place of one of the largest trade fairs in the city, opening on Wednesdays and Saturdays with over 1600 stands offering food items, textiles, shoes and all kinds of fake products. Although the fair as such has been approved and is regulated by the local government, this one has only authorized 600 stands and there is no control on the products sold at it. In fact, it is as though there were two fairs within the same area: one more formal and the 'tail' as they call it, completely informal.

The existence of these informal markets is visible in any undeveloped country and even in some developed ones. What is relevant to our subject here is that there is no formal regulation on the place to be occupied by each trader. All those interviewed by Chávez Molina (2010, p. 153) said the place has to be 'earned,' through the constant participation at the fair and the ensuing relations with other traders. Anyone can set up shop at the fair, starting at the 'tail' which is at the end of the fair or in lateral streets, and only through constant participation and personal relations with established traders will he be able to move to better locations when places are made available. If someone does not show up for a month, no one will question some other trader taking the place, although they may consider situations such as sickness leave.

A side note of interest for Austrian economists derives from this importance of first possession and relates to the need of a formal property title. Most Austrian economists would emphasize the importance of well-defined property rights, but does this require a 'formal' title or just the 'perception of the stability of possession'? In fact, the latter is what the formal title gives. The advantages of a well-functioning registration and titling system have been recognized by Austrians and stressed in De Soto's following book (2002), in this last case pointing to the need of a title to access bank-provided mortgage credit. Empirical studies have also shown the impact of titling in investment (Galiani and Schargrodsky 2005) and also on the quality, size and structure of houses, on children's outcomes, and the formation of beliefs towards property and markets.

Other authors question whether a formal title is needed to secure possession and protect investments, or could other processes achieve a similar result. For example, van Gelder (2010, p. 15) comments:

> Factors such as the official recognition of a settlement, introduction of infrastructure and services, and other factors that could strengthen de facto security of tenure were considered more fundamental than holding a legal document for a plot (e.g., Gilbert, 2002). With respect to accessing credit, titled owners did not take out a bank loan more frequently than residents who lacked title. In El Tala only three people with a property title had taken out a mortgage loan in the previous five years versus two people in the untitled part of that settlement. More people – eight in the titled and five in the untitled areas – had taken out loans at lending institutions that charge high interest rates but do not require property as collateral. In other words, the owners did not pledge their dwellings as collateral to obtain the loans.

Ostuni and van Gelder (2008, p. 205), appeal to a 'subjective construction' or perception of security that could certainly come from a property title but also from the goodwill of government officials, a laissez-faire government policy regarding settlements, or the supply of basic services. Baltrusis (2009, p. 71) reports that prices in informal 'favelas' in Guarulhos, close to Sao Paulo, had an average price of R$ 3,700 in Sao Rafael while those at Cabucú, a recently occupied slum, were only R$ 600.

Regardless of the form it takes, the perception of security is determinative, and adjudicative decisions by mediators or informal judges would therefore tend to stress it. This speaks against a cost/benefit analysis on such decisions since making the allocation of property rights dependent on a judge's evaluation of a net result would bring instability back, a point raised by Block (1995), though also mentioned by Coase.[8]

Rental contracts seem to abide by a strict property right principle: if the tenant cannot pay she must leave the room or house immediately. There is not much flexibility and renegotiation is not usual. Few tenants resist eviction (Cravino 2006, p. 206).

Dispute Settlement

Up to this point, values and visions of slum dwellers seem to be concerned more with 'rights' than 'efficiency' as determinant of dispute settlement. Another source to check on this will come from an unexpected reference for Austrian economists: a Marxian view. Boaventura Sousa Santos (1977) conducted extended research on an alternative legal system in the slums of Rio de Janeiro.[9] In order to study an environment of 'legal pluralism,' Santos presents a model Brazilian slum he names as Pasargada, the name of the ancient Persian capital.

Pasagarda is one of the largest and oldest squatter settlements in Rio de Janeiro. Begun around 1932, it had a population of 18 000 by 1950 and 50 000 by the end of the 70s. It is divided into two parts: one on the hill and the other down the valley where a polluted river runs and the most precarious dwellings are located. Most of the houses are on the hill. The streets, as in many other shanty towns are narrow and muddy with sewage running through them. The houses are mainly made of brick and mortar with electricity and running water, with those who do not have it getting it from public taps or neighbours.

There are several factories in the surrounding areas where many dwellers work, others are entrepreneurs, public officials, municipal workers and odd-jobbers. There is an intense social life channelled through recreational clubs, soccer teams, churches, the electricity commission and a residents'

---

[8]   'It would therefore seem desirable that the courts should understand the economic consequences of their decisions and should, insofar as this is possible without creating too much uncertainty about the legal position itself, take these consequences into account when making their decisions.' (Coase, 1960)

[9]   'Guided by a Marxian theory of society and of law in society, the systematic comparison of the different types of legal pluralism will establish the possible relations between official and unofficial law (vertical or horizontal, integration or confrontation, etc.).' (Sousa Santos 1977, p. 10).

organization. It is clearly one of the informal organizations that De Soto describes for Peruvian informal towns. The association has an elected board and a president, and members pay a monthly fee.

The association, particularly its president and treasurer, the two paid full-time officers, ratify contracts taken to them, particularly on the sale of houses, requesting a proof of ownership and even writing the text in accordance with agreed terms. The contract is read and signed by the two parties and two witnesses, stamped with the association's stamp with copies for both parties and a third is kept on file. The contracts ratified by the resident's association are quite the same as in the formal word, but since the land formally belongs to the state, when a house is sold and bought it is called 'benfeitoria' or improvements over the land. An example considered by Sousa Santos (1977, p 51), reads as follows:

> I, EL [full identification], declare that I sold to Mr. OM [full identification] a *benfeitoria* of my property located at [location]. He paid [amount] as down payment and the balance of the Price will be paid in eight promissory notes beginning [date]. In case Mr. OM defaults in making the payment for three months, this document will be declared invalid. This agreement is free and legal and the property is free of charge and encumbrances. The land does not enter in the transaction because it belongs to the State.
> This contract will be signed by the parties and by two witnesses in two copies, one of which will be kept by the Association for any contingencies that may arise.
> Date:
> Signature:
> Witnesses:

Others include the sale of a room within a house and the right of first refusal in case the new owners want to sell; the sale of a house with the obligation to the buyer of building a wall; the donation of a house; the sale of a house by an illiterate and his son acting as witness but confirming the acceptance of a legitimate heir; and the requirement of the legal spouse's consent. Formal procedures are very important, the president requests proof of ownership and in cases where it is lost the testimony of witnesses.

With regard to the principles applied to dispute settlement, they make no explicit reference to efficiency concerns. Let's consider another of the Sousa Santos cases (1977, p. 61):

Mr. GM comes to the RA with Mr. MT and explains his problem to the presidente.

> MR. GM: You know I own that *benfeitoria* on [location]. I want to sell it to Mr. MT but the problem is that I cannot obtain the consent of my wife. She left home nine months ago and never came back.

PRESIDENTE: Where is she now?

MR. GM: I don't know. Actually I don't think that her consent is very important in this case because, after all, the whole house was built by my efforts. Besides, there is no document of purchase of construction materials signed by her.

PRESIDENTE (silence, then): Well, I know you are an honest person and your wife has behaved very badly. (Silence.) How long has she been away?

MR. GM: Nine months.

PRESIDENTE: That is really not very long. (Silence.) I think that your oldest son should agree to the sale of the *benfeitoria* and sign the document as a third witness.

MR. GM AND MR. BT: We agree.

MR. GM TO MR. BT: We could draft the document right now . . ..

The document is then drafted in the following way:

> I, Mr. GM [full identification], being separated from my wife, who disappeared without notice, and living as a good father with my six children, declare that I sold a *benfeitoria* of my property located on [location] to Mr. BT [full identification]. He will pay immediately [amount] and the balance will be paid on a basis of [amount] per month. We declare that since there are no documents in my wife's name or in mine, I sell this *benfeitoria* without charges or encumbrances. Indeed it was built through my own efforts. I sign this declaration in the presence of two witnesses and in two copies, one of which will be kept in the Residents' Association in case any contingency arises.
>
> Date:
> Signatures:
> Signatures of three witnesses:
> (one of whom is Mr. GM's oldest son)

It could be argued that there is an efficiency justification in allowing the sale to take place since the asset would then go to the most valued use, but although that is the consequence, it is no part of the argumentation on the decision. Acting in 'good faith' is the main principle for the following decision:

> Mr. SB sold his shack to Mr. JQ for Cr\$1,000.53. The purchaser paid half of the price immediately and promised to pay the rest in installments. On the date agreed upon he paid the first installment (Cr\$50). The second installment of Cr\$200 was also paid on time.
>
> However, instead of giving the money to the seller himself, Mr. JQ gave it to the seller's wife. She kept the money for herself and spent it at her pleasure. Besides, she was unfaithful to her husband and had gone to bed with the purchaser's brother. Having learned this, Mr. SB, the seller, killed his wife and demanded repossession of the shack. The purchaser complained that he had duly paid the installments and intended to pay the balance. He had given the second installment to the woman in the belief that she would take it to her husband.
>
> The seller's sister was called to the Association to represent her brother who

could not come since he was being sought by the police. The *presidente* said that it would not be fair to revoke the sale since the purchaser had acted in good faith throughout. On the other hand, the seller should not be injured by the purchaser's failure to tender the money directly to him; therefore the installment in question should not be credited to the balance of the price.

The *presidente* finally decided, and the parties agreed, that the purchaser would pay the balance in six installments, three of Cr$100 and three of Cr$50.

There is no mention here on the different valuations of both parties regarding the shack nor to the allocation towards the most valued use, but a 'classical' approach of defining and allocating rights.

Negligence and 'Coming to the Nuisance'

Similar considerations apply in negligence law, where an 'efficiency' view is derived from the Coase Theorem in the search for a more precise definition of it, embodied in what has been called the Hand formula, an evaluation of the actor's burden against the degree of loss multiplied by the probability of harm (Rizzo 1980). For the same arguments on the subjectivity of value and the impossibility of economic calculation for a planner/judge, Austrians have adhered to a traditional strict liability doctrine which obviates the need for a centralized cost-benefit analysis. The efficiency approach not only demands an evaluation of the defendant and plaintiff's negligence but also, in the case were both were negligent, an evaluation of the 'least cost avoider,' that party that could have avoided the damage at least cost.

At this stage it may be obvious to point out that in the slums cases of accidents are evaluated according to what actually happened, not on a speculation of 'what might have happened in two alternate worlds and then compare the outcomes' (Rizzo 1980, p. 292). Strict liability provides a stable environment for the causal agent that incentives a certain level of analysis on precautionary care,[10] which might be 'efficient' as a result of the accumulated wisdom regarding similar cases. Causal agents are

---

[10]   'In a dynamic world in which the uncertainties of technological change, the ambiguities of foreseeability, and the absence of a unique objective measure of social cost all conspire to make the efficiency paradigm a delusion, the importance of certainty in the legal order is clear. Strict liability obviates or minimizes the need for courts to grapple, if only implicitly, with such impossibly elusive problems as forseeability, cheaper-cost avoider, social cost, and second best. It provides a series of basically simple, strict presumptions. The *prima facie* case is based on straightforward commonsense causal paradigms, whereas the defenses and later pleas minimize the number of issues which must be considered in a given case . . . This greater certainty promotes efficiency in the basic

usually liable for foreseeable types of harm although they may not be held liable for all or some unforeseeable consequences. The simplicity of strict liability as compared to a cheap-cost avoider analysis promotes certainty in the informal legal order and contributes to a better definition of property rights.

The pattern repeats with the doctrine of 'coming to the nuisance' or 'first come first served' in tort law (Cordato 1998). According to it a causal agent should not be liable for the effects of negative externalities towards an un-owned resource if she arrived first and/or the effects were not questioned by a present owner. If efficiency requires determination of who would have been the cheap cost avoider, in this case it requires 'who should have been here first' in order to maximize total social output.

As in the case before, the doctrine would be efficient in a different way, providing a stable legal environment that reduces the costs of uncertainty. Cordato (1998, p. 289) gives the example of a farmer who builds a pig farm with its associated smells spreading towards neighbouring land. If such land has no owner or if the owner does not complain for a certain period of time it is assumed the farmer has homesteaded such a use. If, later, the property is considered for development and the doctrine is in place, prices will reflect the existence of this easement giving information to 'potential comers to the nuisance,'[11] who, in knowledge of the existence of the rule would take that into account in the costing and pricing of the project and may even never file suit. The prevalence of the principle of 'first comer' in slums has already been stated.

CONCLUSION

Slums are informal worlds where the state is absent in many respects, certainly in the prevention and resolution of negative externalities. It is

institutional sense because property rights, in effect, become more clearly or definitely defined.' (Rizzo 1980, p. 317).

[11] 'Such a rule would send important signals to potential comers to a nuisance. In the example, those considering making use of the adjoining property would do so in full knowledge that the farmer has preceded them and, as such, has certain rights with respect to its use. This knowledge, and the certainty about future rights and obligations that it would generate, would be factored into any decisions that are made with respect to the use of the adjacent land, ex ante. Anyone planning to build a house on the land would do so in full knowledge that they would either have to put up with the odors from the pig farm, incur the costs of insulating themselves from the odors, or negotiate a "Coasean" type bargain with the farmer.' (Cordato 1998, p. 289).

an interesting case to find out how dwellers deal with problems of such a nature.

According to Coase, in the absence of transaction costs these problems would be solved and the asset would be allocated to its most valuable use without regard to who has the right. In such case there is no need for governmental solutions; voluntary negotiations would be enough. For Austrians, 'costs' are subjective and are only known as 'revealed preferences.' Life in slums shows that there are many instances where voluntary solutions take place, showing subjective benefits must be higher than subjective costs.

In the case of high subjective transaction costs, an institutional device would help reduce them and slums show such a role is fulfilled by a number of informal organizations, representatives or mediators. However, these do not follow an efficiency rationale, but rely on a classical Lockean view of rights and justice, informal strict liability, and coming to the nuisance doctrines.

Therefore, the normative advice should be taken with a pinch of salt. Does it make sense to advise judges to change the way they have been adjudicating problems of negative externalities when they already have one that has been used for centuries? In a way, 'The Problem of Social Cost' shows that judges seem not to have a clearly defined criteria and they adjudicate sometimes in one direction, then in another. For example, 'Cooke vs Forbes,' 'Bryant vs Lefever' and 'Bass vs Gregory' are all cases of negative externalities through air pollution and Coase (1960) tries to show the different decisions judges make even though circumstances are similar. And if there is no well-established criteria, it may be worthwhile to consider the one of efficiency.

For Austrians, though, 'adjudicating efficiency' is difficult if not impossible and it may be the result of a long and evolved tradition of adjudicating 'rights.'

REFERENCES

Baltrusis, Nelson (2009), 'Mercado informal de terras e vivendas in Sao Paulo,' 15(2) *Revista Bitácora Urbano Territorial*, 55–78.
Block, Walter (1977), 'Coase and Demsetz on Private Property Rights,' 1(2) *Journal of Libertarian Studies*, 111–15.
Block, Walter (1995), 'Ethics, Efficiency, Coasian Property Rights, and Psychic Income: A Reply to Demsetz,' 8(2) *Review of Austrian Economics*, 61–125.
Boettke, Peter J. (1997), 'Where did Economics go Wrong? Equilibrium as a Flight from Reality,' 11(1) *Critical Review*, Winter, 11–64.
Chávez Molina, Eduardo (2010), *La construcción social de la confianza en el mercado informal: los feriantes de Francisco Solano* (Buenos Aires: Nueva Trilce).
Coase, Ronald H. (1960), 'The Problem of Social Costs,' 3 *Journal of Law and Economics*, 1–44.
Cordato, Roy (1992) [2007], *Efficiency and Externalities in an Open-Ended Universe: A*

Modern Austrian Perspective (Auburn, Alabama: The Ludwig von Mises Institute; originally published by Kluwer Academic Publishers, 1992).

Cordato, Roy (1998), 'Time Passage and the Economics of Coming to the Nuisance: Reassessing the Coasean Perspective,' 20 *Campbell Law Review*, 273.

Cravino, María Cristina (2006), *Las Villas de la Ciudad: Mercado e Informalidad Urbana* (Los Polvorines: Universidad Nacional de General Sarmiento).

Cravino, María Cristina (2009), *Vivir en la villa: Relatos, trayectorias y estrategias habitacionales* (Los Polvorines: Universidad Nacional de General Sarmiento).

Demsetz, Harold (1979), 'Ethics and Efficiency in Property Right Systems,' in Mario J. Rizzo, (ed.), *Time, Uncertainty and Profit: Exploration of Austrian Themes* (Lexington, Massachusetts: D.C. Heath and Co.), 97–116.

De Soto, Hernando (1987) in collaboration with E. Ghersi and M. Ghibellini, *El Otro Sendero*, (Buenos Aires: Editorial Sudamericana).

De Soto, Hernando (2002), *El Misterio del Capital. Por qué el capitalismo triunfa en Occidente y fracasa en el resto del mundo* (Buenos Aires: Editorial Sudamericana).

Galiani, Sebastián and Ernesto Schargrodsky (2005), 'Property Rights for the Poor: Effects of Land Titling,' *Documento de Trabajo* 06/2005, Escuela de Negocios, Universidad Torcuato Di Tella, Buenos Aires.

Gilbert, A.G. (2002), 'On the mystery of capital and the myths of Hernando de Soto: What difference does legal title make?' 26 *International Development Planning Review*, 1–19.

Hidding Ohlson, Marcos and Martín Krause (2010), 'La provision de bienes públicos en ausencia del Estado: el caso de La Cava': (unpublished manuscript). Available at: http://works.bepress.com/martin_krause/44/.

Neuwirth, Robert (2006), *Shadow Cities: A Billion Squatters, A New Urban World* (New York: Routledge).

Ostuni, Fernando and Jean-Louis van Gelder (2008), 'No sé si legal. . . ¡pero legítimo es!!: Percepciones sobre la seguridad en la tenencia de títulos de propiedad de barrios informales del Gran Buenos Aires,' in María Cristina Cravino (2008), *Los mil barrios (in)formales: Aportes para la construcción de un observatorio del hábitat popular del Área Metropolitana de Buenos Aires* (Los Polvorines: Universidad Nacional de General Sarmiento).

Rizzo, Mario J. (1980), 'Law amid Flux: The Economics of Negligence and Strict Liability in Tort,' 9(2) *The Journal of Legal Studies*, 291–318.

Smolka, Martim O. and Claudia M. De Cesare (2010), 'Property Tax and Informal Property: The Challenge of Third World Cities,' *Lincoln Institute of Land Policy Working Paper*, WP10MS2 (Cambridge, Massachusetts: Lincoln Institute of Land Policy).

Sousa Santos, Boaventura (1977), 'The Law of the Oppressed: The Construction and Reproduction of Legality in Pasagarda,' 12(1) *Law & Society Review*, 55–126.

Stearns, Maxwell L. and Todd J. Zywicki (2009), *Public Choice Concepts and Applications in Law*, American Casebook Series (Saint Paul, Minnesota: Thomson Reuters).

Tooley, James N. (1999), *The Global Education Industry: Lessons from Private Education in Developing Countries* (London: Institute of Economic Affairs).

Van Gelder, Jean-Louis (2010), 'Tenure Security and Housing Improvement in Buenos Aires,' *Land Lines* (Cambridge, Massachusetts: Lincoln Institute of Land Policy).

Venkatesh, Sudhir Alladi (2006), *Off the Books: The Underground Economy of the Urban Poor* (Cambridge, Massachusetts: Harvard University Press).

Zarazaga, Rodrigo (2010a), 'El Jesuita que desde Harvard estudia las redes clientelares,' Buenos Aires: *La Nación*, 20/6/2010.

Zarazaga, Rodrigo (2010b), 'Entre la ausencia del Estado y la presencia del puntero: racionalidad política en el conurbano bonaerense,' presentation at the *Seminar on Informal Towns*: Buenos Aires, 2/11/2010. Available at: http://ciima.org.ar/2010/11/12/presentaciones-seminario-la-problematica-de-las-villas-en-argentina/.

3. Coase, Posner, and Austrian law and economics *

Peter T. Leeson

1. INTRODUCTION

A hallmark of the Austrian approach to economic science is its emphasis on individuals' beliefs.[1] This emphasis derives from the importance the Austrian approach attaches to subjectivism. According to that approach, to understand observed patterns of human decision making and its results, one must understand the "meanings" humans attach to their actions and the problem situations they confront. Those "meanings" are beliefs.[2]

All beliefs are subjectively true: they're true for the persons who hold them. But not all beliefs are equal. Some of them are "mere opinions;" they have no objective element to them. For example, I believe cigars are divine. This influences how I see the world, the people in it, and how I behave, but my belief is just my judgment. Beliefs such as this are purely subjective.[3]

Other beliefs are understandings about the way the world works that have an objective element to them. Like mere opinions, they're always subjectively true, but objectively, they may be true or false. For example, I believe that milk curdles because microorganisms in it convert lactose into lactic acid, "clotting" the milk. Other persons, certainly historically, and perhaps in some places still today, believe that milk curdles because a witch has given it the "evil eye." My belief is objectively true; the witch's-eye belief is objectively false. Science tells us as much.

The objectively false beliefs individuals hold are called superstitions. Superstitions influence how the persons who hold them see the world, the

---

  * This chapter was previously published as: Leeson, Peter T. 2012. "An Austrian Approach to Law and Economics, with Special Reference to Superstition." *Review of Austrian Economics* 25: 185–98.

  [1] On the importance of subjectivism, "meaning," and thus individuals' beliefs in the Austrian approach to economics, see Boettke (2010).

  [2] Or at least those "meanings" are determined by beliefs.

  [3] Though, admittedly, I find the fact that some people hold the exact opposite view about cigars impossible to understand. Perhaps they are smoking the wrong cigars. As I write this note, I smoke a 2008 San Cristobal. I can assure the reader that it is divine.

people in it, and how persons behave as strongly as their mere opinions and objectively true beliefs. In influencing these things, like other kinds of beliefs, superstitions may also influence institutions.[4]

To the extent that scholarship in law and economics treats individuals' beliefs at all, most of this scholarship proceeds as though individuals' beliefs were either the opinion kind or the objectively true kind. Law and economics has largely ignored superstition. Part of this chapter's purpose is to help remedy that.

My argument is that, contrary to what I suspect is most readers' intuition, many objectively false beliefs *improve* social cooperation and productivity. They make their holders' societies better off. This is not true of all superstitions, of course. But it is true of many of them, including some of those that seem the most ridiculous on the surface. Critically for law and economics, many socially productive superstitions produce their desirable effects by influencing, or "working through," the legal system—the law and institutions of its enforcement.[5]

The other part of this chapter's purpose is to discuss what the components of a specifically "Austrian" law and economics might consist of. Given the importance the Austrian approach to economic science assigns to individuals' beliefs, such a law and economics would necessarily assign beliefs a central place in its study. Further, given that many beliefs influence the legal system, such a law and economics would also seek to analyze the endogenous emergence of legal institutions in light of those beliefs, as well as the endogenous emergence of beliefs in light of legal institutions. My argument is that Ronald Coase's conception of law and economics precludes such analysis. In contrast, Richard Posner's conception facilitates it. An "Austrian" law and economics can't be built on Coasean foundations; it can and should be built on Posnerian ones.

2. COASE, POSNER, AND THE AUSTRIAN WAY

As Coase (1996: 103) points out, there are "two parts" to law and economics. These parts overlap significantly at points; though, in Coase's

---

[4] As I point out below, beliefs may themselves sometimes constitute institutions as well. Thus, I will at points distinguish between belief and non-belief institutions.

[5] This chapter develops thoughts connected to a closely related research project I am currently engaged in that investigates the economics of seemingly absurd legal institutions. Superstition plays a prominent role in much of this work. See Leeson (2011, 2012, 2013a, 2013b, 2014a, 2014b, 2014c), Leeson and Coyne (2012), and Leeson, Boettke, and Lemke (2014).

words, they remain "quite separate." The first branch of law and economics might be called the Coasean one after its founder, Ronald Coase. The second branch might be called the Posnerian one after its founder, Richard Posner.[6] These branches display "sharp differences" (Cameron 1995: 1).

The Coasean branch of law and economics is narrow. It sees the productive and legitimate scope of law-and-economic inquiry as restricted to studying "the influence of the legal system on the working of the economic system" (Coase 1996: 104). This includes, for example, studying how antitrust law affects industrial organization, how labor law affects labor markets, and so on.

The Coasean branch of law and economics' narrowness results from Coase's narrow conception of economics. Coase defines economics, and thus the productive and legitimate scope of economic inquiry, topically. Economics is the study of "the economy"—traditional market decision making, such as that of consumers, independent producers, and firms. As Coase put it, "I think economists do have a subject matter: the study of the working of the economic system, a system in which we earn and spend our incomes" (1998: 93). Or, as he characterized his view elsewhere, "What economists study is the working of the social institutions which bind together the economic system: firms, markets for goods and services, labour markets, capital markets, the banking system, international trade, and so on" (Coase 1978: 206–7).

Because of the Coasean branch's narrow conception of economics, and thus law and economics, that branch precludes institutional endogeneity. It excludes analysis of nonmarket decision making from the realm of productive and legitimate economic analysis and thus excludes economic investigation of the decision making that gives rise to the law and legal (or other) institutions. The Coasean branch of law and economics insists on treating the law and legal institutions as exogenous and given constraints on the decision making of conventional economic actors in conventional markets.

This branch of law and economics not only precludes institutional endogeneity; it considers attempts to use economics to study nonmarket decision making that gives rise to institutions as foolhardy. According to Coase, economists are fundamentally unfit to contribute to the development of knowledge in "nonmarket disciplines," such as law, where their knowledge

---

[6]   On the differences between the Coasean and Posnerian branches of law and economics, see Harnay and Marciano (2009). See also the exchange between Coase (1993a) and Posner (1993a). Coase and Posner have both noted the differences in their respective branches elsewhere too. See, for instance, Coase (1993b) and Posner (1987, 1993c).

is impoverished compared to the scholars who properly occupy them. As he puts it, "an ability to discern and understand these purposes [i.e., those of nonmarket decision makers] and the character of the institutional framework (how, for example, the political and legal systems actually operate) will require specialized knowledge not likely to be acquired by those who work in some other discipline" (Coase 1978: 208).

Coase sees this "fundamental unfitness" as fating attempts to use rational choice theory to understand nonmarket decision making to failure. As he put it, "I would not expect" persons making such attempts "to continue indefinitely their triumphal advance and it may be that they will be forced to withdraw from some of the fields which they are now so busily cultivating." "[T]he movement by economists into the other social sciences which has as its aim, the improvement of these other social sciences . . . seems to me likely to be temporary" (1978: 209; 211). Indeed, according to Coase, economic imperialists' attempts to use the logic of choice to understand nonmarket decision making, such as that which gives rise to legal and other institutions, may simply reflect their inability to make contributions to the study of "the economy" proper. As he put it, these "economists are looking for fields in which they can have some success" (Coase 1978: 203).

The Posnerian branch of law and economics is very different from the Coasean one, and much broader. The Posnerian branch uses economics to study the law and the legal system; it engages in an economic analysis of the law. As Posner (1975: 759) described it, this branch concerns itself with "the application of the theories . . . of economics to the central institutions of the legal system, including the common law doctrines of negligence, contract, and property; the theory and practice of punishment; civil, criminal, and administrative procedure; the theory of legislation and of rulemaking; and law enforcement and judicial administration."

Central to the Posnerian branch of law and economics is the idea that economics is a method of inquiry rather than the topic of one. Similar to the way that Coase's narrow, topical conception of economics drives the Coasean branch's narrow, topical conception of law and economics, Posner's broad, method-based conception of economics drives the Posnerian branch's broad, method-based conception of law and economics. In the Posnerian conception, the economic method is applicable to human decision making in general. It includes narrowly "economic" decision making in the sense that the Coasean branch is concerned with, but it also encompasses human decision making outside this context—nonmarket decision making, for example in the creation of law.

In sharp contrast to the Coasean branch of law and economics, the

Posnerian branch permits, and indeed demands, institutional endogeneity. Nonmarket decision making is as much decision making as that which occurs in the context of conventional, explicit markets. Thus economic analysis of the legal system is not only permissible; if one wants to understand the central phenomena underlying society—not only how social interaction responds to those phenomena but how those phenomena respond to social interaction (i.e., their sources)—economic analysis of legal (and other) institutions is indispensable. As Posner (1972: 439) put it in his statement of the *Journal of Legal Studies'* purpose the founding year of that journal, "economic theory provides a powerful tool not only for the critique of legal institutions (normative analysis) but also for explaining such institutions (positive analysis)."

In one of his earlier articles appropriately entitled "The Economic Approach to Law" (as opposed to, say, "Studying the Law's Impact on the Economy"), Posner (1975) distinguishes between "old" (i.e., pre-1960) and "new" law and economics. The former, he points out, "confined its attention to laws governing explicit economic relationships." The latter "recognizes no such limitation on the domain of economic analysis of law." Ironically, while in one sense Coase is rightly considered the father of the "new" law and economics, the Coasean branch of that law and economics is essentially what Posner describes as the "old" mode. In contrast, the Posnerian branch developed the bulk of the "new" one. Thus, one might substitute "Coasean" for "old" and "Posnerian" for "new" in Posner's sentences and do little violence to the essential distinction he draws, while rendering that distinction in terms that comport more closely with the distinction between the Coasean and Posnerian branches of law and economics I described above.

The Coasean branch of law and economics fits uncomfortably with the Austrian approach to economic science. Indeed, in important respects the Coasean branch is antithetical to it. In contrast, the Posnerian branch of law and economics connects seamlessly to that approach.

The Austrian approach to economic science is rooted in what Ludwig von Mises (1949) called praxeology: the logic of human action. In that approach, *all* purposive behavior falls under the purview of economic study, whether it is the conventionally "economic" kind in markets or some other kind, such as decision making in the political realm, or the legal one. The praxeological perspective seeks to use economics—the logic of choice—to understand purposeful behavior in whatever realm it occurs.[7]

---

[7]   On the use of the logic of choice in applied work per the Austrian approach, see Mises (1957).

In that perspective, economics is everywhere; it is not relegated to a small, confined place called "the economy."[8]

Because of the Austrian approach's praxeological roots, legal institutions occupy a place of particular importance in it. This is true not only because legal institutions influence the incentives and information that individuals confront in their "economic" interactions, i.e., for "Coasean reasons." Equally importantly, legal institutions occupy a place of prominence in the Austrian approach because they are themselves at one level or another the result of purposive behavior, i.e., for "Posnerian reasons." As a consequence, in the Austrian approach, institutions generally, and legal institutions in particular, are objects of praxeological inquiry. They are aspects of decision making properly treated by economic inquiry and thus amenable to investigation using the theory of rational choice.[9]

The praxeological roots of the Austrian approach combined with that approach's insistence on the importance of individuals' "meanings"—their beliefs—for understanding human behavior and that behavior's results means that an Austrian law and economics must, if it is to be in any sense "Austrian," centrally concerned with using the logic of choice to investigate legal institutions' emergence and how individuals' beliefs operate in that logic. In precluding such investigation, the Coasean branch of law and economics precludes the kind of law-and-economic analysis that could in any sense be "Austrian." It cannot serve as a foundation for an Austrian law and economics. The Posnerian branch of law and economics can. By offering the possibility of such an analysis, and making such analysis central to economic study, the latter supplies a suitable framework for an Austrian law and economics. It makes such a law and economics possible.

The discussion that follows sits squarely in the Posnerian branch of law and economics. This is what makes it "Austrian." I limit myself to using economic analysis— rational choice theory—to examine how superstition contributes to and enables the successful operation of legal institutions in four cases. Two of the cases I consider are not original to me. They have been analyzed economically by others, but they supply useful illustrations of the law and economics of beliefs, in particular objectively false ones, and

---

[8]   The Austrian approach to economic science is, in my view, the same one Becker (1976, 1993) articulates. It views economics as a method rather than a subject matter. On the importance of this approach to economics (and Becker more generally) for the development of the Posnerian branch of law and economics, see Posner (1993b).

[9]   That theory is based on the unflinching application of three combined assumptions: maximizing behavior, market equilibrium, and stable preferences. See Becker (1976).

thus useful illustrations of a necessary component of an Austrian law and economics. The other two cases I consider are my own.

My discussion takes the beliefs it considers as given and examines their implications for various aspects of legal systems. However, for reasons I describe below, many beliefs are themselves institutions. Thus, they too should be subjected to the scrutiny of economic analysis and accordingly endogenized through the theory of rational choice. I will make some comments on this enterprise and what it implies for law and economics, and Austrian law and economics in particular, before concluding.

3.   WITCHES AND MAGIC BEANS

Given Posner's approach to law and economics, it should not be surprising that he supplied perhaps the first research one might regard as falling within the domain of the law and economics of belief more generally and the law and economics of superstition in particular. Posner's (1980) contribution was to demonstrate that the objectively false beliefs that permeate some primitive societies perform socially valuable functions, in particular as they relate to improving the operation of law. One such belief is in witches.

A belief in witches—persons who malevolently wield supernatural powers that derive in some way from a close relationship with "evil spirits"—is prominent in primitive societies. No such persons exist; the belief in witches is a superstition. Yet individuals in primitive societies leverage this superstition to facilitate the enforcement of primitive law. Law here should be understood in the broad sense of rules that define acceptable interpersonal conduct: social rules. Primitive societies typically lack anything resembling what, in the developed world, one would describe as government, which might promulgate such law formally. Nonetheless primitive societies have laws. Without them, no society would be possible. Likewise, without some mechanism of enforcing such laws in the absence of government, no society would be possible. It's in this context that the witch superstition is important.

One important law in many primitive societies dictates that individuals share resources with one another. Mother nature-induced vagaries of agricultural production, hunting, and so on subject the members of societies that operate near or not dramatically above the subsistence level to considerable uncertainty. A sensible response to such uncertainty is social insurance.

Under that insurance, primitive producers who generate more than the average produce over some period subsidize the consumption of members of their society who were less fortunate during that period. In turn, lucky producers in period one are subsidized in future periods when they are not so fortunate but their fellow citizens are. This simple redistribution scheme insures primitive producers against uncontrollable misfortunes. Shirking is not a terribly difficult problem under this arrangement, since the members of primitive societies tend to live and work in close physical proximity to one another. This allows them to detect whether a poor yield is the result of the probabilities of mother nature—bad luck—or a producer's laziness or bad decision making.

The law that prescribes the terms of such an insurance system must be enforced to function. If it is not, unfortunate producers in period one who receive consumption subsidies from fortunate producers will be tempted to refuse to provide subsidies to those persons in period two when fortunes change.

In the absence of government, social ostracism of lawbreakers is one means of accomplishing this. But this enforcement technology has limited power. Social ostracism may be costly for certain community members to execute, for example if their close relative or friend is the object of punishment. In this case, a lawbreaker may be able to get away with breaking the law, since he knows he can rely on familial and friend support when he falls on hard times later. Such incentives would restrict effective insurance to arrangements for redistribution to the kin group, weakening its helpful function in proportion to the reduced size of the pool of persons participating in the insurance arrangement.

To avoid this outcome, social ostracism must be made more effective. To do that, the lawbreaker must somehow be rendered more offensive and dangerous to interact with—so offensive and dangerous to interact with that even those persons close to him will be willing to shun him when he breaks the law.

Declaring the lawbreaker a witch accomplishes this. Witches are more dangerous and nefarious than persons who violate laws relating to social insurance. Their connection to evil spirits makes them so. A close relative may be unwilling to cut the lawbreaker off from his support if the lawbreaker is simply a cheater, but he is likely to be willing to do so if the lawbreaker is an agent of something like the devil and therefore by his mere presence threatens to subject his relatives and friends to all manner of dark and nefarious forces. In this way, primitive societies' legal systems leverage their members' objectively false belief in witches to enforce compliance with "social insurance law."

In his analysis of primitive societies, Posner (1980: 7) notes the absence of intellectual property rights in these societies—an absence that, if it really existed, could pose significant problems for their inventive members. Posner is correct to point to the extraordinarily high costs of defining and enforcing intellectual property rights in developed societies, let alone in primitive ones that lack developed societies' enforcement mechanisms. Indeed, primitive societies lack so much as written records that could facilitate this endeavor. However, Posner is incorrect in suggesting that primitive societies have been unable to define and enforce intellectual property rights apart from inventors simply concealing their inventions.

Mark Suchman's (1989) excellent paper, "Invention and Ritual," shows that they have. Individuals in primate societies define and enforce rights to ideas and practices ("trade secrets") by leveraging their societies' belief in magic: spells, potions, talismans, and other manner of supernatural recipes and ingredients. Such belief is superstitious. "Magic," as Suchman defines it, "encompasses any activity that society *construes* as being essential to the success of a technique but that has no *objective* function in the physical mechanics of the process itself" (1989: 1272).

Unlike techniques of production, which are often difficult to conceal and protect, magic is often easy to conceal and protect. For example, many magical formulae ostensibly derive their powers from the "magician"—the magic practitioner—whose ability to practice magic successfully stems from a supposedly age-old, perhaps even quasi-familial, connection to certain helpful spirits with whom the magician has a special relationship. Similarly, unlike the idea it may ultimately protect, a magical talisman is a physical object. Thus it can be easily concealed or kept away from others in the same way as the owner's other physical property.

Though supernatural spells and incantations that invoke magical effects are "ideas" themselves, they too can be monopolized if they are long and elaborate. Certain words must be used; they must be used in the proper order, and they must be delivered in conjunction with the appropriate acts to have force. Unless an observer has an especially good memory or significant practice invoking the supernatural forces that the magical spell entails, he is unlikely to be able to reproduce the magician's incantations exactly, rendering him unable to use the magic successfully.

By tying elements of magic to new production techniques—to inventions— primitive producers can use their ability to enforce property rights over the former to enforce property rights over the latter. Suchman (1989: 1274–5) supplies a nice example to illustrate this logic.

Suppose a primitive producer discovers through costly experimentation that by burying dead fish with his crops, he's able to produce a larger crop yield. In making this discovery the producer has "invented" a new, and very useful, production technology. Such experimentation is socially productive. But the producer's incentive to engage in such experimentation is limited if he knows that if he discovers a useful technology, others can, by observation, copy his invention and in doing so obtain it freely.

To maximize his incentive for socially productive experimentation, the producer must feel confident that he will profit significantly from his costly efforts to improve his yield. He requires intellectual property rights. Intellectual property rights permit him to sell his invention to other producers, allowing him to benefit more significantly from his experimentation. This in turn gives him the incentive he needs to discover new production techniques.

By itself, the invention of burying fish with crop seeds may be an impossible one in which to enforce property rights. But by infusing this production process with superfluous magic, the producer can enforce property rights to his innovation. Having discovered the usefulness of burying fish with his crops, the producer invites others to observe his discovery. However, when demonstrating his invention, the producer buries some "magic beans" along with the fish. The producer tells the observers that it is the combination of the beans and fish that produce the greater yield. And, when some months later the observers see the producer's greater crop yield, the producer offers to sell or rent them his magic beans so that they might enjoy its benefits too.

The producer's property rights may not remain secure forever. Other producers may experiment with planting fish without his magic beans and in doing so discover that the fish alone are enough to generate a greater yield. Still, the magic beans give the producer a stronger intellectual property right over his new production technique than he would have without them. At a minimum, they are likely to allow the producer to earn rents for a longer time than if he did not invoke them at all.

The producer might also engage in other activities that could help prevent others from discovering the truth about his magic beans. For example, before burying the fish, he might shred the them, pulverize them, mix them with some other substance to disguise their odor, or engage in some other act that renders the fish unidentifiable as such to others. He may then mix the beans with the fish and tell others that it is this concoction that has magical properties, which he will sell them if they desire.

This example is hypothetical. Still, it describes in stylized form a process that Suchman (1989) contends comports with intellectual property definition and enforcement in primitive societies where belief in magic is prevalent. These primitive producers leverage their colleagues' objectively false beliefs to create intellectual property rights.

4.   BOILING WATER AND POLYGRAPH TESTS

Medieval European legal systems were more developed than those of primitive societies. The former legal systems had writing, formal laws, formal courts, and formal mechanisms of the law's enforcement. However, they, too, relied heavily on objectively false beliefs to facilitate their legal systems' operation.

Perhaps the clearest example of this is the way in which medieval legal systems' leveraged a then-popular superstition called "iudicium Dei." I have discussed this superstition and how medieval European legal systems exploited it elsewhere (see Leeson 2012). Below I sketch how they did so.

Iudicium Dei is Latin for "judgment of God." According to the iudicium Dei superstition, if priests performed the appropriate rituals, they could call on God to assist them in finding facts in difficult criminal cases. Many criminal accusations that came before medieval courts lacked evidence that would permit justices to determine whether the accused was guilty or innocent of the crime he stood accused of. Witness testimony was usually all justices had to go on, and it was not difficult for parties on both sides of the issue to produce credible witnesses who would swear what they wanted.

This left justices in a quandary. They could simply release the accused, but of course he might be guilty. Such a policy would give incentive to would-be criminals to engage in more crime since they could rest assured that, in many cases at least, they would get off scot free. Alternatively, justices could convict the accused merely because he had been accused, but of course, if he were innocent, this would lead to a miscarriage of justice. Further, convicting every person who was accused of a crime could undermine otherwise law-abiding persons' incentive to remain law-abiding. Without severe restrictions on accusations, nearly anyone might be accused of a crime for any reason, including the innocent. If law-abiding persons were as likely to be accused of crimes as guilty ones, and the legal system condemned them whether they committed crime or not, they might as well commit crimes, or at least would be more likely to do so than if the criminal justice system were functional.

Reasonable criminal justice requires legal systems to sort accused persons by their guilt or innocence and to treat those persons differently. Such sorting requires fact-finding. But how can judges find fact without external evidence? Medieval legal systems' solution to this problem was to find fact with "internal evidence"—evidence of the accused's guilt or innocence supplied by the accused himself.

The key to doing this was tapping into medieval citizens' belief in iudicium Dei. Medieval legal systems' method of doing that was ordeals. Those legal systems used a variety of ordeals for this purpose. Here I restrict my attention to the hot-water ordeal.

In the hot-water ordeal a priest threw a stone or ring into a cauldron of boiling water. The accused was then asked to plunge his arm into the cauldron to fish the object out. The priest would wrap the accused's arm in a bandage and revisit it several days later. If the accused's arm showed signs of having been boiled by the water, the accused was convicted of the crime. If it did not, he was exonerated.

The belief underlying the ordeal was that of iudicium Dei. According to that belief, if the accused were innocent, God would perform a miracle, preventing the water from boiling him, and in doing so evidence the accused's innocence. If the accused were guilty, God would permit the water to boil the accused, evidencing his guilt. Through the ordeal, God would reveal the accused's criminal status to the legal system, which could then proceed to punish or exonerate the accused per the law.

Iudicium Dei was not true. God did not actually intervene in worldly affairs at the legal system's request to find fact when the legal system was unable to do so itself. Yet, precisely because medieval citizens believed God did this, ordeals established the accused's guilt or innocence in such situations nonetheless.

Accused criminals had private information about their guilt or innocence. The "trick" of ordeals was to incentivize them to unwittingly reveal that information to the legal system. Ordeals achieved this by imposing higher costs on guilty persons who were accused of crimes than innocent ones. The reason they were able to do this was citizens' belief in iudicium Dei.

Under that belief, guilty persons expected that if they plunged their arms in the boiling water, God would let the water boil them. Thus, it was better to confess, settle with their accusers, or flee than to undergo the ordeal. Confession, for example, would result in the guilty person's punishment, but that is what the guilty person expected to suffer anyway when he underwent the ordeal and God revealed his guilt. At least by confessing he could avoid being boiled on top of this.

Under the same belief, innocent persons expected the opposite if they plunged their arms in the boiling water. They expected that God would perform a miracle that prevented the water from harming them. This would not only save their arms; it would prove their innocence in the process. Thus, it was better to undergo the ordeal than to confess, settle with their accusers, or flee.

What I have described here is a separating equilibrium. For citizens who believe in iudicium Dei and are innocent, undergoing the ordeal is cheaper than for citizens who believe in iudicium Dei and are guilty. Guilty and innocent persons therefore behave differently when confronted with the specter of the ordeal. In behaving differently, they reveal their private information about their criminal status to the legal system. In this way, through ordeals, the legal system used medieval citizens' superstition to find fact and, in doing so, improved criminal justice.

Primitive and medieval legal systems are not the only ones that leverage objectively false beliefs to improve their operation. Modern legal systems do too. Consider polygraph tests.

By all scientific accounts, "lie detector" tests are incapable of determining whether a person accused of a crime is in fact guilty or innocent of the crime he stands accused of. There is no way to physiologically measure if a person is telling the truth. Precisely for this reason, most (though not all) courts in the United States, for example, bar polygraph results as admissible evidence in criminal trials. But that exclusion may be too hasty. Like iudicium Dei, people's objectively false beliefs—their superstition—that lie detector tests can discern whether they are lying or telling the truth may permit lie detector tests to do precisely that.

Despite overwhelming evidence to the contrary, many Americans believe lie detector tests "work." Thus, the same logic described above in the context of ordeals can be leveraged by law enforcement officials to improve criminal justice and in fact is used by such officials for this purpose, even if it is not typically used by American courts.

Expecting to be "outed" by the polygraph, guilty persons are more likely to decline undergoing lie detector tests than innocent persons. The polygraph imposes different expected costs on guilty and innocent persons. Because of this, guilty and innocent persons choose differently when confronted with the specter of the polygraph. In choosing differently, they reveal something about their guilt or innocence to the polygraph's administrators. In this sense, ordeals were like medieval lie detector tests—or rather modern lie detector tests are like medieval ordeals.

What I have described here and in the previous section is something like an "institutional placebo effect." The effectiveness of legal institutions depends not necessarily, or at least not exclusively, on how well they objectively work, but instead on how well people *believe* they work. People's "meanings," their beliefs—even their objectively false ones—are crucially important to the operation of legal institutions. In terms of policy, ignoring those "meanings" isn't just unproductive; it may be counterproductive. To the extent that legal systems fail to take individuals' beliefs into account, they may end up relying on less effective institutions of law and order.

5. ENDOGENIZING SUPERSTITION

In the foregoing discussion I considered the connection between people's beliefs—in particular their objectively false ones—to the law, taking those beliefs as exogenously given. This is unsatisfactory, or at least highly incomplete, from the Austrian perspective outlined above. To the extent that society's members share certain beliefs and these beliefs influence their expectations about other members' behavior, beliefs form part of society's institutional structure.[10] They count among the institutions that constrain and shape human behavior. Since shared beliefs are themselves institutions, like the legal institutions based on them, they must also come from somewhere. Thus, an "Austrian" law and economics must endogenize persons' beliefs in the same way that it endogenizes non-belief institutions.

Here I make some general remarks about the enterprise of doing so. These remarks parallel in some fashion the "methodological" remarks I made in section 2 regarding Coase, Posner, and the "Austrian way."

There are two broad approaches to thinking about the differences in beliefs we observe across societies. The first approach views those differences as "fundamental," i.e., as reflecting foundational differences in the cultures, preferences, and worldviews of different people. In this view, cross-society differences in beliefs are irreducible and thus inscrutable by economic analysis. They are exogenously given in the same way that my feelings about cigars are.

The second approach to differences in beliefs across societies views those differences—or at least some of them—as reflecting differences in the particular problem situations that people confront in different societies. In this view, beliefs are explicable and understandable in terms of economizing behavior—in terms of the theory of rational choice. Such beliefs reflect institutional responses to the specific problem situations individuals confront in an effort to overcome those situations so as to realize otherwise unrealized gains from social cooperation. Beliefs vary across societies because the natures of particular problem situations vary across them, but the underlying goal of most persons across societies does not. In each case, people seek solutions to obstacles that stand in the way of their ability to exploit the gains from trade.[11]

Social scientists in general, and economists in particular, have become

---

[10] See, for instance, North, Wallis, and Weingast (2006), who make this point. As these authors point out, not all beliefs have this feature. The ones this chapter focuses on do.

[11] The Austrian approach here is, in my view, the same one articulated by Stigler and Becker (1977).

very comfortable with the idea that non-belief institutions—systems of government, law, and so on—might reflect responses to the different obstacles that different societies confront in pursuing this goal. However, social scientists have been much slower or reticent to acknowledge that beliefs themselves may reflect the same. This is unfortunate. Some beliefs clearly evolve to support the operation of non-belief institutions. They have little or nothing to do with fundamental, irreducible worldviews or preferences across different people in different times and places throughout the world.

An example will help illustrate this point. In several societies, people hold a belief—an objectively false one—according to which lawbreakers are in some sense "spiritually contaminated" as a consequence of their lawbreaking and according to which their resulting spiritual contamination is physically contagious (see, for instance, Leeson 2013a). The fundamentalist view of beliefs would maintain that this superstition is prominent in some societies and not in others because people in the former just have different ideas about the way the world works than people in the latter, or they have different preferences that this superstition satisfies.

That people in the former societies have different ideas about the way the world works than people in the latter societies is undoubtedly true. But this does not mean that there is no reason— no economic logic—that gives rise to their different beliefs. The fundamentalist view ignores that we observe other systematic differences—differences in political-economic context—across societies that correlate strongly with differences in the "contagion belief" across them. The contagion superstition is not distributed randomly across peoples. It is prevalent in societies with particular political-economic features, namely a lack formal government and a reliance on multilateral punishment to enforce law.

Correlation is not causation. But, at a minimum, this distribution of beliefs should give belief fundamentalists some pause to consider how political-economic differences across societies may be responsible for differences in those societies' beliefs in much the same way that most would admit that political-economic differences across societies are responsible for the non-belief institutional differences across them. In the case of the contagion superstition, economic logic suggests a ready reason that might account for this belief's correlation with the lack of formal government and reliance on multilateral punishment for legal enforcement.

As indicated above in my discussion of witches, multilateral punishment is most effective when that punishment is maximally multilateral—when every member of society participates in ostracizing lawbreakers. But, as I also discussed above, such ostracism is very costly for certain persons. Thus, to make the multilateral-punishment institution effective, it is important to bring costs to bear on those persons who would not otherwise participate in its application. By rendering the lawbreaker spiritually defiled and his defilement contagious, the contagion superstition accomplishes precisely that. It reflects the emergence of an objectively false belief in response to an institutional problem as a means of overcoming it. The belief is endogenous: it is the product of rational, maximizing behavior given the common problem situation certain societies confront.

6. CONCLUDING REMARKS

An "Austrian" law and economics must be one that, in addition to studying how legal institutions shape individuals' behavior in the marketplace, uses rational choice theory to understand those institutions' emergence. That in turn requires such a law and economics to study the role of beliefs in the logic of choice that gives rise to legal institutions and how legal institutions give rise to beliefs. The Posnerian branch of law and economics, which supplies an economic analysis of the law, achieves this. In doing so, it provides a useful foundation for an Austrian law and economics. The Coasean branch of law and economics, which insists on treating legal institutions as exogenous and has no role for individuals' beliefs other than perhaps as constraints on such institutions' effects on "the economy," eliminates much of the scope for an Austrian law and economics.

This chapter considered some examples of how legal institutional emergence and operation is related to the "meanings" individuals assign to them—i.e., to individuals' beliefs. Hopefully these examples help illustrate the kinds of analyses an Austrian law and economics might be concerned with. In particular, I examined the role that individuals' superstitions— their objectively false beliefs—play in legal institutions' emergence and operation. The examples I considered highlight the perhaps counterintuitive fact that objectively false beliefs can actually improve legal systems' operation and, with it, social cooperation.

REFERENCES

Becker, Gary S. 1976. *The Economic Approach to Human Behavior*. Chicago: University of Chicago Press.

Becker, Gary S. 1993. "The Economic Way of Looking at Life." *Journal of Political Economy* 101: 385–409.

Boettke, Peter J., ed. 2010. *Contemporary Handbook on Austrian Economics*. Cheltenham, UK: Edward Elgar.

Cameron, Alan. 1995. "Coase on Law and Economics." Mimeo.

Coase, Ronald H. 1978. "Economics and Contiguous Discipline." *Journal of Legal Studies* 7: 201–11.

Coase, Ronald H. 1993a. "Coase on Posner on Coase: Comment." *Journal of Institutional and Theoretical Economics* 149: 96–8.
Coase, Ronald H. 1993b. "Law and Economics at Chicago." *Journal of Law and Economics* 36: 239–54.
Coase, Ronald H. 1996. "Law and Economics and A.W. Brian Simpson." *Journal of Legal Studies* 25: 103–19.
Coase, Ronald H. 1998. "The New Institutional Economics." *American Economic Review* 88: 72–4.
Harnay, Sophie, and Alain Marciano. 2009. "Posner, Economics and the Law: From '*Law and Economics*' to *an Economic Analysis of Law*." *Journal of the History of Economic Thought* 31: 215–32.
Leeson, Peter T. 2011. "Trial by Battle." *Journal of Legal Analysis* 3: 341–75.
Leeson, Peter T. 2012. "Ordeals." *Journal of Law and Economics* 55: 691–714.
Leeson, Peter T. 2013a. "Gypsy Law." *Public Choice* 155: 273–92.
Leeson, Peter T. 2013b. "Vermin Trials." *Journal of Law and Economics* 56: 811–36.
Leeson, Peter T. 2014a. "Oracles." *Rationality and Society* 26: 141–69.
Leeson, Peter T. 2014b. "God Damn: The Law and Economics of Monastic Malediction." *Journal of Law, Economics, and Organization* 30: 193–216.
Leeson, Peter T. 2014c. "Human Sacrifice." *Review of Behavioral Economics* 1: 137–65.
Leeson, Peter T., and Christopher J. Coyne. 2012. "Sassywood." *Journal of Comparative Economics* 40: 608–20.
Leeson, Peter T., Peter J. Boettke, and Jayme S. Lemke. 2014. "Wife Sales." *Review of Behavioral Economics* 1: 349–79.
Mises, Ludwig von. 1949. *Human Action: A Treatise on Economics*. New Haven: Yale University Press.
Mises, Ludwig von. 1957. *Theory and History: An Interpretation of Social and Economic Evolution*. New Haven: Yale University Press.
North, Douglass C., John Joseph Wallis, and Barry R. Weingast. 2006. "A Conceptual Framework for Interpreting Recorded Human History." NBER Working Paper No. 12795.
Posner, Richard A. 1972. "Volume One of the *Journal of Legal Studies*—An Afterword." *Journal of Legal Studies* 1: 437–40.
Posner, Richard A. 1975. "The Economic Approach to Law." *Texas Law Review* 53: 757–82.
Posner, Richard A. 1980. "A Theory of Primitive Society, with Special Reference to Law." *Journal of Law and Economics* 23: 1–53.
Posner, Richard A. 1987. "The Law and Economics Movement." *American Economic Review* 77: 1–13.
Posner, Richard A. 1993a. "The New Institutional Economics Meets Law and Economics." *Journal of Institutional and Theoretical Economics* 149: 73–87.
Posner, Richard A. 1993b. "Gary Becker's Contributions to Law and Economics." *Journal of Legal Studies* 22: 211–15.
Posner, Richard A. 1993c. "Nobel Laureate: Ronald Coase and Methodology." *Journal of Economic Perspectives* 7: 195–210.
Posner, Richard A. 1993d. "Reply." *Journal of Institutional and Theoretical Economics* 149: 119–21.
Stigler, George J., and Gary S. Becker. 1977. "De Gustibus Non Est Disputandum." *American Economic Review* 62: 76–90.
Suchman, Mark C. 1989. "Invention and Ritual: Notes on the Interrelation of Magic and Intellectual Property in Preliterate Societies." *Columbia Law Review* 89: 1264–94.

PART III

EVOLUTIONARY LAW

4. Nature as first custom: Hayek on the evolution of social rules[1]

Gerald J. Postema

"Nature is only first custom, as custom is second nature" – Pascal, *Pensees*

Questions about the nature of informal social rules have become a major focus of attention in legal philosophy and legal theory in recent decades. Since Hart insisted that modern municipal law rests on a fundamental *social* rule, the rule of recognition practiced by law-applying officials, it has been a preoccupation of much of analytic legal philosophy to explain the nature of social rules (or "conventions"). More recently, theorists have come to recognize that an understanding of international law cannot proceed very far without a solid understanding of informal rules ("custom"), for customary law still plays an important and foundational role in that domain. Also, in legal theory there has emerged recently a multi-disciplinary study of what are called "social norms," which arguably fall into another species, along with "customs" and "conventions," of the genus "informal social rules." Similar interest in informal social rules can be found in contemporary moral and political philosophy, often drawing conceptual resources and explanatory frameworks from game theory and socio-biology. In these fields, attention has especially turned to explaining how informal social rules emerge and change. An account of the origin and dynamics of such rules is thought to be fundamental to our understanding of how they function, which, in turn, informs our understanding of law, morality, and political institutions. This focus of philosophical attention is not new, of course. One can find at least one especially perceptive antecedent in the eighteenth century in Hume's attempt in his *Treatise of Human Nature* (Hume 1998a) to explain the "origins" of justice and allegiance.

Friedrich Hayek offered, over a large number of works, a systematic explanation of the emergence and dynamics of informal social rules. His theory repays study by those who are interested in contemporary discussions of the evolution of social rules. I begin with an exposition of Hayek's framework for explaining the dynamics of what he calls "grown order,"

---

[1]   Forthcoming in *Research Handbook on Austrian Law and Economics*, Peter J. Boettke and Todd J. Zywicki, eds., Edward Elgar Publishers.

followed by a discussion of problems that threaten to undermine his explanatory scheme.

I.   THE DYNAMICS OF GROWN ORDER: HAYEK'S EXPLANATION OF SOCIAL RULES AND INSTITUTIONS

Central to Hayek's social and legal theory is his explanation of the nature and dynamics of social rules and institutions, especially the market and law, as what he calls *grown orders*. His explanation is multi-layered, accounting for familiar social rules and institutions in terms of deeper levels which are increasingly less obvious to the casual observer. To understand the typical operation and dynamics of social rules, he argued, we must look more closely at the operation and dynamics of rules of the mind. The super-structure, as it were, of social institutions builds on, but never transcends, a rich and layered substructure of more basic rules of conduct and of thought. Our complex social institutions are anchored in this more basic substructure and are radically dependent on it.

Hayek's systematic explanation relies on three fundamental ideas: the idea of a rule (and rule-following), and the "twin ideas" of spontaneous order and evolution, the two components of his idea of grown order. The three ideas are interdependent parts of a single, integrated explanatory scheme, designed to show that key elements of social life are ordered—not the product of some designer, but rather the "unintended consequences" of impersonal and external forces operating on behavior and thought of human beings directed to other ends and purposes. I begin with Hayek's notion of rules, because the other two notions work with an idea of social order regarded as the product of behavior directed by rules.

A.   Hayek on Rules

1.   Rules as subject-grasped and subject-directing patterns
For his purposes, Hayek deploys a very broad concept of a rule. Rules, as he proposes to use the concept, direct both thought and conduct. Rules of thought or mind concern matters of immediate perception, as well as judg-ment and higher order structures like mathematical concepts and abstract theories (Hayek 1967: 23–4, 43–6). Perception, for Hayek, includes every-thing from immediate sensory judgments (e.g., a rhythmic pattern of lights going on and off) to organized, albeit very particular, judgments about one's situation (e.g., the entrepreneur's sense that a certain product might succeed in the current market). Rules falling along this wide spectrum, on

Hayek's proposed understanding, are (i) recognized or *projected patterns*—configurations of items or elements that are grasped (at least in the most basic forms) as a *Gestalt*—that (ii) generate a determinate *response* in the subject (Hayek 1967: 23, 45, 52; Hayek 1973: 75). This proposal needs unpacking. Four elements of this proposal call for our attention.

First, rule-patterns exist only as "recognized" (Hayek 1967: 23, 45), although this "recognition" need not be conscious, let alone articulated by the subject. That is, the patterns may be grasped by the mind of the subject—they are "in" or "of" the mind—at a pre-conscious level, entirely "without intellection," on the one hand, or as matter of conscious mental construction, on the other. Thus, the patterns are not, strictly speaking, detected in the nature we perceive, but rather are responses to encounters with nature and projected onto it. Secondly, rule-patterns are always *abstractions*, patterns resulting from selecting and ordering certain elements of experience and ignoring others (Hayek 1973: 30). Moreover, rule-patterns are, in Hayek's view, *generic* in the sense of being logically universal and in the sense of comprising many real (not merely logically possible) circumstances and instances.

Third, the grasped patterns are always accompanied by *dispositions* of *response*, either a disposition to *see, feel,* or possibly to *judge* something, or a disposition to act in a certain patterned way (Hayek 1973: 75, 79). It is not entirely clear whether Hayek's view is that the pattern causally generates the disposition or that what the subject experiences is a *patterned disposition* to perceive or to act. I suspect that he thinks that, at least at the most basic levels, the latter is true, although at higher levels there may be room to distinguish the pattern grasped and the subsequent judgment or action. In any case, Hayek's rules are not inert: they are *determinants* of thoughts and especially behavior (Hayek 1973: 79). Rules are not merely grasped by the subject, they *direct* the subject.

This supplies the foundation for Hayek's account of rule-following. At its most fundamental level, for Hayek, rule-following is a matter of "know how,"[2] that is, a disposition to act (perceive, judge) in a certain way, arising from a situation that, having grasped its significance, disposes one so to act. Rules, on this view, are never merely regularities or patterns; rather, they are *grasped* patterns that are or give rise to dispositions.[3] Thus, for Hayek, rules are *subject-grasped* and *subject-directing* patterns. Moreover,

---

[2] Hayek draws heavily on Ryle's (1949) distinction between "knowing how" and "knowing that."

[3] In his essay, "Rules, Perception and Intelligibility," Hayek traces our rule-following capacity to our nervous system that acts as both "a movement pattern *detector*," recognizing actions conforming to rules, and "a movement pattern

when we observe rule-generated behavior of things in our environment, including the actions of other agents, we understand each instance of the grasped regularity as having a common cause; not merely presenting us with a pattern, but also manifesting a rule-governed order. Rules manifest themselves in such regularities.

Fourth, since rules of conduct are dispositions to act, rather than actual patterns of actions, it is possible for a subject to be directed to act by a rule and yet not act on the rule. This will occur when the conditions for the realization of the disposition are not met; and, in Hayek's view, among the most important conditions for realization of a rule-disposition is the condition that there is not some other disposition operative in the subject which prevails at the time of action. Not only do rule-dispositions live in subjective environments alongside other rule-dispositions, but, in Hayek's view, rules of thought and conduct always exist together in complex networks. Rules are able to do their work, with subtlety and flexibility, in part because they get their content or meaning from their place in a system of rules, forming "chains" of interconnected meanings (Hayek 1967: 57–8). This is as true of our patterned responses at a very primitive psychological level as it is of sophisticated patterns of reasoning and codes of law.

2.   The primitive evolution of rules of the mind

Rules of thought and action, in Hayek's view, *constitute* the mind of human individuals (Hayek 1973: 18, 30). They are products of the encounters of human individuals with their natural and social environments (Hayek 1973: 17–18). Hayek's account of the basic process by which "rules of the mind" are formed is an early form of what is now called "connectionism" or "neural network" theory (Gaus 2006: 248–52). Roughly, the view is that, at the most primitive level of formation, rules of the mind are the effects of external causes on an individual's sensory apparatus. The external world causes certain neural responses with some determinate configuration. The mind "grasps" a pattern when two events trigger the same configuration and that configuration, further, yields some response on the part of the individual, either a phenomenal experience or behavior. So, for an individual to learn a rule or pattern is just for there to be established in that individual's brain a neural pathway that is triggered by multiple external events.[4] These external, connection-establishing events have their sources

---

effector," generating those actions in appropriate circumstances, or at least disposing us to act in those ways (Hayek 1967: 45).

⁴   Note that on this view we cannot infer that the external world comes already patterned, but only that the mind responds to stimuli by organizing them into patterns. "Abstraction," Hayek insists, is not an advanced activity of the mind but

in the physical environment or the social environment of individuals. We can expect different individuals to have relevantly similar experiences and responses to the external world to the extent that (i) they interact with a similar environment and (ii) the causal mechanism by which neural networks are established works in a similar manner in those individuals.

This potential for overlapping rules of the mind is reinforced by the influence of the social environment on the development of the mind. The root of social "learning" is the inborn capacity of human beings (and other higher animals) to mimic the behavior of those around them (Hayek 1967: 47–8). Following the lead of eighteenth century Scots,[5] Hayek observes that, even very young infants, without the benefit of a mirror to observe their own movements, are able to reproduce the movements or gestures of those around them. These mimicked movements establish a network which is triggered later by other behavior registered by the individual as similar.

This provides the basis for learning of routines of action and of perception and thought. And this learning not only crosses sensory modalities (as in the primitive case across sight and kinesthetic modalities), but also crosses boundaries between persons. Rules are "grasped" simply by being enacted, as it were, in the behavior of the individual learning them, where "enacting" means that a disposition to respond is established by the neural configuration that is established.[6] Moreover, Hayek observes, in our social environments we not only learn certain common behavioral routines, but also their meaning. We perceive in the movements of others their mood or attitude that makes the movements intelligible to us (Hayek 1967: 55, 59). We grasp the behavior as "purposive" rather than random, we do not see just behavior with some regularity, but rule-following behavior. This in turn enables a degree of understanding across minds, a basis for a degree of *Verstehen* (Hayek 1967: 58–60).

---

rather absolutely the most basic and primitive. The mind's initial response to the external world is a pattern-forming response (Hayek 1973: 30).

[5] Hayek cites Dugald Stewart and Adam Smith, but the locus classicus of this line of psychological observation is Book II of Hume's *Treatise of Human Nature* (Hume 1998a).

[6] Hayek does not explicitly acknowledge the further important fact that it is typical of human learning that the "similarity" of the responses is not simply a matter of the events triggering parallel neural configurations, but of those responses being recognized by others and that recognition being recognized by the learner. In this way, a distinctively social form of learning takes place, which is not matched by learning in a subject's physical environment. This, in Hume's view, is one key source of the human capacity for what he calls "sympathy."

3.   The implicit dimensions of rules

A core feature of Hayek's theory of rules is his doctrine, repeated with the frequency of a mantra, that subjects directed by rules of thought and action need not be, and indeed predominantly are not, aware of these rules. The rules are implicit, matters of only tacit understanding. They are, as he says, "known by none, but understood by all" (Hayek 1967: 46). Hayek's doctrine of the implicit dimension of rules comprises several related claims, some based on observation or argument, some asserted but never adequately defended.

He begins from the observation that we are able to act on very sophisticated rules without even the slightest awareness of them. His favorite example is that of children who manage to use language with great facility without any awareness of its rules of diction, grammar and syntax, let alone a capacity to articulate those rules (Hayek 1967: 42–4). He then goes on to maintain repeatedly that this is true about the vast bulk of our (patterned, rule-governed) knowledge of our physical and social world. Moreover, not only are these rules (hence, this knowledge) currently unarticulated, but the vast bulk of it cannot be articulated or even brought to our awareness. This is, in part, due to the fact, as Hayek sees it, that most of these rules are highly localized, restricted to specific times, places, and circumstances of individuals and embedded in the particular activities and skills of their ordinary practical lives. These rules are so deeply embedded in their practice that they cannot be brought to consciousness without distilling away most of their content. The problem, it seems, lies in part in the fact that something can be made explicit to consciousness, in Hayek's view, only if it is articulated linguistically, and we lack the resources to articulate the content linguistically. But it is due even more to the fact that we could not capture it even if our linguistic resources were far more sophisticated, because it is so vast, interconnected, and embedded in practice. Thus, inevitably, a very large part of the whole which gives determinate meaning to any given rule in particular circumstances remains inaccessible to the agent who learns how to follow it. Moreover, since we are unable to make this knowledge explicit, Hayek concludes, we also cannot share it. It is widely dispersed and in very large measure private.

This conclusion rests on a very strong assumption of *subjectivism* (maintained despite the potential for a more modest version represented by his recognition of the possibility of *Verstehen*). This very general and deep assumption takes various forms in Hayek's work. For our purposes it surfaces in two forms. (a) In his epistemology, subjectivism takes the form of the claim that "knowledge exists only as knowledge of [i.e., possessed by] individuals" (Hayek 1960: 24). He rejects any idea of social, shared, or common knowledge.[7] (b) The second form in which subjectivism surfaces is in his understanding of methodology of social explanation.[8] In Hayek's view, our understanding of social rules and institutions must not only start from, but must also always be ultimately reducible to (or brought back home, in some other suitably strong sense) to statements about the mental states of individual subjects. Hayek recognizes that it is possible for us to gain some understanding (*Verstehen*) of each other, but this involves grasping what another mind desires, intends, or "means" (Hayek 1967: 58–60). It is a matter of grasping something in or of the mental state of another person and this grasp will always be subject to very severe limits, because we can only grasp what is conscious to the other person and that, as we have seen, is only a very small portion of the basis of their perceptions, judgments, desires, and purposes.

---

[7]   Although he rejects any notion of shared or common knowledge, he does insist both that widely dispersed and largely private knowledge is nevertheless indirectly *available* to individuals and that this knowledge is *embedded* in rules. The market is Hayek's favorite example of how dispersed and private knowledge is nevertheless socially available. The market is a framework of rules that serves to coordinate the actions and interactions of countless numbers of agents, each market player acting on his or her own local knowledge. The price system does not itself "contain" within its mechanism the knowledge of each player, but it enables each to adjust their decisions to the knowledge abstractly represented by the prices offered. Prices are, as it were, content-independent markers of dispersed knowledge that remains essentially unarticulated and inaccessible in any more direct form. In market economies, knowledge drives activities of parties without the need for any central accumulation of that knowledge. Such knowledge remains dispersed. It is never common.

Similarly, Hayek maintains that knowledge is "embedded" in social rules just in the sense that the process by which they have evolved ensures that they are tested against a wide range of circumstances and have proved to be adequate adaptations (adequate for group effectiveness, as we shall see) to those circumstances. Again, there is, strictly speaking, no accumulated wisdom of the ages stored in these rules; rather, the rules are simply the product of an impersonal (and for that matter, content-independent) process which nevertheless offers promise of a substantial degree of success in day-to-day social interactions.

[8]   A classic statement of Hayek's methodological subjectivism can be found in *The Counter-Revolution of Science*:

> Not only man's actions towards external objects, but also all the relations between men and all social institutions can be understood only in terms of what men think about them. Society as we know it is, as it were, built up from the concepts and ideas held by the people [sc. individually]; and social phenomena can be recognized by us and have meaning to us only as they are reflected in the minds of men. (Hayek 1952: 34–5)

B.   Two Explanatory Models: Spontaneous Order and Evolution

Commentators and critics often treat Hayek's evolutionary explanation of social rules and order as independent of and in competition with explanations drawn from the idea of spontaneous order. This, I think, is a mistake. In Hayek's eyes they are interdependent explanatory schemes.[9] His account of the evolution of social rules depends heavily on the idea of spontaneous order and the role of rules in producing that order; moreover, the sources of disequilibrium, and hence innovation (mutation) and repro-duction (replication), needed for the evolutionary story, occur within the process explained by the spontaneous order scheme. At the same time, the notion of spontaneous order presupposes rules that direct the behavior of individuals from which the order emerges, rules that, on Hayek's account, have emerged from an evolutionary process; moreover, spontaneous order explanations are incomplete explanations of the dynamics of social order and social rules, because (except within certain limits) spontane-ous order explanations are static such that when internal forces no longer suffice to bring the disorder back into disequilibrium spontaneous order explanations run out and the evolutionary account must be deployed to explain how a new order is established. Thus, to understand Hayek's pro-posal for explaining social institutions, we must relate these two explana-tory schemes. Although they are interdependent, it does not distort them too much to view them as working in two stages, following the trajectory of a spiral rather than a vicious circle. The image of a spiral also allows us to capture the idea that the interdependent processes of spontaneous order and evolution build on previous and in some cases more basic stages.

1.   Spontaneous order explanations
We are tempted to regard all manifestations of order in nature and social life as products of design-governed efforts; however, Hayek argues, many ordered structures must be explained as undesigned, endogenous, and self-generating. The "order" or observed pattern emerges from the interaction of a large number of elements responding to their environment (including the behavior of other elements) according to certain forces or rules that direct that behavior. Hayek's model of spontaneous order applies to both natural phenomena like the formation of crystals or patterns of iron filings

---

[9]   This interdependence is clearly evident in Hayek 1967, Ch. 4. Heath (1992) and Gaus (2006) are rare among readers of Hayek to recognize this interdepend-ence and only Gaus, in my view, comes close to understanding the nature of this interdependence.

and social phenomena like a living language or the market (Hayek 1967: 39–40; Sugden 1998b, 485). I will focus here on spontaneous social orders.

To begin, Hayek distinguishes between rules of conduct and the social order that they (indirectly) generate (Hayek 1967: 66–9). "Order" as Hayek understands it, is that "state of affairs in which a multiplicity of elements of various kinds are so related . . . that we may learn from our acquaintance with some . . . part of the whole to form correct expectations with regard to the rest" (Hayek 1973: 36). Social order is an emergent property of the actions and interactions of a large number of agents, that is, it is an abstract pattern manifested in the interactions of particular individuals which may persist even if all the individuals are replaced by others (Gaus 2006: 233–4). This pattern is the product of: (i) the actions of large numbers of individuals; (ii) in an environment of a determinate nature; which (iii) includes the actions of others; all of whom (iv) respond to local knowledge of that environment; (v) from a potentially wide variety of motives; (vi) within the limits defined by the system of rules in force in the group. This order is "spontaneous" because it is the result of individuals arranging themselves according to "forces" (in the social context: motives within the framework defined by rules) in a specific environment. The order is the resultant of the balance of these forces (Sugden 1998b: 487). Because of the interaction among the individuals and the feedback from this interaction, the properties of the order are not simply the aggregate of the properties of individual elements, but rather are emergent from them.

The relationship between the rules operates in a given social context and the order that emerges is indirect and complex, because the order emerges from the combined influence of the rules and the environment on the choices and consequent interactions of the agents. Thus, it is not the case that every set of rules can be expected to produce a corresponding order; indeed, some rules may prevent any order from forming or may produce an order that is dysfunctional from the point of view of the group or of its individual members (Hayek 1973: 43). Also, it is possible that the same social order may be produced by different sets of rules and that the same set of rules may yield different social orders (Hayek 1967: 67–8; Hayek 1973: 43–4). A change in the rules may not result in a change in the social order and rules may produce very different orders in environments that have significantly different properties. The environments in which individuals interact, and the way in which and the extent to which the rules influence the actions of individuals, greatly affect the relationship between rules and the resulting social order or disorder. Finally, a social order may emerge even if the regularities in the behavior of individual members of the group are not uniform. This lack of uniformity can be of two broad kinds. (i) The rules may call for quite different routines of conduct from different people in different roles, stations, or circumstances. What is important for social order is not uniformity of behavior across the membership of the group, but its coordination. Coordination requires only that the rules be broadly compatible, making possible coordinated behavior of those directed by them.[10] (ii) There may be some, perhaps even a substantial, degree of irregularity of behavior (i.e., deviations from the rules) in the group. Just how much irregularity or deviance a social order can tolerate is determined by a wide variety of factors, some environmental, some psychological, some having to do with the internal relations among the rules. Moreover, Hayek realizes that there must be some degree of this kind of irregularity if the social order is to have the flexibility needed to cope with exogenous shocks, and to permit endogenous changes, that cause adaptive changes in the order to occur.[11]

Sugden and Gaus have identified several salient features of spontaneous orders as Hayek conceives of them. First, they are *path-dependent* in the sense that the properties of the order at any point in time depend on its history (Sugden 1998b: 488; Gaus 2006: 233). Second, they *approximate, but never strictly achieve, equilibrium* (Gaus 2006: 234), and this has the result that there is always some greater or smaller degree of disequilibrium in the system. Nevertheless, third, spontaneous orders are, within limits, *self-maintaining* (Gaus 2006: 234); that is, a spontaneous order can survive exogenous and endogenous shocks, restoring its (approximation to) equilibrium. Finally, Hayek recognizes that the spontaneity of a social order is a *matter of degree.*[12] As Sugden points out, spontaneity is a function of at least two properties: dispersion of power and redundancy (Sugden 1998b: 487). If we understand "power" to be the extent to which an individual can influence the properties of the social order, then we can see that the more widely power is dispersed over a population, the less power each

---

[10]   This is a consequence of Hayek's view that rules come linked together in integrated packages, rather than merely aggregated in sets. But the idea is in tension with his official view that rules of spontaneous orders are "abstract" both with respect to the ends served by them and with respect to the agents and circumstances to which they apply (Hayek 1967: 56; Hayek 1973: 50).

[11]   This flexibility, as we shall see, is essential to his scheme of evolutionary explanation, but again this feature is in tension with his frequent insistence that rules must be followed *rigidly* (Hayek 1967: 90–91). The latter dogma expressed here is overly broad and incautiously formulated for his primary purpose, which was to counter the idea that rules are mere rules of thumb for agents who are act-utility maximizers (governed by "expediency" rather than "principle") (Hayek 1973: Ch. 3).

[12]   Hayek 1973: 41–2, 45–6. His penchant for sharp dichotomies, especially between made/imposed order (*taxis*) and grown/self-generating order (*kosmos*), often obscures this fact, perhaps not entirely unintentionally.

individual will have; and, thus, the greater the dispersion, the greater will be the spontaneity of the order. Similarly, spontaneity is in part a function of the density (the number and overlapping nature) of the relations among the members of a group and the interchangeability of the parts. Together, these yield redundancy in a system: the greater the redundancy in a system the less likely is it to be affected by deviations of small numbers of the members. Dispersion of power and redundancy admit of degrees, and, as a consequence, so will the spontaneity of an order. The important conclusion we must draw, although Hayek obscures it, is that we may have to ask what degree of spontaneity of a social order is desirable, and what reasons ought to guide that choice.

With these general features of spontaneous orders in mind we can get a sense of the nature and limits of the dynamic movement within spontaneous orders, as Hayek understands them. First, changes in the environment in which members interact (exogenous shocks) may lead to members adjusting their behavior within the parameters defined by the existing rules, which thereby re-establishes the order. We might call this a case of *simple self-maintenance* of the order. It is also possible that exogenous shocks, or endogenous challenges to the rules, result in change of the rules. If this change does not produce an overall change in the order, we have a more *complex* form of *self-maintenance*; however, if the change of the rules is substantial, the integrity of the social order may be affected. Changes of some rules may bring about shifts in other rules of the system and these adjustments may restore the (near) equilibrium of the order. Other changes in the environment or changes of the rules may require substantial adjustments in the behavior of members of the group thereby altering the nature of their interactions. In that case, the emergent social order will also change, resulting over time either in disorder or the emergence of a new order with different properties.

In each of these cases, individual members may be affected, as may the felicity and fortunes of the group as a whole. Hayek makes clear that the fact that an order emerges spontaneously from the interactions of a group does not guarantee that the order is beneficial, let alone optimal, either to individual members or to the group as a whole (Hayek 1967: 67; Hayek 1973: 43–4). Indeed, it is possible that a set of rules may even prevent order from emerging, or bring about damaging and socially dysfunctional disorder. Hayek's notion of order is entirely value neutral and the fact that an order has arisen spontaneously implies no special value and offers no guarantee of its being in any way beneficial.[13] There is nothing in the idea

---

[13]   Of course, later Hayek seeks to link spontaneous orders with individual freedom, but that is not part of his initial construction of the idea of spontaneous

of spontaneous order to ensure that a coordinated order will be achieved through interactions of individuals (even if they are directed by or act within the limits of rules), neither will it insure that order, once achieved, will be maintained. If social interaction achieves and maintains order, this will be due in part to forces outside those operative within spontaneous orders.

Thus, the idea of spontaneous order provides a model for explaining the emergence and alteration of social rules. On this model, new rules emerge and are altered in response to changing environmental conditions or in response to changes in rules that result from the irregular behavior of some individual members. The balance of forces within the order brings about these changes, without the intervention of any designers who have a view of the whole system of rules and the order it tends to produce. But we are left with several major questions. One question is: where do the rules that initially structure the spontaneous order originate? Another is: what more precisely is the process by which rules are adjusted in response to exogenous and endogenous shocks? How are rules changed? What role does the judgment or practical reasoning of the individual members play in responding to the shocks, or in creating those (endogenous) shocks?[14] And how are rules that actually prevail selected, if, by hypothesis, this is not done by individuals taking account of the impact of changes of the rules on the social order as a whole? What reason have we to think that some order will be achieved and that it will be in some sense beneficial? For answers to these questions Hayek directs our attention to his account of social evolution (Hayek 1973: 44), the necessary complement to the explanatory structure provided by the idea of spontaneous order.

2.   Evolution of social orders and social rules

Hayek's account of the evolution of social rules and institutions is a generalization of the Darwinian account (Hayek 1967: 32), but the precise components and mechanisms of Hayek's account are difficult to pin down. This is largely because never in his many discussions of social evolution does he offer a careful, systematic statement of his theory and it is difficult to reconcile the many different partial accounts one finds scattered in his

---

order as an explanatory device. And this extension of the concept of spontaneous order depends on principles or evaluative premises that are not at the core of the notion itself.

[14]   That is, how do changes in the group's rules occur and to what extent are these changes the product of deliberate choices and actions of members of the group? These questions lie at the core of both Hayek's account of spontaneous order and of the companion theory of the evolution of social rules.

work. This is not the place to attempt to reconcile all these passages; rather, I will offer a reconstruction that seeks to remain faithful to the central motivation of Hayek's account in the hope that this results in a plausible version of that account.

Every evolutionary explanatory scheme must provide (i) a mechanism of selection, including specification of (a) the unit of selection and (b) the basis for selection, and (ii) a mechanism of change, including accounts of (a) the source of innovations or variation ("mutations") and (b) their reproduction ("replication") in the population. Let us look at these elements in order, beginning with the mechanism of selection.

Unit of selection   On Hayek's account, the evolutionary selection of social rules is indirect, the result of evolutionary forces operating on the social order as a whole; that is, the selection of social rules is the result of *competition among social orders* (Hayek 1967: 71). However, this does not yet determine the unit of selection; it does not tell us whether we should look for the effects of changes in the social order on the felicity and functioning of individual members or on that of the group as a whole.[15] Hayek is often criticized for being inconsistent about whether he favors a group or an individual adaptiveness criterion (e.g., Heath 1992: 31–3). Gaus maintains that Hayek embraces both independent accounts and holds that social orders are subject to two competing forces of evolutionary selection (Gaus 2006: 240–46). I believe, however, that Hayek thought that the two elements are closely integrated in a single explanatory account. Impacts on and competition among groups and among individuals are both important for his unified account and inseparable.[16] For, in his view, groups have no aims and enjoy no benefits of their own apart from the aggregate good of individual members. At the same time, individuals benefit—they "succeed" in carrying out their ends and aims, as he likes to put it—only when there is an effective social order that coordinates their efforts and interactions with other members of the group. Moreover, it is judgments of relative "success" of individuals acting within the framework of a given system of rules that are an important part of Hayek's account of the mechanism of change in his evolutionary story. We have no guarantee, of course, that a given social order that functions well for the group as a whole will prove optimal or even beneficial for each individual

---

[15]   It also leaves unspecified how the relevant group is to be determined, but I will ignore this indeterminacy.

[16]   See (Hayek 1973: 18, 80) where the two are closely linked—or, as some critics would have it, confused.

member; so there is room for familiar problems of collective action to complicate the individual/group relationship and critics are quick to point out that the evolutionary process that depends on group selection can be undone by such collective action problems. However, Hayek tends to downplay the potential conflict over the distribution of the benefits of this group success and the possibility of substantial opportunities for individuals to ride free on the cooperation of others. We will explore his reason for doing so in Part II. B.

Putting this issue aside, it is possible to say with reasonable confidence that, although he thought individuals play an important role in the evolutionary process, Hayek took the unit of selection to be the social group (Hayek 1967: 67–8, 71–2; Hayek 1973: 9, 17–19, 74, 99, *passim*). The effects on individual felicity and functioning play an important role in the process, as we shall see, but evolutionary forces of selection work at the group level in Hayek's model.

Basis of selection   Social orders are selected by evolutionary forces, according to Hayek. The basis for selection is primarily and ultimately the "success" or "effectiveness" (sometimes he says "efficiency") of a group relative to and in competition with the relative success of other groups in the vicinity (Hayek 1967: 67, 71–2; Hayek 1973: 11, 17, 80, 99). Hayek does not specify a criterion of "success." We are told that the more successful groups "prevail over" or "displace" their competitors (Hayek 1967: 70; Hayek 1973: 9, 18, 99), or perhaps simply grow and, thereby, are better able to produce wealth and conditions for decent life for their members (Hayek 1973: 80). Some readers contrast group survival with group growth (Heath 32–3; Gaus 2006: 240–43), but Hayek seems to think these are closely related. Groups "prevail" over other groups, he maintains, not necessarily through a clash of forces and the literal destruction of rivals, but rather through doing a better job of enabling individuals to achieve their goals. They, thus, tend to attract members of other groups, leading eventually to the demise of the rival or its assimilation into the more successful group (Hayek 1973: 169 n7). Hayek's basic thought seems to be that it is through doing a better job of guiding expectations and coordinating interactions of individual members than their rivals groups that they grow stronger, wealthier, and more powerful and are then able, either through conquest or through assimilation to win in competition with rival groups. Hayek does not rule out evolution that is red in tooth and claw, but he seems to think that it more typically proceeds in a more pacific manner.

Groups prevail in virtue of the properties of their social orders, properties which are products of interactions structured by the groups' rules of conduct. Thus, social rules are selected for their contribution to the "success" of groups (consisting of the "success" of their members). Notice two key features of this account of the selection of rules. First, it moves entirely without design at the social level (although it may involve a vast number of locally oriented, goal-directed decisions and choices by individuals). Selection operates at group level, but no agent or collectivity of agents decides or acts at that level. Second, rule selection is relative to several conditions: (i) to the system of rules of which it is a part, and hence to the history of the development of those rules; (ii) to the environmental conditions in which the group which practices the rules must function; and (iii) to the other groups that happen to be in the vicinity at the time and that compete with that group. Thus, there is no basis for concluding from the stable existence of a system of rules in a group at a given time that those rules are optimal, or optimal for that group, or even for that group in that environment. For the only rules tested are those that in fact developed historically in the prevailing group and in its rivals. We cannot even conclude from evolutionary success that the rules operative in a group at a given time are superior to those of its past. Past rules might actually be better for the group, but they may no longer available, given the evolutionary history of the group (Gaus 2007: 163–4).[17]

Mechanism of change—the process of innovation and replication Evolution is a dynamic process, so in addition to the mechanism for selection, we need an account of the forces that introduce and replicate changes which then may bring about changes in the social order on which the forces of selection operate. We can gain a sense of what is needed at this point in the explanatory structure by looking at the analog of species evolution. Biological evolutionary forces operate on traits of individuals of a given genotype and changes of the genotype result from mutations of genes in individuals, which are then passed on to other individuals through reproduction. Changes producing individual traits that enable the species better to meet the challenges of its environment are selected; those that do not, die with the individuals and their offspring that carry the mutations. Evolutionary adaptations of a species depend on just enough flexibility of the genetic structure to allow for mutations combined with sufficient rigidity to insure that mutations

---

[17]   Thus, again, if Hayek wishes to draw conclusions about the rationality or merits of evolved rules, he must do so on the basis of premises not included in this explanatory scheme.

are transmitted with fidelity to other individuals of the species. The mutations come from random, exogenous influences on the genes as new individuals are produced.

In Hayek's model of social evolution, social order is the analog of individual traits and rules play the role of genes. Thus, Hayek's model needs: (i) rules with some degree of flexibility; (ii) a process by which variations in rules can arise; and (iii) a process by which variations are transmitted to other individuals in numbers large enough that they can have some impact on the social order as a whole. Hayek has something to offer on each of these points.

First, Hayek maintains that social rules, although they call for strict adherence, are "voluntary" in the sense that deviations are possible and are not so severely sanctioned that individuals never have an incentive to consider deviation (Hayek 1960: 63). Or perhaps we should say that social rules are adaptable to the extent that they enjoy this flexibility. Second, changes in the rules, on Hayek's model, are the results of decisions and actions of individuals seeking to realize their goals with a view only to local circumstances and local effects of their actions within the framework of the established rules. Changes arise from individuals engaging in "trial and error" testing, which can have its roots either in *mistakes* or intentional *experimentation*. Actions that deviate from the rules are assessed in terms of their relative success in furthering the goals of the agent. Deviations have their causes in changes in the environment or in individual's imagining new ways of adjusting to (their local view of) their existing environment. While these changes may influence the social order as a whole, individuals respond only to local conditions without appreciation for such systemic effects.

This account of the initial causes of variations rests on several assumptions about individual agents. First, although they are not equipped with a view of the operation of the social order as a whole, they must be to some degree both self-aware and situation-aware. Moreover, they do not act on established rules entirely uncritically. They appreciate that the rules make a demand on them, which they ignore only at some cost, but they are sometimes willing to risk paying those costs in order to better realize their goals. This judgment of there being a better chance of realizing their goals may be limited to a single rule that seems to stand in their way, but, since rules come in complex packages, it may also involve a more complex assessment that includes awareness of the way that rules interact in particular circumstances to limit or expand opportunities for successful realization of goals. That is, these agents are rule-appreciating, rule-following, self-aware and situation-aware local optimizers (or satisficers), who may also be aware to some extent of how the rules to which they are subject work together to structure the situations and options they face. Hayek's language of "trial and error" is vague, but he must have something along these lines in mind.[18]

How then are these modifications established as rules for the group? We learn from each other by example and imitation, Hayek argues, although neither the teacher nor the pupil may be able to articulate the rule they observe (Hayek 1960: 28–9; Hayek 1973: 19; 1977: 166). Although he insists that learning by experience is "not primarily by reasoning, but rather by observance, spreading, transmission, and development of practices" which prove successful (Hayek 1973: 18), nevertheless, imitation is rooted not in mere (unquestioning) *observance*, but in *observation* of behavior regarded as rule-directed and its local success, (Hayek 1960: 28). Imitation starts small, but through the accumulation of large numbers of such small deviations yielding individual rules ("practices"), which then catch on with others, the rules eventually spread through the group to a point sufficient for them to be established as a group practice and have some influence on the social order as a whole. Moreover, since the rules in question have been taken up and used by lots of people they prove to be serviceable in a wide variety of circumstances (Hayek 1976, 21; Heath 1992, 42). Not all individual rules are imitated, not all imitated rules spread, and not all rules that spread get established in the group as a whole, but some do and among those that do some will introduce changes in the social order that better equip the group to meet its challenges. Of course, some rule-changes may make the group less effective, and in that case rules that catch fire may die with the group that practices them.

---

[18]   I am here drawing out implications of Hayek's vague language of trial-and-error-generated changes in the rules. Hayek frequently claims that this process is unintentional and blind relative to larger purposes and aims. If he means by this that changes in individual rule-following behavior *happen* but the changes are *not made* by the individual, then we must conclude that Hayek has no account of the mechanism of change and his model of social evolution is fatally incomplete. On Hayek's model, mere changes in behavior are not directly selected by evolutionary forces, because those forces operate directly on social orders. The changes in behavior become relevant to evolution only when they congeal into rules which are replicated in the decisions and actions of a number of members of the group sufficient to effect change of the social order. Thus, to save Hayek's account, we must take his talk of the unintentional and blind character of the process to refer to an individual's lack of awareness of systemic effects and purposes at the level of the social order, leaving him space to develop an account of micro-level intentional activities of individuals along the lines suggested above.

II.   PROBLEMS OF IDENTIFICATION AND NORMATIVITY: THE POSSIBILITY OF COMMON SOCIAL RULES

Hayek's explanatory theory, integrating two complementary explanatory schemata, is impressive in its scope and ambition, if disappointing in its lack of rigorously articulated detail. One may wish to challenge the theory at several points, but I propose to inspect just one aspect of the process of emergence of rules on which both schemata depend: the mechanism of change in the evolutionary story which is also the pivot of the equilibrating mechanism of the spontaneous order story. Hayek's discussion at this point is critical for the success of his explanatory account as a whole; it is also the point at which his theory joins issue with recent attempts to explain the nature and dynamics of social rules, conventions, and customs. Let us then take a closer look at Hayek's account of the process of rule-change.

A.   The Tasks

To begin, it is useful to note an important difference between biological and social evolution. Biological evolution proceeds by selecting species physical traits that are expressions of genes. As we have seen, in Hayek's account of social evolution, rules play the role of genes. Social evolution is quasi-endosomatic (or, if we tolerate neologisms, *endopsychic*). I say "quasi," because the rules are rooted in subjective dispositions of thought and action (which, of course, supervene on a somatic base). Hayek's story of social evolution is a story of rule-formation, rule-transformation, rule-transmission, and group rule-adoption. This story introduces a level of complexity and a set of problems not encountered in biological evolution, for what must be explained is the emergence and establishment of rules in the behavior of a group. There are at least four interrelated but distinguishable tasks: to explain (i) how it is that *rules* emerge; which (ii) are *social* rules; and (iii) the *same* rules across individuals; which (iv) then *spread* through the group as a whole. Let us look at each of these tasks.

First, Hayek must explain how it is that *rules* emerge and change through the activities of an individual's "mistakes" or "experimentation." Rules that allow for change are flexible because they are "voluntary." But this flexibility must be of a certain kind. The pattern-consistent behavior now in view is *called for*, not merely produced by, the rules, and off-pattern behavior must be understood to be a *violation* of the rule, not merely a deviation from the pattern. That is to say, the rules now in view have an essential normative dimension. Thus, for an individual to grasp the rule, it is not enough that she behave in rule-consistent way; she must also grasp it *as a rule*. This does not require, of course, that she be able to articulate this recognition, let alone be able to explain its rationale, but it does require that in her practice of the rule she understands both that it is possible to act off-pattern (that her compliance is to that extent voluntary) and that off-pattern behavior is not merely *deviation* but *deviance*—that it is not merely different from what the rule would lead one to expect, but that it *fails* to conform to the rule. For this, the "flexibility" required of the rules is two-fold: deviation must be possible and the individual must have some degree of distance from her disposition, such that the option of deviance is open to her. This distance is even more important if she is to relate consequences of her deviance from the rule to the rule itself in her "trial and error" experimentation. Indeed, on Hayek's model, the individual must be aware of the rule and its suitability for the situation she faces—understanding that situation in terms sufficiently general for her relating consequences back to the pattern which also applies to other situations—and the place of the rule in the complex of rules that gives each rule its meaning.

In addition, individuals must be able to recognize the difference between mere *non-conformity* with a rule and *conformity* to a *different* rule. This generates two problems or tasks. First, if new rules are to be introduced by the behavior of the individual, if only on a trial basis, the individual must have a motive to look to an alternative rule, rather than merely to exploit opportunities for improvement of his condition within the regime of existing rules. Hume's "sensible knave" experiments with various forms of conformity and non-conformity with existing rules, but has no interest in introducing new rules into the regime. He aims only to take advantage of the convenient cooperation of others. Hayek's account needs some answer to the challenge posed by the sensible knave. Second, the rule-tester must have some means of "enacting" or putting in place an alternative rule by means of his deviant behavior. To put the problem in terms familiar to students of customary international law, the question is how is it that *ex iniuria oritur lex*?—how can deviance create new rules? In Hayek's framework, the answer to this must start with the actions or attitudes of the individual rule-innovator, they must choose to "enact" a rule for themselves, and it continues with an account of how this innovation is taken up by others. Unfortunately, Hayek is silent on the initiation of the process. But assuming some account of this process, we must consider the problem of up-take, which has two dimensions: how to establish rules that are rules *for* the group (social rules) and rules *in and of* the group (taken up by the group).

Thus, Hayek faces the task of giving account of the rules as *social rules*; that is, he must explain how rules emerge, not just *personal rules* for the individual who is "testing" the rules, but *rules for the group*. This is necessary because the rules he seeks to explain are rules coordinating complex interactions among agents whose actions are interdependent—the outcomes of the actions of each are the vector sum of the actions of all in a context of limited space, time, and resources—and who must be aware of this fact and of the fact that others are aware of this. That is to say, they must be, at a minimum, strategically rational. This awareness, we must assume, is available to individual rule-innovators because they are aware of their local situations and because these features are impressive, salient features of those situations. So, in circumstances characterized by a high degree of interdependence and the persistence of coordination and cooperation problems, the individual must not view the world as exogenously determined parameters for his own decision, but rather he must look at the whole system of interactions and consider a rule, or a number of subtly interconnected rules, which all those involved in the concrete problem of interaction can jointly follow. In Hume's vivid image, the task for rule-innovating individuals is not that of replacing one brick in a wall with another, but rather replacing a stone in an arch or vault, each stone of which depends on the all the others for the stability and integrity of the vault (Hume 1998b).[19]

The task for Hayek's evolutionary account at this point is to explain how individual rule-testers identify rules of the kind that can perform this complex social function. Moreover, no adequate "test" of such a rule can be performed unilaterally. The rule must be taken up to some degree by others in the group facing the common interaction problem. As Lon Fuller pointed out years ago (Fuller 1969: 4), getting customs or conventions started in conditions of complex social interaction is not like blazing a path through the undergrowth, each successive party treading the path making it more distinct and less formidable. Establishing the rule itself requires coordination.

This brings us to the third task such an account of the emergence of social rules faces. The rules in question must not only be rules *for* a group, they must be rules *in,* practiced by, the group (or some sub-group large enough to provide a good test of the rule). That is to say, the rules must

---

[19]   In game theoretic terms, what the individual seeks is some device that yields a "correlated equilibrium" (see Vanderschraaf 1995; Postema 1998). The rule, "go on green, stop on red" at intersections that have red-green traffic signals is such a rule, as is the rule "yield to traffic approaching the intersection from the right, otherwise proceed." Note that these rules call for different behavior from, i.e., they assign different "roles" to the parties approaching an intersection depending on their relationship to some external feature of their common situation (the traffic signal, e.g., or the spatial relations of the parties).

be passed on, transmitted to others. Hayek's proposal here is that rules are transmitted by "imitation." The suggestion is that an individual enacts a rule in his own behavior (however that is accomplished) and this rule is observed, and its example is followed, by others. For this to happen, the observer must recognize the rule-following behavior of the innovator. Only some behavior responsive to observing the rule-innovative behavior of another agent will result in transmitting the new rule. This problem has two dimensions. First, what must be observed and imitated is not merely deviation from the established rules—e.g., the sensible knave's exploitation of the cooperation of others—but rather behavior conforming to an alternative rule. "Do as I do" in cases of deviation from established rules is crucially ambiguous between these two modes of imitation. This is not a problem of motivation, but rather a problem of interpretation of the "example" set by the observed behavior. Second, if the example is regarded as an example of alternative-rule-following, the pressing problem for the observer is determining what that rule is. What is needed for rule-transmission, on analogy with reproduction of new individuals with mutated genes in the biological case, is that *the same* rule is passed on. This requires that the rule in question be identified. This *problem of identification* bedevils almost all current game theoretic accounts of the evolution of social rules, although the problem is systematically masked by theorists,[20] and it poses a key task for Hayek's theory as well. Imitation may be involved, but we need some reason to think that imitation is a reasonably faithful reproducer of the rules from the rule-introducing member of a group to members.

Finally, since on Hayek's theory rule-innovation begins in small local contexts but, given the nature of spontaneous order, new rules can only influence the social order as a whole if they are practiced widely in the group, he needs an account of how such rule-innovations *spread* through a population. What must be explained is both how the new rules spread and how the changed rules that spread are relatively faithfully reproduced across the larger group population. This magnifies the problems mentioned in the previous paragraph. The mechanism of change must be capable of producing and reproducing social rules in the group with a substantial degree of fidelity, otherwise rule-innovation will only be a cause of noise, disequilibrium, and eventual deterioration of the established rules. Hayek must explain why we can hope that out of the process of individual rule-testing, new regimes of rules *of the group* can emerge.

---

[20]   For a discussion of this problem see Gopal and Janssen (1996), and Sugden (1998a).

B.   Does Hayek's Theory Permit Successful Performance of these Tasks?

Hayek must solve the above four problems if both his theory of spontaneous order and his evolutionary theory are to succeed. They must be solved in order to make plausible his claim that a spontaneous order is self-maintaining and his claim that sometimes disequilibrating forces establish new "orders of action," rather than merely set off a spiral of disorder, which can then be tested on the field of group competition where evolutionary forces work. Of course, for his account to succeed, it is not necessary that all rule-innovative activities of individuals result in establishing new group-wide regimes of rules and corresponding social orders. It will surely be the case that some individual "experiments" amount only to knavish deviance without establishing new rules, and some individual rule-innovations will not be taken up by others or not taken up by a sufficiently large sub-population that the social order is materially affected, and some such group-wide rule-innovations may produce overall disorder rather than new forms of social order. Nevertheless, Hayek must be able to show how each of the above problems can be solved and give us some reason to think that the solutions achieved at each level are frequent enough to provide the mechanism of change that the spontaneous order and evolution explanations rely on. If "solutions" are only random and rare, the proposed explanatory schemata fail. They will not be able to account for the actual emergence, existence, and operation of social rules as it promises.

Hayek's understanding of rules and the agents directed by them to some degree promotes solutions to these problems, but it also puts substantial obstacles in the way of solving these problems. First, his understanding of rules as *dispositions* of thought and action is too limited to permit room for the normative dimension of the rules he seeks to explain. Glass has the disposition to shatter when struck sharply, but should a pane of glass fail to shatter upon being struck sharply, no *violation* of a rule has occurred, only a deviation from the expected pattern of glass-shattering behavior. The deviation calls for a revision of our understanding of the disposition, not for change in the behavior of the glass. This familiar point needs no further elaboration here. The consequence, however, is that the notion of dispositions alone cannot provide the conceptual resources needed to explain normative rules. Equipped only with the notion of dispositions we cannot distinguish deviance from deviations, let alone distinguish conformity to a new rule from mere non-conformity. That is, Hayek's very broad and undiscriminating understanding of rules seems to preclude recognition of their dimension of normativity.

This creates an obstacle to successful performance of the tasks outlined above; however, let us assume Hayek's individuals have the capacity to grasp rules as norms for their behavior and ask whether Hayek has an answer to the knave's challenge. Here the prospects are a bit brighter. The knave's challenge can be seen as two-fold: (i) given the distinction between mere non-conformity and conformity to an alternative rule, the individual rule-tester must have some motivation to test alternative rules, rather than merely to seek opportunities for advantageous non-conformity; and (ii) this alternative behavior must be recognized by others as alternative-rule-following rather than mere advantage-seeking non-conformity. Hayek's response to the first of these challenges rests on his rejection of the conception of human rational agents from which the knave's challenge seems to emerge. Human beings are, first of all, not rational expected-utility maximizers, but rather *rule-following animals,* he insists (Hayek 1973: 11). Of course, they seek to satisfy their desires and realize their aims, but they always do so within a framework of rules. This ordered structure is important to them because the rules provide a source of *intelligibility* in their social lives, which, presumably, Hayek takes to be more fundamental to them than marginal gains from exploiting free-rider opportunities.[21] Thus, rules, for Hayek, must not be conceived as obstacles to achieving maximal utility (more or less useful under some circumstances), but preconditions for effective or "successful" pursuit of ends, and, it must be said, preconditions of having or forming meaningful ends in the first place. In view of this importance to the individual of being able to see his own behavior as rule-governed as well as to see his environment as intelligibly ordered, the individual will not be willing to adopt strategies that significantly risk disorder either at a personal or social level. Thus, while within limits the individual will have an incentive to explore adjustments of the rules to enable him better to realize his aims, he will do so with a keen sense of the need for an ordered structure for this pursuit, both for himself and for others.

Hayek also seems to have resources for answering the second part of the knave's challenge. Again, because of the importance of intelligibility and rule-governed order, individuals, we can assume, will be primed to recognize such behavior in others; moreover, Hayek argues, our foundational mimicking skills make it possible for us to recognize such behavior in others. So, we can conclude that if he has resources for explaining norm-grasping capacities of human beings, Hayek can solve problems posed by the knave.

However, we cannot be as sanguine about his ability to solve the

---

[21] Hayek (1967: 90–91). Hume also seems to have advanced this sort of argument in his reply to the sensible knave (Hume 1998b); or so, at least, I have argued (Postema 1988).

problems posed by the need for common social rules. The device of imitation alone cannot be sufficient to establish *social* rules needed to coordinate behavior in a systematic way, because it is not possible unilaterally to manifest such rules which can then be imitated by others. The problem at this point is that Hayek's story is at least incomplete. We need a richer account of the capabilities and resources on which individuals can draw to grasp and seek to solve problems of complex social interaction. Hayek, however, is reluctant to do so, because that might seem to require of the agent more awareness of the larger systemic situation, and especially of the complex substratum on which rules depend, than he is willing to allow.

His doctrine of the inaccessibility of the substratum of rules of thought and action puts a far more serious obstacle in the way of successful explanation of the emergence of common social rules. This doctrine creates difficulties at two points. First, it makes it very difficult to see how individual rule-innovators can achieve the kind and degree of distance on the rules that direct their behavior that is needed to assess the rules. Second, because this substratum is not only inaccessible to each individual, but also *private*, Hayek is unable to provide a solution to the problem of identification. Hayek allows that there may be some degree of overlap of basic rules of thought and conduct among individuals in a group, since they will have encountered largely the same natural environment and since they will have picked up many of the same behavioral routines through primitive mimicking of the behavior of others in their group. These similarities may fund, to some degree, reliable expectations regarding the regular behavior of others. But Hayek insists that these commonalities are very limited, restricted to routinely occurring circumstances. But novel circumstances and problems of interaction arise constantly and, he believes, we lack the capacities and resources to resolve them spontaneously. This is due, in large part, to the inaccessibility to ourselves, and hence to others, of the vast substratum of experience and knowledge on which our rules are based. Hayek was not forced to this conclusion; indeed, I think he had the resources to explain how a relatively rich "commons of the mind"[22] might develop from the exercise of innate capacities for mimicking and sympathy (as Hume called it) in the thick social environments in which human beings develop, but Hayek refuses to take this route, emphasizing, rather, the inaccessibility and privacy of experience.

It seems, then, Hayek's explanatory project runs aground as a result of two key problems: he cannot account for the normativity of social rules and he cannot solve the problem of identification. Because he cannot

---

[22]   This is Annette Baier's (1997) felicitous phrase.

explain how those observing the behavior of rule-innovators hit upon *the same* rule, he cannot explain how rule changes introduced by individuals are reproduced and spread in the group. The forces of change which drive both spontaneous order and the evolutionary process either grind to a halt or offer no hope that the result of individual rule-innovative activity will not lead predominantly to undermining of social order.

But this conclusion may be too hasty. In fact, Hayek offers an explanation of normativity of social rules which may also enable him to explain how the problem of identification is solved in social groups. Normativity, he maintains, is a dimension of only some rules of thought and action (Hayek 1973: 43, 74–5). Normative rules emerge when individual intellects begin to differ in their perceptions or conduct and there is a felt need to reconcile the differences and to teach and enforce the rules. On this view, appreciation of normativity emerges when individuals observe the possibility of deviations and come to appreciate the need to treat them as violations to be corrected. This much, while rough, is not implausible, but then Hayek's thought takes a surprising turn. Because with the emergence of normative rules comes a felt need for reconciliation of differences regarding the rules, Hayek maintains that this task must be assigned to some agent who can resolve the difference (since members of the group cannot do so on their own). They are, he maintains, assigned to "chiefs," judges, and other authorities who *articulate* the rules and *impose* them on the group (Hayek 1973: 43, 45, 77–8). They express the rules in a form that can then be communicated and explicitly taught and they call upon members of the community to comply with them, backing up their demands with appropriate sanctions. Authorities are not empowered to make any rules they please, he argues, but only to fill gaps in the body of rules already established (in the most primitive instances, presumably, by natural processes). Expectations are shaped and naturally coordinated by implicit common rules and it is the job of authorities to maintain as best they can this structure of coordinated expectations (Hayek 1973: 99–100). Thus, they are called upon to fit their newly articulated rules into the framework of rules already in place, with a view to the system of rules and the resulting order of actions as a whole it makes possible. Their aim, Hayek insists, is to maintain the proper functioning of this order of actions, and the measure of its proper functioning is that satisfaction of legitimate expectations is optimized (Hayek 1973: 86–7, 99–103, 116).

However plausible this story may be as an account of (a certain form of) common law reasoning on which he models this part of his account, it surely cannot help him solve the problems threatening to undermine his spontaneous-order-cum-evolution account of social rules. For at the point of introducing authorities empowered to manage the system of rules and maintain the order of action we have left behind all efforts at explaining the emergence of social rules out of spontaneous, impersonal, and unintentional processes. Authorities, as Hayek describes them, impose explicitly articulated rules where the naturally generated rules run into a swamp of diversity and they do so with the proper functioning of the whole system of rules and the social order they produce fully and explicitly in mind. The order, of course, is thought to have no specific goal other than that of coordinating the expectations of members of the group, but that makes their perspective no less systemic and comprehensive, and their efforts to maintain it no less intentional and "planned." Thus, it is fair to say that Hayek's only developed reply to the problems of normativity and identification is one that does not rescue his favored scheme of explanation, but abandons it. Or at the very least, he must concede that *no* social order is entirely spontaneous and the evolution of social rules is from the beginning assisted by intentional, somewhat system-aware and group-oriented agents of innovation.

REFERENCES

Baier, Annette. 1997. *The Commons of the Mind.* Chicago: Open Court.
Feser, Edward. 2006. "Hayek the Cognitive Scientist and Philosopher of Mind." In *The Cambridge Companion to Hayek.* Edited by Edward Feser. Cambridge: Cambridge University Press, 287–314.
Fuller, Lon L. 1969. "Human Interaction and the Law." *American Journal of Jurisprudence* 14: 1–36.
Gaus, Gerald F. 2006. "Hayek on the Evolution of Society and Mind." In *The Cambridge Companion to Hayek.* Edited by Edward Feser. Cambridge: Cambridge University Press, 232–58.
Gaus, Gerald F. 2007. "Social Complexity and Evolved Moral Principles." In *Liberalism, Conservatism, and Hayek's Idea of Spontaneous Order.* New York: Palgrave Macmillan, 149–76.
Gopal, Sanjeev and Janssen, Maarten. 1996. "Can We Rationally Learn to Coordinate?" *Theory and Decision* 40: 29–49.
Hayek, Friedrich A. 1952. *The Counter-Revolution of Science: Studies on the Abuse of Reason.* Glencoe, IL: Free Press.
Hayek, Friedrich A. 1960. *The Constitution of Liberty.* London: Routledge.
Hayek, Friedrich A. 1967. *Studies in Philosophy, Politics, and Economics.* Chicago, IL: University of Chicago Press.
Hayek, Friedrich A. 1973. *Law, Legislation and Liberty, Volume 1: Rules and Order.* Chicago, IL: University of Chicago Press.
Hayek, Friedrich A. 1976. *Law, Legislation and Liberty, Volume 2: The Mirage of Social Justice.* Chicago, IL: University of Chicago Press.
Heath, Eugene. 1992. "Rules, Function, and the Invisible Hand: An Interpretation of Hayek's Social Theory." *Philosophy of the Social Sciences* 22: 28–45.
Hume, David. 1998a. *A Treatise of Human Nature.* Edited by David Fate Norton and Mary J. Norton. Oxford: Oxford University Press.
Hume, David. 1998b. *An Enquiry Concerning the Principles of Morals.* Edited by Tom L. Beauchamp. Oxford: Oxford University Press.

Postema, Gerald J. 1988. "Hume's Answer to the Sensible Knave." *History of Philosophy Quarterly* 5: 23–40.

Postema, Gerald J. 1998. "Conventions at the Foundations of Law." In *The New Palgrave Dictionary of Economics and Law.* Edited by Peter Newman. London: Macmillan, vol. 1, 465–72.

Postema, Gerald J. 2000. "Objectivity Fit for Law." In *Objectivity in Morality and Law.* Edited by Brian Leiter. Cambridge: Cambridge University Press, 99–143.

Postema, Gerald J. 2008. "Salience Reasoning," *Topoi,* 27: 41–55.

Ryle, Gilbert. 1949. *The Concept of Mind.* Chicago, IL: University of Chicago Press.

Skyrms, Brian. 1996. *The Evolution of the Social Contract.* Cambridge: Cambridge University Press.

Skyrms, Brian. 2004. *The Stag Hunt and the Evolution of Social Structure.* Cambridge: Cambridge University Press.

Sugden, Robert. 1998a. "The Role of Inductive Reasoning in the Evolution of Conventions." *Law and Philosophy* 17: 377–410.

Sugden, Robert. 1998b. "Spontaneous Order." In *The New Palgrave Dictionary of Economics and the Law.* Edited by Peter Newman. London: Macmillan Palgrave, vol. 3, 485–95.

Vanderschraaf, Peter. 1995. "Convention as Correlated Equilibrium". *Erkenntnis* 42: 65–87.

5. The law and economics of rule reform
Christopher J. Coyne

1. INTRODUCTION

Rules find their reason in the need to create parameters on both private and public activity to establish and maintain social harmony and peace (Brennan and Buchanan 1985: ix). Rules can be formal—e.g., constitutions, legislation, etc.—or informal—e.g., norms, beliefs, etc.—in nature. At its core, law and economics is focused on how rules are formed and structured, as well as how different rules affect economic, political, and social outcomes. From the perspective of law and economics, rules serve as prices which influence the net benefit of engaging in certain behaviors. Changes to rules will change the incentive structure facing individuals, ultimately resulting in changes in outcomes. The purpose of this chapter is to highlight how a mix of concepts from traditional law and economics and Austrian economics is crucial to understanding the success and failure of efforts to reform rules.

Rule reform entails making changes to existing rules in order to achieve a preferable state of affairs from the standpoint of the reformer. The law and economics of rule reforms implies that success requires changing existing rules to achieve the desired ends. This, in turn, requires working within the relevant player's goals to find incentives such that the pursuit of those goals will produce behaviors that align with the desired ends of the rule reformers. For example, if the goal of rule reforms is to establish self-sustaining, liberal economic institutions, success requires establishing a set of incentives such that the relevant players prefer those institutions relative to the other alternatives. If such rules can be established, liberal economics institutions will be self-sustaining and self-extending over time precisely because they yield a high net benefit relative to other alternatives.

While establishing the appropriate incentives are necessary for success in rule reforms, they have often proven elusive. For example, empirical evidence regarding efforts to reform political rules through military occupation (Bueno de Mesquita and Downs 2006; Pickering and Peceny 2006; Coyne 2007), spur economic growth through foreign aid driven rule reform (Easterly 2001, 2006), and influence reforms in economic, political, and social rules through sanctions (Pape 1997, 1998) indicates more failures than successes. Further, Scott (1998) and Boettke, Coyne, and Leeson

(2008) provide an array of examples of how government interventions to improve the human condition have failed to achieve the desired ends. Taken together, these examples illustrate how efforts to reform rules to achieve some desired outcome are easier said than done.

While there is an array of potential issues contributing to the difficulty of successful rule reform, one major factor highlighted by those writing in the Austrian tradition is the knowledge constraint facing the designers of reforms (see Mises, 1920; Hayek 1945; Sowell 1980; Lavoie 1985a, 1985b, Boettke 1993, 2002; Ikeda 1997; Coyne 2007). In its broadest form, the "knowledge problem" emphasizes that planners lack the context-specific knowledge to effectively achieve their ends through rational planning. This epistemic constraint manifests itself in numerous ways in rule reforms. For example, in the context of exporting democracy the knowledge problem manifests itself through the limited knowledge of outside reformers in designing effective meta-rules which constrain government (Coyne 2007). The epistemic constraint in the context of rule reforms can be understood as one specific case of the problem facing people in all complex interactions—the problem of discovering and using the relevant knowledge that is dispersed throughout society.

In the following sections I consider how appreciating both the incentive issues (the law and economic focus) and the epistemic issues (the Austrian focus) facing rule reformers can offer insight into the limits of what efforts to reform rules can accomplish in practice. I seek to understand the conditions under which reformed rules will "stick" in the desired manner (Section 2), as well as incentive and epistemic issue of reforming rules due to issues of credible commitment (Section 3). Establishing incentives is crucial, but determining the appropriate incentives is a difficult task given that the perceptions of citizens in other societies are grounded in a cultural context that often cannot be understood by outsiders in a manner that can be effectively incorporated into policies. I pay particular attention to the "knowledge distance" of rule reformers, which refers to the distance between the local knowledge and the knowledge possessed by those design-ing rules. Rules are less likely to stick when they are designed by reformers who are distant from the locus of knowledge associated with the problem they seek to address. Appreciating both the incentive and epistemic aspects of rule reform allows for a better understanding of the limits of such efforts (Section 4).

2.　RULES AND ENFORCEMENT COSTS

2.1　Rules

Economic, political, and social outcomes are a function of formal and informal rules (North 1990, 2005). The "rules of the game" provide incentives which guide behaviors for better or worse. Rule reforms seek to change existing rules or establish new rules. Therefore, a central issue is understanding how rules sustain or change over time. This, in turn, requires an understanding of the relationship between informal and formal rules.

Informal rules refer to the underlying norms, beliefs and attitudes held by people. According to North (2005: 23), "the beliefs that humans hold determine the choices they make that, in turn, structure the changes in the human landscape." When individuals share a similar set of beliefs, or common heritage, it "provides them with a means of reducing divergent mental models. . .and constitutes the means for the intergenerational transfer of unifying perceptions" (2005: 27). Formal rules, in contrast, are codified and therefore constitute written rules.

Prior to North's emphasis on informal rules, Hayek (1988) argued that the "extended order" of human society was largely a spontaneous order which was the result of purposeful human action, but not human design. Specifically, Hayek (1960: 62) emphasized that:

> We understand one another and get along with one another, are able to act successfully on our plans, because, most of the time, members of our civilization conform to unconscious patterns of conduct, show a regularity in their actions that is not the result of commands or coercion, often not even of any adherence to known rules, but of firmly established habits and traditions. The general observance of these conventions is a necessary condition of orderliness of the world in which we live, of our being able to find our way in it, though we do not know their significance and may not even be consciously aware of their existence.

Elsewhere Hayek (1979: 107–8) again emphasized the importance of past experiences and traditions, including the underlying beliefs and dispositions, "which in more fortunate countries have made constitutions work which did not explicitly state all that they presupposed, or which did not even exist in written form." Hayek's point is that a constitution is a codification of the underlying beliefs and traditions of a society which have existed and evolved for long periods of time prior to codifying formal rules. Further, Hayek is highlighting that in order for formal rules to operate as desired, they must be supported by certain belief systems which reduce the enforcement costs of the formal rules. These informal rules are the result of a historical evolutionary process that cannot be grasped even by those how currently follow those rules.

More recently, the recognition of the importance of past experiences manifests itself in the concept of institutional "path dependency," which highlights that the way in which rules and beliefs developed in past periods constrain choices in the present. As a key contributor to the path dependency literature, North (1990, 2005) has emphasized that formal rules are indeed important but must be complemented and reinforced by informal rules in order to operate in the desired manner. Together, the formal and informal rules will operate effectively, but any disjuncture between the two will result in dysfunction.

As noted at the outset of this subsection, North argues that informal rules are the product of the "mental models" of the individuals involved. As such, existing informal rules constrain the set of feasible rules, and thus, political, economic and social rules that function in one society may not be feasible in other societies at some specific point in time. North (2005) also emphasizes that social scientists lack a firm understanding of how informal norms evolve and develop, including how to influence the direction of mental models, and the resulting informal rules, necessary to supplement and reinforce the desired formal rules.

Taken together, the insights of Hayek and North highlight the epistemic aspect of the problem of designing preferable rules. Rules create incentives which guide human behavior, but in order for rules to be effective they must be grounded in informal rules which have emerged as a result of a long and varied process which cannot be fully grasped or comprehended by those involved in that process, let alone by those outside that process. Boettke, Coyne and Leeson (2008) emphasize that the "stickiness" of rule changes is a function of the distance between rule design and the location of the desired institutional take-hold. In this context "distance" refers to the knowledge-distance between the local knowledge and the knowledge possessed by those designing rules. As this distance increases, so too does the likelihood that the designed rules will fail to stick in the desired manner because of the gap between the local knowledge and the knowledge possessed by the rule planner.

The key observation in this discussion is that societies have an existing endowment of informal rules which serves as a constraint on what can be achieved via rule reform. Reforms which attempt to transplant formal rules are not the same thing as transplanting the entire social system that generated that institution in the first place. Absent the complementary informal rules to serve as a foundation, formal rules will be dysfunctional. As Boettke (2001a: 262–3) writes, "When culture and economic logic coincide, commercial experimentation flourishes and material progress lifts the masses of people from subsistence. Absent this coincidence. . .behavior is diverted either into a *sub rosa* existence or manifests itself in counter-productive 'rent seeking' games." This dysfunction will be evident in the enforcement costs associated with formal rules.

2.2   Enforcement Costs

There are two ways that rules can be enforced—self-enforcement and external enforcement. While both means can be effective in enforcing rules, they differ dramatically in the associated costs of enforcement. To understand the differences in these costs, first consider a scenario of "perfect alignment" where people's beliefs perfectly align with the formal rules in a society. In such an instance, enforcement costs will be zero and formal rules would be irrelevant since people will voluntarily follow what the formal rules dictate given that they map perfectly to their underlying beliefs and attitudes. In contrast, consider the other extreme scenario of "perfect opposition" where people's underlying beliefs and attitudes are completely at odds with the formal rules. In such a case, enforcing formal rules will be extremely costly. This relatively high cost will manifest itself both in terms of the resources necessary to maintain order, as well as the level of coercion required to force people to acquiesce to the dictates speci-fied by the formal rules.

Rarely does a society map to one of these extreme categories, but instead operates based on some mix of informal beliefs and formal enforcement to ensure compliance with formal rules. Nonetheless, considering these two conceptual categories highlights the relative costs of enforcement. Where a society is closer to the "perfect alignment" end of the rule-enforcement spectrum enforcement costs will be relatively low as compared to societies closer to the "perfect opposition" end. In such an instance, it is not that deviations from the formal rules never occur, but rather that they are the exception as compared to the norm. In contrast, where a society is closer to the "perfect opposition" end of the rule-enforcement spectrum devia-tions from the formal rules are likely to be the norm, hence the need for the constant threat of coercion to induce coordination and cooperation around formal rules.

From the perspective of rule reform this matters for at least two related reasons. First, rule reform is not simply a matter of "outsiders" designing what they perceive to be the appropriate formal rules. "Outsiders," refers not to some notion of physical distance (e.g., those physically outside the society), but rather to knowledge distance (e.g., those outside of the relevant knowledge context). For example, reform efforts may involve international development advisors working with national leaders to design and implement rule reforms at the local level. Even though the national leaders are citizens of the society being reformed, they may still be outsiders in regards to possessing the relevant knowledge of the local level necessary for effective rule reforms. Boettke, Coyne, and Leeson (2008) emphasize that the relevant issue is the knowledge distance between the planner and the context in which the reform is being implemented. This is important because in order to be effective formal rules must align, to some degree, with underlying beliefs and attitudes. Absent the appropriate beliefs held by citizens to support formal rules, continued coercion will be necessary in the absence of voluntary compliance. Where rule reformers lack the necessary context-specific knowledge (i.e., a significant knowledge distance exists), reforms will be more likely to stick.

Second, recognizing the importance of enforcement costs highlights the trade-off associated with formal rules that deviate with underlying belief systems. This trade-off is captured by the inverse relationship between: (1) the alignment of formal rules with underlying informal rules, and (2) the enforcement costs of formal rules. This is relevant because at some point establishing formal rules becomes too costly relative to the perceived benefits of those rules. Further, this implies that the costs of rule reform are not simply the effort to design and implement rules, but also the cost of enforcing those rules after they have been implemented.

3.   CREDIBLE COMMITMENT AND RULE REFORM[1]

A major issue in changing existing rules, or establishing new rules, is the problem of establishing a credible commitment to change behavior in the future. In general, commitment problems are present in all areas of life where there is a temporal dimension. Wherever a time dimension is present in interactions, those involved must be confident that agreements made in the present will be binding in future periods.

As a simple illustration, consider a credit exchange where the creditor delivers a good in the present period with payment due by the borrower at an agreed upon time in the future. Absent some kind of enforcement mechanism, the issue is that when the payment date arrives it may not be in borrower's interest to make payment. If default is anticipated by the creditor at the time of the initial interaction, the agreement will break down. In

---

[1]   This section draws on Coyne and Boettke (2009).

order to ensure that the initial agreement and transaction take place, the borrower must send a credible signal that they are committed to delivering on their part of the agreement. Similar logic can be applied to a wide array of interactions and in many cases mechanisms emerge to signal credibility (e.g., enforceable contracts, reputation, warranties, external agencies, etc.). However, where mechanisms of credibility are absent, potentially beneficial agreements may not take place.

The credible commitment problem associated with reforming rules is well known among social scientists. Boettke (1993, 2001b) notes how the absence of credible commitments contributed to the failure of reforms in the former Soviet Union. Persson and Tabellini (2000) conclude that the effects of institutional changes vary depending on the ability to make credible promises prior to elections. Kydd and Walter (2002) conclude that extremists are successful in sabotaging the process of peace negotiations when they are able to foster mistrust and uncertainty regarding the credibility of those involved in negotiating and implementing the peace deal. Keefer and Vlaciu (2005) explore how different policy choices across democracies can be explained by the ability of political competitors to make credible commitments to voters prior to elections. In their economic analysis of dictatorship and democracy, Acemoglu and Robinson (2006: 133–72) provide an analysis of the origins of democracy and dictatorship and highlight the importance of credible commitment in the distribution of political power. Keefer (2008) notes that where political leaders lack credibility, they are less able to prevent rebellion because they cannot make binding promises to potential insurgents. Similarly, Flores and Nooruddin (2009) contend that the key to economic recovery in post-conflict societies is a credible commitment to peace because in the absence of such a commitment citizens will fail to make the investments necessary for recovery. They evaluate World Bank assistance programs to post-conflict societies and conclude that the central obstacle to achieving peace among combatants is securing credible commitments. Gehlbach and Keefer (2009) explore how autocracies and weak democracies use institutionalized ruling parties to signal credibility to potential investors. They argue that absent the protections offered to investors under a mature democracy, members of the political elite may invest in sending a credible signal that they will not expropriate the property of investors. Coyne (2007), Coyne and Boettke (2009), and Coyne and Pellillo (2011) all highlight the role that credible commitment problems play in reconstruction and rebuilding efforts during ongoing conflict, as well as when conflict ends.

As this literature suggests the issues of credibility and commitment in the context of rule reform are a central problem facing rule reformers. The success of rule reforms ultimately requires mechanisms that signal a binding commitment on the part of the political elite to abide by the announced rule reforms in future periods. That is, success requires that people have the incentive not only to coordinate around rule reforms, but also to deliver on the promised reforms in future periods. Changes in rules can be understood as agreements to change behaviors in future periods so the parties involved must have the appropriate incentives to deliver on their promises. The failure to appreciate incentives for reforming rules is likely to lead to failure because of a neglect of the importance of signaling a credible commitment.

To further understand why signaling a credible commitment is important in the context of rule reforms, consider the strategic interaction between "rule reformers" and "citizens." From the perspective of rule reformers, a reform that seemed optimal when initially introduced may appear suboptimal in future periods. Without a credible commitment that is binding, rule reformers often have an incentive to renege on the initial agreement.

To provide a basic example, consider a rule reform intended to promote constraints on an existing government. The credible commitment problem in this hypothetical scenario is as follows. Citizens would benefit from these reforms, but members of the existing political elite incur the costs because their power is constrained. Because of the loss of this power, it may be in the interest of the political elite, who initially agreed to the rule reforms, to renege in future periods so they can maintain their hold on power. If citizens anticipate this response on the part of political officials, they will not buy into the initial rule change and efforts at reform will fail.

This hypothetical scenario highlights the importance of signaling credibility in rule reforms. The problem surrounding the sustainability of changes to rules emerges because citizens realize the incentives facing rule reformers. In other words, citizens are able to anticipate that rule reformers will have the incentive to shift their behavior in future periods and renege on agreements made in the present period. Kydland and Prescott (1977) highlighted that current decisions by actors depend critically on expectations regarding future policy and those expectations are influenced by current and past policies chosen. Expectations guide the actions of citizens and absent a credible and binding constraint on the past promises of rule reformers there is a likelihood that those reform agreements will be broken in the future. Given this likelihood, citizens may fail to adopt and invest in the rule reform meaning that it will not take hold in the first place.

The rule reform dilemma described above can be illustrated as follows. Consider a game of complete and perfect information, as illustrated in Figure 5.1 below, where Player 1 is the "rule reformer" and Player 2 is a representative "citizen." The rule reformer may refer to anyone involved in changing existing rules or establishing new rules. This might include

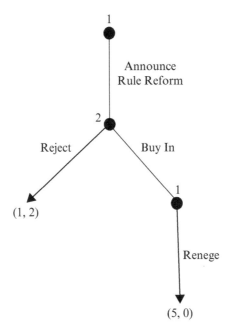

*Figure 5.1   The commitment problem with complete and perfect
          information*

external technocrats, military officials, or diplomats, as well as internal
political elites. Citizens refer to anyone who is not a rule reformer and who
will live under the new rules.

The first step of the game is that rule reformer announces a change to
the rules. The citizen, who chooses second, must decide whether to buy
into the rule reform or reject the rule reform meaning they will not follow
the announced change. Assuming the citizen does buy into the announced
reform, the rule reformer must then decide whether to deliver on the
promised change or renege. Given that the citizens know that the rational
move is for the rule reformer to renege on the announced change in future
periods, their best move is to reject the announced reform after the change
is initially announced. What this basic game illustrates is the fact that
absent a credible commitment which binds rule reformers, the change in
rules will fail to stick.

The unique Nash equilibrium in Figure 5.1 is for the rule reformer to
renege on the announced change to the rules and for the citizen to reject
the rule reform (Renege, Reject). Because of this, the rule reform fails to
"stick" as the citizen knows that the rule reformer will not deliver on their
initial promise in future periods.

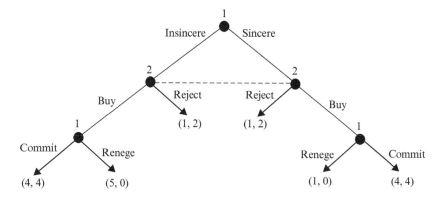

Figure 5.2   The commitment problem with imperfect information

While Figure 5.1 illustrates the basic commitment problem, in reality the situation is even more complex because in many instances citizens cannot be completely sure if the rule reformer is actually credible and sincere in their claim to not only adopt changes to rules, but to follow them in the future. In other words, it is more realistic to ease the assumption of complete and perfect information. Other than easing this assumption, the logic of the game is largely the same as illustrated in Figure 5.2.

Rule reformers (Player 1), announce a rule change which can be either "sincere" or "insincere." Sincerity implies that the rule reformer actually intends to deliver on the promised reform in future periods. The citizen (Player 2) must then decide whether to accept ("Buy In") or reject ("Reject") the announced rule reform. The central issue facing the citizen is that, in the face of imperfect information, they cannot know whether the rule reformer is actually sincere or insincere. The only available information is the rule reformer's past behaviors. The rule reform is intended to create a break from the past, but the citizen must base their expectation of future behavior on past behaviors. If the citizen does decide to "Buy In" to the rule change then the rule reformer must decide whether to deliver on the rule reform or renege on the promised change.

If the rule reformer is "sincere," then the best course of action is for the citizen to buy into the reform. In such an instance both parties will be committed to the rule reform and the change will be self-sustaining over time. Further, note that if the rule reformer is sincere and the citizen buys in, the rule reform will yield a higher payoff for both parties as compared to a scenario where the citizen rejects the reform or where the rule reformer reneged on the promised reform. However, if the policymaker is "insincere" then the best strategy for the citizen is to reject the announced rule reform. This is because in such an instance the citizens would commit to announced reform only to have the rule reformer renege at some point in the future.

In the face of imperfect information regarding the rule reformer's true type, as well as past experience where rule reformers may have reneged, it may be rational for the citizen to assume that the rule reformer will be insincere in their announced commitment to rule reform. Consider that the reason for a rule reform is that there is a perceived problem with the status quo. In order to improve rules they must be perceived as being "broken," or at least not as good as they could be in the wake of reform. This means that there is a high probability that citizens have had a bad experience with the rules or rule enforcers in the past, hence the need for reform. The problem is that citizens base their expectations about the future on past experiences, good or bad, making it more difficult for rule reforms to take hold in cases with dysfunctional rules.

The only way out of this conundrum is to establish a binding and credible commitment. In other words, rule changes must somehow signal credibility regarding the rhetoric of rule reformers regarding their sincerity in future periods. To be clear, the issue is not just a matter of establishing constraints on the future activities of elites. To initiate successful rule changes, rule reformers must establish constraints while simultaneously sending a signal to citizens that the rule reforms are credible.

It is important to note that actual efforts to reform rules are typically more complex than that captured in games presented above. This is because the relevant "rule reformer" is typically some mix of existing, indigenous political elites and "outsiders" (e.g., development experts, foreign advisors, military occupiers, national leaders, etc.) who oversee the design and implementation of reforms. The reason that this adds complexity to the situation is that citizens must not only judge the credibility of a single rule reformer, but rather an array of rule reformers. The presence of numerous layers of overlapping reformers makes the credible commitment problem that much greater.

Recognizing the complexity of the credible commitment problem highlights the epistemic aspect of the issue. The previous discussion focused on the incentive aspects of the problem. Incentives (i.e., constraints) must be established such that elites follow reforms once established. Further, a signal regarding the credibility of those incentives must be established so that citizens have an incentive to "buy in." However, in addition to these incentive issues there is also an epistemic aspect to the problem of credible commitment. The epistemic aspect of the commitment problem arises because in the context of rule reform, credible commitment games are embedded within a cultural context. This means that different players will interpret the issue of credibility in different ways which makes finding a solution that much more difficult. What indigenous citizens view as a signal of credibility may be fundamentally different from what outsides view as legitimate and binding. The relationship between the incentive issue and the epistemic issue can be summarized as follows. While the issue of incentives deals with the structure of the credible commitment game, the epistemic aspect deals with how different players interpret the game.

This implies that getting rule reforms right is not simply a matter of better or more effective planning or design. In order to establish the appropriate incentives and signals, rule reformers have to know what the appropriate incentives and signals are which will be context specific. As noted in Section 2.1, the further removed rule reformers are from the target of their reform, the less likely it is that rule changes will "stick" over time because they will lack the context-specific knowledge necessary to align formal rules with informal rules. Outsiders will often interpret and understand the credible commitment problem in a different manner than insiders. Differences in interpretation can occur through several channels including a misunderstanding of the fundamental commitment problem or a misunderstanding of the overtures necessary to signal credibility. Where such misinterpretations occur, it can result in the failure to signal credibility leading to either higher enforcement costs for rules as discussed in Section 2, or the ultimate failure of rule reforms.

4.   THE LIMITS OF ROMANTIC RULE REFORM[2]

From the foregoing analysis, one might conclude that we are largely helpless to improve the world around us. If rule reform is constrained by informal rules, how can improvements to the status quo ever be made? The beginnings of the answer to this question can be found by appreciating Buchanan's (2004: 133) point that all social analysis must "start from the here and now." We are not helpless to improve the status quo, but we are constrained in what can be accomplished. Buchanan's point is that in order to understand what rule reforms are possible, we must start by appreciating the rules that currently exist. Appreciating the status quo forces one to recognize the existing institutional constraints, and hence the feasible alternatives for changes.

Buchanan (1986) further develops this point in attempting to reconcile a tension that he sees in the writings of F.A. Hayek. Buchanan points out

---

[2]   This section draws on Coyne (2011).

that Hayek is simultaneously a harsh critic of "rational constructivism"—
the idea that the world can be constructed as desired according to human
reason—while simultaneously endorsing major reforms to improve the
world, such as the denationalization of money, which are both constructivist and based on reason. Buchanan (1986: 323) notes that it is not so
much "rational constructivism" that Hayek is warning against, but instead
"romantic constructivism" which attempts to design rules while ignoring
"culturally evolved rules for human behavior that constrain the set of
institutional alternatives. . ." (Buchanan 1986: 319; see also Vanberg 1983).
These insights allow us to establish the existing status quo as the "outer
bound" for the reform of rules. Rule reforms that fail to appreciate this
outer bound will be more likely to fail in their desired end as compared to
those that appreciate existing constraints.

Within the constraints of the status quo, rule reforms must appreciate the importance of belief systems and informal rules as discussed in
Section 2. Rule reforms, which appear preferable from the standpoint
of the designer, will fail to operate in the desired manner the further
removed they are from underlying beliefs and informal rules. Even if
these interventions are motivated by the best of intentions, they will fail
if designed rules are at odds with the underlying realities of the society in
which they are imposed. In this context, appreciating informal rules is not
necessarily the same as understanding those rules. Indeed, as discussed,
a key part of appreciating informal rules is recognizing that in many
cases they are beyond the comprehension of a single mind, or group of
minds.

The recognition of the limits of what can be rationally designed is
recognized by Fukuyama (2004: 31–2), who focuses on the "components
of institutional capacity" and the transferability of knowledge associated
with each component as illustrated in Table 5.1.

One could disagree with the transferability which Fukuyama assigns to
each institutional component. However, the power of his schemata is that
it emphasizes that the transferability of institutional capacity is a function
of the ability to formalize the knowledge associated with the institutional
component. The formalization of knowledge is important for its communication in different contexts. Where knowledge cannot be formalized, it
becomes difficult, if not impossible, to transfer. The extreme case of this is
Hayek's (1945) notion of context specific knowledge of "time and place"
which cannot be formalized let alone transferred to different contexts.
Given this, the knowledge associated with the first component, organizational theory, is typically the most easy to formalize and, hence, the
most transferable across societies. As one moves down the list of institutional components, it becomes increasingly difficult to transfer knowledge

Table 5.1   *Example of transferability of components and institutional capacity*[3]

Component	Transferability
Organizational design and management	High
Institutional design	Medium
Basis of legitimization	Medium to low
Social and cultural factors	Low

because the nuances of the component are more difficult to formalize in any meaningful way.

The implications are as follows. Reforms which aim to influence the organizational design and management of rules are the most likely, although by no means guaranteed, to succeed because they require the least amount of context-specific knowledge. In contrast, interventions aimed at influencing embedded social and cultural factors—i.e., informal rules—are the least likely to succeed because they tend to require knowledge which cannot be easily understood, let along formalized. In general, while determining the transferability of different rules and "institutional components" is not always easy, thinking about rule reforms in these terms provides a starting point which appreciates the limits of what can be constructed through human reason.

In sum, a basic appreciation for the status quo places limits on utopias by shifting focus from what "ought" to be done in an ideal world to what "can" be accomplished in actuality. This is crucial for adopting rule reforms that have a realistic chance of working. More importantly, recognizing constraints on what can be designed is central to ensuring that interventions undertaken to improve the lives of people in other societies do not have the opposite effect by causing significant harm.

5.   CONCLUDING REMARKS

Traditional law and economics focuses on rules as prices which influence the net benefit of engaging in certain behaviors. While fully appreciating the importance of incentives, those writing in the Austrian tradition also emphasize the knowledge constraint facing those who seek to improve the world through rationally designed interventions. While the

---

[3]   Source: Fukuyama 2004: 31.

issue of incentives deals with how rules influence behaviors, the epistemic aspect focuses on how people interpret those rules. This chapter has combined these insights to understand some of the limits of rule reform aimed at establishing the conditions for economic growth and development.

The overarching implication is that there are significant constraints on what rule reforms can accomplish. In focusing on the constraints of what can be designed through human reason, the analysis developed in this chapter indicates that first-best, and often the second- and third-best policies, will not be realistic given the incentives and knowledge limitations. This implication may appear obvious, but as the numerous examples of failed rule reforms indicate, these lessons have yet to be sufficiently internalized. The failure or success of future rule reforms will depend on the appreciation of basic incentives and constraints including the status quo. This is important precisely because failed rule reforms are not simply a matter of wasted resources and efforts, but instead can impose significant costs on ordinary citizens who must live under the dysfunctional rules. Some of these harms could be avoided with a simple shift in primary focus from attempting to design reforms to improve the world, to a deeper appreciation of the limits of what can be designed through human reason.

REFERENCES

Acemoglu, Daron and James A. Robinson. 2006. *Economic Origins of Dictatorship and Democracy*. Cambridge, MA: Cambridge University Press.

Boettke, Peter J. 1993. *Why Perestroika Failed: The Politics and Economics of Socialist Transformation*. New York, NY: Routledge.

Boettke, Peter J. 2001a. "Why Culture Matters," in Peter J. Boettke, ed., *Calculation and Coordination*. New York, NY: Routledge.

Boettke, Peter J. 2001b. "Credibility, Commitment, and Society Economic Reform," in Peter J. Boettke, ed., *Calculation and Coordination*. New York, NY: Routledge.

Boettke, Peter J. 2002. "Information and Knowledge: Austrian Economics in Search of its Uniqueness," 15 *Review of Austrian Economics* 263–74.

Boettke, Peter J., Christopher J. Coyne and Peter T. Leeson. 2008. "Institutional Stickiness and the New Development Economics," 67 *American Journal of Economics and Sociology* 331–58.

Brennan, Geoffrey and James M. Buchanan. 1985. *The Reason of Rules: Constitutional Political Economy*. Cambridge, MA: Cambridge University Press.

Buchanan, James. M. 1986 [2001]. "Cultural Evolution and Institutional Reform," in Charles K. Rowley, ed., *The Collected Works of James M. Buchanan, Volume 18, Federalism, Liberty, and the Law*. Indianapolis, IN: Liberty Fund, Inc.

Buchanan, James M. 2004. "The Status of the Status Quo," 15 *Constitutional Political Economy* 133–44.

Bueno de Mesquita, Bruce and George W. Downs. 2006. "Intervention and Democracy," 60 *International Organization* 627–49.

Coyne, Christopher J. 2007. *After War: The Political Economy of Exporting Democracy*. Stanford, CA: Stanford University Press.

Coyne, Christopher J. 2011. "Constitutions and Crisis," 80 *Journal of Economic Behavior and Organization* 351–7.

Coyne, Christopher J. and Peter J. Boettke. 2009. "The Problem of Credible Commitment in Reconstruction," 5 *Journal of Institutional Economics* 1–23.

Coyne, Christopher and Adam Pellillo. 2011. "Economic Reconstruction Amidst Conflict: Insights from Afghanistan and Iraq," 22 *Defence and Peace Economics* 627–43.

Easterly, William. 2001. *The Elusive Quest for Growth*. Cambridge, MA: The MIT Press.

Easterly, William. 2006. *The White Man's Burden*. New York, NY: Penguin Press.

Flores, Thomas E. and Ifran Nooruddin. 2009. "Democracy Under the Gun: Understanding Post-Conflict Economic Recovery," 53 *Journal of Conflict Resolution* 3–29.

Fukuyama, Francis. 2004. *State-Building: Governance and World Order in the 21st Century*. Ithaca, NY: Cornell University Press.

Gehlbach, Scott and Philip Keefer. 2009. "Investment Without Democracy: Ruling-Party Institutionalization and Credible Commitment in Autocracies," Mimeo, Department of Political Science, University of Wisconsin, Madison.

Hayek, F.A. 1945. "The Use of Knowledge in Society," XXXV *American Economic Review* 519–30.

Hayek, F.A. 1960. *The Constitution of Liberty*. Chicago, IL: The University of Chicago Press.

Hayek, F.A. 1979. *Law, Legislation, and Liberty, Volume III: The Political Order of a Free People*. Chicago, IL: The University of Chicago Press.

Hayek, F.A. 1988. *The Fatal Conceit: The Errors of Socialism*. Chicago, IL: The University of Chicago Press.

Ikeda, Sanford. 1997. *Dynamics of the Mixed Economy: Toward a Theory of Interventionism*. New York, NY: Routledge.

Keefer, Philip. 2008. "Insurgency and Credible Commitment in Autocracies and Democracies," 22 *The World Bank Economic Review* 33–61.

Keefer, Philip and Razvan Vlaicu. 2005. "Democracy, Credibility and Clientelism," 24 *Journal of Law, Economics, & Organization* 371–406.

Kydd, Andrew and Barbara F. Walter. 2002. "Sabotaging the Peace: The Politics of Extremist Violence," 56 *International Organization* 263–96.

Kydland, Finn E. and Edward C. Prescott. 1977. "Rules Rather than Discretion: The Inconsistency of Optimal Plans," 85 *Journal of Political Economy* 473–91.

Lavoie, Donald. 1985a. *Rivalry and Central Planning: The Socialist Calculation Debate Reconsidered*. New York, NY: Cambridge University Press.

Lavoie, Donald. 1985b. *National Economic Planning: What is Left?* Cambridge, MA: Ballinger.

Mises, Ludwig von. 1920 [1935]. "Economic Calculation in the Socialist Commonwealth," in F.A. Hayek, ed., *Collectivist Economic Planning*. London: George Routledge & Sons.

North, Douglass C. 1990. *Institutions, Institutional Change and Economic Performance*. New York, NY: Cambridge University Press.

North, Douglass C. 2005. *Understanding the Process of Economic Change*. Princeton, NJ: Princeton University Press.

Nooruddin, I. and T.E. Flores. 2009. "Financing the Peace: Evaluating World Bank Post-Conflict Assistance Programs," 4 *Review of International Organizations* 1–27.

Pape, Robert. 1997. "Why Economic Sanctions Do Not Work," 22 *International Security* 90–136.

Pape, Robert. 1998. "Why Economic Sanctions Still Do Not Work," 23 *International Security* 66–77.

Persson, Torsten and Guido Tabellini. 2000. *Political Economics: Explaining Public Policy*. Cambridge, MA: The MIT Press.

Pickering, Jeffrey and Mark Peceny. 2006. "Forging Democracy at Gunpoint," 50 *International Studies Quarterly* 539–60.

Scott, James. 1998. *Seeing Like a State: How Certain Schemes to Improve the Human Condition Have Failed.* New Haven, CT: Yale University Press.
Sowell, Thomas. 1980. *Knowledge and Decisions.* New York, NY: Basic Books.
Vanberg, Viktor. 1983. "Libertarian Evolutionism and Contractarian Constitutionalism," in Svetozar Pejovich, ed., *Philosophical and Economic Foundations of Capitalism.* Lexington, MA: Lexington Books.

6. Legal process for fostering innovation
Henry N. Butler and Larry E. Ribstein

INTRODUCTION

This chapter shows that innovation depends at least as much on how laws are made as on *a priori* analyses of the optimal content of those laws. Legal process therefore is critical to the development of efficient policies for fostering innovation and growth. Of particular importance is whether the U.S. legal system promotes an efficient market for law. Our analysis builds on central insights of Austrian economics and the role of institutions in supporting market processes. We begin with a brief introduction to Austrian economics. We then show how, in the light of these basic principles, particular legal institutions can foster innovation by supporting a market for law. The remainder of the chapter illustrates this theory with specific examples.

Austrian Economics and Legal Institutions

Austrian economic theory shows how market-based institutions enable prices to reveal preferences and thereby guide the behavior of economic actors toward greater efficiency. Austrian economists created a theory of competition as a process of dynamic efficiency characterized by discovery and creativity. A key aspect of this theory is Ludwig von Mises's (1949) conception of the market as continual human action which can shift the production possibility curve and not just move prices toward equilibrium as in traditional market theory. Schumpeter (1975) conceived the notion of "creative destruction" to describe such economic shifts. Kirzner (2000) added a focus on the entrepreneur's role in coordinating social action by finding arbitrage opportunities.

An Austrian economic concept that has particular importance for this chapter is Frederick von Hayek's (1945) insight that experts, academics, and lawmakers lack the necessary knowledge to make decisions about which legal and regulatory structures maximize welfare. Hayek emphasized that even the most brilliant and thoughtful policymakers cannot take account of the enormous number of political, social, technological and economic variables that determine how their plans will operate in the unknowable real world of the future. In order to deal with this knowledge problem, Hayek championed the market system as a vast network that can produce the necessary information.

Austrian-type market processes must be supported by appropriate legal institutions. First, legal processes need to be able to harness market-like mechanisms to create an information network that leads to the discovery of better policies over time. Second, legal institutions can encourage entrepreneurial activity by reducing incumbent firms' control of the political process. We show how both objectives can be achieved by enhancing the potential for jurisdictional competition.

Law Markets and the Information Problem

To understand the scope of the information problem involved in regulatory design, consider the broad array of approaches to regulating contracts – mandatory vs. default rules, opt-in vs. opt-out, disclosure vs. substantive duties. In general, legal rules must be designed to balance solutions to specific problems in the market against the need to allow parties the freedom to engage in innovation. These rules should sometimes restrict opportunistic conduct in order to encourage trade or investment while at other times enabling the parties to craft their own agreements. Legal rules also can reduce information costs or transactional frictions and increase property rights. Individual policymakers, however, lack the knowledge or foresight to see all the potential alternatives or figure out which should be adopted in particular circumstances. Among other things, they cannot determine all of the immediate costs of regulation, the interaction among rules, the effect on incentives, or the long-run value of prohibited conduct.

The knowledge problem is particularly challenging in determining how to maximize long-term growth. Indeed, short-term efficiency-enhancing rules may prove to be wealth reducing in the long term. For example, even if intellectual property rights clearly promote innovation now, locking up ownership rights in those innovations for long periods may have unpredictable effects on the production of new information and products that build on existing information. These questions can be addressed only by experimenting with and observing the effects of different rules over time.

In order to solve the knowledge problem and to create efficient legal technologies, the legal system can use the same competitive process that encourages innovation in the private sector – that is, competition among suppliers of law. As we will see, this entails enforcing contracts among the parties regarding the applicable law. The greater the knowledge problem the more necessary it is to unleash markets for law to solve the problem.

Enhancing Entrepreneurship

Legal process can enhance entrepreneurship by reducing incumbents' ability to block the path of new entrepreneurs that are essential to Austrian-style dynamic efficiency. This can be done by supplementing the "voice" of the political process with the power of exit, drawing from Hirschman's (1970) famous analysis. The political process tends to favor the interests of today's economically powerful firms over the small and not-yet-existing (or yet-to-be relevant) innovators of tomorrow's potentially leading firms. Incumbent firms not only have significant resources to fund political activities but also a strong incentive to spend those resources so as to block innovation. After all, these firms are threatened much more by potential extinction by brand new industries and technologies than they are by their competitors' potential erosion of their share of the existing market.

It is difficult to give future firms more voice without significantly altering the political system. But firms also can influence policymaking by deciding where to locate their businesses. A firm's exit or potential exit can activate interests in the state who would be injured by this exit, including suppliers, customers, lawyers and workers. These groups would then enter the political mix in opposition to the incumbent pro-regulatory interest groups. Through this process exit expands the political voice to include actors who will engage in efficiency-driven economic policy.

Balancing Costs and Benefits of Jurisdictional Competition

Critics of enhancing jurisdiction choice point out that it can lead to a "race to the bottom" in which jurisdictions enact laws that favor particular parties rather than enhancing social wealth. For example, if the rules on jurisdictional choice emphasize enforcement of the parties' contracts for the applicable law, laws might favor expert and economically powerful manufacturers and sellers and undermine efficient state laws aimed at these parties. Jurisdictional choice also may favor economically mobile capital and systematically harm less mobile labor. Jurisdictional choice therefore could replace the defects of political choice with a different set of defects associated with exit.

There are several responses to these criticisms of enabling more jurisdictional choice. A first potential response is to emphasize the problems of enforcing restrictions on jurisdictional choice. In particular, if states or other jurisdictions can override choice and impose their regulation on parties they can haul into their courts, the determination of which laws to apply could depend on considerations such as plaintiffs' trial lawyers' decisions where to sue. This could introduce different but equally perverse legislative incentives.

A second response to criticisms of jurisdictional choice is that a system that favors the dynamic growth potential of the firms empowered by greater jurisdictional choice may increase social welfare more than a system that focuses on avoiding static inefficiency caused by wealth-transferring regulation. Even if economically powerful incumbent firms could gain from greater ability to avoid regulating states, these firms already have leverage in crafting regulation, and sometimes use this leverage to increase costs for potentially innovative competitors. Increasing innovative firms' ability to choose the applicable law therefore may increase the political power of these firms relative both to incumbent firms and to other pro-regulatory groups, thereby leveling the political playing field. Also, because growth has a potential multiplier effect on social wealth, the positive effects of systemic rules that enhance growth may swamp their negative effects from short-term deadweight losses.

Third, and most importantly, criticism of jurisdictional choice must proceed against a background of inevitable jurisdictional choice and competition in a multi-jurisdictional world. No single jurisdiction can reach all transactions in a global economy. Nor would we want it to, for the result would be duplicative regulation and chaos. Economic actors therefore inevitably can choose the jurisdiction whose laws govern their transactions. Thus, the relevant question is how to establish the best possible system of jurisdictional choice for maximizing growth in a multi-jurisdictional system.

LAW MARKET INSTITUTIONS THAT COULD BOOST INNOVATION

Our proposal for institutional reform to enhance jurisdictional choice draws on earlier work concerning a particular mechanism for jurisdiction-selection—that is, contracts for the applicable law (O'Hara and Ribstein, 2009). Specifically, we suggest harnessing the power of jurisdictional competition among the states through a federal law enforcing contracting parties' choice of law except to the extent states legislatively override the choice of law and regulate local transactions. This proposal is "Austrian" in that it provides a mechanism for experimentation and discovery while preserving space for entrepreneurs to enhance dynamic efficiency.

Our proposal seeks to set the stage for jurisdictional competition to help discover efficient institutions by balancing the benefits of exit and jurisdictional competition against those of empowering governments to address local problems. By preserving a space for regulation, our proposal protects innovation by government as well as by the private sector. At the same time, the proposal uses both exit and voice mechanisms to discipline inefficient regulation.

In order to provide context for our suggested reform, this section discusses specific aspects of the system for choosing the law applicable to particular disputes. We focus on the particular context of the U.S. federal system. This system's general features illustrate basic issues regarding jurisdictional choice, including the existence of multiple jurisdictions from which economic actors can choose, individual jurisdictions' incentives to favor local interests over systemic benefits of jurisdictional choice, the role of alternative adjudication mechanisms as a way of alleviating these problems, and the potential for coordination by a federal government or equivalent institution.

State Choice-of-Law Rules

Choice-of-law rules focus on two types of decisions. Under conventional choice-of-law rules, courts choose which law applies to a particular transaction "ex post" when litigating a case arising out of the transaction. U.S. courts generally apply vague choice-of-law rules with results parties cannot reliably predict prior to litigation. These rules enable courts to apply local law, which effectively lets whoever controls the litigation forum—usually the plaintiff—choose the law. Plaintiffs' lawyers accordingly have an incentive to promote rules that encourage lawsuits in the states where they are licensed, and perhaps also rules that make these suits more costly for defendants. Courts and legislatures, in turn, have an incentive to come up with rules that cater to this powerful interest group. The only qualification is that states would not want the rules to be so harsh to defendants that firms would avoid jurisdictional contacts that subject them to suit in the state.

By contrast, changing the rules to focus on "ex ante" choice of law involves enforcing contracts that choose the governing law at the time when the parties make their deal. States that enforce these contracts have an incentive to design their laws so as to attract as residents and litigants parties who value contract enforcement. By enforcing property rights and contracts, these laws provide a secure basis for innovation and a potential escape route from other states' excessive regulation of contracts. The problem with contractual choice of law is that it can enable evasion of rules intended to protect the contracting parties or non-parties. The competition facilitated by ex ante choice of law therefore may turn into a "race to the bottom" where jurisdictions adopt socially inefficient rules to appeal to the parties that control the contracting process.

The alternative approaches to choosing the applicable law raise the question whether the inefficiency resulting from empowering trial lawyers under ex post choice is greater than the potential inefficiency from a race to the bottom that might result from ex ante choice. Moreover, whatever the answer to this question, it is difficult for states on their own to avoid both horns of the dilemma. Parties always have some power to avoid subjecting themselves to the jurisdiction of heavily regulating states, while states have some power to avoid applying the law selected by contractual choice-of-law clause entered into by parties that are subject to their jurisdiction. As discussed below, it may be necessary for the federal government to act as an umpire to guide the system toward efficient outcomes.

Federal Substantive Regulation

One approach to resolving the problems with multiple state laws would be to apply a single federal standard and thereby eliminate the inefficient outcomes of state choice of law discussed above. However, the application of a single federal law inhibits the potential for state law competition and discovery that is essential to support Austrian market processes.

To be sure, enactment of a federal statute is followed by a common law process of judicial interpretation which has elements of an Austrian discovery process. Statutes can be designed with this process in view (Hylton, 2003). However, such a process brings problems of its own. First, the interpretation process is tethered to the statute and therefore may allow less discovery and innovation than the sort of competition among multiple jurisdictions that can occur under an efficient state law system. Second, even a federal law designed to enable evolution may inhibit entrepreneurship by protecting incumbent firms. Third, a federal statute designed to maximize common law development may provide less certainty than state legislation coupled with a federal choice-of-law statute as discussed below.

State Initiatives

Federal substantive law is not the only way to improve state legal competition. Individual states have incentives to engage in process innovations that attract firms to locate headquarters or factories in their states in order to increase the possibility that their cases will be litigated in the innovating state's courts. The innovators here are legislators, individual lawyers and bar associations who essentially serve as legal entrepreneurs. Arbitration and business association law have developed partly as a result of this legal entrepreneurship. Several states have adopted choice-of-law statutes which clarify that choice-of-law clauses will be enforced in certain types of contracts, mainly large commercial contracts.

The potential for process innovation by the states is indicated by a Delaware court rule (Delaware Chancery Court Rules 96–98 (February 1, 2010)). The rule essentially turns Delaware's respected Chancery Court judges into private arbitrators. Contracting parties can agree to have their case governed by the new procedures before a Delaware chancellor with direct appeal to the Delaware Supreme Court. The new rules represent a convergence of private arbitration and public judicial procedures.

This state-private convergence theoretically could be taken a step further by Delaware judges retiring from Delaware public life and going private. Other states also might hire the judges and adopt Delaware law, thereby competing with both Delaware law and infrastructure. Perhaps a central agency could be developed for accrediting roving judges. As more states have an opportunity to become viable competitors in the law market, they have greater incentives to change the choice-of-law rules to better accommodate state competition.

A problem with all state initiatives, however, is that they are ultimately subject to being trumped by uncooperative states. As long as a plaintiff can get jurisdiction in a state that has not signed onto the procedure, the forum state has some power to disregard the contract's choice of the innovative state in favor of enforcing local regulation. This suggests that federal law, despite its potential for inhibiting state experimentation, may have an important role to play in providing the institutional base for Austrian-style legal market processes.

Federal Choice-of-Law Statutes

Instead of providing for specific regulation, federal law can promote discovery and innovation by harnessing the state law process while ameliorating its worst problems. This could be done through a federal statute that provides for the enforcement of contracts regarding the applicable law.

One approach is for federal legislation designating the types of choice-of-law contracts that are or are not enforceable. But designing this regulation would implicate the knowledge constraints on policymaking discussed above.

Federal law could instead impose procedural constraints on state laws blocking enforcement of choice-of-law contracts. In particular, a federal statute could specify that choice-of-law contracts can be invalidated only pursuant to state legislation and not by judicial decisions (O'Hara and Ribstein, 2009, Ch. 10). This would serve two purposes. First, using the legislative process would promote robust competition among interest groups, which in turn can maximize welfare (Becker, 1983). Specifically, as discussed above, interest groups who are hurt by firms' exit would join in opposition to the regulation with those more directly injured by it.

A second advantage of the proposed approach is that requiring clarification of the rule by embodying it in legislation would better enable firms to select jurisdictions in which to do business based on their enforcement of choice-of-law contracts. This would encourage jurisdictions to take firms' interests into account when deciding on enforcement.

Although this approach would enable states to inhibit experimentation and discovery by imposing regulation, the procedural limitations suggested above would interact with other limits on state regulation to move the system toward efficiency. First, as noted above, firms would retain their ability to avoid states that impose excessive regulation, thus forcing states to choose between regulating and enabling exit.

Second, the federal choice-of-law solution could encourage interstate recognition of contractual choice of law if the federal law were backed by an implicit threat of federal regulation and preemption of state law if the states insist on promoting parochial local interests and refuse to enforce even reasonable sister state laws that parties select in their contracts. The crafting of preemption to further markets for law is discussed below.

A potential problem with the above proposal is that giving legislatures the exclusive opt-out power foregoes the benefits from judicial decisions whose random mutations can spur efficient legal evolution (Butler, 2006). However, these beneficial mutations are more likely with respect to complex substantive issues than for the relatively simple question of whether or not to enforce contractual law. In any event, these potential benefits of judicial mutation must be balanced against the costs of lower predictability, notice and political transparency.

Federal Choice of Forum and Arbitration

Parties can help ensure enforcement of their choice-of-law contracts by avoiding non-enforcing courts. They can do this not only by avoiding contracts with non-enforcing jurisdictions, as discussed above, but also by contracting for adjudication of their disputes by pro-enforcement courts or arbitrators. As with choice-of-law contracts, choice-of-forum and arbitration contracts help motivate courts to maximize the welfare of all contracting parties rather than just the party that makes the ex post litigation decision. Rules regarding the enforcement of choice-of-forum and arbitration agreements therefore are a potentially important part of the institutions supporting Austrian law market processes.

Choice-of-forum and arbitration contracts may seem to raise the same issues as choice-of-law contracts in that courts that do not want to enforce the latter also will not enforce the former. However, contracting for the forum adds two new dimensions to jurisdictional choice. First, some courts that are not willing to enforce law-choice contracts may be willing to enforce forum-choice contracts because the latter do not require the court to choose between two competing state policies.

Second, federal law enters the picture with respect to forum choice through the Federal Arbitration Act, which itself was a response to global trade competition. Arbitration has become a powerful mechanism for supporting jurisdictional choice and furthering the Austrian discovery process. However, pro-litigation and consumer groups are now lobbying to reduce the role of arbitration, particularly of consumer contracts. Regulation of arbitration should take account of arbitration's benefits in promoting the law market.

Federal Preemption Rules

A final institution for promoting jurisdictional choice is the judicial rules for deciding on the extent to which federal statutes preempt state law under the Supremacy Clause of the Constitution. When a federal statute conflicts with state law, as long as the statute is within Congress's constitutional power it is the supreme law of the land and takes precedence over state law. Congressional intent as to the existence of a conflict with state law is often ambiguous and courts have taken a variety of approaches to resolving the ambiguity.

An approach to determining the scope of preemption that resonates with Austrian market processes is to interpret the federal law in light of the overall goal of achieving efficient jurisdictional choice (O'Hara and Ribstein, 2011). Specifically, as long as the states offer efficient jurisdictional choice, the courts should presume against applying the federal statute to override state law. On the other hand, where the federal law provides for choice-of-state law, or where the state choice-of-law rule does not enable efficient jurisdictional choice, these would be circumstances favorable for preemption. These results are grounded in the reasonable assumption that the U.S. federal system is designed to enable efficient jurisdictional choice, and therefore that Congress should be presumed to be crafting its law consistent with this design.

Private Law

Even given the potential for jurisdictional competition, the effects of this competition may be limited by public lawmakers' weak incentives to innovate. Private parties' production of laws may usefully supplement public lawmaking (Hadfield and Talley, 2006). However, private lawmaking, like jurisdictional competition, requires appropriate legal institutions.

In this case the main institutional aid is giving private lawmakers greater property rights in law (Kobayashi and Ribstein, 2011). Under current law, private lawmakers may not obtain patent or copyright protection for their creations that are embodied in law (Copyright Act §105). Nor can they contract for substitute contractual protection because of legal restrictions on law firm non-competition agreements. Without such property rights, private lawmaking may be confined to interest groups which would limit the availability of efficient forms. Conversely, additional intellectual property rights in law could enhance the development of an Austrian-style market for law.

SPECIFIC APPLICATIONS OF THE MARKET FOR LAW

This part applies the above general principles to a few areas of the law that significantly affect innovation. The following discussion attempts to capture the range of applications in terms of the feasibility of applying law market principles. Such applications illustrate the myriad of ways in which changing the legal process can encourage innovation and entrepreneurship toward economic growth and prosperity.

Business Associations

Efficient business structures are vital to innovation. For example, capital-intensive firms need outside investors. These investors want rules that balance the benefits of empowering managers to run the firm against the need to hold them accountable for their actions. Given the almost infinite combinations of rules that are possible in structuring the governance of a business association, the market for state law is especially important in designing efficient business structures. Since large firms can have owners in many states, each of which can exercise jurisdiction over suits regarding the firm's governance, any market for corporate governance law would be infeasible in large firms unless firms could choose a single state's law to control their governance. Also, in situations involving long-term contracts governing parties whose needs may change and involving litigation that may arise multiple times during the life of the firm, parties have strong reasons for choosing not only a particular law but also a particular jurisdiction with reliable courts, lawyers, and legislature.

These conditions justify the strong U.S. rule providing for enforcement of firms' choice of the state law applicable to their governance contracts (O'Hara and Ribstein, 2009). Under the so-called "internal affairs doctrine," the parties to a firm can organize in any state and have the rules of the state of organization apply to their firm's internal organization regardless of where they live or where the firm is based. The internal affairs doctrine has facilitated the evolution of the corporation from the era of special chartering, when firms had to seek legislatures' permission to form, to the adoption throughout the U.S. of general incorporation laws giving the parties full contractual freedom to decide on governance rules appropriately tailored to fit their specific needs (Ribstein and O'Hara, 2008). Broad application of the internal affairs doctrine to small and unincorporated firms has facilitated efficient contracting for incentives and governance in these firms. This is significant for present purposes because small firms are an important source of innovation and growth.

These considerations support continued encouragement of the corporate law market not only by enforcement of the internal affairs doctrine at the state level, but also by limiting the effect of federal securities and tax laws that can constrain the state law market. A positive development along these lines was the promulgation of the "check the box" tax classification rules, which permitted small firms to choose their business form irrespective of their tax status as corporations or partnerships (Treas. Reg. § 301.7701-1-3 (2004)). On the other hand, the expansion of federal law into the details of corporate governance in both the Sarbanes-Oxley Act of 2002 and the Dodd-Frank Wall Street Reform and Consumer Protection Act of 2010 significantly reduced the ability of the state market for law to experiment with governance provisions and discover the most efficient provisions. Such preemptive prevention of experimentation is not conducive to a system of legal competition allowing room for innovation and economic expansion.

Law Firms

Law firms are an important exception to firms' general freedom to choose the appropriate state governance law. As part of their power to regulate the legal profession, states limit the types of business structures lawyers practicing in the state can use for the practice of law. Because these rules apply to all lawyers practicing in the state, lawyers may not choose to organize under the law of State A while practicing in State B. National law firms therefore must abide by the laws of all of the states in which they practice. This rule effectively requires the legal profession to function under uniform laws proposed by the American Bar Association. Uniformity, in turn, bars law practice from the competitive lawmaking process that has enabled the evolution of business associations discussed in the previous section.

The purported rationale for having a distinct choice of law rule for law practice is that states have a special need to regulate the legal profession. Even if this is true, however, it does not clearly justify regulating law firms' structure, as distinguished from lawyers' and law firms' conduct. Firms generally are free to choose their business structure to best facilitate their business operations, including the firms' compliance with applicable regulation of business practices. It is not clear why the same principle should not apply to law firms.

Law firm governance illustrates the significance of jurisdictional choice in encouraging entrepreneurship. The existing regulatory structure of the legal profession is controlled by factions that exercise power in the American Bar Association. These groups seek to limit competition with lawyers by those who do not pay the entrance fee of a license to practice law and by lawyers who do not play by the existing rules of the game. A simple business-association-type rule that allowed national law firms to choose their state of organization could have profound effects in enabling entrepreneurship in the legal profession.

The availability of a competitive market for law firm governance is particularly important now because of the pressures facing law practice. Law firms confront unprecedented challenges to their business model because, among other things, of changes in technology and increased global competition. Innovations in business structure facilitated by legal competition would enable the legal services business to better respond to these challenges (Ribstein, 2010a). This, in turn, would not only facilitate growth of the legal services industry but also provide incentives for the development of more efficient legal information and services that could support growth throughout the economy.

An important example of the need for innovation in law firm structure concerns the sale of equity shares in law firms to non-lawyers. In the U.S. only lawyers may own law firms (Model Rules of Professional Conduct Rule 5.4). This means that law firms, the largest of which are multi-billion-dollar operations, can obtain financing only from their lawyers and bank loans. This limitation effectively forces firms to operate hand-to-mouth, and can result in their swift unwinding under financial pressure. It also prevents law firms from financing new lines of business such as investments in the research and development of new legal technologies and from fully realizing potential synergies from combinations with non-lawyer professionals.

A competitive law market for law firm governance would promote the development of financing structures that would meet the special challenges of non-lawyer financing of law firms. Law firms need new structural rules that balance outside investors' demands for power to protect their investments against lawyers' need for sufficient control to assure clients and regulators that the firm will maintain professional standards. These structures raise new issues and the potential problems are unforeseeable. Effective solutions call for the same sort of discovery process as the competition for business association laws under the internal affairs doctrine.

While jurisdictional competition for law firm structures would encourage beneficial innovation, it is also necessary to preserve some role for efficient state regulation of law firm structure. These objectives could be accomplished through a default rule of enforcing interstate law firms' choice of state law subject to each state's power to enact laws regulating local lawyers (Ribstein, 2001).

Internet Law

The Internet can be a powerful medium for communicating and gathering information. Because websites place unique identifying numbers called "cookies" on the hard drives of consumers who browse the Internet, web operators can gather information from consumers who visit their sites. This enables the operators to know which pages consumers visit and how long they spend on each page and potentially to link this information with customer identifying information such as email addresses, passwords, and credit card numbers. This technology offers significant opportunities to reduce transaction costs and increase information. At the same time, it poses potential problems by enabling sellers to invade consumers' privacy.

Balancing these competing concerns raises issues as to what the applicable rules should be, whether they should be default or mandatory, whether it is enough to let consumers opt-out of default rules, or whether consumers should have to opt-into rules that enable sellers to invade their privacy. The answers to these questions depend to some extent on how individual consumers weigh privacy interests against the convenience of visiting websites that know their preferences. Different types of transactions and goods and different types of consumers may call for different rules.

Developing a competitive legal process would enable experimentation and discovery necessary to determine the mix of rules that would enable efficient innovation. Each firm could choose the set of rules that best fits its business model. The industry could innovate based on these secure and suitable legal platforms. At the same time, enabling jurisdictional choice would offset the political power of powerful industry incumbents.

A fully competitive legal process in this area entails enforcement of choice-of-law contracts. If each state can apply its law under general common law choice-of-law rules to transactions that are connected to the state (which connections states can determine through modern geographic filtering technologies), sellers might not know which law applies to any of their transactions and may have to comply with the strictest rule (Kobayashi and Ribstein, 2002). This would discourage legal innovation and deny firms the secure legal platforms they need for growth.

The National Conference of Commissioners of Uniform State Laws attempted to achieve interstate enforcement of choice of law contracts by promulgating the Uniform Computer Information Transactions Act, section 109(d) (UCITA) of which would enforce a choice of law clause in electronic consumer sales unless the contract would vary a mandatory rule in the seller's state. Like the internal affairs doctrine applicable to business associations, the choice-of-law contract would be enforceable without regard to the seller's or transaction's relationship with the state whose law is selected in the transaction. This would free sellers to choose the law of any state. If there is a restrictive law in the seller's home state, the seller can avoid the restriction simply by relocating to another state. A similar rule could be applied to the "cookies" context.

Only two jurisdictions adopted the UCITA provision and several adopted "bomb shelter" provisions that explicitly invalidated choice-of-law clauses choosing UCITA-based laws. This leaves firms subject to more open-ended default choice-of-law rules. This result arguably indicates the futility of relying on the uniform lawmaking process to encourage the efficient evolution of state law. States rejected contractual choice of law that was tied to an objectionable uniform law. Contractual choice might work if states were free to develop laws that met sister state objections rather than being bound to a single "uniform" solution.

The states' rejection of contractual choice in the Internet setting also might reflect the states' inherent inability to coordinate on this issue, perhaps because local business interests are able to override those of out-of-state firms competing on the Internet. The appropriate solution might be a federal law mandating enforcement of choice-of-law clauses, except to the extent enforcement is explicitly prohibited by a state statute. This could enable a competition among state laws which over time discovers the right balance between permissive and mandatory rules.

Non-competition Clauses

Contracts restricting competition by former employees can significantly affect innovation. On the one hand, non-competition agreements protect employers' rights in intellectual property and thereby potentially encourage investments in creating that property and therefore innovation. On the other hand, non-competition agreements can inhibit the movement of knowledge, skills, and information among firms and thereby discourage innovation that depends on new combinations of these resources. Individual firms may be tempted to ignore the effect of their contracts on innovation because they incur all of the costs of losing control over intellectual property while capturing only some of the benefits of innovation. Such experimentation and competition is precisely what Austrians like Schumpeter emphasize as critical to a flourishing economy.

The problem of determining the appropriate regulatory approach to non-competition agreements illustrates how the law market can promote innovation while allowing space for reasonable regulation. The dynamic and long-term social costs and benefits of rules protecting property rights or encouraging the spread of knowledge are beyond the knowledge or foresight of any individual lawmaker. Indeed, it is likely that no single rule is appropriate. California's law making these clauses unenforceable has been heralded as spurring the growth of Silicon Valley (Gilson 1999). On the other hand, non-competes may be critical in industries in which developments take longer and patents and copyrights are less available to protect intellectual property. The law market provides a way to experiment with a variety of regimes to achieve the optimal pro-growth/pro-innovation policy.

Insurance

The insurance industry would seem to be ripe for innovation of numerous kinds of contracts that protect from a variety of risks. However, the industry is particularly stymied by the choice-of-law problem. The McCarran-Ferguson Act of 1945 prohibits federal regulation of the insurance business, thus leaving regulation up to the states. The states, for their part, are particularly reluctant to cede their regulatory power through enforcement of choice-of-law contracts, given concerns about the complexity and take-it-or-leave-it nature of insurance contracts and consumers' inability to judge insurers' solvency. Moreover, many states prohibit arbitration clauses in insurance contracts, thereby blocking an important mechanism for promoting enforcement of choice-of-law and choice-of-forum clauses.

There is currently a move toward repealing McCarran-Ferguson and federalizing insurance law. This would protect insurers from duplicative state regulation and consumers from inadequate state regulation. However, as discussed throughout this chapter, federal regulation would eliminate the potential for experimentation and discovery of superior regulatory solutions through state competition. Dodd-Frank made a move toward federalization but stopped with the creation of some oversight through a new Federal Insurance Office.

As with the other contexts discussed above, the various relevant interests could be addressed through a federal law that requires state courts to enforce choice-of-law provisions in insurance contracts unless a statute in the state where the policy is sold explicitly bars such enforcement (Butler and Ribstein, 2008). This would enable firms to choose the law that suits their business and encourage states to adopt the laws firms prefer. States could compete to lead the competition, which is significant in this area given the complexity of insurance law and the need for regulatory expertise. States' ability to specialize may increase the quality of regulation compared to the current system of regulation under which parties cannot choose the applicable law. Also, states' power to adopt legislation applying local law to local insureds would help prevent a "race-to-the-bottom" in insurance law. At the same time, repealing McCarran-Ferguson and paving the way for potential federal regulation would discipline the states by exposing them to the threat that excessive regulation could lead to broad federalization of insurance law.

Property Law

Rights concerning real property, including rules regarding use, ownership and transfer of the property, are subject only to the law of the state where the property is located. This clear "situs" rule at least reduces the potential for applying multiple state laws at the time of litigation to a single transaction. However, the application of a single rule also prevents the operation of a competitive process that can lead to the discovery of the most efficient menu of rules. As land use is subject to increasing stresses of laws relating to such matters as the environment, historic preservation and restrictions on growth (Garnett, No Reference), there is a special need for a discovery process with respect to the development of new legal technologies for real property. (Morriss 2010, 116) A competitive law process could further this development by making it easier for property owners to choose among rights available in various states (O'Hara and Ribstein, 2009, Ch. 8).

Conservation easements illustrate how such a lawmaking process could facilitate property rights' innovations (Ribstein, 2010b). These instruments enable property owners to lock in particular uses of their property in perpetuity. Many states have adopted laws providing for these easements, spurred by a federal tax break for conservation easements. The complexity and novelty of these property rights and the federal tax law have induced states to widely adopt the Uniform Conservation Easement Act. Letting property owners enter into easements provided for by the law of states other than where the property is located could spur a competitive lawmaking process and legal innovations. As with the other areas discussed above, states would retain the ability to legislatively block local property owners from adopting certain types of laws. This combination of competition and mandatory rules could lead to the discovery of more efficient rules regarding this relatively new property right.

Products Liability

Nowhere is there a greater need for legal process to pave the way for innovation than with regard to products liability law. Manufacturers may be significantly discouraged from innovating because new products pose new risks of liability to consumers for product injuries. The expansion of tort law is sometimes viewed as a failure of state law that calls for federal safety regulation to preempt the states. But before sacrificing the benefits of the market for state law, it is worth trying the choice-of-law alternative.

Current choice-of-law rules generally let plaintiffs choose to litigate in states with the most pro-plaintiff laws. Changing the prevailing rule to one that always applies the law where the product is manufactured could be too favorable to manufacturers. Applying the law of the state where the product is first sold might be a reasonable compromise because firms could determine their prices based on the product liability laws in each state where the product is sold. However, no states apply such a rule.

A possible solution, as with the other areas discussed above, is a federal law enabling the parties to contract for the applicable state's product liability law. Consumer groups might fear that this would cause a "race to the bottom" toward the laxest standards because consumers could be expected to shop on the basis of the applicable state law. However, states would have an interest in protecting their own residents from unsafe products rather than just being states chosen in product liability contracts. Also, manufacturers of high-quality goods have an incentive to avoid choosing very lax laws because of the negative signal this could send as to product quality. Consumers can rely on the press, blogs and consumer watchdogs to alert the market of very pro-manufacturer state laws and the large consumer product firms that adopt them.

Even if consumers cannot rely fully on the market, the system applied throughout this chapter—that is, enabling states to enact statutes blocking enforcement of contractual choice—could provide fallback protection. States could decide whether they want to adopt relatively lax product standards and enforce contractual choice in order to attract manufacturers into the state or adopt strict laws that protect consumers. The federal government could provide discipline by standing ready to supplant state law if states prove too obedient to trial lawyers or manufacturers. Conversely, courts could interpret federal laws narrowly to avoid preemption of state laws that enable efficient jurisdictional choice.

This approach would enable states to experiment with various legal rules and to discover policies that optimally balance the costs and benefits of product innovation. Although this system may not yield perfect results, it is important to keep in mind the costs of the alternatives—a chaotic state system that exposes manufacturers to the rules of all of the states in which they sell products, or a one-size-fits-all federal rule that preempts state law and precludes experimentation.

Franchise Regulation

Franchising is a potentially valuable form of contracting and an important pathway for innovations in distributing products and services. However, state regulation has limited the usefulness of franchising by restricting franchisors' ability to terminate franchisees, thereby undercutting franchisors' most important mechanism of policing franchisees' attempts to cheat on quality. Proponents of the regulation argue that the laws are necessary to prevent franchisors from opportunistically using termination provisions to take over the locations that prove most profitable (i.e., "cream-skimming").

State franchise regulation has been tested in the market for state law. Franchisors have struck back against the regulation by inserting choice-of-law and choice-of-forum clauses in their contracts that avoid the most onerous state regulation. Regulating states counter-attacked by enacting laws invalidating these provisions. Theory predicts that franchisors would then avoid the states that insist on applying the most onerous laws. This, in turn, could set off a political backlash by workers, suppliers and customers in the state who are injured by the departure of the franchises.

Indeed, there is direct evidence of the reduction of outlets in regulating states, and indirect evidence of this reduction based on reduced employment in franchise industries. These effects are greatest in states that invalidate choice-of-law and choice-of-forum contracts (Klick, Kobayashi, and Ribstein, 2006, 2009). These data indicate that the market for state law can enable innovation by limiting the effect of regulation.

Our proposed federal law mandating enforcement of choice-of-law clauses subject to states being free to opt-out through legislation again provides a useful compromise between the market for law and state regulatory interests. This approach is particularly valuable in a context such as franchise regulation where the interest groups that would face off in the legislature are closely matched and the threat of franchisor exit could influence the legislative decision. As discussed in the Klick, Kobayashi and Ribstein article above (2006), franchise regulation went through a period of back-and-forth between judicial decisions and legislation that left the law unclear and muted interest group competition. A clear rule providing for enforcement of choice of law clauses subject to state legislative opt-out could have shortened the period of uncertainty, helped ensure a regulatory outcome that best reflected all political interests, and encouraged growth-enhancing developments in franchising.

CONCLUSION

Austrian economics stresses the importance of market processes continually discovering valuable information and entrepreneurship that discovers new and more efficient ways of doing business. Markets can be as important to the development of efficient legal frameworks as they are to business. Markets in both areas require the support of legal institutions. This chapter suggests how the market for state law could be designed to produce a process for discovering efficient rules. Even if the suggested approach is not adopted, the main lesson of this chapter is that any regime for encouraging growth must take account of the existence of multiple jurisdictions and the potential for jurisdictional choice and competition.

REFERENCES

Becker, Gary S. "A Theory of Competition Among Pressure Groups for Political Influence." (1983) 98(3) *Quarterly Journal of Economics* 371–400.

Butler, Henry N. "Smith v. Van Gorkom, Jurisdictional Competition, and the Role of Random Mutations in the Evolution of Corporate Law." (2006) 45(2) *Washburn Law Journal* 267–82.

Butler, Henry N. and Larry E. Ribstein. "A Single-License Approach to Regulating Insurance." (2008) http://ssrn.com/abstract=1134792.

Gilson, Ronald J. "The Legal Infrastructure of High Technology Industrial Districts: Silicon Valley, Route 128, and Covenants Not to Compete." (1999) 74(3) *New York University Law Review* 575–629.

Hadfield, Gillian and Talley, Eric. "On Public versus Private Provision of Law." (2006) *Journal of Law, Economics and Organization* 414.

Hayek, Frederick von. "The Use of Knowledge in Society." (1945) 35(4) *American Economic Review* 519–30.

Hirschman, Albert O. *Exit, Voice and Loyalty.* Cambridge, Mass.: Harvard University Press, 1970.

Hylton, Keith N. *Antitrust Law: Economic Theory and Common Law Evolution.* New York: Cambridge University Press, 2003.

Kirzner, Israel. *An Entrepreneurial Theory of the Firm.* London and New York: 2000.

Klick, Jonathan, Bruce H. Kobayashi and Larry E. Ribstein. "The Effect of Contract Regulation: The Case of Franchising." (2006) 13 December. http://ssrn.com/abstract=951464.

Klick, Jonathan, Bruce H. Kobayashi, and Larry E. Ribstein. 2009. "Federalism, Variation, and State Regulation of Franchise Termination." University of Pennsylvania Law School Faculty Scholarship Paper 1127.

Kobayashi, Bruce H. and Larry E. Ribstein. "State Regulation of Electronic Commerce." (2002) 51(1) *Emory Law Journal* 1–82.

Kobayashi, Bruce H. and Larry E. Ribstein. "Law as a Byproduct: Theories of Private Law Production." (2011) 9 *Journal of Law, Economics and Policy* 521.

Morriss, Andrew P. "The Role of Offshore Financial Centers in Regulatory Competition." In *Offshore Financial Centers in Regulatory Competition*, by Andrew P. Morriss, ed., pp. 102–46. Washington, D.C.: AEI Press, 2010.

O'Hara, Erin A. and Larry E. Ribstein. "Exit and the American Illness." Illinois Program in Law, Behavior and Social Science Paper No. LBSS11-08, 2011.

O'Hara, Erin A. and Larry E. Ribstein. *The Law Market.* Oxford, New York: Oxford University Press, 2009.

Ribstein, Larry E. "Ethical Rules, Law Firm Structure and Choice of Law." (2001) 69(4) *University of Cincinnati Law Review* 1161–203.

Ribstein, Larry E. "The Death of Big Law." (2010a) 3 *Wisconsin Law Review* 749–815.

Ribstein, Larry E. "The Market for Conservation Law." (2010b) 17 May. http://ssrn.com/abstract=1609793.

Ribstein, Larry E. and Erin A. O'Hara. "Corporations and the Market for Law." (2008) *Illinois Law Review* 661–729.

Schumpeter, Joseph A. *Capitalism, Socialism and Democracy.* New York: Harper, 1975.

von Mises, Ludwig. *Human Action.* New Haven, Conn.: Yale University Press, 1949.

7. Customary commercial law, credibility, contracting, and credit in the high Middle Ages
Bruce L. Benson

Writing around 1020, Alpert of Metz described merchants in the town of Tiel as "men unaccustomed to discipline, who judge suits not according to law but according to inclination. . ." (Pertz 1925: 118). In other words, merchants did not follow what Alpert considered to be law.[1] If merchants were lawless, however, they were not *rule-less*, as a monk writing around 1000 A.D., Notger of St. Gallen, suggested. He explained that 'negotiale' referred to a situation in which a "dispute which arise about custom: as merchants maintain that a sale made in a fair should be binding, whether it is just or unjust, since *it is their custom*" (translated and quoted by Volckart and Mangels 1999: 439; emphasis added).[2] Quoting from eleventh century Maghribi documents, Greif (2006: 70) similarly stressed that:

> Given the state of communication and transportation technology in the eleventh century, it is not surprising that the Maghribi traders . . . employed a set of cultural rules or behavior – merchants' law .. . .
> The importance of the merchants' law in determining expectations about and attitudes toward an agent's behavior is reflected in the letter written by Maymum ben Khalpha to Naharay ben Nissim. In discussing the conflict between Naharay and his agent, Maymum justifies the agent's actions by arguing that the agent "did something which is imposed by the trade and the communication [system; what you asked him to do] contradicts the merchants' law.". . .. In

---

[1] Perhaps Alpert was referring to Canon law, manorial law, local customary law, or early royal law (see Berman (1983) for discussion of the variety of legal systems emerging in Europe during the twelfth century). Alpert, who was a monk, clearly did not understand the rules that formed the basis of merchant dispute resolutions [nor did he approve of merchants, noting that "They begin their drinking bouts at the crack of dawn, and the one who tells dirty jokes with the loudest voice and raises laughter and induces the vulgar folks to drink gains high praise among them" (Pertz 1925: 118)]. Most writing during this period was by monks and other clerics, of course, and they probably had little incentive to concern themselves with the rules and processes of merchant law unless they observed something that was considered to be in violation of the Church's law.

[2] Volckart and Mangels (1999: 439, note 41) suggested that the monk was referring to "just prices" rather than legalities.

another letter a "very angry" merchant accused his business associate of taking "actions [that] are not those of a merchant."

Greif (2006: 71) also noted that numerous early documents indicate that Islamic law was not applied to merchants because merchants were subject to the "custom of the merchants." There are even earlier documents from the first half of the ninth century suggesting that merchants in parts of Europe were using different legal procedures than those employed in local communities (Kadens 2004: 43, note 17). Clearly, even if merchants did not follow law as Alpert saw it, some kind of *law-like* institutional arrangements existed in much of Europe and the Middle East by the beginning of the high Middle Ages (roughly 1000 A.D. to 1300 A.D.) that merchants considered to be relevant to their dealings. At least some non-merchants also realized that such institutions were important. These institutional arrangements continued to evolve throughout this period, resulting in a system of rules and procedures that is usually referred to as *Lex Mercatoria*, or the "Law Merchant" in much but not all of the relevant literature, although writings about or from the medieval period often use other terms, such as "merchants' law," "custom of merchants," "customary law of merchants," "method of merchants," "the way of the trade," and "law of the fair."[3] Hayek (1973: 83) contended that: "It is in the . . . law merchant, and the practices of the ports and fairs that we must chiefly seek the steps in the evolution of law which ultimately made an open society possible."

There is a very large literature devoted to describing and analyzing the medieval *Lex Mercatoria*,[4] much of it supporting Hayek's contention, but

---

[3]   In the mid-1950s, *Lex Mercatoria* also began to be used as a label for certain rules and procedures of modern international commercial activity that arise through contracting.

[4]   The oldest English treatise on *Lex Mercatoria*, a chapter in *The Little Red Book of Bristol,* was written sometime around 1280 (Bickley 1900 [c.1280], Teeter 1962, Basile 1998 [c. 1280]), but the earliest known "analytical" examinations of the Law Merchant in England did not appear until the seventeenth century, with publication of Malynes (1622), Marius (1651), and Zouch (1663) [Stracca (1553) appeared earlier, in Italy]. This is not surprising since merchants themselves really had no incentive to produce or encourage such analysis. Something else had to create incentives to do so, and this occurred in England when the competition between common law and the prerogative or civil law courts was at its peak [see Zywicki (2003)]. This was part of the competition for power between the Crown and Parliament, as the common law courts were aligned with Parliament and prerogative courts were associated with the Crown. The common law jurists attempted to assert jurisdiction over all law in England (including merchant law) during the late sixteenth and seventeenth centuries, while the civil law courts

there also is an expanding literature, particularly over the last decade, that is critical of the medieval Law Merchant story.[5] Volckart and Mangels (1999: 436) [hereafter VM] contended, for instance, that: "As late as the **high and late Middle Ages** ... nonsimultaneous commercial transactions were rare if they occurred at all. Simultaneous exchanges had, however, one advantage: there was no dispute over the date of payment, the conditions of payment and so on" (emphasis added). In other words, they contended that issues such as credibility of promises and enforcement of contracts were not relevant, making it "highly problematic to speak of a medieval *lex mercatoria* when the term is meant to denote an 'international system of commercial law' (Benson 1989: 645) or an 'integrated, developing system, a *body* of law' (Berman 1983: 333, italics added)" (VM 1999: 442).[6] Sachs (2006: 690) was even stronger in his critique, stating that: "the historical experience of medieval mercantile law has been grossly misconceived. The Romantic interpretation is deeply inaccurate, at least as applied to the experience of medieval England, and provides a prime example of the misuse of historical evidence in support of political ends." The purpose of this chapter is to address some of these criticisms.[7]

The medieval Law Merchant was a system of "customary law" (Benson

---

tried to support what they considered to be their own jurisdictions. Advocates for both sides produced "scholarly" arguments in an effort to substantiate their jurisdictional claims. Zouch was an Admiralty Court Judge, for instance (Coquillette 2004: 318). Admiralty was one of the prerogative courts, and Zouch (1668 [1663]) offered a detailed argument to support Admiralty's jurisdiction over merchant disputes, contending that the relevant rules were supplied by the Law Merchant. Descriptions and interpretations (based on various documents and on reasoning by analogy) of the medieval Law Merchant have continued to appear since then. For a few examples, see Mitchell (1904), Bewes (1923), Trakman (1983), Berman (1983), Benson (1989, 1990, 1999, 2010, 2011), and Milgrom, et al. (1990). Numerous modern legal scholars accept the description provided by this literature, including Johnson and Post (1996), Mallat (2000), Zywicki (2003), Callahan (2004), Belhorn (2005), and Levit (2005).

[5] For instance, see Volckart and Mangels (1999), Donahue (2004), Fassberg (2004), Kadens (2004), Drahozal (2005, 2008), and Sachs (2006). Criticisms not addressed here are being examined in detail in a book manuscript (Benson 2016) nearing completion.

[6] VM (1999) drew this conclusion despite the fact that they described how such a system can grow and expand, first through the development of trust and reputation effects within small groups of traders, and then through the development of intergroup reputation and support arrangements. They even cite several sources referring to the differential "legal" treatment of merchants and non-merchants.

[7] Sachs (2006) makes so many incorrect criticisms of the Law Merchant literature that they cannot even begin to be addressed here, but an attempt to correct his errors is made in Benson (2016) where numerous other critiques are also examined.

1989, 1999, 2010, 2011), and many of the criticisms of the Law-Merchant literature appear to reflect a severe lack of understanding of the concept of "customary law" as the term is used in that literature.[8] Therefore, Section I below explains this concept and its implications for interpretation of historical evidence. An overview of the medieval *Lex Mercatoria* is then provided in Section II. While the system has been described numerous times, the description provided here is intended to stress the roles of contracting and credit in trade during the high Middle Ages in order to address the VM contention cited above, while simultaneously emphasizing certain characteristics of the customary Law Merchant that apparently have not been understood [or perhaps, have not been adequately explained], given some of the other recent criticisms of the medieval Law Merchant literature. Section III concludes with an examination of various relationships between the medieval Law Merchant and other legal systems that existed in or were developing during the high Middle Ages, as these relationships also have proven to be significant sources of some misunderstandings underlying some criticisms.

I.   CUSTOMARY LAW[9]

The term, customary law, has been used in many different ways (Pospisil 1971, 1978),[10] but it is defined here to be a system of rules of obligation and governance arrangements that spontaneously evolve from the bottom up within some community (Pospisil 1978) rather than being imposed from the top down.[11] As Hayek (1973: 96–7) explained, many issues of "law" are not:

---

[8]   Much of the controversy over the Law Merchant actually is definitional (Coquillette 1987: 291–2; Donahue 2004: 27; Epstein 2004: 3–4). Basic concepts like law, customary law, and *Lex Mercatoria* itself, have been given multiple definitions (Epstein 2004, Kadens 2004, Drahozal 2005, 2008, Sachs 2006), and many of the critics define one or more of these terms differently than do the targets of their criticisms. A definition of the Law Merchant is provided below, but the alternative definitions are not addressed. Instead, criticisms arising because of definitional issues are considered in Benson (2016).

[9]   This section draws freely from Benson (2010, 2011, 2016).

[10]   The term often refers to rules that are not codified, for instance, and that have been relied upon by the members of a group, unchanged "from time immemorial." This condition often has been required for judicial recognition of customary underpinning of the common law, but this definition is not applied here. That is, customary law does not refer to the customary rules recognized by a sovereign or a court in this presentation.

[11]   This means that some systems of rule referred to as custom, such as "feudal custom", are not "customary law" as defined here, because these rules have a

whether the parties have abused anybody's will, but whether their actions have conformed to expectations which other parties had reasonably formed because they corresponded to the practices on which the everyday conduct of the members of the group was based. The significance of customs here is that they give rise to expectations that guide people's actions, and what will be regarded as binding will therefore be those practices that everybody counts on being observed and which thereby condition the success of most activities.

In this light, in the following presentation a "rule of behavior" refers to a behavioral pattern that individuals within a community are expected to adopt and follow in their various interdependent activities and actions. The rules individuals are expected to follow influence the choices made by other individuals: rules coordinate and motivate interdependent behavior. Thus, Fuller (1981: 213) noted that;

> We sometimes speak of customary law as offering an unwritten code of conduct. The word <u>code</u> is appropriate here because what is involved is not simply a negation, . . . but of this negation, the meaning it confers on foreseeable and approved actions, which then furnish a point of orientation for ongoing interactive responses.

Customary law involves more than rules of behavior, however (Pospisil 1978, Benson 1988, 1989, 1990). Indeed, customary rules and procedures often can be characterized as "legal systems" from Hart's (1961) positivist perspective, with primary rules of obligation, as well as secondary rules of change, adjudication and recognition (Benson 1989, 1990). In fact, for instance, change in primary rules often characterizes bottom-up customary-law systems (Pospisil 1971, Fuller 1981, Benson 1988, 1989, 1990). If conditions change and a set of individuals decide that, for their purposes, a new behavior rule will support the pursuit of their interdependent objectives better than the current rule, they can voluntarily agree to follow (contract to adopt) the new rule within their own interactions. Thus, an existing rule is replaced by a new obligation, but importantly, only for the contracting parties. This change occurs without prior consent of, or simultaneous recognition by, any other members of the relevant community beyond recognition of the rights individuals have to contract. Individuals who interact with these parties learn about their contractual innovation, however, and/or members of the community observe its results. If the results are more desirable than outcomes under older custom, the new rule can be rapidly emulated. As Fuller (1981: 224–5) explained, "If we permit ourselves to think of contract law as the 'law' that parties themselves bring

---

top-down component. Pospisil (1978) labels top-down rules based on coercion and command as "authoritarian law," a distinction employed here.

into existence by their agreement, the transition from customary law to contract law becomes a very easy one indeed." In fact, contract and custom are tightly intertwined and often inseparable:

> if problems arise which are left without verbal solution in the parties' contract these will commonly be resolved by asking what "standard practice" is with respect to the issues. . . In such a case it is difficult to know whether to say that . . . the parties became subject to a governing body of customary law or to say that they have by tacit agreement incorporated standard practice into the terms of the contract.
> . . . [Furthermore,] . . . the parties may have conducted themselves toward one another in such a way that one can say that a tacit exchange of promises has taken place. Here the analogy between contract and customary law approaches identity. (Fuller 1981: 176)

Negotiation (contracting) also is the most important method for initiating change in customary law (Fuller 1981: 157).

A gap in existing customary rules can also be revealed because a dispute arises. Negotiation is the primary means of dispute resolution, of course, reinforcing the contention that contracting is a primary mechanism for initiating change in customary law. If direct negotiation fails, however, the parties to a dispute often turn to community-based arbitration or mediation. Many different procedures are observed in different customary communities (Benson 1990), so rather than explore all possibilities, medieval Law Merchant procedures are described in Section II. Nonetheless, a new customary rule might be suggested by resulting third-party dispute resolution (Fuller 1981: 110–11). Unlike modern common law precedent, however, the resolution only applies to the parties in the dispute, just as contracts only apply to the parties to the contract. If it suggests behavior that effectively facilitates desirable interactions, the implied rule can be adopted and spread through the community. In situations where contract is widely employed, however, adjudication can be a trivial source of change. Arbitrators may look to existing practice and usage or to contractual terms, but if this does not provide guidance, they may simply apply general default rules based on equity considerations while contracting serves as the primary procedure for the initiation of new rules. This appears to be the case for much of the changes in rules of obligation in the medieval Law Merchant, as suggested below.[12]

---

[12]   There are other ways for new customary rules to be initiated as well. An individual may simply begin to behave in a recognizable way when she is engaged in a particular type of interaction with others, for instance, and after noticing this behavior others are likely to begin expecting it from her. The behavioral pattern

Both "positive" and "negative" incentives to recognize rules and accept dispute resolutions arise in customary law. The sources of such incentives vary (e.g., family ties, friendship, common religious and/or ethnic backgrounds), but they clearly include bilateral repeated dealing which creates both trust and the ability to threaten punishment with tit-for-tat strategies. More importantly, multilateral webs of interactions based on reciprocities accompanied by development of communications mechanisms and investments in reputations also enhance the potential for voluntary interaction. Such multilateral webs of interaction and communication simultaneously provide large benefits from cooperation in economic, social, and/ or cultural (e.g., religious) activities and create threats of punishment by the spread of information about misbehavior, leading to social sanctions including ostracism. Examples are detailed in Section II.

Institutionalized rules and procedures also can facilitate the expansion of inter-community interaction, but communities need not formally "merge" and accept a common set of rules that govern all interactions (Benson 1988; Pospisil 1971). Individuals from different communities only have to expect each other to recognize specific rules pertaining to the types of inter-group interactions that evolve. Indeed, a "jurisdictional hierarchy" often arises wherein each group has its own rules and procedures for intra-community relationships while a separate and possibly different set of rules and procedures apply for inter-group relations (Pospisil 1971; Benson 1988, 1990). This hierarchy does not create top-down law (e.g., through appellate courts), however, as the inter-group institutions have no role in intra-community relationships (other than possibly by revealing potential rules and procedures that might be observed and emulated). Customary law, therefore, often is "polycentric," with multiple parallel "local" (i.e., community-level) jurisdictions, as well as overlapping jurisdictions supporting various kinds of inter-community interactions. Two communities can have very different community level rules and procedures, and the inter-community arrangements may involve still different rules and procedures (people from different groups often independently come up with similar solutions to the same problem, however, and furthermore, over time, comparisons of many rules are likely to occur with the most effective rule for a particular activity being emulated), but the communities can still capture benefits of voluntary inter-community interactions despite such differences.

Customary communities also can (and generally do) become mutual

---

is not a general rule, however, as the expectation only applies to one individual. If others emulate the behavior and it is widely adopted, then everyone will be expected to conform to that behavioral pattern under similar circumstances.

support groups with reciprocal obligations to assist each other in the pursuit of justice against outsiders. While this may simply involve mutual defense or mutual support in pursuit and prosecution of outsiders who commit offenses against insiders, it can also facilitate voluntary inter-group activities. For instance, communities can develop surety arrangements when cooperative inter-group interactions become desirable. Members insure one another in order to assure outsiders who might be victimized, intentionally or accidently, by a member of the group that they can expect compensation from the entire community if a community member who is the offender cannot or will not pay. The offender who initiates the inter-community conflict generally will be expected to compensate those who pay, of course, through contractual (indentured) servitude if other means are not available. This serves as a means of maintaining a group's reputation, and increasing the credibility of members' promises to outsiders. It also illustrates that intra-group institutions can differ from intergroup institutions. Intra-community recognition is largely based on trust, reciprocities, and individual reputations, while inter-group recognition may also require group reputations, surety commitments and/or bonding.

A crucial implication of this discussion is that understanding customary law requires consideration of different sources of information than those used to understand modern state-produced law, including common law. Unfortunately, some of the most ardent critics of the Law Merchant literature (e.g., Donahue 2004; Sachs 2006) fail to recognize this. A relatively good picture of state-imposed rules might be obtained by reading legislation, administrative documents, and/or court records or opinions, but customary rules generally are not recorded, either as statutes or as judicial opinions. Some obligations may appear as contract clauses, but contracts typically do not specify widely understood practices and usage (Fuller 1981: 176). There is no reason to do so when the contracting parties recognize the same set of customary rules. Therefore, behavior itself has to be observed to conceptualize customary rules. When observation is not possible (e.g., historical systems like the medieval Law Merchant), the best one can generally do is to read contracts, and probably more importantly, letters and other documents that can reveal actual behavioral patterns beyond those specified in contracts. Such documents only provide an incomplete snapshot of customary law, however, so even if they are available, a more complete understanding requires theoretical analysis informed by examinations of other customary law systems.[13]

---

[13]   See Benson (1990) where well-documented customary systems are discussed to establish basic principles about customary law, before examining historical

Custom Versus Authority

Pospisil (1971, 1978) distinguished between "legal" arrangements that evolve from the top down through command and coercion, which he called "authoritarian law," and customary law systems that evolve from the bottom up through voluntary interaction. Similarly, Hayek (1973, 82) distinguished between "purpose-independent rules of conduct" that evolve from the bottom up, and rules that are designed for a purpose and imposed from the top by "rulers." Both Hayek's and Pospisil's distinction suggests that customary law may conflict with authoritarian law. Indeed, as Hayek (1973, 82) stressed, "the growth of the purpose-independent rules of conduct . . . often have taken place in conflict with the aims of the rulers who tended to turn their domain into an organization proper." When this occurs, an authority backed by coercive power may attempt to assert jurisdiction over a customary community, but this will have very different impacts depending on the options available to members of the customary-law community. If the authority is strong enough, the customary community might be forced to accept the commands. Another possibility is that customary rules and procedures evolve that allow the customary community to avoid some and perhaps most authoritarian supervision (Bernstein 1992, Benson 1995, 2006). This may involve moving "underground," making the customary rules and procedures difficult to observe, in order to raise the costs of enforcement for the authority. If the customary community (and its wealth) is geographically mobile, however, members may simply move outside an authority's jurisdiction. The threat to move can significantly constrain authoritarian attempts to displace a customary system. If the sovereign wants to avoid an exodus for some reason, such as availability of tax revenues, she may even offer to assist in enforcing the customary rules, or explicitly codify them. Indeed, a sovereign may offer special privileges to members of a highly mobile customary community in order to capture benefits including revenues, perhaps directly from tribute or taxes on the customary law community, but also indirectly because of a positive impact that this community has on other less-mobile sources of wealth (e.g., land) that can more easily be controlled and taxed. Once customary behavioral rules are absorbed, and the customary procedures atrophy, an authority may amend or replace customary rules, although the

---

systems including the medieval Law Merchant. VM (1999) do something similar by looking first at the modern international Law Merchant before interpreting the medieval system, but they focus on differences rather than similarities, and they do not consider the actual behavior of merchants suggested by documents such as those examined in Face (1958, 1959) and Greif (1989, 1993, 2006).

ability to do so depends on the costs of reinvigorating customary institutions, on the mobility of members of the community, and on the value of the privileges granted to the community's members.

One of Berman's (1983) primary purposes was to illustrate that there was a plurality of distinct but interdependent legal systems in Europe during the high Middle Ages, some predominantly authoritarian and some predominantly customary, and that an understanding of their various behavioral implications provides important insights about the interactions between these systems and the influence each had on the others (Berman 1983: 10):

> The very complexity of a common legal <u>order</u> containing diverse legal <u>systems</u> contributes to legal sophistication. Which court has jurisdiction? Which law is applicable? How are legal differences to be reconciled? Behind the technical questions lay important political and economic considerations. ... The pluralism of . . . law, . . . has been . . . a source of development, or growth -- legal growth as well as political and economic growth.

Also note that many of these evolving medieval legal systems, both customary and authoritarian, were polycentric. Different royal law, manorial law, urban law, local custom and merchant law applied in different areas although similar rules also were shared, and rules to facilitate intergroup interaction also were common. The impact of the interdependence of legal systems on the medieval Law Merchant is examined below, but first it is important to understand *Lex Mercatoria* itself, as in Berman (1983).

II.   *LEX MERCATORIA*: CUSTOMARY LAW, CREDIBILITY, CONTRACT AND CREDIT IN THE HIGH MIDDLE AGES[14]

Substantial change occurred in Europe during the eleventh, twelfth and thirteenth centuries, the period often referred to as the high Middle Ages. With regard to economic activities and wealth creation, technological progress in agriculture (Mokyr 1990) meant that less labor was needed to produce sufficient food and clothing, individuals increasingly specialized, and many moved into towns. Trade accompanied specialization, and both production and trade expanded substantially between 1000 A.D. and 1300 A.D.[15] As wealth increased, demands for spices, dye-stuff, cordovan and

---

[14]   This section draws on material also presented in Benson (2010, 2011, 2016).

[15]   Many other factors also supported the increase in productivity, specialization and trade. Population increased with increased agricultural production. In addition, the Viking threat declined dramatically, making travel safer. The Viking

other "luxury" items available in the Mediterranean (generally through trade with Middle-Eastern merchants) increased in other parts of Europe. Similarly, demand for wool and linen cloth (and some other products, such as furs) from Northern Europe increased in more southerly regions. As long-distance trade in these goods expanded, growing numbers of merchants from widely dispersed parts of Europe began trading with one another at fairs (Face 1958).[16] These merchants often had different cultural and ethnic backgrounds and different native languages. In addition, geographic distances often inhibited direct communication between merchants, as agents frequently represented them at fairs (see discussion below). Such transactions costs had to be reduced so merchants could insure credibility of promises and engage in contractual trading.

---

age had militarized much of Europe, however, and military leaders (knights) often turned their objective to one of subjugation of local communities (essentially protection rackets) when the foreign threat declined. These local "lords" also were in a position to threaten merchants, but merchants travelled together and often hired their own protection (VM 1999), and they often could avoid the jurisdictions of particularly aggressive lords. Localized powers also wanted traders to offer goods within their jurisdictions, after all, so the competition to attract fairs (discussed below) probably constrained aggression against merchants. The subjugation efforts of the local lords also created incentives for people to escape to the urban areas where they had to find work in non-agricultural production, and as these urban areas grew they became increasingly powerful and often developed their own law. In 1095 the first of the Crusades was launched, attracting many knights who joined the effort with much of their military power, reducing the localized threats against producers and merchants. In addition, new knowledge was introduced to Europe from the Middle East (e.g., better medical practices) because of the Crusades, as were enhanced tastes for the spices and other "luxuries" available in the Muslim world. The Crusades also illustrate the influence of the Roman Church on Europe's population, including those with military power. Because of the strength of Christian beliefs, the "threats" the church could bring to bear (excommunication, the wrath of the Saints) served as a counter force to the secular powers that could mitigate at least some of their locally focused violence. The Church's monasteries and abbeys were also major producers and they were anxious to engage in trade, so they also offered safe havens for fairs and supported merchants in other ways (see the discussion of adjudication below). The point is that a number of important changes occurred in Europe just before or during the early years of the high Middle Ages that enhanced both the desire for and ability to trade.

[16] Fairs took place much earlier. For instance, a document from Migne (1850, 510) reproduced in Cave and Coulson (1036 [1965], 114–15) suggests that Dagobert, King of the Franks, granted a Fair to the Monks of St. Denis in 629 (there is some question about the authenticity of this document, but the Fair at St. Denis was one of the earliest in Western Europe). Fairs became more prevalent, larger, and more important during the high Middle Ages.

As Greif (2006: 56) noted, "Markets do not necessarily spontaneously emerge in response to opportunities for profitable exchange. For exchange to transpire, institutions that protect property rights and provide contract enforcement must be in place."

Sachs (2006: 706–12) contended that merchants depended on coercive authorities to provide recourse and enforcement,[17] but as VM (1999: 435) noted, to the degree that anything like a state existed as Europe moved into the high Middle Ages, these kinds of localized authoritarian organizations were "unable to supply the basic services of the state," including enforcement of fundamental property and contract law. In this context, Berman (1983: 333) contended that it was during the eleventh and twelfth centuries "that the basic concepts and institutions of . . . *lex mercatoria* . . . were formed."[18] Indeed, credibility can be established through knowledge, trust, or recourse (Benson 1999), and merchants pursued improvements in all three.[19]

---

[17]   The bases for his contentions are discussed in notes 19 and 20. VM (1999: 437–40), appear to agree as they imply that guilds and the urban commercial towns had to arise before merchants were able to develop non-simultaneous transactions and that contracting did not occur until after permanent market towns developed legal arrangements. See note 24 in this context. Also see Benson (2016) for a detailed rebuttal of both VM's and Sachs' contentions about the requirement for authority, whether from an urban government or a powerful lord, for the Law Merchant to succeed.

[18]   This should not be taken to imply that the medieval Law Merchant arose out of nothing or that it arose immediately. As Bewes (1923: 8–11) noted, while the "great commercial development was new in European hands, it was of centuries standing in the hands of the Eastern nations. . . . [So] Europe may be indebted to the East for the earliest form of shipping documents, as well as for the law merchant generally." In addition, as Berman (1983: 339) and Benson (1989: 169) both pointed out, the medieval Law Merchant also was influenced by Roman commercial law [Roman commercial law was also customary law rather than authoritarian state-made law (Leoni 1961: 83; Bewes 1923: 7–8)]. The point made by Berman (1983), Benson (1989 and elsewhere), Trakman (1983), and others is that the Law Merchant began to evolve and change relatively rapidly during the early high Middle Ages, becoming more prominent and more widely known by non-merchants as well as merchants over a period of perhaps 100 to 200 years.

[19]   While the following discussion has examples of innovations to increase knowledge and enhance trust, the focus is on recourse: law, essentially to substitute for limited knowledge and trust.

Credible Promises: Repeated Dealing, Information Networks, and Reputation

A key to understanding the incentives for medieval merchants to live up to their contractual promises and behave as expected given the behavioral rules that evolved, primarily through negotiation and emulation, is that information was spread rapidly through processes that evolved as other parts of the Law Merchant were evolving (Milgrom, et al. 1990). Thus for instance, "For diversification, traders were associated with many traders residing in different trade centers [in the eleventh-century Mediterranean]. It was [or, at some point, became] customary for merchants to supply their business associates with trade-related information, which was crucial to business success" (Greif 2006: 64). This implies that incentives to behave as expected by other merchants become stronger as information about behavior spread more effectively and more widely, so behavioral rules and resulting expectations tended to spread through a merchant network. In addition, a reputation for honesty became valuable.

Consider the group of Jewish merchants who moved to Tunisia, part of the Maghrib or Muslim West, in the tenth century because of political insecurity in Baghdad. When the Maghrib capital relocated to Cairo near the end of the tenth century, the Jewish traders who followed became known as Maghribi traders. They deposited thousands of contracts, price lists, letters between traders, accounts and other documents in the *geniza* of a synagogue in Fustat (old Cairo). Greif examined these documents, and in discussing relationships between Maghribi merchants and agents, he (2006: 62–5) noted that there could have been a serious credibility problem: a merchant's agents were located in distant locations so monitoring agents conducting business with the merchant's capital was costly, creating an opportunity for agent embezzlement. The flow of information mentioned above provided a means of reducing these transactions costs, however, in part by providing a mechanism for agents to signal honesty. "Eleventh-century Maghribi agents generally conducted important business in the presence of other coalition members. In their reports they included the names of witnesses the merchant knew, thus enabling the merchant to verify the agent report" (Greif 2006: 65). Merchants hired the same agents repeatedly as long as information indicated agent honesty.

The importance of information and reputation went further, however, as it provided an opportunity for spontaneous, uncoordinated but effective punishment. Maghribi traders "share the belief that coalition merchants . . . will reward his agent enough to keep him honest. All coalition merchants, however, are expected never to employ an agent who cheated while operating on behalf of a coalition member" (Greif 2006: 66). Greif (2006: 69) stressed that this ostracism process was not an intentionally-created and coordinated process, however; it was an "uncoordinated response of the merchants located in different trade centers." It arose as a result of the common practice of sharing information, and the behavioral reactions of merchants when they received information about dishonesty. Despite the lack of a coordinated response, Greif (2006: 66–9) cited several Maghribi documents illustrating this unorganized sanction's impacts. For instance, letters written in 1055 discussed an agent in Jerusalem accused of embezzling from a Maghribi trader. As word spread, merchants "as far away as Sicily" canceled their agency contracts with the individual.

These Maghribi practices help explain why Sachs (2006: 706) was wrong. He based his claims that merchant enforcement was essentially non-existent and that merchants depended on coercive authorities on the fact that "the fair court rolls [from one fair, St. Ives, during a very short time frame around the end of the high Middle Ages, 1270–1324] contain no evidence that such ostracism was institutionalized;. . ."[20] Sachs (2006: 706) cited Benson's (2002) brief discussion of ostracism as a sanction to motivate his attack on the idea of merchant enforcement through ostracism threats, but Benson has repeatedly described the evolution of ostracism as a uncoordinated spontaneous process (e.g., 1989, 1990, 1995, 1999), as suggested by Greif, and never claimed that ostracism was "institutionalized" in the sense that it was ordered by the fair courts discussed below.[21] Benson (e.g., 1995, 1999) does explain that a formal organization like a modern trade association can impose formal boycott sanctions, including expulsion from the organization, thereby increasing the strength of the

---

[20]   Sachs (2006: 706) continued this sentence with "indeed given that some defendants appear repeatedly in the rolls, one infers that they lived to trade again." There are a number of flaws in this argument too. First, if an individual is repeatedly involved in disputes that go before a merchant court (adjudication processes are discussed below) but he always accepts and complies with the court ruling, he is in compliance with the Law Merchant. Second, even if the repeated defendant is perceived to be an opportunist, or as someone who imposes extra costs on trades because issues repeatedly have to be settled by a trial, the fact that an individual is able to continue to trade does not mean that he can continue to trade on the same terms. Conditional ostracism can apply, as discussed below, forcing the individual to pay higher (or accept lower) prices, or put up larger and larger bonds. Ultimately, the individual may be unable to compete and go out of business, resulting in an outcome essentially identical to ostracism.

[21]   Similarly, Benson did not contend that medieval merchants engaged in "collective action" (Sachs 2006: 706) in order to create an "organized boycott" (Sachs 2006: 707), and he never suggested that boycotts were initiated by "organizers" (Sachs 2006: 708).

threatened sanction, but that was clearly not his contention in his writings on the medieval Law Merchant.[22]

The effectiveness of the reputation (ostracism) threat is revealed by the fact that Maghribi agents and merchants were willing to sacrifice immediate gains to maintain their reputations. One revealing incident involved a contract for flax purchase. The parties' agreed price was 13 dinar per load, but before the flax arrived, the price fell to eight dinar. The buyers initially refused to pay 13 dinar, but ultimately did so. Greif (2006: 68) quoted a seller's letter: "if not [for their fear of losing their] honor . . . we wouldn't have received a thing." Similarly, a merchant had two loads of pepper to sell, one that he owned, and one owned by a temporary partner. The pepper price in the port where the merchant was selling was very low and falling, so he sold his partner's load for 133 quarter dinars, but did not sell his own load. The night before his pepper was to be shipped to another location, new buyers arrived, bidding up the price, and he sold at 140–142 quarter dinars. He shared the profit with the partner even though the partnership agreement did not specify doing so, and it was not being renewed: "the merchant acted honorably solely to maintain his reputation with other coalition members" (Greif 2006: 69). Greif (2006: 63) also reported that "Despite the many opportunities for agents to cheat, only a handful of documents contain allegations of misconduct."

While the Maghribi traders quickly boycotted dishonest merchants and agents, partial or conditional ostracism also was possible and probably practiced in some merchant communities, just as it is today.[23] Merchants can continue trading with someone accused of misbehavior, but only if certain conditions are met that reduce the expected risk, perhaps by demanding relatively high returns (e.g., requiring higher prices if selling, or lower prices if buying) or that bonds be posted. These conditions sanction

---

[22]   This mistake by Sachs (2006) is one of many that arises because of his lack of understanding of customary law, and resulting assumption that looking at a single court's records (St. Ives in England) is an appropriate, and indeed sufficient, method for understanding the Law Merchant, not only during the period of the records he examined (1270–1324) but apparently for everything that came before, including the eleventh through the thirteenth centuries discussed by Berman (1983) and Benson (1989). Benson (1989, 1990) discussed later years as well but in the context of his examination of the absorption of the law merchant into authoritarian law systems. See Benson (2016) for refutation of many other errors by Sachs (2006).

[23]   A modern example is the eBay reputation mechanism where sales, prices, and survivability vary significantly across sellers, depending on their feedback records, with negative feedback producing significant "punishment" but not immediate ostracism (Cabral and Hortacsu 2004: 1–2).

the offender by raising his costs of doing business. In all likelihood the degree of ostracism imposed by individual merchants varied based on their individual knowledge, risk preferences and business opportunities, but importantly, both complete and partial ostracism ultimately can put a merchant out of business, and repeated instances of non-cooperative behavior is likely to do so quite quickly. More importantly, however, positive incentives associated with reputation building and/or reciprocities, and the expanding opportunities for profitable trade, were the primary reasons for recognition of the Law Merchant (Trakman 1983: 10), not threats of punishment.

In a general way, VM's (1999) arguments about the development of reputation sanctions within guilds is consistent with Greif's (2006) evidence about the Maghribi traders. They recognized that within-group trust and reputation mechanisms can arise to facilitate non-simultaneous trade. There are important differences between VM's and Greif's descriptions, however, as VM contended that "Merchants were itinerant" (VM 1999: 436) and that the "merchants . . . formed communities to travel together [and] to protect the property rights of their members vis-à-vis non-members" (VM 1999: 437). VM suggested that they were focusing on merchant groups that formed between the Rhine and the Seine, but they clearly assumed that their arguments applied to trade throughout Europe. It was not necessary for Maghribi traders to be itinerant, however, because they contracted with distant agents and with partners. Furthermore, while the purposes of this organization may have included the protection of property rights while travelling together, this does not appear to be paramount. The Maghribi traders and their agents were dispersed throughout the Mediterranean in order facilitate trade between different locations. Given the flow of information, traders were able to learn about trading opportunities and presumably non-Maghribi traders' reputations within other dispersed networks. Indeed, the Maghribi traders or agents in each location presumably developed repeated dealing arrangements with local non-Maghribi traders, and local reputation presumably became valuable. In this way they became members of two merchant groups, the local market and the Maghribi network. A linked web of interactions based on repeated dealing and reputation would be a natural development.

An obligation to spread information was not the only rule that helped deter misbehavior. Reciprocal support in the pursuit of justice against offenders from outside a group was apparently an intra-group obligation. Thus, as *The Little Red Book of Bristol* explained, a "hue and cry" could be raised if an offender refused to abide by an adjudication decision, resisted efforts to collect debts, removed or reduced the value of disputed assets, or fled (Basile 1998 [c. 1280]: 25). Such cooperation did not mean that the relevant threat was violent physical punishment, however, as the purpose was to induce performance of promises or payment of compensation.

As communications about reputations become more effective and mutual support arrangements developed, much larger inter-community trading networks developed. Trade between members of different groups presumably made tit-for-tat and ostracism threats relatively weak, and VM contended that it did so to the degree that intergroup trade was always simultaneous rather that contractual. This was not the case, as demonstrated below. For one thing, with the potential for intergroup trading, the reputation of trading communities also became valuable, creating incentives to develop surety arrangements to protect group reputations and increase the credibility of members' promises. As Malynes (1622: 93) explained,

> Faith or trust is to be kept between merchants, and that also must be done without quillets or titles of the law to avoid interruption of traffic, where in his Suretiship is to be considered according to the promise; for if it be conditional if such a man do not pay, the other to pay the same within a time, or to save him harmless: it is first to be demanded of the Principal, and if he do not pay, the Surety is to pay it without any course of law, unless he be ordered by the Court of Merchants to perform the same. . .[24]

VM believe that these kinds of group-level arrangements to make inter-group promises credible could not develop, however, because the transactions costs involved with inter-group trade could not be overcome (1999: 442):

> We demonstrated [actually, they made some assumptions and derived some conclusions, but the assumptions were flawed so the conclusions were not valid] that it was extremely difficult for merchants to enforce institutions regulating nonsimultaneous transactions between them and members of another guild or outsiders. To solve these problems, a number of political and social changes had to come about, which resulted in towns developing from feudal or ecclesiastic administrative centers into autonomous political organizations.

---

[24]   VM (1999: 445) referred to such arrangements as the application of "joint liability" for merchant groups under urban law. "Joint liability" under a coercive system of law is not the same as mutual insurance based on reciprocities under customary law, however, even though Sachs (2006: 709) assumed they are identical. In fact, joint liability imposed coercively is clearly not likely to be appreciated by foreign merchants [apparently it was widely reviled when it was demanded under urban law (VM 1999: 445; Sachs 2006: 709–10)], but it may have been an easy concept to develop for the domestic merchants who controlled urban law, because they observed and perhaps even participated in mutual insurance arrangements where a group came to the rescue of a member. Equating surety arrangements and imposed joint liability, however, reflects a misunderstanding of customary law.

VM's subsequent description of the gradual displacement of the older guilds (and probably other merchant communities) by the institutions of market towns is quite good, as explained in the conclusion, but the contention that merchants could not solve the transactions costs of intergroup trading until market towns gained political power is demonstrably false. What VM failed to recognize is that the developments of market towns and relationships between them that they accurately describe do not mean that the developments described by the medieval Law Merchant literature did not also arise. That this is in fact the case can be seen by considering VM's alleged demonstration (1999: 436) that:

> merchants could not afford to specialize in specific goods. As late as the high and late Middle Ages, they used to deal with anything promising a return. Given high transport and transactions costs, most merchandize consisted of luxury goods. Long distance trade in mass products did not exist. Transactions were concluded at yearly fairs, such as the one at St. Denis near Paris, or at naturally favored locations where traders met accidentally (e.g., river crossings).
>
> Because of unstable political situations, merchants found it difficult to keep dates: The likelihood of meeting a specific partner again was low. Under such conditions, nonsimultaneous commercial transactions were rare if they occurred at all. Simultaneous exchanges had, however, one advantage: there was no dispute over the date of payment, the conditions of payment and so on.

In reality, however, non-simultaneous trade between different merchant groups was the norm within the fairs (i.e., outside the jurisdictions of market towns) in much of Europe long before the end of the high Middle Ages.[25] Disputes arose and were resolved, and there were many relatively specialized traders.

---

[25]   At times it is actually difficult to know precisely when VM contended that various developments occurred. Some statements appear to apply to the entire high Middle Ages and even later, while in other passages they discussed developments in the tenth and eleventh centuries that are quite consistent with the story told by various authors they attack. For example, VM (1999: 439–40) claimed that "sources indicating that nonsimultaneous transactions occurred between merchants of different organizations . . . are scarce and moreover ambiguous." They make this claim after discussing sources from around 1000 to 1020 A.D. (see notes 3 and 4 above), so if this is the period they are referring to, there is no quarrel in this regard: sources are indeed scarce. It does not follow that such nonsimultaneous trade did not arise, of course, but more importantly, contributors to the literature on the Law Merchant, such as Mitchell (1904: 7–9), Bewes (1923: 138), Berman (1983: 342, 350–55), and Benson (1989: 649), all clearly contend that the law merchant arrangements they discuss were largely in place around the end of the twelfth century, not the beginning of the eleventh.

Non-Simultaneous Inter-Group Trade, Credit and Contracting

Consider the Champagne Fairs, probably the most important fairs during much of the high Middle Ages. Face's (1958, 1959) examination of twelfth- and thirteenth-century notarial documents from Genoa and Marseilles demonstrated that non-simultaneous trade between Northern and Southern European merchants in the twelfth century (and thirteenth century) was the overwhelming dominant practice at these fairs. Indeed, Face (1958: 428) contended that:

> Even the most superficial examination of the Genoese documents . . . indicates that as early as 1180 [the oldest documents Face found] . . . the yearly cycle of the six fairs of Champagne was fully developed, and that the internal divisions of the order of business at each of these fairs had been *evolved at some time long before*, and continued to regulate and to dominate all business activity. (emphasis added)

The cycle of six Fairs in different Champagne towns, each lasting about 52 days, took place every year. Note in this regard that while each fair occurred once a year, six fairs in reasonably close proximity occurred sequentially so that a fair was occurring someplace in Champagne for over 300 days each year. These fairs all were organized as follows:

(1)   eight days of "entry" when merchants set up their shops;
(2)   ten days during which only cloth was traded;
(3)   11 days during which cordovan (leather) goods were traded;
(4)   19 days for the trading of goods that were sold by weight, such as spices and dye-stuffs, and when accounts also began to be settled; and
(5)   four days during which the "letters of the Fair" [credit instruments; e.g., to deal with unsold goods that might be stored, or individuals who purchased more than their revenues would cover] were drawn (Face 1958: 427 and note 2).[26]

French, German, English or Flemish merchants from Northern Europe selling cloth to buy spices, dyes or cordovan from Southern European merchants accepted some sort of promissory note or letter of credit as payment during the first period of trading at the fairs when cloth was sold, or they simply accepted the promise to pay later made by a merchant from the Mediterranean region, sealed by a handshake or a godspenny (Kadens

---

[26]   Some other goods also were bought and sold at the Champagne fairs, such as silk. Similarly, furs which travel both north (e.g., from Spain, Africa, and Southern France) and south (martin, rabbit, and other northern furs) were bought and sold.

2004: 57). The notes or promises could then be converted into goods from the South later during the next two trading periods, or they could be retained for later use. Similarly, the merchants from Genoa (as well as Asti, Arras, Piacenza, Lucca, Florence and other Italian commercial cities as well as other Mediterranean merchants) selling spices, dyes, or cordovan, had to buy the Northern cloth before they sold their goods, so they offered promises, promissory notes or letters of credit from money lenders to buy the cloth. These notes and letters of credit were negotiable so merchants from the North could use them to buy from any merchant from the Mediterranean region. They did not have to buy from the same merchant who purchased their cloth. The end of the fair was dedicated to balancing all of the books: "it marked the climax to which the extensive buying and selling, the criss-crossing of financial exchange, had been building up, in Champagne and in far distant places as well. The floating promises generated on all sides were now liquidated" (Face 1958: 437). Clearly, trading on credit was the norm at these fairs well before the end of the high Middle Ages, in apparent contrast to VM (1999: 436).[27] Commercial contracting was even more widespread, however, and more dependent on credit devices to facilitate non-simultaneous trade, than just the practices at these fairs.

Italian "caravan" merchants who traded at the Champagne Fairs where highly specialized, again in contrast to the VM (1999: 436) claim that "merchants could not afford to specialize in specific goods." They purchased spices, dyes and/or cordovan in the Italian ports, transported those goods to the Fairs and sold them, and purchased woolen or linen cloth from Northern Europe, transported the cloth back to Italy and sold it to "*draperii*." Furthermore, Face (1958: 429) discovered documentation demonstrating that Genoese caravan merchants bought spices, dyes and cordovan on credit from merchants trading between the Middle East and Italy (e.g., Maghribi traders). When they returned after a fair, they made large numbers of sales of cloth to Italian *draperii*, again on credit. Since these exchanges often occurred within the market cities, VM's contention that they were under the jurisdiction of those towns may be accurate (but

---

[27] The evolution of credit arrangements was important for reasons beyond their value in facilitating non-simultaneous trade. As Jones (1987: 93) noted, for instance, the invention of the bill of exchange made:

> capital mobile and free. Sudden debasement of the coinage were rendered useless or counter-productive because extensive foreign exchange dealing and arbitrage would follow at once, more swiftly than when traders had been obliged to denote debts in kind in order to escape using debased coin. In this brave new world only good government could bring prosperity to the prince.

see further discussion below suggesting otherwise). If so, these urban jurisdictions did not back the use of credit at the fairs, however, and as explained below, the fairs did not fall under any other authority until the end of the high Middle Ages, in contrast to Sachs (2006).

Documents also suggest that merchants from England, Flanders and other Northern European countries did the opposite, buying cloth, transporting it to Champagne, selling it, buying spices, dyes and/or cordovan to transport back North to be sold, almost entirely through the use of credit. As Benson (1989, 1990) and Berman (1983) both stressed, the commercial revolution of the high Middle Ages was built on credit, not cash [and definitely not on simultaneous barter or gift exchange, in contrast to what VM (1999: 436) apparently assumed].

Even more contractual complexity is illustrated by the documents that Face (1958, 1959) examined. For instance, Genoese caravan merchants often did not even arrive at the Fair in time to buy cloth. Instead, the earliest documents Face reported on (recorded in the last two decades of the twelfth century and more than a century before the end of the high Middle Ages) demonstrated that merchants generally contracted with agents or partners, just as the Maghribi did in the Mediterranean, and these individuals often reached a fair well in advance of the merchants themselves (Face 1958: 433).[28] Indeed, they often simply stayed in Champagne moving from one fair to another, representing the Italian merchants with whom they had contracts, and furthermore:

> There is no contract or credit instrument pertaining to the fair trade or to the cloth trade found in any notarial cartulary which does not indicate that the debt or settlement to a question might be paid to the creditor's agent, to his '*certo nuncio*' or '*certo misso*'. Every merchant had his agent, or perhaps several, to act in his place, to fulfill old obligations, and in many cases to undertake new ones. Agency in this sense was from the very beginning of our records employed in both Genoa and Champagne. The words '*tibi vel tuo certo misso dare et solvere promitto per me vel meum missum*' are found in contracts drawn on the fairs themselves, as well as in credit instruments payable in Genoa.
>
> The evidence demonstrating the use of partnerships among the caravan merchants is equally extensive. "*Socii*" were frequently related, and a general participation in the family business was very common. But partnerships were by no means limited to siblings. . . even though the family business was the natural affiliation, and usually the most enduring, these independent arrangements were frequently outstanding. It would of course, be unnecessary in any such

---

[28]   The eleventh century Maghribi traders in the Mediterranean also employed numerous agents (Greif 2006: 58–62). The *Little Red Book of Bristol* (Basile 1998 [c. 1280]: 11 & 16) similarly noted that agents were employed by merchants. Also see note 26.

arrangement for both partners to be present at the same time, either in Genoa or in Champagne. (Face 1958: 431)

The Genoese documents also illustrated that Northern merchants contracted with agents to represent them in Champagne (Face 1958: 433). Therefore, a merchant did not have to arrive on a specific date to engage in non-simultaneous trade, as VM (1999: 436) assumed when they contended that "The likelihood of meeting a specific partner again was low." A merchant's representative was at the fair with time to spare, and the caravan merchant simply had to arrive sometime before the goods he took to the fair were to be sold (if he attended the fair at all, as suggested below).

Merchants who traveled to the fair also left agents or partners to tend their affairs in Genoa. In addition, Genoese caravan merchants had several partners on a relatively permanent basis. They also had agents and procurators representing them in various places in the North in addition to Champagne (Face 1958: 432). In fact, documents suggest that at least some merchants simply stayed in Genoa, month after month, while continually selling Northern cloth, and also making large purchases of spices and other commodities on credit to send by caravans to Champagne (Face 1959: 245), once again in contrast to VM (1999: 436) when they suggest that all merchants were itinerant.[29] This was possible, in part because the merchants had contracts with partners or agents in Champagne and other important trading locations.

Merchants also had to move their goods to and from the fairs. Not surprisingly, as Face (1959) detailed, drawing on notarial records from both Genoa and Marseilles, there was widespread merchant contracting

---

[29]   The same is true for other merchants in other locations who sent their agents out to buy or sell goods. For instance, the following is a 1248 contract written by an agent acknowledging an order on goods to be sold elsewhere (Blancard 1884, Vol. II: 232, as reprinted in Cave and Coulson 1936 [1965]: 109–10):

June tenth. In the year of the Incarnation of the Lord 1248. I, Bartholomew, son of the late Benedict of Lucca, confess and acknowledge to you Rolland Vendemmia, of Lucca, that I have had and received from you as an order twenty-three pounds and ten solidi (Genoese currency), invested in armor and in prepared silk and gold wire from Lucca and in two cross-bows, renouncing, etc.

With that order I shall go, God willing, on the next journey I make to Montpellier, by sea or by land, for the purpose of selling the said things, with God's favor and at the risk of the sea and to your profit. I promise by this agreement to repay you all the capital and the profit of the said order, retaining for myself what I expend for the transport and sale of the goods, pledging all my goods, etc.

with professional freighters or *"Vectuarii"* who specialized in the transportation of trade goods to and from the fairs. Contracts between merchants and freighters, called *"lettres de voiture,"* were very common long before the end of the high Middle Ages. Documents from the twelfth century indicated that a substantial overland freight business existed [Face (1959, 242) cited several 1191 documents]. In these contracts, the freighter acknowledged receipt of specified goods and promised to transport them to a specified destination and to reach the destination on or before some specified time (VM's contention that "merchants found it difficult to keep dates" (1999: 436) has to at least be questioned given the willingness of freighters to make such promises and merchants to accept them). The mode of transportation was specified and the contracts often indicated that the goods were to be delivered to a particular person, generally the merchant's agent or partner. Freight charges were specified and paid in advance. An example of such a contract is from Blancard (1884, Vol. II: 109, as reprinted in Cave and Coulson 1936 [1965]: 159–60):

> April twenty-fourth in the year of the Incarnation of the Lord 1248.
> We, Eustace Cazal and Peter Amiel, carriers, confess and acknowledge to you, Falcon of Acre and John Confortance of Acre, that we have had and received from you twelve full loads of brazil wood and nine of pepper and seventeen and a half of ginger for the purpose of taking them from Toulouse to Provence, to the fairs of Provence to be held in the coming May, at a price or charge of four pounds and fifteen solidi in Vienne currency for each of the said loads. And we confess we have had this from you in money, renouncing, etc. And we promise by this agreement to carry and look well after those said loads with our animals, without carts, and to return them to you at the beginning of those fairs and to wait upon you and do all the things which carriers are accustomed to do for merchants. Pledging all our goods, etc.; renouncing the protection of all laws, etc.

Note that contract also explicitly states that other customary duties would be performed, without specifying those duties, and that the agreement was outside the "protection of all laws"; that is, it was written in light of the customs of merchants (the Law Merchant) rather than recognized authoritarian legal arrangements such as royal or Cannon law. Clearly, the freighters' promises to deliver were credible since these terms were present in virtually all *lettres de voiture* (Face 1959: 239). And importantly, many contracts like this one:

> contained a clause indicative of a long tradition, an established customs which governed the relationship between caravan merchants and *vectuarius.* . ..
> A clause of this kind, repeated word for word in four separate contracts, seems a reliable indication that by 1248 a substantial and generally known set of obligations existed to which *vectuarii* were required to adhere by custom, if

not by law, in their professional dealings with merchants. . ... The very existence, therefore, of an acknowledged set of rules and regulations, such as that implied by the clause quoted above, makes it quite impossible that the *vectuarii* appeared suddenly in the middle of the thirteenth century as full-blown specialists in the medieval business world. (Face 1959: 240–41)

Over time, new clauses were added to these contracts. For instance, the freighter might guarantee that the goods would arrive undamaged, and that the packages or bales would not be opened, as well as the number of days for the journey, and perhaps the actual route to be taken. Generally, the merchant bore the risk of loss or theft, but in some contracts, freighters took on this risk.

While VM (1999: 440) recognized that merchants used gossip to initiate within-community (e.g., guild, caravan) sanctions, information flows served many more purposes, and formal mechanisms to transmit information developed quite early. In order to learn about market conditions and coordinate activities in multiple locations with freight haulers, agents and partners, for instance, the Italian caravan merchants had to transmit information relatively quickly, and:

The only feasible answer to this need was a courier service, a kind of "pony express" to race back and forth on a regular schedule between the fair towns in Champagne and the chief commercial cities of northern Italy and the Mediterranean coast. Such a service existed in the second half of the thirteenth century. . ... Italian business houses whose representatives frequented the fairs could avail themselves of this service on a kind of subscription basis, but in addition, both business houses and Italian cities maintained their own courier service. . ... Furthermore, the evidence is altogether convincing about a second point of great significance: that between 1190 and 1290 nothing new had been added to the pattern of the fair trade which would have made the services of couriers indispensable in 1290, but entirely unnecessary one hundred years earlier. . ... Indeed, the whole pattern of the trade, tied so closely to the order of business at the fairs, demanded the services of this courier from the start. (Face 1958: 434–6)

Clearly, with dispersed agents and partners communicating through a network of couriers, merchants were able to gather a large amount of information. No doubt, much of this information was about purchases, sales, credit arrangements, estimates of demand and supply, and other factors directly related to the technical side of trade. However, it was obviously possible for merchants to gather a good deal of information about potential trading partners' reputations and/or their trading organization (e.g., guild, caravan), the trading practices and usage that applied in particular fairs, and other factors related to the personal and legal aspects of commerce.

Face (1958: 427) pointed out that "it has been difficult not to form an inaccurate and almost naïve image of the merchant who frequented these fairs." It appears that VM (1999: 436) [and Sachs (2006)] formed such an image, as their assertion that there was virtually no non-simultaneous exchange between members of different trading communities (guilds, caravans, ethnic groups such as the Maghribi traders) unless the trade took place under the jurisdiction of a market town is clearly wrong:

> The whole complex structure of the commerce centering about the fairs of Champagne with its extensive use of agency and partnership, its reliance on professional freighters, and its attendant system of couriers, was based entirely on credit. Every document employed in the reconstruction of the pattern of this trade records a credit transaction; no other evidence survives. The records of merchants in Italy show that at the wholesale level only the smallest fraction of the total business done was conducted for hard cash. . .. But the vast majority of these documents took for granted payment by paper. This is true for as early as we have any records at all, and must therefore be true for some time prior to our earliest records. . .. One must look far behind that date [1180] to discover the origin of these practices. The pattern of the fair trade, with all its concomitant devices of business and financial organization, was worked out some time too early for any written records to have survived. (Face 1958: 437)

The formation of trade networks and the spread of rules of contract certainly did not occur overnight. Merchant communities and their contractual arrangements evolved as commerce developed, so they evolved at different rates in different areas as commerce emerged and spread. The "commercial revolution" of the tenth through the thirteenth centuries involved tremendous changes in trading arrangements and conditions, as VM recognized, but the institutional developments to support expanding commerce through between-group non-simultaneous trade occurred earlier than they claimed, and did not require the institutional developments they contended were necessary. Face (1958: 430) suggested that twelfth- and thirteenth-century merchants employed:

> A group of advanced and polished techniques of business [that] enabled them to carry out a seemingly impossible task with the utmost regularity and precision. These techniques are hinged on three factors: first, the ingenious use of partnerships, agency, and procuration; second, the integration of these devises with communication and transportation; and third, the extensive use of credit instruments in the trade.[30]

---

[30]   Indeed, one means of obtaining credit was to form a partnership with a money lender. This is illustrated by a contract provided in Blancard (1884, Vol. 1: 137, as reprinted in Cave and Coulson 1936 [1965]: 186–7):

These techniques clearly had to be based on contracts, and a commercial system based on contracting had to have mechanisms in place to ensure that most promises were credible. As Face (1958: 428) stressed, such developments had to occur much earlier than the period depicted by the records he studied (part of the twelfth and thirteenth centuries) in order for the "advanced and polished techniques" to be so well established. Face's research is not the only source of evidence about such developments either.[31]

All of these developments certainly do not mean that opportunism never occurred, of course. Furthermore, one individual might accuse another of misbehavior and the other might deny it. This could occur because a guilty party denied guilt, or simply because the two parties disagreed about what rule should apply or how to deal with an unanticipated contingency. In either case, the availability of impartial third-party dispute resolution could reduce the costs of such disagreements, and therefore, encourage contracting. After all, violence is likely to be the means of resolution in the absence of third-party options, but more importantly, violence can be a very costly method for resolving disagreements, so reliance on violence for this purpose implies that individuals would be much less likely to enter into contractual arrangements.

In the name of the Lord. In the year of the Incarnation 1240, May eighth. Let it be known to all hearing this document read that I, Nicholas Dangiers, confess and acknowledge to you, John de Manduel, that I have had from you, by reason of our partnership, thirty pounds in royal crowns. . . . These thirty pounds, according to the agreement had or made between you and me I ought to look well after, and to do business with them as well as I am able, and as well as I know how in pursuit of my business of cooper, by buying and selling to your advantage and to mine. And I promise to repay to you, John de Manduel, the said thirty pounds with one half of all the profit, agreeing to pay it peaceably and without molesting you throughout the whole month of August next coming; and for the completing of this agreement I pledge to you, John de Manduel, all my goods, at present or in future in my possession, renouncing the twenty days and four months and all other delay.

This same source provides other examples of merchant partnerships to obtain capital, as well as other contracts from the first half of the thirteenth century, generally involving Marseilles-based merchants.

[31] As the *Little Red Book of Bristol* (Basile 1998 [c. 1280], 11), written around 1280, stated, "it is well known to all that merchants sell their goods and merchandize on credit more frequently without tallies and writings than by tallies or writing . . . and also that servants and apprentices of such merchants [sell on credit] the goods and merchandise of their lords to other men in the same way" (parenthetic phrase in the translated quote). Also see notes 29 and 30.

Third-Party Dispute Resolution for Merchants in the High Middle Ages

"As any practicing commercial lawyer knows, there are many ways of enforcing fair practices, and punishing unfair practices, outside the [government's] courtroom. These patterns of informal enforcement are 'law' to those who operate in that context, and have been called 'law' for centuries" (Coquillette 2004: 298). For instance, arbitrators, generally chosen from the merchant community, were an important option (Malynes 1622 [1686]: 447–54). Not surprisingly, merchants could and did insert arbitration clauses into contracts. Face (1959: 243) discussed two fairly complex contracts from 1191 involving an individual who rented horses to a caravan merchant, for example; these contracts specified that if a horse was injured the degree of injury was to be determined by a board of arbitrators. Arbitration also was chosen after disputes arose. Consider the "Memorandum of Arbitration Concerning a Freight Charge" about a 1229 dispute in Marseilles (Blancard 1884, Vol. 1: 29, as reprinted in Cave and Coulson 1936 [1965]: 157–8):

> Upon the complaint or petition which existed between Martin Castagne . . . and Stephen de Manduel. . . on behalf of himself and his son Bernard, about the freight charge of thirty-one bundles of skins, which belonged to Paul Sicard, concerning which skins the said Martin and his associates said that they had retained them until the charge they demanded was paid; but on the other hand the said Stephen said that the charge should be paid by Paul Sicard, or by someone on his behalf, and that Bernard de Manduel, son of Stephen, had bought or otherwise acquired the said thirty-one bundles free from freight charges . . . and free from all other burdens, for which charge Stephen placed twenty-four pounds in the keeping of Bernard Peter . . . This money ought to be in the possession of Bernard Peter, for the charge on the thirty-one bundles if it appears that the said charge was not paid. For this charge or for the complaint about the charge Stephen and Martin have agreed before Bernard Peter and John of St. Maximin, judges chosen freely by both contestants . . . both promised to submit to the judgment or decision of the judges, however the judges might wish to settle the matter according to equity, requiring the truth, and, according to what appeared from the hearing of the complaint, to disregard the due order of legal process and the solemnity of the law. The said judges, having required the truth, and having heard the testimony . . . according to the wish of both parties, and having . . . the said judges agreed and gave their decision as below . . . according to what seemed just and honest to them. Wherefore the said Bernard Peter and John of St. Maximin, the said judges . . . absolved Stephen for himself and his son from paying the freight, ordering besides that the twenty-four pounds, which Bernard Peter had in his possession, should be restored to Stephen by Bernard, without objection by any one. . .
> This decision was made by the said judges in the shop of William Aicard. . ..

This is a relatively unusual document since, as Malynes (1622 [1686]: 450) noted, medieval "Arbitrators have a determinate power to make an end of controversies in general terms, without declaration of particulars." This was the case because of the merchants' need for quick solutions to their disputes, as discussed below, and the fact that arbitrators chosen to resolve disputes had "skill and knowledge of the Customs of Merchants, which always does intend expedition" (Malynes 1622 [1686]: 450).[32]

Participatory merchant courts were also established at many fairs, particularly during the early years of the medieval Law Merchant. While the origins of these fairs courts, called *Piepoudre* or Pie Powder courts in some places, are difficult to determine, surviving records from the tenth through the twelfth century do not indicate that kings or local lords created them (Bewes 1923: 14). Each group of merchants at a fair (e.g., caravan group) generally appointed a captain or consul to perform various administrative duties such as determining where merchant stalls would be located, but as a group, these consul also could serve as the fair court (these individuals also were often chosen to arbitrate disputes between their own group's members) (Bewes 1923: 14; Kadens 2004: 59). As with arbitrators, Pie Powder courts did not leave significant records, but this is not surprising since their purpose was to provide quick and equitable dispute resolution. Merchant judges had no precedent setting power, so as with arbitrators, these judges had "a determinate power to make an end of controversies in general terms, without declaration of particulars" (Malynes 1622 [1686]: 450).

The Little Red Book of Bristol, c. 1280 (Basile 1998) stressed that one important difference between the Law Merchant and England's royal law was that Law Merchant disputes were resolved quickly because most merchants had to complete transactions at one fair quickly to move to the next. This was one reason for choosing Pie Powder judges or arbitrators from among merchants attending the fair (e.g., group captains/consuls). Another was that clerics, lawyers, local lords, and royal judges often had little knowledge of many commercial issues, so the risk of judicial error was lower with merchant judges, particularly when highly technical commercial issues were involved. In addition, non-merchant judges might not accept evidence that merchant judges and arbitrators respected, as Zouch (1663 [1686]: 128) observed:

> At the Common Law no mans Writing can be pleaded against him, as his Act, and Deed, unless the same is sealed, and delivered: But in Suites between

---

[32]   Malynes (1622 [1686]: 447) discussed methods of choosing arbitrators to insure unbiased adjudicators with appropriate expertise. Such expertise was also important in merchant arbitration because "good orders and customs are to be maintained as laws, and nothing is to be admitted that may infringe the Law of Merchants" (Malynes 1622 [1686]: 452).

Merchants, Bills of Lading, and Bills of Exchange, being but Tickets, without Seals, Letters of advice, and Credence, Policies of assurance, Assignments of Debts, all which are of no force at the Common Law, are of good credit and force by the Law-Merchant. To which may be added, what Malines observes, that the bearer of such Bills, by the course amongst Merchants, shall be admitted to demand, and recover the Contracts, without Letters of Attorney, which is not admitted in the Common Law.

Consideration of such documents is illustrated in a 1242 arbitration decision regarding a 1235 contract between a Jewish merchant and a Christian merchant in Barcelona. The details of the contract and dispute are available from Arxiu Capitular de Barcelona (1-6-3475), but the final paragraph of the document illustrates the dispute resolution process and the evidence considered:

> Over all of these issues and over the arguments made by both parties after the claims were made, we Guillem Ponç and Gerald de Marnia, jointly accepted arbitrators, having examined the proofs as they appear in the acts which were received, and having looked at Solomon's bill of sale made by Berenguer Bailiff for the quarter share of the mills, and the notes in the relevant notebook of the notary Pere Carbonell which Berenguer Bailiff made for Ramon de Plegamans of the mills and another note of the purchase which Arnau D'Arlet made from Ramon for one year, . . . having made a valid and accurate calculation of the profit of the said mills, [and having judged how much] Solomon lost from the profit which Arnau D'Arlet and his partner made in the said mills through the fault of Berenguer Bailiff, we sentence the said Berenguer de Valle and Joan de Banyeres and their wives to give Solomon and his agent 10 pounds 5 solidi which it seems to us according to the evidence that Solomon is owed from the profit for that year through the fault of Berenguer Bailiff, absolving both sides of all other claims. This sentence was given on the Kalends of September, A.D. 1242.

Many of the local authorities who successfully attracted important annual fairs over time allowed Pie Powder courts and arbitrators to function without interference. The Champagne fair courts operated for at least a century (and probably longer), for instance, before the Count appointed wardens to deal with administrative and judicial issues that the consul had been performing, an action that helped set the decline of these fairs in motion, as explained below. Similarly, Piergiovanni (1995, 1998), drawing on information from fifteenth century *consiia,* concluded that merchant courts in Italy operated independently from other tribunals, following their own procedures, and that this apparently did not change significantly until the sixteenth century.

Kadens (2004: 64) noted that, "merchants, at least in Northern Europe, also used a second sort of court – that of the town, the prince, or the Church, in other words, noncommercial court." Some of the other legal systems that were evolving during the medieval period [see Berman (1983)] had relevant rules in common with the Law Merchant, or their judges offered to apply Law Merchant rules, so if a non-merchant court was willing to try the case quickly, and the court had a reputation for fair unbiased decisions, merchants certainly could and did choose to use it. Ecclesiastical courts were often available, for instance, because many of the major fairs were held at important priories and abbeys. Furthermore, as Bewes (1923: 9) noted:

> the Canon law . . . was the prevailing authority and would tend . . . to favour simple good faith unhampered by formalities, and thus would extend its influence to the law merchant which, until damaged by legislation, rested on mutual confidence and good faith to an extent unknown in civil life. In this connection it should be remembered that in the Middle Ages the Church was a very considerable trader.

Indeed, it was in the interests of church's leaders to maintain good relationships with merchants by offering them quick and equitable dispute resolution. There were some differences between cannon law and merchant law, however, so ecclesiastical courts were not attractive alternatives for all merchant disputes.

As suggested above by the appointment of wardens for the Champagne fairs, Pie Powder courts also were taken over by authorities such as "a mayor of a corporate town. Sometimes they belonged to a lord" (Holdsworth 1903: 331). Even when Pie Powder courts were explicitly replaced by a manor (or urban) court, however, merchants often dominated dispute resolution, as the *Little Red Book of Bristol* (Basile 1998 [c. 1280]: 20) explained:

> In every market court, every judgment ought to be rendered by Merchants of the same court and not by the mayor or by the seneschal of the market.
> And if such a mayor and seneschal take it upon themselves in any way to render judgments, although judgments do not belong to them in a court of this court, and [if] they execute the judgments or have them executed in any way whereby anyone feels aggrieved by such judgment and its execution, whether the judgment was just or unjust itself . . ., the aggrieved person should have his recovery both against the mayor, seneschal, or other reeve of the same market who acted thus and against those who execute such a judgment on their order, by a writ of trespass of the lord king, as of a matter done of their own wrong and against law and custom and against mercantile law.

A local lord might have imposed his court on a fair, but resolved merchant disputes quickly using merchant juries, or at least, advice from merchants. He might also have enforced the court rulings. Merchants were often more than willing to have authorities enforce their law, thereby reducing costs that they might bear personally (Benson 1989), like responding to the hue and cry.[33]

Various local authorities may have imposed some modification over time, such as fines paid to the authority. The magnitude of the modifications probably depended on the availability of, and competition from, other potential trading locations, as well the relative attractiveness of the various locations. An authority with a particularly attractive fair location could probably depart from the Law Merchant, at least to a degree, as discussed below, capturing some of the location rents. Kings often "granted" rights to hold a fair, however, and in doing so, stated that the Law Merchant must apply.[34] For instance, when Frederick I Barbarossa

---

[33] Such courts should not always be characterized as Law Merchant courts, however. In fact, as commerce developed and merchant communities gained wealth, local authorities and Kings increasingly attempted to assert authority over various aspects of commerce, including merchant courts, in order to increase their abilities to collect revenues or other benefits. This process is discussed further below.

[34] Many examples of royal recognition of a Law Merchant have been cited in the Law Merchant literature. Sachs (2006: 780–88) misinterpreted much of the literature on this point, however, as noting the indisputable fact that various kings referred to the Law Merchant in statute often was simply intended to illustrate that there must have been something called the Law Merchant for them to refer to. Authors like Berman, Benson and Trackman did not contend that "the charter [*Carta Mercatoria*] or the statute [Statute of Staples] guaranteed a more rapid method of dispute resolution, which followed the various uses and customs of the commercial towns and fairs." In fact, Benson (1989, 1990) argued just the opposite: that these actions were part of the process of absorbing the Law Merchant into royal law and changing it in various ways to allow more royal control over commerce. Interestingly, Sachs (2006: 726, note 128) actually recognized this point but took it out of context to support another point taken out of context. In this case he accused Trakman and Benson both of contending that merchant court decisions were "unreviewable by existing authorities" (Sachs 2006: 726). In this context, he quoted a partial statement from Benson (2002) including the phrase, "appeal was forbidden." Benson was referring to appeal from one Law Merchant court to some other Law Merchant court, however, not appeal to an authoritarian court. In other words, as far as the merchant community was concerned, arbitration and Pie Powder court decisions were final. This certainly did not mean, and was never intended to mean, that a merchant could not go to an authority and ask that authority to retry the case. This would violate Law Merchant norms, as explained below, but if an authority with coercive power wanted to accept such a case, the merchant community did not have the police force or army that would be needed to prevent such a trial. Sachs also cited Benson's brief discussion of the Statute of Staples and claims that Benson was "erroneously arguing that royal courts gained appellate jurisdiction only after the 1353 Statute of Staples" (Sachs, 2006: 726, note 128). No such claim was made in Benson, who was simply trying to illustrate royal actions that gradually led to the absorption of the Law

"granted" Aachen the right to hold two fairs in 1166, the grant document stated (quoted in Menadier 1913: 58 as reprinted in Cave and Coulson 1936 [1965]: 121):

> And so, on the advice of our nobles, we have given, out of respect for the most holy lord, the Emperor Charlemagne, this liberty to all merchants—that they may be quit and free of all toll throughout the year at these fairs in this royal place, and they may buy and sell goods freely just as they wish.
> *No merchant, nor any other person, may take a merchant to court for the payment of any debt during these fairs*, nor take him there for any business that was conducted before the fairs began; *but if anything be done amiss during the fairs, let it be made good according to justice during the fairs*. (emphasis added).

These grants may have deterred local legal arrangements (manorial law, urban law) from interfering with the market, at least to a degree, essentially recognizing the temporary jurisdiction of the Pie Powder court. Deterrence is never perfect, of course, so such grants do not mean that such interference never happened. While merchant "justice during the fairs" often was available and recognized by royal authority to have exclusive jurisdiction, however, it should not be inferred that royal "backing," or the backing of some other authority, was necessary for such courts to judge or for merchants in general to execute the Law Merchant.

The Kings benefited from having fairs within their jurisdictions so they could collect tolls, and in some cases, taxes or fees. As commerce developed and merchant communities gained wealth, however, local authorities and Kings increasingly attempted to assert authority over various aspects of commerce, and over merchant courts, in order to increase their abilities to collect revenues, and/or to eliminate competitors for such revenues. Before considering this issue, however, one other point deserves attention.

Universal and Polycentric

Recall VM's (1999: 442) statement that it is "highly problematic to speak of a medieval *lex mercatoria* when the term is meant to denote an 'international system of commercial law' (Benson 1989: 645) or an 'integrated, developing system, a *body* of law' (Berman 1983; 333, italics added)." Similarly, after discussing the fact that the Statute of Staples refers to both the law merchant and the "law of Staple," Sachs (2006: 784) stated that "The Conceptual plurality of these laws and usages does not sit easily with the

---

Merchant. This is not surprising since, as Berman (1983) explained, royal law was just beginning to develop in the tenth through the twelfth centuries.

vision of a single *invariant* law merchant" [emphasis added].[35] Universality is not synonymous with "invariant," of course, but it must be recognized that the market system consisted of many parallel-evolving-interrelated-overlapping markets, and similar polycentric arrangements characterized the evolving medieval Law Merchant system (Benson 1999). At any point in time, variation in some rules and practices existed across merchant communities, just as they do today (Benson 1999, Kadens 2004). Some of these groups were ethnic and/or religion based, others were geographic, and still others were both (e.g., the German merchants who ultimately formed the Hanseatic League, the Jewish, Muslim and Italian merchants in the Mediterranean). The medieval Law Merchant was polycentric (Benson 1999), made up of similar but certainly not identical or "invariant," parallel, interdependent and overlapping merchant communities. This does not mean that the most important principles of the Law Merchant were not universal, however, as Epstein (2004: 8–9) explained:

> . . .within the appointed area of the Law Merchant no one wants to depart from the norm of freedom of contract. . . With that concurrence as to ends, huge sources of potential disagreement just disappear from view. . . There might not be perfect agreement among the practitioners of the art as to how the Law Merchant came about or what ideal customs are. But this fundamental

---

[35]   In his critique of the Law Merchant literature, Sachs (2006) appears to have assumed that statements by Berman, Trakman, Benson and others about universality imply absolutely identical rules about everything everywhere. This is clearly not true. First, the authors subject to his attack all recognized that merchant law varied over space and time. After all, these authors explained that the evolution of the major tenets of the Law Merchant took at least 200 years (e.g., Berman 1983: 333). To my knowledge, none of the modern authors contended that the Law Merchant was "invariant." Second, it must be noted that the context of Sachs' criticism is rather odd given the literature he attacked. Berman's (1983) book was about the "plurality" of law, after all, and one type of law that he discussed was urban law (presumably "the law of staples" refers to the law of the staples market towns). Similarly, Benson (1989, 1990, etc.) and Trakman (1983) both discussed the competition between legal systems (plurality of law), Holdsworth (1903) emphasized that urban law dominated by merchant guilds often stifled trade and discriminated against foreign merchants, and so on. Beyond that, of course, the Statute of Staples is a "statute." It is authoritarian law imposed from the top, and while it clearly had an impact on merchants, it was not part of the Law Merchant created through merchant interaction. Sachs (2006: 786) also contended that the "drafters of the statute – even the merchants for whom it was enacted – had specific principles in mind." I cannot say what the drafters had in mind, but I can say that the assumption that the statute was imposed primarily for the benefit of merchants in general is highly suspect. No doubt, some merchants had some influence over parts of the statutes (primarily those who dominated the governments of the staple towns), but the statute was also intended to benefit the crown (Benson 1989: 652).

agreement on ends was universal . . . Any differences in local culture could not push anyone away from basic principles. They only influenced the second-tier questions of formality and procedure. . . .
. . . . [T]he trick is to increase the number of contracting opportunities. The Law Merchant does that in line with the time-honored principle too easily forgotten, that the extent of the market determines the division of labor.

This point is very consistent with Berman, since he suggested that the "basic concepts and procedures" of the Law Merchant were in place as part of a "developing system" of law. He did not contend that all rules were the same everywhere. It is quite normal to discuss the common law system, for instance, while simultaneously recognizing that there are differences in various doctrines across states. Indeed, Benson (1989: 648, note 4) noted that variations persisted across space even after 200 years of evolution. Kadens (2004) echoed Epstein but with some additional specificity that is quite consistent with Berman (1983), Benson (1989, 1999) and others. She depicted the customs of the medieval merchant community as layered, and contended that the "top layer" was "similar across Europe" (Kadens 2004: 56; citing Fagniez 1898: 116). In this context, she noted that merchant disputes pretty much everywhere were resolved quickly "from day to day or from tide to tide" and that they did not employ some of the trial procedures common in other legal systems of the day, such as ordeal or trial by battle (Kadens 2004: 56–7). These procedural uniformities reflected the desire for speedy and informal dispute resolution while striving to achieve equitable solutions to problems arising from incomplete contracts. This in turn reinforced incentives to contract and trade.

One very common trial procedure in law at the time, trial by oath, was allowed, but this was not the only method of "proof" under the Law Merchant. While this method of trial appears to be unsophisticated,[36] it actually was quite reasonable for the time and place. Essentially, it relied

---

[36]   Sachs (2006: 687) asked in passing, as he develops his criticism of the Medieval-Law-Merchant literature, how "the 'law merchant' could possibly have retained a consistent meaning across more than seven centuries. How could any institution that required oath-helpers of Gerard of Cologne [in 1270] also provide a model for the transnational regulation of Internet 'bots'?" Apparently he did not realize that trial by oath, or compurgation, was a common practice under many legal systems in the medieval period, including the common law. Trial by oath was used in the English Ecclesiastical courts until the seventeenth century. It was substantially abolished as a common law defense in felonies by the Constitutions of Clarendon (1164), but it was still permitted in civil actions for debt. In fact, it was not officially abolished for civil trials in England until 1833, by 3 and 4 William IV, c. 42, s. 13 (Lea 1996: 75). So Sachs also should have asked, how could the common law, a system that required oath-helpers for many trials in the medieval

on local knowledge (in the Law Merchant it depended on the reputation of merchants). Oath-helpers knew the character of the person they were helping and were likely to know the facts of the case better than anyone else. Furthermore, individuals who had strong religious beliefs were very reluctant to swear an oath before God that was actually false. It also must be stressed that Law Merchant courts and arbitrators did not rely exclusively on trial by oath. Testimony, various documents, and other forms of evidence were considered when available. Indeed, the Law Merchant recognized a good deal of documentary evidence that royal and ecclesiastical courts would not, as noted above (Zouch 1663 [1686]: 128; Arxiu Capitular de Barcelona 1-6-3475).

The importance of equity implied substantively significant similarities across Europe as well, and it is clear that many fundamental rules were widespread. Thus, while merchants in a particular location, or exclusively trading in certain markets or fairs, may not have known that many of the local rules were similar to or identical to those accepted elsewhere, there can be little doubt that merchants did, over time, find similar solutions for similar problems. As an example, Kadens (2004: 57) cited several sources to conclude that merchants throughout the major Northern and Southern trading areas indicated that a deal had been made by putting down a godspenny or by handshake. She also noted that merchants "all used some forms of credit, though the variety of monetary instruments employed may best be described as unity in diversity. In the south, merchants preferred bills of exchange or letters of credit, while in the North they used primarily letters of obligatory until the fifteenth century" (Kadens 2004: 57–8). Kadens also noted that there were some variations in how these instruments were used in different local communities, a point also recognized by Trakman (1983: 20–21) and Benson (1989: 648). Nonetheless, "the law, in its broad lines, as laid down by the merchants . . . was necessarily of the international character" (Bewes 1923: 299).

Berman (1983: 350) concluded that, "a great many if not most of the structural elements of the modern system of commercial law were formed" during the high Middle Ages. Berman's (1983: 341) conclusion that the rights and obligations of merchants in their dealings with each other "became substantially more objective and less arbitrary, more precise and less loose" by 1200, and probably by 1150, appears to be quite consistent with the evidence provided by Face (1958, 1959) and Greif (1989, 1993, 2006), despite what Berman's critics have claimed. Importantly,

---

period, and allowed them in some situations until 1833, maintain a consistent meaning across the centuries?

universality of all of the specific substantive rules is not necessary for Berman's (1983) contention to be true. As the trading range of most merchants and merchant communities were limited, all it required was that the statement applied within the various communities and for intercommunity trades between specific communities like the merchants who traded in the Champagne fairs. For this to occur, information had to be provided to foreign merchants so they could behave according to local expectations. A widely accepted (universal) set of fundamental rules substantially lowered the cost of interpreting other rules, because all of the local practices and usage could be expected to be consistent with the fundamental overarching rules. Many of the local practices and usage also would have been very similar, if not identical, particularly after inter-community trade had been going on for a while, as profit-seeking merchants naturally looked for the rules that minimized their transactions costs.[37]

While merchants within various communities tended to travel together, form partnerships, and engage in various kinds of mutual support, much of the merchant trade was between members of different groups. Most trade between merchants occurred at fairs when commerce began to emerge from the dark ages, and merchants from different communities clearly came together at the major fairs, as explained above. As a result, it should not be surprising that over time many of the rules and practices of one community could be observed by members of other communities. Within-group rules evolved as merchants emulated relatively effective practices they observed. Those rules that proved to be the most effective at facilitating commercial interaction tended to supplant those which were less effective. Nonetheless, at any point in time considerable variety in rules across communities probably was the norm. Two different rules might be equally effective for instance. Also, as new issues called for solutions, they might have developed in a particular community first, so that community might have had a standard practice to deal with the issue long before another community even faced the issue. In additions, merchants predominantly trading in one area or one commodity faced different kinds of issues than merchants trading mostly in another area.[38] Nonetheless, as Kadens (2004: 62–3) explained,

---

[37]   The increasing interest in commerce from those with coercive power, or with sufficient political influence to benefit from such power, also was an important reason for differences in the Law Merchant's local rules. See the concluding section of this chapter, and note 46 in particular.

[38]   Consider wool, for instance [this discussion paraphrases Kadens (2004: 60)]. Wool from England was baled in amounts of standard size. During the bale-packing process, a sworn wool-sorter sorted the wool according to quality,

The fact that customs were local or trade-specific did not mean that they had no effect on commerce in general. The Italian wool buyer in England followed English custom; the Fleming who purchases a bill of exchange in Paris followed the local *usance*. One of the prevailing tropes in works by merchants on trade practices is the discussion of the rules one must follow in different locales. Knowing those rules and working within them was part of how a trader abided by the law merchant. When disputes arose about customs, whether the nearly universal or the local ones, courts assumed that the merchants parties had knowledge of the practices. Consequently, they believed that they could rely on merchant experts to give them guidance on how to resolve the disagreement.

In fact, since some rules varied from place to place, itinerant consul often travelled with groups of traders of a particular nationality, specializing in determining the rules and practices in the markets and fairs they visited, and watching over the community's interests (Bewes 1923: 85). In some large markets and fairs, permanent consul representing particular nationalities apparently attended to the needs of travelling merchants, offering their services regarding local legal issues and disputes [they also apparently were sources of information about reputations: before finalizing a contract, each merchant was free to check with a consul about the behavior and reputation of the other party in the exchange (Milgrom, et al. 1990: 10–14)]. In addition, merchants also retained agents who spent much more time at particular fairs and in particular locations than the merchants themselves (Face 1958, Greif 2006), so these agents also were sources of information.

This brings up an apparent misinterpretation by Sachs (2006). He appears to believe that if the medieval Law Merchant existed then the rules of the Law Merchant (or at least many of its rules) should have been created and imposed by merchant courts as if they were modern precedents, and that fair courts should, therefore, have referred to other fair courts' rulings. After actually admitting that it is "difficult to make any conclusions about national or international similarities based primarily on court records from only one area (the fair of St. Ives) and period of time (1270–1324)" (Sachs 2006: 762), he went on to do so at great length, contending, for instance, that: "one can examine the alleged university of the law merchant in reverse: rather than ask whether courts resembled

---

marked each bale to indicate the wool merchant involved, the quality of the bale, the place of origin for the bale, and a specific bale number. The individual who created these bales sold them to buyers who generally did not inspect each bale. Instead, a sample out of a set of bales was examined. The expectation was that all similarly marked bales were of similar quality. These bales would then be sold to others based on the verbal guarantee of the merchant. These markings and verbal guarantees were unique to the wool trade, so they were irrelevant to other traders.

St. Ives, one can inquire to what extent St. Ives sought to follow other courts" (Sachs 2006: 763). He then contended that: "The merchant courts functioned on an almost entirely independent basis; each court considered itself competent to decide cases from anywhere in the world, and showed no hesitation in doing so" (Sachs 2006: 763). Similarly, the court appears to have been reluctant to issue a "general ruling" (Sachs 2006: 757), and:

> if the mercantile courts were partners in the administration of a universal law merchant, one might expect some sort of organized division of labor among them. This is especially true given that cases in the St. Ives court might be simultaneously litigated elsewhere. . ... What principle mediated the contacts between St. Ives and its sister courts, and how were conflicts between them resolved? Some occasional mentions of external courts appear in the St. Ives rolls. However, such examples are exceedingly rare, and generally represent other aspects of court process rather than true collaboration. (Sachs 2006: 765)

And again:

> Although the St. Ives court was willing to pass judgment on controversies arising out of foreign cities and fairs, it did not appear to recognize the courts of those areas as participating in a special and shared transnational jurisdiction. Decisions reached in the courts of other cities or communities could be challenged and even reversed in the fair court. (Sachs 2006: 765–6)

Several similar statements could be cited, but the fact is that what Sachs observed is precisely what should be expected with a polycentric customary law system. Since true merchant courts had no authority to create or impose rules, all they really did was resolve disputes by offering default rules that could be ignored in future contracts.[39] A decision might have occasionally suggested a useful rule that might then be adopted, but no merchant court considered its rulings to be binding on any other court or on any merchant other than the parties in the dispute for the term of the contract. Furthermore, a decision might not have been consistent with another court's decision, but that did not mean that the other court's ruling was "reversed." The decision was different, but neither applied as a

---

[39]   Similarly, strong precedents observed in common law today were not part of the medieval common law. Zywicki (2003) explained that common law dispute resolutions were actually similar to Law Merchant dispute resolutions—decisions did not create hard precedent, but instead, essentially suggested default rules that people could contract around. If precedents are necessary for a system to be law, then medieval common law was not law either.

universal principle unless or until it was voluntarily adopted within the relevant community. In fact, local rules were understood to apply in a market or fair as long as those local rules were consistent with the overarching universal rules of the Law Merchant (see below). Merchants were free to write contracts that addressed the issue in ways that were consistent with either court's decision or inconsistent with both—the "principles" of freedom of contract and that local rules applied in local transactions "mediated the contacts between St. Ives and its sister courts."[40] Unlike modern common law courts, merchant courts had no legislative authority,[41] and they were not "partners" engaged in "collaboration" to create an "invariant" Law Merchant.

The preceding discussion reveals many of the universal rules of the Law Merchant (and helps distinguish these rules from the many non-Law-Merchant rules that were imposed on merchant activity over time, as explained below). The following list is my characterization of such rules. It is not a list derived from a medieval source, although it reflects information from such sources, other secondary sources, and a detailed examination of literature about other customary law systems. In fact, merchants may not have consciously recognized these rules, or been able to articulate them. That is often the case with customary law. Nonetheless, by 1200 merchant behavior in commercialized Europe implies that they generally acted under universal rules such as:

(1) respect other merchants' property rights;
(2) respect freedom of contract, as well as freedom not to contract (thus, for instance, a contract agreed to under duress was not valid);
(3) be honest in dealings with other merchants: for instance, accurately represent merchandize when negotiating an exchange (therefore, a contract agreed upon because of fraudulent misrepresentation was not valid);

---

[40] Merchant courts apparently communicated with one another for advice on occasion. Another potential reason for inter-court communications was to prevent filing the same suit in more than one court:

> Here let us remember the controversy between two brothers ... who went to law in Brabant for many thousand pounds, and afterwards one of them did commence suit in Flanders being another jurisdiction, whereupon he was compelled to pay a forfeiture of 4000 pounds; for in truth good orders and customs are to be maintained as laws and nothing is to be admitted that may infringe the law of Merchants (Malyne 1622 [1686]: 452).

[41] Sachs (2006: 761) believes he identifies a precedent-setting decision of the St. Ives court, but it will be evident below that the court's decision is consistent with widespread and longstanding practice and usage.

(4) do what you promised to do in a valid agreement, unless a subsequent agreement voluntarily alters the first contract (e.g., do not engage in opportunistic behavior by demanding changes in a contract to capture a larger portion of the gains from trade);

(5) provide truthful information to other merchants about observed behavior of individual merchants, and if requested, provide such information under oath (see number 10 below);

(6) learn and follow local practice and usage when trading, unless all parties to an exchange agree to behave otherwise for the term of their contract;

(7) when trading locally with foreign merchants or domestic merchants from other regions, provide accurate information about local practice and usage relevant to the transactions;

(8) treat all merchants attending a fair or market equitably, whether foreign or domestic;

(9) if a dispute arises that cannot be resolved through negotiation, take the dispute to an arbitrator(s) or judge(s) who is either agreed upon by both parties (e.g., an ecclesiastical court, a merchant arbitrator) or chosen by the relevant group of merchants (e.g., those attending a fair); do not use violence to resolve the dispute unless the other party refuses to accept fair arbitration;

(10) accept an arbitrator(s) or judge(s) who is a reputable merchant or other adjudicator(s) (e.g., an ecclesiastical court) who will resolve the dispute quickly and equitably after considering the relevant evidence (documented terms of a contract, related documents, testimony of witnesses of an agreement) if such evidence is available; whose dispute resolution will be consistent with the customs, practices and usage that each party should have been familiar with—the universal rules that everyone knows (such as those suggested here), along with relevant local practices and usage; and who will, if necessary to reach a quick decision, recognize evidence about the reputations of the parties (oaths—recall number (5)—with the number of oath-helpers established according to local practices regarding relevant circumstances);

(11) if a dispute is taken to an arbitrator(s) or judge(s), accept and abide by the resolution proposed within the confines of the contract that generated the dispute; the same dispute is not to be taken (appealed) to another adjudicator, but the resolution need not affect future contracts with the same or another party;

(12) the terms of a particular contract and the resolution of a particular dispute do not impose rules on you or other merchants that must be followed in future interactions or contracts (although they may

suggest beneficial practices for future interactions or contracts that you may choose to adopt);[42]

(13) support the reputable merchants in your own merchant community (guild, caravan, ethnic or national group) if called upon to protect property or assist in pursuit and collection efforts (the hue and cry); and

(14) provide financial backing to reputable merchants from your community, and if any surety loan of this type is provided to you by others, repay or work off the loan in a timely fashion.

As with any legal system, rules were violated. Appeals to some authoritarian courts occurred, fraud was practiced, domestic merchants did not always inform foreign merchants about local practices and usage, and so on. The flow of information about such violations was vital [number (5)], as this allowed individual merchants to decide how to treat violators (e.g., ostracize, demand bonds or other terms of a contract). There were probably other universal rules, and the importance of some of those listed probably varied over time and space. Significantly, by accepting these kinds of fundamental overarching general rules, many more specific behavioral requirements could be generated through negotiation and contracting.

III. CONCLUSIONS: COMPETITION FOR JURISDICTION, AND ALTERATIONS IN THE LAW MERCHANT

As long as most trade took place at numerous temporary fairs, the incentives for local powers (and domestic merchants) to try to control trade were relatively weak. However, as trade expanded, some locations that had particular geographic advantages for either production or trade (e.g., access to raw materials such as ore deposits or coal, a good harbor, a relatively large cluster of wealthy customers such as a royal court), local powers realized that they could extract some of the locational rents. Domestic merchants and craftsmen, also attempting to extract locational rents, might choose to settle permanently in some of these locations, making them permanent market towns. Many grew rapidly, becoming cities of significant political importance. Politically important market towns were governed, for the most part, by merchant and craft guilds whose members located in them.

---

[42] This was also the case for common law courts during the early centuries of its development (Zywicki 2003).

Many of the rules that had evolved through Law Merchant processes were adopted by local authorities trying to attract merchants to their fairs, and by the market towns dominated by commercial interests. In fact, Kings often recognized ("granted") legal authority (coercive power) to politically important urban governments and to other local authorities, like barons and abbots. The powers granted to recognized local authorities often included the power to set up their own courts.[43] When coercive power is established in a jurisdiction, however, it becomes possible to impose discriminatory rules from the top down (Benson 1999, 2001). And as Hayek (1973, 10) noted, "the growth of the purpose-independent rules of conduct ... often have taken place in conflict with the aims of the rulers who tended to turn their domain into an organization proper." Many urban governments dominated by local merchants and guilds began discriminating against various foreign trading communities (Jewish traders were favorite targets) while simultaneously granting other trading groups special privileges (e.g., treating them as if they were local merchants) in exchange for similar privileges in the local bases of those groups. As Holdsworth (1903, 302) explains, when this occurred:

> It was only those who belonged to the Guild Merchant who could trade freely within the town. Its conduct was sometimes so oppressive that trade was driven from the town. In fact all the various privileges, jurisdictional and administrative, which the towns possessed could be, and often were used in a manner adverse to the commercial interests of the country. The foreign merchant was hampered at every turn by the privileges of the chartered towns. They were averse to allowing him any privileges except those which they had specifically bargained to give him.

Reciprocal agreements between market towns became increasingly common with each agreeing to grant certain exclusive privileges to merchants from the other. Some of these agreements developed into multilateral and geographically extensive coalitions that discriminated in favor of merchants from the towns in the coalition. The most obvious example

---

[43]   This recognition often was accompanied by some sort of "grant" of the privilege to maintain local law and hold local courts, but this does not necessarily imply that Kings could have provided and enforced law in these localities. Local lords maintained military forces that Kings required in order to pursue their wars, and commerce was necessary in order for kings to raise funds through taxes and loans, so jurisdictional "grants" were virtually always "exchanges." In order to maintain the military support of local lords and encourage commerce despite the taxes collected, kings recognized various privileges for lords and urban powers, including legal authority in local jurisdictions. Recall the discussion of the mobility of merchants as a constraint on local authoritarian power.

are the Hanseatic Cities of Northern Europe that establish near-exclusive control of trade throughout the Baltic for German merchants (Dollinger 1970).

Kings also used their coercive powers to extract revenues or political benefits from fairs, and commerce in general. As royal power expanded, for instance, French kings appointed "jurists, who, having recommended the study of Roman law, supported the royal claims by the Digest of Justinian" (Bewes 1923: 105), displacing the Law Merchant, at least to a sufficient degree that commercial activity in France declined, shifting eastward to the Rhine and westward to direct sea routes between Northern and Southern traders.[44] Kings also found it beneficial to sell exclusive monopoly franchises, and exclude specified merchant groups such as Jewish traders, thereby gaining the support of the powerful domestic merchants who captured monopoly rents and shared them with the Kings (through franchise fees, taxes, etc.).

Some writers apparently assume that authoritarian law imposed on merchants was the Law Merchant or vice versa (e.g., VM 1999, Sachs 2006). Equating these systems is inappropriate. Citing letters reported in *The Little Red Book of Bristol (c. 1280),* Coquillette (1987: note 21) explained that "surviving correspondence forms between one fair court and another, even fair courts of different countries, show a formula that

---

[44]   The Count of Champagne did not interfere with the fairs through most of the twelfth century, but toward the end of that century this began to change. Wardens were appointed to deal with administrative and judicial issues. These wardens were supported by serjeants to deliver summons, serve as night watchmen or guards, and enforce orders of the court (Kadens 2004: 53). These courts apparently continued to apply merchant law. Some historians have dated the beginning of the decline of the Champagne fairs to the conquest of Champagne by Phillip the Bold in 1273, but in 1285 Champagne became dependent on the King of France, and Abu-Lughod (1991, 58) contended that this is when "the Champagne fairs lost their edge." The institutions established by the Count became the King's, and fiscal exactions increased. Then in the fourteenth century, the Hundred Years War started. It continued from 1336 to 1453 although the political buildup to the war started several years earlier. The French kings required revenues to maintain their war efforts and the fairs were seen as a source of revenues. In addition, the Black Death plague hit Europe shortly before the middle of the fourteenth century. Jews were widely blamed for the plague, and Jewish merchants were expelled from many fairs and markets, including those of Champagne. The result of the displacement of merchant law, the extraction of war revenues, the Jewish expulsion and other authoritarian controls over these fairs, along with the dangers for merchants traveling during the war, was that over time "The Rhone was deserted for the Rhine the caravan for the convoy, and so the Flemish and British markets were reached. . . but this is but a partial account of the change in the course of trade, for . . . the greatest part of this trade became waterborne and direct" (Bewes 1923: 111).

clearly distinguishes between the law merchant . . . and the town customs."
While urban and manorial (and royal) law supported many Law Merchant
rules, they also imposed top-down authoritarian and discriminatory additions or alterations to extract revenues and/or provide special procedures,
privileges and powers to selected individuals or groups.[45]

In conclusion, let us summarize the characteristics of the medieval Law
Merchant as described in Bewes (1923), Berman (1983), Trackman (1983),
Benson (1989, 1990, 1995, 1999, 2002, forthcoming), Johnson and Post
(1996), Mallat (2000), Zywicki (2003), Callahan (2004), Belhorn (2005),
Levit (2005), and many others. *Lex Mercatoria* of the high Middle Ages was:

(1)   a distinct (but not independent) system of polycentric customary law
      which arose and continued to evolve spontaneously from the bottom
      up through the interactions of merchants in pursuit of universal
      objectives to enhance the opportunities for contract and trade, and
      maintain freedom of contract; consisting of:
(2)   primary rules of obligation including both longstanding custom and
      evolving commercial practices and usage that supported freedom of
      contract and increased opportunities to contract by increasing the
      credibility of promises; as well as secondary rules of:
(3)   change initialized through negotiation (contracting), and perhaps
      dispute resolution, followed by voluntary emulation of those prac-
      tices that best enhanced opportunities to engage in contractual trade
      and support freedom of contract;

---

[45]   The success of authoritarian efforts to capture benefits by controlling commerce, including merchant law, depended on several factors, including the degree
of competition between jurisdictions (the availability of fairs or markets in other
jurisdictions which were more receptive to the Law Merchant), the mobility of
merchants and their wealth, and the locational advantages enjoyed by particular
markets or fairs. If competition was severely limited, merchants might be forced to
use authoritarian courts despite a preference for some other method of dispute resolution. As Jones (1987: 89–90) explained, however, "the ability of the market to free
itself from the worst interferences by the authorities" was a distinctive characteristic
of European trade. Arbitration could be used, for instance. Also recall that ances-
tors of the Maghribi traders moved from Baghdad to Tunisia in the tenth century
because of the political situation in Baghdad (Greif 2006: 61). Similarly, German
merchants representing the Hanseatic League moved out of Bruges, the Flanders
trading hub, in 1288 because Bruges' appointed weighers fraudulently falsified
weighings (Kadens 2004: 51). Bruges' government had to promise to prevent the
fraud in order to get the German merchants to return. A more significant example
of merchant mobility probably is the decline of the fairs of Champagne as some
trade moved east and maritime trade increased to the west – see note 44. Also see
note 46 and the discussion of underground activities such as smuggling.

(4) adjudication through processes such as mediation, arbitration, participatory courts and other courts willing to resolve merchant disputes quickly and equitably; and:

(5) recognition arising from positive incentives to expand contracting opportunities (and merchant well-being) through maintenance of repeat-dealing and reputation benefits, along with negative incentives created by spontaneous sanctions such as varying degrees of ostracism; but:

(6) this distinct system also interacted, in various complementary and/or competitive ways over time and space, with other distinct polycentric legal systems that often had objectives differing from those of the Law Merchant; and as a result:

(7) its primary and secondary rules influenced and were influenced by other legal systems.

Over time the Law Merchant was absorbed in varying degrees by the urban and royal legal systems evolving within European states (urban law was also largely absorbed by national law in parts of Europe), at times with the consent and support of domestic merchants and at times, despite merchant resistance. This absorption often altered or replaced Law Merchant rules and procedures to the detriment of commercial activity (Trakman 1983, Benson 1989, 1990). International trade continued, to a substantial extent, to be ruled by the Law Merchant, however, as did trade within various commercial organizations and trade associations which have become increasingly prominent over the last two centuries (Benson 1995, Bernstein 1992). Over the centuries, Law Merchant rules and procedures have changed to reflect the changes in market organizations and practices, and its polycentric nature has become more pronounced (Cooter 1994, Benson 1999). Indeed, new Law Merchant systems have been severely undermined in some places and driven underground,[46] only

---

[46] Even when royal or urban authorities declared various trading activities illegal and undermined incentives to be productive, illegal trading generally developed. The illegal traders followed practices and usage developed under their own Law Merchant processes. This underground Law Merchant would not be easily observable, of course. Leeson's (2007) examination of the rules and procedures employed within pirate communities illustrates that illegal activities are not "lawless" even though they may be engaged in activities that are illegal under the laws of nation states. The underground practices and usage were also probably stifled in various ways, and the resulting Law Merchant system may have been relatively less effective than systems that arose in environments where trade was much freer and less controlled [e.g., see de Soto's (1989) insightful discussion of the rules and processes governing the "informal" sector in Peru]. Nonetheless, as

to arise and evolve again whenever market systems are able to emerge (Benson 2016).

REFERENCES

Abu-Lughod, J. L. (1991) *Before European Hegemony: The World System A.D. 1250–1350.* New York: Oxford University Press.
Arxiu Capitular de Barcelona 1-6-3475, E. Klein (trans. from P. Halsall, ed.) (2006) *Internet Medieval Sourcebook*, Fordham University for Medieval Studies, http://www.fordham.edu/halsall/source/1242barcelonabusagreement.html (last visited February 4, 2010).
Basile, M. ed. ([c. 1280] 1998) "*Lex Mercatoria* from *The Little Red Book of Bristol*," in *Lex Mercatoria and Legal Pluralism: A Late Thirteenth Century Treatise and its Afterlife.* Cambridge: The Ames Foundation.
Belhorn, S. (2005) "Settling Beyond the Shadow of the Law: How Mediation Can Make the Most of Social Norms," 20 *Ohio State Journal on Dispute Resolution* 981–1026.
Benson, B. (1988) "Legal Evolution in Primitive Societies," 144 *Journal of Institutional and Theoretical Economics* 772–88.
Benson, B. (1989) "The Spontaneous Evolution of Commercial Law," 55 *Southern Economic Journal* 644–61.
Benson, B. (1990) *The Enterprise of Law: Justice Without the State.* San Francisco: Pacific Research Institute.
Benson, B. (1995) "An Exploration of the Impact of Modern Arbitration Statutes on the

---

Nee (1998: 88) explained, "opposition norms" inevitably evolve as the incentives created by formal institutions and sanctions are weak relative to the incentives to pursue personal interests. For instance, as European governments attempted to establish control over maritime trade in order to tax it or to protect powerful domestic merchants' franchises and privileges, the "average merchant and seaman responded with piracy and smuggling, and a substantial part of maritime commerce was carried out in violation of the laws of some nation-state" (Rosenberg and Birdzell 1986: 92–6). Furthermore, the middle and even the upper classes willingly wore, drank, and ate smuggled goods (Rosenberg and Birdzell 1986: 93). Clearly, the royal and urban courts would not consider contract disputes involving smuggled goods that undermined their tax collection activities and/or the privileges they had given to various individual merchants, domestic merchant groups, and guilds. Contracts still arose, no doubt subject to an underground Law Merchant. Similarly, while craft guilds attempted to monopolize (cartelize) production within particular urban markets, illegal production of the goods the guild supposedly had exclusive rights to produce often occurred outside the urban boundary, with illegal (counterfeit) goods then sold to both city residents and alien merchants (Jones 1987: 99). As Jones (1987: 96) noted;

> Rigidities impeding the movement and use of goods and factors of production had to be removed for economies to work efficiently. The lure of profit was sufficient in already commercialized economies to bite into the "cake of custom" or to get around the regulations. Rigidities were less of a bar to development than residual arbitrariness, though the course of market expansion through the maze of inconveniences was not quite as that might suggest.

Development of Arbitration in the United States," 11 *Journal of Law, Economics, & Organization* 479–501.

Benson, B. (1999) "To Arbitrate or to Litigate: That is the Question," 8 *European Journal of Law and Economics* 91–151.

Benson, B. (2001) "Knowledge, Trust, and Recourse: Imperfect Substitutes as Sources of Assurance in Emerging Economies," 21 *Economic Affairs* 12–17.

Benson, B. (2002) "Law Without Government: The Merchant Courts of Medieval Europe and Their Modern Counterparts," in *The Voluntary City: Choice, Community, and Civil Society*, D. Beito, P. Gordon, and A. Tabarrok, eds. Ann Arbor, MI: University of Michigan Press.

Benson, B. (2006) "Contractual Nullification of Economically-Detrimental State-Made Laws," 9 *Review of Austrian Economics* 149–87.

Benson, B. (2010) "It Takes Two Invisible Hands to Make a Market: *Lex Mercatoria* (Law Merchant) Always Emerges to Facilitate Emerging Markets," 3 *Studies in Emergent Order* 100–128.

Benson, B. (2011) "The Law Merchant Story: How Romantic is it?," in *Law, Economics and Evolutionary Theory*, Gralf Calliess and Peer Zumbansen, eds. Cheltenham UK, Northampton MA: Edward Elgar.

Benson, B. (2016) "Yes Virginia, there is a Law Merchant," Working Manuscript, Department of Economics, Florida State University.

Benson, B. (forthcoming) "International Economic Law and Commercial Arbitration," in *Economic Analysis of Law: A European Perspective*, Aristides N. Hatzis, ed., Cheltenham UK, Northampton MA: Edward Elgar.

Berman, H. (1983) *Law and Revolution: The Formation of Western Legal Tradition*. Cambridge, MA: Harvard University Press.

Bernstein, L. (1992) "Opting Out of the Legal System: Extralegal Contractual Relations in the Diamond Industry," 21 *Journal of Legal Studies* 115–58.

Bewes, W. (1923) *The Romance of the Law Merchant: Being an Introduction to the Study of International and Commercial Law With Some Account of the Commerce and Fairs of the Middle Ages*. London: Sweet & Maxwell.

Bickley, F. ed. (c. 1280 [1900]) *The Little Red Book of Bristol*. Bristol.

Blancard, L. ed. ([1884] 1965) *Documents Inédits sur le Commerce de Marseille au Moyen Age*. Marseilles: Barlatier-Feissat, Pere et Fils, in *A Source Book for Medieval Economic History*, R. Cave and H. Coulson, eds. (1936 [1965]) Milwaukee, The Bruce Publishing Co., reprint ed., New York: Biblo & Tannen, from P. Halsall, ed. (2006) *Internet Medieval Sourcebook*, Fordham University for Medieval Studies, http://www.fordham.edu/halsall/ source/ with the following endings for specific material 1230freight-abrit.html, 1240pship2. html, 1248billoflading.html, and 1248sale-ack.html (last visited February 4, 2010).

Cabral, L. and A. Hortacsu (2004) "The Dynamics of Seller Reputation: Theory and Evidence from eBay," *National Bureau of Economic Research*, Working Paper 10363.

Callahan, D. (2004) "Medieval Church Norms and Fiduciary Duties in Partnerships," 26 *Cardozo Law Review* 215–87.

Coquillette, D. (1987) "Ideology and Incorporation III: Reason Regulated – The Post-Restoration English Civilians, 1653–1735," 67 *Boston University Law Review* 289–361.

Cooter, R. (1994) "Structural Adjudication and the New Law Merchant: a Model of Decentralized Law," 14 *International Review of Law and Economics* 215–31.

de Soto, H. (1989) *The Other Path: The Invisible Revolution in the Third World*. New York: Harper & Row.

Dollinger, P. (1970) *The German Hansa*. Stanford CA: Stanford University Press.

Donahue, C. Jr. (2004) "The Empirical and Theoretical Underpinnings of the Law Merchant: Medieval and Early Modern Lex Mercatoria: An attempt at the probatio diabolica," 5 *University of Chicago Journal of International Law* 21–37.

Drahozal, C. (2005) "Competing and Complementary Rule Systems: Civil Procedure and ADR: Contracting out of National Law: an Empirical Look at the New Law Merchant," 80 *Notre Dame Law Review* 523–52.

Drahozal, C. (2008) "Busting Arbitration Myths," 56 *Kansas Law Review* 663–77.

Epstein, R. (2004) "The Empirical and Theoretical Underpinnings of the Law Merchant: Reflections on the Historical Origins and Economic Structure of the Law Merchant," 5 *University of Chicago Journal of International Law* 1–20.

Face, R. (1958) "Techniques of Business in the Trade Between the Fairs of Champagne and the South of Europe in the Twelfth and Thirteenth Centuries," 10 *Economic History Review* 427–38.

Face, R. (1959) "The *Vectuarii* in the Overland Commerce Between Champagne and Southern Europe," 12 *Economic History Review* 239–46.

Fagniez, G. (1898) 2 *Documents Relatifs à l'Histoire de l'industrie et du Commerce en France.* Alphonse Picard et Fils.

Fassberg, C. (2004) "The Empirical and Theoretical Underpinnings of the Law Merchant: Lex Mercatoria—Hoist with Its Own Petard?" 5 *University of Chicago Journal of International Law* 67–82.

Fuller, L. (1981) *The Principles of Social Order.* Durham, NC: Duke University Press.

Greif, A. (1989) "Reputation and Coalitions in Medieval Trade: Evidence on the Maghribi Traders," 49 *Journal of Economic History* 857–82.

Greif, A. (1993) "Contract Enforceability and Economic Institutions in Early Trade," 83 *American Economic Review* 525–48.

Greif, A. (2006) *Institutions and the Path to the Modern Economy: Lessons from Medieval Trade.* New York: Cambridge University Press.

Hart, H.L.A. (1961) *The Concept of Law.* Oxford, UK: Clarendon.

Hayek, F. (1973) *Law, Legislation, and Liberty*, Vol. 1. Chicago: University of Chicago Press.

Holdsworth, W. (1903) *A History of English Law*, Vol. 1. London: Methuen & Co.

Johnson, D. and D. Post (1996) "Surveying Law and Borders – Law And Borders – The Rise of Law in Cyberspace," 48 *Stanford Law Review* 1367–402.

Jones, E. (1987) *The European Miracle.* Cambridge, UK: Cambridge University Press.

Kadens, E. (2004) "The Empirical and Theoretical Underpinnings of the Law Merchant: Order within Law, Variety within Custom: The Character of the Medieval Merchant Law," 5 *University of Chicago Journal of International Law* 39–65.

Lea, H. (1996) *Superstition and Force: Torture, Ordeal, and Trial by Combat in Medieval Law.* New York: Barnes and Noble.

Leeson, P. (2007) "An-arrgh-chy: The Law and Economics of Pirate Organization," 115 *Journal of Political Economy* 1049–94.

Levit, J. (2005) "A Bottom-Up Approach to International Lawmaking: The Tale of Three Trade Finance Instruments," 30 *Yale Journal of International Law* 125–209.

Leoni, B. (1961) *Freedom and the Law.* Los Angeles: Nash Publishing.

Mallat, C. (2000) "Commercial Law in the Middle East: Between Classical Transactions and Modern Business," 48 *American Journal of Comparative Law* 81–141.

Malynes, G. (1622 [1686]) *Consuetudo, vel, Lex mercatoria or, The ancient law-merchant, in three parts, according to the essentials of traffick: necessary for statesmen, judges, magistrates, temporal and civil lawyers, mint-men, merchants, mariners, and all others negotiating in any parts of the world.* London: Printed for T. Basset, R. Chiswell, M. Horne, and E. Smith.

Marius, J. (1651) *Advice Concerning Bills of Exchange wherein is set forth the nature of exchange of monies, the several kinds of exchange in different countries, divers cases propounded and resolved, objections answered, &c.: With two exact tables of old and new style.* Philadelphia: Re-printed by D. Humphreys, Front-Street, near the drawbridge, 1790.

Menadier, J. ed. (1913) *Die Aachener Münzen.* Berlin: W. Pormetter.

Migne, J.P. ed. (1850) *Patrologiae Cursus Completus*, Vol. LXXX. Paris. in *A Source Book for Medieval Economic History*, R. Cave and Coulson, eds. (1936 [1965]) *A Source Book for Medieval Economic History.* Milwaukee, The Bruce Publishing Co., reprint ed., New York: Biblo & Tannen, from P. Halsall, ed. (2006) *Internet Medieval Sourcebook*, Fordham University for Medieval Studies, http://www.fordham.edu/halsall/source/629stdenis.html (last visited, February 4, 2010).

Milgrom, P., D. North, and B. Weingast (1990). "The Role of Institutions in the Revival of Trade: the Law Merchant, Private Judges, and the Champagne Fairs," 2 *Economics and Politics* 1–23.

Mitchell, W. (1904) *Essays on the Early History of the Law Merchant*. New York: Burt Franklin.

Mokyr, J. (1990) *The Lever of Riches: Technological Creativity and Economic Progress*. Oxford, UK: Oxford University Press.

Nee, V. (1998) "Norms and Networks in Economic and Organizational Performance," 88 *American Economic Review Papers and Proceedings* 85–9.

Pertz, G. ed. (1925) *Monumenta Germaniae Historica, Scriptorum Tomus IV.* Hanover: Hahn.

Piergiovanni, V. (1995) "Statito. Diritto Commune e Processo Mercantile," in *El Dret Comu I Catalunya: Actes del VII Simposi International.* Barcelona: Fundacio Noguera.

Piergiovanni, V. (1998) "Diritto e Giustizia Mercantile a Genova ne XV Secolo: I Consilia di Bartolomeo Bosco," in *Consilia im Spaten Mettlelalter: zum Histoischen Aussagewert einer Quellengattung.* I. Gaumgartner, ed. Thorbecke, 13 Schrifenreihe des Deutschen Studienzentrums in Venetia.

Pospisil, L. (1971) *Anthropology of Law: A Comparative Theory.* New York: Harper and Row.

Pospisil, L. (1978) *The Ethnology of Law.* 2nd Edition, Menlo Park, CA: Cummings Publishing.

Rosenberg, N. and L. Birdzell, Jr. (1986) *How the West Grew Rich: The Economic Transformation of the Industrial World.* New York: Basic Books.

Sachs, S. (2006) "From St. Ives to Cyberspace: The Modern Distortions of the Medieval Law Merchant," 21 *American University International Law Review* 685–812.

Stracca, B. (1553) *De Mercatura seu Mercatore Tractatus.* Venice, Italy: Michael Bonellum.

Teeter, R. (1962) "England's Earliest Treatise on the Law Merchant: The Essay on Lex Mercatoria from The Little Red Book of Bristol (Circa 1280 AD)," 6 *American Journal of Legal History* 172–210.

Trakman, L. (1983) *The Law Merchant: The Evolution of Commercial Law.* Littleton, CO: Fred B. Rothman and Co.

Volckart, O. and A. Mangels (1999) "Are the Roots of the Modern *Lex Mercatoria* Really Medieval?" 65 *Southern Economic Journal* 427–50.

Zouch, R. (1663) *The jurisdiction of the Admiralty of England asserted against Sr. Edward Coke's Articuli admiralitatis, in XXII chapter of his jurisdiction of courts.* London: Printed for Francis Tyton and Thomas Dring.

Zywicki, T. (2003) "The Rise and Fall of Efficiency in the Common Law: A Supply-Side Analysis," 97 *Northwestern Law Review* 1551–634.

8.   Self-governance, property rights, and illicit commerce*
David Skarbek

1.   INTRODUCTION

Governance institutions provide rules of the game that facilitate human interactions, and they vary in their form and effectiveness. When governance institutions work well, people engage in economic exchange. When these institutions operate poorly, markets fail and costly disputes over property rights occur. Legal centrism argues that the government 'is the exclusive creator of property rights' (Ellickson 1989) and 'that rational law cannot arise spontaneously from human interaction, but instead requires deliberation and debate. . .and that laws must be made deliberately to be rational' (Cooter 1993, 417, 427). Government, therefore, must provide governance.

This chapter challenges the legal centrism hypothesis by examining the internal governance institutions of prison gangs, arguing that order and property rights can emerge without the state. The *Nuestra Familia* prison gang in California operates without reliance on contract law or government protection of property rights, yet the group develops effective self-enforcing internal governance mechanisms to limit opportunistic and shirking behavior. Despite its status as an outlaw group, it successfully operates large-scale criminal enterprise.

2.   LITERATURE REVIEW

Groups of individuals need rules to govern interactions among themselves and with other groups. Government can provide these rules through the legal system, but under many conditions, privately produced, self-enforced governance institutions can operate effectively. As a positive research question in political economy, 'analytical anarchism' focuses on identifying the institutional mechanisms that facilitate self-governance in different

*   The author gratefully acknowledges the generous support of the Searle Foundation.

contexts (Boettke 2005). An extensive literature on the historical operation of private law and self-governance finds that order without law is often both possible and profitable (Stringham 2015).

This literature focuses on two environments of self-governance. Intragroup governance coordinates joint activity to achieve commonly desired ends within a defined group of self-identified members. Intergroup governance, on the other hand, facilitates cooperative interactions between people of different groups. The ability for governance mechanisms in either environment to arise outside of a centralized and consciously designed government institution depends, in part, on the demographics of the community's population. The more trustworthy people are and the lower their discount rates, the easier it will be to deter defection and punish it when it occurs. The more hostile, non-cooperative, and impatient people are, the less likely it will be that self-enforcing governance mechanisms will generate beneficial outcomes.

Institutions are not robust if they can only come into existence when people act ideally or in ideal situations (Pennington 2011). Past work provides evidence about how robust self-governance mechanisms can be to various environmental and population characteristics. Consider Figure 8.1 below: the rows distinguish between intragroup governance and intergroup governance in peaceful and hostile contexts; the columns identify whether the state suppresses the self-governing community.

The most well researched context of self-governance focuses on self-enforcing commercial exchange (category III, Figure 8.1). Intergroup governance of commercial traders (a peaceful context) allows widespread and long-distance trading to flourish in the absence of government with the aid of a diversity of commitment mechanisms and signaling strategies (e.g. Benson 1989; Clay 1997; Schaeffer 2008). Avner Greif's work (1989) on the Maghribi Traders is a well-known example. Empirical work on cults, communes, and other collective groups (Iannaccone 1992), such as

		Government suppression	
		Absent	Present
Type of group governance	Intragroup	I Orthodox Jews	II Pirates
	Intergroup (peaceful)	III Maghreb traders	IV Medieval temples
	Intergroup (hostile)	V Anglo-Scottish borderland	VI The Mexican Mafia

Figure 8.1   Examples of self-governance under different conditions

Orthodox Jews (Berman 2000) and charitable organizations (Skarbek, forthcoming), shows that intragroup governance can limit free riding and facilitate internal governance when government suppression is absent (category I, Figure 8.1).

Self-governance is less likely to be effective when the participants are biased to be uncooperative, have high discount rates, or are actively suppressed by the government. However, recent research documents the mechanisms operating in particular places and times to show how self-governing communities overcome these problems. Intragroup governance in the presence of government suppression (category II, Figure 8.1) was possible for 18th century pirates who developed a self-enforcing constitution to prevent internal predation by a ship's captain (Leeson 2007). Medieval temples and monasteries provided Japanese landowners an alternative to the government for conflict adjudication in commercial disputes and protection from external threats (Adolphson and Ramseyer 2009), showing that intergroup governance mechanisms can effectively protect people engaged in peaceful exchange from predatory states (category IV, Figure 8.1). Groups that are free of both government suppression and governance can still create rules to govern interactions (category V, Figure 8.1). For example, hostile groups along the Anglo-Scottish borderland in the 16th century developed rules that limited violence (Leeson 2009). The diversity of historical examples suggests that self-governing mechanisms that establish property rights can be quite robust.

The current chapter examines the remaining category: instances in which groups that are hostile to each other are interacting in the face of government suppression (category VI, Figure 8.1). One example in the literature is the Mexican Mafia prison gang, which protects property rights and mediates conflict between rival street gangs in Los Angeles in the face of active government suppression. It is willing and able to do so because its ability to tax drug dealers transforms it into a stationary bandit (Skarbek 2011; 2014).

Compared with the literature on self-enforcing commercial exchange, there is relatively little research on intragroup governance mechanisms in the presence of government suppression. Just as businesses in traditional markets devise mechanisms for overcoming organizational costs arising from transaction costs (Milgrom and Roberts 1992; Miller 1993), the mechanisms developed in illicit groups depend on the context. For example, one drug-dealing street gang overcame significant monitoring problems with careful accounting, and motivated employees with the potential for promotion into high-paying positions (Levitt and Venkatesh 2000). The following sections contribute to this literature by examining the incarceration context, where communicating information about peoples' actions and reputations is especially costly. Given these costs, establishing information transmission mechanisms is crucial to success. The Nuestra Familia prison gang defines and enforces property rights in prison, facilitates illicit trade, and directs criminal regiments outside of prison from behind bars.

3.   THE NUESTRA FAMILIA PRISON GANG

3.1 Brief Overview

Since the 1960s, the Nuestra Familia (NF) prison gang has played a prominent role in the criminal underworld in Northern California. It is the second largest prison gang in the California corrections system, and in addition to being a major source of drug trafficking behind bars, it engages in robbery, extortion, and murder for hire. It recruits members primarily in prison. Members swear lifetime allegiance to the gang, and when released from prison, gang members are required to continue working for the gang in specific geographic regions (Federal Bureau of Investigation 2009, 13). NF has become a highly profitable criminal enterprise with several hundred members and thousands of associates who facilitate its operations. A former Federal prosecutor describes the NF as being as sophisticated as a Fortune 500 company (60 Minutes 2005, see also Lewis 1980; Koehler 2000; United States v Rubalcaba et al 2001; Fuentes 2006; Skarbek 2010; 2012).

The California Department of Corrections and Rehabilitation actively disrupts NF operations. When gang members are identified, they are held in restrictive cellblocks, and the highest-ranking members usually reside in super-max facilities or a secure housing unit where they are locked in their cells for up to 23 hours a day. Law enforcement organizations regularly investigate NF members outside prison and prosecute them for narcotics trafficking, home invasion robberies, and murder. Because they are engaged in illegal activities, intragroup governance cannot rely on courts of law to protect their property rights, and employment law cannot govern the relationship between gang leaders and members.

In 1967, the NF formed and outlined its original internal governance system in a written constitution (Fuentes 2006, 3–11; Skarbek 2010; 2014). Since then the constitutional rules have changed in several ways. Some of the positions have been altered or renamed and various subsidiary groups have been created and terminated to aid NF. Robert Gratton, a member of the gang who became an informant for the Federal Bureau of Investigation, provided written correspondences between gang members, including orders from incarcerated leaders (Fuentes 2006; also see United States v Rubalcaba et al 2001, 4). These messages contain information about how the gang implemented the organizational structure outlined in its written constitution. These internal communications and the gang's constitution explain how NF uses information transmission mechanisms to provide protection of property rights behind bars and allows incarcerated gang leaders – who face high information costs – to monitor and direct gang activity in the free world.

3.2   NF Protects Property Rights and Facilitates Exchange

Legal centrism argues that only the state can define and enforce property rights, but this does not imply that the state always can and will do so (Stringham 2015). Correctional officers frequently are incapable of obtaining the information needed to punish or deter inmate-on-inmate harm. First, correctional officers often do not believe inmate claims of victimization. Inmates file false complaints for numerous reasons, including getting time away from prison jobs, moving to different cellblocks, avoiding other inmates to whom debts are owed, and as a means of entertainment. Second, even when correctional officials believe an inmate has been victimized, the anti-snitching culture that exists in prison often prevents collection of evidence and witness statements. When correctional officials do obtain evidence, they must convince the local district attorney to file charges. A former San Quentin Prison official estimates that, over the course of a year and a half, the local district attorney pursued three out of 100 cases that they submitted (Porter 1982, 16).

It is also important to ask how reliable state enforced property rights will be. Correctional officers are not perfectly monitored by their superiors, and they may lack the motivation needed to investigate a complaint or punish the victimizer. One sociologist describes correctional officers as passive victimizers, noting that in contemporary prisons, they have 'withdrawn to the walls, leaving inmates to intimidate, rape, maim, and kill each other with alarming frequency' (Irwin 1980, vii). To the extent that guards actively influence the inmate social system, they may exhibit bias. In the 1960s and 1970s, penologists argued that many guards held prejudiced racial views and gave preferential treatment to white inmates (Irwin 1980, 124–9). Although not representative, news accounts regularly report on correctional officers who neglect their duties, smuggle contraband into the facility, and victimize inmates (for example, Piller 2010). In the 1990s in California's Corcoran Prison, numerous correctional officers were reportedly 'staging [involuntary] inmate fights, sometimes wagering on the outcome and then, when those fights got out of control, of shooting the inmates involved. . .[and correctional officers also] allowed inmates to be raped by other inmates, as retaliation against those who had gotten out of line' (60 Minutes 1999; also Arax 1996). Although this is not the typical behavior of correctional officers, the worst outcome of state-enforced property rights appears to be the active violation of those rights and the abuse and killing of inmates.

State-based protection of property rights for inmates is incomplete or absent, and prison gangs formed to fill this need. A federal indictment explains that NF 'provided protection and security for its members and associates from rival organizations and gangs both inside and outside California correctional institutions' (United States v Rubalcaba et al 2001, 2). According to prison gang members, the original founders of NF grouped together to provide protection for Hispanic inmates from rural areas in California from predatory inmates (Fuentes 2006; see also Porter 1982, 10; Camp and Camp 1985; Mendoza 2005, 22; Morales 2008, 7). Members of another prison gang, the Mexican Mafia, had frequently victimized these inmates. The abuses included theft, assault, intimidation, and murder. Inmates who were not affiliated with a gang had 'to surrender their prison luxuries and items of comfort such as wrist watches, rings, shoes and anything that could either be enjoyed by [the Mexican Mafia] or sold on the prison black market' (Mendoza 2005, 22–3). These 'attacks aroused and consolidated a large number of "independent" Chicanos, who planned to eliminate the [Mexican] Mafia members' (Irwin 1980, 190; also Morales 2008, 20–23, 56–8). The prison gang's earliest written constitution outlines its intentions and internal organization, explaining that the 'primary purpose and goals of this O[rganization] is for the betterment of its members and the building up of this O[rganization] on the outside into a strong and self-supporting *familia*' (Fuentes 2006, 5). Former inmate and anthropologist Robert Koehler explains that NF 'provides Familianos with physical protection from rival gangs and supplies them with store goods at low cost or on low credit, and Familia serves as their emotional family' (Koehler 2000, 174).

Prison gangs generally perform two related and important functions: the protection of property rights and facilitation of illicit trade (Skarbek 2014). A correctional officer with 25 years of experience in California writes, 'most gangs in prison originally started out as protection groups' (Morales 2008, 6). A Black Guerrilla Family prison gang member explains that joining the gang provided benefits, as they 'controlled the line there by offering protection of numbers, protections of comradeship' (Porter 1982, 14). In 1985, the Department of Justice conducted a national study on prison gangs and found that their 'purposes range from mutual care-taking of members to large profit-making criminal enterprises' (Camp and

Camp 1985, 1). The gang maintains its power by providing 'protection for its members and the exploitation of others – and through its ability to acquire and distribute goods within the prison – primarily drugs' (Camp and Camp 1985, 42).

Since they cannot use state-based institutions to deter defection and opportunism in illicit exchange, inmates rely on prison gangs to do so. Koehler explains that 'the basis of Familia is capitalism. . .economic ventures allow Familia to counter the perceived hegemony of the guards/ prison system and the threat of rival prison gangs' (2000, 170–71). NF members arrange for the importation of drugs into the prison system and they act as either wholesaler or retailer in the narcotics market behind bars. In fact, one of the primary reasons that correctional facilities try to prevent the formation and operation of prison gangs is because they are the primary source of drug trafficking. A survey of prison wardens reports that drug trafficking is the second most frequent criminal activity engaged in by prison gangs and they are in charge of the majority of drug trafficking (Camp and Camp 1985, 44–5, 52–3). Gangs created a credible threat of violence to protect themselves, and once they accomplished this, they could credibly threaten people acting opportunistically during illicit trade.

The provision of protection and facilitation of exchange by organized criminal groups is actually quite common. Gambetta (1993) and Bandiera (2003) document how the early Sicilian Mafiosi protected land and enforced contracts. Organized criminal groups protect businesses and property in Japan (Milhaupt and West 2000), post-Soviet Russia (Varese 2005), Northern Italy (Varese 2006), and around the world (Varese 2011). Recent research finds that membership in Los Angeles street gangs is a response to violence rather than preceding it. This suggests that people join gangs for protection rather than as a vehicle for engaging in violence (Sobel and Osoba 2009). Research in criminology finds that protection is a common reason given by youth for their choice to join a gang (Melde, Taylor, and Esbensen 2009), and ethnographic research finds that protection is one of the most common services that members enjoy (Jankowski 1991, 122–3).

Correctional officials failed to establish and protect property rights in prison, so inmates created their own governance mechanisms to do so. As a former inmate-turned-criminologist explains, prison gangs in California 'control the contraband distribution systems, prison politics, the public areas of the prison, and any pan-prison activities. . .[and] to circulate in this world. . .one must. . .with a few exceptions, have some type of affiliation with a powerful racial clique or gang' (Irwin 1980, 195). For Hispanic inmates in particular, 'Chicanos in large California prisons – Soledad, San

Quentin, Folsom, and Tracy – must have at least a loose affiliation with one of the Chicano gangs' (Irwin 1980, 206).

3.3   Information Transmission Mechanisms

The information costs associated with impersonal exchange and large-scale enterprise is a notable challenge in self-governing communities. How does NF overcome this problem, which is especially severe given the constraints of the incarceration context? It faces two related problems. First, it must be able to identify who is associated with the gang and has a claim to the group's protective services. There are currently roughly 170,000 inmates in 33 CDCR prisons; thousands of new inmates enter each month; and officials regularly transfer inmates to different facilities. How do NF-affiliated inmates that arrive at a new prison prove their membership? Second, the gang must prevent individual members from misusing the gang's threat of violence or weakening the gang's reputation. The NF addresses these problems by developing an explicit process to obtain information about inmate activity, authenticate it, and communicate it to higher-ranking gang members. Information transmission mechanisms allows it to identify which inmates to protect and give gang leaders information for monitoring member activity.

NF assigns a leader in each correctional facility to organize Hispanic inmates into protective associations and to oversee their operations. A former NF member describes the responsibility of one particular gang leader, 'Castillo was also authorized as the overall authority in charge of the Monterey County Jail, responsible for establishing a functioning household and making sure all NF members and associates were operating according to established procedures and recruiting' (Fuentes 2006, 121). When inmates arrive at a facility, the NF has protocols for obtaining information about the new inmate. Gangs send a questionnaire to an arriving inmate asking about his name, nickname, date of birth, neighborhood, street gang affiliation, criminal charges, associates who are incarcerated, and where he has served time in the past (Balassone 2010). The questionnaire becomes more thorough at state prisons than at county jails because the gang can rely less on local social connections for information about new inmates. Correctional gang investigators describe one such note found in an inmate's cell, 'Further on in the notes, [inmate] gives a brief history of himself and identifies numerous other identified NF and NS associates and members. It appears that [inmate] is informing the security or squad leader who [inmate] is and what he has done or accomplished' (Fuentes 2006, 84). The questionnaire is also often followed up with a face-to-face meeting with gang members (Fuentes 2006, 63–6).

NF members cross-reference the questionnaire with the 'bad news list,' which records people who have been marked for punishment because of bad past behavior. A high-ranking member in each facility holds the bad news list, and other gang members often hold additional copies. The list typically includes names of gang dropouts, rapists, informants, and other inmates who have violated accepted rules of behavior. The bad news list details what type of punishment the inmate deserves, which can range from assault to murder.

New inmates usually have to wait several days before having their status cleared with the gang, at which time they can begin to integrate themselves more fully into the inmate social system. The NF may place inmates on a probationary period for several months (Fuentes 2006, 80). Prison gangs educate new inmates about their history, purpose, and goals, including requiring that they memorize written rules of behavior (Fuentes 2006, 66). One of the more prominent written guidelines for inmates is the '14 Bonds,' which outlines the permitted, forbidden, and obligated behaviors for a Hispanic inmate from Northern California while incarcerated.

When a gang member transfers to a new cellblock or facility, he provides information to the ranking gang members in the new facility about the status and activities of the gang in his former location. For example, when an inmate moved within a facility to a new secure housing unit he filed 'a report with the NF's overall authority in charge of that unit' (Fuentes 2006, 84), and when he was transferred to a new facility he 'filed a full report pertaining to himself and his NF status, as well as a mandatory update regarding [California State Prison] – Corcoran' (Fuentes 2006, 88).

By establishing an explicit process for obtaining, authenticating, and communicating information, prison gangs can more effectively control inmates. They have well-established methods of keeping track of who does not adhere to accepted behavioral rules and what level of punishment violations warrant. They know which inmates violate property rights and act opportunistically in illicit trade. Prisons are by no means perfectly safe, nor are prison gangs benevolent and always respectful of the property rights of gang members and other inmates. However, given the context of incarceration and the state's inability or unwillingness to provide all of the governance that inmates demand, prison gangs provide an important service in the inmate social system.

4. NF OPERATES OUTSIDE CORRECTIONAL FACILITIES

In addition to providing governance behind bars, the NF extends its criminal enterprise to the outside world. A federal grand jury indictment describes the NF operation in the 1990s: 'Outside of penal facilities, the Nuestra Familia was divided into geographic 'regiments' managed by 'regiment leaders'; these regiments served as the basic unit or crew through which the Nuestra Familia conducted much of its criminal activity' (United States v Rubalcaba et al 2001, 3). These street regiments are in charge of accumulating and investing funds, supporting the incarcerated members of the gang, and carrying out the organization's business.

Each geographic region establishes a 'regiment familia bank' (FBI 2009, 9–10). Regiment familia banks integrate paroled NF members into profitable criminal activities. A summary of an informant interview explains the process:

> an NF member getting out of jail is normally set up with a car, a gun, drugs, and some money. This 'set up' is supposed to get the NF member 'on his feet' and in business for himself. Those who do not take advantage of this opportunity risk severe discipline (Fuentes 2006, 231).

Facilitating communication was a central part of NF operations, especially for monitoring its non-incarcerated members. A federal indictment explains:

> Maintaining discipline within, and allegiance to, the Nuestra Familia Organization was a constant concern and preoccupation of the Nuestra Familia leadership. . .To maintain discipline and allegiance, the Nuestra Familia leadership in Pelican Bay State Prison demanded frequent communication by members through assigned 'channels'. . .Through such communication, the Nuestra Familia leadership remained abreast of the activities of members and associates inside and outside of correctional facilities and issued new rules and directives' (United States v Rubalcaba et al 2001, 4).

Smuggling letters and notes about gang activity into prison is one method of communication. The gang also structures its leadership positions to reduce shirking. They have established ex-post punishments, including both monetary fines and physical assaults, for members who did not actively engage in gang business once released from prison (Fuentes 2006, 248).

In addition to integrating released members into productive activities, the regiment bank pays wages and provides for medical and legal expenses to NF members in that local regiment. In return, members must deposit a portion of their profits from both legal and illegal endeavors into the regiment familia bank. A federal indictment explains that all NF members and associates were required to pay 25 per cent of proceeds from robberies, drug deals, and other crimes into the bank (United States v Rubalcaba et al 2001, 6). Regiment leaders have the responsibility to ensure that soldiers acquire 'at least two firearms (one of which would be donated to the regimental armory), [obtain] a cellular phone, and [accumulate] no less than $500 on a monthly basis, which [is] put towards building the regimental bank' (Fuentes 2006, 173–4). Gang correspondence explains, 'Those who are appointed to function as [a regiment commander] are also responsible for the building up of a familia bank, with no less than a $10,000 minimum' (Fuentes 2006, 90). The NF leadership requires regiment commanders to meet fixed percentage goals of growth for the regimental bank, creating an incentive for regiment captains to monitor the productivity of lower-ranking members.

An important component of the regiment commander's job is to monitor the activities of lower-ranking members on the streets and communicate incarcerated leaders' orders and policies (Fuentes 2006, 173). Regiments are constrained to a particular geographic region, so regiment leaders can observe operations and access local social networks to obtain information on members' productivity. Correspondence between two high-ranking NF leaders explains that it is the regiment commander's job to 'see that all ventures undertaken are planned effeciently [sic]' (Fuentes 2006, 90).

Regiment leaders have authority to mediate conflict within the organization. High-ranking members 'were responsible for establishing regiments and gang policy, resolving intra-gang disputes among members and associates of the Nuestra Familia, approving new memberships in the organization and authorizing significant actions by members of the Nuestra Familia and Nuestra Raza, including the commission of murder' (United States v Rubalcaba et al 2001, 3–4). Internal conflict is costly because members use resources to transfer wealth from other members (or defend against wealth transfers) instead of engaging in criminal profit seeking. The regiment captain, who has relatively good information about the personalities of his members and the details of the circumstance, can effectively adjudicate intra-group conflict. The incarcerated leadership sets broad guidelines that limit the discretion of the regiment leaders and guide their managerial actions. In one instance, for example, the gang's leadership demoted a regiment leader who was not strict enough and replaced him with a more disciplined member (Reynolds 2008).

5. CONCLUSION

The legal centrism hypothesis argues that the state is required to define and enforce property rights, and that in the absence of doing so, self-governing groups will be unable to engage in economic exchange and extended commercial operations (Stringham 2015). The success of the Nuestra Familia prison gang provides evidence to the contrary. This group is composed of people who have high discount rates and are actively disrupted by the government, yet it secures property rights for many inmates behind bars and effectively conducts business outside prison.

Most of economic research assumes that property rights are clearly defined and fully enforced. Research in law and economics has brought this assumption into the foreground and analyzed it explicitly. Related work from a market process perspective emphasizes two concepts that are usefully studied in illicit contexts. First, the market process focuses on exchange behavior and the institutions in which it takes place. Because criminal groups cannot rely on state-based institutions, they must devise their own governance solutions. This provides the opportunity to understand when institutions succeed and why they fail. Studying how people capture the gains from trade and how it differs across contexts suggests the robustness of self-enforcing exchange institutions. Second, social institutions are often the result of human action but not human design. In the incarceration context, the conditions that led to the rise of prison gangs resulted unintentionally by the actions of numerous people. Choices made about the capacity of correctional facilities, federal and state laws about what is a crime and how it will be punished, the composition of inmates, and correctional officers daily actions led to an environment where inmates lacked secure property rights. Prison gangs formed first to protect themselves, but once they were able to do this, they found that they had an advantage in engaging in illicit trade. Given the constraints, prison gangs were the most effective providers of governance in the inmate social system.

REFERENCES

60 Minutes. 1999. 'A Brutal Prison' Airdate: 04/06/1999.

60 Minutes. 2005. 'Maximum Security?' Airdate: 05/15/2005.

Adolphson, Mikael and J. Mark Ramseyer. 2009. 'The competitive enforcement of property rights in medieval Japan: The role of temples and monasteries' 71(3) *Journal of Economic Behavior and Organization* 660–68.

Arax, Mark. 1996. 'Tales of Brutality Behind Bars: Five officers claim staging of 'gladiator days,' other abuses at Corcoran State Prison,' *Los Angeles Times*, August 21.

Balassone, Merrill. 2010. '2 Will Stand Trial in Turlock Rapper's Killing,' *The Modesto Bee*. December 30.
Bandiera, Oriana. 2003. 'Land Reform, the Market for Protection, and the Origins of the Sicilian Mafia: Theory and Evidence' 19(1) *Journal of Law, Economics, and Organization* 218–44.
Benson, Bruce. 1989. 'The Spontaneous Evolution of Commercial Law' 55(3) *Southern Economic Journal* 644–61.
Berman, Eli. 2000. 'Sect, Subsidy, and Sacrifice: An Economist's View of Ultra-Orthodox Jews' 115(3) *Quarterly Journal of Economics* 905–53.
Boettke, Peter J. 2005. 'Anarchism as a Progressive Research Program in Political Economy' in *Anarchy, State and Public Choice*, Edward Stringham, ed., Edward Elgar Publishing, pp. 206–19, 2005.
Camp, George M. and Camille G. Camp 1985. *Prison Gangs: Their Extent, Nature and Impact on Prisons*. U.S. Department of Justice. Federal Justice Research Program.
Clay, Karen. 1997. 'Trade without Law: Private Order Institution in Mexican California' 13(1): *Journal of Law, Economics & Organization* 202–31.
Cooter, Robert D. 1993. 'Against Legal Centrism' 81 *California Law Review* 417–29.
Ellickson, Robert C. 1989. 'A Hypothesis of Wealth-Maximizing Norms: Evidence from the Whaling Industry' 5(1) *Journal of Law, Economics, & Organization* 83–97.
Federal Bureau of Investigation. 2009. Freedom of Information and Privacy Acts. Subject File: Mexican Mafia (File 1).
Fuentes, Nina. 2006. *The Rise and Fall of the Nuestra Familia*. Know Gangs Publishing.
Gambetta, Diego. 1993. *The Sicilian Mafia: The Business of Private Protection*. Cambridge, MA: Harvard University Press.
Greif, Avner. 1989. 'Reputations and Coalitions in Medieval Trade: Evidence on the Maghribi Traders' 49(4) *Journal of Economic History* 857–82.
Iannaccone, Laurence R. 1992. Sacrifice and Stigma: Reducing Free-riding in Cults, Communes, and Other Collectives' 100(2) *Journal of Political Economy* 271–91.
Irwin, John. 1980. *Prisons in Turmoil*. Little, Brown.
Jankowski, Martin. 1991. *Islands in the Street: Gangs and American Urban Society*. Berkeley, CA: University of California Press.
Koehler, Robert. 2000. 'The Organizational Structure and Function of La Nuestra Familia within Colorado State Correctional Facilities' 21 *Deviant Behavior* 155–79.
Leeson, Peter T. 2007. 'An-arrgh-chy: The Law and Economics of Pirate Organization' 115(6) *Journal of Political Economy* 1049–94.
Leeson, Peter T. 2009. 'The Laws of Lawlessness' 38(2) *Journal of Legal Studies* 471–503.
Levitt, Steven D. and Sudhir A. Venkatesh. 2000. 'An Economic Analysis of a Drug-Selling Gang's Finances' 115(3) *Quarterly Journal of Economics* 755–89.
Lewis, George H. 1980. 'Social Groupings in Organized Crime: The Case of La Nuestra Familia' 1 *Deviant Behavior* 129–43.
Melde, Chris, Terrance J. Taylor, and Finn-Aage Esbensen. 2009. 'I Got Your Back': An Examination of the Protective Function of Gang Membership in Adolescence' 47(2) *Criminology* 565–94.
Mendoza, Ramon A. 2005. *Mexican Mafia: From Alter Boy to Hitman*. Corona, CA.: Ken Whitley and Associates.
Milgrom, Paul and John Roberts 1992. *Economics, Organization, and Management*. Prentice Hall.
Milhaupt, Curtis J. and Mark D. West. 2000. 'The Dark Side of Private Ordering: An Institutional and Empirical Analysis of Organized Crime' 67(1) *University of Chicago Law Review* 41–98.
Miller, Gary J. 1993. *Managerial Dilemmas: The Political Economy of Hierarchy*. Cambridge, UK: Cambridge University Press.
Morales, Gabriel C. 2008. *La Familia – The Family: Prison Gangs in America*. San Antonio, TX: Mungia Printers.
Pennington, Mark. 2011. *Robust Political Economy: Classical Liberalism and the Future of Public Policy*. Cheltenham UK, Northampton, MA: Edward Elgar Publishers.

Piller, Charles. 2010. 'California Senate Probe Rips Prison Watchdogs' *The Sacramento Bee.* December 7.

Porter, Bruce. 1982. 'California Prison Gangs: The Price of Control' 8(6) *Corrections Magazine* 6–19.

Reynolds, Julia. 2008. 'Gang Leader Took Unusual Route to the Top' *Monterey County Herald*, February 10.

Schaeffer, E.C. (2008). 'Remittances and Reputations in Hawala Money-transfer Systems: Self- enforcing Exchange on an International Scale' 24(1) *Journal of Private Enterprise* 95.

Skarbek, David B. 2010. 'Putting the "Con" Into Constitutions: The Economics of Prison Gangs' 26(2) *Journal of Law, Economics, & Organization* 183–211.

Skarbek, David B. 2011. 'Governance & Prison Gangs' 105(4) *American Political Science Review* 702–16.

Skarbek, David B. 2012. 'Prison Gangs, Norms, and Organizations' 82(1) *Journal of Economic Behavior & Organization* 96–109.

Skarbek, David B. 2014. *The Social Order of the Underworld: How Prison Gangs Govern the American Penal System.* New York: Oxford University Press.

Skarbek, Emily C. 2015. 'Aid, Ethics, & the Samaritan's Dilemma: Strategic Courage in Constitutional Entrepreneurship' *Journal of Institutional Economics*, forthcoming.

Stringham, E.P. (2015). *Private Governance: Creating Order in Economic and Social Life.* Oxford University Press.

Sobel, Russell, and Brian Osoba. 2009. 'Youth Gangs as Pseudo-Governments: Implications for Violent Crime' 75(4) *Southern Economics Journal* 996–1018.

United States v Rubalcaba et al. 2001. Indictment. Federal District Court, Northern District of California. April.

Varese, Federico. 2005. *The Russian Mafia: Private Protection in a New Market Economy.* Oxford, UK: Oxford University Press.

Varese, Federico. 2006. 'How Mafias Migrate: The Case of the Ndrangheta in Northern Italy' 40(2) *Law & Society Review* 411–44.

Varese, Federico. 2011. *Mafias on the Move: How Organized Crime Conquers New Territory.* Princeton, NJ: Princeton University Press.

9. Austrian law and economics and efficiency in the common law
Todd J. Zywicki and Edward P. Stringham*

I. INTRODUCTION

The common law, the body of principles and rules of action "which derive their authority solely from usages and customers of immemorial antiquity, or from the judgments and decrees of courts recognizing, affirming, and enforcing such usages and customs; and, in this sense, particularly the ancient unwritten law of England" (Black 1910: 227), has been subject to much praise from economists in both the neoclassical and Austrian traditions. Where Richard Posner (1979) famously declared that the common law helps maximize wealth, Friedrich Hayek (1973: 107) has stated that the common law is "purpose independent" and helps "maximize the possibility of expectations in general being fulfilled." Where Posner (1983: 114) stated that the common law was shaped during "a period when economic values were an important part of the prevailing ideology," Murray Rothbard (2009: 749) states: "The common law has often been a good guide to the law consonant with the free market." None of these authors claimed that the common law is perfect, but their overall positive views could lead one to believe that they supported the common law for similar reasons. Leeson (2012), although not addressing the common law specifically, suggests that the schools are similar enough that an Austrian law and economics be based on Posnerian foundations.

Despite their apparent agreement, most neoclassical economists and Austrian economists evaluate the law in very different ways. Where neoclassical economists evaluate efficiency of the common law from the perspective of whether it helps maximize wealth measured in dollar terms (Kaldor-Hicks efficiency), Austrians typically adopt various non-cardinal standards. We suggest that common law judges and procedures be evaluated similar to how most Austrians evaluate other market products, specifically how well the suppliers (the judges) meet the needs of those

* The authors thank seminar participants at the Research Roundtable on Austrian Law and Economics at the Law and Economics Center at George Mason University for helpful comments and suggestions.

demanding their products (those requesting help resolving a dispute). Although litigants in a dispute often have conflicting interests, when both parties must agree to enter a forum they demonstrate that forum is ex ante value enhancing to all involved. Joint agreement on forums was common in much of the history of the common law (and it is common with arbitration and mediation today) and it meant that judges must serve parties with rules and procedures that are ex ante mutually beneficial to all. When free choice is lacking, then the law can be used to advance various political goals including redistribution. We conclude that "the good parts" of the common law are those that developed when the common law was a more competitive and voluntary system.

Our chapter proceeds as follows. Section II reviews the neoclassical arguments about whether or not the common law maximizes economic efficiency. Section III discusses Austrian arguments about the desirability or undesirability of the common law. Section IV then describes why Hayek praised the common law as a type of spontaneous order, why his view was somewhat limited, and how his perspective can be augmented by focusing on historical competition among common law judges.

II.   ARGUMENTS FOR AND AGAINST THE EFFICIENCY IN THE COMMON LAW HYPOTHESIS

(a)   Neoclassical Arguments for the Efficiency of the Common Law Hypothesis

Posner (1979) first hypothesized that that the common law is efficient (Kaldor-Hicks efficient) because judges view wealth maximization as a normative ideal.[1] Posner argued that during the formative period of the common law, English judges implicitly adopted the utilitarian philosophy

---

[1]   Useful prior surveys of some of the literature discussed here can be found in Rubin (2005a), Parisi (2004), Aranson (1986), and Kornhauser (1980). For a discussion and summary of critiques of Posner's early hypothesis, see Zywicki (2003). This theory cannot explain the apparent trend of recent years for the common law to depart in many areas from the promotion of efficiency to the apparent motivation to satisfy other social goals, such as redistribution and the apparent growth in the number of judges dedicated to the promotion of redistributive goals for law (Krier 1974). Even if judges are constrained in their ability to engage in systematic wealth redistribution, they nonetheless appear to have increased their desire and efforts to do so.

of 19th century English liberalism and that adopting rules consistent with wealth maximization was their best proxy. To the extent that the common law has deviated from this orientation, it could be a reflection of the changing philosophical orientation of judges during the 20th century toward other goals like redistribution or social engineering (Priest 1991, Priest 1985, Priest 1987a, Priest 1987b). Later, however, Posner hypothesized that even if judges theoretically prefer other normative values, they nonetheless pursue wealth maximization as the most practical to accomplish. Unlike redistributive goals, which are more contested as a social matter, efficiency (even if not the only social goal) is a more widely held social goal and, all else equal, judges prefer rules resulting in more wealth. To Posner, judges have limited tools to engage in consistent wealth redistribution, because most common law rules are default rules that parties can alter by contract or relative price adjustments. Posner (2007: 252) concludes that because judges "cannot do much . . . to alter the slices of the pie that the various groups in society receive, they might as well concentrate on increasing its size."

Others who believe that the common law is efficient have come up with hypotheses other than that judges prefer to maximize wealth. Rubin (1977) and Priest (1977) offer what may be considered invisible hand theories where processes of selective re-litigation of precedents lead to economically efficient outcomes. In these models, a tendency toward efficiency will be observed regardless of judicial tastes or preferences. Rubin argues that expenditures influence outcomes and people with more at stake will invest more in litigation. The potential for establishing precedent will encourage even more investment. But to Rubin this is a good thing. Rubin (1977: 53) writes, "If rules are inefficient, there will be an incentive for the party held liable to force litigation; if rules are efficient there will be no such incentive. Thus, efficient rules will be maintained, and inefficient rules litigated until overturned." Priest (1977) offered a complementary story arguing that inefficient rules will tend to produce more societal conflict which, because litigation only arises when parties' expectations clash, will lead to more litigation involving those rules than efficient rules. He postulates that even if judges reverse precedents at a stochastic rate, the tendency for inefficient rules to arise more frequently in litigation will lead to them being disproportionately overruled relative to efficient precedents (which are tested less often). This largely random process will thus lead to a tendency for inefficient rules to be tested, and thus corrected, more often than efficient rules.

(b)   Neoclassical Arguments Against the Efficiency of the Common Law Hypothesis

Of course, not all neoclassical economists agree about whether the common law maximizes wealth. Usually their motivation is to propose small (or large) changes to push the common law toward greater efficiency. Cooter and Kornhauser (1980) argue that invisible hand mechanisms within the common law have at best a very weak tendency toward producing efficiency, and Hirshleifer (1982) argues that evolutionary models provide little reason to believe that there will be any strong tendency toward efficiency. Hathaway (2001) and Stearns (1995) argue that aspects like *stare decisis* can lead to lock-in or path-dependency in the common law. Wangenheim (1993) argues that potential future innovators are unable to organize now and thus have little ability to influence the law today. Giving judges more discretion or having more oversight to avoid suboptimal outcomes are a couple of possible solutions.

Others highlight public choice problems with the common law. Elhauge (1991) argues that judicial processes are subject to the same sorts of interest-group pressures as legislatures, and Rubin's model simply highlights how concentrated interests will have more power. Well-organized groups may influence judicial appointments (Zywicki 2000; Rubin 2005b) or work to prevent "bad" cases from establishing undesirable precedents (Stearns and Zywicki 2009).[2] Rubin, Curran, and Curran (2001) and Osborne (2002) argue that that interest groups weigh using litigation versus legislative lobbying for rent seeking, and Crew and Twight (1990) provide a comparative analysis of rent-seeking in the common law and legislative processes. Litigants may seek to use the law to extract resources from others and forum shopping enables litigants to look for judges or venues that will be more favorable to them (Zywicki 2006; DiIanni [forthcoming]; Stringham and Zywicki 2010). Judges who favor expanded liability will have more cases filed in their court, providing them with more cases on which to imprint their stamp on the law (Fon and Parisi, 2003).

Tullock argues that the adversarial feature of common law adjudication is fundamentally a rent-seeking and rent-dissipating system (Tullock 1997; Tullock 2005). Parties only care about whether they win but not whether their lawsuits are wealth maximizing overall. The system creates incentives

---

[2]   Rubin and Bailey (1994: 814–17) have noted that one reason trial lawyers have been effective in changing tort law in recent decades has been their considerable ability to organize and to engage in strategic litigation through organizations such as the American Association for Justice (formerly the Association of Trial Lawyers of America).

for both to enter an arms race with lots of wasteful spending.[3] The fact that precedents are binding also can encourage rent-seeking through the legal system. While strict *stare decisis* can theoretically increase the predictability of the law (although this is not clear [Zywicki, 1996; Leoni, 1991]) and reduce administrative costs associated with re-litigating issues until established as precedent, when one case establishes a binding precedent with just one favorable decision (as under *stare decisis*), this provides a target for interest groups to shoot at in seeking to establish a favorable precedent. Moreover, stronger *stare decisis* doctrine increases the implications of rent-producing precedents by making overruling more difficult, and thus simultaneously increases the value of the prize ex ante by increasing the precedent's lifespan. Law and economics scholars like Tullock propose moving away from the traditional common law with its system of precedents. To neoclassicals the debate is almost always whether adjusting the legal system will help bring about more or less efficient results.

(c)   Austrian Arguments Against the Efficiency of the Common Law Hypothesis

Austrian theories of the common law are grounded in significantly different assumptions and methodologies than those that drive the standard neoclassical model of efficiency in the common law (Zywicki and Sanders 2008). With a few exceptions like Leeson (2012), Austrian economists reject Kaldor-Hicks efficiency as a guide for judges, and focus on the problems facing judges who seek to even determine, much less to implement, the most economically efficient rules. Austrians focus on how value and costs are subjective and that prevents judges from peering into the minds of litigants to estimate willingness to pay associated with different outcomes (Stringham 2001; Stringham and Zywicki, 2011b; Zywicki 1996). Willingness to pay only makes sense within the context of a market, because as market conditions change, so does willingness to pay. Judges sitting in a courtroom have little ability to estimate a litigant's net willingness to pay associated with a given outcome, and much less ability to estimate society's net willingness to pay associated with all different outcomes.

O'Driscoll (1980), Rizzo (1980b), Aranson (1992), Sima (2004), and

---

[3]   Luppi and Parisi (2010) also note that because one source of rent-seeking in Tullock's model of the adversary system is the ability of parties to externalize some of their costs on their rivals, this problem can be alleviated by adopting the British "loser pays" that requires the losing party to pay the attorneys' fees and expenses of the prevailing party, thereby forcing parties to internalize a greater share of the costs of meritless litigation.

Zywicki and Sanders (2008) highlight the challenges that a judge would confront if they sought to even identify, much less to implement, economically efficient legal rules. To consciously determine the wealth maximizing legal rule or allocation of rights in any given case presents challenges very similar to that of a Soviet-style economic central planner. The problem becomes even more complicated when one recognizes that changes in legal rules (even small ones) affect willingness to pay and that can change the outcome with the highest willingness to pay associated with it. As Scitovsky (1951) and others (Rizzo 1980b) have pointed out, as one changes the distribution of property rights the economically "efficient" outcome can change, leading to a non-commensurability of different regimes. Measurements of what law leads to the "wealth maximizing" outcome has to assume away the important problem of wealth effects (Rizzo 1980b). Hadfield (1992) argues that even if judges sought to improve the operation of the law through conscious effort, they would be unable to do so coherently because the cases that come to trial are such a small and non-random sample of all of the interactions in society. Rules are intertwined with the myriad of other rules so changing any particular rule that comprises the legal system may have profound implications for other rules within the legal system. For instance, a movement from contributory to comparative negligence may have implications not only for other elements of the tort system (such as liability rules or damages), but also contract law, procedure, and remedies. Tweaking is not so simple.

Judges aiming at maximizing wealth would need to constantly optimize by reevaluating and reallocating rights and responsibilities over time. But Austrian economists point out that the world is in a state of constant change as billions of consumers around the world continually adjust to shocks (Zywicki and Sanders 2008). As Mario Rizzo (1980a) writes, law exists "amid flux" (see also Rizzo 1987). How easy would it be for judges to make these decisions and adjustments that affect outcomes for everyone?

III. AUSTRIAN PERSPECTIVES ON THE COMMON LAW

(a) Arguments for Stability or Non-economic Evaluation of the Common Law

Given the dynamic and constantly changing nature of the economy and the limited ability of government to measure and implement the most economically efficient set of rules, what is the alternative? Different Austrian economists present different perspectives. Many Austrians focus on law's primacy in providing a stable rule-bound framework within which people can coordinate their individual plans. Equilibrium, Hayek (1981) argues, cannot describe the world in the abstract, but is rather a relationship that describes the ability of individuals to mesh their particular plans at any given time and to form expectations about how parties will perform in the future. In this view, the primary purpose of the law is not to try to impose rules that bring about the wealth maximizing "outcome," but instead to provide a stable institutional framework that will enable individuals to plan and coordinate their affairs in a world of constant dynamism.

The focus should be on clear, stable rules that enable people to predict one another's behavior, rather than judicial tinkering and fine-tuning. Hayek (1973) and Epstein (1980) argue that clear and stable rules create boundaries for property rights and other legal obligations that enable individuals to adapt their behavior to the ever-changing world. Adding a constantly-changing legal system—even if in the name of modernization or updating—adds uncertainty and undermines the ability of individuals to coordinate plans. As Zywicki (1998) also notes, one benefit of clear, intuitive, bright-line rules, is that they allow ordinary people have some degree of confidence in the content of the law without needing to consult lawyers or run across an unexpected legal obligation, thereby enabling radical and efficient decentralization of decision-making authority to individuals who have the tacit and local knowledge most relevant to the particular decision. The role of the judges and the law should be to establish a clear, predictable legal framework that encourages consensual exchanges with a minimum of judicial intervention (Aranson 1990).

Another strand of arguments popular among many who are Austrian is to evaluate law using extra-economic means (Block, 1995, 2000; Stringham and White, 2004). Austrian economics is a positive discipline that does not say what any given policy or any given law should or should not be. One can be an Austrian economist and hold any number of normative perspectives. To Kirzner (2000: 85) laws must be evaluated using non-economic criterion so to him there is a "need for society-wide acceptance of shared ethical perspectives." To Rothbard (1981: 164):

> It is a happy accident of history that a great deal of private law and common law is libertarian, that they elaborate the means of preserving one's person and property against "invasion." But a good deal of the old law was anti-libertarian, and certainly custom cannot always be relied on to be consistent with liberty.

What these theorists have in common is to not evaluate and tinker with the law in order to maximize Kaldor-Hicks efficiency.

(b) Hayek's Praise for the Common Law

Hayek provides one of the more in-depth economic analyses of the common law from an Austrian point of view. We believe that Hayek said a lot of great but also some inconsistent things so we are not trying to put him on a pedestal. But we believe he had a lot of insight, so we would like to outline Hayek's ideal view of the common law and then discuss possible ways it might be realized today. To Hayek the relevant level of analysis and selection for evaluating the law is at the level of the legal *system* or collection of relevant rules rather than at the level of any particular rule studied in isolation (Zywicki and Sanders 2008). Hayek (1973) likened the common law to a spontaneous order in which the doctrines and principles of the law were emergent properties of individual judges deciding individual cases.[4] Hayek analogized the common law process to the market process: just as the prices for various goods and services that emerge from the "market" are really the byproduct of millions of individual consumer decisions, he argues that the legal principles that emerged under the classical common law reflected the decentralized decisions of many litigants and judges acting independently over time. Thus, just as no single person sets the price of apples, no single person makes the body of law that comprises contract or tort law, or even the concepts that lie within them, such as consideration, negligence, or strict liability.

This decentralized process of law-making has two key elements that support a general preference for the common law over centralized legislative rule-making or the quasi-legislative rule-making of a Posnerian judge seeking to maximize social efficiency. First, it draws on the local and decentralized knowledge of many judges and litigants resolving many cases in concrete factual disputes that arise from particular conflicts. Second, because of the decentralized nature of the rule-production process, there is no central decision-maker for interested parties to capture who can then impose a rule that will generate long-term rents thereby reducing the opportunity and incentive for rent-seeking litigation. This combination of the benefits of decentralization of local knowledge and insulation from rent-seeking litigation was reinforced by the common law's traditional reliance on custom as a source of legal principles, which manifests these characteristics in an even more robust manner than the traditional common law itself. (Zywicki 2003; Pritchard and Zywicki 1999; Parisi 1995).

---

[4] Leoni (1991) argued that the classical Roman law had similar spontaneous order properties.

Hayek (1973) applied much of the same terminology that he used for markets to law. He argued that judges decided concrete disputes based on their detailed, albeit often intuitive tacit and local knowledge. Hayek also argued that although each case was a judicial resolution of particular disputes in concrete factual contexts, the common law itself was abstract in nature, as coherent, abstract principles emerged from the aggregation of many decentralized judicial decisions. But these abstract articulated principles are emergent from many particular judicial decisions, not their genesis.[5] Hayek claimed that the law must gradually evolve depending on what will help keep people's expectations relatively stable. The role of the judge, Hayek argued, is not to "make" the law, such as by articulating the "best" rule according to some external standard of value, but to "discover" the law in this imminent consensus of norms and expectations that underlie a given community (Zywicki and Sanders, 2008). To Hayek (1973: 118), this judge-made law is part of the spontaneous order.[6]

Hayek (1973: 72) argued that law "has never been 'invented' nor can it be 'promulgated' or 'announced' before hand" (1973: 118). He says the role of the judge is to *discover* the law and apply it to a particular concrete dispute, not to create or impose the law. He wrote:

> While the process of articulation of pre-existing rules will thus often lead to alterations in the body of such rules, this will have little effect on the belief that those formulating the rules do no more, and have no power to do more, than to find and express already existing rules, a task in which fallible humans will often go wrong, but in the performance of which they have no free choice. The task will be regarded as one of discovering something which exists, not as one of creating something new, even though the result of such efforts may be the creation of something that has not existed before. (1973: 78)

Hayek's use of the term discover to describe the task of the judge in the common law system is almost certainly deliberate in the sense that it is

---

[5] Hayek (1973: 86) wrote: "The chief concern of a common law judge must be the expectations which parties in a transaction would have reasonably formed on the basis of the general practices that the ongoing order rests on." He thought that "in an ever changing society" judges must seek to find rules that will "aim at securing certain abstract characteristics of the overall order of our society that we would like it to possess to a higher degree" (Hayek 1973: 105).

[6] Hayek (1973: 123) wrote;

> The difference between the rules of just conduct which emerge from the judicial process, the nomos or law of liberty—and the rules laid down by authority. . .lies in the fact that the former are derived from the conditions of a spontaneous order which man has not made, while the latter serve the deliberate building of an organization serving specific purposes.

meant to invoke Hayek's notion of competition as a discovery process articulated in his economic theory. Still further, Hayek's description of the iterative process of legal discovery by judges, of trial-and-error efforts to better articulate the underlying norms and expectations of justice of those in a given society, strongly resembles the market-discovery process that he has previously described. Furthermore, this sense of the law is oftentimes tacit (Zywicki, 1998); it exists in customs and conventions that evolve over time, in Hayek's framework an intuitive knowledge of what the rules are even if it is difficult to state or define the rules precisely.

Discovery of legal rules takes place on several different levels. We do not know what principles a society should adopt to realize the end of overcoming the knowledge problem. From this perspective, the principles that guide a society will not be known ahead of time. Rather, Hayek claims that they spontaneously emerge from the ongoing interactions of individuals. Some general truths or laws may exist, but those that best encourage cooperation must be mixed with local elements such as culture, religious beliefs, climate, or land as well (Rosser and Rosser, 2008). No one can be certain beforehand of the exact institutions that will allow each specific society and each individual within the society to make the best use of his knowledge of his local situation. As Hayek stated:

> The rules under which the citizens act constitute an adaptation of the whole of society to its environment and to the general characteristics of its members. . . The rules may have come to exist merely because, in a certain type of situation, friction is likely to arise among individuals about what each is entitled to do, which can be prevented only if there is a rule to tell each what his rights are. (Hayek, 1960: 157)

Because this law is a convention created to meet the needs of the individuals in a society, it will never be completely static. Rather, it will change as human needs change, and the application of the general principles to specific cases will also change over time. In general, however, the overall principles will remain relatively constant. These general laws that develop are basically unarticulated beliefs that will differ in minor ways from society to society, depending on the local circumstances in which a society finds itself. The law of a society is given its content by the individuals that comprise this society. These rules, however, are not arbitrary; they are general ideas that emerge to resolve conflict and promote coordination. As society becomes larger, more complex, and more heterogeneous, it becomes necessary to verbalize and articulate these intuitively understood rules and case law helps guide future decisions. Judges can rely on previous cases and existing precedent in much the same way that individual producers in markets rely on prices.

(c) Some Missing Pieces in Hayek's Analysis of the Common Law

But Hayek's analysis has been criticized as being incomplete (Hasnas, 2005; Rothbard, 1997: 149; Stringham and Zywicki, 2011a). Rowley (1989: 372) wrote that Hayek has not "presented a convincing explanation as to why, or through what mechanism, the judiciary should be supportive of the law of liberty or the law of efficiency in a largely monopolistic court bureaucracy such as that which characterizes twentieth century Britain and the U.S." Even though Hayek talked about decentralized judges, Hayek viewed decentralized judges as all working for a legal system controlled by government. Hayek believed that ultimately judges must be subservient to the legislature which can step in to alter the law when common law reaches a "dead end" through adherence to precedent or when the law develops in ways that are inconsistent with the market economy.

But putting government (whether judges or legislatures) in a position where they can "improve the law" introduces all of the same problems faced by the judges in Posner's system. Hayek never explains how judges or legislatures will know when to improve matters and how they will know whether their changes are appropriate. Because Hayek ultimately believed in a system of government judges, the feedback that he praises elsewhere when talking about markets is absent with judges. At the outset even well-intentioned judges will have little idea if they are discovering the type of laws people support in society, just as a well-intentioned economic planning board will lack the knowledge to discover the appropriate prices of goods and services in the economy without competition and market feedback. Although judicial decisions will be subject to critique and analysis by other judges and scholars, that intellectual critique is only tangentially related to the real measure of judicial success—whether the judicial decision dovetails with existing societal expectations and whether the decision promotes social and economic coordination. The real test of the usefulness of a legal rule is found in the *unseen* effects of the rule in terms of the number of accidents avoided or conflicts averted, not the *seen* effects of the cases that come before the judge. On this question the judge will have almost no relevant knowledge or, crucially, a way of possibly acquiring the relevant knowledge to make that assessment (Stringham and Zywicki, 2011a).

Without any measurement of market demand, judges will be unable to determine whether their decisions are really right or wrong as measured by whether they actually do reflect parties' expectations and social consensus. Judges will also be vulnerable to mistakes in articulating the unarticulated law. Hayek recognizes that this process of articulation may oftentimes be inaccurate and supports minimizing it. But with a monopoly and no feedback mechanism, how will the judges know initially or as consumer demands change whether a particular decision or verbal articulation is consistent with underlying expectations? Hayek's *nomos* or law of liberty is ever-changing, so even if a monopolistic legal system could discern the content of the law, the specifics would be useful for only a short period of time. Hayek also gives us no theory of why government judges will want to discover the law of liberty and what will happen to them if they pursue other interests.

(d)   The Importance of Competition for the Common Law

We believe that Hayek was onto something when he talked about discovery in the law, but his discussion of a decentralized but governmental system does not provide the answer of how it comes about. Instead we want to highlight the fact that much of the common law that Hayek praises was developed when there was a large degree of competition in law. Berman (1983), Benson (1990) and Stringham and Zywicki (2011b) outline that the legal order during the formative centuries of the English common law system, was in many ways a competitive and non-coercive legal order. During the Middle Ages multiple courts with overlapping jurisdictions existed side-by-side throughout England including: ecclesiastical (church) courts, law merchant courts, local courts, the Chancery court, and three different common law courts, the King's Bench, the Court of Common Pleas, and the Exchequer Courts. For many legal matters a litigant could bring her case in several different courts. For instance, church courts had jurisdiction over all matters related to testamentary succession, but if the deceased owed a debt at the time of his death this suggested the possibility of jurisdiction in other courts as well.

Rothbard (2009: 1051) wrote that "much of the common law began to be developed by privately competitive judges, who were sought out by litigants for their expertise in understanding the legal areas involved." Judges were paid in part from the litigant filing fees, thus providing competitive incentives respecting the scope of jurisdiction and expansion of judicial dockets. This encouraged judges to compete for litigants. Depending on the institutional context, competition could provoke judges to compete either by offering pro-plaintiff or pro-efficiency law. As Adam Smith (1976: 241–2) observed, the competition of the Middle Ages generally encouraged the production of good law:

> The present admirable constitution of the courts of justice in England was, perhaps, originally in a great measure, formed by this emulation, which anciently took place between their respective judges; each judge endeavouring

to give, in his own court, the speediest and most effectual remedy, which the law would admit, for every sort of injustice.

Smith also noted that requiring judges to compete for fees motivated them to work harder and more efficiently, thereby removing incentives for judges to shirk or to indulge their personal preferences. Stringham and Zywicki (2011b) claim that this judicial competition helped improve the law as courts competed to provide the law and procedures most appropriate to parties' needs.

The choice of court was often explicitly made at the outset of the contract (for example, church courts encourage people to swear an oath to God at contract if they wanted the option of having their case heard in the church court) and many of these courts provided law rooted in principles of reciprocity derived from merchant custom or religious belief. Many of these substantive and procedural rules were incorporated into the common law and equity courts during the mid-19th century. In fact, many of the doctrines that are often identified as demonstrating the efficiency of the common law, especially contract law, were originally created in these non-common law courts and incorporated into the common law by judges such as Mansfield.

The competitive system allowed dissatisfied parties to opt out of disadvantageous legal regimes and into preferable ones. For instance, merchants rarely resorted to the official common law courts, opting instead for law merchant courts, thus limiting the reach of sometimes archaic common law rules in commercial transactions. The coercive element necessary for judicial rent seeking was largely absent, giving potentially burdened parties an exit option. For parties to successfully rent-seek via litigation it is necessary for beneficiaries of wealth transfers to be able to involuntary capture the wealth of otherwise unwilling parties to provide the transfer. Authors such as Benson (1990) describe how many of these courts did not involve compulsion but judgments were enforced by threat of ostracism and reputational sanctions. In this sense, choice among competing courts can be thought of as a radical form of federalism, providing a heightened version of the exit and matching (Tiebout) functions of federalism (Stearns and Zywicki, 2009).

Over time the law became more monopolized and in these areas one should expect more problems. The reduced ability of litigants to choose their court or to exit expropriatory courts dampened the incentives for judges to be responsive to parties' needs, raised the agency costs associated with judicial decision making, and increased the incentives and opportunities for rent-seeking litigation. Under a monopolized system judges have a much greater ability to infuse ideology, such as redistributive goals, into their judicial opinions and to respond to pressures for rent-seeking litigation.

IV.   CONCLUSION

Austrian and neoclassical law and economics scholars evaluate the common law from very different perspectives. Where neoclassical economists find praise or faults in the common law based on how well it brings about Kaldor-Hicks efficiency, Austrian economists reject Kaldor-Hicks efficiency and must judge the common law using other criteria. One way to evaluate the common law is how much it serves the consumer and the best way to know that is if we observe consumers choosing it. Just as competition enables discovery and innovation in markets, competition enables discovery and innovation in law, too. When what is the law moved away from a more competitive system, many of the beneficial aspects of the common law eroded.

Those who take Hayek's discussion of the importance of discovery through competition seriously, should question the idea that the state must provide law centrally. Centralized law enforcement faces knowledge and accountability problems similar to those of central economic planners. Applying Hayek's insights about the knowledge problem in the economy to the workings of the legal system, leads to the conclusion that law, like other goods and services, should be provided competitively. Whether the competition takes place alongside government law, as with modern arbitration, mediation, and other forms of alternative dispute resolution (Benson, 1998; Caplan and Stringham, 2008), or whether the competition is completely free of government (Friedman 1979; Benson 1990; Anderson and Hill, 2004; Curott and Stringham, 2010), we can see private legal bodies providing different rules and procedures dependent on time and place. A centralized system of law is one-size-fits-all (Hasnas 1995), and everyone receives rules and procedures regardless of whether they are being served. But in a system in which people are allowed to select from many competing providers of law, individuals can have the set of rules and enforcement procedures that they actually value.

REFERENCES

Anderson, T.L. and P.J. Hill. 2004. *The Not So Wild, Wild West: Property Rights on the Frontier*. Stanford, CA: Stanford University Press.

Aranson, Peter H. 1992. "The Common Law as Central Economic Planning." *Constitutional Political Economy* 3(3): 289–319.

Aranson, Peter H. 1990. "Federalism: The Reasons of Rules." *Cato Journal* 10(1): 17–38.

Aranson, Peter H. 1986. "Economic Efficiency and the Common Law: A Critical Survey." In *Law and Economics and the Economics of Regulation*, J.-Matthias Graf von der Schulenburg and G. Skogh, eds., 51–84. Boston, MA: Kluwer Academic Publishers.

Arrow, Kenneth J. 1963. *Social Choice and Individual Values*. 2nd ed. New York, NY: John Wiley & Sons.

Bailey, Martin J. and Paul H. Rubin. 1994. "A Positive Theory of Legal Change." *International Review of Law and Economics* 14: 467–77.

Benson, Bruce. Forthcoming. "The Law Merchant's Story: How Romantic Is It?" In *Law, Economics and Evolutionary Theory*, Gralf Calliess and Peer Zumbansen, eds., 68–87. Cheltenham, UK: Edward Elgar Publishing.

Benson, Bruce. 1998. *To Serve and Protect: Privatization and Community in Criminal Justice*. New York, NY: New York University Press.

Benson, Bruce. 1990. *The Enterprise of Law*. San Francisco, CA: Pacific Research Institute for Public Policy.

Berman, Harold. 1983. *Law and Revolution: The Formation of the Western Legal Tradition*. Cambridge, MA: Harvard University Press.

Black, Henry Campbell. 1910. *Law Dictionary*. Saint Paul, MN: West Publishing.

Block, Walter. 2000. "Private Property Rights, Erroneous Interpretations, Morality and Economics: Reply to Demsetz." *Quarterly Journal of Austrian Economics* 3(1): 63–78.

Block, Walter. 1995. "Ethics, Efficiency, Coasean Property Rights and Psychic Income: A Reply to Demsetz." *Review of Austrian Economics* 8(2): 61–125.

Caplan, Bryan, and Edward Peter Stringham. 2008. "Privatizing the Adjudication of Disputes." *Theoretical Inquiries in Law* 9(2): 503–28.

Cooter, Robert, and Lewis Kornhauser. 1980. "Can Litigation Improve the Law Without the Help of Judges?" *Journal of Legal Studies* 9: 139–63.

Crew, Michael A. and Charlotte Twight. 1990. "On the Efficiency of Law: A Public Choice Perspective." *Public Choice* 66(1): 15–36.

Curott, Nick, and Edward Peter Stringham. 2010. "The Historical Development of Public Policing, Prosecution, and Punishment." In *Handbook on the Economics of Crime*, Bruce L. Benson and Paul R. Zimmerman, eds., 109–26. Cheltenham, UK: Edward Elgar Publishing.

DiIanni, Isaac. Forthcoming. "The Role of Competition in the Market for Adjudication." *Supreme Court Economic Review*, Vol. 19.

Elhauge, Einer R. 1991. "Does Interest Group Theory Justify More Intrusive Judicial Review?" *Yale Law Journal*, 101(1): 31–110.

Epstein, Richard A. 1980. "The Static Conception of the Common Law." *Journal of Legal Studies* 9: 253–75.

Friedman, D. 1979. "Private Creation and Enforcement of Law: A Historical Case." *Journal of Legal Studies* 8, 399–415.

Fon, Vincy and Francesco Parisi. 2003. "Litigation and the Evolution of Legal Remedies: A Dynamic Model." *Public Choice* 116: 419–33.

Hadfield, Gillian K. 1992. "Incomplete Contracts and Statutes." *International Review of Law and Economics* 12(2): 257–9.

Hasnas, J. 2005. "Hayek, the Common Law, and Fluid Drive." *New York University Journal of Law and Liberty* 1: 79–110.

Hasnas, J. 1995. "The Myth of the Rule of Law." *Wisconsin Law Review* 199–233.

Hathaway, Oona A. 2001. "Path Dependence in the Law: The Course and Pattern of Legal Change in a Common Law System." *Iowa Law Review* 86: 601–65.

Hayek, F.A. von. 1981. "Economics and Knowledge." In *L.S.E. Essays on Cost*, James M. Buchanan and G.F. Thirlby, eds., 31–50. New York, NY: New York University Press.

Hayek, F.A. 1973. *Law, Legislation, and Liberty: Rules and Order*, Vol. 1. Chicago, IL: University of Chicago Press.

Hirshleifer, Jack. 1982. *Research in Law and Economics: Evolutionary Models in Economics in Law*, 4: 1–60. Greenwich, CT: JAI Press.

Kirzner, Israel. 2000. *Driving Force of the Market: Essays in Austrian Economics*. London: Routledge.

Kornhauser, Lewis A. 1980. "A Guide to the Perplexed Claims of Efficiency in the Law." *Hofstra Law Review* 8: 591–639.

Krier, James E. 1974. "Book Review." *University of Pennsylvania Law Review* 122: 1664–706.

Leeson, Peter T. 2012. "An Austrian approach to law and economics, with special reference to superstition." *The Review of Austrian Economics* 25(3): 185–98.

Leoni, Bruno. 1991. *Freedom and the Law.* 3rd ed. Indianapolis, IN: Liberty Fund.

Luppi, Barbara and Francesco Parisi. 2010. "Litigation and Legal Evolution: Does Procedure Matter?" University of Minnesota Law School, Legal Studies Research Paper Series, Research Paper No. 10-09.

O'Driscoll, Gerald P. 1980. "Justice, Efficiency, and the Economic Analysis of Law: A Comment on Fried." *Journal of Legal Studies* 9(2): 355–66.

Osborne, Evan. 2002. "What's Yours Is Mine: Rent-Seeking and the Common Law." *Public Choice* 111(3/4): 399–415.

Parisi, Francesco. 2004. "The Efficiency of the Common Law Hypothesis." In *Encyclopedia of Public Choice*, Charles K. Rowley and Friedrich Schneider, eds., 519–522. New York, NY: Kluwer Academic Publishers.

Parisi, Francesco. 1995. "Toward a Theory of Spontaneous Law." *Constitutional Political Economy* 6: 211–31.

Posner, Richard A. 2007. *Economic Analysis of Law.* 7th ed. New York, NY: Aspen Publishing.

Posner, Richard A. 1983. *The Economics of Justice.* Cambridge, MA: Harvard University Press.

Posner, Richard A. 1979. "Utilitarianism, Economics, and Legal Theory." *Journal of Legal Studies* 8: 103–40.

Priest, George L. 1991. "The Modern Expansion of Tort Liability: Its Sources, Its Effects, and Its Reform." *Journal of Economic Perspectives* 5(3): 31–50.

Priest, George L. 1987a. "The Current Insurance Crisis and Modern Tort Law." *Yale Law Journal* 96(7): 1521–90.

Priest, George L. 1987b. "Puzzles of the Tort Crisis." *Ohio State Law Journal* 48: 497–502.

Priest, George L. 1985. "The Invention of Enterprise Liability: A Critical History of the Intellectual Foundations of Modern Tort Law." *Journal of Legal Studies* 14(3): 461–527.

Priest, George L. 1977. "The Common Law Process and the Selection of Efficient Rules." *Journal of Legal Studies* 6(1): 65–82.

Pritchard, A.C. and Todd J. Zywicki. 1999. "Finding the Constitution: An Economic Analysis of Tradition's Role in Constitutional Decision-Making." *North Carolina Law Review* 77: 409–521.

Rizzo, Mario J. 1987. "Rules versus Cost-Benefit Analysis in the Common Law." In *Economic Liberties and the Judiciary*, James A. Dorn and Henry G. Manne, eds. Fairfax, VA: George Mason University Press.

Rizzo, Mario J. 1980a. "Law Amid Flux: The Economics of Negligence and Strict Liability in Tort." *Journal of Legal Studies* 9: 291–318.

Rizzo, Mario J. 1980b. "The Mirage of Efficiency." *Hofstra Law Review* 8: 641–58.

Rosser, J.B., Jr. and M.V. Rosser. 2008. "A Critique of the New Comparative Economics." *Review of Austrian Economics* 21: 81–97.

Rothbard, Murray N. 2009. *Man, Economy, and State and Power and Market.* Auburn, AL: Mises Institute.

Rothbard, Murray N. 1997. *The Logic of Action: Method, Money, and the Austrian School.* Cheltenham, UK: Edward Elgar Publishing.

Rothbard, Murray. 1981. "Review of Bruno Leoni's Freedom and the Law." In *New Individualist Review*, Ralph Raico, ed., 163–6. Indianapolis: Liberty Fund.

Rowley, Charles K. 1989. "Common Law in Public Choice Perspective: A Theoretical and Institutional Critique." *Hamline Law Review* 12(2): 355–84.

Rubin, Paul H. 2005a. "Why Was the Common Law Efficient?" In *The Origins of Law and Economics: Essays by the Founding Fathers*, Francesco Parisi and Charles H. Rowley, eds., Cheltenham, UK: Edward Elgar Publishing.

Rubin, Paul H. 2005b. "Public Choice and Tort Reform." *Public Choice* 124(1): 223–36.
Rubin, Paul H. 1977. "Why Is the Common Law Efficient?" *Journal of Legal Studies* 6: 51–63.
Rubin, Paul H. and Martin J. Bailey. 1994. "The Role of Lawyers in Changing the Law." *Journal of Legal Studies* 23: 807–31.
Rubin, Paul H., Christopher Curran, and John F. Curran. 2001. "Litigation Versus Legislation: Forum Shopping by Rent Seekers." *Public Choice* 107(3/4): 295–310.
Scitovsky, Tibor. 1951. "The State of Welfare Economics." *American Economic Review* 41: 303–15.
Sima, Josef. 2004. *Introduction to the Logic of Social Action: Law and Economics Primer*. Prague: Vysoká Škola Ekonomická v Praze.
Smith, Adam. 1976. *An Inquiry into the Nature and Causes of the Wealth of Nations*. Edward Cannan, ed. Chicago, IL: University of Chicago Press.
Stearns, Maxwell L. 1995. "Standing Back from the Forest: Justiciability and Social Choice." *California Law Review* 83(6): 1309–414.
Stearns, Maxwell L. and Todd J. Zywicki. 2009. *Public Choice Concepts and Applications in Law*. Saint Paul, MN: West Publishing.
Stringham, Edward Peter. 2010. "Economic Value and Costs Are Subjective." In *The Handbook on Contemporary Austrian Economics*. Peter Boettke, ed. Cheltenham, UK: Edward Elgar Publishing.
Stringham, Edward Peter. 2001. "Kaldor-Hicks Efficiency and the Problem of Central Planning." *Quarterly Journal of Austrian Economics* 4(2): 41–50.
Stringham, Edward Peter, and Mark White. 2004. "Economic Analysis of Tort Law: Austrian and Kantian Perspectives." In *Law and Economics: Alternative Economic Approaches to Legal and Regulatory Issues*. Margaret Oppenheimer and Nicholas Mercuro, eds. New York, NY: M.E. Sharpe.
Stringham, Edward Peter, and Todd J. Zywicki. 2011a. "Hayekian Anarchism." *Journal of Economic Behavior and Organization* 78(3) May: 290–301.
Stringham, Edward Peter, and Todd J. Zywicki. 2011b. "Rivalry and Superior Dispatch: An Analysis of Competing Courts in Medieval and Early Modern England." *Public Choice* 147: 497–524.
Tullock, Gordon. 2005. "Technology: The Anglo-Saxons Versus the Rest of the World." In *The Selected Works of Gordon Tullock*. Charles K. Rowley, ed., 291–308. Indianapolis, IN: Liberty Fund.
Tullock, Gordon. 1997. *The Case Against the Common Law* (Issue 1, Blackstone Commentaries Series). Durham, NC: Carolina Academic Press.
Wangenheim, Georg von. 1993. "The Evolution of Judge-Made Law." *International Review of Law and Economics* 13: 381–411.
Zywicki, Todd J. 2006. "Is Forum-Shopping Corrupting America's Bankruptcy Courts?" *Georgetown Law Journal* 94: 1141–95.
Zywicki, Todd J. 2003. "The Rule of Law, Freedom, and Prosperity." In *Supreme Court Economic Review: The Rule of Law, Freedom, and Prosperity*, 10: 1–26.
Zywicki, Todd J. 2000. "Public Choice and Tort Reform." George Mason Law & Economics Research Paper No. 00-36 (October 2000).
Zywicki, Todd J. 1998. "Epstein & Polanyi on Simple Rules, Complex Systems, and Decentralization." *Constitutional Political Economy* 9: 143–50.
Zywicki, Todd J. 1996. "A Unanimity-Reinforcing Model of Efficiency in the Common Law: An Institutional Comparison of Common Law and Legislative Solutions to Large-Number Externality Problems." *Case Western Reserve Law Review* 46(4): 961–1031.
Zywicki, Todd J. and Anthony B. Sanders. 2008. "Posner, Hayek, and the Economic Analysis of Law." *Iowa Law Review* 93: 559–604.
Zywicki, Todd J. and Edward P. Stringham. 2010. "Common Law and Economic Efficiency." George Mason Law and Economics Research Paper No. 10-43.

10. Dispute resolution when rationalities conflict: cost and choice in a mixed economy

Richard E. Wagner

A considerable literature exists on the settlement of legal disputes as an alternative to going to trial, as illustrated by Bebchuk (1984), Cooter and Rubinfeld (1989), Hughes and Snyder (1995), Hylton (1993), Micelli (2005), Priest and Klein (1984), and Shavell (1995). This literature operates within a context of private property and a market economy, along with the associated calculus of residual claimancy where people have ownership over the value consequences of their actions. A century ago when governments in the US occupied less than 10 percent of GDP, such a market-grounded calculus would cover the bulk of legal disputes. But when governments occupy more than 40 percent of GDP, a market-based theory can give only an incomplete account of the organization of economic activity, including the resolution of disputes, because much economic activity and interaction is organized through collective and not private property, as Wagner (2007, 2012) explains. Politically based enterprises operate within a framework of collective or common property that promotes a different substantive rationality than that pertaining to market-based enterprises. This conflict between rationalities generates societal tectonics whereby what is commonly misidentified as market failure is actually a systemic property of the conflicting rationalities that characterize modern mixed economics.

This chapter starts by exploring how different institutional arrangements promote differences in the substance of rational action even as all those actions can be brought within the purview of a generic and purely formal rationality. After reviewing the standard framework of dispute settlement within a market context of rational action grounded on private property, the chapter explores how the substantive character would proceed differently when one of the parties operates within a framework of common or collective property. When action takes place inside a societal architecture that contains entangled relationships among entities organized in market squares and public squares, a conflict-laden political economy results that bears a family resemblance to what Jane Jacobs (1992) described as "monstrous moral hybrids" in her treatment of entanglement between carriers of commercial and guardian activity. With private ordering, social relationships are dyadic and are governed exclusively by principles of private property. When public ordering intrudes, social relationships become triadic and, more significantly, conflicting principles of rational action characterize social interaction. This alternative societal architecture intensifies conflict within a society, and also leads to a misidentification of societal turbulence as indications of market failure when that turbulence is really a systemic property of the conflict between rationalities. While this conflict might be mitigated through an appropriate constitutional architecture, it is doubtful that it can be eliminated.

1.   TWO RATIONALITIES FOR HUMAN GOVERNANCE

Economists typically work with a purely formal notion of rationality as conveyed by a pure logic of choice where agents are presumed to make consistent choices that maximize given utility functions. But rationality can also be treated in a substantive manner. In this respect, rationality is concerned with the use of reason as a tool to operate successfully in the particular social area in which an actor is situated. Rationality thus pertains to practical action as a logic of practice (Bourdieu 1990, 1998) as conveyed by the idea of praxis or praxeology. With respect to human practice there can be different rationalities, as Alasdair MacIntyre (1988) explains in his examination of the contrasting rationalities of excellence and effectiveness. This contrast is also explored to charming effect in Robert Pirsig's (1974) *Zen and the Art of Motorcycle Maintenance*, and also in Matthew Crawford's (2009) *Shop Class as Soulcraft*.

With respect to arenas of human practice, this chapter treats commerce, politics, and the intersection of the two as conveyed by the hybrid term political economy. A logic of practice is still an abstraction from the practice itself, yet practitioners should be able to recognize some contours of their activities within the theoretical framework being presented. Such an approach to theorizing seeks to penetrate reality rather than to disengage from reality, to use a distinction that Elinor Ostrom used to describe her work when interviewed by Aligica and Boettke (2009: 142–59). Economics is thus the science that studies the practice of commerce and industry while political science is the science that studies the practice of governing. The compound term political economy would thus denote the practice of acting within the intersection of those two arenas. I should perhaps also note that the relevant human actions, when economics is treated as a genuine social science as distinct from being treated as a science of rational action (Wagner 2010), are not decisions or choices as such but are transactions or interactions between or among people, which is reminiscent of Commons's (1934) treatment of a transaction as the basic unit of analysis and also Buchanan's (1964) treatment of economics as centered on exchange and not on choice.

These contrasting rationalities of action and interaction play out in terms of two distinct institutional configurations or arrangements, both of which are presented as ideal types. One is private property, which is the abstract framework within which the theory of markets has been developed. To speak of a market economy is to invoke an abstraction wherein people relate to one another through the principles of private property and freedom of contract and association. In no society are human relationships governed exclusively by this framework, for societies also entail a collective commons, with actions undertaken on that commons often though not always trumping actions undertaken within the framework of private property. To think of commons is, of course, almost instantly to think of tragedy (Hardin 1968), though it should also be noted that the tragedy of the commons has a long lineage in economic theory, as illustrated by Knight (1924) and Gordon (1954). Ostrom (1990) explains that numerous commons settings operate without tragedy because the participants have developed methods, institutions, and practices of governance that avoid tragedy. What is particularly notable about the commons that Ostrom examines is that their governance arrangements were fashioned through private ordering. With private ordering, participation within an enterprise must be secured by attracting participants. With public ordering on the collective commons, however, much participation is commanded and not attracted.

The requirements of practical action and interaction differ when human relationships are governed by the principles of private property than when they are governed by the principles of common or collective property. What is rational at the level of practical action depends on the context within which action occurs. What comprises rational practice differs when people act within a setting of private property than when they act within a setting of common property. For instance, Angello and Donnelley (1975) found that people act differently when they farm oysters within a framework of common property than when they farm them within a framework of private property. In dredging oysters, immature oysters as well as deposits of rock and shell (cultch) on which oysters grow are collected along with mature oysters. To separate mature oysters from immature oysters and cultch is a costly activity. Taking time to separate and return cultch and immature oysters takes time away from dredging for oysters. When oyster beds are held privately, the farmer who returns the cultch and immature oysters will be able to harvest those oysters at a later date when they have matured. Should oysters be harvested under common property, however, the increased value of future harvests will no longer be something the acting farmer can rely upon because any future farmer can harvest them. If there are 100 farmers who work the bed under common property, an individual's gain from returning cultch and immature oysters will be but 1 percent of the total gain. Yet the farmer will bear 100 percent of the cost of returning immature oysters and cultch. In comparing these settings, Angello and Donnelley estimated that conversion of common property to private property would increase by about 50 percent the present value of the output from farming oysters.

Private ordering provides a framework under which commercial plans are pursued by attracting participation. Someone who has an idea for an enterprise must attract numerous participants if that enterprise is to be successful. Figure 10.1 below presents a simple schematic of such a plan. It bears some analogies to a road map, with a point of departure and a point of destination. What is shown are four sets of intermediate points numbered one through four. To arrive at the destination, the plan must pass through one option at each point. For instance, point one might denote a location for the place of business. Shown in Figure 10.1 are two potential locations. To pass through either location requires the owner of the plan to secure permission from the owner of the land and premise. As shown in the sketch, the lower circle is closer to the point of departure than is the upper circle. This might denote a locational preference, and yet the upper point might be chosen because its price is less. The central point in any case is that the plan proceeds through voluntary participation where entrepreneurs must attract people to participate in their plans. With a location selected, other inputs must be assembled, as illustrated by points two, three, and four. At each such point the entrepreneur faces options, some superior to others in the entrepreneur's judgment but perhaps not available at a price the entrepreneur is willing to pay. At the final stage, customers must also be enlisted in support of the entrepreneur's plan if the plan is to succeed. Using the analogy to the road map, the distance traveled between departure and destination might not be the minimum distance but it will be the most economical distance in light of the voluntary character of purely private ordering.

With private ordering, every entrepreneurial plan is a node in someone else's plan. The plan depicted in Figure 10.1 might represent a new breakfast cereal. The destination of that plan is a presence in grocery stores and purchase by customers. Before arriving at that destination, the entrepreneur must assemble a set of inputs from among options at several stages in the production process. To the cereal entrepreneur, the world resembles the network depicted by Figure 10.1. To other people, however, the entrepreneur's network is but one node in their plans. For instance, a landowner wants to put his land holdings to substantive use and faces options in this respect, with one of those options being lease of the land and building to the cereal entrepreneur. Similarly, grocery stores have limited shelf space and face options about how to use that space. For a grocery store, the plan of the cereal entrepreneur is but one option among many from which the grocery store must select in pursuing its commercial plan. By continuing this line of reasoning, it becomes quickly apparent that a market economy assembled through private ordering is an ecology of plans, along the lines sketched in Wagner (2012a).

This situation changes when public ordering intrudes into private ordering, as explained by Littlechild (1978) and Ikeda (1997). With public ordering, participation is not attracted but is commanded. Figure 10.1 shows one black node at point G. Merely showing the G node is not to illustrate how public ordering alters the ecology of plans, but it can be used to point in that direction. Referring again to the road map analogy, public ordering represents a point of monopoly within the ecology of plans because plans cannot go forward without passing through this node. To be sure, it is possible to imagine numerous different ways such a node might operate and different places it might be located. In actuality, there are numerous nodes of public ordering that plans must pass through. It is possible to imagine nodes that occupy central locations and facilitate passage, just as someone traveling from New York to Los Angeles might be required to pass through Saint Louis. But it is also possible that public ordering could establish nodes that warp commercial plans considerably, as by requiring the traveler from New York to Los Angeles to pass through Detroit and then San Antonio.

What is of particular significance for economics as a social science is the human faculties that are strengthened or weakened in consequence of different arrangements for ordering human interaction, as Crawford (2009) recognizes with particular lucidity. With private ordering people must enlist voluntary participation in the activities they are sponsoring. To do this it is necessary to listen to the people whose participation you are seeking to attract and to convince them to participate in your plan. Social interactions within a system of private ordering are among equals in that each person can choose whether to give or withhold consent. In contrast, with public ordering listening is no longer necessary because command replaces consent. Social interactions entail status relationships in the presence of public ordering. The traveler from New York to Los Angeles has no option but to pass through Detroit and San Antonio. With private ordering, by contrast, the intermediate points through which a plan passes is determined through negotiation among the affected parties.

2.   DISPUTE RESOLUTION WITHIN A FRAMEWORK OF PRIVATE ORDERING

Prah v. Maretti (321 N.W. 2d 404 (1982)) involved a dispute between adjacent landowners. Prah complained that the house Maretti was planning to build would interfere with the solar panels on his house. While Maretti offered to move the house a bit, he would not move it sufficiently to satisfy Prah because he did not want to lose his view of a nearby lake. So the case went to trial, with the trial court finding for Maretti and the appellate court reversing the trial court.

The setting for this case offers a framework for exploring dispute resolution in a manner that will be amenable to reconsideration in the presence of public ordering. Suppose a large marina at the edge of a lake derives much of its energy from solar panels. On adjacent land to the south, someone plans to build a hotel, the height of which would put much of the marina in shade much of the day. When the marina owner complains to the hotel owner, the hotel owner offers to move the hotel 100 feet but claims that he would require $20 million to do so for a variety of reasons: significant grading of the alternative land would be required, the original architectural plans would have to be revised, and the opening of the hotel would be delayed by several months. The marina owner refuses to make the payment, so sues the hotel owner.

To illustrate settlement under private ordering before turning to public ordering, suppose each party expects its legal expenses to be $2 million. Further suppose for now that each party thinks its chance of success at trial is 50 percent. For the plaintiff, the expected value of going to trial is the expected award to be received from winning the trial less the legal expenses resulting from going to trial. With the amount at issue being $20 million, the expected value of going to trial for the plaintiff is $8 million, which is 50 percent of the $20 million minus the $2 million of litigation expenses. For the defendant, the expected value of going to trial is the payment that could be avoided. This expected value is likewise $8 million: a 50 percent chance of avoiding the $20 million payment less legal expenses of $2 million. For each party, the value of going to trial is $8 million or $16 million in the aggregate. Yet the trial itself is expected to return an award of $20 million, so $4 million is dissipated through litigation. This amount represents the potential gain that can be captured by settling the case without trial as a form of Coasian (1960) resolution.

To be sure, the presumption that each party thinks the outcome of a trial is equivalent to some such random process as a flip of a coin, where the sum of the probabilities equals one, drives this particular outcome. It is not necessary that each party thinks its probability of success is 50 percent;

what is necessary is only that the sum of the perceived probabilities equals one. For instance, the plaintiff could think its probability of success is 60 percent, which means the defendant thinks its probability of success is 40 percent. In this case, the expected value of going to trial for the plaintiff is $10 million, while for the defendant it is $6 million. The aggregate of the expected values is still $16 million, which again indicates the presence of a $4 million settlement range. The only difference between the two settings is that settlement is likely to shift in favor of the plaintiff when both parties concur in the 60–40 likelihood relative to the 50–50 likelihood.

There is, of course, no reason for the perceptions by the litigants to map into a presumption that the sum of both parties' beliefs about success at trial is unity. Both parties could be optimistic about their chances of success. Suppose each party thought it had an 80 percent chance of success. For each of them, the expected value of going to trial would be $14 million, which would give an aggregate value of $28 million. Yet the trial will award only $20 million, so there is no region of settlement where each party can anticipate gaining relative to going to trial. Perceptions are clearly significant in this situation. While there is surely basis for thinking that such procedures as discovery and deposition help to narrow differences between the perceptions, there is no reason to think that these will lead to a common perception. The settlement of disputes within a framework of private property is economically intelligible but it is not economically necessary. So some disputes will be taken to trial.

For purposes of this chapter, what is particularly significant about this formulation is that both parties operate within a framework of private property and private ordering. The choice between settling a dispute and taking it to trial bears a family resemblance to a situation where both parties are gambling with their own money. But what if one of the parties to the dispute is a public entity which gambles with someone else's money? Rather than the hotel owner facing a marina owner who objects to the degradation of his solar panels, suppose the hotel owner faces an environmental agency that objects to various features of the proposed hotel's design and insists on changes that will raise the hotel's investment by $20 million, but without that added investment generating any kind of return to the hotel. Rather than operating on the market square where residual claimancy is present, public agencies operate on the public square where it is absent. This distinction between contexts of operation leads to differences in the substance of rational conduct. Behind the pure form of rational action there resides multiple specific contexts for rational action. There is a general form to which rational conduct conforms but there are also multiple rationalities of practical action. A public litigant faces a different rationality of practice than a private litigant, and this difference generates a form of societal tectonics (Young 1991) in contrast to equilib-rium-based presumptions of societal harmony illustrated by presumptions that societal observations pertain to Nash equilibriums.

3.   DISPUTE RESOLUTION WITHIN A MIXED ECONOMY

Any choice entails the displacement of an alternative action that could have been chosen, with cost being the valuation placed by the chooser on the option not chosen, as Buchanan (1969) explains. While economists speak of the chosen option as being preferred to the option not chosen, it is important to note that the valuations the chooser places on those options are acts of imagination and not realized experiences, as George Shackle (1979) explains. A choice between settling a suit and going to trial will be made according to a formal calculus of cost-and-gain. The substantive content of that calculus, however, depends on the context within which choice occurs, as illustrated by harvesting oysters in settings of private and common property. It should also be noted that it is people and not organi-zations *per se* who choose whether or not to settle a dispute. Cost is faced by those who are responsible for making choices and not by organizations with which those choosers might be associated. This holds regardless of whether those organizations operate within a framework of private or common property. What differs between those types of organizations is the nature of the connection between individual choosers and the organiza-tions in whose name they choose.

While no one claims that agency relationships work perfectly to harness actions to the service of principal interest, it is well recognized that private property and its associated conventions makes possible a framework of governance that does this pretty well (Manne 1965; Meckling and Jensen 1976; Fama and Jensen 1983). For the marina deciding whether to settle a case with the hotel, the relevant bearer of cost is the party that makes the decision. To the extent corporate officers operate within well-working agency relationships, the action taken by the legal office will be that which produces the higher anticipated present value for the firm. The value of the firm, moreover, has real existence within a framework of private property. The reality of firm value means that judging choices in terms of their probable impacts on firm value is a reasonable activity even if it might be difficult and subject to error. The reality of firm value makes it possible to question commercial decisions on the basis of the standard of firm value which all owners of the firm accept, and to do so within a context where there is unanimity among suppliers of capital to the firm, as De Angelo (1981) and Makowski (1983) explain.

It is easy enough to imagine how agency issues might arise in this setting. An attorney to whom this action is delegated might recommend settlement even though there might be strong grounds for thinking that trial offers higher net worth for the firm. While trial might portend higher firm value, the agent's share of that higher value might not be sufficient to offset the personal cost of cancelling a planned family vacation. While such outcomes are imaginable, they are surely rarities in well-governed corporations due to the ability of private property and its conventions to inject economic calculation (Boettke 2001) at myriad points within commercial organizations, as illustrated by mergers, take-over efforts, forms of executive compensation, and competitive tournaments.

This situation changes with public organizations, as explored in the several papers collected in the symposium devoted to Timothy Besley's (2006) *Principled Agents* and published in volume 23 (2009) of the *Review of Austrian Economics*. For one thing, there is no firm value, so it is impossible to offer plausible conjectures about how different actions will affect firm value. Public agencies receive budgetary appropriations as a remote form of faux-market process, as Wagner (2012b) explains, but the informational content of this process is weak compared with market processes. Furthermore, there are no explicit investors who own a public agency. There are *de facto* owners of public agencies who derive cash flows from the enterprise, but the suppliers of capital to public agencies are often forced and not willing investors. Without unanimity among suppliers of capital, agency principles cannot be brought to bear directly on the activities of public agencies because there is no longer agreement among providers of capital as to what comprises better or worse agency performance. The formal language of agency can be used, but the substance evaporates when the real quality of firm value gives way to an ideology that offers conjectures about "social value."

When both parties to a dispute operate within a framework of private property, they both speak the same language of profit-and-loss. For instance, the defendant might be the hotel owner after renovation and the plaintiff might be the owner of an adjacent marina who complains that height of the hotel blocks a view of the setting sun, thereby degrading the value of the rooftop restaurant. Both participants speak the language of profit-and-loss. While each would have understandable incentives to exaggerate their cases, that exaggeration is limited by their positions of residual claimants and the possibility that settlement might lead to higher net worth than trial.

The setting changes if the plaintiff is a public agency. Now it is only the hotel that speaks the language of profit-and-loss. The public agency speaks a different language, one that refers to social value that cannot materialize in anyone's account in particular. This language advances ideological appeals that resonate with the sentiments held by pertinent interest groups, in contrast to the commercial calculus that would be in the foreground of discussions in the presence of private ordering. In Vilfredo Pareto's (1935) treatment of ideology, some public choice implications of which are explored in Backhaus (1978), ruling elites sought to articulate ideological frames of reference that would resonate so strongly with widely-held sentiments that people would support actions that they would have been rejected in the presence of truly rational deliberation. Pareto's framework, the gist of which is presented lucidly in Aron (1967: 101–76) and explored carefully in McLure (2007), distinguishes among actions, residues, and derivations. We observe actions, as illustrated by settling a dispute or going to trial. We also observe derivations, which are the justifications people give when asked about their actions. We do not observe residues, which are the real sources of or motivations for action. In this respect, Pareto often remarked that residues are remarkably constant while derivations are highly volatile, meaning that people were capable of rationalizing nearly anything if the incentive were sufficiently strong.

Within a setting where both parties act within a framework of private ordering, it is reasonable to expect that the gap between residues and derivations is relatively narrow. Both the hotel and the marina are concerned about the value of their enterprises, and there is no need to disguise or conceal this concern. They speak the same language. It is understandable that each party would engage in strategic posturing and exaggeration, and yet neither party has any reason to be ashamed of trying to promote the value of their enterprise. The situation changes if the plaintiff is a public agency which files suit against the hotel and advances derivations based on claims of promoting "social good." The agency cannot claim to be trying to capture lost profits, and in this it is speaking truthfully because there are no profits that it can capture due to its status as a non-profit entity. But in speaking of securing the social good, it is advancing a proposition that is incapable of *ex post* falsification. While a public plaintiff does not have a residual claim to legal expenses, such a plaintiff can use legal expenses as a form of investment in seeking higher office or otherwise pursuing particularly favored causes through the attention-gathering and publicity-generating potential of going to trial. If so, the suit offers the head of the agency an opportunity to invest at public expense in achieving that desired outcome, though, of course, no person with such aspirations would ever make such a declaration. In a suit between market participants, both parties can be honest and open in their aspirations; but when one party is a public entity, such rectitude necessarily and understandably recedes.

Yet both parties interact on the same societal space, so the two distinct practical rationalities collide, resulting in a form of societal tectonics along the lines sketched in a different context by Robert Young (1991). In this respect, Maffeo Pantaleoni (1911) described a society as containing two conflicting price systems, a system of market prices and a system of political prices. Consistent with the economic theory in play when he wrote, Pantaleoni characterized market prices as being equal to marginal costs and so were constant across buyers. In contrast, political prices were discriminatory and with the type of price discrimination depending on the type of tax system in place. Under a flat-rate tax on income, political prices would vary in proportion to income. Under a progressive income tax with a significant level of exemption, moreover, a considerable number of people would face political prices of zero, which would lead them to support satiation levels of public spending on desired objects and programs.

A further feature of Pantaleoni's analysis is the parasitical character of political pricing. Action within a framework of collective property cannot generate prices because the generation of prices requires exchange and the alienability of property rights. Within this framework where a society operates with both market and political pricing, there will always exist margins of activity where the two pricing systems collide. What results is a form of predator-prey relationship as noted in Wagner (1997), where increased use of political pricing degrades the market pricing that is necessary for the political price system to operate. It should be noted in this respect that taxes are expressed and collected in terms of observed market prices. Without market prices, there could be no income tax, sales tax, or any other form of tax. Hence, a system of market pricing is necessary to host a parasitical system of political pricing, so political pricing necessarily distorts market pricing but at the same time requires market pricing as an object to which it can attach.

Disputes involving both private and public parties entail a form of Faustian bargain. Public parties can sue private parties without having to face the constraints upon the power to sue that private property imposes on market participants. In some instances, reasonable public purposes might be secured by the deployment of that power. But that power can also be employed in the pursuit of the private advantages of those who wield that power, as perhaps illustrated by an attorney general who is able to parlay legal expenditures into investments in an effort to seek higher elected office.

It is doubtful that there is any resolution to this particular Faustian bargain. This form of the bargain bears a family resemblance to the problem of statistical decision theory as illustrated by Jerzzy Neyman's (1950) treatment of the problem of the lady tasting tea. In that problem, a lady claims to be able to tell whether milk is added to tea that is already in the cup or whether tea is added to milk. In the nature of the problem setting, perfection is impossible. The greater the effort made to avoid granting the lady's claim when she really cannot distinguish between the methods, the greater the frequency with which her claim will be rejected even though she can distinguish between the methods. All choices will thus be subject to error even if the chooser is a disinterested truth-seeker trying to implement the common desire of principals. In Neyman's presentation, the person who was judging the claim was presumed to be an impartial spectator, which made sense in light of Neyman's interest to present his approach to statistical decision theory. While such impartiality might well be a characteristic of private ordering when the parties to a dispute agree upon a judge or judges who will decide the dispute, such impartiality seems unlikely to be a characteristic of public agencies that pursue disputes with market-based firms.

Following Epstein (1985), a public agency might take private property under eminent domain, claiming that it had good public reason for doing so. After all, what else could it claim? The Fifth Amendment to the US Constitution requires that such takings be for public purposes only and that any such taking be accompanied by just compensation. It is easy enough to give a Coasian gloss on this procedure. The ability of the hotel to build upward might destroy scenic opportunities elsewhere that are valued more highly than what is created by adding to the height of the hotel. There is a simple market test for this proposition. But in the absence of a market test, the burden falls on the public processes through which agency actions are determined. Some of those processes might be more market conformable than other processes. In any case, relationships between market-based and public-based entities create a source of turbulence that is not present in relationships between market-based entities, due to differences in the substantive content of rational action.

4. A FUNDAMENTAL AMBIGUITY IN THE NOTION OF A MARKET SYSTEM

The credit market turbulence that became visible in 2008 has spawned intense controversy over whether that turbulence reflects market failure that calls for new regulation or whether it reflects government failure that might call for less regulation. Throughout these discussions and debates, the participants mostly speak as though a market is a precise entity that exists independent of institutional arrangements in society. Hence the entire set of interactions among participants engaged in credit transactions is referred to as the "credit market." A set of dyadic transactions between borrowers and lenders might be aggregated and the outcome designated as being the outcome of the credit market. Within this framework of wholly private ordering, all terms of contract, as well as whether or not agreements are reached in particular instances, will be decided through interaction between borrowers and lenders. Contemporary credit markets, however, are not dyadic; they are triadic, and with one of those participants being a public agency (actually, numerous public agencies). Dyadic and triadic markets entail distinct architectures and have different performance properties. In the presence of public ordering, a fundamental ambiguity arises in the very notion of a market system.

Figure 10.2 below illustrates the distinction I have in mind between dyadic exchange governed by private ordering and triadic exchange where public ordering is present. The left panel denotes dyadic exchange with private ordering. The two large circles denote market participants who engage in an exchange that offers anticipated gains to each participant, with those gains illustrated by the smaller subtended circles of profit coming out of the larger circles. The terms of trade, and whether an agreement is reached in the first place, is for the parties alone to decide. The triangle inscribed inside the exchange is meant to denote the conventional position of law as an umpire that supports the intentions of the participants, as conveyed perhaps by images of a night-watchman state.

A credit contract is a form of rental contract where a lender transfers temporary custody of an asset to a borrower. All rental situations entail possible asset conversion by borrowers, against which lenders will seek protection. Within a framework of private law, credit transactions are wholly a matter between borrower and lender. Such terms of contract as rate of interest, provisions for repossession, procedures for settling disputes, among numerous other possible terms of contract are matters of interest only to the parties to the contract. The set of transactions made within this framework of wholly private law could be designated as a credit market. The place of the public agency denoted by the triangle inside the dyadic exchange is merely to support agreements made by the parties. For instance, both parties might agree to repossession in the event payment becomes 60 days late. Yet the borrower might resist giving up the asset. The public agency denoted in the left side of Figure 10.2 would support the lender, and would equally support the borrower should the lender seek unilaterally to change some condition in the contract. To be sure, this does not mean that the presence of some public agency is necessary, for the parties to the contract could agree upon some private adjudicator of disputes, but is only to provide a context for a public presence within a framework of private ordering of credit relationships.

It is worth noting that in the presence of private ordering, *ex ante* Ricardian equivalence characterizes each credit relationship and so is a quality of the entire set of credit transactions. Ricardian equivalence means simply that each party expects to gain from the relationship. If Ricardian equivalence did not characterize a transaction, the transaction would not truly be a transaction. It would be either charity or a gift, but it would not be an economical transaction. As an *ex post* matter, however, not all transactions will turn out as the parties anticipated when they entered into the transaction. This is an unavoidable feature of all economic action, where resources are committed to a plan today based on projections about how that plan will turn out. But plans do not always turn out as projected, in which case failed plans create economic debris of lesser value than what was initially anticipated, with that debris to be spread among negatively affected participants through commercial reorganization.

These days, however, credit arrangements are governed only partially by private law, as public ordering also intrudes into credit markets. Yet we still describe those arrangements by the generic term "credit market." Hence, the term "market" has no precise meaning, as what people mean when they speak of markets varies with the institutional arrangements that govern transactions. Market is thus used as an invariant feature of societies independent of institutional arrangements, which means in turn that the term conveys no precise meaning. Among other things, this common usage makes market failure a meaningless term because it conveys no knowledge about just what it is that is thought to have failed. Failure might be attributed to some quality of private ordering, but it could also be attributed to the public ordering component of actual market arrangements, or yet again to some emergent feature of interaction stemming from the confluence of particular instances of private and public ordering.

In contemporary economies, a particular credit contract is never between a borrower and lender only. At multiple places third parties inject their interests into credit contracts. Many of these third-party interests take shape through regulation. For instance, lenders are often required to demonstrate various "fairness" characteristics within their portfolio of loans, which operate to change the pattern of loans from what they would otherwise have been. A different set of credit transactions arise in the presence of public ordering than would have arisen in the presence of private ordering alone. It is still possible to speak generically of a market for credit, only the framework of rules that governs those transactions is an admixture of private and public ordering. What results is a type of regulation-induced tie-in sale where it is no longer the case that Ricardian equivalence pertains *ex ante* to each transaction. The unavoidable turbulence that accompanies private ordering will be intensified through the alternative pattern of credit relationships that public ordering promotes.

Once various fairness or distributive requirements are imposed on the loan portfolios of market-based providers of credit, credit transactions are no longer the province of the borrower and lender. As a purely formal matter, the two parties must still agree to the transaction. Only now a lender's denial of credit does not end the matter because a denied borrower can seek reversal by appealing to a collective entity that is not a residual claimant to the transaction, though actually in many cases such appeal will be forestalled in advance through regulation and associated inspection and auditing activities. The imperative of rational conduct will typically differ for the representative of that collective entity than the rational imperative that guides action within a framework of private ordering. To the extent collective property trumps private property, market transactions will take on different patterns than would otherwise have prevailed.

For instance, people who are judged by lenders to be bad credit risks and so might be rejected for credit might be granted credit under regulation even though Ricardian equivalence does not characterize that transaction *ex ante*. To provide a simple illustration, suppose a bank has deposits of $1,000, chooses to keep reserves of $400, and lends out $600 in six loans of $100 each. Further suppose that all borrowers have net worth above $X, or have posted equivalent collateral. In contrast, those who were denied credit all had net worth below $X. Within a framework of private ordering, that would end the matter. To be sure, private ordering is consistent with rejected borrowers offering to pay higher interest to increase the willingness of lenders to accept their proffers. The response of the lender to such a proffer would be for the lender to determine, and would do so as governed by the principle of residual claimancy. Still, within a framework of private ordering some people would receive loans and others would be denied.

To simplify the point, suppose all those who were denied credit had net worth below $X. Further suppose that public ordering requires that any bank's portfolio must have at least 20 percent of its volume extended to loans where borrowers have net worth below $X, and with banks being prohibited from charging differential interest rates between the two categories of borrower. For borrowers below the regulatory threshold, Ricardian non-equivalence would be expected *ex ante*. The price charged to borrowers above the threshold would also rise to reflect the higher cost of doing business, leading to a regulation-induced decrease in the total volume of credit, as well as a shift in the pattern of credit transactions. Ricardian equivalence would still exist at the aggregate level of the bank, but it would no longer pertain to individual loans.

Furthermore, banking under the mixed scheme of private and public ordering would exhibit more turbulence than banking organized fully under private ordering, especially once it is recognized that borrowers insert their loan proceeds into an ecology of plans, thereby influencing other participants within that ecology by changing the web of expectations that is in play within that ecology. To be sure, private ordering would still exhibit turbulence within the ecology of plans, but the intrusion of public ordering would increase the turbulence because public ordering increases riskiness in the operation of banks. To be sure, the intrusion of public ordering is invariably justified on the grounds of reducing riskiness. As Pareto recognized, the challenge faced by governing elites is to craft derivations that resonate sufficiently with prevailing sentiments to lead people generally to support actions they would reject if they were faced directly with the choice. An ideological framework that treats all so-called market outcomes as if they were products of private ordering when they are not is one that feeds the appetites of governing elites, as Pareto would surely have appreciated.

5. A CONSTITUTIONAL ARCHITECTURE FOR A MIXED ECONOMY

In her perceptive treatment of *Systems of Survival*, Jane Jacobs (1992) explained that well-working societies operated with a delicate balance between what she described as commercial and guardian moral syndromes. While her distinction was not identical to the distinction between commerce and government, it was close. She also explained that when the carriers of those syndromes commingle excessively, what she termed "monstrous moral hybrids" can arise as illustrations of the dynamics of the mixed economy (Ikeda 1997). The central issue that arises in the presence of such commingling is whether it supports or undermines the character of the economic order. While democratic systems are based on a norm of equality and mutuality, there are plenty of analytical grounds for recognizing that they also face pressures leading toward a re-feudalization of the economy where relationships based on contract give way to relationships based on status. It was to forestall such re-feudalization that Walter Eucken (1952) articulated the principle of market conformability, wherein state action would be constrained to act congruently with the central operating principles of private ordering and a market economy.

How a state might be so constrained is an open and difficult question to answer. The Fifth Amendment to the American constitution fits the idea of market conformability. The Amendment does not prohibit states from taking private property, but only puts constraints on such takings that would render takings market conformable. Hence, takings would be limited to public purposes and would be accompanied by just compensation. As articulated by Epstein (1985), this constraint on government would induce governments to act pretty much in a manner compatible with the assembly of property through market transactions. At the same time, however, the substance of Epstein's book was devoted to a recitation of a century of cases where any reasonable notion of market conformability, which Epstein denoted as "forced exchanges," was violated repeatedly by legislatures and with those violations supported repeatedly by judges. To similar effect, David Primo (2007: 109) noted that in 1978 the US enacted a law which was known as Byrd-Grassley, which required a balanced budget by 1981, and with this law never having been rescinded. It is easy enough to articulate constraints on government, both legislative and constitutional, but such articulation does not itself assure the effectiveness of those constraints.

The rampant fiscal irresponsibility that has been a democratic disease of increasing intensity over the better part of a century is a manifestation of the monstrous moral hybrid that can result from excessive commingling between commercial and guardian activity. Politicians manage their personal budgets in responsible fashion but fail to do so in their public capacities. This is not so much a personal failing on their part as it is a reflection of their being caught up in the tragedy of a democratic budget commons. Political enterprises unavoidably engage in commercial types of activity, but they lack the tools to do so with full commercial responsibility. The more fully governments undertake such commercial-type activity as engaging in credit market activity, the more fully fiscal irresponsibility will engulf democratic budgeting. To be sure, the commingling of commercial and governmental activity is not a product of travel along a one-way street. The traffic flows in both directions, as many commercial entities also scramble for positions close to political power to gain competitive advantage. Whether those entities do so out of an effort to preempt what they anticipate will be rent extraction (McChesney 1997) or whether they do so to gain advantage over competitors is probably an undecidable question, as the tendency for such commingling probably inheres in human nature, as illustrated by Vincent Ostrom's (1987, 1997) treatment of the difficulty of sustaining self-governing republics.

There is a path to remedy for fiscal irresponsibility, though that path is surely narrow and steep. Following that path starts with recognition that guardian-type activities are distinct from commercial-type activities. While there necessarily will be points of contact, the challenge of good governance is to keep those points of contact from dissolving into rampant commingling where governments engage in commercial activities and where commercial entities seek commercial advantage from public entities. It might be acceptable for governments to police commercial agreements, but it is easy for policing to morph into faux-commercial activity when the policing agency can compel performance as against having to attract it. As governments become increasingly involved in commercial-like activities, fiscal irresponsibility will unavoidably intrude because the commercial tools that facilitate responsible action do not operate with public ordering.

Even worse, governments have strong reasons to degrade commercial activity through regulation to render commerce duplicitous with its own fiscal irresponsibility. Hence, governments do such things as modify the operation of credit markets to complement their own faux-commercial activities, just as major firms in the provision credit have welcomed the receipt of support from governmental agencies. A constitution of liberty must be based in some manner on recognition of the principles that Jane Jacobs subsequently articulated. Those principles imply an architectural organization of governments that would limit if not eliminate the commingling of commercial and guardian activities. Over the past century or so, that architecture has been undergoing demolition. The result of this demolition to date is not pretty. Restoration of a constitution of liberty, however, will not be easy, and not just because of such things as faction and rent seeking and rent extraction, but also because of the growing sickness of the people that seems apparently to have weakened desires and capacities for self-governance. Any effort at restoration must include recognition that the fiscal problems we are coming increasingly to experience do not reflect some kind of technical failure or weakness. To the contrary, they reflect a systemic quality of life on a democratic commons which worsens as the commons expands. In short, governments will accomplish more to facilitate a robust civic life as they recede from faux-commercial activity.

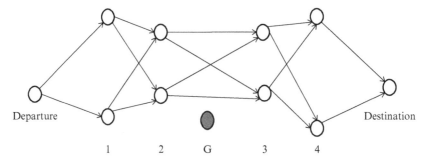

Figure 10.1   Commercial Plans: Private vs. Public Ordering

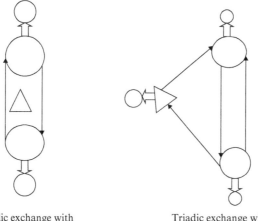

Dyadic exchange with   Triadic exchange with mixed
wholly private ordering   public and private ordering

Figure 10.2   Dyadic vs. Triadic Exchange

REFERENCES

Aligica, Paul D. and Boettke, Peter J. 2009. *Challenging Institutional Analysis and Development: The Bloomington School*. London: Routledge.

Angello, Richard J. and Lawrence P. Donnelley. 1975. "Property Rights and Efficiency in the Oyster Industry." *Journal of Law and Economics* 18: 521–33.

Aron, Raymond. 1967. *Main Currents of Sociological Thought II: Durkheim, Pareto, Weber*. Translated and edited by R. Howard and H. Weaver. New York, NY: Basic Books.

Backhaus, Jürgen G. 1978. "Pareto and Public Choice." *Public Choice* 33: 5–17.

Bebchuk, Lucian. 1984. "Litigation and Settlement under Imperfect Information." *Rand Journal of Economics* 15: 404–15.

Besley, Timothy. 2006. *Principled Agents? The Political Economy of Good Government*. Oxford: Oxford University Press.

Boettke, Peter J. 2001. *Calculation and Coordination*. London: Routledge.

Bourdieu, Pierre. 1990. *The Logic of Practice*. Stanford, CA: Stanford University Press.

Bourdieu, Pierre. 1998. *Practical Reason: On the Theory of Action*. Stanford, CA: Stanford University Press.

Buchanan, James M. 1964. "What Should Economists Do?" *Southern Economic Journal* 30: 213–22.

Buchanan, James M. 1969. *Cost and Choice*. Chicago, IL: Markham.

Coase, Ronald H. 1960. "The Problem of Social Cost." *Journal of Law and Economics* 3: 1–44.

Commons, John R. 1934. *Institutional Economics: It's Place in Political Economy*. Madison, WI: University of Wisconsin Press.

Cooter, Robert and Daniel Rubinfeld. 1989. "Economic Analysis of Legal Disputes and their Resolution." *Journal of Economic Literature* 27: 1067–97.

Crawford, Matthew B. 2009. *Shop Class as Soulcraft: An Inquiry into the Value of Work*. New York: Penguin Press.

De Angelo, Harry. 1981. "Competition and Unanimity." *American Economic Review* 71: 18–27.

Epstein, Richard A. 1985. *Takings: Private Property and the Power of Eminent Domain.* Cambridge, MA: Harvard University Press.

Eucken, Walter. 1952. *Grundsätze der Wirtschaftpolitik.* Tübingen: J.C.B. Mohr.

Fama, E.F. and M.C. Jensen. 1983. "Agency Problems and Residual Claims." *Journal of Law and Economics* 26: 327–49.

Gordon, H. Scott. 1954. "The Economic Theory of a Common Property Resource: The Fishery." *Journal of Political Economy* 62: 124–42.

Hardin, Garrett. 1968. "The Tragedy of the Commons." *Science* 162: 1243–8.

Hughes, James and Edward Snyder. 1995. "Litigation and Settlement under the English and American Rules." *Journal of Law and Economics* 38: 225–50.

Hylton, Keith. 1993. "Asymmetric Information and the Selection of Disputes for Litigation." *Journal of Legal Studies* 22: 187–210.

Ikeda, Sanford. 1997. *Dynamics of the Mixed Economy.* London: Routledge.

Jacobs, Jane. 1992. *Systems of Survival.* New York, NY: Random House.

Knight, Frank H. 1924. "Some Fallacies in the Interpretation of Social Cost." *Quarterly Journal of Economics* 38: 582–606.

Littlechild, Steven C. 1978. *The Fallacy of the Mixed Economy.* London: Institute of Economic Affairs.

MacIntyre, Alasdair. 1988. *Whose Justice? Which Rationality.* Notre Dame, IN: University of Notre Dame Press.

Makowski, Louis. 1983. "Competition and Unanimity Revisited." *American Economic Review* 73: 329–39.

Manne, H. 1965. "Mergers and the Market for Corporate Control." *Journal of Political Economy* 73: 10–20.

McChesney, Fred. 1997. *Money for Nothing: Politicians, Rent Extraction, and Political Extortion.* Cambridge, MA: Harvard University Press.

McLure, Michael. 2007. *The Paretian School and Italian Fiscal Sociology.* Basingstoke, UK: Palgrave Macmillan.

Meckling, W.H. and M.C. Jensen. 1976. "Theory of the Firm: Managerial Behavior, Agency Costs, and Ownership Structure." *Journal of Financial Economics* 3: 305–60.

Miceli, Thomas J. 2005. "Dispute Resolution." In Jürgen G. Backhaus, ed., *The Elgar Companion to Law and Economics,* 2nd ed. Cheltenham, UK and Northampton, MA: Edward Elgar Publishing.

Neyman, Jerzzy. 1950. *First Course in Probability and Statistics.* New York, NY: Henry Holt.

Ostrom, Elinor. 1990. *Governing the Commons: The Evolution of Institutions for Collective Action.* New York, NY: Cambridge University Press.

Ostrom, Vincent. 1987. *The Political Theory of a Compound Republic,* 2nd ed. Lincoln, NE: University of Nebraska Press.

Ostrom, Vincent. 1997. *The Meaning of Democracy and the Vulnerability of Societies: A Response to Tocqueville's Challenge.* Ann Arbor, MI: University of Michigan Press.

Pantaleoni, Maffeo. 1911. "Considerazionisulleproprieta di un sistema di prezzipolitici." *Giornaledegli Economisti* 42: 9–29, 114–33.

Pareto, Vilfredo. 1916 [1935]. *The Mind and Society: A Treatise on General Sociology.* New York, NY: Harcourt Brace.

Pirsig, Robert. 1974. *Zen and the Art of Motorcycle Maintenance.* New York, NY: William Morrow.

Priest, George and Benjamin Klein. 1984. "The Selection of Disputes for Litigation." *Journal of Legal Studies* 13: 1–55.

Primo, David M. 2007. *Rules and Restraint: Government Spending and the Design of Institutions.* Chicago, IL: University of Chicago Press.

Shackle, George L.S. 1979. *Imagination and the Nature of Choice.* Edinburgh: Edinburgh University Press.

Shavell, Steven. 1995. "Alternative Dispute Resolution: An Economic Analysis." *Journal of Legal Studies* 24: 1–28.

Wagner, Richard E. 1997. "Parasitical Political Pricing, Economic Calculation, and the Size of Government." *Journal of Public Finance and Public Choice* 15: 135–46.

Wagner, Richard E. 2007. *Fiscal Sociology and the Theory of Public Finance*. Cheltenham, UK and Northampton MA: Edward Elgar Publishing.

Wagner, Richard E. 2010. *Mind, Society, and Human Action: Time and Knowledge in a Theory of Social Economy*. London: Routledge.

Wagner, Richard E. 2012a. "A Macro Economy as an Ecology of Plans." *Journal of Economic Behavior and Organization* 82: 433–44.

Wagner, Richard E. 2012b. *Deficits, Debt, and Democracy: Wrestling with Tragedy on the Fiscal Commons*. Cheltenham, UK and Northampton MA: Edward Elgar Publishing.

Young, Robert A. 1991. "Tectonic Policies and Political Competition." In Albert Breton, et al. eds., *The Competitive State*, 129–45. Dordrecht: Kluwer Academic Publishers

PART IV

BASIC LAW

11. Sparks cases in contemporary law and economic scholarship
Eric R. Claeys

INTRODUCTION

In any academic discipline, a scholar may classify different normative theories by whether they assume what Thomas Sowell calls "constrained" or "unconstrained" priors. (Sowell, 2002, pp. 9–34). "Constrained" theories assume that human knowledge is relatively limited and that people are relatively resistant to attempts to transform their preferences or behavior by political or social control. Constrained theories focus on identifying the goals that decision makers can know, with practical certainty, to be feasible and likely to contribute to the well-being of the members of the community in question. Such theories tend to support strong individual rights and private ordering. In contrast, "unconstrained" theories tend to assume that decision makers can know most of what they need to know to plan centrally, and/or that human behavior is relatively pliable and responsive to socialization. Unconstrained theories facilitate more ambitious government planning, and they justify case-specific administration of particular resource disputes. In case it needs saying, among normative economic theories, Austrian theories of economics fall on the constrained side of the spectrum.

Constrained and unconstrained approaches vie with one another in American law and economic scholarship. For example, in 2001, Thomas Merrill and Henry Smith wondered why "economists" and "economically oriented lawyers [had] los[t] sight" of very basic aspects of property rights. Their answer: "[M]odern legal economists [had become] interested not in the problem of order but in the maximization of welfare." Merrill and Smith deplore this tendency; they think it "overlooks . . . that the refined problems of concern in advanced economies exist at the apex of a pyramid, the base of which consists of the security of property rights." (Merrill and Smith, 2001, p. 398). Following Merrill and Smith's usages, in this entry, a "welfare-maximizing" approach assumes and applies unconstrained priors to economic analysis of law, while an "order-securing" approach assumes and applies constrained priors.

This entry uses "sparks cases" to illustrate the contrast between welfare-maximizing and order-securing legal theories of regulation—and to suggest possibilities for further scholarship deepening and extending the case for theories in the latter group. "Sparks cases" refer to common law tort cases between rail engine ("train") operators and the owners of land lots adjacent to railroad rights of way. It may seem parochial or narrow for a scholarly work to focus on sparks cases. The issues raised in such cases are technical, and the cases are hardly ever litigated anymore. (In the United States, most sparks cases were litigated between 1860 and 1920.) Nevertheless, sparks cases provide an excellent point of contact for our interests here. Contemporary American legal scholars often cite Ronald Coase's *The Problem of Social Cost* (1960) ("*Social Cost*") as paving the way for welfare-maximizing approaches to economic analysis of law. Coase used the sparks fact pattern as one of several key examples illustrating *Social Cost*'s main insights. Law and economic scholars often use the sparks fact pattern to illustrate new theoretical insights about the economic analysis of tort doctrine; many of those insights illustrate the preference for welfare-maximization criticized by Merrill and Smith. By the same token, leading sparks cases apply, in a rights-based vocabulary, many assumptions about legal rights and regulation operationally similar to key tenets of Austrian economics. Austrian economics cannot influence American legal scholarship without engaging legal doctrine, moral concepts, and economic analysis on the terms on which *legal* scholars are accustomed to engaging them. The following study of sparks explains and concretely illustrates the terms of engagement legal scholars expect.

I.   SPARKS CASES IN LEGAL DOCTRINE

Trains driven by coal-powered steam engines emit sparks, cinders, ash, and burning embers. These flammable emissions ("sparks" for short) can ignite grass on the train operator's right of way, and such fires can spread to nearby properties. Sparks can also float tens or even hundreds of feet from a railroad track, and then ignite nearby crops, grass, haystacks, or other materials on private property. When claims for property damage are made by the owners of land adjacent to railroad rights of way, the owners initiate sparks cases.

   Doctrinally, sparks cases have raised two main questions. First, when sparks ignite materials on private property, should the train operator be held strictly liable for any property damage—or should the land-owning plaintiff be required to prove that the operator negligently took substandard precautions against sparks fires? Different authorities have taken different approaches to this question. In England, in the 1860 case

Vaughan v. *Taff Vale Railway Co.*, Baron Bramwell, sitting as the trial judge in the Exchequer Court, instructed the jury to find the operator negligent if its engine was dangerous to adjacent property even if the train was operated with the utmost skill and care. "The defendants come to the [plaintiff's land]," Bramwell reasoned, with the plaintiff "being passive, and do it a mischief." The judges in the Exchequer Chamber, however, overruled Bramwell. Baron Cockburn and his colleagues believed that, when Parliament enacted a law authorizing the construction and operation of the rail line, the authorization had the effect in law "that if damage results from the use of the [authorized] thing independently of negligence, the party using it is not responsible."[1] In the 1880 case *Powell* v. *Fall*, however, the Queen's Bench tried another sparks case, found the train operator strictly liable for fire damage, and rejected the statutory argument that Cockburn and his colleagues had found decisive in *Vaughan*. This judgment was affirmed unanimously, and Baron Bramwell (now on the appellate court) specifically pointed out that 20 years of time had hardened his conviction that the Exchequer Chamber had decided *Vaughan* wrongly.[2] In the early nineteenth century, many American state courts required a sparks plaintiff to prove negligence. Gradually, however, state legislatures preempted such common law holdings. Some legislatures enacted statutes requiring that, if a land-owner proved he suffered property damage caused by a sparks fire, the court should presume the railroad operator liable unless it could disprove its negligence. Other statutes instituted strict liability. By the end of the nineteenth century, these relatively strict (and land-owner-favoring) legal rules prevailed over (railroad-favoring) negligence standards. (Ely, 2001, pp. 1234.)

Second, assuming that the railroad operator is *prima facie* liable, may the operator excuse that *prima facie* liability by proving contributory negligence—i.e., by blaming the land-owning plaintiff for negligently failing to move crops, haystacks, etc out of harm's way? Case law split on this issue as well. Hornbook law held that the land-owning plaintiff owed no duty to prevent contributory negligence. Since the "use of the land [by the plaintiff] was of itself a proper use"—that is, "it did not interfere with nor embarrass the rightful operation of the railroad"—the owner should not be "subject in its use to the careless as well as the careful operation of the [rail] road."[3] In a substantial number of cases, however, judges or courts

---

[1] *Vaughan* v. *Taff Vale Railway Co.*, 157 Eng. Rep. 667, 671 (Exch. Ct. 1858), overruled, 157 Eng. Rep. 1351, 1354 (1860).

[2] *Powell* v. *Fall*, Q.B. 597, 601 (1880).

[3] *LeRoy Fibre Co.* v. *Chicago, M. & St. P. Ry. Co.*, 232 U.S. 340, 349 (1914); see *Kellogg* v. *The Chicago & N.W. Ry. Co.*, 26 Wis. 223 (1870).

resisted applying this principle categorically. In the case just quoted (the 1914 U.S. Supreme Court decision *LeRoy Fibre Co.* v. *Chicago, Milwaukee & St. Paul Railway Co.*), Justice Oliver Wendell Holmes concurred separately to warn that this field of law turned on "differences of degree," it was at least possible that "a man [could] stack[] his flax so near to a railroad that it obviously was likely to be set fire to by a well-managed train," and a jury should thus be free to find the man contributorily negligent and disentitled from recovery.[4] Holmes described this hypothetical land-owning plaintiff as being negligent, but another court (the Kansas Supreme Court, in the 1877 case *Kansas Pacific Railway Co.* v. *Brady*) portrayed the same point as a matter of causation:

> If the defendant was negligent at all as against the plaintiffs, it was really as much because said hay was stacked in a dangerous place, and because dry grass was allowed to intervene all the way from the stack to the railway track, as because said fire was permitted to escape.[5]

II. SPARKS CASES IN "THE PROBLEM OF SOCIAL COST"

Whether readers find sparks cases interesting or quaint, in contemporary legal and economic scholarship they have become a stock example. They were made most popular by "Social Cost." In that article, Coase critiqued a conventional assumption shared among economists at the time: When an entity creates a negative externality for neighbors in the course of conducting a productive activity, the entity should be excluded from, made liable for, or taxed for creating the externality. Coase made four main arguments in response.

First, every negative externality created by an economic activity may be paired to a reciprocal externality that occurs if the government stops or penalizes the activity. As the Kansas Supreme Court had treated haystacks and sparks as reciprocal negative externalities, so Coase generalized: "We are dealing with a problem of a reciprocal nature. To avoid the harm to B would inflict harm on A." (Coase, 1960, p. 2.)

Second, if there were no transaction costs or resource constraints, and if actors pursued their rational economic interests, it would not matter how legal decision makers assigned starting legal rights. Neighbors with resource disputes would bargain to conduct activities at levels that would

---

[4] *LeRoy Fibre Co.*, ibid., 352–4 (Holmes, J., concurring).
[5] *Kansas P. Ry.* Co. v. *Brady*, 17 Kan. 380, 386 (1877).

maximize their joint product. Here, "joint product" means the difference created by subtracting, from the sum of the values of their productive activities, the sum of the externalities associated with both activities. If one party stood to generate a large surplus from its activity, it could pay the other from its surplus to reach that maximum joint product. (Coase, 1960, pp. 2–15.)

Third, however, because transaction costs do exist and vary in many ways, in practice, it might make a significant difference how legal decision makers initially assign legal entitlements relating to the activity. (Coase, 1960, pp. 15–42.) So, fourth and finally, before deciding that a tax, a liability system, a shut-down, or any other remedy will optimally induce a polluting entity to internalize negative externalities, an economist must consider, on one hand, all the ways in which parties might bargain around such legal rules and, on the other hand, all the ways in which transaction costs might distort such attempts to bargain.

To illustrate these arguments, Coase analyzed the facts of a sparks dispute at length. A.C. Pigou's economics textbook (1932) illustrated the conventional assumptions Coase was challenging. Pigou had used sparks as an illustration of the conventional approach. When train sparks inflicted damage on adjacent woods, Pigou had argued, an economist could not sum up the total net social product without subtracting for the losses wood owners suffered by sparks fires. (Pigou, 1932, p. 134). Coase concluded that Pigou's economic analysis had been faulty.

Coase developed several counter-examples illustrating problems in Pigou's analysis. Coase supposed that a railway, *not* liable for sparks fires, had the choice to run two trains per day with the following profit function:[6]

Table 11.1

	Value of services performed	Cost to railroad of operation	Net value
Train 1	$150	(−$50)	$100
Train 2	$100	(−$50)	$50
Trains 1 and 2	$250	(−$100)	$150

He then supposed that each train would inflict $60 of crop or other property damage per run. That property damage diminishes the value of each railroad run:

---

[6] In all of the following tables, negative numbers are indicated with parentheses and also a negative sign.

Table 11.2

	Value of services performed	Cost to railroad of operation	Cost to farmers	Net value
Train 1	$150	(−$50)	(−$60)	$40
Train 2	$100	(−$50)	(−$60)	(−$10)
Trains 1 and 2	$250	(−$100)	(−$120)	$30

If these figures were accurate, Coase acknowledged, it would be better if train 2 did not run. Yet Coase doubted that these figures would be accurate or complete in real life. The figures assume that owners with land near train tracks would not generate any income from their crops unless they received damage payments from the railroad; in real life, farmers could sell (unburnt) crops on the market. Pigovian payments could distort farmers' incentives to sell crops in competitive markets. If the railway were liable, farmers would be indifferent whether they received revenue for their crops from sale or from liability payments from the railroad. If the railway were *not* liable, the farmer would take out of cultivation land that would not be cost-justified to farm when the costs of expected crop damage were factored in. Liability would generate more crops—and more liability payments by the railroad.

Coase assumed more hypothetical data to illustrate his points. On one hand, he assumed that, if the railroad was held liable for crop damage, the liability rule would encourage farmers to double their crop production. Under that assumption, if the railroad were required to pay some sort of Pigovian payment, no railroad runs would generate positive joint product:

Table 11.3

	Value of services performed	Cost to railroad of operation	Cost to farmers	Net value
Train 1	$150	(−$50)	(−$120)	(−$20)
Train 2	$100	(−$50)	(−$120)	(−$70)
Trains 1 and 2	$250	(−$100)	(−$240)	(−$90)

On the other hand, Coase insisted, a full analysis would also need to consider the possibility that the coming of the railroad might *deter* farmers from planting and raising crops on some parts of their land. Farmers would lose value from farming these parts, but make it up by switching to the next best uses of the land abandoned. Coase illustrated as follows:

Table 11.4

	Value of services performed	Cost to railroad of operation	Cost to farmers from crop damage	Cost to farmers from not farming	Value of farmers' next best uses	Net value
Trains 1 and 2	$250	(−$100)	(−$120)	(−$160)	$150	$20

With these assumed figures, if the railroad were not held liable for crop damage, the railroad would increase joint product by operating. Since Pigovian payments would generate negative joint product (by stimulating an increase in crop damage, see Table 11.3), Coase concluded "that it is better that the railway should not be liable for the damage it causes, thus enabling it to operate profitably. Of course, by altering the figures, it could be shown that there are other cases in which it would be desirable that the railway should be liable for the damage it causes." For Coase's purposes, it did not matter what the relevant data indicated in real life; the important point was "that, from an economic point of view, a situation in which there is 'uncompensated damage done to surrounding woods by sparks . . .' is not necessarily undesirable." (Coase, 1960, pp. 33–4; see also pp. 28–34).

When he made arguments like the ones just recounted, Coase was not necessarily prescribing that legal entitlements be assigned in the manner most likely to maximize net joint product. Coase wrote "Social Cost" to economists, to challenge conventional assumptions (which he attributed to Pigou) about the relationship between economic activity and government fines or regulation. In the above passages, Coase was careful to specify that his prescriptions were all made "from an economic point of view." And, he reminded economist readers, "that the immediate question faced by the courts is *not* what shall be done by whom *but* who has the legal right to do what." (Coase, 1960, p. 15).

Nevertheless, in law and economic scholarship, *Social Cost* has been read to justify and anticipate legal scholars' prescribing legal entitlements based on economic analysis. (I will refer to this reading of Coase as "the Coasean Coase." Merrill and Smith, 2011; Claeys, 2010a, p. 1387). In arguments like the ones just recounted, "Social Cost" portrayed economic analysis as determinate, careful, and open to considering the future consequences of legal rules. In other parts of "Social Cost," Coase portrayed standard judicial legal reasoning as indeterminate and thoughtless. For example, after reporting and analyzing several nuisance cases, Coase described "[t]he reasoning employed by the courts in determining legal rights" as seeming "strange to an economist," and he described one judicial argument as "about as relevant as the colour of the judge's eyes." (Coase, 1960, p. 15; see Merrill and Smith, 2011; Merrill and Smith, 2001).

III.   SPARKS CASES IN LAW AND ECONOMIC SCHOLARSHIP

A substantial segment of law and economic scholarship equates "Social Cost's" argument with the approach associated with the Coasean Coase. This scholarship applies "Social Cost's" insights in the opposite direction from Coase's argument—i.e., it uses economic analysis to prescribe substantive legal entitlements.

In legal scholarship, sparks cases are used in two main ways. In more general scholarship, authors use sparks cases simply to illustrate "Social Cost's" main lessons. Richard Posner (2011, p. 63) uses a sparks fact pattern in this manner, to illustrate the basics of regulating what he calls "incompatible uses." Posner does not generate any hard and fast prescription about incompatible-use regulation; instead, he works through several different approximations, each highlighting important factors a thorough economic analysis would consider. When one considers Posner's presentation in its entirety, however, it strongly suggests that judges can administer incompatible uses, while taking account of extremely detailed, party- and context-specific information, to maximize the joint utilities of the regulated parties.

Posner starts with two inversely-related curves, one for the railroad's marginal profits per extra train and another for farmers' marginal costs per extra train. In stage 1, Posner suggests that the socially-optimal "uses" of trains and crops occur at the point where the curve for the railroad's (decreasing) marginal profit per train crosses the curve for the farmers' (increasing) marginal cost per train. Here, Posner is not yet making prescriptions for judges; he is identifying an economic ideal state. As "Social Cost" teaches, this state is the optimum to which the parties would bargain if transaction costs are not prohibitively large. Note, however, that *if* a court did try to require parties to reach this ideal state, the trier of fact would need to learn and grasp the railroad's profit curve and the farmers' cost curve. The trier of fact would also need to administer both parties' operations in as much detail as a public utility regulator regulates the prices and services of a railroad or a cable company.

As stage 2, Posner starts to make legal prescriptions. He qualifies the presentation in stage 1, for situations in which transactions costs prevent the parties from bargaining. In such cases, "efficiency is promoted by assigning the legal right to the party who would buy it" if the judge or regulator (mistakenly) assigned the relevant legal right to the wrong party at stage 1. Here, Posner assumes a judge or regulator can identify the most likely impediments to market bargaining. At stage 3, Posner then calls into question the assumptions crucial to stages 1 and 2. At stage 3, he exposes "the costs of administering the property-rights system, which might be lower under a simpler criterion for assigning rights," and he acknowledges that "it is difficult to apply in practice" the (stage 1) ideal of requiring the parties to use their properties at the levels where the railroad's marginal profit curve intersects with the farmers' marginal cost curve.

At stage 3, Posner acknowledges that, in practice, it might be difficult for courts to conduct the analyses he has suggested in stages 1 and 2. Among other things, public decision makers must choose among an "endless" list of possible of combinations of farmer and train activities. "[I]t is unrealistic to expect courts to discover the optimum one – and uneconomical to make them search too hard for it!" Nevertheless, without any explanation, Posner immediately disregards these practical problems: "[I]n most cases, and without excessive cost, [courts] may be able to approximate the optimum definition of property rights, and these approximations may guide resource use more efficiently than would an economically random assignment of rights." (Posner, 2011, pp. 66–7.)

Separately, sparks cases are used in law and economics scholarship to illustrate different economic insights about accident precautions. Consider for example Cooter (1985). In this article, Cooter highlights a theoretical paradox. On one hand, whenever a party can take precautions to diminish losses created by an incompatible-use conflict with another party, it is efficient to make that party liable for all harm caused. On the other hand, if both parties to a bilateral dispute can take precautions against losses, there is no way to make them both take efficient precautions. The more the law makes one party responsible, the more it encourages the other to leave precautions to the first party. Cooter modeled the paradox formally and suggested that the most likely way to achieve the efficient levels of precautions and losses was to condition each party's recovery or responsibility on its taking reasonable (i.e., legally non-negligent) precautions. Although Cooter illustrated with several examples, his lead example consisted of sparks cases. A railroad can take precautions against a sparks fire by installing a sparks arrester, by ordering trains to run more slowly, or by running fewer trains—but farmers can plant their crops elsewhere, plant crops unlikely to burn, or leave their fields fallow.

In the same spirit, Grady (1988) surveyed American sparks cases to corroborate observations about strategic behavior by parties in cases in which both could take precautions against accidental losses. According to Grady, a party may take precautions against incompatible-use losses in any of three periods. The first is a "preparation period," when the party is trying to protect his own person or resources in advance, without knowing what precautions other individuals will take against accidental loss. The second is a "reaction period," when the accident is occurring and the party is trying to avoid further loss to himself or his property. The last is a "mitigation period," in which the accident has ended but the party may reduce its adverse consequence to himself or others. In Grady's interpretation, American sparks cases applied different doctrines of negligence as appropriate to incentivize railroads and land owners each to take the efficient precautions available in each period. Courts held railroads liable for failing to install adequate protections against sparks fires (like arresters) and also for failing to take reasonable care to keep tracks and rights of way free of combustible materials. Courts required landowners, as a condition of recovering for sparks damage, to take preparation-period precautions— e.g., not to build structures too near rights of way, and not to leave wood shavings or other combustibles near rights of way. Courts did not require landowners, however, to take reaction-period precautions—e.g., to tamp down fires as soon as they started.

In law and economic scholarship on the private law, authors are not always entirely clear about the precise contributions they intend their works to make. Some economically-oriented works of legal scholarship make "full-blown normative arguments." More, however, "(implicitly) advanc[e] a limited and contingent normative argument ... 'To the extent that you care about efficiency as a value, you should care about the following conclusions.'" (Craswell, 2003, p. 906.) Cooter (1985) is better read as making a limited and contingent normative argument: if efficiency has normative value, then the policy maker must consider how general efficiency-based prescriptions about precautions may be difficult to apply when both parties may take precautions. In contrast, Grady (1988) clearly makes full-blown normative arguments. In normative terms, Grady assumes that tort doctrine promotes efficiency if it forces parties to take precautions feasible in one of his three periods. As he read the facts of the cases he presented, courts did require parties to take precautions when (judging the facts as reported) such precautions seemed feasible. So in positive terms, Grady concludes that the relevant tort law was in fact efficient. (In its treatment of sparks cases, it is difficult to pin down Posner (2011) along this spectrum.)

IV. AUSTRIAN REACTIONS TO WELFARE-MAXIMIZING LAW AND ECONOMIC SCHOLARSHIP

Law and economic analysis has brought great insights to law, and law and economic works have provoked helpful debate about the foundations of property rights, liability in tort, and public law alternatives to both. In particular, works like those just recounted help identify important consequences of alternative legal rules. Such works create heuristics; whatever their other limitations, at least those heuristics force legal decision makers to consider trade-offs.

In analyzing those consequences and trade-offs, however, the works just recounted make important assumptions and normative arguments characteristic of welfare-maximizing economic analysis. Scholars sympathetic to Austrian economics have noticed those assumptions and arguments—and criticized them. Such Austrian sympathizers, however, have made their criticisms generally and abstractly—*not* by engaging particular legal doctrines or economic analyses, at the level of particularity to which legal scholars are accustomed.

For example, Rizzo (1980, p. 641) advanced two main arguments: "if the normative case for common law efficiency has any validity at all, it can only be for concepts of efficiency for which the information requirements are exceedingly high," and "partial efficiency is insufficient as a basis for constructing any persuasive normative argument." Rizzo proved these theses with several different arguments. First, analyzing leading hypotheses about the relation between law, efficiency, and wealth, Rizzo concluded that none of them could make clear positive prescriptions or normative arguments without collapsing into tautology or non-verifiability. Second, Rizzo sketched several general reasons why wealth-maximizing theories could not produce or validate a coherent theory of legal rights: wealth effects, relative price effects, and problems measuring wealth across societies with substantially different rights. Similarly, Rizzo suggested several reasons why it might be difficult or impossible to explain what it means to make a "marginal" change in legal rules, or to predict whether legal rules supply *"ex ante"* compensation.

Cordato (1992) attempted to work out the implications of Austrian economics for law and economics at some length. Cordato argued that it was impossible for economic analysis to identify legal arrangements that are efficient in relation to social welfare—i.e., they allocate resources to their highest and best use more effectively than alternative arrangements. To make this argument, Cordato relied on primary Austrian themes: time and change; the limits of the knowledge of actors and regulators; and the subjectivity of value. As an alternative to efficiency defined in relation to social welfare, Cordato proposed that Austrian economics focus on promoting what he called "catallactic efficiency," an arrangement in which individuals, in a social community but with different individual goals, may accomplish their own goals more effectively than they could in alternative arrangements. A political community could achieve catallactic efficiency, Cordato continued, *not* by having legal decision makers allocate resources as they thought most likely to maximize social welfare, but rather by enforcing basic rules of property and contract. Such rules embody and implement an "ideal institutional setting" (or "IIS"), a set of conventions which members of the political community intuitively judge by how well it frees them all use property or make promises to satisfy their own preferences. (Cordato, 1992, pp. 4–10, 57–68, 99–105).

Cordato did apply these general arguments to a case example—Coase's treatment of sparks disputes. "The principle question that a judge must ask in resolving this dispute is not whether the farmer or the railroad contributes more to the social value of output, but who owns the land that is acting as a receptacle for the sparks." (Cordato, 1992, p. 100). In Coase's portrait, this issue is "unimportant." In Cordato's view, by contrast, the most important and useful function a legal decision maker may perform is uphold the IIS—by enforcing the conventions members of the society have adopted to give specific content to property and contract rights. For example, sparks cases arise against a backdrop in which land-owners are entitled to exclude most trespassory invasions from their lots. Decision makers should hold railroads strictly liable for sparks damage because injurious sparks constitute invasions of the sort that deprive land-owners of their property. Judges promote catallactic efficiency not directly, by reasoning about what efficiency requires, but rather by enforcing legal rights grounded in common political and ethical commitments to the IIS. (Cordato, 1992, pp. 100–103). (Drawing on non-economic legal tort scholarship, Cordato called this approach "corrective justice." See Epstein, 1979, 1973). In other words, judges can only, and should only, focus on securing the conditions of private ordering.

Finally, some Austrians have gone even farther than Cordato—by suggesting that the analysis of law should be treated as basically separate from economics. Here, Rothbard (1982) is instructive. Rothbard confronted Coase and in particular Coase's use of sparks hypotheticals—among other reasons because his approach, while "pretending to be value-free ... in reality import[s] the ethical norm of 'efficiency,' and assert[s] that property rights should be assigned on the basis of such efficiency." Rothbard proposed instead to ground legal analysis in self-ownership, the principle that "[n]o action should be considered illicit or illegal unless it invades, or aggresses against, the person or just property of another." (Here, "justice" entitles every person to be a "self-owner, having absolute jurisdiction over his own body.") (Rothbard, 1982, pp. 59–60).

Rizzo (1980) criticized assumptions central to the welfare-maximizing tendencies in contemporary law and economics. Yet he did not illustrate any of his criticisms with particular case examples (like train sparks) or theoretical examples (like analysis of efficient precautions). However appropriate Rizzo's criticisms are, they are formal, and not likely to engage economically-oriented legal scholars in the manner to which they are accustomed.

Cordato and Rothbard referenced sparks cases and other similar cases. Yet they focused primarily on sketching how such cases could and should be decided by principles of justice—in Rothbard's case, a libertarian theory of self-ownership or, in Cordato's case, a theory of corrective justice implementing and enforcing the IIS. Neither Cordato nor Rothbard considered welfare-maximizing economic analyses of sparks cases at length.

* * * * *

In short, Austrian scholars have responded to welfare-maximizing law and economic scholarship in at least two significant ways. One has been to criticize the epistemological and economic priors of that scholarship's economics. The other has been to change the subject, to explain and justify law and legal rights in theories of justice independent of economics. Each of these responses will be considered (respectively) in each of the next two parts.

V.   AN AUSTRIAN CRITIQUE OF PREVIOUS ANALYSES OF SPARKS DISPUTES

There is considerable force to Austrian critiques of the economic priors of welfare-maximizing law and economic scholarship. To be sure, to date, the critiques have not resonated in American legal scholarship. Among other reasons, criticisms like Rizzo's and Cordato's have not been made using more legal examples, and they have not considered welfare-maximizing scholarly works on those works' own terms. This Part illustrates how Rizzo's and Cordato's criticisms could be articulated, to make the criticisms more immediately relevant to the criteria by which law and economic scholarship is judged.

A.   Property, Rights, Harm, and Causation in Legal Doctrine

The first place to focus is on the conceptual structure of the common law. Although law and economic scholarship tends to stress "economics" over the "law," the scholarship suffers significantly if it does not respect legal doctrine and institutions as they exist in real life. Posner, Cooter, Grady, and the Coasean Coase all portray basic common-law concepts in a manner alien to social practice and the common law.

Most important, there is a huge gulf between the meanings of a property "right" at common law and in "Social Cost"-inspired law and economic scholarship. (Claeys, 2011, 2010a, pp. 1432–7; Merrill and Smith, 2001). In the latter, "property" means neither "ownership" nor "using [an asset] as a factor of production" but rather "a right to carry out a circumscribed list of actions." (Coase, 1960, p. 44). Implicitly, a "right" is an entitlement, conferred by the government, to carry out a particular use at levels and subject to conditions spelled out by the state. A *property* right consists of such an entitlement when it relates to an external asset.

By contrast, at common law and in common morality, "rights" refer to domains of freedom or decisional authority. Such domains are structured to give many different individuals authority to decide—simultaneously, each right-holder for himself—how to use a given resource for his own individual benefit. That is the meaning the U.S. Supreme Court assumed in *LeRoy Fibre*, when it observed that the land-owning plaintiff's land use "was of itself a proper use—it did not interfere with nor embarrass the rightful operation of the railroad." It is also the meaning that Baron Bramwell assumed in *Vaughan*, when he assumed that Vaughan deserved a right to enjoy the "natural and proper" "use" of his land free from trespassory invasions creating fires or other risks of accident. In both cases, the plaintiffs enjoyed a general domain of freedom to decide how to use their land. That freedom was subject to outer boundaries, so that neither the plaintiff nor any other land-owner could assert decisional freedom inconsistent with or greater than the general freedom enjoyed by every other resident. Conduct that claimed greater freedom than allowable would (in *LeRoy Fibre*'s terms) "interfere with [or] embarrass" neighbors.

When they neglect or reject this understanding of rights, Posner, Cooter, and the Posnerian Coase then invert the conceptual structure of "harm." If *A* and *B*'s "rights" refer to incompatible and reciprocal permissions to engage in two particular conflicting uses, then it makes sense to assume, as "Social Cost" does, that "[t]o avoid the harm to *B* would inflict harm on *A*." Harm is not reciprocal, however, if a property right refers to a domain of freedom or legitimate decisional authority. Then, conceptual "harm" occurs only when one party's use exceeds the proper bounds of his decisional authority, and diminishes the corresponding authority of another party.

This relation is easiest to see not in property disputes but in personal disputes involving physical violence. Assume that B injures A while successfully repelling A's attempt to hold him up. In Coase's framework, the injuries B inflicts on A are reciprocal negative externalities on A's desire for money from B. In common sense, B has a right to bodily security and liberty, A's hold-up threatens B's security and liberty, and B inflicts no moral or legal harm on A because he acts legitimately to repel a threat to his own rights. With appropriate adjustments, the same relations apply to property disputes. Even if B planted crops where A's cinders could burn them, if A was the only party who invaded someone else's rights, A is the sole "cause" of recognized social "harm." (Claeys, 2010a, pp. 1393–4, 1405–14). The common law structures and protects land-owners' legitimate decisional authority by protecting them from unconsented particulate entries across their boundaries. The physical-invasion test endows owners with freedom to choose how to use their land, more or less as a physical-touching test protects people's rights to deploy their bodies toward goals of their own choosing. On that basis, one land-owner "harms" another *not* by diminishing the economic value of activities on the other's land, but rather by diminishing that owner's zone of free choice. That understanding explains why, in *LeRoy Fibre Co.*, the Court spoke of the "harm" as follows: "That one's uses of his property may be subject to the servitude of the wrongful use by another seems an anomaly." The land-owner had a right to set the "uses" of his property; the railroad engaged in conduct "wrongful" because it diminished that right. That understanding also explains the contrast Bramwell drew between Vaughan's "passive" use of his land and the railway company's "mischievous" use of its right of way. Even conceding that a railway constitutes a valuable activity, it inflicts more physical disruptions on neighbors than the other way around, and it diminishes neighbors' spheres of free and equal choice how to manage their lots than they do to it.

The same contrast recurs in scholarly treatments of legal causation. The Kansas Supreme Court made a conceptual mistake when it equated the harm caused by sparks with the harm caused by putting haystacks in the likely path of sparks. Conceptually, a party "causes" harm only if it causes a *harm*—i.e., a significant setback to a party's moral interests. And such harms cannot be ascertained without knowing which interests inhere in the party's moral rights. That is why the U.S. Supreme Court assumed that the railroad was the "immediate cause" of moral and legal harm to the land-owner but not vice versa.[7] The Kansas Supreme Court's portrait makes more sense in a context like "Social Cost"—where the legal rights are taken as givens and the focus is on transacting with the rights given. It makes much less sense when the rights are the object of focus—as they are for Cooter, Grady, Posner, and the Coasean Coase.

As just recounted, in lay discourse and in law, the terms "right," "harm," and "cause" all assume and contain implicit moral content. Some scholars may think that the reciprocal negative externality framework avoids that moral content—and find the framework preferable because it avoids moral issues. Yet the externality framework is confused practically and philosophically—and the confusions seem likely to have the effect of obscuring the issues that seem most salient from a commonsensical moral perspective. A railway company inflicts a loss on an adjacent farm when sparks from its trains ignite crops or personal articles on the farm. The farm, by itself, does not inflict any corresponding loss on the railway. The farm owner may petition a legal official to enjoin trains or impose liability on the railway company, and these legal orders may inflict losses on the company. But the harms or externalities that the government causes when it orders the railway company to stop violating property rights are conceptually and normatively different from the losses the parties' conflicting land uses impose on one another. (Coleman 1980, pp. 235–6.) The government should not be allowed to limit the freedom of the railway or take money from it unless it can show that it has legitimate authority to do so—as it would if the farmer has legitimate property rights and the government is protecting them. Similarly, the railway company should not be allowed to inflict losses on the farmer unless it can show that it inflicts those losses in the legitimate exercise of a right. A defendant could make such a showing if the plaintiff and the defendant were competitors and the plaintiff suffered losses because the defendant sold a better product. Or if (as in another of Coase's examples) the defendant inflicted losses on the plaintiff in the course of repelling back to the plaintiff pollution originally emitted from the plaintiff's property.[8] From a conceptual perspective, however, when the losses going each way are classified as reciprocal negative externalities, that classification obscures what in law and morality are the most salient questions: whether the railway company has a general right to emit sparks, whether the farmer has a general right to farm free from risk-threatening trespasses, and whether the government has justification to intervene to protect one or the other party's rights.

---

[7] *LeRoy Fibre Co.*, 348, 349.
[8] See *Bryant* v. *Lefever*, 4 C.P.D. 172 (1878–79), cited in Coase 1960, 11–13.

To be sure, even if one has a sound grasp of the concepts "right," "harm," and "causation," these concepts do not by any stretch determine the scope of the "rights" and "wrongs" relevant to property law. River water, personal articles, land, trade secrets, patents, and copyrights all confer different domains of decisional authority. Yet there are obvious normative reasons why the possessory interest for land should be extremely broad: privacy, personal autonomy, security of investment, and clarity of rights for the purposes of transaction. Presumptively, any unconsented entry onto land—by a person, by a projectile, or by a spark or another low-level physical invasion—diminishes land-owners' presumptive freedom to decide how their lots should be used. Many presumptive invasions end up being excused at common law because the invasions do not threaten and perhaps even encourage common uses of land. Nuisance law excuses barbeque smoke and the noises from lawn-mowing, in the expectation that neighbors bothered by these low-level nuisances will benefit reciprocally when *their* neighbors are bothered by their music-playing or lawn-mowing. However, sparks cannot be excused with such a justification. They create a risk of fire and property damage to land-owners, but land-owners do not generate reciprocal risks of accidents on railroad rights of way that could be excused like low-level nuisances.

That normative justification for land rights then explains the character of sparks law. In principle, any invasion by a spark onto land wrongfully diminishes land-owners' rightful control to decide how to use their land. Sparks law excuses harmless sparks invasions for administrative reasons. When sparks inflict actual property damage, however, this excuse ceases to apply. At that point, the railroad should be deemed strictly liable. Furthermore, since the wrong from the spark is its disruption to the land-owner's freedom to decide how to use his land, it is indeed an "anomaly" to say that the land-owner owes a duty to anticipate and take counter-measures against the possibility of property damage from sparks fires.

B. Time, Ignorance, Subjectivity, and Sparks

In short, the concept of a "reciprocal negative externality" delinks the analysis of a sparks dispute from contexts presumed in law and common sense discourse. Legal and common sense link the dispute to the relevant legal right, namely the right of the land-owner to determine how his land will be used. That right is structured as it is to fulfill a few different over-determining goals. Many of those goals assume that, other things being equal, in a broad range of situations, the land-owner is better situated than the train operator, other non-owners, or courts and juries how his land may best be used.

Austrian economics can flesh out the links in this argument. Austrian economics have a lot to say about the last link (about which party is best situated to manage a resource and know its best uses) and also about the limits of attempts by outside lawyers or economists to forecast a resource's highest and best use. In different ways, the works recounted in the last Part all study in isolation a few practical policy issues raised by sparks cases—and then jump to the conclusions that their studies of *parts* of the relevant issues are relevant to knowing how the *whole* should be regulated in practice. For Austrian economists, the trick is to identify all the policy issues relevant to the whole any legal doctrine tries to regulate—and then to show how limited the partial contributions are.

Grady's study illustrates. Grady derides the concepts discussed in the last section much as Coase did—as "rigid," and in the grip of a "pristine idea of right colliding with wrong." (Grady, 1988, pp. 30, 33). This criticism assumes that an economist or a court can maximize the joint social product of a railroad and the activities of one or a few land-owners, and criticizes a legal approach that declines to increase welfare where it can. The common law, by contrast, prefers to focus on securing the minimal conditions of order. For example, in *LeRoy Fibre*, when the U.S. Supreme Court rejected contributory negligence, it insisted: "Depart from the simple requirement of the law, that everyone must use his property so as not to injure others, and you pass to refinements and confusing considerations."[9] The Court justified the common law not in terms of efficiency or welfare but justice and rights—in particular, "property" grounded in each owner's having a right of free "use" choice structured to give other members of the community equal rights of similar use choice. (Claeys, 2010a, pp. 1398–407.) When the Court spoke of the dangers of "refinements" and "confusing considerations," however, it voiced practical concerns that may be explained in economic terminology.

To be sure, Austrian economics is not absolutely indispensable to explaining these concerns in economic terms. After all, Coase was not an Austrian, and yet he warned against taking his insights about the economics of resource disputes too seriously as a guide to resource administration. Such administration "would require a detailed knowledge of individual preferences and I am unable to imagine how the data needed for such a taxation system could be assembled," and "the proposal to solve . . . smoke-pollution and similar problems by the use of taxes bristles with difficulties: the problem of calculation, the difference between average and marginal damage, the interrelations between the damage suffered on

---

[9]   *LeRoy Fibre Co.*, 350.

different properties, etc." (Coase, 1960, pp. 41–2). Nevertheless, Austrian economics deserves pride of place in any discussion of the limits of economic analysis. Temporal change, limits in human knowledge, and the subjectivity of value capture the problems that plague welfare-maximizing law and economic analysis.

Change, knowledge limits, and the subjectivity of value all constrain how much public decision makers can know about the operations of the railroad and land-owner: about their profit functions, the costs from accidents or corresponding liability payments, or the costs of implementing precautions. The analyses in Parts II and III assume that these figures are knowable—knowable enough to depict in tables like Tables 11.1 through 11.4 or in a graph (like Posner's) of marginal profit and cost curves. Yet it is at least possible, and from everyday life it seems quite likely, that these various costs and profits fluctuate drastically depending on many factors. It also seems possible and even likely that the land-owner and the railroad will value the different profits and costs extremely differently. If so, then it is inappropriate to depict the various costs in terms of things like repair costs, and it is inappropriate to depict profits in simple monetary terms. Indeed, it is inappropriate to depict the profits and costs with *single figures*. The railroad probably values all the profits and costs extremely differently from the land-owner. In addition, time and change may complicate analysis further. The land-owner and railroad's valuations may change depending on how markets for crops, transportation service, fuel, and other factors change. In addition, if both act in an economically rational manner, each should behave game-theoretically. Each should increase or decrease precautions when the other does the opposite. Accident losses should vary across time for similar reasons; the more trains the railroad runs, the fewer crops the farmer may plant (Claeys, 2010a, pp. 1437–40).

By contrast, when legal rights are keyed toward physical invasions, these informational problems are diminished significantly.[10] Decision makers only need to inquire whether owners have suffered physical invasions, whether they have suffered harm as a result of the invasions, and whether

---

[10]   The problems are "diminished," not eliminated. Many items listed in text do get considered in common law—later, if a defendant is liable and the court must determine the appropriate damages or other remedies. Even so, this process simplifies the common law's decisional process. *Prima facie* theories of liability rely on simple boundary rules and invasion tests to specify the content of legal rights. Courts consider more party-specific information only when they have concluded that defendants have wronged plaintiffs' rights. That conclusion simplifies what courts do with party-specific information; they inquire mainly what relief is necessary to restore plaintiffs to their rights.

the invasion and harm may be excused by reciprocal invasions running in the other direction. These tests *avoid* forcing decision makers to identify party-subjective value. The tests leave all property owners free to enjoy and protect their subjective values in the land uses closest and most tangibly *on* their properties—on condition that they all also waive rights to claim value in land uses remote from or physically removed from their properties.

These subjectivity, informational, and game-theoretic difficulties seem severe enough when the public decision maker is trying to administer a pure bilateral dispute. They seem exponentially more severe when the decision maker is trying to administer a dispute with many parties—say, many railroads using the same track, and all the owners with land along the track. Different legal entitlements differ in the information costs they impose on third parties. (Merrill and Smith, 2011, pp. S91–S92; Merrill and Smith, 2000). Furthermore, in sparks cases, courts and regulators settle disputes *ex post*, after losses have occurred. The information costs are even greater *ex ante*—if a railroad commission is trying to settle disputes prophylactically, or if a train operator is trying to identify thousands of farmers along a right of way, determine whether it will be liable, and if so head off litigation by purchasing pollution easements. By contrast, boundary rules simplify the determinations judges or regulators must make to determine legal liability, and they also simplify the forecasts any railroad must make about whether it will be liable to any particular owner.

Yet temporal change and the subjectivity of value can have even more far-reaching influence—on the content of legal property rights. Although boundary rules and invasion tests help steer owners' control over the use of their assets, they are also structured to be apolitical. Triers of fact must determine only: where boundaries lie; whether a defendant's conduct invades those boundaries; and (in some doctrines, like nuisance) whether the invasions may be excused on the ground that they are characteristic of a class of reciprocal invasions incidental to beneficial land uses common in the area. Farmers, railroads, or other constituencies may consider lobbying the legislature to preempt the common law and to institute a new rule more partial to their particular factional interests—but clear and simple rules may seem fair and stable enough that the disputants leave well enough alone.

But assume that, in sparks cases and in many other trespass, accident, or pollution disputes, public decision makers maximize the social products of the parties with the strongest interests in the disputes. Such a standard requires parties to submit more information to the decision maker. The facts to be found require decision makers to make more judgments, and judgments that are more subjective and contestable, than the factual findings involved in boundary rules and invasion tests. When legal standards are open-ended and indeterminate, disputants will submit more partisan information, about their costs, profits, precautions, and so forth. The less clear the rules, the more likely it is that polluters will refuse to bargain early or settle quickly, knowing that they are *prima facie* liable; instead, they will be more likely to litigate, in the hope that they can persuade a trier of fact that their activities generate great social wealth, that the owners suffering pollution are better cost-avoiders or precaution-takers, and so forth. And if parties are dissatisfied with indeterminate and politicized decision making by common law courts, they are more likely to lobby legislators. Indeed, if the relevant legal standards are indeterminate, the law may encourage disputants to believe that they are *entitled* to legal rights, ones which guarantee to them what they subjectively believe to be the true values of their assets and those assets' uses. The more disputants litigate and lobby for preferential legislative regulation, the less property rights are respected, the less parties bargain in markets, and the more they divert resources, which might have been invested in crop production, hay supply, or so forth, instead on further litigation and lobbying. (Claeys, 2010a, pp. 1441–2).

C.   The Limits of Welfare-Maximizing Law and Economic Methodologies

None of the foregoing predictions or analyses are obviously right. Yet none of them are obviously wrong. At a minimum, there is a huge gulf between the accounts of sparks disputes (recounted in Part III) by welfare-maximizing law and economic scholars and the account given in the last section. That gulf illustrates, in a very concrete way, the way in which unconstrained and constrained priors drive different economic analyses of law to sharply different approaches and conclusions.

In addition, there are also reasons for preferring the Austrian analysis sketched in the last section over the accounts recounted in Part III. If Austrian priors about change, the limits of human knowledge, and the subjectivity of value seem generally more faithful to how people process social knowledge than their opposites, then the predictions and analyses supplied in the last section are more persuasive than mainline, welfare-maximizing law and economic analyses like those by Posner, Cooter, and Grady.

In addition, law and economic scholars often judge economic analyses of law by the extent to which they conform to existing doctrine. Analyses like those in Part III and the last section make "claims [that] are implicitly empirical but not capable of precise justification." In the absence of such justification, law and economic scholars accept as a tiebreaker whether a given explanation is consistent with "the very strong set of practices in legal systems," in the expectation that a "judgment has been made" in favor of that explanation, "perhaps unconsciously, by large numbers of persons who have been forced to confront" law's economic tradeoffs. (Epstein, 1997, p. 2095). The account supplied in the last section explains not only how the relevant common law doctrines treat sparks cases but also how they regulate land-use disputes generally. (Claeys, 2010a, 1398–430). By contrast, while Posner and Cooter use sparks disputes to illustrate their approaches to economic analysis, neither discusses whether their analyses conform to existing law. Grady (1988) claims that his analysis fits the case law; although courts may have insisted on strict property boundaries and physical-invasion tests in cases like *LeRoy Fibre*, he argues, in practice courts behaved more like the *Kansas Pacific Railway v. Brady* court when strict boundary rules really mattered. Here, the positive question (how did courts really decide sparks cases) becomes intertwined inextricably with the deep methodological, epistemological, and normative questions that distinguish welfare-maximizing and order-securing theories of economics. If one accepts welfare-maximizing priors, courts could and should focus on precautions—and thus legal scholars may and should treat cases like *Kansas Pacific Railway* as the general-rule cases. If one prefers order-securing priors, *Kansas Pacific Railway* and similar cases should be regarded as aberrational decisions; they gamble that they can enlarge the net joint product of a few specific parties without destabilizing property rights generally.

The same gulf also helps expose and highlight limits in traditional welfare-maximizing law and economic methodologies. Grady's analysis is the most ambitious, but it is the most contestable for the reasons just recounted: Because it focuses on a few retail-level consequences issues (about precautions in sparks disputes), it does not consider whether wholesale-level concerns (about the clarity and security of property rights) dwarf retail-level consequences. The analysis of Posner is similar to Grady's. Posner assumes in the first instance that courts can forecast which legal assignment of rights will maximize joint social product, and save the parties the transaction costs of bargaining to that assignment. He qualifies this assumption out of respect for "the costs of administering the property-rights system, which might be lower under a simpler criterion for assigning rights"—but then, without elaboration, assumes "in most cases, and without excessive cost, [courts] may be able to approximate the optimum definition of property rights." (Posner, 2011, pp. 66–7). Like Grady, Posner does not explain why retail-level analysis of joint product will not be overwhelmed by wholesale problems that come with maintaining a system of property rights and markets.

In contrast, Cooter (1985) makes the most cautious, limited, and contingent claim: if efficiency is a value worth considering while setting legal doctrine, then the problems that arise when both parties can take precautions count as one of several factors that decision makers should consider in the course of setting doctrine. If information is limited, change is the rule and not the exception, and party values are subjective and heterogeneous, however, then in practice it is impossible for a decision maker to know how much weight to give Cooter's analysis of double-precaution problems. Cooter's work deserves credit for its elegance and insight about one retail-level effect. If Austrian priors are correct, however, this effect contributes extremely little to the factors on which legal decision makers can realistically focus in practice. Decision makers may and should disregard Cooter's precaution effect, on the ground that the best they can do is to institute legal rights that encourage apolitical decision making and steer to owners control over property use, planning, and bargaining.

VI. THEORIES OF JUSTICE, LAW, AND AUSTRIAN ECONOMICS

Recall that Cordato and Rothbard suggested that legal rights should be treated as being largely autonomous from economic analysis. The issues these scholars raise have not been developed adequately in contemporary American legal scholarship, and in any case this collection is an encyclopedia not of Austrian philosophy but Austrian *economics*. That said, a few general observations may be in order.

First: some recent legal-philosophy scholarship confirms Cordato and Rothbard's basic point—that there is and should be some separation between economics and law—but for reasons different from those scholars themselves articulated. Some legal philosophers have taken law and economic methods on their own terms, and identified shortcomings or unexamined premises in those methods. (See, e.g., Coleman, 1980.) George Fletcher (1996, pp. 155–70) used *Vaughan* and the sparks fact pattern in this spirit, to suggest that Posner and other law and economic scholars use the Kaldor-Hicks criterion in efficiency analysis far more often than may be warranted. In Fletcher's interpretation, the Pareto superiority criterion applies with the most moral justification to transactions when the parties have well-defined and justified rights to the resources they intend to transact, they are capable of consenting to the transaction, and they have sharply different personal interests and preferences. The paradigm case where Pareto superiority applies is a simple contractual exchange. The Kaldor-Hicks criterion applies with the most justification when a party who may lose from a transaction has a bad or problematic claim to the entitlement threatened. Kaldor developed what became the Kaldor-Hicks criterion to study protectionist tariffs on corn, and Hicks generalized to all systems protecting imperfect competition. (Hicks, 1939; Kaldor, 1939.) The sparks fact pattern fits the Pareto paradigm better; the right to determine the uses of one's land is a far more solid and convincing right than a continued expectancy that one's country will continue to impose tariffs on grain imported from another country. Posner and other law and economic scholars use Kaldor-Hicks criteria anyway. When they do so, the economic analysis that follows "restate[s] the utilitarian principle that in a dispute about property rights, the courts should make the decision that would promote the interests of society as a whole." (Fletcher, 1996, p. 162.) Austrian economics supplies normative arguments and empirical generalizations why such utilitarian analysis is unlikely to succeed. In particular, as applied to a sparks dispute, Kaldor-Hicks analysis will founder when the economist is forced to make interpersonal comparisons about the subjective values of the farmer and the train operator. But such economics acquire much more traction once a legal scholar has, like Fletcher, showed how this problem arises from the choice to apply Kaldor-Hicks and not Pareto.

Second: non-economic legal scholars have raised sharp questions about whether law and economic scholarship can supply a satisfactory account why efficiency is normatively attractive in the kinds of ways that make it capable of justifying law. Law is distinct from many other institutions because it coerces people, and that coercion is problematic normatively unless defenders of the legal system can supply a justification showing how the coercion protects just freedoms and a just conception of the general welfare. (See Raz, 1979, pp. 29–30.) Legal philosophers wonder whether efficiency links to any normative value capable of supplying such a justification. Law and economic scholars have suggested three main possibilities—preference utilitarianism, wealth, and consent imputed from Pareto superiority—but all three suffer from major problems. (See Coleman, 2003, pp. 1514–23; Shapiro and McLennen, 1998.) Austrian economics expresses, in economic language, why efficiency analysis may founder in making estimates about subjective value problems, change, and information limits. These critiques parallel moral arguments about why people deserve freedom to decide what resources and activities they value, and freedom to decide how to pursue those sources of value. But Austrian critiques may gain further traction if the similarities and differences with moral critiques of efficiency are explored.

Last: assume, as Cordato and Rothbard do, that the common law is not informed directly to a significant degree by economics and that it is layered on a common political morality focusing on rights, duties, and justice. Cordato and Rothbard both refer to such a layered approach as a "corrective justice" approach. Given these assumptions, where does the common political morality come from? Legal and political philosophers could answer this question in a range of ways; Cordato and Rothbard's answers illustrate the two ends of that range. Cordato's answer is relatively general and universal: different political communities are likely to converge on a common IIS. In relation to the use of external assets, for example, people have similar needs for them and (after making appropriate adjustments for differences in economic development across different societies) people's likely intended uses of such assets should be relatively similar across different societies. It could well be that, notwithstanding their economic, political, cultural, or religious differences, many cultures institute very similar protections for tangible property, relying on boundary rules, strict-liability tests, and so on. This answer could be right, but it has not yet been proven to be right. To determine whether it is right would require comparative-law scholarship, canvassing how different legal systems protect property rights for important test cases—like the accidental fire damage in sparks disputes. Or, a scholar might conduct similar anthropological or economic inquiries, studying how land and other common objects of property ownership are used and protected in different societies.

By contrast, Rothbard illustrates the other end of the range of acceptable answers: to interpret and justify the common political morality in a very particular theory of justice. Rothbard favors a libertarian theory of justice, grounded in such principles as self-ownership and autonomy. (Rothbard, 1982; see Nozick, 1974). This libertarian theory generates strong individual rights of liberty and control over property; corrective justice then requires citizens to rectify interferences they make with the liberty and property of others. This strategy requires considerable focus on political and legal philosophy, answering questions such as the following: Are libertarian theories of self-ownership and autonomy internally coherent? Do the policies they prescribe seem just? Do they adequately accommodate the rights-claims of individual citizens and the common interests those citizens share? How do they propose to settle sparks cases and other hard cases, and can they respond adequately to the theoretical objections legal and economics scholars associate with those hard cases?

Another possible source of a theory of justice consists of flourishing-based theories of natural law (Claeys, 2010b; Gordley, 2007), and political and legal theory by John Locke, William Blackstone, and other natural rights political theorists and jurists (Claeys, 2010a, pp. 1398–430). Many of these sources do not elaborate about what they mean when they say that a legal right is grounded in natural law or rights. Yet some do. In these sources, what is "natural" is usually defined to be what contributes to human flourishing. In the more explicit and better-reasoned sources, however, the "natural" is defined in relation to universal human psychological tendencies and motives to action, realistic limits on what people can know about the future and about the happiness of others, and realistic expectations about politics given human selfishness.

For example, property rights may be justified by Locke's account of the natural right to labor. In that account, "labor" refers to purposeful and intelligent activity generating goods contributing to the survival or improvement of the actor. (Locke, 1689, II.26–II.27, pp. 304–6; see Buckle, 1991, p. 151). Locke structured "labor" in such a manner (among other reasons) in response to epistemological limitations. Human knowledge of practical action, Locke believed, was limited to a "state of mediocrity," such that man could only ever have "judgment and opinion, not knowledge and certainty"—in contrast with the knowledge he could acquire over the "figures ordinarily considered in mathematics." (Locke, 1700, Bk. IV, Ch. 3, sec. 19, Bk. IV, Ch. 2, sec. 10, pp. 550, 645). Within these limitations, Locke believed, it was politically prudent to ground property rights in a low but solid moral good. In practice, government actors cannot forecast reliably the best particular uses of things for particular people; they can forecast reliably that most people will want to apply similar acquisitive and productive passions to do different things with assets. Locke structured the natural right to labor to capture the common acquisitive and productive tendencies, without getting them mired in the different particular uses different owners might make of their assets. (Claeys, 2010a, pp. 1400–401). A justification like this defends, on a combination of moral argument and broad empirical generalizations, concerns quite like Austrian concerns about time, ignorance, and subjective value.

CONCLUSION

This chapter has used sparks litigation as a case study. The case study illustrates how property rights and regulation are structured and justified in Austrian economics, welfare-maximizing law and economic scholarship, several different rights-based theories of justice—and in Anglo-American common law.

This case study does not generate policy prescriptions immediately relevant to any contemporary important political or regulatory dispute. Sparks disputes never were of crucial importance, and in any case the applicable principles of law were settled almost a century ago. Instead, the case study should illustrate, in a very concrete way, the most effective and profitable avenues for scholars to transplant themes from Austrian economics to contemporary American legal scholarship.

The most straightforward avenue is to critique contemporary welfare-maximizing scholarship using tenets of Austrian economics. Here, if the scholarship covering sparks is representative, existing Austrian economic scholarship has critiqued the relevant law and economic scholarship on Austrian terms but not on law and economic terms. In other words, Austrian scholars have criticized law and economic scholarship for not taking change, relative ignorance, or the subjectivity of value seriously enough. Yet Austrian scholars have not explained how these themes limit the ability of policy makers to gather the kinds of information law and economic scholars are accustomed to discussing: about the costs of accidents, precaution costs, party profit functions, and social responses to legal rules. Nor have Austrian scholars focused enough on how basic private-law doctrines and structures reflect change, ignorance, or the subjectivity of value: especially the structure of a property "right" and the nature of legal "causation."

Alternately, Austrian scholars may explore rights-based accounts of the private law, on the suspicion that law is largely autonomous from economics and other social sciences. If they pursue this avenue, Austrian scholars will need to engage issues raised in contemporary conceptual, legal, and political philosophy.

All of these questions may be explored and answered. Whether "Austrian" themes will influence American legal scholarship a generation from now depends in large part on whether scholars interested in those themes answer the relevant questions in terms that American legal scholars are accustomed to following.

REFERENCES

Buckle, Stephen. 1991. *Natural Law and the Theory of Property: Grotius to Hume.* Oxford: Clarendon Press.

Claeys, Eric R. 2010a. "Jefferson Meets Coase: Land-Use Torts, Law and Economics, and Natural Property Rights," 85 *Notre Dame Law Review* 1379–446.

Claeys, Eric R. 2010b. "The Private Law and the Crisis in American Catholic Scholarship in the American Legal Academy," 7 *Journal of Catholic Social Thought* 253–87.

Claeys, Eric R. 2011. "Bundle-of-Sticks Notions in Legal and Economic Scholarship," 8 *Econ Journal Watch* 205–14.

Claeys, Eric R. 2012. "Exclusion and Private Law Theory: A Comment on *Property as the Law of Things*," 125 *Harvard Law Review Forum* 133–50.

Coase, R.H. 1960. "The Problem of Social Cost," 3 *Journal of Law and Economics* (Oct.): 1–44.

Coleman, Jules L. 1980. "Efficiency, Exchange, and Auction: Philosophic Aspects of the Economic Approach to Law." 68 *California Law Review* 221.

Coleman, Jules L. 2001. *The Practice of Principle.* Oxford: Oxford University Press.

Coleman, Jules L. 2003. "The Grounds of Welfare." 112 *Yale Law Journal* 1511.

Cooter, Robert. 1985. "Unity in Tort, Contract, and Property: The Model of Precaution," 73 *California Law Review* 1–51.

Cordato, Roy E. 1992. *Welfare Economics and Externalities in an Open Ended Universe: A Modern Austrian Perspective*. Norwell, MA: Kluwer Academic Publishers.

Craswell, Richard. 2003. "In That Case, What Is the Question? Economics and the Demands of Contract Theory," 112 *Yale Law Journal* 903–24.

Ely, James W. 2001. *Railroads and American Law*. Lawrence, KS: University Press of Kansas.

Epstein, Richard A. 1973. "A Theory of Strict Liability." 2 *Journal of Legal Studies* 151–204.

Epstein, Richard A. 1979. "Nuisance Law: Corrective Justice and Its Utilitarian Constraints." 8 *Journal of Legal Studies* 49–102.

Epstein, Richard A. 1997. "A Clear View of the Cathedral: The Dominance of Property Rules," 106 *Yale Law Journal* 2091–120.

Fletcher, George P. 1996. *Basic Concepts of Legal Thought*. Oxford: Oxford University Press.

Gordley, James. 2007. *Foundations of Private Law: Property, Tort, Contract, and Unjust Enrichment*. Oxford: Oxford University Press.

Grady, Mark F. 1988. "Common Law Control of Strategic Behavior: Railroad Sparks and the Farmer," 17 *Journal of Legal Studies* 15–42.

Hicks, Cecil R. 1939. "The Foundations of Welfare Economics," 49 *Economic Journal* 696.

Kaldor, Nicholas. 1939. "Welfare Propositions of Economics and Interpersonal Comparisons of Utility." 49 *Economic Journal* 549.

Locke, John. 1689. *Two Treatises of Government*, ed. Peter Laslett. Cambridge, UK: Cambridge University Press, 1960.

Locke, John. 1700. *An Essay Concerning Human Understanding*, ed. Peter H. Nidditch. Oxford: Clarendon Press, 1975.

Merrill, Thomas W. and Henry E. Smith. 2000. "Optimal Standardization in the Law of Property: The *Numerus Clausus* Principle," 110 *Yale Law Journal* 1–70.

Merrill, Thomas W. and Henry E. Smith. 2001. "What Happened to Property in Law and Economics?" 111 *Yale Law Journal* 357–98.

Merrill, Thomas W. and Henry E. Smith. 2011. "Making Coasean Property More Coasean," 54 *Journal of Law and Economics* S77–S104.

Nozick, Robert. 1974. *Anarchy, State, and Utopia*. New York: Basic Books.

Pigou, A.C. 1932. *The Economics of Welfare*, 4th ed. London: Macmillan & Co.

Posner, Richard A. 2011. *Economic Analysis of Law*, 8th ed. United States: Aspen Publishers.

Raz, Joseph. 1979. *The Authority of Law*. Oxford: Oxford University Press.

Rizzo, Mario. 1980. "The Mirage of Efficiency," 8 *Hofstra Law Review* 641–58.

Rothbard, Murray N. 1982. "Law, Property Rights, and Air Pollution," 2 *Cato Journal* 55–99.

Shapiro, Scott and Edward McLennen. 1998. "Law-and-economics from a Philosophical Perspective," *The New Palgrave Dictionary of Economics and the Law*. London: MacMillan Reference Ltd. Vol. 2, 460.

Sowell, Thomas. 2002. *A Conflict of Visions: Ideological Origins of Political Struggles*, USA: Basic Books.

12. Austrian economics and tort law
Michael E. DeBow

Scholars associated with the Austrian School—either as card-carrying members or as fellow-travelers—have written more about tort law than any other subfield of "law and economics." However, after Mario Rizzo's multiple contributions in the 1980s the field went dormant, more or less, for a couple of decades. Recently Austrian writers have returned to tort law, sparking a revival of interest in the Austrian view of this subject. This chapter offers a survey of the literature, and a few modest suggestions for those who might wish to contribute to it.

The chapter proceeds as follows—Part I offers a brief historical overview of American tort law and introduces some essential terms; Parts II through IV survey the Austrian economics literature on intentional and unintentional torts and products liability; and Part V urges Austrians to keep an eye on and respond to lawyers' efforts to expand the outer boundaries of tort liability.

I. AMERICAN TORTS: AN OVERVIEW

Contemporary American tort law is a vast enterprise. A widely-cited annual study estimated the total cost of the tort system in 2010 at $264.6 billion, or 1.82 percent of U.S. GDP (*U.S. Tort Cost Trends*, 2012, 3, 5).[1] In 2000 there were approximately 700,000 new tort suits filed in state courts and 37,000 filed in federal courts. Four years earlier, in the 75 most populous counties in the country, the largest categories of tort cases were automobile-related injuries (49 percent of the total), premises liability (22 percent), and medical malpractice (12 percent) (Beider and Elliott, 2003). Given tort law's scope it is not surprising that several aspects of it generate spirited debate — most notably products liability, medical malpractice,

---

[1] *U.S. Tort Cost Trends* (2012, 3, 5). The estimate includes three components of the costs incurred by insurance companies and self-insured entities: the benefits paid or expected to be paid by insurance companies to third party claimants, defense costs, and administrative expenses. (Ibid. at 8.) For another easily accessible source of statistical information on American tort law, see *Economic Report of the President* (2004, 203–21).

punitive damages, and so-called mass tort claims. Tort reform proposals are perennial items on both state and federal legislative agendas.

Tort law has proven to be a protean concept in large part because of its open-endedness. The standard definition of tort as the law of non-contractual civil wrongs[2] stakes out a potentially huge territory for it. The boundaries that separate tort from other areas of law, particularly contract law, are thus frequently contested, with the plaintiff's bar working diligently in recent years to expand the domain of tort law. (Rubin and Bailey, 1994; Zywicki, 2003; Rubin, 2005b; *Trial Lawyers Inc.*).

As currently constituted American tort law consists primarily of three subfields: intentional torts, unintentional torts (accidents), and products liability. Intentional tort and product liability claims are dealt with using different types of "strict liability" analysis, while unintentional torts are dealt with using "negligence" analysis. Understanding this tripartite arrangement requires a bit of history.

At the time of the Founding, the newly independent American states adopted the English common law, which allowed only a very limited scope for the law of civil, noncontractual wrongs. There was "'a residual category of noncriminal wrongs not arising out of contract,' which were litigated under the old common-law write system as 'trespass' or 'trespass on the case,'" but English law did not treat torts as "an autonomous branch of law." (Hall, Finkelman and Ely, 2005, 203) "Blackstone did not use the word 'torts' to describe a legal category at all." (Witt, 2009, 474.) Thus, the "private wrongs" recognized by early American law included assault, trespass, and libel—causes of action based on intentional actions by a defendant (Hall, Finkelman and Ely, 2005, 203). Under the strict liability standard for intentional tort claims, once the plaintiff establishes that the defendant's deliberate actions fit the definition of the tort (for example, that defendant did in fact trespass on plaintiff's land), liability follows automatically unless the defendant can successfully plead and prove a recognized defense, such as consent, self-defense, or necessity.

Although the intentional tort/strict liability rubric was a satisfactory arrangement for a largely rural, agricultural America, as the 19th century wore on the inherited English causes of action proved inadequate to deal with the conflicts generated by increasing urbanization and industrialization. Technological breakthroughs, including railways and (later)

---

[2]   As in *Black's Law Dictionary* (2009): "A civil wrong, other than breach of contract, for which a remedy may be obtained, usu. in the form of damages; a breach of a duty that the law imposes on persons who stand in a particular relation to one another."

automobiles, led to a dramatic increase in the number of accidental injuries involving people who were previously strangers to one another. This in turn gave rise to an increase in suits brought by accident victims, whose injuries were the unintended consequences of defendants' acts.[3]

The expansion of tort litigation was illustrated by the publication of the first English-language treatise on torts in Boston in 1859, which cited more than 5,000 cases. (Witt, 2009, 474; Hall, Finkelman and Ely, 2005, 203) As a matter of logistics, the American courts' handling of this growing caseload was made possible by the replacement of the old writ system with new, modernized rules of civil procedure. As a matter of doctrine, the disposition of lawsuits involving unintentional torts was guided by the judges' creation (or recognition, if you prefer) of a new cause of action for negligence. Legal historian Lawrence Friedman (2005, 351) explains negligence as:

> . . . a law about carelessness, about not living up to standards. It was about those who inflicted harm—but not on purpose. It was about lapses in judgment. Liability for negligence was not absolute; it was based on fault. What was expected was not perfection, but the vague, subtle standard of the "reasonable man." Fault meant a breach of duty to the public, meant that the defendant had not done what a reasonable person should do.

The defendant in a negligence case will ordinarily try to convince the trier of fact—typically a jury—that his action was not negligent at all, that he behaved as a "reasonable person" would have behaved under the circumstances. Even if the defendant loses the argument as to his own negligence, he may still argue that his negligent act was not the "cause-in-fact" or the "proximate cause" of the plaintiff's injury, or that the plaintiff had assumed the risk of injury through her own actions, or that the plaintiff's own negligence acts had contributed to the accidental injury she sustained. All of these questions in negligence cases are (usually) treated as questions of fact rather than questions of law, and thus are decided by the jury (or, if no jury is requested by the judge sitting as the trier of fact).

Another example of 19th century judicial creativity came in the form of decisions that expanded the scope of strict liability to cover accidental injuries due to "ultrahazardous activities" such as blasting or maintaining reservoirs. The creation of modern negligence doctrine and the expansion of strict liability provide strong support for Friedman's assessment that,

---

[3]   We will ignore the difficulties encountered in analyzing reckless acts, which may be argued to involve some element of intentionality.

"For the nineteenth century, it is hard to think of a body of judge-made law more striking than tort law" (Friedman, 2005, 350).[4]

The third principal subfield of American tort law, products liability, is a product of the 20th century. A number of judicial decisions prior to World War II eliminated the requirement of privity of contract between plaintiff and defendant in cases involving product-related injuries, thus opening the way for consumers to sue manufacturers. Post-World War II academic criticism set the stage for another series of innovative judicial decisions in the early 1960s.[5] Key events included a 1960 decision of the New Jersey Supreme Court that swept away long-standing contract rules that had governed express product warranties, in favor of judicially-created implied warranties more protective of the consumer. This dramatic change in the law was justified by the court on the ground that mass consumer contracts are take-it-or-leave-it offers from manufacturers who enjoy an unfair quantum of "bargaining power" over consumers. (*Henningsen v. Bloomfield Motors*, 1960, 95) This decision was followed by other state courts eager to expand the domain of tort while shrinking the domain of contract. Two years later the California Supreme Court explained its embrace of products liability as a means to "insure that the costs of injuries resulting from defective products are borne by the manufacturers that put such products on the market rather than by the injured persons who are powerless to protect themselves" (*Greenman v. Yuba Power Products*, 1962). Indeed, the most remarkable feature of the *Greenman* decision is its failure to consider the likelihood of the cost of additional safety measures being passed through to consumers in the form of higher prices.

A milestone was reached in 1964, when the American Law Institute announced a new rule for products liability cases in the second Restatement of Torts. Section 402A declares that the seller of a product that was "in a defective condition unreasonably dangerous to the user or consumer or to his property is subject to liability for physical harm hereby caused. . ." The Restatement is clear that liability should be imposed on a seller even if he "exercised all possible care in the preparation and sale of his product. . . ." State supreme courts across the country adopted this approach rather quickly: 28 states did so by 1971, 41 by 1976, and 48 by 1991. (Priest, 1991, 37)

---

[4] For a recent contribution to the history of tort law in the 19th century, see Shugerman (2008).

[5] This history is well-known. See Priest (1985), Huber (1988), Priest (1991), White (2003), and Zywicki (2003).

Although the new products liability is sometimes referred to as "strict liability," that term is somewhat misleading when applied to Section 402A. Specifically, the requirement that the product be shown to have been "unreasonably dangerous" is an echo, however faint, of negligence law's concept of a "reasonable person." Defendants, however, soon learned that judges were not eager to interpret this requirement in a way that helped them avoid liability. Rather, as Grant Gilmore put it, judges "manipulate[ed] the new catchwords in such a way as considerably to increase the liability of manufacturers and other commercial sellers to the users of their products." (Gilmore, 1974, 93–4) In many states, this requirement morphed into the so-called "risk-utility test," with juries instructed to impose liability if "the risk of product injuries given current product design exceeds the product's utility." (Priest, 1991, 40)

Epstein (2008, 724) sees a "constant string of plaintiffs' breakthroughs . . . between 1965 and 1980," but also that "as a doctrinal matter, the last generation has been a period of consolidation, if not some modest retrenchment" in products liability law. Significantly, the third Restatement of Torts, announced in 1998, involves a significant rethinking of the field and is having its own effect on state courts in the present time.

The cumulative impact of the revolution in products liability law is succinctly explained by Zywicki (2003, 1623): "The whole point of strict product liability . . . was to supplant [the common law's traditional] regime of default rules with a network of immutable rules that parties were specifically forbidden to contract around."

With this brief overview of intentional and unintentional torts and products liability in mind, we now turn to the Austrians' contributions to tort scholarship.

II.   INTENTIONAL TORTS

The core of the law of intentional torts protects an individual's interest in bodily integrity (by providing a remedy for assault) and her property rights (by providing remedies for trespass and conversion). This mission obviously overlaps, to one degree or another, with the non-aggression axiom of libertarianism. Perhaps not so obviously, the mission may also overlap with the philosophical underpinnings of Austrian economics. The only law review article to survey Austrian law-and-economics scholarship maintains that "The central value premise embraced by Austrians is individual freedom from domination, which they regard as best furthered by pervasive and clearly demarcated private property rights and reliance upon market processes for social organization" (Crespi, 1998, 331). This raises the question of whether and to what extent Austrian and libertarian views on the law of intentional torts coincide.

Murray Rothbard analyzes a number of intentional torts from a libertarian perspective in Rothbard (1982). He defines law as "a set of 'ought' or normative propositions" and "the true jurist or legal philosopher" as one who "sets forth what the law should be, difficult though that might be" (Rothbard, 1982, 56). He then criticizes the claim that custom is a reasonable basis for law, stating that "common law judges, who are merely interpreting the custom of the . . . society, cannot escape normative judgments. . . .*Why* must the rules of custom be obeyed?" (Rothbard, 1982, 57 (emphasis in original)).

Rothbard asserts that the basic normative principle for law is the libertarian non-aggression axiom: "No action should be considered illicit or illegal unless it invades, aggresses against, the person or just property of another." Moreover, "[t]he invasion must be concrete and physical" (Rothbard, 1982, 60). He contrasts his position with that of John Stuart Mill, who substitutes "[t]he vague concept of 'harm' . . . for the precise one of physical violence" (Rothbard, 1982, 61).

After setting out these basic parameters of his preferred tort regime, Rothbard freewheels from one topic to another, arguing:

- for the superiority of strict liability over negligence
- for allowing the victim of any physical attack to use deadly force in self-defense
- for using the criminal law standard of "proof beyond a reasonable doubt" in tort cases
- against vicarious liability, and
- for a "homesteading," first-in-time treatment of previously unowned resources (including rights to pollute or to be free from pollution).

Rothbard discusses trespass and nuisance law to set the stage for his discussion of air pollution. He argues that it should be treated as strict liability tort, but would require a plaintiff to clear a number of high hurdles, including a showing of "strict causality from the actions of the defendant to the victimization of the plaintiff" beyond a reasonable doubt. Rothbard states that none of the existing statutes and regulations dealing with air pollution are permissible "under libertarian legal theory" (Rothbard, 1982, 89). Neither is it permissible for public officials to bring suit against polluters on behalf of the public. And;

> if there is no such entity as society or the state, or no one except the victim that should have standing . . . this means that the entire structure of criminal

law must be dispensed with, and that we are left with tort law, where the victim indeed presses charges against the aggressor. (Rothbard, 1982, 91)

There is much more in the article, but this description should satisfy the reader that Rothbard provides plenty of food for thought. The problem is that Rothbard proceeds in such a peremptory fashion that he illustrates Crespi's criticism that "the Austrian normative literature has a strangely disembodied, ex cathedra quality to it . . . ." (Crespi, 1998, 338).

At the least, Rothbard's article raises the question of the relationship between "libertarian legal theory" and an Austrian economics-informed legal theory.[6] Libertarian legal theory has remained underdeveloped, according to Kinsella (2009). On the other side of the question, it seems unlikely that a single, unified Austrian legal theory will develop, given intramural divisions among Austrians. For example, Rothbard's views on custom are certainly at odds with Hayek's (see Zywicki and Sanders, 2008, 565, 599–602). Further, Rothbard's plans for dismantling criminal law should strike most (if not all) Hayekians as much too constructivist. Might Austrians today productively address these differences in opinion — or is this more likely a dead end?

One more recent article that bears on this subject is Stringham and White (2004), which commends Kantian ethics to Austrian economists. They argue inter alia that the dominant Chicago School approach to law and economics is utilitarian at its core, and is thus subject to the same philosophical criticisms as utilitarianism itself. The rights-based ethical writings of Immanuel Kant constitute "an alternative for those who reject the consequentialist ethics upon which neoclassical law and economics is based" (Stringham and White, 2004, 382). "Such a program would emphasize the constraints placed on judges, both to acknowledge the informational difficulties of ambitious decisionmaking and to respect the rights of individuals, more than the ends the judges would attempt to achieve" (Stringham and White, 2004, 386).

Austrians who wish to follow Stringham and White's advice will need to familiarize themselves with the philosophical literature on torts. Good introductory surveys include Coleman and Mendlow (2010) and Goldberg (2003). Particular attention is probably due "corrective justice theory," which Coleman and Mendlow describe as "the most influential non-economic perspective on tort law." For a portal into the Kantian literature

---

[6] Stephan Kinsella has recently begun to work on a libertarian theory of tort (Kinsella, 2009).

on torts, including the widely discussed work of Ernest Weinrib, see Perry (2008).

Eric Claeys's recent article, "Jefferson Meets Coase: Land-Use Torts, Law and Economics, and Natural Property Rights," is also a must-read for Austrians interested in intentional torts. Claeys "compares standard economic analysis of [trespass and nuisance] against an interpretation that follows from the natural-rights morality that informed the content of these torts in their formative years." He concludes that "'Jeffersonian' natural-rights morality predicts the contours of tort doctrine more determinately and accurately than 'Coasian' economic analysis" (Claeys, 2010, 1379).

III. UNINTENTIONAL TORTS

The impressive Austrian literature discussing accident law originated in the long-running debate in the 1970s and 1980s over the relative strengths and weaknesses of negligence and strict liability in dealing with accidental injuries. Participants in this debate—dubbed "the cold war in torts" by Zipursky (2010)—addressed "[t]he problem . . . that nowhere have the courts decided precisely where the principles of negligence should dominate and where they should not." (Epstein, 1973, 153 n.2)

A quick overview of the cold war in torts will help place the Austrian contribution in context. The debate begins with several articles published in the 1960s by Guido Calabresi that argued for the superiority of strict liability. Calabresi (1970) pulls together the (partially) economic case he made that "sophisticated and wealthy market actors . . . are better situated than ordinary individuals to make risk-reducing and risk-spreading decisions" such that tort law should be transformed into "de facto third party insurance" via the use of strict liability. (Zipursky, 2010)

In a famous exchange of articles in the *Journal of Legal Studies*, Posner (1972b) defended negligence as the more efficient approach, and Epstein (1973) offered a brief for strict liability on grounds different from Calabresi's.

Posner's defense of negligence was a key element in his early work, which advanced the positive claim that traditional common law rules possess an inherent economic logic. In short, "The common law method is to allocate responsibilities between people engaged in interacting activities in such a way as to maximize the joint value, or, what amounts to the same thing, minimize the joint cost of the activities." (Posner, 1972a, 98) Posner was especially appreciative of Judge Learned Hand's apparent anticipation of Posner's views in the opinion Hand wrote for the Second Circuit in *United States v. Carroll Towing* (1947). The case involved a maritime accident in

New York harbor which resulted in the sinking of a barge and the loss of its cargo. Numerous issues in the case were decided under a negligence standard, but only one of these is relevant here. The captain of the barge that sank left it unattended for 21 hours prior to the accident. The court concluded that the barge's cargo would have been saved if the captain had been aboard at the time of the accident. This raised the question whether the barge owner had been negligent in not taking steps to require the captain to remain on board.

Judge Hand explained the negligence standard as an exercise in cost-benefit analysis, in a passage that contains the Hand Formula for negligence:

> Since there are occasions when every vessel will break from her moorings, and since, if she does, she becomes a menace to those about her, the owner's duty, as in other similar situations, to provide against resulting injuries is a function of three variables: (1) The probability that she will break away; (2) the gravity of the resulting injury, if she does; (3) the burden of adequate precautions. Possibly it serves to bring this notion into relief to state it in algebraic terms: if the probability be called P; the injury, L; and the burden, B; liability depends upon whether B is less than L multiplied by P: i.e., whether $B < PL$. (United States v. Carroll Towing, 1947, 173)

Although the Second Circuit did not have before it any numbers to be plugged into the Formula, it nonetheless concluded that the defendant had been negligent in not having the captain on board at the time of the accident.[7] Of course, judges and juries will seldom if ever have the data necessary to use the Hand Formula in a rigorous, mathematical way.[8] In spite of this, the Hand Formula impressed then-Professor Posner as a near-perfect example of the predicted common law tropism toward efficiency, and a good reason to favor negligence over strict liability as the governing standard of behavior. Posner cast the Hand Formula in both positive and normative terms: it was Hand's "attempt to make explicit the standard that the courts had long applied" and it specified what "the judge (or jury) should attempt to measure. . ." (Posner, 1972b, 32).

It is precisely the information required for a judge or jury to assess the presence or absence of negligence that troubled Mario Rizzo (1980a, 292): "To make [the Hand Formula] operational the analyst must be able to measure, with tolerable accuracy, the relevant social costs. This is no simple task; and if our thesis is correct, it is fundamentally intractable." This echo of the Austrian impossibility thesis from the socialist calculation debate

---

[7] Because the suit was in admiralty, no jury was involved.
[8] England (1991, 415–19) discusses several judicial opinions which wrestle with the Hand Formula.

comes through more clearly at later points in the article, such as (Rizzo, 1980a, 299):

> The costs that we use to explain certain legal rules must be measurable outside of the "market" that produces those rules. This is the crux of the problem: in many cases the relevant social costs are revealed with any degree of accuracy only through the legal system they are relied upon to explain.

When Rizzo moves from the static analysis of negligence to analyze the dynamics of the doctrine, the information problem is compounded. For example:

> In the dynamic framework ... the problem of determining the time frame in which a given party is the cheaper-cost avoider becomes even more severe [than in static analysis]. A world in which technological change is permitted involves infinitely greater informational problems. (Rizzo, 1980a, 307)

Although the greater part of the article is devoted to his critique of negligence, Rizzo spends the last two sections explaining the superiority of Epstein's vision of a strict liability regime—as explicated in Epstein (1973, 1974, and 1975). Rizzo explains that although Epstein's case for strict liability does not rely on economic analysis, it "may, in fact, promote efficiency by providing an institutionally more stable environment in which economic decision making can take place," with efficiency defined in "a more general, long-run sense" than Posner uses (Rizzo, 1980a, 311). Epstein's version of strict liability:

> obviates or minimizes the need for courts to grapple, if only implicitly, with such impossibly elusive problems as foreseeability, cheaper-cost avoider, social cost, and second best. It provides a series of basically simple, strict presumptions. The *prima facie* case is based on straightforward commonsense causal paradigms, whereas the defenses and later pleas minimize the number of issues which must be considered in a given case. (Rizzo, 1980a, 317)

In short, Rizzo argues the superiority of rules over standards, of bright lines over balancing tests—a thoroughly Austrian insight.[9]

In the final paragraph Rizzo argues that since Posner's:

> "fine-tuning" paradigm is a mere delusion, the only basis on which the "efficiency" of systems can be compared is on a fundamental institutional level. The *central* question is then: which legal framework provides a more stable environment for individuals to pursue their own ends in harmony with each other? Ironically, it is precisely because we live in a dynamic world where the informa-

---

[9]   Rizzo (1985, 879) describes Epstein's version of strict liability as "precisely the kind of rule-based abstract order about which Hayek has written."

tion needed by the "fine-tuners" is not available that the answer must be the antiquated and static system of strict liability. (Rizzo, 1980a, 318)

Although Rizzo makes a strong case for strict liability in terms of both the information problem that plagues negligence and strict liability's superiority in promoting plan coordination among individuals,[10] the Epstein-Rizzo view of torts lost out in the marketplace of ideas.[11] As noted above, the development of products liability law seems to have plateaued about 1980 and, in any event, that law differs significantly from the Epstein-Rizzo version of strict liability. Moreover, tort law after 1980 did not see judicial creation of new areas of strict liability. Rather, "the new frontiers of tort liability are being explored primarily though extensions of concepts that stem from negligence. Thus, courts are today hearing and sometimes endorsing a wide variety of innovative claims for negligent failure to warn, negligent marketing, negligent infliction of emotional distress and economic loss." (Feldman, 2003) More recently Zipursky (2010) says that "it is quite clear that negligence has been more dominant in courts than strict liability and Posner and the Posnerites have been more dominant in the law school classroom." Consistent with this judgment, the Restatement (Third) of Torts has adopted the Hand Formula as its definition for negligence. Finally, according to Zipursky, "[e]fforts to cover tort theory with a single principle, buttressed by economic theory, are largely part of our intellectual history."

Even though we have witnessed the apparent triumph of the Hand-Posner conception of accident law, Mario Rizzo's work in this area remains important for Austrians interested in law because his tort scholarship, rooted in the Austrian side of the socialist calculation debate, actually provides the basis for a critique of the entire Posnerian law-and-economics project. Rizzo presents his broader critique of Posner in Rizzo (1980b and 1985) — both of which make extensive use of tort examples.[12] Rizzo's broader attack on Chicago law-and-economics is beyond the scope of this chapter, but its principal points—including most importantly the information requirements facing Posnerian judges (or jurors, or legislators for that matter)[13] and law's importance for plan coordination—are most clearly illustrated in his torts scholarship.

---

[10] For another sketch of Rizzo's analysis, see Stringham and White (2004, 3758).

[11] Epstein revisits the cold war in Epstein (2010).

[12] Aranson (1992) builds on and extends Rizzo (1980b and 1985).

[13] Appreciating this point allows the student of law and economics to recognize the hubris one encounters in some law-and-economics writing, such as the

Present-day Austrians might consider extending Rizzo's work to cover the current controversies in negligence law mentioned above—negligent failure to warn, marketing, and infliction of emotional distress, as well as the recovery of economic losses in negligence cases.[14]

Before leaving negligence, mention should be made of a recent article by Alexander Volokh (2011) raising both positive and normative objections to cost-benefit analysis in general. Volokh cites several Austrian authors and notes that cost-benefit calculation typically puts the bureaucrat who attempts it in the position of "essentially rediscovering the socialist calculation problem." He also gives brief attention to the "natural-rights libertarian" objections to cost-benefit analysis. This article and Perry (2008) provide a starting point for Austrians interested in further critiquing the use of cost-benefit analysis in law.

IV. PRODUCTS LIABILITY

As explained in section I, the revolution in products liability law depended on judges' willingness to turn their backs on the long-standing contract law governing product warranties and take on themselves the job of specifying implied terms of warranty. The judges' rationale for this convulsive change had several elements. Corporations were said to be in "a better position" to deal with product risk and could "spread" the costs of improvements in safety across all their customers. Consumers were uninformed about risk, could not bargain with large corporate sellers, and (apparently) were uninsured. In rescuing consumers from this awful plight, the judges seemed to think that they could force manufacturers to bear the increased costs associated with it. This was not the case, of course. Price increases followed, and the result was that consumers in effect buy both a product and a government-mandated mini-insurance policy to go with it.

Viewed in cost-benefit terms, products liability law looks like a poor

---

statement in an undergraduate textbook that "In analyzing the [economic] model [of accidents], we first derive the socially efficient level of precaution, defined to be the level that would be chosen by a social planner." (Miceli, 2009, 19) See also Calabresi (1970, 26): "I take it as axiomatic that the principal function of accident law is to reduce the sum of the costs of accidents and the costs of avoiding accidents."

[14]   Rizzo has written on the economic loss doctrine (Rizzo 1982), but the article does not use obviously Austrian analysis. Similarly, Rizzo's work on causation in tort (Rizzo 1981) is concerned primarily with probability theory rather than Austrian themes.

bargain for consumers. Priest (2000, 578) reports that "no single study has been able to demonstrate any consequent improvement in safety or reduction in the accident rate. . ... [T]here has been no additional increase in safety or in accident reduction that can be attributed to the expansion of liability." Polinsky and Shavell (2010) observe that price increases due to expanded product liability chill otherwise desired purchases, and consumers often carry insurance that compensates them for some or all of their losses from accidents. Everyone recognizes the high administrative costs of current products liability law. Zywicki and Sanders (2008, 568) argue that recent experience gives "good reason to conclude that strict liability has proven less efficient in the long run than the evolved regime it replaced and that the unanticipated consequences and individual responses have illustrated the perils of judicial central planning, rather than its promise."

Consideration should also be given to the role of juries in product liability cases.[15] Most such cases settle, of course. For example, one study found that of only 3 percent of the tort cases terminated in federal court in 2000 were decided in trials. (Beider and Elliott, 2003). However, all the settlement negotiations in tort litigation take place in the shadow of potential jury deliberations. Some observers make a strong case that over the last 50 years or so juries have become much keener to impose liability on defendants, and that the imprecision of the terms used in tort doctrine give juries the latitude to indulge their appetite for redistribution in favor of injured plaintiffs. George Priest, a well-known proponent of this view, describes the change in the jury's role in product liability cases this way (Priest, 2000, 576):

> Today, in the products field, as a general matter, the only question for the jury is whether a safer product could have been designed or built that would have prevented the accident . . ..This is not the standard that prevailed prior to the 1960s . . ..Nor is it the standard promoted by economic analysis which evaluates whether some greater level of consumer or producer investment at the margin would have prevented the accident. . ..The adoption of the new approach — generated by the culture of the law, not by the legal rule itself—is responsible for the transformation of product suits from trial over manufacturing normalcy to trials over the disparate claims of product design experts.

Presumably some consumers would prefer to avoid all this and buy (lower-priced) products without also being required to buy the implied product insurance and the ticket to the litigation lottery that is mandated by current products liability law. Returning warranty law to the domain of

---

[15] Hetcher (2003) is an interesting discussion of the jury function in tort litigation, and the fact that little attention is paid to it by "leading tort theorists."

contract would allow such consumers the freedom to opt out of the current paternalistic regime, thus shrinking the domain of tort while increasing the domain of personal autonomy, responsibility and freedom.

The "tort reform by contract" proposed by Paul Rubin would provide that "[w]here there is a prior relationship between injurers and victims (product liability, workplace injury, medical malpractice[16]) the parties should be allowed to specify by contract or warranty the types of damages for which injurers will be liable" (Rubin, 1993). To the extent that a seller's liability exposure is reduced, price would adjust accordingly. As sensible and straightforward as this idea seems, it and other such proposals encounter very effective opposition from the plaintiffs' bar. As Rubin sees it, "much of the modern law of torts has been shaped by special interest lobbying efforts and rent seeking by the trial lawyers." (Rubin, 2005b, 223) The plaintiff's bar can thus be counted on to oppose tort reform consistently and tenaciously. In addition, judges benefit in various ways from increased legal complexity (Barton, 2010, 271–7) and thus some (perhaps many) judges will be inclined to favor the status quo in products liability for that reason.

Tort reform thus seems to merit active Austrian support, inasmuch as the movement of the tort-contract boundary in the direction of contract would be consistent with Austrians' "central value premise" (noted earlier) of "individual freedom from domination." Austrians might be able to articulate the freedom argument for product liability reform in a way that appeals to the general public. Additional empirical research on the topic is always helpful, as is research that increases our understanding of the politics of tort reform. As to the latter, Rubin (2005b, 233–4) contains a list of possible topics for future research, including several questions about the political realities of tort reform efforts, successful and unsuccessful. Products liability reform thus presents a grand opportunity for Austrians and public choice scholars to find common ground as urged by Boettke and Lopez (2002) and Ikeda (2003).

V.   TORT LAW AND TOTAL JUSTICE

Writing more than a quarter-century ago, Lawrence Friedman declared, "There has developed in this country what I call here a general expectation of justice, and a general expectation of recompense for injuries and loss.

---

[16]   For an argument by a law and economics scholar against contracting with regard to medical malpractice, see Arlen (2010).

Together, these make up a demand for what will be called 'total justice.'" (Friedman, 1985, 5) Many in the plaintiff's bar see it as a, if not the principal, supplier of total justice. It is thus not surprising that in 2006 the American Trial Lawyers Association changed its name to the American Association for Justice.

Changes in tort law feature prominently in the plaintiff's bar's story of itself and the march to total justice. This dovetails with George Priest's claim that "the conception underlying the culture of modern tort is almost infinitely expandable." (Priest, 2000, 577) At the outer edges of tort law some members of the plaintiff's bar have recently shown quite a talent for innovation. The state lawsuits against the tobacco industry in the mid-1990s provided a template for the later federal tobacco suits and for similar suits brought by cities, states, public unions and other plaintiffs against firearms and lead paint manufacturers. These cases often included tort claims, although, as tobacco litigation mastermind Dickie Scruggs once admitted, "it really doesn't matter what legal theory we use" (*Panel Three: Audience Discussion*, 1997, 510). (For more on these cases, see Task Force on Tobacco Litigation, 1996; Levy, 2000; Krauss, 2000; DeBow, 2001) The successes won by plaintiffs' lawyers in some of these cases strongly suggest that the trial bar will continue to test the outer limits of tort litigation in the future. While it may not be possible to predict all the features of the trial bar's next attempt at public policy innovation, it is fairly easy to predict that any changes they seek in tort law will involve more in the way of collectivization, income redistribution, and infantilization than does current law.

Austrians who are comfortable with the normative side of their tradition and thus committed to "individual freedom from domination" as the primary goal should help monitor the ever-contested tort-contract boundary. These scholars may well have something quite valuable to say about the best future for tort law.

REFERENCES

Aranson, Peter H. 1992. "The Common Law as Central Economic Planning," 3 *Constitutional Political Economy* 289–319.

Arlen, Jennifer H. 2010. "Contracting Over Liability: Medical Malpractice and the Cost of Choice," 158 *University of Pennsylvania Law Review* 957–1023. http://www.pennumbra.com/issues/article.php?aid=255.

Barton, Benjamin H. 2010. *The Lawyer-Judge Bias in the American Legal System.* New York: Cambridge University Press.

Beider, Perry, and Cary Elliott. 2003. *The Economics of U.S. Tort Liability: A Primer.* Washington, DC: Congressional Budget Office. http://www.cbo.gov/ftpdocs/46xx/doc4641/10-22-Tortreform-study.pdf.

Boettke, Peter J., and Edward J. Lopez. 2002. "Austrian Economics and Public Choice," 15
    Review of Austrian Economics 111–19.
Calabresi, Guido. 1970. *The Costs of Accidents: A Legal and Economic Analysis.* New Haven:
    Yale University Press.
Claeys, Eric R. 2010. "Jefferson Meets Coase: Land-Use Torts, Law and Economics, and Natural
    Property Rights," 85 *Notre Dame Law Review* 1379–1446. http://www.nd.edu/~ndlrev/
    archive_public/85ndlr4/Claeys.pdf.
Coleman, Jules, and Gabriel Mendlow. 2010. "Theories of Tort Law," *Stanford Encyclopedia
    of Philosophy*, http://plato.stanford.edu/entries/tort-theories/.
Crespi, Gregory Scott. 1998. "Exploring the Complicationist Gambit: An Austrian Approach
    to the Economic Analysis of Law," 73 *Notre Dame Law Review* 315–83.
DeBow, Michael E. 2001. "The State Tobacco Litigation and the Separation of Powers in
    State Governments: Repairing the Damage," 31 *Seton Hall Law Review* 563–97.
Economic Report of the President. 2004. Washington: U.S. Government Printing Office.
    http://www.gpo.gov/fdsys/browse/collection.action?collectionCode=ERP.
Englard, Izhak. 1991. "Law and Economics in American Tort Cases: A Critical Assessment
    of the Theory's Impact on Courts," 41 *University of Toronto Law Journal* 359–430.
Epstein, Richard A. 1973. "A Theory of Strict Liability," 2 *Journal of Legal Studies*
    151–204.
Epstein, Richard A. 1974. "Defenses and Subsequent Pleas in a System of Strict Liability," 3
    Journal of Legal Studies 165–215.
Epstein, Richard A. 1975. "Intentional Harms," 4 *Journal of Legal Studies* 391–442.
Epstein, Richard A. 2008. *Cases and Materials on Torts.* New York: Wolters Kluwer.
Epstein, Richard A. 2010. "Toward a General Theory of Tort Law: Strict Liability in
    Context," 3 *Journal of Tort Law* art. 6.
Feldman, Heidi Li. 2003. "Symposium: The New Negligence," 91 *Georgetown Law Journal*
    511.
Friedman, Lawrence M. 1985. *Total Justice.* New York: Russell Sage Foundation.
Friedman, Lawrence M. 2005. *A History of American Law.* New York: Touchstone.
Gilmore, Grant. 1974. *The Death of Contract.* Columbus: Ohio State University Press.
Goldberg, John C.P. 2003. "Twentieth-Century Tort Theory," 91 *Georgetown Law Journal*
    513–83.
Greenman v. Yuba Power Products, Inc. 1962. 377 P.2d 897 (Cal.).
Hall, Kermit L., Paul Finkelman, and James W. Ely, Jr. 2005. *American Legal History: Cases
    and Materials.* New York: Oxford University Press.
Henningsen v. Bloomfield Motors, Inc. 1960. 161 A.2d 69 (N.J.).
Hetcher, Steven. 2003. "The Jury's Out: Social Norms' Misunderstood Role in Negligence
    Law," 91 *Georgetown Law Journal* 633–58.
Huber, Peter W. 1988. *Liability: The Legal Revolution and Its Consequences.* New York: Basic
    Books.
Ikeda, Sanford. 2003. "How Compatible are Public Choice and Austrian Political Economy?"
    16 *Review of Austrian Economics* 63–75.
Kinsella, Stephan. 2009. "The Libertarian Approach to Negligence, Tort, and Strict Liability:
    Wergeld and Partial Wergeld," StephanKinsella.com http://www.stephankinsella.com/20
    09/09/the-libertarian-approach-to-negligence-tort-and-strict-liability-wergeld-and-partial-
    wergeld/.
Krauss, Michael I. 2000. *Fire and Smoke: Governments, Lawsuits and the Rule of Law.*
    Oakland, CA: Independent Institute.
Levy, Robert A. 2000. "The War on Tobacco," in Roger Pilon, ed., *The Rule of Law in the
    Wake of Clinton.* Washington, DC: Cato Institute.
Miceli, Thomas J. 2009. *The Economic Approach to Law.* Stanford: Stanford University
    Press.
"Panel Three: Audience Discussion." 1997. 41 *New York Law School Law Review* 507–12.
Perry, Ronen. 2008. "Re-Torts," 59 *Alabama Law Review* 987–1035.
Polinsky, A. Mitchell, and Steven Shavell. 2010. "The Uneasy Case for Product Liability,"

123 *Harvard Law Review* 1437–92. http://www.harvardlawreview.org/issues/123/april10/Article_6968.php.

Posner, Richard A. 1972a. *Economic Analysis of Law*. Boston: Little Brown.

Posner, Richard A. 1972b. "A Theory of Negligence," 1 *Journal of Legal Studies* 29–96.

Priest, George L. 1985. "The Invention of Enterprise Liability: A Critical History of the Intellectual Foundations of Modern Tort Law," 14 *Journal of Legal Studies* 461–528.

Priest, George L. 1991. "The Modern Expansion of Tort Liability: Its Sources, Its Effects, and Its Reform," 5:3 *Journal of Economic Perspectives* 31–50.

Priest, George L. 2000. "The Culture of Modern Tort Law," 34 *Valparaiso University Law Review* 573–9.

Rizzo, Mario J. 1980a. "Law Amid Flux: The Economics of Negligence and Strict Liability in Tort," 9 *Journal of Legal Studies* 291–318.

Rizzo, Mario J. 1980b. "The Mirage of Efficiency," 8 *Hofstra Law Review* 641–58.

Rizzo, Mario J. 1981. "The Imputation Theory of Proximate Cause: An Economic Framework," 15 *Georgia Law Review* 1007–38.

Rizzo, Mario J. 1982. "A Theory of Economic Loss in the Law of Torts," 11 *Journal of Legal Studies* 281–310.

Rizzo, Mario J. 1985. "Rules Versus Cost-Benefit Analysis in the Common Law," 4 *Cato Journal* 865–84. http://www.cato.org/pubs/journal/cj4n3/cj4n3-10.pdf.

Rothbard, Murray N. 1982. "Law, Property Rights, and Air Pollution," 2 *Cato Journal* 55–99. http://www.cato.org/pubs/journal/cj2n1/cj2n1-2.pdf.

Rubin, Paul H. 1993. *Tort Reform by Contract*. Washington, DC: AEI Press.

Rubin, Paul H. 2005a. "Micro and Macro Legal Efficiency: Supply and Demand," 13 *Supreme Court Economic Review* 19–34.

Rubin, Paul H. 2005b. "Public Choice and Tort Reform," 124 *Public Choice* 223–36.

Rubin, Paul H., and Martin J. Bailey. 1994. "The Role of Lawyers in Changing the Law," 23 *Journal of Legal Studies* 807–31.

Shugerman, Jed Handelsman. 2008. "A Watershed Moment: Reversals of Tort Theory in the Nineteenth Century," 2:1 *Journal of Tort Law* art. 2.

Stringham, Edward Peter, and Mark D. White. 2004. "Economic Analysis of Tort Law: Austrian and Kantian Perspectives," in Margaret Oppenheimer and Nicholas Mercuro, eds., *Law and Economics: Alternative Economic Approaches to Legal and Regulatory Issues*. http://www.sjsu.edu/stringham/docs/Stringham.and.White2005.pdf.

Task Force on Tobacco Litigation. 1996. "Report of the Task Force on Tobacco Litigation," 27 *Cumberland Law Review* 577–652.

Trial Lawyers Inc. New York: Manhattan Institute. http://www.triallawyersinc.com/.

United States v. Carroll Towing Co. 1947. 159 F.2d 169 (2d Cir.).

U.S. Tort Cost Trends: 2011 Update. 2012. New York: Towers Watson. http://www.towerswatson.com/assets/pdf/6282/Towers-Watson-Tort-Report.pdf.

Volokh, Alexander (Sasha). 2011. "The Positive and Normative Flaws of Cost-Benefit Analysis," 48 *Houston Law Review* 79–98.

White, G. Edward. 2003. *Tort Law in America: An Intellectual History*. New York: Oxford University Press.

Witt, John Fabian. 2009. "Tort: United States Law," in Stanley N. Katz, ed., *Oxford International Encyclopedia of Legal History*. New York: Oxford University Press.

Zipursky, Benjamin C. 2010. "Richard Epstein and the Cold War in Torts," 3 *Journal of Tort Law* art. 5.

Zywicki, Todd J. 2003. "The Rise and Fall of Efficiency in the Common Law: A Supply-Side Analysis," 97 *Northwestern University Law Review* 1551–633.

Zywicki, Todd J., and Anthony B. Sanders. 2008. "Posner, Hayek and the Economic Analysis of Law," 93 *Iowa Law Review* 559–603.

13. Antitrust and competition from a market-process perspective
Donald J. Boudreaux

[C]ompetition is the more important the more complex or "imperfect" are the objective conditions in which it has to operate.

F.A. Hayek[1]

I.

On no topic in microeconomics does the Austrian approach differ so profoundly from that of mainstream neoclassical economics as it does on the topic of competition. And because sharp differences in understandings of "competition" (and, hence, of "monopoly") promote different attitudes toward commercial practices and market arrangements, it is no surprise that Austrian assessments of antitrust policy differ strikingly from typical mainstream assessments.[2]

Unlike the great majority of economists outside the Austrian tradition, Austrians reject the argument that antitrust is needed to keep markets competitive or that antitrust can be reliably used to increase markets' competiveness, inventiveness, and efficiency. Three separate reasons justify this deep Austrian skepticism of antitrust, although any one reason standing alone would be sufficient to justify this rejection.

First, government will not administer antitrust free of political influences—influences that will often distort its application. For my purposes here I need mention this public-choice point only in passing, but its practical importance looms large. Governments have a long history of granting special privileges to politically influential producers. (Think of tariffs.) The prospect, therefore, of government deploying its antitrust

---

[1] Hayek (1948, 103).
[2] The classic text that explores in most detail the flaws in American antitrust theory and enforcement from an Austrian perspective is Armentano (1982). Although more than 30 years old, this text remains timely and no less relevant today than when it was first published. Kirzner (1973) offers a profound, if more abstract, analysis of competition from a market-process perspective.

powers to grant favors to politically influential producers ought not be overlooked simply because antitrust regulation is explicitly justified on pro-consumer, pro-competition grounds. And antitrust's actual history supplies ample reason to fear that antitrust enforcement will indeed generally subvert rather than promote competition.[3]

Second, Austrians are deeply skeptical that even apolitical and highly intelligent government authorities can apply antitrust legislation in ways that improve the operation of markets over time. We can be thankful that the best non-Austrians are sensitive to what Judge Richard Posner describes as "the daunting challenge of designing antitrust remedies that are effective without being anticompetitive" (Posner 2001: ix). But Austrians go further. They insist that the challenge is not simply daunting; it is practically impossible to meet. Government officials do not and cannot ever know enough about the countless, ever-changing, and all-important details of markets to intervene in ways that make markets more competitive and better able to satisfy consumer demands.

The illusion that helpful intervention is possible is perhaps conjured by mistaking models of the economy for the economy itself.[4] Not only are the two not the same thing, but even the most useful economic models necessarily capture only a razor-thin slice of the individual adjustments and manifestations of creativity that make market economies work. Unlike, say, a visual model of the solar system, even unmistakably *micro*economic models of the economy are constructed mostly of large aggregate concepts ("*the* price of wheat" or "*the* Hirschman-Herfindahl Index number for *the* market for wheat") that very much are artifacts of the modeler's own mind or of conventional classifications that economists or statisticians have come to accept over time. These concepts have neither the objectiveness nor the distinctiveness of the sort that both Jupiter and the sun have as the former orbits the latter.

This observation is no prelude to a call to reject economic models. Far from it: it is, however, a plea for greater appreciation of the limitations of economic models. The extraordinary abstraction from details that is required to construct useful economic models—and the frequent need to rely upon artifactual statistical constructs (such as "the HHI for industry X")—results in models that necessarily ignore the countless on-going

---

[3]   See Armentano (1982), Bork (1978), and McChesney and Shughart (1995).

[4]   Among the reasons that Richard Posner gives for his lack of sympathy with calls "to curtail antitrust enforcement drastically or even to repeal the antitrust laws altogether" is his assessment that "economics is an improving discipline." Hence, in Posner's estimation, economics is increasingly able to wisely guide antitrust enforcers (Posner 2001: x).

individual actions that give rise to the more aggregative phenomena featured as variables in the models.[5]

Yet it is only at this deeply micro level that individuals perceive profit opportunities and act to seize them. Analysts' knowledge of the vast array of the countless particular facts that are at every moment the ones to which economic actors must adjust is so skimpy and abstract that we must concede that mastery of economic theory is not even remotely identical to mastery of the economy itself or of enterprise. The capacity for models to inform economists and government officials of what are the best ways for firms to meet consumer demands—and of what are the best organizational forms for markets to facilitate the maximization of consumer welfare—is very limited.

A third and related reason for skepticism of antitrust is that markets are much more robustly competitive than mainstream economic theory reveals them to be. The remainder of this chapter is devoted to explaining why this robustness is real and how mainstream scholars have been misled—and, hence, mislead—by their failure to appreciate this robustness.

II.

For the past century, mainstream economists have defined "competition" as an equilibrium state of affairs. In the mainstream view, market competition is an *outcome*—or, alternatively, competition is a set of equilibrium conditions in which each seller of some given good or service maximizes its profits by producing that volume of output at which marginal cost equals price. In the Austrian view, market competition is entirely different. Competition is a *process*. Competition is a time-embedded

---

[5]   There is, in fact, no single price of wheat, if for no reasons other than there is neither a single type of wheat nor a single point in time in which wheat is bought and sold. And each market identified and modeled does not—unlike a planet orbiting the sun—have definite-enough boundaries that distinguish it clearly enough from phenomena apart from itself. The market for wheat might well, for some purposes, best be thought of as being a distinct market unto itself. For other purposes it might be best to reckon the market for wheat as part of the market for wheat, corn, and barley. And for yet other purposes as being part of the market for all grains. Nothing about objective reality makes clear what are the boundaries of the market(s) in which wheat farmers compete. That people can usefully talk about "the" price of wheat, and that economists can measure with fine precision the HHI for the wheat industry, does not give these things an objectiveness and a distinctiveness of the sort that is possessed (at least from the perspective of humans) by planets and stars.

complex of activities, many of which are incompatible with each other, in which entrepreneurs continually—and often quite creatively—vie to raise the net present value of their firms. If no special protections or privileges are available from the state, this competitive process plays out exclusively in the form of entrepreneurs struggling to increase their efficiencies and to raise the attractiveness (to consumers) of their product offerings.[6]

As many Austrians have noted, no actual competition—as that term is popularly understood—occurs in perfectly competitive markets. To attract more customers, no perfectly competitive firm must cut prices, advertise, or build a better mousetrap. Each firm that manages to keep its unit cost low enough to be covered by the market price of its output can sell as much as it wants. All that each firm in perfectly competitive markets must do is to choose its level of output. And even that choice is mechanical: expand the rate of output produced per period of time up to, but not beyond, the rate at which marginal cost is made equal to the externally determined and fully known market price.

Matters are similar for consumers in perfectly competitive markets. These consumers simply are *assumed* to be fully (or at least always adequately) informed about prices, product quality, and product availability. Also, consumers' demands simply are *assumed* somehow to prompt firms to produce that mix of outputs which optimally satisfies those demands. There is in the theory of perfect competition no organization, agent, or process that *discovers* what consumers do, or might, demand. There are no active economic agents who catalyze inchoate consumer preferences into economically meaningful, concrete consumer demands.[7] And there are certainly no agents who create, intensify, reduce, refine, distort, or otherwise change those demands.

Consumers and firms in this theory are mechanical and utterly artless computing devices. Consumers are mere vessels of utility functions that, when mixed with consumers' incomes, are (somehow) transformed into demand schedules for various goods and services. Firms are nothing more than devices for transforming inputs into outputs that satisfy these given and fixed demands. For consumers and firms alike, then, all demand under

---

[6] This conclusion does not rely upon the implicit assumption that firms never seek monopoly power by engaging in the likes of price-fixing or horizontal mergers. As I explain below, however, the market-process understanding of markets reveals that such efforts to monopolize will fail, with either the monopoly-seekers going bankrupt or unintentionally *improving* consumer welfare in their ultimately futile quest for monopoly power.

[7] My own modest attempt to model competition in both price and non-price dimensions is Boudreaux (1994).

perfect competition exists prior to market activity. Consumer preferences that give rise to demands are given to the system and are not affected by it in any way.

Likewise for costs. By assumption, firms are fully informed about production functions and about input prices. Nothing need be discovered, for there is nothing *to* discover.

In short, because in a perfectly competitive world there is no error, misinformation, or yet-to-be exploited (or even perceived) profit opportunities, there is no entrepreneurship or economic growth in such a world. There is not even any recognizable human activity that adjusts prices upward or downward to the equilibrium levels identified in the model (Arrow 1959). In a perfectly competitive world, all that entrepreneurs do in the real world—even something as simple as actually adjusting prices—is already done.[8]

III.

Of course, every theory is unrealistic in that each one abstracts from many features of reality in order to focus attention on those few features judged to be most relevant for the purposes at hand. Unrealism, in this sense, is indispensable to any useful theory. The theory of perfect competition is no exception. As a tool for sharpening our insight into the likely consequences of certain exogenous changes—for example, how increases in consumer demand for product X affect the price and output of product X if product X is sold by many different sellers—this theory works well enough.

Trouble arises, instead, out of a confusion borne largely of its name. The theory of perfect competition is not a theory *of* competition. We learn nothing from this theory about how firms actually compete. Beyond the positive relationship between the number of competitors and the intensity of price competition—a relationship that is simply assumed rather than demonstrated—this model is silent about the kinds

---

[8]   See, e.g., Demsetz (1997, 137):

> [P]erfect competition, the central model of neoclassical economics, does not really involve competitive pricing activity. The equilibrium market clearing price that emerges from the perfect competition model may be termed a competitive price, but it results from mysterious market clearing forces and not the competitive pricing activities of firms. . .. Competition in the perfect competition model is nothing more or less than the undertaking of profitable *imitative* output responses to given market prices, and is best described just so (emphasis added).

of competitive activities that real-world firms might practice under different market conditions. And it sheds no light on the many different modes of competition that we actually do observe in reality *except* that none of these modes will ever happen under the conditions assumed in the theory of perfect competition.

No competitive activities of the sort that we routinely observe in the real world occur in the model that economists (the experts!) call *perfect* competition. From the confines of that model, activities such as advertising, price discrimination, and product differentiation are naturally viewed as suspect—as evidence either of existing monopoly power or of attempts to secure monopoly power. What else can such activities be from the perspective of the model of perfect competition? When markets are perfectly competitive, consumer welfare *by assumption* is maximized when firms are price takers, securing maximum profit exclusively by adjusting their rates of output in response to observed exogenous changes in the market prices or costs of production that these firms confront. Any other activities violate the conditions of perfect competition.

From this neoclassical vantage point it is a short leap to the conclusion that the real world is chock-full of markets that are not ideally competitive. The verdict seems clear: real-world markets, because they differ so starkly from perfectly competitive markets, are infused with elements of monopoly power and, hence, generate imperfect outcomes that are at least potentially correctable by policies that make real-world markets more closely resemble perfectly competitive ones.

Theories of imperfect competition do nothing to change this line of reasoning. Although more realistic than the theory of perfect competition, the welfare conclusion that falls out of imperfect-competition theories is that markets perform worse the more their conditions differ from those of perfect competition. The imperfections—or "monopolistic"—elements identified as such in theories of imperfect (and monopolistic) competition are precisely those features of reality that cause, or permit, real-world market activities to differ from those that prevail in a world of perfect competition.

The realism introduced by such theories is the assumed fact that real-world markets swarm—lamentably—with monopoly power. Ideal competitive conditions might be practically unobtainable, and so theories of imperfect and monopolistic competition more accurately describe real-world markets than does the theory of perfect competition. But for all of these theories the ideal is unquestionably perfect competition. Perfect competition sets the standard against which the competitiveness of real-world markets is judged.

IV.

Austrians reject this neoclassical theorizing about competition. They do so not because such theorizing abstracts from some features of real-world markets, but because it abstracts from the very features of real-world markets that are most in need of being explained by any theory of competition. In the Austrian understanding, the discovery of consumer demands—discovery not only by producers, but also by consumers themselves—is an important function of real-world markets. Likewise the discovery of lower-cost methods of production. Likewise the discovery of information about (often rapidly changing) prices, product qualities, and availabilities of products and inputs. Likewise the potential for producing and selling entirely new products. In reality, none of this knowledge is ever given or fixed. It must be discovered. And competition—real-world competition, the struggle among producers to increase their profits by better appealing to consumers in any ways that they can—is chiefly a process of such discovery.

Clearly, this entrepreneurial discovery process differs greatly from the "competition" that occurs in neoclassical models. In Austrian accounts, types and qualities of outputs are never given. Nor are demands. Nor are prices. Nor is knowledge of prices. Nor are production functions, costs, and knowledge of input availability. These economic phenomena are all understood to be, at least in large part, discovered—or even created by—entrepreneurial actions of the sort that are assumed away in the model of perfect competition.[9]

One result of this difference is that many real-world activities that either do not occur in the theory of perfect competition or that are plainly at odds with the assumptions of that theory are, in the Austrian view, revealed as being at least potentially pro-competitive. Many of the "monopolistic" elements or "imperfections" that mainstream economists see in real-world markets are, through Austrian lenses, seen as manifestations of well-functioning and creative competition.

For example, a firm that builds a better mousetrap gains for itself, if only temporarily, a greater ability to increase its profits by raising its price above marginal cost. The mainstream economist focuses on the absence of instantaneous forces to compel this innovative firm to sell its better mouse-

---

[9]   From the vantage point of the theory of perfect competition, no one can make sense of Shlomo Maital's (1994, 169) observation that "Good executives create customers. Great ones create markets." In contrast, from the standpoint of reality—and from economic history—Maital's observation makes perfect and profound sense.

trap at a price equal to marginal cost; therefore, this economist identifies the innovation as introducing a quantum of monopoly power into the mousetrap market. The Austrian, in contrast, focuses on the unquestionable increase in consumer welfare brought about by the entrepreneur's successful effort to improve the product varieties available to consumers. No consumer, after all, was forced to abandon the old mousetrap for the new mousetrap.

Such product experimentation is necessary in a world in which consumer demands are not fully known to suppliers—and, as is also likely, also are not fully known even to consumers themselves. The typical consumer might well be unaware that he is willing to purchase Z amount of new product X at price $\$Y$ until he actually first sees product X displayed on a retailer's shelf and priced at $\$Y$. Even though the assumption that each consumer knows his demands fully is useful for several purposes, its use in a theory of competition masks an important function of competition— namely, to help consumers themselves discover the specific features of their demands.

If demands and products are not given and fixed, the prospect for earning, at least for a short time, profits above normal by being able to charge prices higher than cost is surely a principal lure to entice entrepreneurs to experiment with different product offerings. Therefore, neither above-normal profits nor P>MC any longer serves as an unambiguous marker or signal of monopoly power. On the contrary, both become potential pieces of evidence of intense competition.

Austrians see no reason to classify product differentiation differently from price-cutting: both actions are competitive in the popular *and proper* sense of the term; both are done for self-interested commercial reasons; and both improve consumer welfare *relative to* what that welfare would otherwise be (Boudreaux 1994).

V.

Austrians thus reject most of the mainstream markers of monopoly power—markers such as P>MC, profits greater than normal, high market concentration, and price discrimination. These mainstream signs of monopoly power are, instead, at least as likely to be evidence of on-going competitive struggles among firms each to better position itself to "win" more consumer patronage.

For Austrians, competitive markets exist as long as there are no *artificial* barriers to production and exchange. The range of actions available to entrepreneurs and consumers in a market is, in fact, open-ended, and therefore the range of observed arrangements and market "outcomes" that are consistent with competition is also open-ended. What might well appear to an economist trained only in mainstream models to be evidence of monopoly power is perhaps, in reality, evidence of the market's creative way of groping toward greater efficiencies.

Obviously, a question is raised by the statement "competitive markets exist as long as there are no *artificial* barriers to production and exchange." What, exactly, is meant by "artificial barrier"? The answer—or, *my* answer—is a barrier to production and exchange is artificial if it results from legislative or regulatory power targeted to give differential advantage to a particular product, person, firm, industry, or region. That is, a barrier is artificial only if it springs from the discriminatory application of force in favor of certain market participants.

In the absence of government favoritism (and of the outright breaking of foundational common-law prohibitions, such as those against vandalism and theft), a firm can increase its profits only by achieving greater efficiencies in production and distribution, or by enhancing the attractiveness of its product in the minds of consumers. The resulting continual and creative struggle among entrepreneurs for maximum profits will result in a variety of experiments—some successful, some not—across the spectrum of possible ways to organize firms and industries. For Austrians, the test of whether or not markets are competitive is not how well markets conform to some external criteria imposed by economists, courts, legislators, or government administrators. Rather, that test is whether or not artificial barriers exist. Period.

The mainstream economist objects, along with advocates of vigorous antitrust enforcement: "This Austrian definition of 'artificial barriers' simply assumes away the possibility that such barriers can arise in free markets." But this objection misses the larger picture. Economic theory—mainstream as well as Austrian—has at its foundation the assumption that entrepreneurs are forever searching for opportunities to earn profits as large as possible *and* that consumers are forever searching for opportunities to increase their utility as much as possible.[10] With these assumptions, economists readily recognize that (say) an unexpected increase in the demand for bananas relative to that for papayas will prompt producers to supply fewer papayas and more bananas. In this case no one frets that

---

[10]   Indeed, the assumption that producers are forever on the lookout for new ways to maximize their profits is critical to the case for antitrust. It is that single-minded and cunning quest for profit that fuels producers' efforts to collude, merge-to-monopoly, predate, and otherwise suppress competition.

consumers will not be supplied with more bananas, or that consumers will long pay exorbitant prices for bananas. Freedom to enter the banana market is recognized as sufficient to ensure that the current higher-than-"competitive" price for bananas (and the current lower-than-"competitive" quantity of bananas supplied) will be corrected by increased production of bananas.

Importantly, in such a case as that of an increased demand for bananas, no mainstream economist worries if told that the production functions of each existing banana producer make it unprofitable for *these* producers to increase *their* production of bananas even at the higher price of bananas. The reasonable assumption in this event is that, absent government-imposed restrictions on entry into the banana industry, the higher demand for bananas would then be met exclusively by new entrants.

This same set of assumptions and train of reasoning that apply in the case of an exogenous increase in consumers' demand for bananas should apply also in the case of the most widely condemned violations of antitrust legislation, namely, horizontal collusion and horizontal mergers. If in the absence of government-imposed restrictions on entry a rise in the price of bananas caused by increased consumer demand for bananas attracts new entrants into the banana market, why suppose that in the absence of government-imposed restrictions on entry horizontal collusion or horizontal mergers among banana producers that restrict output and raise prices will not do the very same—namely, attract new competitors? No good reason exists.

It will not do to insist that a relevant distinction is found in the fact that horizontal collusion or consolidation is initiated by producers while rising consumer demand (as in the banana example) is not. If new entry is assumed possible and effective when the latter occurs, it must be assumed possible and effective when the former occurs. In both cases, new entrants are self-interestedly seeking profits in response to current patterns of prices above costs and not in response to the motives or reasons that give rise to these patterns.

Nor will it do to assert that, unlike rising consumer demand, horizontal agreements that restrict output and raise prices serve no legitimate economic function and, therefore, ought not be tolerated. First, scholars have identified plausible situations in which even successful collusion promotes consumer welfare over the long run (see, for example, Dewey 1979 and Bittlingmayer 1982). Second and more importantly, as long as there are no government-erected barriers to entry, the most reliable test for what arrangements best promote long-run consumer welfare is the market test. If a particular horizontal arrangement survives in the face of entry, or the possibility of entry, we are not scientifically entitled to assume that

that arrangement is undesirable. Our presumption must run in the other direction. The same intellectual humility that obliges us to regard the continuing supply of vanilla ice cream, in a market free of artificial barriers, as serving consumers' best interests also obliges us to regard a successful collusive agreement or horizontal merger, in a market free of artificial barriers, as serving consumers' best interests.

Put differently, the potential for entry that is free of obstruction by artificial barriers is sufficient to discipline producers to continually experiment with organizational arrangements and contractual practices that improve their abilities to serve consumers. Arrangements and practices that serve consumer interests poorly relative to other arrangements and practices will over time be displaced in competition with those other arrangements and practices.

To most economists and legal scholars this Austrian position seems extreme. When the complexity and dynamism of the economy is reckoned properly, however, the Austrian position is seen to be more realistic than the position staked out by the mainstream. What F.A. Hayek (1948: 80) famously called "the particular circumstances of time and place" are all-important. It is *these* details that must be reckoned with, moment to moment without end, by people on the spot. It is these details that furnish hints only to close-in observers—only to those people on the spot—for how resources might be reallocated, or how organizational forms and practices might be altered, to generate more profit. Using antitrust legislation to prevent experimentation with organizational forms and practices short-circuits competition among organizational forms and practices. Even if antitrust enforcement results in more intense price competition (and, hence, lower prices), it will do so by weakening other forms of competition.

VI.

Before turning to an example of how a market-process perspective promotes analyses different from those that typically issue from the mainstream, a few words must be said about the modern Chicago/UCLA School. While more neoclassical than Austrian in method—and while not going as far as Austrians in rejecting many mainstream conclusions— modern Chicago and UCLA economists have contributed impressively to a more realistic and much-improved assessment of market processes and of antitrust policy. Research done by these scholars, especially from the 1950s through the early 1990s, was a shot across the bow of mainstream antitrust research.

This Chicago/UCLA scholarship shares much with Austrian scholarship.

Like Austrians, Chicago/UCLA scholars understand that competition is a discovery procedure—and, hence, they understand the importance of entrepreneurship; they understand that heuristic models are neither descriptions of, nor prescriptions for, reality; and they treat seriously the subjectivity of tastes and costs. It is fair to say that the bulk of Chicago/ UCLA insights into industrial organization and antitrust policy is a product of that school's embrace, however unconsciously or imperfectly, of concepts that form the core of Austrian scholarship.

Lester Telser's (1960) work on vertical restraints; John McGee's (1958) and Frank Easterbrook's (1981) work on predatory pricing; George Bittlingmayer's (1982) work on horizontal collusion; Harold Demsetz's work on barriers to entry (1982)—these are just some examples of pioneering research that, although these works "feel" more neoclassical than Austrian, their authors are highly sensitive to the reality of phenomena such as dispersed and ever-changing knowledge, subjective preferences, and the open-endedness of genuinely competitive markets.[11]

It is an interesting question (although one that I do not explore here) why Chicago/UCLA scholars have been more effective than self-identified Austrians at changing antitrust policy for the better. Whatever the answer, the fact remains that Austrian analyses of antitrust policy overlap greatly with Chicago/UCLA analyses.

The distinctiveness of this Austrian/Chicago/UCLA-style market-process tradition in antitrust is seen clearly in analyses of predatory pricing.

VII.

In neoclassical theory, a price is predatory if it is below marginal cost. To this requirement for finding unlawful predation, American antitrust doctrine adds the additional requirement that the firm that initiates the below-cost price-cutting do so as a result of that firm's intent to gain monopoly power or to increase whatever monopoly power it already enjoys.

In a world, though, in which competitive firms (certainly no less than predatory-pricing firms) cut prices in order to attract more buyers, predatory price-cutting is strikingly similar to competitive price-cutting. The test, therefore, of whether a low price is predatory or competitive is whether or not that low price is below some relevant measure of cost. Theoretically,

---

[11] This Chicago/UCLA antitrust scholarship is eloquently summarized and brilliantly applied to the American experience in Bork (1978).

that relevant measure is the price-cutting firm's marginal cost. But marginal cost is notoriously difficult to measure practically. To relieve courts of the nearly impossible tasks of divining defendants' intent and of measuring marginal costs, Phillip Areeda and Donald Turner (1975) devised a cost-based test that allegedly offers courts an objective and sufficiently reliable way to identify predation. Under the Areeda-Turner test, prices above average total cost (ATC) are *per se* legal, prices lower than ATC but not below average variable cost (AVC) are presumptively non-predatory, and prices below AVC are presumptively predatory.

While the Areeda-Turner test improved courts' treatment of predation claims by shifting attention away from the economically irrelevant belligerent language ("Let's crush our competitors!" "Our goal is to destroy our rivals!") often found in internal company memoranda (Elzinga and Mills 1994), this test is fundamentally flawed. From the market-process perspective, *all* pricing practices should be *per se* legal. The reasons are four: (1) misidentifying competitively low prices as predatory chills competitive behavior; (2) costs are inherently difficult to measure; (3) firms will almost never pursue even temporary enhancements of their market power by using price cuts because such a strategy is too unlikely to be worth the costs to firms of pursuing it; and (4) the relationship between price and cost at any moment says nothing about predatory intent or likelihood of predatory success.

The first two reasons are widely recognized even outside the Austrian and Chicago/UCLA traditions. I will therefore not discuss them. And although a great deal has been written about the third reason,[12] still more can be said. But saying more requires first an understanding of the fourth reason—that is, why the relationship between price and cost yields no information about predatory intent.

The Areeda-Turner test rests squarely on the belief that P<AVC conveys relevant information about the firm's predatory designs (or likely monopolistic future consequences). The reason P<AVC is believed to announce that a firm has predatory designs is that such a price causes unnecessary losses for the firm and, hence, an unreasonable and socially damaging way for it to increase profits. Because a firm in mainstream theory likely has no good reason to charge prices below AVC, a firm observed charging such a low price is probably doing something other than maximizing its profits during the current period. That something else is concluded to be attempted monopolization.

As Herbert Hovenkamp (2005: 341) explains, it is "generally true" that

---

[12]   The classic studies here remain McGee (1958) and Easterbrook (1981).

"dropping a price below short-run marginal cost is not reasonable profit-maximizing behavior, unless the resulting losses are more than offset by future monopoly profits."[13] If firms intend their below-cost pricing to promote their monopoly power, therefore, they are socially harmful predators.

This conclusion (which is of a type that philosophers call "the fallacy of the residual") is invalid. Due to its unavoidably limited scope, the partial-equilibrium model at the heart of theories of perfect competition and of imperfect competition defines only a limited number of economically sound reasons for firms to cut prices below AVC (or below MC). So it hardly follows that an observed price cut that is inexplicable when analyzed using this mainstream model is predatory.

As explained above, the mainstream model of markets (upon which the Areeda-Turner test is built) is designed to explain pricing and output decisions by firms producing given products to satisfy given demands, all within the confines of well-defined and given constraints on resource availability, knowledge, and production techniques. In reality, though, firms must decide which kinds and qualities of products to produce as well as how to market these products. If pricing decisions are part of a firm's product-development and marketing plan, prices below conventionally measured costs (whether marginal or average variable) are not validly classified as predatory simply because the mainstream model has no room for such pricing practices. Such prices might, in reality, be a legitimate investment in marketing or product or firm development.

For example, a firm might decide that if it can today develop long-lasting consumer loyalty, construction tomorrow of a larger and more-efficient factory will be justified. But how to develop such loyalty? One way might be to charge, for a time, prices below conventionally measured AVC (or MC). Yet under the Areeda-Turner test, such prices are presumptively predatory.

Suppose, however, that the firm seeks to engender consumer loyalty by some means other than pricing below cost, such as by spending extra funds training sales clerks to be singularly friendly, knowledgeable, and helpful. There is no economically relevant difference between these alternative means of building consumer loyalty. In each case, the firm "loses"—more accurately, invests—money today in the hope of recouping these "losses" tomorrow. Also in each case, rivals are harmed if the firm succeeds; in each

---

[13] Hovenkamp (2005: 341) continues: "Marginal cost pricing is consistent with competition; supramarginal cost pricing is consistent with monopoly. But prices lower than marginal cost are consistent with neither."

case, rivals might even be bankrupted and the successful firm left for a time to enjoy "monopoly" power. And yet predation is declared only in the case in which the firm spends money charging prices below cost. If training sales clerks is presumed to be a wholesome competitive exercise, it is utterly unclear why pricing below cost is presumed to be pernicious. Both activities involve investments by the firm designed to increase its net present value *through means that will work only if consumers voluntarily respond positively to those means*. Both activities help the firm, harm rivals, and benefit consumers (at least until the firm becomes a monopolist as a result either of its excessively low prices or its staff of unusually competent and agreeable sales clerks). Because the Areeda-Turner test and the mainstream theory upon which it rests are largely blind to possible efficiency justifications for prices below AVC, that test and mainstream theory are too quick to label all such prices as predatory.

None of the foregoing denies that a firm's pricing practices *can* ruin rivals and leave the firm with a monopoly. Yet it does point out the fact that prices below AVC are an investment that differ in no economically relevant way from other indisputably competitive investments that firms use to attract consumers. And nothing in even mainstream theory justifies the conclusion that investments in the form of price-cutting are any more (or less) likely than are other investments to result in monopolized markets. Mainstream theorists simply assume that these different kinds of investments have very different likely consequences for the competitiveness of markets. A plausible theory of predation, though, must realistically distinguish investments that are likely to result in welfare-reducing monopolies from investments that are unlikely to do so. Focusing on the relationship of price to cost does not help in finding such a distinction.

There are now, indeed, several well-known reasons for doubting that attempts to monopolize *ever* take the form of predatory price-cutting (Easterbrook 1981). To these well-known reasons I add others. These other reasons are suggested by a market-process perspective—a perspective that reveals that firms' efforts to compete legitimately for consumers' patronage span a far larger range of activities than is revealed by the price-obsessed mainstream models.

So, firms intent on securing monopoly power are unlikely, for the following three reasons, to use predatory *price* cutting;

(1) Non-price improvements are more difficult than are price cuts for rivals to mimic. What can be easier to imitate than a price cut? No special skill, experience, or organizational sophistication is required to cut prices to meet lower prices charged by a rival. Entrepreneurs and business executives need to know only how to read numbers.

In contrast, matching an improvement in product quality or in the efficiency of production or distribution techniques *does* require real skills on the part of rivals—skills much more scarce than the ability to read numbers. While the dullest rival will have no trouble matching a price cut exactly, some rivals might never be able to match a non-price change in a competitor's offering or method of production.

(2) Non-price improvements take more time to match than do price cuts. The longer it takes for rivals to match a predator's actions, the greater are rivals' losses during the period of predation. Thus, compared to a predator that merely slashes prices, one that employs non-price tactics to damage rivals—say, a firm that seeks monopoly power by building a better mousetrap—will oblige its rivals to exit the market more quickly. In addition, re-entry into the monopolized industry will be slower if the monopoly was won through non-price tactics rather than through simple price-cutting. Because (in analyses of predatory pricing) rivals of the predator are assumed to be efficient participants in the industry, only a genuine non-price improvement has any chance of giving the predator a durable advantage over rivals—an advantage that not only is difficult or impossible to match today, but might well be difficult or impossible to match also in the future.

(3) Unlike with predatory pricing, non-price improvements might yield profits to the predator even before rivals exit the industry. An improvement in product quality by a predator might increase consumer demand for its output so substantially that the predator recovers all costs of the product improvement even before all rivals are driven from the industry. No such profits are available during predatory-price wars. Moreover, future demand for the product might be higher when the predator improves the quality of its product than when it simply charges below-cost prices.

In short, *if* there is predation, it almost certainly will not be carried out with easy-to-mimic price cuts. Savvy predators will instead choose non-price tactics to harm rivals.

Of course, because Austrians have good reason to doubt that a market can be monopolized for any length of time in the absence of artificial barriers to entry, I do not mean by the above Austrian-inspired comparison of non-price predation to predatory pricing to suggest that non-price predation is a real problem worth worrying about. Rather, that comparison is meant to reveal how mistaking a theory of *pricing* for a theory of *competition* can mislead competent scholars to reach mistaken conclusions—conclusions whose faults are clearly visible from a market-process perspective.

VIII.

The bottom line to the above market-process analysis is radical. It is that any particular profit-seeking activity in private markets is just as appropriately reckoned to be an attempt to "monopolize" as it is to be "vigorously competitive." Every firm (or so we can realistically assume) does *all* that it does in the hope that its efforts—individually and as a group—increase its net present value as much as possible. The firm that cuts its prices to match a rival's lower prices no less than the firm that cuts its prices to undercut its rival's prices—and no less than the firm that builds a better mousetrap or that spends more on advertising to make availability of its mousetraps better known to potential buyers—hopes that the result of its action will be as much "market power" as can possibly be had.

There is no justification for pretending that firms sometimes want, or are content, only to "compete" while at other times—overcome with anti-social profusions of greed, guile, or other grasping motives—they seek instead to be monopolists. Firms simply and always do whatever they can to increase their NPVs as much as possible. No separate mental, psychological, *or economic* category exists for "competitive" as distinct from "monopolizing" actions within markets. To repeat: the only goal for each profit-seeking firm is to increase as much as possible its NPV. Period. That's all. And to increase its NPV as much as possible each firm experiments with different arrays of pricing and non-pricing options, none of which can be known in the abstract, independently of actual competitive market process, to be worthwhile or not. The only activities of firms that can legitimately be called predatory are those activities that either violate existing tenets of property and contract law—for example, Jones's Restaurant hiring a vandal to slash the tires on the cars of patrons of Smith's Restaurant—or those activities that seek to persuade government officials to use force to artificially reduce consumer demand for rivals' offerings (or to artificially raise rivals' costs). All activities that do not forcibly reduce consumer options (either directly or indirectly) are best regarded, by economists no less than by government officials, as part of the healthy and competitive market process. Antitrust regulation, therefore, is certainly unnecessary and all too likely harmful.

REFERENCES

Areeda, Philip and Donald F. Turner. 1975. "Predatory Pricing and Related Practices Under Section 2 of the Sherman Act," *Harvard Law Review*, Vol. 88, Feb., pp. 697–733.

Armentano, Dominick T. 1982. *Antitrust and Monopoly: Anatomy of a Policy Failure* (New York: Wiley).

Arrow, Kenneth J. 1959. "Toward a Theory of Price Adjustment," in Moses Abramovitz, ed., *The Allocation of Economic Resources* (Palo Alto: Stanford University Press), pp. 41–51.

Bittlingmayer, George. 1982. "Decreasing Average Cost and Competition: A New Look at the Addyston Pipe Case," *Journal of Law & Economics*, Vol. 25, October, pp. 201–29.

Bork, Robert H. 1978. *The Antitrust Paradox* (New York: Basic Books).

Boudreaux, Donald J. 1994. "Schumpeter and Kirzner on Competition and Equilibrium," in *The Market Process: Essays in Contemporary Austrian Economics*, Peter J. Boettke and David L. Prychitko, eds. (Cheltenham, UK, Edward Elgar), pp. 52–61.

Demsetz, Harold. 1982. "Barriers to Entry," *American Economic Review*, Vol. 72, March, pp. 47–57.

Demsetz, Harold. 1997. *The Economics of the Business Firm* (New York: Cambridge University Press).

Dewey, Donald. 1979. "Information, Entry, and Welfare: The Case for Collusion," *American Economic Review*, Vol. 69, September, pp. 587–94.

Easterbrook, Frank. 1981. "Predatory Strategies and Counterstrategies." *University of Chicago Law Review*, Vol. 48, Spring, pp. 263–337.

Elzinga, Kenneth G. and David E. Mills. 1994. "Trumping the Areeda-Turner Test: The Recoupment Standard in *Brooke Group*," *Antitrust Law Journal*, Vol. 62, Spring, pp. 559–84.

Hayek, F.A. 1948. *Individualism and Economic Order* (Chicago: University of Chicago Press).

Hovenkamp, Herbert. 2005. *Federal Antitrust Policy*, 3rd edition (Saint Paul, MN: Thomson West).

Kirzner, Israel M. 1973. *Competition and Entrepreneurship* (Chicago: University of Chicago Press).

Maital, Shlomo. 1994. *Executive Economics* (New York: Free Press).

McChesney, Fred S. and William F. Shughart, eds. 1995. *The Causes and Consequences of Antitrust* (Chicago: University of Chicago Press).

McGee, John S. 1958. "Predatory Price Cutting: The Standard Oil (N.J.) Case," *Journal of Law & Economics*, Vol. 1, October, pp. 137–69.

Posner, Richard A. 2001. *Antitrust Law*, 2nd edition (Chicago: University of Chicago Press).

Telser, Lester G. 1960. "Why Should Manufacturers Want Fair Trade?" *Journal of Law & Economics*, Vol. 3, October, pp. 86–105.

14. Civil procedure reconsidered
Jeffrey S. Parker*

The economic analysis of civil procedure can be enriched by a more thorough consideration of the productive functions of civil adjudication. The previous literature has recognized that civil adjudication does have products—conventionally described as dispute resolution services, plus precedents for future cases—but otherwise has tended to treat civil litigation as a tax on productive activity, or, worse yet, as unproductive or counter-productive rent-seeking activity.

While all of those perspectives can have their uses in certain contexts, they are all incomplete, because none captures an essential function of civil litigation within the legal system, which is *learning*, meaning the production of new knowledge or information, and not merely the exchange or revelation of pre-existing knowledge or information. Adding this perspective profoundly changes the economic analysis of civil litigation, which cannot thereafter be treated merely as a zero-sum (or negative-sum) game of strategic posturing and bargaining.

A more thorough consideration of the information-production function of civil adjudication presents a difficult and daunting task, because it requires more searching consideration of an obvious fact that has been recognized but not fully developed in the previous literature, which is that procedural law and substantive law act as both complements and substitutes for one another.[1] This means that a full economic analysis of procedural law necessarily must account for its interactions with the substantive law that is sought to be enforced, and also account for the temporal interaction between ex ante and ex post investment in new knowledge.[2]

* Research assistance was provided by Ashley Finnegan, and research support by the Law and Economics Center at George Mason University School of Law. I am grateful for comments on earlier drafts from Todd Zywicki, Bruce Kobayashi, Henry Manne, Derek Yonai, and the other participants at the Research Roundtable on Austrian Law and Economics, sponsored by the Law and Economics Center at George Mason University School of Law, on April 25, 2013.

[1] This point is developed somewhat in Lewisch and Parker (2016).

[2] Differential information costs, including the ex ante/ex post distinction, previously have been identified as a basis for selecting among types of legal rules and remedies. *See* Wittman (1977); *see also* Brown (1972); Calabresi and Melamed (1972), and Cooter (1984). The advance of this chapter is to develop the

Both are highly complex undertakings, which tend to frustrate the instinct of analysts in all fields, which is to carve up the subject of study into more easily digestible parts for examination.

Therefore, the primary objective of this chapter is to show in a simple way that it is essential to consider the substance-procedure interaction and the temporal interaction in order to arrive at useful results. The implications are profound, because these interactions expose the information-production function that lies at the heart of the civil adjudicative process: because neither parties nor tribunals nor the legal system can "know" anything precisely until the point of definitive adjudication, the adjudicative process itself functions creatively and productively, much like the price system in markets. Moreover, as adjudication is a substitute for as well as a comple-ment to substantive law (or ex ante contracting), decisions to defer (or not defer) information production into the adjudicative stage themselves are productive decisions of economic moment. Therefore, the tradeoff between ex ante investment (as through contractual provisions, rules of substantive law, or parties' decisions regarding their primary conduct) and ex post investment in adjudicative fact-finding is in no sense neglectable in the economic analysis of procedural law, but rather may be the single most important question to be examined.

In developing that thesis, this chapter draws upon the insights of the Austrian economists, most notably Mises and Hayek. However, this is not a special "Austrian" perspective only, but a completely general point: once it is recognized that civil litigation creates a product in the form of new knowledge, then decisions to invest in litigation (versus its alternatives) must be treated not merely as "rent-seeking," but also as embodying some element of innovation, and thus are analogous to other investments in new knowledge, such as research and development, or exploration for natural resources. Because the incentives affecting such investment decisions necessarily will affect the supply and price of new knowledge, then the rules of civil adjudication, no less than those of any other legal regulatory structure, will affect welfare through their effects on the creation and pro-duction of new information through litigation, or its alternatives. To the extent that rules of procedural law influence those investment decisions toward less productive uses, they can reduce welfare.

---

endogeneity of the choice of rules or specifications ex ante with the information costs of litigation ex post.

I.   RETURNING TO FIRST PRINCIPLES

Why is there procedural law? Conventionally, this question is answered by a trite truism that procedural law exists to enforce or carry out substantive law, and hence the older term for procedure of "adjective" law. However, this conventional answer masks the dual nature of procedure: yes, it carries out substantive law (a complement), but it also may replace a rule of substantive law (a substitute).

The easiest illustration can be drawn from a simple two-party contract. In a sense, the terms of the contract are the rules of "substantive" law for the contracting parties. But the parties may or may not be able to agree ex ante on all of the terms of the contract, or—more to the point of this chapter—they may decide jointly that it is not worthwhile for them to specify all of the details of their bargain in advance. Instead, they may specify a process or procedure to address such questions as may (or may not) arise in the future. The contracting parties may explicitly appoint some third party to resolve a future contingency, or agree to submit to an arbitral agency, or, in default of those options, implicitly agree to litigate in the event of a future dispute. In each case, if the bargain underlying the contract is a productive activity, then so also are the parties' joint decisions on how to invest in ex ante specification versus ex post disputation—these are decisions about investment in information.

Thus, the superficial appearance of civil adjudication as simple state-sponsored coercion can be misleading. In the contractual context, parties easily may avoid the coercive process by contracting away from it, or simply not contracting at all. Few would argue that the complete absence of enforceable contracts is an acceptable state of affairs. It is true that there are extra-legal enforcement alternatives, both coercive and non-coercive, such as mutual forbearance, reputational markets, moral suasion, or self-help, violent or otherwise. There are also contractual alternatives, such as insurance. However, for some parties, those alternatives will not maximize their joint interest in contracting. Instead, some contracting parties could agree in their mutual interest ex ante to appoint a third party to adjudicate ex post disputes, with the possibility of coercive enforcement of the result. In that context, civil adjudication in public courts is only another option in an array from which the parties may choose, in their joint interest. And each of those choices, including ordinary civil litigation, can be a productive choice. Therefore, to the extent that rules of civil litigation may affect the parties' choices, those rules may divert economic resources from one investment to another, for good or ill.

While this effect is most transparent in the case of a simple two-party contract, actually it is entirely general. For what is "substantive" law aside from a specified set of consequences when certain events occur? The major bodies of non-contract law, such as tort, property, crime, and various public-law regulations, all follow that pattern. Similarly, the distinction between questions of law and questions of fact is another extension of the same continuum: whether a given question of fact has significance is a function of the "rules" of law, which usually are only partially specified in advance. So, nearly every question in actual adjudication is a "mixed" question of whether a particular event took place and what legal consequence (if any) that event connotes. Going back to the example of the two-party contract, any question of fact can be converted into a question of law by contractual provisions specifying the lack of legal consequence to a given fact, or entire sets of facts. The same is true of other bodies of substantive law.

II. PREVIOUS ECONOMIC TREATMENTS OF CIVIL PROCEDURE

Previous economic treatments of civil procedure largely ignore or suppress the information-production function of civil adjudication.

One large body of literature is concerned primarily with a descriptive characterization of civil litigation as a strategic bargaining process, considering such matters as decisions to file suit, to settle or go to trial, and the like.[3] As the central feature of this literature is mutual estimates of expected outcomes in litigated matters, it is called here the "expected outcome" literature. To the extent that this literature considers information economics at all, it is in terms of exchange or revelation of information held by each party, or the effects of asymmetrical information. However, revelation is not learning in the sense used in this chapter, which is the creation of information that neither party may have possessed ex ante lite. And in these models, the only value of information lies in predicting what the third-party adjudicator may do. There is little attention to the problem of error by the adjudicating authority.

Another large body of literature has grown up around a pioneering 1973 article by Richard Posner,[4] which postulates a more normative model of the welfare consequences of civil litigation. In Posner's model, the "efficiency"

---

[3] For an early survey of this literature, see Cooter and Rubinfeld (1989). More recent summaries can be found in Kobayashi and Parker (2000); and in Sanchirico (2012). Another source of more selective but excellent development of both this literature and the Posner model of direct and error costs is Bone (2003).

[4] Posner (1973); and see the summary sources cited in note 2, above.

of procedure is seen as requiring the minimization of the sum of "direct" costs and "error" costs, both of which have both private and social dimensions. In this framework, the recognition of "error" costs at least concedes that adjudicators may err, but it actually does not explain how such a thing might be observed, and the existing literature only partially develops the welfare consequences of both private and social error costs.

Similarly, Gordon Tullock's famous critique of the adversarial system, published in 1980 as *Trials on Trial*,[5] appears to take information supply as given exogenously to the litigation problem. In Tullock's model, every civil lawsuit has a "Mr. Right" and a "Mr. Wrong," and thus he criticizes adversarial procedure as inefficient because "in adversarial proceedings, a great deal of the resources are put in by someone who is attempting to mislead." (Tullock (1980), p. 96). But he does not explain how observers know which is "Mr. Right" and "Mr. Wrong," nor even how the parties themselves know. In effect, Tullock assumes that this information somehow is provided exogenously to the litigants' decisions, perhaps by an idealized judge in the inquisitorial system. But the judge has to learn, too. How does the judge do so, and how do we know whether the judge is right or wrong?

In fairness to Tullock, he was making only a limited comparative point. Even that point is subject to substantial doubt.[6] However, the major contribution of Tullock's work has been in stimulating further thought—some critical and some supportive of Tullock[7]—that is beginning to identify the information-production features of civil litigation.

A following literature comparing the properties of adversarial versus inquisitorial procedure has produced important insights.[8] Adversarial procedure possesses an obvious resemblance to competition in the marketplace,[9] and following this analogy has produced a series of papers drawing on game-theoretic models to challenge Tullock by showing the comparative superiority of competitive production of the information supplied to tribunals, beginning with a 1986 paper by Milgrom and

---

[5] Tullock (1980).

[6] My own experiments with Michael Block and others have shown that the actual structures of both the process and information production were more complex than previously appreciated. See Block, Parker, Vyborna, and Ducek (2000). Further results from this series were reported in Block and Parker (2004), and Parker and Lewisch (1998).

[7] Among the supportive papers, see Zywicki (2008) and Parisi (2002). However, as discussed below, considering the cost of evidence production and the nature of the decision-maker can change the picture.

[8] An excellent summary of this literature is given in Froeb and Kobayashi (2012).

[9] See Fuller (1978).

Roberts, as extended in papers by Froeb and Kobayashi (1996 and 2001), and supplemented in papers by Shin (1998), Dewatripont and Tirole (1999), Sanchirico (2001a), and Yonai (2012). The important advances in these models are in the recognition that information supply is a costly activity, and that both tribunals and litigants can be uninformed and imperfect. But perhaps the most important insight is that the information-supply properties of civil adjudication, especially in the competitive adversarial form, can replicate the information-impacting effects of free competition on the supply and price of commodities in the marketplace. Like other products, information supplied to litigation is not a free lunch, either. These insights lead directly to a consideration of the economics of information, as developed most notably by Hayek, discussed in the next section.

In a somewhat parallel development coming from the opposite direction of contract law and economics, papers by Scott and Triantis (2006) and by Sanchirico and Triantis (2008) have begun to develop the tradeoff between ex ante contract specification and ex post disputation. This insight calls attention to the importance of opportunity costs and subjective valuation: because parties may differ in their ex ante ability to anticipate future disputes—and their opportunity costs of doing so—then the tradeoffs involved would seem to be inherently subjective. Thus, a one-size-fits-all approach to rules of civil adjudication, and especially those affecting the parties' incentives to produce information, seems unlikely to be universally satisfactory.

While the recognition remains imperfect, the more recent literature is beginning to come to grips with the profound effects of recognizing the information-production function of civil litigation. What this means is that the temptation to treat civil litigation as essentially a tax (as in Posner) or simple rent-seeking by one or another party (as in Tullock), must be rejected. Moreover, because information supplied to litigation is not only costly to produce (thus affecting the incentives to supply) but also diffused in nature, in the baseline case it cannot be "known" exogenously to the litigation process, but rather is learned through that process. In terms of Tullock's model, observers cannot "know" which is "Mr. Right" and "Mr. Wrong," and even the litigants themselves may not "know." In other words, there is such a thing as an honest dispute in which neither side may know who is "Mr. Wrong," because it was not worthwhile to invest in that question ex ante. Finding out ex post is an important part of what civil litigation produces, for the parties as well as the legal system. And, like commodities prices in the market, that knowledge is a particular of time and place, which neither the parties nor the legal system have adequate incentive to learn until the transaction—i.e, the adjudication—actually takes place.

III.   THE ECONOMICS OF INFORMATION, SUBJECTIVE VALUATION, AND OPPORTUNITY COSTS

One of Hayek's great contributions to economics was to characterize the nature of information supply in the marketplace. His paper on *The Use of Knowledge in Society* shows that the precise information needed to determine prices is never possessed by a single individual, and in fact is generated only by transactions in the marketplace. For this reason, valuation and allocation decisions by a central planner, no matter how well-informed, are all inferior to market transactions. The argument of this chapter is that adjudicative facts are analogous to prices determined in the market, and thus are subject to the similar economic effects of diffused information.

At first blush, readers may resist this analogy, because one of the most cherished myths about adjudication is that there is some absolute "truth"— or perhaps a monopoly "truth"—to which the adjudicative process aspires. This is not even formally correct: what litigation actually does is to generate the information necessary to ascertain the legal rights and obligations of the parties, under some pre-existing set of rules or standards, which has very little to do with anyone's version of either "truth" or "justice." In fact, the material standards of adjudication may have less to do with historical accuracy than with generating optimal incentives for ex ante conduct.[10] And even when they have to do with historical events, and do not depend on the sometimes narrow perspectives of the substantive legal regime, those facts may themselves be inherently subjective, at least in the sense that they are meaningful only to the immediate parties. And even when meaningful to the immediate parties, they may not be meaningful unless and until a dispute arises.

Again the simple two-party contract helps to illustrate the point. Assume a contract for the sale of raw materials suitable for use in a manufacturer's unique process, and a dispute arises as to the suitability of a given shipment. The actual quality of the material probably is a matter of complete indifference to the rest of society, and may even be a matter of indifference to the contracting parties until a disruption of the manufacturer's operation occurs. It is hard to find any "objective" element in this dispute; the actual question for the legal system is what did the contracting parties "intend." Our current law may seek to objectify certain aspects of the

---

[10]   For an excellent paper developing this point in the context of evidentiary rules, see Sanchirico, (2001b); see also Parker (2007).

dispute in order to make it more tractable,[11] but, in pure economic theory, the "right" answer is the one that reflects the parties' subjective intent.[12] And, for purposes of this chapter, the key point is that the parties themselves may not have "known" ex ante which qualities of the raw material rendered it suitable to the manufacturer's needs, because it was not worth it to the parties themselves to invest in that information until the problem arose. In this sense, the parties' dispute in adjudication is analogous in Hayek's terms to a particular marketplace transaction, and is essentially subjective, in that it means something only to the immediate parties and only by their (perhaps) idiosyncratic standards.

There are two further consequences. First, given the inherently subjective nature of the inquiry, there is unlikely to be any dominantly optimal rule of either substantive contract law or civil procedural law to govern the parties' decisions to invest either ex ante or ex post in the information. As a first approximation, the parties themselves, and neither a future tribunal nor "society" in general, are likely to be in the superior position to make those investment decisions. Furthermore, those decisions are likely to be subjectified by the unique opportunity costs of each party.[13] Suppose, in the example, that the manufacturer is a baker uniquely skilled in the baking art but technically deficient in specifying the technical characteristics of suitable flour, which are known (if at all) only to the supplier. In that instance, it may not be worthwhile for the parties to specify the flour characteristics beyond "suitable," and certainly neither the legal system nor a later adjudicating tribunal is in a position to second-guess that decision. Perhaps it is the case that developing technical specifications for the flour will require costly investments in new chemical or biological knowledge. If, at the time of ex ante contracting, future disputes over suitability were considered unlikely, then it would have been wasteful for the parties to invest in developing a new science of flour specification; perhaps, such an investment would have overwhelmed the productive margins of the contracting

---

[11]   Perhaps in an explicit or implicit effort to account for the information costs encountered in ex post litigation, modern contract law has evolved from a "subjective" to an "objective" theory of contract. To the extent that this is driven solely by the ex post needs of adjudicating courts, it may be economically inefficient.

[12]   The example chosen actually represents one of the relatively few instances in which a highly subjective standard is recognized in our law, as through the Uniform Commercial Code's warranty of "fitness" for a particular purpose. U.C.C. § 2-315.

[13]   One of the best early treatments of opportunity costs is von Mises (1949). An excellent development of the concept as foundation for economic theory is Buchanan (1969).

parties. The ex post fact that the unlikely dispute arose does not show that the parties' ex ante decisions were misguided, but only that the unlikely contingency occurred.

Second, and despite the subjective nature of the costs involved, the future shadow of civil procedure rules as affecting the nature and cost of both ex ante and ex post information investments will affect the available quality and supply of information to any ex post dispute.[14] To take an extreme example from familiar civil procedure, the famous "work product" rule of *Hickman v. Taylor*[15] is based upon the Supreme Court's very explicit consideration of the effect that the opposite rule would have on the quality of information produced by the parties within the civil litigation itself, by undermining the parties' incentives to invest in new knowledge ex post. The traditional distinction in the federal civil discovery rules is between obtaining access to pre-existing data held by the opposing litigant and premature discovery of the opposing litigant's "case" (i.e., its work product of creative inputs generated by the dispute itself). In both respects, the rules create (or destroy) incentives to create and preserve information.

Going back to the example of the baker and the flour supplier, allowing the potential investment in new flour science to be deferred to the time of the contingent dispute can permit both parties to invest elsewhere, and perhaps more productively, at the time of the original transaction. There does not appear to be any a priori reason to believe that the rules of adjudication should be structured in such a way as to force such an investment into the earlier period, either for some or all parties. Given the subjective nature of the investment, the parties may differ in their cost of investment. Given the contingent nature of the future dispute, any premature investment in that information may be wasted, because the dispute may never arise.

IV.   A THOUGHT EXPERIMENT IN COASIAN ENFORCEMENT: THE CASE OF THE FRACTIONAL COW

This section attempts to make the insights of the previous three sections less abstract by applying them to a motivational example inspired by Coase's famous paper on *The Problem of Social Cost*. Using Coase's systematic treatment of opportunity costs helps to show the generality of

---

[14]   On the general point, see Hirshleifer (1971).
[15]   329 U.S. 497 (1947).

the points being made here, as it can be used as a basis for expanding the model beyond a simple two-party contract into other fields of law. The example also helps to fill two gaps left by Coase: one is costly enforcement of "Coasian bargains," which are suppressed in his analysis; the other is costly information, which he notes but sets aside. The thesis here is that the two are related to one another, and together they serve to illuminate the previously-neglected function of civil adjudication in creating new knowledge.

My example of "The Case of the Fractional Cow" is inspired by Coase's hypothetical of the adjoining farmer and cattle rancher whose land uses influence one another. Specifically, Coase postulated that the size of the rancher's herd of cows affected the incidence or magnitude of the "externality" that the rancher's cows would escape from the ranch, stray over to the adjoining farm, and damage the farmer's crops. Coase's purpose was to show that the joint product of the conflicting uses could be maximized under opposite legal entitlements respecting the "externality," provided that positive transaction costs did not prevent the rancher and farmer from reaching an optimal "Coasian bargain." Thus, whether ranchers were liable for straying cows or farmers were required to absorb their losses, under those conditions the parties could still maximize their joint product by contracting away from the starting rule of law.

My example writes a sequel to one variation of the "Coasian bargain," where the prospect of enforcement arises under that bargain. This highlights two aspects of the solution that Coase did not consider explicitly. First, while suppressing both transaction costs generally and information costs between the conflicting parties, Coase's statement of the problem assumes positive costs of legal policy formulation, in that the law can err in assigning the original legal entitlement. Second, what happens after the "Coasian bargain" is reached? In particular, what happens if one of the parties fails to live up to the Coasian bargain? Coase seemed to assume that the enforcement of both the original entitlements and the Coasian bargains between the parties were perfect and costless. Relaxing those assumptions is what begins to characterize the problem of civil procedure.

The most interesting case is where both of the extreme structures of the beginning legal entitlement—either that ranchers were liable for all crop damage caused by straying cows, or that farmers were required to absorb those costs—were sub-optimal, because joint product was maximized by an agreement to control the size of the rancher's herd at some level above zero. So, let us assume that the optimal herd size is two cows, because increasing the herd to three cows increases marginal crop loss more than marginal ranch product, and similarly, a decrease in herd size reduces marginal ranch product more than marginal crop loss. This solution also assumes (as did Coase) that regulating herd size is the least-cost method of controlling the "externality." However, because the parties have chosen the intermediate solution, crop loss from cow straying is not reduced to zero, but presumably is compensated ex ante in the consideration paid in order to reach the Coasian bargain.

Now, what happens if one of the parties accuses the other of breaching the Coasian bargain? Suppose that the farmer sues or threatens to sue the rancher, claiming that the rancher exceeded the contractually-specified herd size, thus producing "excess" crop loss. This is where the characteristics of the procedural system, in a world of positive information costs, begin to have an effect.

In procedural systems featuring "strict" pleading rules that require plaintiffs to state the factual grounds of their case with particularity, the farmer may not have a litigable case at all, if the farmer knows only that his crops were trampled down. If the strict pleading rules block the farmer's access to information through the pretrial discovery process in litigation, this will produce an ex ante incentive for the farmer to bargain for pre-dispute access to the necessary information, because the ex post rules now threaten to deprive the farmer of the benefit of his bargain. We can think of many potential contractual provisions that may assure that the farmer will be able to monitor the rancher's herd size, such as regular reports from the rancher, an inspection right in the farmer, or other monitoring technologies. But none of this will be free to either the farmer or the rancher. At the limit, these additional costs may be a form of transaction cost that prevent the Coasian bargain from being struck in the first instance. We cannot say whether parties may preserve their joint product more efficiently by deferring the monitoring costs into the future phase of contingent disputation.

In systems with more "liberal" pleading rules and a right to pretrial discovery, the farmer may be allowed to bring his case and might actually win, if it turns out to be true that the rancher exceeded the agreed herd size. On the other hand, it could be argued that "liberal" pleading rules might encourage "frivolous" litigation, as the farmer's crops could have been trampled by vandals, or by one of the farmer's careless farm workers. Or the same case may present both possibilities simultaneously: the rancher may have run too many cows, but the actual trampling of the crops was caused by a farm employee. In that case, both parties would have an interest in pretrial discovery from the other. These possibilities present problems of asymmetric information as to the actual merits of the case, and raise substantial questions as to the tradeoff between accuracy or "justice" on the one hand, and speed and expense of adjudication on the other.

But these are only the obvious, first-order problems. More subtle problems may appear. Depending upon the structure of the adjudication system, the decision-maker may or may not be willing to explore some of the more exotic possibilities, such as whether the crops were trampled by incompetent crop-circle hoaxers, or whether scientific analysis of the crop field could distinguish cow-trampling from other forms of trampling. And there could be issues of credibility: the farmer may actually believe that the cows trampled his crops, and therefore failed to question his farm workers; or, the farmer may simply be a lying rent-seeker, who deliberately trampled his own crops, after they failed from some other cause, such as unfavorable weather. Or, the credibility of the rancher, and his business records, could be in question: if the rancher were deliberately cheating on the bargain, he may be unlikely to make an honest record of his cheating. Should he be permitted to present his own business records as proof that he observed the herd limitation? Should non-parties who dealt with the rancher be subpoenaed to produce records and testimony? Who is in the better position to decide whether to pursue these avenues of proof, and to assess the credibility of the results?

But even these questions are relatively conventional. Suppose that informational asymmetries and credibility problems are overcome, and the facts, as developed, show that the rancher actually ran three cows on his property for one-quarter of the year. This is the "fractional cow" problem, as we now have two-and-a-quarter cows per year.[16] The ex ante bargaining of the parties may or may not have considered the "fractional cow" in specifying the contractual two cows. In that case, how is the contract to be construed? It is easy enough to say that the "intent of the parties" should govern. But how is that intent to be found? Is it subjective intent, as would be suggested by economic analysis? Or is it objective intent? And how much of that choice is influenced by information costs associated with ascertaining the parties' intent? If the parties actually never foresaw the "fractional cow" problem, then this question may not be answerable ex post. This raises the question, often encountered in procedural systems, of just how such a question should be resolved. Should the court pretend that it is simply determining an historical fact? Or, should it recast the substantive rule, because the pre-existing rule is too costly to enforce with tolerable accuracy? Or, should it pretend that the question of fact is actually a question of law? Or, should it dismiss the case because the parties, or one of them, has failed in the burden of proof? These are all variations that are observed in practice.

From the economic point of view, the best solution to the "fractional

---

[16]   Assuming an annual contract simplifies the example. Obviously, assuming multi-period contracts would complicate the problem.

cow" problem may have been for the parties to recognize and agree on a solution ex ante. If information and transaction costs are negligible, this could be the efficient solution. But in a world of positive transaction and information costs, it is a costly activity, and incurring that cost could exceed the benefits of a more precisely-specified contract. For example, suppose that the "fractional cow" was a new calf. Did the parties mean to include calves in cows? If they failed to foresee that contingency, who should bear the resultant loss? Is there actually any way to "find" what the parties' ex ante intent was, or would have been?

Moreover, the parties' incentives to solve the problem ex ante are given in part by the features of the ex post procedural system, or, in other words, the assumed ex post procedural system is endogenous to the contracting parties' choices. In this respect, the procedural system can reduce economic efficiency by being either too inexpensive or too expensive. If it is the case that efficiency would be promoting by ex ante bargaining to this level of detail, then the provision of an expeditious and inexpensive procedural system ex post reduces economic efficiency, because it still may be more costly in the deeper sense that coercive litigation can never replicate the exact result of ex ante bargaining. On the other hand, an unduly expensive or unreliable litigation system may impair efficiency by encouraging parties to over-specify their ex ante bargains in terms of improbable contingencies.

The law and economics literature only recently has begun to address some of these problems, by developing in the contractual context the general proposition of substitution between substantive law (or contract terms) and procedural law, as a way of optimizing the endogenous tradeoff between ex ante bargaining and ex post litigation costs by the contracting parties.[17] However, including this perspective introduces an array of new considerations that have yet to be worked out completely.

In particular, considering the substitution of procedural rule specifications for substantive contract terms introduces a third party into the analysis—the adjudicating authority itself. If the contracting parties fully internalize all of the litigation costs, including those borne by the adjudicating authority, then private contracting can provide the efficient solution. In this situation, it seems that the parties' solution is efficient by hypothesis because it is Pareto-optimal, regardless of how outlandish it may appear to outside observers. Thus, the parties may decide to solve the case of the fractional cow by commissioning expensive new scientific research on distinguishing cow crop-trampling from other crop-trampling,

---

[17]   *See* Section II, above.

or, at the other end of the spectrum, they may agree to be bound by local customs or mythologies, such as whether the crop-trampling occurred during a full moon. Either way, social policy would seem to have very little to say.

However, the parties' intent may not be so apparent. Moreover, the parties may well evince an intent to rely on the presumed expertise of an established tribunal (not necessarily a public court), which could be efficient to the parties (and to society), if the adjudicating tribunal faces lower marginal costs than the contracting parties themselves in selecting and implementing efficient procedural rules.

In contrast with the pure case where the adjudicating tribunal is merely a private agent for the contracting parties, most adjudicating tribunals in fact are repeat players who specialize in dispute resolution, spread their production costs over a number of disputes, and thus have a comparative advantage over the contracting parties who, by definition, specialize elsewhere (farming and ranching, in Coase's example).

To see the effect, we need not resolve the question whether dispute resolution is a public good that is more efficiently provided on a social scale, although that is one of the standard explanations for the public provision of courts to resolve civil disputes. Even private arbitral tribunals may provide economies of scale and skill in providing dispute-resolution services. Those economies may require that the tribunal adhere to repeat patterns of procedure. To take a crude example, suppose that the adjudicating tribunal has chosen the English language for its adjudications. If the parties instead choose Mandarin as their optimal language of ex post disputation from their point of view, the tribunal may be unable to provide the dispute-resolution services at a cost that the parties are willing to bear, simply because there are not enough disputants to justify a tribunal using Mandarin. This puts the contracting parties back into the problem of contracting under constraints imposed by the available adjudication choices ex post.

In the case of publicly-provided courts, this problem becomes even more severe. Publicly-provided systems vary in their amenability to contractual specification of procedural rules, but nearly all of them will draw the line somewhere, in order to maintain their basic competency as tribunals. Actual functioning systems are likely to have even more complex pricing structures. For example, public "common-law" courts in the Anglo-American system specialize in part in providing rules of law—substantive and procedural—for the benefit of the larger society. A large part of the "price" paid by litigants for access to the publicly-subsidized courts may be the parties' provision of the facts of their dispute—or a certain quality of factual dispute—in exchange for the publicly-subsidized resolution.

However, as the public courts become less flexible in terms of the contracting parties' preferences for procedural rules, this reduces the range of choice available to the parties ex post. As contracts and disputes become more diverse, then it would seem that also becomes the optimal ex post procedure for each given dispute. Reducing the range of choice among ex post procedural systems can also constrain the range of contractual choice ex ante, and thereby reduce the efficiencies obtainable in the joint product of ex ante bargaining and ex post disputation.

From this point of view, civil procedure rules applicable in public courts would appear to involve a tradeoff between the presumed social benefits of the provision of disputes for public adjudication versus the potential costs to litigants in the form of too much rigidity in the ex post procedures applied. As indicated above, there is likely to be a wide range of optimal dispute-resolution procedures for a given dispute, and only limited public interest in choosing among them, except perhaps to the extent that the parties' choices are so idiosyncratic as to impair the comparative advantage of the tribunal or produce relative underpricing. But if that is the case, it would seem to call for some pricing structure whereby the parties jointly could purchase "custom" procedures, even within the publicly-provided system.

So far, the discussion in this section is limited to the hypothetical Coasian contracting situation. However, just how different are other areas of civil litigation? The discussion of ex post bargains between the parties respecting litigation rules would seem to apply with equal force to any form of civil litigation, whether over torts, contracts, property, or any other subject. Especially in the context of pretrial discovery procedures, if the parties wish to take a more extensive or leisurely course, then why should even the public tribunal care? Except in the case of discovery disputes, there is little to no spillover to the tribunal.

At first blush, the non-contractual areas would appear to differ in terms of the ex ante/ex post tradeoff between information investments. However, this is not necessarily true: areas of tort or regulatory law certainly can involve ex ante agreements as to litigation procedures, including arbitral tribunals, or "assumption of risk" agreements, among others. Moreover, the same temporal dynamic applies to all fields: even as default rules, the rules of civil procedure can relatively encourage or discourage parties ex ante to invest in information that may be useful either in future litigation, or in deciding whether to undertake a given activity or level of activity.

This is the frontier of future research on the economics of civil procedure: working out whether and under what circumstances the existing rules or supposed "reforms" to civil procedure actually have adverse consequences for the primary activities of potential litigants. As this chapter shows, that question extends far beyond the rules themselves or the interest groups that influence most procedural rules.

V. SOME IMPLICATIONS FOR CURRENT DEBATES

This section seeks to apply the information-production perspective briefly to some current topics in civil procedure, primarily for the purpose of stimulating further research. As will be shown, applying that perspective can have dramatic effects on the terms of debate.

A. Adversarial versus Inquisitorial Procedure and "Managerial Judging"

The discussion above has considered the debate between adversarial versus inquisitorial procedure, which appears to have been the first one now profoundly affected by the information-production perspective, and in this sense is a paradigm for future research on a variety of topics in civil procedure.

The most recent research would seem to support the traditional American "adversarial" system, which gives extensive party autonomy and requires each party to bear its own costs of litigation. Only the immediate parties can know what is optimal procedure for their own dispute, which under subjective valuation is unique to them. There are two qualifications: (1) public subsidy, which seems minor; and (2) ex post strategic behavior, which is potentially significant, but could be excluded in cases of mutual agreement, either ex post or ex ante, and in other instances could be distinguished or regulated without restricting the parties' range of choice.

Law-and-economics researchers should take note that the current trend of our literature is somewhat at odds with the general trend in recent "reforms" to civil procedure, especially at the U.S. federal level, which for the past 35 years at least have reflected an incessant march towards more "managerial" judging and the suppression of some margins of party autonomy, especially in pretrial discovery.[18] There also is a longer-standing drive toward more "uniformity" in civil procedure, first at the national level and more recently at the international level.[19] The information-production

---

[18] Since 1980, successive amendments to the Federal Rules of Civil Procedure, especially those in 1980, 1983, 1993, 2000, 2006, 2010, and 2015, have progressively restricted the parties' autonomy and enhanced the regulatory role of the federal district judge, essentially pushing the parties jointly to use less time and effort in developing their cases.

[19] For an analysis of the recent international trends, see Parker (2009).

perspective developed in this chapter indicates that these trends probably are misguided.

All of these trends overlook the basic insight from Hayek's work on information diffusion and production. In those cases (not all) where there ultimately is a "Mr. Right" and a "Mr. Wrong," that characterization itself may be an exogenously imposed construct of the legal system, and thus represent social friction rather than "justice." Moreover, even in such cases where it does represent the joint subjective valuation of the parties, "Mr. Wrong" does not necessarily know that he is "Mr. Wrong" ex ante lite. Like a consumption decision in the marketplace, an adjudicatory fact that one of the litigants is a "Mr. Wrong" is a particular of time and place, which neither party may have an adequate incentive to learn until the dispute actually arises. Thus, the essence of the civil litigation process, much like market processes, is to learn (i.e., to produce) information that did not previously exist. In that context, economics would suggest that the competitive production of such information represented by an adversarial system with sharp incentives and some symmetrical access (perhaps through pre-trial discovery) produces a superior outcome to an inquisitorial system that more nearly resembles central planning or monopoly.

Furthermore, much of the brief for "inquisitorial" procedure seems to rest on the supposed "sophistication" of the career judge decision-maker, as opposed to "naive" jurors or Anglo-American judges, who are vaguely accused by innuendi of being dilettantes in the judging business, as they are appointing from the practicing bar.[20] But the "sophistication" of the decision-maker does not seem crucial to the relative performance of the rule systems.

At some level of competitive information production, the answer will become clear to all, and the danger with "expert" decision-makers is precisely their sophistication, or what I have called the "Judge Judy" effect.[21] After all, what is an "expert" other than one who believes that she already "knows" the facts without thorough investigation of the particulars of the case? The more control by the "expert" decision-maker, the more tendency there will be to substitute pre-judgment for the actual facts of the controversy. At the limit, this would entirely defeat the information-production function, which in essence is a learning function, that lies at the heart of civil adjudication.

---

[20]   See Langbein (1985).
[21]   See Parker (2009).

B.   Contracting for Procedural Rules and Fora

A related point concerns the surprising degree of hostility, even within American courts, toward accepting litigants' efforts to customize the civil procedure rules of the public courts for their particular dispute. There appear to be very limited grounds for courts to resist such efforts, and yet they do so.

Extending the previous discussion of party control, why not treat all rules of civil procedure as "default" rules rather than "mandatory" rules? This is not the current practice in American courts, and still less so elsewhere. Under current American rules, contracting parties may choose arbitration ex ante, and all parties generally (with some exceptions) may choose arbitration ex post. But they have only limited rights to "customize" the public rules for their own dispute. The rationale for this position presumably is that the parties somehow do not internalize the efficiency losses (e.g., less precedent, less familiarity of judges with the chosen rules), and therefore are taking more than their "fair share" of the public facility. But why not allow the parties jointly to "bargain" with the court over applicable rules? Judges may be bad agents for the public interest, but they are likely to be better than centralized rule-makers, if left to their own devices. Unfortunately, under recent trends of procedural rule-making, judges increasingly are instructed to "manage" the litigants by demanding faster and more summary dispositions.[22]

A "second-best" solution to the foregoing problems is provided by expanded enforcement of choice-of-forum clauses, as well as choice-of-law clauses. In a sense, the inclusion of both types of clauses reflects the joint maximization of the ex ante and ex post perspectives. Choosing law may be one way of economizing on the costs of ex ante contractual specification, and choosing both law and forum reflects the ex ante/ex post tradeoff of substance versus procedure. All other things being equal, the broader the range of both substantive law and procedural system choice available to the parties, the more efficient will be the resolution of disputes.

In this respect, any move toward "harmonization" of procedural systems across jurisdictional boundaries would be a step in the wrong direction. Part of the idea of enforcing choice-of-forum clauses is to promote inter-jurisdictional competition in procedural systems; eliminating diversity in procedural systems undercuts that benefit.

The public courts' reticence to accept customization of procedure may be the same as any incumbent monopolist: innovation is a threat to the

---

[22]   See the discussion below in subsection E.

monopoly. But particularly when coupled, as it is in the United States, with a willingness to accept agreements to arbitrate outside the courts on a broad range of subjects,[23] it would seem to be a losing strategy. Perhaps that is the entire point—to drive most private civil adjudications out of the public courts.

The welfare implications of these trends are ambiguous. If left unmolested by public law, perhaps the private markets can succeed in producing a sufficient range of diverse procedural systems to give litigants effective choices. On the other hand, withdrawing the public courts from the competition may undermine the legal regularity of the system and reduce choices available in the marketplace.

We can see both trends together in the Supreme Court's 2008 decision in *Hall Street Associates, LLC v. Mattel, Inc.*,[24] where the Court held that the Federal Arbitration Act's limited grounds for modifying or setting aside an arbitration award were exclusive and could not be varied by contract to require the strict application of law by arbitrators. While that ruling was confined to the federal statutory procedures only, the implication, if extended more generally, would be to limit parties' ability to contract for more court-like procedures even within arbitration. This could reduce the parties' range and continuity of choice in procedural rules and decision standards, and thereby reduce efficiency.

More broadly, one is left to contemplate what would be left in the public courts if private adjudications largely were driven out. Especially in the federal courts, this would make public enforcement actions (i.e., those initiated by federal government agencies and officers), both criminal and civil, the predominant form of litigation in those courts. This could produce a fundamental change in the nature of civil adjudication as it has been known for most of our legal history.

---

[23]   For at least the last 30 years, American courts, and especially the federal Supreme Court, have been highly receptive to the enforcement of agreements to arbitrate private disputes, even those involving issues of public law. *See, e.g., Dean Witter Reynolds, Inc. v. Byrd,* 470 U.S. 213 (1985); *Mitsubishi Motors Corp. v. Soler Chrysler-Plymouth, Inc.*, 473 U.S. 614 (1985); *Shearson/American Express Inc. v. McMahon,* 482 U.S. 220 (1987); *Rodriguez de Quijas v. Shearson/American Express Inc.*, 490 U.S. 477 (1989) (overruling *Wilko v. Swan,* 346 U.S. 427 (1953)). More recent decisions have extended this position to the waiver of class action rights, culminating in *AT&T Mobility LLC v. Concepcion,* 563 U.S. 333 (2013), which held that the Federal Arbitration Act preempted state law selectively limiting class action waivers.

[24]   552 U.S. 576 (2008).

C. External Preclusive Effects from Civil Adjudications

The analysis of this chapter would seem to disfavor giving any external effect (i.e., impact on third parties) of civil adjudications. This would call the current law of non-mutual collateral estoppel into question.[25] As a general proposition, most adjudicative facts would appear to be particularized to the context of the immediate parties' dispute. Creating an artificial "externality" in the form of non-mutual estoppel effects usable by nonparties would impair the efficiency of the immediate litigants' efforts to specify rules and procedures governing their own dispute, either ex ante or ex post.

While certain types of issues commonly encountered in non-mutual estoppel (e.g., product defects and patent validity) might appear to have external significance in themselves, the existence of external preclusive effects could bias the immediate parties' incentives in a direction that may serve neither the immediate parties nor the external interests. When one of the litigants is likely to be a repeat player (such as a product manufacturer or a patentee), while the other is not (injured customer or accused infringer), the existence of external effects introduces asymmetric stakes and prevents the immediate parties from reaching a convergent agreement upon how much to invest in the current dispute. As a result, the repeat litigant has an incentive to over-invest in the current litigation, which may bias the outcome against the non-repeat litigant, who is faced with a coordination problem in which the externally-benefitted non-parties may attempt to "free ride" on a favorable outcome but assume no risk of an unfavorable one. On both sides, the full internalization of stakes is frustrated by the non-mutual estoppel rule.

A similar analysis may call into question the doctrine of precedent (except in those cases of mutual repeat litigation),[26] and suggest that private arbitration should be preferred. As with external estoppel effects, the lack of full internalization of the value of precedent-setting to non-repeat litigants may induce them to under-invest in a "legal" resolution of their dispute.

To the extent that civil litigants mutually choose the public courts over private alternatives, it raises the question whether there is a "free rider" problem, i.e., whether there is underpricing to the immediate parties. The alternative explanation is that prior precedent has more value to

---

[25] For an economic analysis of external effects, see Kobayashi (1996), pp. 17–49, which is further extended in Kobayashi and Parker (2000).

[26] See Rubin (1977).

the current litigants than the marginal costs of litigating in the public courts. These would appear to be fruitful competing hypotheses for future research. At present, there is only a very small public expenditure on the apparatus of civil procedure, and therefore most of the costs are borne by the parties (excluding external effects). Accordingly, even small changes in public adjudication rules may have dramatic effects on parties' choices of public versus private fora. We already know that there is extensive "forum shopping" within the public courts.

D.   Remedial Structures

The information-production and subjective valuation aspects of this chapter can help to achieve some analytical advance in distinguishing both substantive and procedure law on the one hand from what I will call "remedial structure" on the other.

To some extent, "remedial structure," i.e., the form and valuation of remedies given in civil litigation, as between damages and injunctive relief, is an established concept in the law-and-economics literature, usually framed as "property rights" (i.e., injunctive relief and specific performance), versus "liability rules" (damages).[27] The importance of subjective valuation tends to favor the "property rights" type. However, there are two important qualifications in the ex post world: (1) strategic behavior by one or both litigants; or (2) exogenous change from ex ante conditions. The first problem seems endemic to torts, but it is possible that damages rules could be re-framed to more closely approach ex ante subjective valuations (e.g., insurance rates).

The new contributions made by this chapter are two-fold. First, ex ante specifications, such as liquidated damages clauses or exclusions of certain types of remedies, should be favored by the courts, as they generally are. Second, explicitly distinguishing "remedial structure" from either substantive or procedural law as such helps to clarify several current debates that ostensibly are about "civil procedure reform," but in reality are problems of the remedial structure itself and therefore cannot be solved by changes to procedural rules. Several examples of this effect are developed in the following subsection.

---

[27]   In particular, this taxonomy is associated with the 1972 paper by Calabresi and Melamed, which itself has stimulated an extensive following literature.

E.   The Scope and Expense of Pretrial "Discovery"

For the last several decades, there has been a constant drumbeat of criticism about the American system's proclivities toward "overdiscovery." Rules amendments since 1980 have sought to "limit" or "manage" discovery in various ways. However, it has not been shown that this is a serious social problem, either empirically or in theory. Costs of litigation, including discovery costs, can go up simply due to changes in substantive or remedial law, or from exogenous changes in information technology, rather than any procedural dysfunction.

Instead, the problem (if there is one) may lie in the remedial structure (remedies and their "objectified" measures) rather than the rules of procedure. If the remedial structure were consistent with subjective valuation (and if third-party preclusion benefits are excluded), then each side should have the appropriate incentive to request such discovery as is justified by its own subjective valuation of its case, provided that the requesting party internalized the full cost of its request. So, the real debate reduces to one of two things: (1) the remedial structure is mis-specified, in which case this is not a "procedure" problem as such, and no amount of procedural rule-changing can address it; or (2) the system is not sufficiently internalizing the costs of discovery to the requesting litigant, such that discovery requests are being used as extortion devices.[28] Assuming the second of these two problems, shifting discovery costs to the requester would seem to be the solution.

However, it has been suggested (e.g., Allen and Guy) that the procedural system is unable to shift costs accurately.[29] That may be true, but perfect accuracy is not necessary. As in other cases of moral hazard, it would seem that even partial "co-insurance" can help to mitigate the problem. Moreover, even though subjective, some of the opportunity costs of the responding party can be estimated with tolerable accuracy, or at least more accurately than the central-planning-style solutions that have been suggested to date.[30]

Many of the rule changes indicate that court-assisted coercion of one party by the other is not the fundamental problem. As noted above, the rise of "managerial judging" to trump the mutually-agreed preferences of opposing litigants is entirely inconsistent with the extortion hypothesis.

---

[28]   Bruce Kobayashi recently has published a paper that begins to get at this problem; *see* Kobayashi (2014).

[29]   Allen and Guy (2010).

[30]   See Redish and McNamara (2011).

Also, certain traditional discovery devices—such as the oral deposition—appear to have very little potential for unchecked abuse, because the bulk of the costs are borne by the discovering party, and the imposition on the opposing party (essentially, the opportunity costs of its deponent and lawyer) are observable on the basis of marketplace transactions. And yet, there appears to be equal emphasis on limiting the scope of both the more and less abusive methods of discovery. This suggests that the stronger explanation for the many recent discovery rule changes rests in public choice analysis of the pressure groups influencing the rule-making outputs rather than the transaction costs of adjudication itself.

Much of the push to this style of "reform" seems to stem from the idea that litigants *jointly* would spend "too much" on their own litigation. If true, this may not be a problem of the procedural system, but rather a problem of lawyer agency costs or the substantive law's remedial structure, which in neither case can be solved by procedural rule change. Moreover, it seems unlikely to be caused by lawyer agency costs, as the provision of litigation representation is a highly competitive explicit market with widely observable results and strong reputation effects. This points to remedial structure (i.e., the nature and number of legal obligations imposed, or the measurement of the remedies applied, such as punitive damages) as the more fundamental problem.

A second-order problem is created by the possibility of counter-strategies on the part of some litigants to deliberately raise the cost of their own discovery response, in order either to exploit a discovery cost-shifting system (the "moral hazard," in reverse), or, under the current system, as a device to defeat discovery requests. A more complex system of cost-shifting may be necessary to defeat these strategies, but here again, the system need not be perfect in order to realign incentives.

As both subjective valuation and the information-production perspective seem to be important arguments against the assertion that there is "overdiscovery," then one answer may be that even tort litigation is partly the product of voluntary decisions to engage in a more or less litigation-producing activity. But if so, then the analysis here would suggest that this is not a problem for procedural law reform. Again in this case, the appropriate inquiry is more likely to focus on substantive law or remedial structure rather than procedural law as such. In general, the cash subsidy to civil litigation in terms of public expenditure is quite small relative to public expenditures generally, and therefore an efficiency case must rest on the idea that some feature of the litigation system has created an adverse selection of disputes. So far as I am aware, no one has made that identification. And, as developed in the next section, most of the recent attention has been given over to creating a new problem rather than solving an old one.

F.   Newly "Heightened" Standards of Pleading

Recent developments in federal law have produced a controversial new "plausibility" standard of pleading, generally known as the *Twombly-Iqbal* standard,[31] which appears to be justified primarily by the concerns about "overdiscovery" noted above. However, from the information-production perspective, the entire doctrine seems misguided, as it suppresses or denies the creation of new knowledge through litigation.

As noted above, the "overdiscovery" critique itself is overdrawn. Moreover, if there are problems in the current system, they may be driven by problems of remedial structure rather than anything to do with procedural law. Instead, *Twombly-Iqbal* standard appears to add a new problem without solving a pre-existing problem. Basically, the "plausibility" standard prevents any learning within the litigation process, by blocking the development of cases unless the plaintiff already possessed sufficient pre-complaint facts to plead its case.

Deciding in the abstract, and without discovery, whether the plaintiff's claims are "plausible" turns Hayek upside down, by removing the decision-maker even farther away from the particulars of time and place, and relying on what amounts to nothing more than generalizations that, even if well-intentioned, are likely to be wrong.

Indeed, we are fairly confident that they will be wrong, because of the well-known selection effects in litigation: filed cases are not representative of all disputes; cases that proceed to advanced stages are even less so; and cases that proceed to trial are likely to be both unusual and, by the selection effect, "close calls,"[32] in the sense that more information—not less—is needed to resolve the dispute justly. Thus, truncating the process at an earlier phase will have a disproportionate effect on precisely the cases that need the most development.

Instead, the new standards of "plausible" pleading introduce a new problem of asymmetric error, by potentially generating a higher level of false negatives, in which necessary evidence is held by the defending party. In contrast with the criminal procedure system, which assumes a high false negative rate, this type of asymmetric error creates serious problems for civil procedure. To the extent that the litigants deal with one another ex ante lite, it increases the incentive for either or both to "pre-discover" evidence that may or may not be needed for a future litigation that may

---

[31]   So named after the two leading Supreme Court cases, *Bell Atlantic Corp. v. Twombly*, 550 U.S. 544 (2007), and *Ashcroft v. Iqbal*, 566 U.S. 662 (2009).

[32]   This is the basic hypothesis advanced by Priest and Klein (1984).

or may not take place, or to take other costly steps to insure that they are a prospective defendant rather than a prospective plaintiff. Moreover, like other procedural rules, the new pleading standards do not appear to be variable by contract, certainly not ex ante or perhaps not ex post, if a "managerial" judge wishes to assure that this is a "plausible" case.

Let us draw out the economic implications by taking a case like *Twombly*, which involved an alleged geographic market-division cartel among the regional Bell operating companies that succeeded to the previously-integrated AT&T. The effect of the *Twombly* ruling is to raise the risk that customers in similar circumstances could face an unremediated cartel in the telephone services market. Ex ante, this provides an increased incentive for customers to demand further assurances of non-collusive behavior among the service providers. But these increased transaction costs may preclude such arrangements. Nevertheless, there will be economic consequences. Without the prospect of either ex post litigation or ex ante assurance, customers may switch to other sources of communications services less prone to geographic market division, perhaps cell phones or satellite-internet phones. It may be possible that marketplace competition is more efficient than antitrust litigation in policing cartels, but if that were true, then perhaps the antitrust claim should not exist at all.

But what the case actually does is to increase the relative costs of ex post enforcement of antitrust claims differentially, by insulating the more clandestine cartels, which in turn increases the payoff to ex ante secrecy by the cartel members. What is gained through such a decision? Unless the "heightened" pleading standard reduces the costs of false positive claims by more than the losses imposed by raising the false negative rate, then the net result would appear to be negative for social welfare. But the mechanism seems ill-chosen for this purpose: the Court suggests no reason why the likelihood of a true-positive is positively correlated with the obviousness of the claim, which is what "plausibility" seems to connote. If anything, and given the nature of the violations involved here, the opposite would seem more likely.

But in any event, the pleading standard seems designed to prevent the civil litigation process from generating any new knowledge at all. The standard truncates the continuum representing the tradeoffs between ex ante and ex post information investments. Ex ante investments may or may not be more efficient, and the heightened pleading standard does nothing to distinguish those cases. If ex ante investments are more efficient, then the pleading standard will not screen out those cases. If ex ante investments are not more efficient, then both true and false positive cases will be screened out at the same rate. The pleading standard does enhance, artificially, the incentive to invest ex ante, but cannot make that investment the efficient choice. Given the diffused and subjective nature of the information costs involved, it seems doubtful that any directive standard of pleading can make the necessary distinction.

G. Class Actions

The recent efforts to promote the use of class actions and other types of "aggregate" or "mass" litigation would seem generally to be inconsistent with the perspective developed here. With the exception of the derivative suit (which harnesses the organizing force of business entities), most of these types of litigation are inefficient because they fail to account for particularized information and subjective valuation. The problem is exacerbated by such things as the "opt-out" rule for the formation of litigant classes, and the heavy-handed control exercised by the adjudicating judge. Here again, there is a false economy in coerced joinder, and mismatched means for solving the agency costs problems between the class and its lawyers, and within the class members themselves.

Unlike the previous applications, it would appear that the federal case law in general has taken the appropriate line of development, by insisting upon a strong indication of joint versus individualized interests before class certification is granted. The 2011 decision in *Wal-Mart Stores, Inc. v. Dukes*[33] represents this trend.

VI.   CONCLUDING COMMENTS

Developing the information-production perspective on civil procedure can help to distinguish between two visions of the social role of civil litigation. As originally developed and practiced for most of the history of Anglo-American law, civil procedure was designed primarily to provide *an* available means, always readily displaced by mutual consent, for redressing disputes between private individuals concerning their respective rights and obligations. In terms of both information-generation and law formulation, it worked incrementally, giving coercive solutions only as a last resort and only as necessary.

Of course, there were always some exceptions to the private-dispute-resolution model, as in constitutional litigation or in private litigation that raised questions of public authority. However, within the past half-century, civil litigation increasingly has come to be used as a tool of public policy,

---

[33]   131 S. Ct. 2541 (2011).

especially at the federal level. Perhaps for that reason, the rules of civil procedure today are increasingly viewed as involving public interests of aggregate welfare, and, in many instances, the underlying substantive law applied itself is designed to vindicate public rather than private interests. And yet, this same system continues to serve its traditional private dispute-resolution function. We may have come to a point where most private disputes perhaps will be committed to a separate set of tribunals that are designed to serve only this traditional function. Civil litigants themselves may be recognizing this fact, by increasingly choosing arbitration over litigation. The next phase in this development, perhaps presaged by some of the trade- or industry-based arbitration systems, may be the development of more general private systems of private law.

As discussed above (Section V.B), this development may or may not be favorable to economic efficiency, depending upon how the public courts mesh with the increasing use of private systems of adjudication. If the public courts act to limit the range of private adjudicative choice—as by confining the private sector to truly "arbitrary" private dispute resolution—the results could be negative for both economic efficiency and the rule of law. Even they do not interfere with the private alternatives, the retreat of the public courts from the business of private civil adjudication is ambiguous in its implications. However, to the extent that public courts continue to evolve toward suppressing the knowledge-creation function of civil litigation, they marginalize themselves in all types of civil cases.

The analysis presented here represents only the first step toward a new direction of research on the economic analysis of civil procedure, whether public or private. But it is important to take that new direction. Analyses that treat civil litigation as merely a tax on productive activity, or purely rent-seeking behavior, miss an important creative and productive aspect of both the litigation process and its alternatives. Ignoring that aspect of the process when considering current and proposed rules of civil procedure is likely to produce the wrong policy judgments.

REFERENCES

Allen, Ronald J. and Alan E. Guy, "Conley as a Special Case of Twombly and Iqbal: Exploring the Intersection of Evidence and Procedure and the Nature of Rules," 115 *Penn St. L. Rev.* 1 (2010).
Block, Michael K. and Jeffrey S. Parker, "Decision Making in the Absence of Successful Fact Finding: Theory and Experimental Evidence on Adversarial versus Inquisitorial Systems of Adjudication," 24 *Intl. Rev. L. & Econ.* 89–105 (2004).
Block, Michael K., Jeffrey S. Parker, Olga Vyborna, and Libor Ducek, "An Experimental Comparison of Adversarial versus Inquisitorial Procedural Regimes," 2 *Am. L. & Econ. Rev.* 170–94 (2000).

Bone, Robert G., *Civil Procedure: The Economics of Civil Procedure* (West: 2003).

Brown, John Prather, "Toward an Economic Theory of Liability," 2 *J. Legal Studies* 323 (1972).

Buchanan, James M., *Cost and Choice* (University of Chicago Press: 1969).

Calabresi, Guido, and A. Douglas Melamed, "Property Rules, Liability Rules, and Inalienability: One View of the Cathedral," 85 *Harvard Law Review* 1089 (1972).

Coase, R.H., "The Problem of Social Cost," 3 *J. Law & Econ.* 1–44 (1960), *reprinted in* R.H. Coase, *The Firm, the Market, and the Law*, pp. 95–156 (University of Chicago Press: 1988).

Cooter, Robert D., "Prices and Sanctions," 84 *Colum. L. Rev.* 1523 (1984).

Cooter, Robert D. and Daniel L. Rubinfeld, "Economic Analysis of Legal Disputes and their Resolution," 27 *Journal of Economic Literature* 1067–97 (1989).

Dewatripont, Mathias and Jean Tirole, "Advocates," 107 *J. Pol. Econ.* 1 (1999).

Froeb, Luke M. and Bruce H. Kobayashi, "Naive, Biased, yet Bayesian: Can Juries Interpret Selectively Produced Evidence?" 12 *J. L. Econ. & Org.* 257–75 (1996).

Froeb, Luke M. and Bruce H. Kobayashi, "Evidence Production in Adversarial vs. Inquisitorial Regimes," 70 *Econ. Letters* 267–72 (2001).

Froeb, Luke M. and Bruce H. Kobayashi, "Adversarial versus Inquisitorial Justice" in *Procedural Law and Economics*, C. Sanchirico (ed.), pp. 1–18 (Edward Elgar: 2012).

Fuller, Lon L., "The Forms and Limits of Adjudication," 92 *Harvard Law Review* 353 (1978).

Hayek, F.A. *The Use of Knowledge in Society*, 35 *Am. Econ. Rev.* 519 (1945).

Hirshleifer, Jack, "The Private and Social Value of Information and the Reward to Inventive Activity," 61 *Am. Econ. Rev.* 561 (1971).

Kobayashi, Bruce R., "Case Selection, External Effects, and the Trial/Settlement Decision" in *Bridging the Settlement Gap*, D.A. Anderson (ed.), pp. 17–49 (JAI Press: 1996).

Kobayashi, Bruce R., "Law's Information Revolution as Procedural Reform: Predictive Search as a Solution to the *In Terrorem* Effect of Externalized Discovery Costs," 2014 *U. Ill. L. Rev.* 1473.

Kobayashi, Bruce R. and Jeffrey S. Parker, "Civil Procedure: General" and the companion chapter by Parker and Kobayashi on "Evidence," in *Encyclopedia of Law and Economics*, Bouckhaert and deGeest (eds.) (Edward Elgar: 2000).

Langbein, John H., "The German Advantage in Civil Procedure," 52 *U. Chi. L. Rev.* 823 (1985).

Lewisch, Peter and Jeffrey S. Parker, "Procedure" in *Law and Economics in Europe and the U.S.: The Legacy of Jurgen Backhaus*, A. Marciano & G. Ramello (eds.), pp. 185–210 (Springer: 2016).

Milgrom, Paul and John Roberts, "Relying on the Information of Interested Parties," 17 *Rand J. Econ.* 18–32 (1986).

Mises, Ludwig von, *Human Action: A Treatise on Economics* (Yale: 1949).

Parisi, Francesco, "Rent-seeking Through Litigation: Adversarial and Inquisitorial Systems Compared," 22 *International Review of Law and Economics* 193–216 (2002).

Parker, Jeffrey S., "Economics of Evidence and Proof," in *Encyclopedia of Law and Society* 524–27, David S. Clark (ed.) (Sage: 2007).

Parker, Jeffrey S., "Comparative Civil Procedure and Transnational 'Harmonization': A Law-and-Economics Perspective" in *Economic Analysis of Civil Procedure* 387–421, Bork, Eger and Schaefer, pp. 410–12 (Mohr Siebeck: 2009) (Proceedings of the 2008 Travemunder Symposium).

Parker Jeffrey S. and Peter Lewisch, "Materielle Wahrheitsfindung im Zivilprozess", in 100 Jahre ZPO: Ökonomische Anlayse des Zivilprozesses, P. Lewisch and W. Rechberger (eds.) (Manz: 1998).

Posner, Richard A., "An Economic Approach to Legal Procedure and Judicial Administration," 2 *J. Leg. Studies* 399–458 (1973).

Priest, George L. and Benjamin Klein, "The Selection of Disputes for Litigation," 13 *J. Legal Studies* 1 (1984).

Redish, Martin H. and Colleen McNamara, "Back to the Future: Discovery Cost Allocation and Modern Procedural Theory," 79 *George Washington L. Rev.* 773 (2011).

Rubin, Paul H., "Why is the Common Law Efficient?" 6 *Journal of Legal Studies* 51–63 (1977).

Sanchirico, Chris William, "Relying on the Information of Interested—and Potentially Dishonest—Parties, 3 *Am. L. & Econ. Rev.* 320 (2001a).

Sanchirico, Chris William, "Character Evidence and the Object of Trial," 101 *Colum. L Rev.* 1227 (2001b).

Sanchirico, Chris William and George Triantis, "Evidentiary Arbitrage: The Fabrication of Evidence and the Verifiability of Contract Performance," 24 *J. L. Econ. & Org.* 72 (2008).

Sanchirico, Chris William (ed.), *Procedural Law and Economics* (Encyclopedia of Law and Economics, 2nd edn, Vol. 8) (Edward Elgar: 2012).

Scott, Robert E. and George G. Triantis, "Anticipating Litigation in Contract Design," 115 *Yale L. J.* 814 (2006).

Shin, H.S., "Adversarial and Inquisitorial Procedures in Arbitration," 28 *Rand J. Econ.* 378 (1998).

Tullock, Gordon, *Trials on Trial* (Columbia University Press: 1980).

Wittman, Donald. "Prior Regulation versus Post Liability: The Choice Between Input and Output Monitoring," 6 *J. Legal Studies* 193 (1977).

Yonai, D.K., "Trials as Markets for Truth: A Catallactic Approach to Comparative Legal Procedures" (Draft paper, April 2012, Lundy-Fetterman School of Business, Campbell Univ.).

Zywicki, Todd J., "Spontaneous Order and the Common Law: Gordon Tullock's Critique," 135 *Public Choice* 35–58 (2008).

15. An Austrian analysis of contemporary American business law
Peter G. Klein and Thomas A. Lambert

I. INTRODUCTION

Economic analyses of law have typically relied on models from mainstream, neoclassical economics. This approach assumes that individuals act "rationally," that they are fully informed, and that all-important phenomena can be described in formal equilibrium models. In the last couple of decades, a number of legal scholars have attempted to incorporate "behavioral" economic analyses of legal rules, jettisoning the assumption of *homo economicus* and considering how welfare calculations change if individuals are not rational, self-interested maximizers but instead exhibit predictable irrationalities (e.g., the endowment effect) or tendencies toward non-self-interested behavior (e.g., the "fairness" tendencies exhibited in the Ultimatum Game). Indeed, some scholars have referred to behavioral law and economics as the "growth stock" of legal academia (Choi and Pritchard, 2003).

Whereas behavioral economics has made significant inroads into legal analysis, another group of heterodox theories, those associated with Austrian economics, have rarely been explicitly invoked in economic analyses of law.[1] This chapter begins to fill that gap in one area: American business law. We begin by setting forth some Austrian insights that are particularly relevant to an analysis of business law. We then examine a number of business law doctrines—some from corporate law, others from business-related fields such as agency and antitrust—and demonstrate how they cohere or conflict with Austrian insights.

---

[1]   Exceptions include the essays collected in Rizzo (2011), along with important papers by Block (1977), Kirzner (1979), Rothbard (1982), Hoppe (2004), and Hülsmann (2004).

II.   RELEVANT CONCEPTS IN AUSTRIAN ECONOMIC AND LEGAL THEORY

Austrian thinking on the nature of the firm is the obvious starting point for an Austrian analysis of business law. But Austrian insights on business cycles and on the nature of law itself also shed light on the propriety of the rules governing business structures and operations. We therefore begin with a brief summary of Austrian thought on the nature of the firm, business cycle theory, and the propriety of different types of legal rules.

a.   An Austrian Theory of the Firm?

The early Austrians did not develop an explicit theory of the business firm, though their works are rife with insights on the organization of production (Foss and Klein, 2010). More recently, a number of distinct Austrian theories of the firm have emerged, emphasizing characteristically Austrian ideas about property, entrepreneurship, economic calculation, tacit knowledge, and the temporal structure of capital.[2]

i.   Insights from the socialist calculation debate

Austrian economists are perhaps best known for their role in the early 20th Century "socialist calculation" debate. Pointing to instances of crushing poverty and severe wealth inequality during and following the Industrial Revolution, socialists, Marxists, and other critics of *laissez faire* contended that free markets had effectively failed and that wise and benevolent governments could allocate resources in a more efficient and equitable manner. A number of theorists now associated with the Austrian school took up the cause of *laissez faire*, contending that markets allocate resources better, or at least no worse, than even the best-run governments could do.

Ludwig von Mises (1920) launched the debate with his argument that rational economic planning requires private property in factors (the "means of production"). Economists had already recognized the role of the price mechanism in allocating resources to high-valued uses, but had not spelled out the legal foundations for this procedure. Mises pointed out that if all factors are owned collectively—by a socialist dictator, or even a voluntary collective with democratic voting—then there can be no exchange markets for factors, and thus no market prices for these

---

[2]   See, for example, the papers collected in Foss and Klein (2002) and the references cited therein, along with more recent works by Adelstein (2005), Casson (2005), Langlois (2007), Pongracic (2009), and Foss and Klein (2012).

factors. Central planners can assign their own "prices," but these are just meaningless, arbitrary numbers. Without real markets and real prices, it is impossible for entrepreneurs to form judgments about the relative scarcities of various factors and the expected profitability of combining them in various combinations in their attempts to produce goods and services consumers want (and are willing to pay for). Because factors are heterogeneous, it is impossible to quantify, add up, and compare them without prices (bushels of wheat cannot be added to tons of steel or man-hours of labor to see which combinations are the least costly for producing particular outputs). Mises's argument was essentially about the need for cost accounting with numbers that accurately reflect real-world economic conditions (Klein, 1996).

Mises (1951) also emphasized the role of factor markets, and the profit-and-loss mechanism more generally, in selecting among more and less able entrepreneurs. Without markets for inputs and outputs, there can be no economically meaningful profits and losses, and no way for the competitive process to shift resources from less to more valuable uses (i.e., from less to more able entrepreneurs).

F.A. Hayek interpreted Mises's argument in terms of the "knowledge problem"—the fact that the information required to allocate productive resources to their highest and best ends is not readily available to any individual or central authority, because it is widely dispersed among individuals throughout society and frequently idiosyncratic, tacit, and otherwise unarticulable (e.g., Hayek, 1945). Socialist planners, Hayek emphasized, lack access to value-relevant information (including information about individuals' subjective preferences for different uses of productive resources) and could not effectively process all those frequently conflicting bits of information even if they were accessible—hence the failure of centralized economic planning.[3]

Austrian thinkers further emphasized that the factors affecting the value any allocation of resources will generate are constantly changing. Mises, for example, insisted that "the problem of economic calculation is of economic dynamics; it is no problem of economic statics" (Mises, 1922, p. 121). Hayek later added that "economic problems arise always and only in consequence of change" (Hayek, 1945, p. 82). To allocate resources efficiently, socialist planners would have to keep abreast of a multitude

---

[3]   There is a lively debate within and outside the Austrian school about whether Mises's and Hayek's arguments are slight variations on a common theme, or reflect important differences about value, prices, and equilibrium. This variety of perspectives and interpretations is reflected in the applied Austrian literature on the business firm.

of changing facts, many of which (such as individuals' changing preferences for products and services) cannot be directly observed. In a market economy, by contrast, value-relevant changes continually affect prices, which in turn motivate the "man on the spot" to alter his behavior in a salutary direction. Thus, in Salerno's (1994, p. 121) words, Mises "makes it crystal clear that the static prices mathematically imputed from perfect knowledge of the economic data would not lead to a dynamically efficient allocation of resources. The latter can only be achieved by the entrepreneurially appraised prices that are generated by the historical market process."

Austrian defenders of *laissez faire* also noted the incentive problems besetting socialism. A right to at least a portion of the residual value occasioned by their superior allocation decisions, even the most highly competent socialist planners with complete knowledge about the relative value of competing resource allocations would have little incentive to allocate resources to their highest and best ends, especially if they could attain personal benefits from suboptimal resource allocations. Actual and proposed socialist systems generally did not, however, grant planners any ownership stake in the value they generated. Moreover, such systems generally conferred tremendous power and discretion on planners, so much so that they could easily enrich themselves by personally usurping resources or channeling them so as to earn kickbacks or other perquisites. Accordingly, socialist planning faced an incentive problem as well as a knowledge problem.

As explained below, these three insights from the socialist calculation debate—the knowledge problem, the ubiquity and significance of change, and the importance of incentives in economic planning—contribute to a distinctly Austrian theory of the firm.

ii.   Entrepreneurship
The ubiquity of change, Austrian thinkers recognized, creates a constant need for resources to be reallocated (i.e., redirected in their use) in a manner that will unlock greater value. A key figure in any capitalist system, then, is the entrepreneur—an agent who, in the face of uncertainty and widely dispersed knowledge, seeks to discover and take advantage of opportunities to create value and profit by moving capital and resources from less valuable to more valuable uses. Entrepreneurs are constantly alert to opportunities to discover and exploit maladjustments in resource allocation. By engaging in the activities Kirzner termed arbitrage (instantaneous exploitation of price differentials), speculation (arbitrage through time), and innovation (the creation of a new product, productive method, resource use, or organization different from the usual one), entrepreneurs

constantly reallocate resources toward higher and better ends, creating value and earning personal profit in the process (Kirzner, 1985, pp. 84–5).

One way entrepreneurs create value is by experimenting with capital assets. As Barzel (1997) observed, capital assets are distinguished by their "attributes," which are the assets' characteristics, functions, and possible uses, as perceived by an entrepreneur. Asset attributes exist not objectively, but subjectively in the minds of entrepreneurs who employ the assets in various lines of production. This implies that asset attributes are manifested in production decisions and are realized only *ex post*, after those decisions have generated profits or losses. Entrepreneurship is thus not merely a matter of deploying, in a "risky" manner, assets with *given* attributes; it involves experimentation to discover those attributes under conditions of uncertainty.

Because an entrepreneur is a speculator who operates under conditions of true "uncertainty," where not even the probability of success may be determined,[4] he cannot easily be hired. Entrepreneurial judgment cannot be assessed in terms of its marginal product and therefore cannot be valued *ex ante* for purposes of ascertaining a wage. Accordingly, there is no market for the judgment that entrepreneurs rely on, and exercising such judgment may require the person possessing it to start a firm. Klein (2008) therefore asserts that "[f]irms exist not only to economize on transaction costs, but also as a means for the exercise of entrepreneurial judgment, and as a low-cost mechanism for entrepreneurs to experiment with various combinations of heterogeneous capital goods."

iii. Institutions

A final concept that should be included in any Austrian theory of the firm is the notion that social order tends to emerge from the voluntary, decentralized interactions of individuals pursuing their own interests without necessarily trying to create any sort of social order. While very much a feature of Scottish Enlightenment thinking, as exemplified by Adam Smith's "invisible hand" (Smith, 1776, Book IV, Ch. II, para. IX) and Adam Ferguson's reference to establishments that "are indeed the result of human action, but not the execution of any human design" (Ferguson, 1767, Part III, Section II), this concept was embraced by Hayek, building on Menger's distinction between "pragmatic" and "organic" institutions,

---

[4]   *See* Knight (1921), pp. 19–20, distinguishing "risk," which is quantifiable, from "uncertainty," which is not, and Foss and Klein (2012, Ch. 4) on the implications of the Knightian distinction for the theory of the firm. Mises (1949) emphasized a similar distinction between "class probability" and "case probability" (Klein, 2009).

in which the former are the result of "socially teleological causes" while the latter are "the unintended result of innumerable efforts of economic subjects pursuing individual interests" (Menger, 1883, p. 158). Menger's (1892) famous analysis of the origin of money is the best-known example of such a process. Hayek similarly focused on this distinction between "planned" and "spontaneous" orders, going so far as to distinguish between the rules giving rise to a spontaneous order and those supporting a planned order (Hayek, 1973). (His distinction between types of rules is considered below.)

iv.   Synthesis

At first glance, many of the hallmarks of Austrian thought—the impossibility of centralized economic planning, the central role of prices created through decentralized exchange, the general superiority of organic institutions over those resulting from conscious design—seem inconsistent with the notion of planned, structured business firms. Consider, for example, Coase's (1937, p. 389) famous observation that "the distinguishing mark of the firm is the supersession of the price mechanism" and his attempt to define the firm by pointing to its opposite, the unplanned allocation of resources in a free market:

> Outside the firm, price movements direct production, which is coordinated through a series of exchange transactions on the market. Within a firm, these market transactions are eliminated and in place of the complicated market structure with exchange transactions is substituted the entrepreneur-coordinator, who directs production. (Coase, 1937, p. 388)

In light of these observations, one may query whether Austrian thought can accommodate a view that recognizes business firms as instances of central planning—"islands of conscious power," as Coase called them—yet regards them as salutary components of a market economy. It can and does.

As an initial matter, the notion of economic planning itself is not inconsistent with Austrian thought. Austrian economists have long recognized that such planning must exist in any economic system. Hayek, for example, emphasized that "all the dispute about 'economic planning'" in the socialist calculation debate was "not a dispute about whether planning is to be done or not"; rather, it was "a dispute as to whether planning is to be done centrally, by one authority for the whole economic system, or is to be divided among many individuals" (Hayek, 1945, pp. 519–20).

While planning and conscious power will appear in any economic system, there is a difference between *state* planning and that which occurs within organizations that are created voluntarily via contract in a system of private ownership. State planners possess presumptively legitimate power to coerce using force, and are often far-removed (both geographically and temporally) from the situations they govern, and usually face little competition. The "planners" within a contractually created business entity, by contrast, cannot forcefully coerce their subjects (they must procure consent from resource providers), are typically "closer to the action" than state planners, face significant competition from other individuals and contractual entities, and hold residual control rights over the resources they own and manage. Planning within a voluntary association, then, is not the same as state economic planning.

Business entities that allocate resources via managerial fiat regularly emerge in free societies and should thus be regarded as instances of spontaneous order. The Coasian explanation of why they emerge—i.e., because "there is a cost of using the price mechanism" to allocate productive resources—is consistent with Austrian thinking. But Austrian ideas may helpfully supplement the Coasian account. Thus, as Foss and Klein have explained, one may develop a "uniquely 'Austrian' approach to the firm" by "start[ing] with the basic contractual approach, and the Coasian *explananda* of the firm's existence, boundaries, and internal organization, and add[ing] concepts of entrepreneurship, economic calculation, the time-structure of production, and other elements of the Austrian tradition" (Foss and Klein, 2010, p. 287).

In this approach, the firm is a manifestation of entrepreneurial judgment, a nexus of contracts voluntarily entered into by resource owners and suppliers of labor seeking to reduce various costs (e.g., transaction costs, costs stemming from "hold-ups" occasioned by asset-specific investments, agency costs, etc.). In addition, however, firms tend to emerge as the means by which entrepreneurs may secure compensation for their judgments. Because entrepreneurs operate under conditions of true uncertainty (as opposed to predictable risk), the value of their efforts cannot be predicted *ex ante*, and they therefore cannot easily be hired at pre-determined wages. They will often prefer to structure arrangements so that their compensation comes in the form of the residual income stream occasioned by their entrepreneurial judgments, and this will require them to establish a firm.

Austrian insights from the socialist calculation debate, then, shed light on the internal characteristics of the nexus of contracts that constitutes a firm. While resource-owning entrepreneurs hold residual decision rights over the use of the firm's assets, these entrepreneurs will typically delegate specified decision rights to subordinates to take advantage of local knowledge and high-powered incentives (i.e., moving some day-to-day decision-making away from far-removed capital providers and toward hands-on managers, who more closely resemble Hayek's "man on the spot"). Given the need to align the incentives of managers and suppliers of capital,

Austrian thought predicts that the parties to firms will recognize duties from managers to residual claimants and will impose liability on managers who benefit themselves at the expense of those claimants. Because change is both ubiquitous and important, the posited duties should be somewhat flexible, perhaps conceived of as "standards" of care whose contours are fleshed out ex post, rather than "rules" of behavior, which are specified *ex ante*. (In Foss, Foss, and Klein's (2007) terminology, these managers exercise a subordinate form of judgment that is "derived" from the "original" judgment rights of owners.)

In Part III, we consider the degree to which American business law coheres with this somewhat general Austrian theory of the firm. First, though, we consider two other concepts that are relevant to an Austrian analysis of business law principles.

b.   Business Cycle Theory

Although an in-depth consideration of Austrian business cycle theory is beyond the scope of this chapter, Austrian insights on the causes of recessions and depressions are useful in analyzing some key securities law doctrines, and we therefore provide a cursory overview of Austrian thinking on business cycles.[5]

The Austrian theory differs from mainstream accounts of business cycles in its emphasis on resource heterogeneity (Foss et al., 2007; Agarwal et al., 2009). In a modern, industrial economy, consumer goods result from complex, multi-stage production processes. Entrepreneurs purchase capital and labor in the present, in anticipation of the receipts from selling products (to consumers or to entrepreneurs at the next production stage) in the future. Entrepreneurs are continually adjusting the economy's inter-temporal production structure, or capital structure, based on their knowledge of past and present technology and resource availability and their expectations about future market conditions. Because production takes time, interest rates are essential for coordinating activities across production stages.

In an economy with a central bank (such as the US Federal Reserve System), interest rates are affected not only by the rates at which individuals save (by deferring current consumption in favor of future consumption) and at which entrepreneurs borrow (to invest in production), but also by the government's monetary policy. If the central bank increases the supply

---

[5]   For more detailed treatments see Hayek (1931), Rothbard (1963), and Garrison (2001). For practical implications see Klein (2014).

of loanable funds (e.g., by purchasing bonds), market interest rates fall, and entrepreneurs borrow to finance new projects that would not have been profitable at higher interest rates. Because time-consuming and temporally remote projects tend to be most sensitive to interest rate changes, those newly funded projects are often "higher-order" projects that are somewhat far-removed from finished consumer goods—e.g., construction projects, mining, new capital equipment, or purchases of raw materials.

This process is appropriate where the growth in funds available for borrowing occurs because of increased saving. Members of the public, by their savings decisions, have indicated a willingness to forego current consumption in favor of future consumption. The public's saved resources provide the wherewithal to see the long-term investment projects through to completion, so the long time horizon of the newly funded projects presents no problem. Market-determined interest rates therefore send appropriate signals, encouraging entrepreneurs to undertake long-term projects only when the public has set aside the funds necessary to finance them.

The situation is different, though, when interest rates drop because the central bank has increased the money supply. In those circumstances, the public has not set aside the resources necessary to make possible the newly initiated projects, and those resources do not magically appear as a result of the central bank's creation of new fiat money. Thus, the lower interest rates resulting from the central bank's actions encourage entrepreneurs to invest in long-term projects and discourages saving by individuals, when the public has not actually set aside the resources required for long-term investment projects. The result is malinvestment—i.e., the allocation of productive resources *away* from their highest and best ends. As Mises (1949, p. 549) puts it, credit expansion by the central bank "falsifies economic calculation." When it becomes clear that the factors do not exist in sufficient quantities to make all the newly initiated projects profitable, the low interest rate-fueled boom turns into a bust, during which malinvestments are liquidated, resources are re-directed to more value-productive ends, and the economy readjusts itself. Government efforts to interfere with this painful process of readjustment—e.g., propping up malinvestments rather than allowing their liquidation—only prolong the economic hardship or sow the seeds for a future boom-bust cycle.

As explained below, Austrian thinking on business cycles is relevant to an analysis of securities regulation, for some aspects of the securities laws encourage the overvaluation of equity and impede price correction, leading corporate managers to make analogous value-destructive malinvestments.

c.   The Nature of Law: *Nomos vs. Thesis*

A final concept that is relevant to an Austrian analysis of business law is Hayek's distinction between the types of legal rules (Hayek, 1973). Some legal rules are general in their application, are "purpose-independent" (meaning that the law-giver is not seeking to achieve some specific social outcome but is instead endeavoring to posit the means for resolving disputes in accordance with the parties' settled expectations), and have the effect of setting clear expectations so that parties may confidently predict outcomes in structuring their affairs. Hayek referred to these sorts of rules as *nomos*. Other legal rules are more akin to specific orders from a central authority seeking to achieve some specific purpose. Such "teleological" rules Hayek labeled *thesis*.

In light of his emphasis on the knowledge problem and the impossibility of effective central planning, Hayek contended that the rules that legitimately constrain individuals in their interactions with each other are *nomos*. *Thesis* should be (but often is not) limited to the context of intragovernmental administration. The common law, rendered by judges resolving specific disputes among parties and looking to precedent for guidance, is generally *nomos*. Most (but not all) legislation is *thesis*. The characterization of any piece of legislation will depend on whether it amounts to specific orders aimed at achieving a set purpose (e.g., the recently enacted federal health care law), in which case it is *thesis*, or is instead simply seeking to codify purpose-independent rules that settle parties' expectations and enable them to order their affairs in light of the information to which they alone are privy (e.g., the Uniform Commercial Code), in which case it is *nomos*. As explained below, some business law doctrines are *nomos*-like; others are plainly *thesis*.

III.   AN AUSTRIAN ANALYSIS OF SELECTED BUSINESS LAW FEATURES AND DOCTRINES

Having set forth some key insights from Austrian thought, we turn now to an analysis of some specific aspects of American business law. We first consider features that cohere with Austrian thinking on the limits of centralized economic planning and the entrepreneurial function of firms. We then consider various features that conflict with Austrian insights on those matters. (Our lists of coherent and conflicting features are, of course, far from complete. Our goal is not to provide an exhaustive Austrian analysis of business law, but instead to highlight doctrines and features that appear to be particularly coherent or in conflict with Austrian thinking.)

a. Coherent Features

i. Acknowledging the limits of centralized economic planning

A number of features of contemporary business law display a sensitivity to Hayekian thinking on the difficulty of centralized economic planning in light of dispersed knowledge and constant change. Most notably, the very structure of most business organizations' statutes (e.g., state corporation statutes, the Uniform Partnership Act, state limited liability company acts) reflects skepticism about central economic planning. In general, those statutes simply posit sets of tailorable default rules that will determine relations among the participants in a business organization *if those participants do not specify otherwise*. Section 18 of the Uniform Partnership Act (1914), for example, sets the rules that govern how general partners will share profits, losses, and management authority, but it expressly makes those rules "subject to any agreement between [the partners]." By providing rules on a number matters, the state business organization statutes settle expectations among the parties, permitting them to arrange their affairs with some confidence about outcomes. By allowing parties to alter those rules, the statutes enable parties to craft their relationships in light of their private knowledge (including knowledge about parties' subjective values), information to which legislators and regulators could never be privy. State business organization statutes are thus *nomos*-like, purpose-independent rules that eschew central planning and facilitate the emergence of spontaneous orders that reflect local conditions and participants' subjective values.

A similar solicitude for private ordering is evident in the legal doctrines employed to control agency costs, the inevitable losses that occur when a self-interested agent purports to act on a principal's behalf.[6] The law has generally sought to constrain agency costs by saddling agents with fiduciary duties—broad, amorphous obligations whose specific contours are fleshed out *ex post*. Many of these fiduciary duties are tailorable so that they are, in effect, default contract terms between principal and agent. For example, a number of fiduciary duties preclude an agent from earning any "secret profits" from his agency (i.e., any compensation other than that specifically agreed upon with the principal). For the most part, though, those duties apply "except as otherwise agreed" (see, for example,

---

[6] The agent, who does not capture all the benefit of his diligent service to the principal, has an incentive to shirk and/or act opportunistically. The principal, knowing her agent's tendencies, has an incentive to expend resources monitoring the agent. The combined losses from the agent's shirking and opportunism and the principal's monitoring constitute agency costs.

Restatement (Second) of Agency Sections 1958, 387–398). Thus, we again see *nomos*-like rules that facilitate planning but permit parties to tailor relationships in light of their private information.[7]

A particularly interesting aspect of fiduciary duties is the remedy provided for breach. When an agent somehow profits from his breach of fiduciary duty to his principal, the law requires that he "disgorge" his gain, *even if* the breach of duty did not injure the principal and the principal could not have earned the profits herself. This is a somewhat curious doctrine. Most breaches of fiduciary duty could alternatively be analyzed as breaches of contract (either express or implied contracts), and a punitive disgorgement remedy would never be allowed if the breach were so analyzed.[8] It might seem odd to permit the principal to collect what are effectively punitive damages by pleading her claim as a breach of fiduciary duty rather than a breach of contract. The disgorgement remedy for breach of fiduciary duty makes sense, though, as an information-forcing "penalty" default. The idea is that the law should encourage agents who know of potential side businesses in which they could earn additional profit to disclose those opportunities to their principals, bargain over them, and strike mutually beneficial deals in which the opportunities are exploited and the profits shared in whatever proportion makes most sense, given the information to which only the principals and agents themselves are privy. If the default rule "punishes" agents who have private information about potential business opportunities by requiring them to disgorge any profits they earn exploiting such opportunities, it encourages agents to share that information and tailor mutually beneficial arrangements. Because the disgorgement remedy (1) recognizes and seeks to harness the value of private information and (2) facilitates private ordering, it appears to cohere with Austrian insights.

Recent developments in antitrust law also seem to recognize the value of allowing business persons to structure their relations as best they see fit given their private information. Until the mid-1970s, antitrust doctrine was quite hostile to "vertical intra-brand restraints"—i.e., manufacturer/distributor agreements under which the distributors promise not to sell the manufacturers' goods on certain terms. Both vertical price restraints

---

[7]   Note that the law has deemed some fiduciary duties to be non-waivable. Corporate directors, for instance, may not contract out of their duties to shareholders in a way that would permit the directors to engage in insider trading. Mandatory, "tort-like" fiduciary duties would seem to be inconsistent with Austrian thought.

[8]   Contract doctrine rejects punitive damages for breach of contract because they deter efficient breaches.

(e.g., resale price maintenance agreements under which a retailer may not sell a manufacturer's product below a certain price) and vertical non-price restraints (e.g., agreements under which a retailer is forbidden to sell a manufacturer's product outside a specified geographic region) were per se illegal. Manufacturers were therefore limited in their ability to distribute their products through dealers while simultaneously exercising control over how those dealers distributed their products. Instead, manufacturers generally confronted a stark "make or buy" decision with respect to product distribution: They could either "make" product distribution by distributing their products themselves (i.e., by vertically integrating) or "buy" it by selling through distributors, over whom they could assert little control. Limiting manufacturers' freedom to engage in partial vertical integration by outsourcing distribution but then contractually controlling their distributors' conduct conflicted with the Austrian notion that decisions about distribution arrangements are best left to the "man on the spot," who should be free to tailor his distributor arrangements in whatever way he believes, based on his private information, will maximize total sales of his product.

In the last few decades, antitrust doctrine has become far less hostile to vertical intra-brand restraints. All such restraints—both non-price and price—are now judged under a rule of reason that recognizes that contractual arrangements achieving a partial vertical integration are generally output-enhancing and should be permitted. Of course, the ability of the courts to decide which vertical restraints promote efficiency (and thus should be permitted) and which are aimed at building, protecting, or extending market power (and thus should be forbidden) violates the idea that business arrangements are best left up to market participants. More generally, Austrians reject the neoclassical economics notion of "perfect competition" that underlies conventional antitrust analysis, tending to view a market as competitive as long as there are no governmental restrictions on entry (Armentano, 1996; Salerno, 2003). Still, contemporary antitrust permits more of the sort of private ordering favored by Austrian thinkers than was the case before the 1980s.

ii.   Furthering the entrepreneurial function of the firm

As explained above, Austrians recognize that firms not only economize on various costs, they also provide a vehicle for the exercise of entrepreneurial judgment, which involves experimentation with novel asset allocations in an attempt to create value (and profits).[9] A chief function of the Austrian

---

[9]   Given that value is subjective and change ubiquitous, wealth may be created (and profit earned) by deploying assets differently over time. Entrepreneurs

firm, then, is to foster entrepreneurial uncertainty-bearing. This understanding of the firm provides theoretical support for two central features of corporate law: limited liability and the business judgment rule.

Austrian writers such as Israel Kirzner have distinguished sharply between the "pure entrepreneur" who owns no capital and the "entrepreneur-capitalist" who does, while others have insisted that the exercise of entrepreneurial judgment involves ownership.[10] In either case, entrepreneurs typically rely on outside investors for additional capital. Limited liability—the legal doctrine that, for some types of firms (e.g., corporations), limits an individual investor's liability for firm debts and obligations to the amount of his investment in the firm—facilitates capital formation by entrepreneurs. The business judgment rule—the doctrine that precludes courts from second-guessing business decisions by managers who acted loyally, in good faith, and on a reasonably informed basis—encourages firm managers to take significant business risks. Collectively, limited liability and the business judgment rule enable firms to act as vehicles for entrepreneurial judgment.

The most obvious way limited liability encourages capital formation is by permitting investors to externalize some of the cost of their firms' activities.[11] This somewhat troubling "externalization of cost" effect, though, does not fully account for limited liability's role in facilitating capital formation[12] (Bainbridge, 2002). Limited liability enables passive investment because investors need not monitor firm managers as closely as they would if their entire fortunes were at stake. The possibility of passive investment, then, permits investors to diversify their investment portfolios, thereby reducing unsystematic investment risk. Limited liability also renders equity investments "fungible," because investors need not adjust

---

continually experiment with asset allocations, hoping to discover new allocations to which consumers will attach a high value. Because entrepreneurs accomplish this task under conditions of true uncertainty, it is impossible to evaluate and provide compensation for their entrepreneurial judgments *ex ante*, and their best option for compensation is to establish firms in which they are residual claimants.

[10]　Compare, e.g., Kirzner (2009) and Foss and Klein (2012).

[11]　If, for example, a firm creates tort liability of $2 million but has assets of only $1 million, the investors effectively foist $1 million of the cost of the firm's activities onto the tort claimants.

[12]　Limited liability's externalization of cost effect is likely less significant than it initially appears. Contract creditors dealing with limited liability firms can and usually do bargain for protection from externalization (e.g., a higher interest rate, a guaranty from investors). Reputational considerations and, for closely held limited liability entities, the possibility that courts will "pierce the corporate veil" provide a good deal of protection for potential tort victims.

their valuation of an investment to account for the risk that a creditor will pursue their personal assets. This fungibility permits equity investments to be traded on highly liquid markets, which in turn makes those investments particularly attractive to suppliers of capital. By encouraging passive investment, enabling diversification, and facilitating the creation of highly liquid equities markets, limited liability assists entrepreneurs in raising capital for their risk-taking ventures.

The business judgment rule, then, assures that firm managers—who may not themselves hold equity stakes—are willing to bear uncertainty, making them act more like entrepreneur-owners. The rule holds that absent fraud, self-dealing, bad faith, or gross negligence in becoming informed, courts will abstain from assessing the merits of business decisions that lose money for investors. Oft-stated rationales for the rule are that judges are not business experts and that the rule encourages individuals to serve as corporate managers by insulating them from liability for decisions that turn out badly. Those explanations, though, are incomplete. In other contexts, courts routinely assess the merits of complicated decisions, even when they lack expertise and might dissuade qualified individuals from serving in high-risk roles. In medical malpractice cases, for example, courts regularly review treatment decisions, despite the facts that judges and jurors lack medical training and that potential malpractice liability discourages qualified individuals from becoming doctors.

The business judgment rule is thus better understood as a doctrine aimed at encouraging managerial risk-taking. In larger, more mature business organizations, most business decisions are made by professional managers (e.g., corporate directors and officers), who tend to be more risk averse than equity investors. Professional managers are usually fully compensated when a firm breaks even (i.e., earns no economic profit) but stand to lose their career if the firm fails or suffers a large loss. Equity investors, by contrast, receive no payout at all if the firm merely breaks even and lose only the value of their investment, which is typically held as part of a diversified portfolio, if the firm fails. Relative to managers, then, equity investors have a much stronger preference for high-risk, high-reward decisions. By assuring managers that their loyal, good faith, and reasonably informed business decisions cannot create legal liability even if they turn out miserably, the business judgment rule encourages managers to take greater business risks and thereby facilitates the firm's role as a vehicle for entrepreneurial uncertainty-bearing.[13]

---

[13]   Delaware courts have explicitly acknowledged how the business judgment rule's leniency enables corporations to embrace risk and thereby fulfill their

b. Conflicting Features

While the business law features discussed above seem consistent with Austrian insights on the limits of centralized planning and the entrepreneurial function of the firm, other features of contemporary American business law conflict with those ideas.

i. Discounting the limits of centralized economic planning and the crucial role of prices in allocating resources appropriately

Unlike state business organization statutes and many fiduciary duties, which largely consist of *nomos*-like, purpose independent rules that facilitate private ordering, numerous aspects of contemporary business law ostensibly seek to achieve some pre-determined end state and therefore resemble Hayek's *thesis*. Among the many examples of such "purposive" legal features are federal laws and regulations on shareholder voting rights, rules mandating particular firm structures, attempts to regulate executive compensation, and efforts to assure a level playing field among investors by restricting insider trading. These and similar purposive legal features, often adopted as a political response to some sort of business crisis, are generally insensitive to Austrian insights on the knowledge problem, the ubiquity of change, the limits of centralized economic planning, and the importance of prices.

If they were free to structure their relations as best they saw fit, investors and corporate managers might well decide that broad investor voting rights are not cost-justified. Shareholder voting, after all, is quite

---

entrepreneurial function. Consider, for example, the following discussion from the 1996 *Caremark* decision of the Delaware Court of Chancery:

> Where review of board functioning is involved, courts leave behind as a relevant point of reference the decisions of the hypothetical "reasonable person", who typically supplies the test for negligence liability. It is doubtful that we want business men and women to be encouraged to make decisions as hypothetical persons of *ordinary* judgment and prudence might. The corporate form gets its utility in large part from its ability to allow diversified investors to accept greater investment risk. If those in charge of the corporation are to be adjudged personally liable for losses on the basis of a substantive judgment based upon what persons of ordinary or average judgment and average risk assessment talent regard as "prudent" "sensible" or even "rational", such persons will have a strong incentive at the margin to authorize less risky investment projects.

In re Caremark International Inc. Derivative Litigation, 689 A.2d 959, __ n. 16 (1996).

costly, and shareholders tend to be rationally ignorant about a great many issues facing the corporate enterprise. Shareholders might thus prefer to have only a cheap "exit" option, foregoing a relatively costly "voice" option in order to preserve corporate resources. Several aspects of federal law, though, limit the ability of investors and corporate managers to order their relations in a manner limiting the investors' abilities to vote on certain matters. Securities Exchange Act Rule 14a-7, for example, requires corporations to assist certain shareholders seeking to mount proxy contests by either distributing the shareholders' proxy materials or providing them with a list of the names and addresses of shareholders of record. Rule 14a-8 requires corporate managers to go further with respect to some voting matters, actually including on the company's own proxy form certain shareholder proposals. The newly enacted Dodd-Frank law will require corporations to permit some shareholders to nominate directors to be included in the company's proxy solicitation materials and to give shareholders a nonbinding "say on pay" made to certain executive officers. These and similar voting rules, ostensibly designed to give shareholders more say in corporate governance, conflict with the Austrian notion that investors and managers should be free to arrange their relationships as best they see fit given their private information and subjective values.

So do a number of recently enacted "reactive" rules on corporate governance and executive compensation. In the wake of massive financial frauds at Enron and Worldcom, for example, Congress enacted legislation and the securities exchanges (with congressional encouragement) adopted listing standards that mandate certain governance structures for public corporations and dictate who may serve in certain capacities (e.g., only independent directors may serve on audit committees).[14] These and similar mandatory governance rules, which ostensibly aim to reduce financial fraud, limit the ability of business planners to set up governance structures in light of the information to which they alone are privy.

In recent months, Congress has embarked on an effort to combat excessive corporate risk-taking by regulating executive compensation. Section 956 of the new Dodd-Frank law requires "appropriate federal regulators" to require disclosure by financial institutions of the structures of

---

[14] The Sarbanes-Oxley law requires that public corporations establish audit committees comprised exclusively of independent directors and empower those committees with direct and unfettered responsibility for the hiring, firing, and compensation of auditors. Listing standards for the New York Stock Exchange and NASDAQ go even further: a majority of members of the board itself must meet independence standards, and all members of the audit, compensation, and newly mandated nominating committees must be independent.

all incentive-based compensation, so that the regulators can determine whether such compensation is "excessive," or could lead to a material financial loss by the financial institution. These and similar mandatory governance rules, which ostensibly aim to reduce financial fraud, limit the ability of business planners to set up governance structures in light of the information to which they alone are privy.

Perhaps no feature of American business law conflicts more starkly with Austrian thinking on the desirability of private ordering and the importance of prices than the federal ban on insider trading. Imposed out of a desire to ensure some sort of level playing field among investors, the insider-trading ban precludes corporate managers from trading in their own companies' stock on the basis of material, non-public information. Absent the ban, some firm planners might opt to allow managers to trade on the basis of inside information. As Henry Manne first observed, such trading could constitute an efficient compensation mechanism for managers and would also tend to make the corporation's stock price, influenced by highly informative insider trades, more reflective of the corporation's true business prospects (i.e., more efficient) and thus a less risky prospect for investors (Manne, 1966). As corporations experimented with different insider trading policies, capital markets would tend to punish those that were value-destructive and reward those that were value-enhancing. By imposing a uniform insider trading policy in a quixotic attempt to assure a level playing field among investors, the federal securities laws likely preclude the sort of value-enhancing private ordering favored by Austrian thinkers.[15]

The insider-trading ban is also inconsistent with the Austrian emphasis on the crucial role of prices in assuring efficient resource allocation. When corporate insiders purchase or sell their own company's stock, thereby betting their own money that the stock is mispriced, they convey valuable information to the marketplace. Assuming their trades somehow become public, other rational investors will likely follow their lead, which will cause stock prices to reflect more accurately the underlying value of the firm. More efficient stock prices, then, will lead to a more appropriate allocation of investment capital throughout the economy. The insider-trading ban thwarts this process.

Finally, the insider-trading ban, as implemented in concert with the rest of securities regulation, is inconsistent with the Austrian concern that an

---

[15]   The insider trading ban conflicts with Austrian thought even if one construes the ban as a means of protecting the corporation's property rights in information (see, e.g., Bainbridge, 2002). While the Austrians would certainly support policies that clarify who owns corporate information, they would oppose policies mandating that the ownership right be non-transferable from corporation to managers.

excess of fiat money will generate value destruction. Under the prevailing regulatory regime, the groups primarily responsible for identifying and correcting instances of stock mispricing are corporate managers and sell-side stock analysts. Both groups are substantially more likely to take steps to correct undervaluation than overvaluation—corporate managers because their jobs depend on maintaining a high stock price, and analysts because they usually work for investment banks that make most of their money advising corporations on deals and thus have an incentive not to "talk down" a potential client's stock. Equity mispricing, then, tends to be more in the direction of over- than undervaluation (Finn, 1999). This means that corporate managers, who can issue stock of overvalued firms at unduly high prices or use overvalued stock to fund acquisitions and other projects, frequently have access to an artificially high level of capital for corporate investments. As Michael Jensen has observed (Jensen, 2005), this dynamic can create significant "agency costs of overvalued equity" as corporate managers use their overvalued equity to make value-destructive acquisitions (Moeller et al., 2005) and pursue investment projects with a negative net present value (Polk and Sapienza, 2004). Eventually, managers of overvalued firms, hoping to delay the day of reckoning on their firm's stock price, will tend to engage in earnings management, delay investments with a positive net present value in order to meet analysts' earnings expectations (Graham et al., 2005), and eventually resort to accounting fraud (Jensen, 2005). This spiral of value destruction resulting from mal-investments occasioned by inflated stock prices should look familiar: it is closely analogous to Austrian business cycle theory's predictions about inflated money supplies. And it is facilitated by the prohibition on insider trading, perhaps the most effective means of correcting equity overvaluation (Lambert, 2006).

ii.   Hindering the entrepreneurial function of the firm

As explained, Austrian thought ascribes a key role to the entrepreneur. Often operating through firms, entrepreneurs constantly look for ways to earn supra-competitive returns by allocating resources in novel ways that consumers value. Much of modern antitrust doctrine, however, focuses solely on static efficiency, attempting to eliminate supra-competitive pricing even though such pricing likely enhances dynamic efficiency by spurring innovation. The relentless pursuit of static efficiency at the expense of dynamic efficiency through enhanced innovation conflicts with Austrian thinking on the importance of entrepreneurship.

Take, for example, antitrust's treatment of price discrimination. By varying consumer prices according to consumers' willingness to pay for the product at issue (i.e., charging higher prices to consumers who value a product more, less to those who value it less), producers can enhance their gain from selling a product. And with certain types of price discrimination ("third-degree" price discrimination, in which the seller divides consumers into groups according to likely willingness to pay and then charges a different uniform price per group), neoclassical price theory predicts that this reallocation of surplus may actually cause a static efficiency loss. In dynamic terms, though, the freedom to price discriminate enhances overall well-being by encouraging firms to innovate. By allowing the entrepreneur to capture more of the surplus her innovation creates, price discrimination encourages innovation by increasing the reward for developing a unique product or service for which consumers are willing to pay above-cost prices (Klein and Wiley, 2003; Semeraro, 2009). Innovation, a central determinant of economic growth, tends to be retarded by the fact that innovators generally capture only a fraction of the surplus their efforts produce (Baker, 2007; Bresnahan, 2003; Griliches, 1992). Price discrimination helps alleviate this wealth-reducing positive externality. Antitrust, though, has frequently been hostile to price discrimination. The Robinson-Patman Act prohibits much price discrimination outright, and antitrust courts have often pointed to price discrimination effects as grounds for restricting business practices such as tying. Such hostility to price discrimination, a consequence of focusing on static efficiency without regard to dynamic considerations, conflicts with Austrian thinking on entrepreneurship and innovation.

In recent years, the Supreme Court has suggested a willingness to take a more dynamic point of view in evaluating antitrust challenges. In its 2004 *Trinko* decision,[16] the Court conceded that monopoly pricing, which occasions static efficiency losses, is key to motivating the sort of entrepreneurial innovation that creates dynamic efficiencies. The Court observed: "The opportunity to charge monopoly prices—at least for a short period—is what attracts 'business acumen' in the first place; it induces risk taking that produces innovation and economic growth."[17] Then, in its 2007 *Independent Ink* decision,[18] the Court suggested that price discrimination is consistent with competitive markets and is not, in itself, enough to warrant antitrust's ire.[19] These developments suggest a move toward an antitrust policy that is more consistent with Austrian thought.

---

[16]   *Verizon Communications Inc. v. Law Offices of Curtis v. Trinko*, LLP, 540 U.S. 398 (2007).

[17]   Ibid. at 407.

[18]   *Illinois Tool Works Inc. v. Independent Ink, Inc.*, 547 U.S. 28 (2006).

[19]   Ibid. at 45 (observing that "it is generally recognized that [price discrimination] also occurs in fully competitive markets").

IV. CONCLUSION

It would be impossible, in a short book chapter, even to set forth the principles of Austrian thought that would be relevant to an Austrian analysis of business law, much less to conduct such an analysis in any but a cursory fashion. We therefore view this chapter not as a final word, but as a conversation starter. By setting forth the aspects of Austrian thought we believe to be most relevant to an analysis of American business law and analyzing some key business law features in light of those insights, we have shown that this rich body of thought that has proven so useful in analyses of institutions (e.g., the socialist calculation debate) and monetary and fiscal policies (e.g., Austrian business cycle theory) has much to offer the economic analysis of discrete legal rules. We hope the conversation continues.

REFERENCES

Adelstein, Richard, *Knowledge and Power in the Mechanical Firm: Planning for Profit in Austrian Perspective*, 18 REVIEW OF AUSTRIAN ECONOMICS 55 (2005).

Agarwal, Rajshree, Jay B. Barney, Nicolai Foss, and Peter G. Klein, *Heterogeneous Resources and the Financial Crisis: Implications of Strategic Management Theory*, 7 STRATEGIC ORGANIZATION 467 (2009).

Armentano, Dominick, ANTITRUST AND MONOPOLY: ANATOMY OF A POLICY FAILURE (1996).

Bainbridge, Stephen, CORPORATION LAW AND ECONOMICS (2002).

Baker, Jonathan B., *Beyond Schumpeter vs. Arrow: How Antitrust Fosters Innovation*, 74 ANTITRUST L. J. 576, 576 (2007).

Barzel, Yoram, ECONOMIC ANALYSIS OF PROPERTY RIGHTS (1997).

Block, Walter E., *Coase and Demsetz on Private Property Rights*. 1 THE JOURNAL OF LIBERTARIAN STUDIES: AN INTERDISCIPLINARY REVIEW 111–15 (1977).

Bresnahan, Timothy F., *The Mechanisms of Information Technology's Contribution to Economic Growth*, in Jean-PhillipeTouffut, ed., INSTITUTIONS, INNOVATION AND GROWTH: SELECTED ECONOMIC PAPERS 135–7 (2003).

Casson, Mark, *Entrepreneurship and the Theory of the Firm*, 58 JOURNAL OF ECONOMIC BEHAVIOR & ORGANIZATION 327 (2005).

Choi, Stephen J. and A.C. Pritchard, *Behavioral Economics and the SEC*, 56 STAN. L. REV. 1, 7 (2003).

Coase, Ronald H., *The Nature of the Firm*. 4 ECONOMICA 386–405 (1937).

Ferguson, Adam, AN ESSAY ON THE HISTORY OF CIVIL SOCIETY (1767).

Finn, Mark T. et al., *Equity Mispricing: It's Mostly on the Short Side*, 55 FIN. ANALYSTS J. 117 (1999).

Foss, Kirsten, Nicolai J. Foss, Peter G. Klein, and Sandra K. Klein, *The Entrepreneurial Organization of Heterogeneous Capital*, 44 JOURNAL OF MANAGEMENT STUDIES 1165 (2007).

Foss, Kirsten, Nicolai J. Foss, and Peter G. Klein, *Original and Derived Judgment: An Entrepreneurial Theory of Economic Organization*, 28 ORGANIZATION STUDIES 1893 (2007).

Foss, Nicolai J. and Peter G. Klein, ENTREPRENEURSHIP AND THE FIRM: AUSTRIAN PERSPECTIVES ON ECONOMIC ORGANIZATION (2002).

Foss, Nicolai J., and Peter G. Klein, *Austrian Economics and the Theory of the Firm*, in Peter G. Klein and Michael E. Sykuta, eds, ELGAR COMPANION TO TRANSACTION COST ECONOMICS (2010).

Foss, Nicolai J. and Peter G. Klein, ORGANIZING ENTREPRENEURIAL JUDGMENT: A NEW APPROACH TO THE FIRM (2012).

Garrison, Roger, TIME AND MONEY: THE MACROECONOMICS OF CAPITAL STRUCTURE (2001).

Graham, John R., Campbell R. Harvey, and Shivaram Rajgopal, The Economic Implications of Corporate Financial Reporting tbl.6 (Nat'l Bureau of Econ. Research, Working Paper 10550, 2005), available at http:// ssrn.com/abstract=491627.

Griliches, Zvi, *The Search for R&D Spillovers*, 94 SCANDINAVIAN JOURNAL OF ECONOMICS S29 (Supp.) (1992).

Hayek, F.A., PRICES AND PRODUCTION (1931).

Hayek, F.A., *The Use of Knowledge in Society*, 35 AMERICAN ECONOMIC REVIEW 519 (1945).

Hayek, F.A., LAW, LEGISLATION AND LIBERTY, VOLUME I: RULES AND ORDER (1973).

Hoppe, Hans-Hermann, *The Ethics and Economics of Private Property* in COMPANION TO THE ECONOMICS OF PRIVATE PROPERTY (Enrico Colombatto. ed. 2004).

Hülsmann, Jörg Guido, *The A Priori Foundations of Property Economics*. 7 QUARTERLY JOURNAL OF AUSTRIAN ECONOMICS 41–68 (2004).

Jensen, Michael C., *Agency Costs of Overvalued Equity*, 34 FIN. MGMT. 5, 5–6 (2005).

Kirzner, Israel M., *The Perils of Regulation: A Market Process Approach*, Occasional Paper, Law and Economics Center, University of Miami School of Law (1979).

Kirzner, Israel M., DISCOVERY AND THE CAPITALIST PROCESS (1985).

Kirzner, Israel M., *The Alert and Creative Entrepreneur: A Clarification*, 32 SMALL BUSINESS ECONOMICS 145 (2009).

Klein, Benjamin, and John Shepard Wiley, Jr., *Competitive Price Discrimination as an Antitrust Justification for Intellectual Property Refusals to Deal*, 70 ANTITRUST L. J. 599, 619 (2003).

Klein, Peter G., *Economic Calculation and the Limits of Organization,* 9 REVIEW OF AUSTRIAN ECONOMICS 51 (1996).

Klein, Peter G., *Opportunity Discovery, Entrepreneurial Action, and Economic Organization,* 2 STRATEGIC ENTREPRENEURSHIP JOURNAL 175 (2008).

Klein, Peter G., *Risk, Uncertainty, and Economic Organization*, in Jörg Guido Hülsmann and Stephan Kinsella, eds, PROPERTY, FREEDOM, AND SOCIETY: ESSAYS IN HONOR OF HANS-HERMANN HOPPE (2009), 325–37.

Klein, Peter G., *Information, Incentives, and Organization: The Microeconomics of Central Banking,* in David Howden and Joseph T. Salerno, eds, THE FED AT ONE HUNDRED: A CRITICAL VIEW ON THE FEDERAL RESERVE SYSTEM (2014).

Knight, Frank, RISK, UNCERTAINTY, AND PROFIT (1921).

Lambert, Thomas A., *Overvalued Equity and the Case for an Asymmetric Insider Trading Regime*, 41 WAKE FOREST L. REV. 1045 (2006).

Langlois, Richard N., *The Austrian Theory of the Firm: Retrospect and Prospect*, REVIEW OF AUSTRIAN ECONOMICS (2007).

Manne, Henry, INSIDER TRADING AND THE STOCK MARKET (1966).

Menger, Carl, INVESTIGATIONS INTO THE METHOD OF THE SOCIAL SCIENCES, WITH SPECIAL REFERENCE TO ECONOMICS (1883).

Menger, Carl, *On the Origin of Money*, 2 ECONOMIC JOURNAL 239 (1892).

Mises, Ludwig von, *Economic Calculation in the Socialist Commonwealth*, in COLLECTIVIST ECONOMIC PLANNING (F.A. Hayek. ed. 1920).

Mises, Ludwig von, SOCIALISM: AN ECONOMIC AND SOCIOLOGICAL ANALYSIS (1936).

Mises, Ludwig von, HUMAN ACTION: A TREATISE ON ECONOMICS (1949).

Mises, Ludwig von, *Profit and Loss* (1951), in Mises, PLANNING FOR FREEDOM (1952).

Moeller, Sara B., Frederik P. Schlingemann, and René M. Stulz, *Wealth Destruction on a Massive Scale? A Study of Acquiring-Firm Returns in the Recent Merger Wave*, 60 J. FIN. 757, 760 (2005).

O'Driscoll, Gerald P., and Mario J. Rizzo, THE ECONOMICS OF TIME AND IGNORANCE (1985).

Polk, Christopher, and Paola Sapienza, *The Real Effects of Investor Sentiment*, NBER Working Paper No. 10563 (2004).

Pongracic, Ivan, EMPLOYEES AND ENTREPRENEURSHIP: CO-ORDINATION AND SPONTANEITY IN NON-HIERARCHICAL BUSINESS ORGANIZATION (2009).

RESTATEMENT (SECOND) OF THE LAW OF AGENCY (1958).

Rizzo, Mario J., ed. AUSTRIAN LAW AND ECONOMICS (2011).

Rothbard, Murray N., AMERICA'S GREAT DEPRESSION (1963).

Rothbard, Murray N., *Property Rights, and Air Pollution.* 2 CATO JOURNAL 55–99 (1982).

Salerno, Joseph T., *Reply to Leland B. Yeager on "Mises and Hayek on Calculation and Knowledge",* 7 REVIEW OF AUSTRIAN ECONOMICS 111 (1994).

Salerno, Joseph T., *The Development of the Theory of Monopoly Price: From Carl Menger to Vernon Mund,* Working paper (2003).

Semeraro, Steven, *Should Antitrust Condemn Tying Arrangements that Increase Price Without Restraining Competition?* 123 HARV. L. REV. F. 30 (Dec. 2009).

Smith, Adam, AN INQUIRY INTO THE NATURE AND CAUSES OF THE WEALTH OF NATIONS (1776).

UNIFORM PARTNERSHIP ACT (1914).

16. Firms without boards: unleashing the Hayekian firm
M. Todd Henderson

Every publicly traded corporation in the United States is managed by a group of individuals known as a "board of directors." This is most likely an artifact of law. Many other institutional forms through which business is conducted—partnerships, limited liability companies (LLCs), sole proprietorships, and so on—are managed in other ways, often by a single individual or by owners acting directly. But law compels publicly traded companies (at least) to be managed collectively by a group of non-professional managers, known as directors. While state law allows some variation in terms of governance, federal law (both securities law and tax law) and the listing requirements of the various stock exchanges effectively require firms be governed by multi-member boards. Even where state law tolerates deviations from the board governance model, the entire body of state corporate law is premised on board control.

This governance structure is not at all obvious in terms of economics or organizational theory. If it were, then we would expect group authority to be more universal. While group decision making has defenders in general and in the corporate law specifically,[1] many non-corporate organizations eschew the idea of decisions being made by a board of experts.[2] Individuals run many organizations de facto, if not de jure. The president, not a board of executives, runs the executive branch of government; a single individual, known as the administrator, runs the EPA; platoons are run by captains, not a board of officers; and so on. Sometimes groups are used in these areas: other administrative agencies of the government are headed by groups (e.g., the five commissioners of the SEC); the legislative branch uses group decision making; the judicial branch sometimes uses individuals (district courts) and sometimes groups (appellate courts); and the military uses groups for some decisions (e.g., the Joint Chiefs of Staff). The point is that one model does not dominate as a matter of theory, even within common areas.

---

[1] See, e.g., Stephen M. Bainbridge, *Why a Board? Group Decisionmaking in Corporate Governance*, 55 VAN. L. REV. 1 (2002).

[2] See, e.g., LARRY RIBSTEIN, THE RISE OF THE UNCORPORATION (2009).

Although some firms are undoubtedly best managed by a group of part-time directors, it is unlikely this is the local maximum for all firms in terms of governance. (At the very least, we cannot be sure in light of the legal requirement to use a board.) Trying to fit all firms into this model may make firms and society worse off. It may be, for instance, that board management leads to both private and social resources being devoted to governance that is not worth the cost; or it could be that this type of governance generates outcomes that are worse than other types of governance would generate.

For instance, board members do not have as strong incentives to maximize firm value as full-time managers of the firm, and their downside risk (in terms of liability and job security) is also much less. In addition, elaborate rules and vague standards, known as "fiduciary duties," make board governance extremely costly. To be sure, there are costs of managing a firm without board oversight, but the question is whether the additional benefit of a board outweighs the cost. This is, of course, an empirical question, but one that the law currently does not allow to be determined because it rigidly prescribes a single form of governance.

Scholars have started to make noises about getting rid of, or at least deemphasizing, boards. In *Other People's Money*, Douglas Baird and I proposed replacing the role played by board fiduciary duties with contracting among various firm stakeholders.[3] We argued the costs of vague, court-enforced duties for board members were outweighed by the benefits, and imagined a world in which individual firms were free to structure their own governance model based on contracts. More ambitiously, in a series of articles following from this work, Kelli Alces proposed doing away with the current conception of a board, replacing it with either a board of firm stakeholders (an "investor board") or an equity trustee.[4] The motivation behind both sets of work is a belief that the current legal regime establishing a one-size-fits-all approach to governance and creating a series of requirements, such as off-the-rack fiduciary duties, minimum numbers of "independent" directors, and so forth, is inefficient. Boards could be thought to be both ill-suited for the complex task of running firms (because they are staffed by part-time outsiders who operate with less information and lower-powered incentives) and insufficiently accountable for the decisions they make (because board members are the major

---

[3]   See, Douglas G. Baird and M. Todd Henderson, *Other People's Money*, 60 STAN. L. REV. 1309 (2008).

[4]   See, Kelli Alces, *Beyond the Board of Directors*, 46 WAKE FOREST L. REV. 783 (2011); Kelli Alces, *The Equity Trustee*, 42 ARIZ. ST. L. REV. 717 (2010).

way for law to impact firm governance but board members are rarely, if ever, held personally liable).

In *Boards-R-Us: Reconceptualizing Corporate Boards*, Stephen Bainbridge and I describe the weaknesses of current boards, and propose a simple legal reform that would allow firms to provide board services to other firms. Although firms provide legal, consulting, accounting, and other services to businesses, state law requires individuals to provide board services. We argue that this requirement is unjustified. The potential economies of scale and scope in the board services industry (including vertical integration of consultants and other board member support functions), as well as the benefits of risk pooling and talent allocation, mean that large professional director services firms may arise, and thereby create a market for corporate governance distinct from the market for corporate control. More transparency about board performance, including better pricing of governance by the market, as well as increased reputational assets at stake in board decisions, means improved corporate governance, all else being equal.[5]

This short chapter takes this line of thinking a step further, by imagining a world in which firms may be able to do away with the board of directors all together or dramatically alter and reduce its role. My goal is not to make the argument in full, but rather to raise the possibility in a way that hopefully encourages others to think about what the Austrian School can teach us about corporate governance and what role law should play in mandating certain governance arrangements or encouraging innovation in governance.

The best defense we can probably make of board-mandated governance is that a group of decision makers helps solve the collective action problem of disperse ownership by shareholders and a complicated mix of other firm stakeholders (such as creditors, employees (both pensioners and current employees), customers, and so on). But the idea of a group of "experts" making these decisions seems to run squarely afoul of the central teachings of the Austrian School—that is, the importance of tacit knowledge and spontaneous order in generating efficient outcomes and social welfare.[6] It is ironically within America's corporations that some of the last bastions of central planning reside. F.A. Hayek's observations about the shortcomings of command and control, and top-down governance seem as applicable to Verizon as they do to Venezuela.

---

[5] For a proposal that board services be provided by firms instead, see, Stephen M. Bainbridge and M. Todd Henderson, *Boards-R-Us: Reconceptualizing Corporate Boards*, 66 STAN. L. REV. 1051 (2014).

[6] See, e.g., F.A. Hayek, *The Use of Knowledge in Society*, 35 AM. ECON. REV. 519 (1945).

To be sure, firms exist within markets of various kinds (e.g., product, capital, and labor markets), and these provide a locus for the Hayekian discipline of many minds and Schumpeterian creative destruction, but technology is enabling the market to move inside the traditional firm to unlock the knowledge and information of employees and other firm stakeholders. Today, law requires that a group of part-time experts serve the role of aggregating all the information within a firm to make crucial decisions about who to hire and fire to manage the firm, how and how much the CEO should be compensated, whether to engage in mergers or acquisitions, whether laws were violated or shareholders' rights infringed by firm decisions, and so on. This role of aggregating and processing information held in disparate minds and locations could alternatively be done in intra-firm markets, facilitated by advances in information technology and new markets for predicting future events. This chapter imagines a world in which boards are a thing of the past and argues that law should enable experimentation with what we might call the Austrian model of corporate governance.

WHY BOARDS

A board of directors governs every public company in the United States. In this sense, corporate governance is remarkably uniform, despite the huge differences across firms, industries, times, and so forth. This part discusses the reason, both legally and practically, why boards of directors govern firms.

Law

The place to start for all matters of corporate governance is state law. In this regard, there appears to be some variation on the necessity of managing a firm via a board of directors. About two dozen states use a variant of the Model Business Corporation Act (MBCA), and it mandates that boards of directors manage firms. For example, section 8.05 of the Illinois Business Corporation Act of 1983 provides: "each corporation *shall* have a board of directors and the business and affairs of the corporation shall be managed by or under the direction of the board of directors."[7] Importantly, the MBCA provides an exception to this for small, privately held corporations that elect to be deemed "close corporations." These

---

[7]　See, 805 ILCS 5/8.05 (emphasis added).

firms can opt for management directly by shareholders, so long as they comply with restrictions on the transferability of shares.[8] The idea is that small firms, like a dry cleaner or nursing home, may have only the number of shareholders that would typically constitute a board, and therefore requiring them to call themselves a "board" is simply nomenclature. But for all intents and purposes, any large business, and especially any publicly traded business, in Illinois and the other states that have adopted the MBCA, must be managed by a collective group of individuals known as a board of directors.

Delaware, the most important corporate law state and the state of incorporation for about half of the Fortune 500 companies, has a slight variation on this requirement, although the practical effect is largely the same due to the overlay of federal law. Section 141(a) of the Delaware General Corporation Law provides: "The business and affairs of every corporation organized under this chapter shall be managed by or under the direction of a board of directors except as may be provided in this chapter [under rules governing close corporations] . . . ."[9] If it stopped there, Delaware would be the same as the MBCA. But it continues: ". . . or in its certificate of incorporation."[10] Consistent with other aspects of freedom of contract in Delaware corporate law, this seems to leave open the prospect of innovation and local variation. In the absence of any other rules, such as the federal and exchanged-based ones discussed next, we might expect to see some. This is especially true given the fact that businesses organized under Delaware's LLC statute and elsewhere often opt for a non-board governance model.[11]

There are, however, overlays on Delaware (and MBCA) law that preclude public companies from experimenting with their approach to governance. Tax law limits the use of pass-through taxation (and thus various uncorporate forms) to cases in which firms are earning "qualifying income," such as interest, dividends, and capital gains.[12] Publicly traded companies therefore

---

[8]   See, Sec. 2A.45 ("Management by shareholders").

[9]   See, DEL. CODE ANN. tit. 8, § 141 (2001 & Supp. 2006).

[10]   See, ibid. The statute provides that;

If any such provision is made in the certificate of incorporation, the powers and duties conferred or imposed upon the board of directors by this chapter shall be exercised or performed to such extent and by such person or persons as shall be provided in the certificate of incorporation.

[11]   See, e.g., RIBSTEIN, RISE OF THE UNCORPORATION, *supra* note 2.

[12]   See IRC §§ 7704(c)–(d) (defining passive and "qualifying" income); for a general discussion of the limits on the use of "uncorporate" entities, see RIBSTEIN, ibid.

will be corporations, at least as far as taxes are concerned. Moreover, securities law and the listing requirements of the various stock exchanges mandate that firms be governed by boards of directors. For instance, the Sarbanes-Oxley Act amended the Securities Exchange Act to mandate a rule requiring the exchanges to prohibit the listing of firms without a fully independent audit committee of a board of directors.[13] More generally, the New York Stock Exchange requires that "[l]isted companies must have a majority of independent directors."[14] These and other rules make it impossible for a publicly traded firm to operate without a board of directors, despite the possibility being left open by some state laws.

Theory

There are several theoretical accounts for why this de facto requirement might be the case. Melvin Eisenberg believes boards serve as monitors on behalf of shareholders to try to reduce agency costs.[15] Eisenberg believes managers, specifically the CEO, need a boss, and therefore the "role of the board is to hold the executives accountable for adequate results (whether financial, social, or both). . . ."[16] In this account, the board is about *reducing* agency costs, so that corporate owners can expect managerial decisions to better track their interests. It should be noted that Eisenberg does not fully articulate why boards do not need bosses or why the boss need be a group as opposed to an individual.

An alternative approach is that taken by Margaret Blair and Lynn Stout. They argue for a model of the firm with the board serving as a central mediator of various forces pulling at the firm (e.g., shareholders demanding more risk, employees demanding good working conditions and more job security, creditors demanding less risk, and so on) in order to maximize the value of the "team."[17] In this account, the board is not about reducing

---

[13]   See section 301 of the Sarbanes-Oxley Act of 2002 (the "Sarbanes-Oxley Act"),15 U.S.C. 78j–1(m)(1), which required the SEC to direct the national securities exchanges "to prohibit the listing of any security of an issuer that is not in compliance with several enumerated standards regarding issuer audit committees." http://www.sec.gov/rules/final/33-8220.htm#P77_5902.

[14]   See, e.g., NYSE Listed Company Manual, § 303A.01 "Independent Directors", available at http://nysemanual.nyse.com/LCMTools/TOCChapter.asp?manual=/lcm/sections/lcm-sections/chp_1_4/default.asp&selectedNode=chp_1_4.

[15]   See, Melvin Eisenberg, The Structure of the Corporation: A Legal Analysis (1976).

[16]   Ibid. at 165.

[17]   See, Lynn Stout and Margaret Blair, *A Team Production Theory of Corporate Law*, 85 Va. L. Rev. 247 (1999).

agency costs (as in Eisenberg), but rather *increasing* them. The idea is that a board, like the saucer-cup role played by the Senate, cools the passions of the various competing stakeholders and mediates them in ways that, in the long run, enhance the overall value of the firm to everyone. Missing from their account, as it was in Eisenberg's, is a rigorous defense of why a board, as opposed to another individual or a different type of technology altogether, must serve this role. Perhaps this is because the question these scholars were addressing is what the board does, not why we have boards in the first place.

Stephen Bainbridge tries to directly answer this question in a series of papers espousing what he calls "director primacy."[18] Drawing on the psychology and decision-making literatures, Bainbridge concludes that two heads (or maybe ten) are better than one. He cites various studies of college students making decisions individually and in groups, noting that in general the studies find that groups are better.[19] Summarizing the findings of several experiments, Bainbridge concludes: "groups appear to outperform their average member consistently, even at relatively complex tasks requiring exercise of evaluative judgment."[20] He argues not that boards should focus on this or that, whether it is strategy or monitoring, but rather that the statutes that grant decision making authority in boards are sensible as a matter of organizational theory.

Group decision making may be better or it may not be, either for college students deciding which survival items to take with them after a hypothetical plane crash or for boards making corporate decisions. But extrapolating from a set of experiments to the real world may be dangerous.[21] Conclusions might be based on experimental artifacts or may not otherwise reflect real world results. It is also doubtful that one size fits all. Individuals might make some decisions better, while groups might make others better. Consider, for instance, the fact that nearly all corporate decisions are made by the CEO, who is an individual person, rather than the board. Or consider judicial decisions: individual trial court judges make most decisions, but groups (appellate court) judges make some. Referees in sports sometimes act individually while other times they act in groups. If groups were always better, then why would we elect one

---

[18]   See, e.g., Stephen M. Bainbridge, *Why a Board? Group Decisionmaking in Corporate Governance*, 55 Van. L. Rev. 1 (2002).

[19]   Ibid. at 19.

[20]   Ibid.

[21]   See, e.g., Steven D. Levitt and John A. List, *What Do Laboratory Experiments Tell Us About the Real World?* 21 Journal of Econ. Perspectives 153 (2007).

president instead of two (as in the Roman Republic, at least for a time) or ten?

But in corporate decision making, the law effectively requires group decision making for certain tasks, like hiring and firing the CEO, setting CEO pay, negotiating mergers and acquisitions, and so on. It might be that an individual—the super CEO—or shareholders or employees, would make better decisions. Unfortunately, the law forecloses the possibility of any experimentation by firms with governance. It is, of course, impossible to know in advance in every case whether one model of governance is superior over another, especially in the absence of wide scale experimentation.

It is impossible even to say on average or in the bulk run of cases what a superior model is—we just do not have the information to make such an assessment. We might feel comfortable saying that watching firms in practice come to a settled model would tell us something about the most efficient form of governance, but, as noted above, law intervenes in ways that dampen, if not prevent, experimentation. And since firms are only competing with each other and there is complete transparency about and no intellectual property in governance, there is not a strong incentive to lobby for changes to such laws. Moreover, even if we knew what was the best governance model on average, it is quite an additional leap to a universal answer to what might be a local problem. Even if there were evidence that firms with boards outperformed firms without boards along some metric, we could not take from this a policy prescription that firms can increase value by adopting a board. It might be that there exist local maxima, such that the average and the specific values deviate significantly.

WHY *NOT* BOARDS

There are many arguments against boards, some of which are briefly mentioned here. But, importantly, none of these must necessarily be true or an accurate account of board governance in order for us to doubt the wisdom of requiring all firms to use boards. So long as there are any shortcomings of boards that outweigh their value in individual cases, then a rule requiring them may be suboptimal.[22] Interestingly, most of the arguments identifying board pathologies propose board-based reforms instead of

---

[22]   There may be, for instance, value from a mandatory rule if firms would not choose the optimal board structure in all cases based on their private assessment of the costs and benefits of governance structure. The only way this would not be the case is where the market does not price governance or where the managers were not property incentivized to choose the optimal structure.

jettisoning the board entirely. A reasonable read of the corporate governance literature is that boards are dysfunctional in some or many instances, but that with the wisdom of reformers, they can be made to work better.

Perhaps the most powerful criticism of board governance (at least as practiced) comes from law professors Lucian Bebchuk and Jesse Fried. In their book *Pay Without Performance: The Unfulfilled Promise of Executive Compensation*, they put forward a "managerial power" theory of executive pay in which the board is, at best, a lap dog to CEO power.[23] They argue that boards are ineffective at controlling runaway CEO pay because of a variety of factors:

(1) the power of the CEO over the appointment of directors;
(2) the ability of the CEO to reward cooperative directors;
(3) the social and psychological influences the CEO has over directors, such as the power of friendship, loyalty, collegiality, and authority;
(4) the cognitive biases of directors that come from being CEOs or former CEOs themselves; and
(5) the time and informational barriers most directors face to making an informed and reasoned decision about pay.[24]

In other words, boards do not work effectively to oversee the decision making of executives. The net result, writes one critic who has seen the compensation negotiation process from the inside, is that "the negotiations between a CEO and the outside directors who sit on the compensation committee can hardly be called negotiations at all."[25]

One need not buy into the Bebchuk and Fried critique to see the shortcomings of boards. I for one have written several critiques of their general conclusion that the dynamic they describe as systematic and explains the patterns of compensation we observe.[26] But my work is sort of beside the point, since I believe the board dynamic they describe is true in some, if not many, cases, and we may therefore have a false confidence in boards and board-centered governance in such cases or in other areas of decision

---

[23]   LUCIAN A. BEBCHUK AND JESSE M. FRIED, PAY WITHOUT PERFORMANCE: THE UNFULFILLED PROMISE OF EXECUTIVE COMPENSATION (2006).

[24]   Ibid. at 25–53.

[25]   Charles M. Yablon, *Overcompensating: The Corporate Lawyer and Executive Pay*, 92 COLUM. L. REV. 1867, 1873 (1992) (reviewing GRAEF CRYSTAL, IN SEARCH OF EXCESS (1991)).

[26]   See, M. Todd Henderson, *Paying CEOs in Bankruptcy: Executive Compensation When Agency Costs Are Low*, 101 NORTHWESTERN UNIVERSITY LAW REVIEW 1543 (2007); M. Todd Henderson, *Insider Trading and CEO Pay*, 64 VAND. L. REV. 505 (2011).

making. Moreover, the monies spent on boards, both directly and indirectly (such as litigation, extra process, and so on), may be wasted if the board is not doing much valuable work. There are, after all, many cases where boards were doing what they were supposed to be doing, and utterly failed. The Enron board, like that of WorldCom, MF Global, Lehman Brothers, AIG, and countless other corporate failures were stocked with industry experts and smart, diligent individuals, including numerous Nobel laureates. In addition, best we can tell, they were all compliant with the countless rules and regulations governing proper board governance. This may be because, as Eisenberg noted in his study of boards in the 1970s, boards are not professional managers, are not devoted full time to the firm, are not paid as high-powered incentives as managers, and are far less accountable, either legally or practically in terms of job security, as managers. Legions of law review articles and news stories recount the failures of boards, and of our system of corporate governance to adequately address the issues of potentially excessive risk taking and malfeasance by corporations.

As Stephen Bainbridge has noted, there is also what Theodore Geisel, writing as Dr. Seuss, referred to as the Bee-Watcher-Watcher problem.[27] You see the bee that the town relied on did not work as well without being watched, so the town hired a bee-watcher. But the bee-watcher was also a slacker, so they hired a bee-watcher-watcher and so on. Whenever authority is delegated to someone else, the issues giving rise to the delegation are merely displaced: in Seuss's case, from the bee to the various watchers, or, in the corporate context, from the CEO to the board.

The typical academic response is to try to improve the board, by making it more independent, as the Sarbanes-Oxley Act did, or to involve shareholders (the watchers of the board) more directly, as the Dodd-Frank Act did by requiring non-binding, episodic shareholder votes on pay. Corporate crusaders also want to empower internal forces within the firm, known as whistleblowers, to reveal information up the chain of command, and perhaps outside it, in order to improve corporate governance. As Jonathan Macey notes in his extended treatment of corporate governance, "The intuition that directors add value is strong and deeply held."[28] Thus, reforms want to preserve it, but by improving it with various tweaks.

---

[27] See, Stephen M. Bainbridge, Corporation Law and Economics (2002).
[28] Jonathan Macey, Corporate Governance: Promises Kept, Promises Broken (2008).

AN AUSTRIAN CRITIQUE

All of these proposed reforms may be good or bad, but there is an alternative to tweaking the board-centered model of governance. The way to see it is to go to the problem at the heart of the board model: the problem of information aggregation and processing. The argument against boards is an Austrian one, and the core is Hayek's insights about tacit knowledge and spontaneous order. Here is Hayek from his classic article, "The Use of Knowledge in Society":

> The peculiar character of the problem of a rational economic order is determined precisely by the fact that the knowledge of the circumstances of which we must make use never exists in concentrated or integrated form but solely as the dispersed bits of incomplete and frequently contradictory knowledge which all the separate individuals possess. The economic problem of society is thus not merely a problem of how to allocate "given" resources—if "given" is taken to mean given to a single mind which deliberately solves the problem set by these "data." It is rather a problem of how to secure the best use of resources known to any of the members of society, for ends whose relative importance only these individuals know. Or, to put it briefly, it is a problem of the utilization of knowledge which is not given to anyone in its totality.[29]

Hayek was writing about national economic systems, but the same problem about dispersed information exists at the firm level. The thousands of employees, shareholders, and other firm stakeholders are analogous to the citizens of a country, while the managers, be they a board of directors or otherwise, are analogous to political leaders and policy setters. Hayek and other Austrian writers noted the importance of markets at revealing, aggregating, processing, and disseminating information.

Thomas Sowell summarizes nicely how markets, using the price mechanism, can efficiently aggregate, process, and reveal valuable information held by all individuals—what F.A. Hayek called "tacit knowledge."[30] Sowell writes:

> Knowledge is one of the scarcest of all resources and a pricing system economizes on its use by forcing those with the most knowledge of their own particular situation to make bids for goods and resources based on that knowledge, *rather than on their ability to influence other people in planning commissions, legislatures, or royal palaces.*[31]

---

[29]   Hayek, *The Use of Knowledge in Society*, *supra* note 6.
[30]   See F.A. HAYEK, THE FATAL CONCEIT (1988).
[31]   THOMAS SOWELL, BASIC ECONOMICS (2007) (emphasis supplied).

Boards could be thought of as a nod in the direction of the Austrian contribution to decision making. After all, as Bainbridge notes, in complex decisions, many heads may be better than one. But more heads might be even better. Journalist James Surowiecki presented a popular account of this possibility in his book *Wisdom of Crowds*,[32] describing the various situations in which the aggregation of tens or hundreds of non-expert opinions outperform smaller groups of experts. Decision-making theorists describe this process as aggregating mundane knowledge, information about time and place, and bringing non-expert information together in dynamic ways that can get at expert questions. In many instances, the benefit of aggregation and processing is akin to making a mosaic, in which individuals with "small bits and pieces of relevant information[, which] exist[] in the opinions and intuition of individuals who are close to an activity," put it together in ways unaware to any of them individually but that creates a complete picture.[33]

The trick for corporate governance is encouraging the creation of this mosaic—that is, defining the structure of information flows for key decisions in ways that generate the best possible outcomes. Firms have strong incentives to get this information structure as optimally designed as possible (given transaction costs) when it comes to core business functions, like financing, design, manufacture, marketing, supply chain management, customer relations, and so on. There is little theorists, and especially lawyers, could possibly add that would help in solving these problems. But when it comes to corporate governance and the decisions that currently are made by boards, there is again the problem of law mandating a particular approach, which even if largely ignored in practice, generates large costs. For instance, if the law requires the board to decide if and when to sell the company, and at what price, then putting authority here when it should reside elsewhere generates costs, including the cost of deciding, the cost of making a mistake, the costs of ex post litigation about these decisions, and so forth. Relying on boards when they are not reliable may also generate false confidence and hide problems that would be more apparent in a different governance model. At the very least, a non-board model would have the potential to create greater accountability for failures. Only a handful of board members in history have had to pay monetary damages for the decisions, and the reputational effects from being a board member who failed are doubtful.

---

[32]   JAMES SUROWIECKI, THE WISDOM OF CROWDS (2004).

[33]   See, e.g., Kay-Yut Chen and Charles R. Plott, *Information Aggregation Mechanisms: Concept, Design and Implementation for a Sales Forecasting Problem* 13 (Cal. Inst. Tech., Social Sciences Working Paper No. 1131, 2002), available at http://www.hpl.hp.com/ personal/Kay-Yut_Chen/paper/ms020408.pdf.

When discussing corporate governance, Hayek uncharacteristically noted that hierarchical, collective, command-and-control decision making by a board of directors is generally "adequate," and where it is not, the solution is a powerful, singular individual.[34] Hayek argues that "the man of independent means" is essential in "reforming and redirecting organizations" by starting new ventures that refresh and advance the competitive environment. New entry funded by rich individuals prevents the "ossification of the whole corporate structure." Here, Hayek has in mind something like the modern venture capital industry, which is simply an intermediated form of this phenomenon. Hayek then goes on to apply a similar principle of importance for powerful figures for existing organizations:

> And this superiority of individual over collective decisions is not confined to new ventures. However adequate collective decisions of a board may be in most instances, the outstanding success even of large and well-established corporations is often due to some single person who has achieved his position of independence and influence through the control of large means.[35]

At first, this seems difficult to square with what are viewed as Hayek's central contributions—the notions of "tacit knowledge" and "spontaneous order." If decisions about the economy or public policy are best left to dispersed forms of knowledge and unplanned coordination, why would the same not be true for business decisions?

For Hayek, the answer seems to be because of the different levels of competitive intensity faced by firms and governments. In other words, market forces are less needed internally to a particular institution, be it a business firm or a government, when that institution operates in a robust external market. Hayek argues "the whole system of private enterprises" offers "both employees and consumers sufficient alternatives to deprive each organization from exercising coercive power."[36] In other words, tacit knowledge exists outside a firm, and firms are competing in markets driven by spontaneous order, so there is little reason to bring these forces inside firms. One can conceptualize this point of view as akin to seeing firms like individual humans operating in the market. Hayek does not argue for the bringing of market forces inside individuals, since by definition a person is a singular entity incapable of a many-minds approach. So in corporate law, Hayek echoes Coase, who *defined* the boundaries of a firm as the place

---

34   F.A. HAYEK, THE CONSTITUTION OF LIBERTY: The Definitive Edition 190 (2011).
35   Ibid.
36   Ibid.

where the costs of market forces operating exceeded their benefits.[37] The Coasian/Hayekian conception of the firm, therefore, frames the issue as one in which internal decision making is necessarily based on command and control, be it from a board or otherwise.

But this just begs the question of whether Coase's definition of a firm is rich enough. There may be instances where a firm is held together by forces other than the virtues of a particular type of hierarchical decision making. There may be, in other words, opportunities for the tacit knowledge and spontaneous order *within* firms to create value that could not be achieved by housing this information processing outside of the firm's boundaries.

UNLEASHING THE HAYEKIAN FIRM

Individual governance and board governance, are just two discrete options in the spectrum of choices available for decision making. But this dichotomous view has broken down in the face of organizational innovation and technological developments in the area of prediction markets. Many firms are developing ways of aggregating information, processing it, and making decisions that do not involve a single decision maker or a small group, but rather replicate a market for information in which decisions are made by the collective wisdom of all stakeholders. Just as the price of milk is not set by a single individual or a group of experts, but rather the decisions of millions of people, be they suppliers, shippers, retailers, or customers, so too can prices inform decision making within firms. Following on the success of public information markets at predicting event outcomes, firms have created highly specialized internal markets to elicit and aggregate information from employees, both to improve internal forecasting and decision making and to allocate resources.

The most famous set of prediction markets is the Iowa Electronic Markets (IEM), which offers the opportunity to essentially bet on the outcomes of U.S. Presidential and Congressional elections, as well as a host of other issues of wide public interest.[38] IEM election markets are set up as futures markets, trading contracts whose payoffs depend on the outcome of future events. The simplest case is a tradeable contract that pays $1 in the event a future event comes to pass and $0 if it does not. The event could be

---

[37] See Ronald Coase, *The Nature of the Firm*, 4 ECONOMICA 386 (1937).

[38] Other IEM markets include the Federal Reserve Monetary Policy Market and the 2012 Republican Nomination Market. *See* Iowa Electronic Markets, available at http://tippie.uiowa.edu/iem/index.cfm (last visited June 8, 2012).

anything that is reasonably definable ex ante. For instance, one could trade contracts on a contract "Barack Obama will be reelected president in 2012" or on a contract "the average daily high temperature in Chicago in August 2013 will be greater than 82 degrees Fahrenheit." The price of these contracts would roughly correlate with the probabilities of the outcome coming to pass.[39] And, the contract prices should adjust to reflect the average belief of market participants. For instance, if the Obama contract were trading at $0.56, and one had information or belief that Romney was very likely to win, then it would make sense to "sell" shares at $0.56. This could cause the price to drop, and in this way the market would aggregate this information.

Prediction markets like IEM have bested expert opinion in their predictive accuracy in a variety of contexts, including elections,[40] the performance of Hollywood films (both in awards and box office receipts),[41] and the winners of NFL games.[42] An Irish company, Intrade, ran an online marketplace in which hundreds of prediction contracts were traded, often with great accuracy.[43] These successes encouraged private companies to construct their own internal prediction markets. Hewlett-Packard, an early adopter, found that employees trading in their internal prediction market generated more accurate forecasts of printer sales than the firm's bureaucracy.[44] Google runs dozens of internal markets to forecast product demand, internal performance, and industry events.[45]

---

[39]   Justin Wolfers and Eric Zitzewitz, *Prediction Markets*, 18 J. ECON. PERSP., 107, 110 (2004).

[40]   See, ibid. See also, Joyce Berg, Robert Forsythe, and Forrest Nelson, *Results from a Dozen Years of Election Futures Markets Research*, in HANDBOOK OF EXPERIMENTAL ECONOMIC RESULTS (Charles Plott and Vernon Smith, eds. Amsterdam: Elsevier; Joyce Berg, Forrest Nelson, and Thomas Rietz, 2006).

[41]   David Pennock, Steve Lawrence, Finnrup Nielsen and C. Lee Giles, *Extracting Collective Probabilistic Forecasts from Web Games*, in PROCEEDINGS OF THE SEVENTH ACM SIGKDD INTERNATIONAL CONFERENCE ON KNOWLEDGE DISCOVERY AND DATA MINING, 174–83 (2001).

[42]   Emile Servan-Schreiber, Justin Wolfers, David Pennock and Brian Galebach, *Prediction Markets: Does Money Matter?* ELECTRONIC MARKETS, 14(3), 243–51 (2004).

[43]   Unfortunately, Intrade shut down in part because of a ban by U.S. regulators. See Steve Schaefer, *Intrade Closes To U.S. Bettors, Bowing to Pressure from Regulators*, FORBES, Nov. 27, 2012, available at http://www.forbes.com/sites/steve-schaefer/2012/11/27/cftc-takes-aim-at-intrade-files-suit-going-after-prediction-ma rket/.

[44]   Kay-Yut Chen and Charles Plott, *Information Aggregation Mechanisms: Concept, Design and Implementation for a Sales Forecasting Problem*, Caltech (2002).

[45]   Bo Cowgill, et al., *Using Prediction Markets to Track Information Flows: Evidence from Google*, NBER Working Paper, Jan. 2009, at 6 and tbl. 1.

In addition to predicting events, firms use internal markets to allocate resources, including labor. British Petroleum has used internal electronic trading to allocate carbon dioxide emission permits among business units.[46] Intel has experimented with internal markets to allocate manufacturing capacity, allowing plant managers, sales representatives and other employees to trade futures contracts for specific products.[47] Hewlett-Packard has experimented with informal internal markets for assigning workers to projects.[48] Researchers have also modeled internal allocation markets, identifying design features important to their success.[49]

These markets can be used to do much if not most of the work currently done by boards. But there are two obvious threshold issues. First, to achieve any of this, the law must get out of the way, since currently publicly traded companies cannot do away with their boards. Second, much more work needs to be done: some by thinkers applying the lessons of the Austrian School, but much more by doers.

Notwithstanding the modest aim of this chapter to merely raise the possibility of firms without boards, what follows are some ideas for how prediction markets within firms can serve as a board substitute. A few crucial board functions will be discussed briefly to illustrate the potential for Austrian thinking to revolutionize corporate governance. These are: monitoring, deciding whether to engage in fundamental transactions, hiring and firing the CEO, and paying the CEO. These activities are the core duties of boards, and if they can be done in other ways, may suggest the lack of a need for a board. (These ideas are explored more fully in a paper I wrote with Michael Abramowitz, *Prediction Markets for Corporate Governance*.[50])

Board Monitoring

Monitoring is an essential board function. Professor Eisenberg believes it is the primary job of the board, and the modern trend in board practice,

---

[46] Thomas W. Malone, *Bringing the Market Inside*, HARV. BUS. REV. 107 (Apr. 2004).

[47] Ibid. at 110; David McAdams & Thomas W. Malone, *Internal Markets for Supply Chain Capacity Allocation* 6 (MIT Sloan Working Paper 2005).

[48] Malone, *supra* note 46, at 109.

[49] Stanley Baiman, Paul Fischer, Madhav V. Rajan and Richard Saouma, *Resource Allocation Auctions within Firms*, 45 J. ACCTG. RSC. 915 (2007); McAdams and Malone, *supra* note 47; James B. Bushnell and Shmuel S. Oren, *Internal Auctions for the Efficient Sourcing of Intermediate Products*, 12 J. OPER. MGMT. 311 (1995).

[50] See, M. Todd Henderson and Michael Abramowitz, *Prediction Markets for Corporate Governance*, 82 NOTRE DAME L. REV. 1343 (2007).

described as moving from a strategic board to a compliance board, seems to support this claim. Putting aside the bee-watcher-watcher problem described above, it is easy to see why: the board's many eyes and various expertise and perspectives, backed by the threat of reputational sanctions and legal liability provide a check on potential cheating or shirking by managers. Section 404 of the Sarbanes-Oxley Act, for instance, mandates that the board put in place "internal controls" designed to ensure that information about firm activities flows to the board so that it can monitor firm activities. Similarly, the independence requirements for the audit committee of the board of directors is premised on a belief that the board is best positioned to detect and remedy potential accounting fraud. But what if monitoring could be done without a board?

Prediction markets are a potential alternative. Instead of the board, through the audit committee, engaging in oversight and conducting investigations into potential accounting fraud, why not deploy the power of internal markets to serve this function. Independent board members may have the advantage of being unbiased (subject to the capture story told by Bebchuk and Fried), but they have the disadvantage of being outsiders with less information and motivation. For instance, Nobel Prize-winning economist Paul Krugman, who rails against shady corporate accounting and practices, was on the board of Enron. Although this is just an anecdote, it points to the larger problem identified in the academic work cited above.

What would a market like this look like? Take the case of accounting fraud. Most simply, the firm could run a market that was designed to predict whether the firm would be required to restate its earnings over some period of time, or what the firm's final statement of earnings will be. The contract could pay $1 if "Firm X restates its earnings at any point in the next year" and $0 if it does not. The trading price of these contracts should reflect the probability of a restatement coming to pass.[51] Because most frauds materialize eventually, traders could profit on markets with sufficiently long time horizons. Everyone at the firm, including external auditors and maybe even suppliers and customers, could participate in the market, and therefore the market price would reflect the probabilities of wrongdoing. Not only would this alleviate the need for a centralized group of experts to monitor accounting practices, but it would likely be superior at detecting fraud, since all information could be processed into the monitoring instead of simply what information was spoon-fed to the board. For

---

[51]   For a discussion of the potential for manipulation and the likely efficacy of such markets, see, ibid.

instance, in the case of channel stuffing, a common accounting fraud of the 1990s and 2000s, there were undoubtedly people throughout the firm and the supply chain who knew about the illicit practice, but the boards of the companies, either out of ignorance, sloth, or complicity, failed to detect and do anything about it. A market for accounting fraud would give individuals, perhaps far down in the hierarchy, financial incentives to reveal the fraud.

If such markets were effective at revealing misconduct, be it accounting or otherwise, then the need for board oversight will be reduced. Of course, if the goal is for the board to oversee the CEO and the CEO is the one who is most likely to be cheating, then the market might not arise in the first place. This could be easily solved by either public disclosure of the existence of such markets, thus allowing the market to price governance in a way that would punish firms without them. A government mandate might work as well, but it wouldn't obviously be necessary, since CEOs who were not planning on cheating would have incentives to create such markets, and therefore enjoy cost advantages in markets for labor, capital, and so on.

Mergers and Acquisitions

Prediction markets might be useful not only as a means of policing mis-behavior but also in deciding whether a corporation should engage in par-ticular "fundamental" transactions, such as mergers, acquisitions, or asset sales. This is an area where, for the most part, shareholder participation—in the form of a vote—is required by state law. For example, in the case in which one firm wants to acquire another firm through a statutory merger, all states require the majority consent of the target firm's shareholders.[52] But under prevailing state law, boards are responsible for deciding when to buy and sell, and at what price. They have enormous discretion.

Instead of vesting the power to determine value and police potential manager deviations from wealth maximization (say, because of a time horizon mismatch with shareholders or a desire to maximize private wealth instead of firm wealth), an alternative approach would be to use predic-tion markets to predict the value of proposed transaction for the acquirer and/or target, allowing each shareholder to receive an assessment of the value that is not biased by private values, short-term liquidity positions, or undisclosed interests that may conflict with the valuation assessment. For example, a conditional market could assess the value of any consideration

---

[52]   See, e.g., DEL. CODE ANN. tit. 8, § 251(c) (2001 & Supp. 2006).

received for the target's shares at some point in the future after consummation of the transaction being considered.

In theory, prediction markets could solve the long-standing debate about defensive tactics and the duties of the board in fundamental corporate transactions. Using prediction markets to predict the value, other than private value, that each shareholder will receive if an acquisition is or is not accepted has at least some advantages over alternative approaches. Unlike a shareholder vote, there is no danger that different intensity of preference will lead to an embrace of inefficient transactions. At the same time, participants in the prediction market would not be making individual decisions about whether to tender securities, and so prediction markets would not present any conflict in which an individual tender decision might conflict with the individual's preferences. Participants in the prediction market would have incentives to consider that if a particular bid were denied, the bidder or some third party might offer a higher bid.

Markets in the takeover context are particularly useful because they help constrain corporate actors to act in the interest of shareholders. But markets are also useful for the general reason that they reduce the costs and distortions of information flows within a firm, allowing decision makers better access to valuable information necessary to make reasoned and fully informed decisions. Commentators frequently point to the merger transaction process as evidence of broken corporate governance. The CEO of a firm has proposed to the board a merger with a competitor. The board must decide whether to approve the merger and on what terms. The board, however, is composed of part-time employees without day-to-day experience or access to information except through the CEO. The CEO "can thus present a . . . merger in a way so as to avoid or undermine any board critical evaluation of it."[53] Recognizing this limit on their ability to gauge the true value of the merger, and recognizing that the public market's reaction includes the noise of self-interested arbitrageurs, short sellers, speculators, and profit takers as well as long-term holders of the firm's equity, the board could construct a prediction market to process its informational decision more effectively.

Hiring and Firing the CEO

In "The Prime Directive," Douglas Baird argued that the most important job of the board of directors is the decision about who to hire to be CEO,

---

[53]   See, James A. Fanto, *Breaking the Merger Momentum: Reforming Corporate Law Governing Mega-Mergers*, 49 BUFF. L. REV. 249, 293 (2001).

how to pay them, and when to fire them.[54] The board currently does these things, but it is possible that they could be done via market mechanisms. Where specific candidates have been widely speculated about, a corporation (or a group of interested shareholders) might use prediction markets to make an assessment about the value of particular candidates for the top job. For instance, one could run a conditional market that trades contracts tied to the value of the firm in one year if individual X were CEO, and then compare this with individuals Y, Z, and so on. Choosing the next CEO could then simply be a matter of looking at these prices.

There are many more possibilities of differing degrees. A corporation also might run a prediction market with participation limited to members of a search committee or search firm, to improve the chance that the search firm in fact recommends the candidate that members of the committee believe most likely to increase shareholder welfare. Prediction markets can be designed to give small numbers of individuals incentives to share their reasons for particular positions, and so a market can serve as the locus of small group deliberation. Prediction markets also might be used to select among possible search firms or search committees.

Markets could also be used to assess the impact of the departure, voluntary or involuntary, of an executive, such as the CEO. In this case, the identity of the relevant official is already obvious, and so there is no difficulty associated with secrecy. The magnitude of the impact is also potentially very large, based on recent high-profile CEO departures. The problem for firms, which prediction markets can solve, is that this impact was seen only *after* the decision was announced. While a firm may have had some information, based say on interviews with investment bankers or analysts, that the stock price would increase after the decision, prediction markets would provide a powerful tool that would increase, on the margin, the number of cases in which firms could make a value-increasing decision about which manager to run the firm.

Such markets in effect would provide a real-time continuous measurement of the market's assessment of the expected future performance of a particular official. While the general stock price measure of a firm may help discipline CEO actions, making officials less likely to make value-decreasing decisions, prediction markets focused directly on the CEO could be considerably more powerful. Such markets would assess the degree to which a corporation's future anticipated success is dependent on a particular official. Even the CEO of a corporation that happens to be

---

[54]   See, Douglas G. Baird and Robert K. Rasmussen, *The Prime Directive*, 75 UNIV. CINC. L. REV. 921 (2007).

successful for reasons having little to do with the CEO would have to strive to establish personal value.

Compensating and Incentivizing the CEO

Prediction markets could be used to assess the value of a particular executive, and therefore to set the executive's compensation. Conditional prediction markets provide a way of measuring the value of executives relative to the next best alternatives. This may be valuable in deciding how much to pay particular executives. For example, if a prediction market estimates that the stock price would increase upon an executive's departure, it would suggest that the executive was overpaid. If, on the other hand, the market predicts a stock price decrease upon an executive's departure, it suggests that the executive is not overpaid.

Prediction markets also might be used to assess the possibility of making discrete changes in compensation packages, for particular employees. For example, a corporation might use a conditional prediction market to assess the impact on stock price of different possible changes to compensation, including different levels of decreases and raises and different baskets of cash, stock options, and perks.

As Bebchuk and Fried argue at length, there are some potential problems with CEO pay being set by a board appointed by the CEO. To solve this problem, scholars have proposed reforming the board, such as requiring a fully independent compensation committee. But if markets can be established in which firm shareholders, internal managers, and other stakeholders can estimate the marginal product of individual executives, then this would effectively automate compensation decisions. Such a market might trade a conditional market designed to estimate the stock price (and hence market value of the firm) at some future time based on particular individuals being in executive positions. A well-designed contract would give a market-based assessment of the marginal contribution from an individual executive, and this could inform, if not determine, that executive's compensation. Although this may sound somewhat fanciful, it is no more fanciful than a small group of individuals making the decisions based on a limited amount of information and the constraints identified by Bebchuk and Fried. If large groups of fair goers or economists can outperform experts, there is reason to believe the same might be true for corporate decisions.[55]

---

[55]   SUROWIECKI, THE WISDOM OF CROWDS, *supra* note 32.

* * *

One might argue that there must be someone to create, monitor, and implement these markets, and then logically believe this must be a board. While one can imagine a board serving this role, this need not be the case. An individual inside or outside the firm could play this role, on either a full or part time basis. Firms could arise to run these markets for other firms. Or individuals could specialize in running governance prediction markets and selling their services to firms. Or the pressure of disclosure and transparency could simply cause firms to establish such markets to automatically address certain questions. For example, venture capitalists managing a new firm could put in place prediction markets that would inform shareholders about the value of different firm choices, be they about personnel, compensation, or otherwise. The firm via its charter could also specify how the prediction markets would inform decisions. They could be self-executing, meaning that the decision of the market would be the decision of the firm. Or, the market could simply inform a shareholder vote about a particular issue. There are countless choices along this spectrum, including the use of part-time, issue-specific deciders, be they boards or individuals, self-executing markets with a shareholder veto, and so on.

CONCLUSION

Large, publicly traded companies in the United States are all governed by a small group of part-time "experts." Although much day-to-day power resides with a single individual, known as the chief executive officer, the board is responsible for oversight and fundamental decisions, like who the CEO is, how much he is paid, when he should be fired, and whether to sell the company, to whom, and at what price. The board is also the primary mechanism for legal control of the corporation—inquiries about firm compliance with the law generally focus on whether board members complied with their fiduciary duties.

If this state of affairs were the result of market forces—that is, the decisions of thousands of firms and millions of individual investors—then we might conclude that it is the efficient arrangement from an organizational perspective. But we cannot be confident about this because the board is a legally required governance form in every state. These laws may be wise or not; it is an empirical question. The recent spate of corporate failures, including many traceable to board failures, gives us reason to doubt the model is optimal in general, let alone for every firm.

So what might a firm without a board look like? The idea would be to replace the command-and-control aspect of board governance with a more market-based approach in which firms reallocated some of the information aggregation and processing functions done by boards to dispersed stakeholders acting through various prediction markets. Austrian critiques of centralized economic planning tell us about the power of markets in addressing questions of resource allocation. These arguments seem to be as powerful for firms as they are for governments. It may be that some firms would retain boards, while others might have boards with different roles, such as designing, interpreting, and applying the results of various prediction markets. The law must first get out of the way and allow experimentation and innovation in governance.

17. Bankruptcy judge as a central planner
*Todd J. Zywicki and Shruti Rajagopalan**

> The statesman who should attempt to direct private people in what manner
> they ought to employ their capitals, would not only load himself with a most
> unnecessary attention, but assume an authority which could safely be trusted
> to no council and senate whatever, and which would nowhere be so dangerous
> as in the hands of the man who had folly and presumption enough to fancy
> himself fit to exercise it.
> Adam Smith, Wealth of Nations, 1776

1. INTRODUCTION

Chapter 11 details the U.S. Bankruptcy procedure for restructuring and
rehabilitating financially distressed firms. The existence, function and
performance of Chapter 11 reorganization was hotly debated over the last
few decades[1] and has taken on new significance with increased filing rates
given the current economic crisis.

Chapter 11 filings increased dramatically in the 2006–08 period with
an unprecedented 60 percent increase in filing from 2008 to 2009, a trend
has slowed only since late 2010.[2] Apart from the increase in filing rates
(or perhaps because of it) there is an increase in state subsidies and bailouts for troubled firms and industries. In these troubled times, some have
recommended restructuring under Chapter 11 as the panacea for large
troubled firms over other alternatives such as liquidation or government
bailouts (Levine 2008, Zingales 2008, and Rauh and Zingales 2009).

Yet the question over the performance of Chapter 11 is not settled.

---

* The author would like to thank Simon Bilo, Peter Boettke, Chris Coyne,
Peter Leeson, Mario Rizzo, Virgil Storr, Richard Wagner, Larry White, and the
participants of the Graduate Student Paper Workshop and the NYU Colloquium
on Market Institutions & Economic Processes for comments. The standard dis-
claimer applies.

[1]   Most notable of these exchanges was Baird (1987a) and Warren (1987). See
Warren (1992) response to Bradley and Rosenzweig (1992). Also see Tabb (2002)
for a summary of the debate.

[2]   Data from US Courts accessed at http://www.uscourts.gov/News/NewsView/
11-02-15/Growth_in_Bankruptcy_Filings_Slows_In_Calendar_Year_2010.aspx.

The analysis of the theory and performance of Chapter 11 is divided into two camps. The "free-market critics" such as Baird (1986), Jackson (1986), Adler (1993) have been critical of Chapter 11 reorganization on counts of its inefficiency, high cost, time delays and inaccurate valuations of firms and have called for some a repeal of Chapter 11 (Bradley and Rosenzweig, 1992). "The traditionalists" defend the traditional Chapter 11 process either on the normative basis that the purpose of Chapter 11 is not economic efficiency alone but to preserve value by keeping a firm together. Warren (1992), and Schwartz (1993) articulate this approach to bankruptcy reorganization.

While the two camps disagree on the purpose, function, goals and performance of Chapter 11 reorganization,[3] both have acknowledged the economic inefficiency of the current Chapter 11 system. The free market critics have called for a repeal or restructuring of Chapter 11 on the basis of such inefficiency (Bradley and Rosenzweig 1992); while the traditionalists have justified the inefficiency as a reasonable trade-off in light of other redistributive goals in society (Warren 1992: 467).

Among the free market critics, there seems to be much agreement on the inadequacies of the current Chapter 11 reorganization regime. It is rightly blamed for errors in valuation of firms in bankruptcy courts, which impede the flow of resources to their highest valued use (See Baird 1986, Bebchuk 1988, Bradley and Rosenzweig 1992, Roe 1983). While all these scholars have persuasively pointed out that the problem with Chapter 11 is one of incorrect valuation; this large literature provides no explanation for why the reorganization process does systematically worse than the market process in the valuation of an insolvent firm.

In this chapter we provide an explanation for the inaccurate valuation in the Chapter 11 reorganization process relative to the market process. This is a crucial step towards reforming the current bankruptcy regime to ensure that resources flow to their highest valued use in the economy.

Our critique here is a complement to, but more fundamental than, the argument of the free market critics of Chapter 11. We argue that one should neither be surprised by the abysmal success rate of Chapter 11 reorganization or its high cost, which are inevitable problems that cannot be eliminated from the Chapter 11 reorganization process. The flaws in Chapter 11 reorganization are inherent in the task of the bankruptcy judge. The reorganization process fundamentally requires bankruptcy judges to serve as economic central planners, which is an impossible task. Reorganization takes place in a market institutional vacuum where relevant prices are

---

[3]   For a summary on these fundamental differences see Baird (1998).

suppressed, yet the bankruptcy judge is required to decide whether a given firm should be reorganized in whole, part, or simply liquidated.

We argue here that the information problem in bankruptcy simply cannot be solved, just as it could not be overcome in Socialist planned economies. Indeed, the problems are identical. To understand why, it is necessary to understand the nature of the knowledge problem as articulated by Ludwig von Mises and F.A. Hayek in response to the arguments of socialist economic planners in the 1930s. In this chapter we provide an explanation for the systemic inaccurate valuation in the reorganization process relative to the market and argue that the inferior results and higher cost of the Chapter 11 process are inevitable byproducts of the process. Bankruptcy judges can no more outperform the market than a Soviet-style central planner could outperform markets. Indeed, if bankruptcy judges *could* outperform markets then there would be little reason to restrict them to such a modest role of determining whether to salvage a particular distressed firm. Instead, we could simply eliminate venture capital and other financial capital and labor markets and replace those decentralized decisions with opinions of bankruptcy judges as to the optimal deployment of economic resources through the economy via a bankruptcy-like procedure. That such a proposal seems absurd with respect to decision-making outside bankruptcy hints at its absurdity inside bankruptcy.

Given the impossibility of market allocation by the judge, political and judicial allocation act as substitutes and bring with them the problems of rent-seeking as in the case of Soviet central planning. Such rent-seeking, which is inherent to the reorganization process, causes much loss in efficiency.

In Section 2, we discuss the theory, practice and critique of the existing Chapter 11 regime. In Section 3 we discuss the dilemma of a common law judge in determining awards and damages with different levels of availability of market data. We provide a theoretical explanation for why the systemic problem of valuation is faced by judges in the reorganization process. In Section 4 we highlight the difference in the incentives of a judge and an entrepreneur and its effect on Chapter 11 reorganization. In Section 5 we analyze that political allocation is used in Chapter 11 reorganization, since the judge cannot perform market allocations in his institutional vacuum. In Section 6 we provide alternatives to Chapter 11 and in Section 7 we conclude.

2. CHAPTER 11

2.1 Theory

The purpose of Chapter 11 reorganization policy "is to restructure a firm's finances so that it may continue to operate, provide its employees with jobs, pay its creditors, and produce a return for its stockholders."[4] The U.S. Supreme Court has seconded this view and held that "the fundamental purpose of reorganization is to prevent a debtor from going into liquidation, with an attendant loss of jobs and possible misuse of economic resources."[5] Therefore, the purpose of Chapter 11 is to preserve the going-concern value of a firm by keeping its assets intact rather than liquidating the firm and channeling those assets elsewhere in the economy. The argument regarding presence of a going-concern surplus rests on the assumption that the current deployment of human, physical, and financial capital is more valuable than the opportunity cost of each in its next-best alternative usage.

For instance, reorganization arose in the late 19th century when creditors of railroads unable to meet their debt obligations threatened to tear up their tracks, melt them down, and sell the steel as scrap to recover their claims. But judges and other stakeholders recognized that solving the collective action problems to keep the railroads running and producing revenues to pay them off would help the creditors recover more.

To accomplish this, the judge must decide if a firm is merely financially distressed or if it is economically distressed. An economically distressed firm is one that has no market, and its assets would be worth more allocated in some other use. A financially distressed firm on the other hand is an economically viable enterprise but is unable to meet its financial obligations. If a typewriter manufacturer were to file for bankruptcy today it likely would be considered an economically failed enterprise. The market for typewriters is small and shrinking, and the manufacturer's financial, physical and human capital would probably be better redeployed elsewhere, such as making computers. A financially failed enterprise, on the other hand, is worth more alive than dead. Chapter 11 exists to allow it to continue in business while reorganizing (Zywicki 2008).

Ideally, firms that are economically viable, but in temporary financial distress should be preserved or reorganized and firms that are not economically viable should be liquidated.

---

[4] H.R REP. NO. 595, 95th Cong., 1sr Sess. 220 (1997), reprinted in 1978 U.S.C.C.A.N. 5963, 6173.
[5] *NLRB v Bildisco & Bildisco* 465 U.S. 513, 528 (1983).

Another rationale for using Chapter 11 reorganization instead of going concern sales is that finding third-party buyers is difficult. The biggest hurdle for third-party buyers is high information costs faced by buyers and their inability to accurately value the insolvent firm. The problem of accurate valuation by third-party buyers ratifies reliance on non-market valuation, where a bankruptcy judge helps preserve the value of the firm more accurately through the reorganization process.

Importantly, the supporters of Chapter 11 must implicitly assume that the bankruptcy judge does not face the same information costs and problems of valuation that plague third party buyers (See Jackson 1986: 210–11). Or that the bankruptcy judge as an ideal observer of market data can improve on the inaccurate valuation by third-party buyers in the liquidation process.

2.2 Performance

While reorganization with the hypothetical sale against the claims of creditors seems plausible, the empirical reality of Chapter 11 reorganizations is far from perfect. The evidence on plan confirmation by creditors, feasibility of the confirmed plan as well as the re-filing rate casts serious questions on Chapter 11 reorganization.

Chapter 11 reorganization is an administratively costly and time-consuming exercise. Average time from filing for Chapter 11 to confirmation of the plan was 740 days, the median was 656 days and almost two-thirds of confirmations were in the second and third years after filing (Flynn 1989). Moreover, bankruptcy proceedings are often enormously expensive, consuming millions, or even hundreds of millions of dollars of assets in the form of administrative costs for lawyers, bankers, accountants, and others, that might otherwise be available to pay creditors.[6]

However, even after the lengthy process, confirmation does not imply success for the financially distressed firm. Previous studies have shown that the probability of confirmation of plan in Chapter 11 reorganization is approximately 17 percent. Further, only 10–12 percent of the confirmed plans result in a successful reorganization of the business. (Flynn 1989).

A large majority of small businesses filing for Chapter 11 fail to obtain confirmation of a Chapter 11 plan and typically end up in liquidation. And fewer than 10 percent of small to medium-size firms (assets under $500,000) emerge from Chapter 11 as going concerns (Baird 1993). This

---

[6] In the Enron case, for example, professional and other administrative fees exceeded $1 billion.

is especially a problem since the vast majority of business bankruptcies involve small and midsized firms.[7]

Even in studies on large companies[8] with assets over $100 million; the results are mixed. While the confirmation rate in these cases is a high 96 percent; post confirmation performance is poor. Over 32 percent of these cases refile for bankruptcy after emerging from Chapter 11 (LoPucki and Whitford 1993).

A study by Jenson-Conklin (1992), also known as the Poughkeepsie Study, focused on how the plan-confirmed cases of small companies played out in reality. According to the study, a Chapter 11 debtor has a 6.5 percent chance of confirming and consummating a plan as well as surviving as a rehabilitated entity post confirmation. For the creditor (if we also include cases that were liquidated); there is a 10 percent chance of receiving a distribution promised in the confirmed Chapter 11 plan.

Another study examining the post bankruptcy performance of 197 firms found that over 40 percent experience operating losses in the three years following bankruptcy. And 32 percent of the firms re-enter bankruptcy or privately restructure their debt (Hotchkiss 1995).

This brings us to the question of how to interpret these numbers and judge the performance of Chapter 11.

One possible way to judge the performance of Chapter 11 is a comparative analysis of Chapter 11 with other jurisdictions. Comparing reorganization in Canada and the U.S. reveals that in Canada reorganization plans have a higher rate of acceptance, confirmation and consummation. And a firm that has emerged from the Canadian reorganization process is eight times more likely to emerge from Chapter 11 and survive as an on-going concern (Fisher and Martel 1999). One of the reasons the authors suggest is that the Canadian system allows for less intervention from the judge and procedures such as *cramdown* are not part of the Canadian system.

Though these results tell us about Chapter 11 in practice, and there seems much consensus that these numbers reflect the poor performance of Chapter 11 in the U.S.; there is no *real* benchmark for comparison. The reason for this is that the only comparison would be to see how the market performs and in the market process it is not entirely clear if a liquidated firm is categorized as a success or as a failure. One plausible way is to compare filing rates on the market with the filing rates of firms already

---

[7]   Only 20 percent of Chapter 11 cases filed since 1979 involved assets of $1 million or more.

[8]   A review of Chapter 11 filings for big businesses during 1980–2010 show that during this period 898 cases were filed. Lynn M. LoPucki's Bankruptcy Research Database available at http://lopucki.law.ucla.edu/index.htm.

reorganized. In general, when the filing rate of the economy is compared with the re-filing rate of cases that have emerged from that court; the re-filing rates are higher. The most notorious state in this regard is Delaware (LoPucki and Kalin 2001). Even this is not a conclusive judge of Chapter 11 performance; but given that evidence of market performance necessarily precludes Chapter 11 reorganization, a perfect comparison of the two is impossible to obtain.

2.3   Critique

The cause for such performance of Chapter 11 reorganization is blamed on forum shopping, inadequate negotiation between creditors and debtors, high-profile tort litigation, pensions, or in some cases a very speedy reorganization (LoPucki 2006). Further costs of legal and accounting fees and disruption of a firm's business throughout the process have been highlighted as the problem. (Adler 1993). Others (Bradley and Rosenzweig 1992) blame the perverse incentives faced by the incumbent management for reorganization failures. In his seminal article on Chapter 11 reorganization, Baird (1986) faults the valuation process used by the bankruptcy judge within Chapter 11 for the reorganization failures. The "free market critics" propose various alternatives to the traditional Chapter 11 reorganization process, such as a mandatory and prompt sale of the bankrupt firm as a going-concern (Baird 1986), the automatic conversion of bondholders into equity holders upon a firm's insolvency (Adler 1993) to avoid problems of valuation and long delays in bankruptcy courts.

On the other hand, Warren believes that the foremost function of Chapter 11 is to preserve, enhance and redistribute the value of a failing firm among various participants, where Chapter 11 balances the interests of these participants (creditors, debtors, tort victims and unions etc.) (Warren 1993). And the complexity of this task requires evaluation on grounds other than economic efficiency. Warren believes that while Chapter 11 performs poorly when narrowly judged on grounds of economic efficiency, it is a success, if all other interests in society are considered (Warren 1992).

While we agree with Warren on the complexity of the task of reorganizing a failed firm; we believe the task is impossible to accomplish given the information and incentives of the judge and must therefore be left to the market process. Our critique is a complement to Baird's critique, as we provide a theoretical explanation for Baird's critique regarding the cause of inaccurate valuation, and we come to the same conclusion as Baird suggesting going-concern auctions as an alternative to Chapter 11.

3.   THE BANKRUPTCY JUDGE'S DILEMMA

Scholars have suggested judicial allocation as a viable alternative to market allocation in situations of incomplete information or high transaction cost (Posner 1998; Cooter 2000). But these suggestions create a dilemma for a judge who must make optimal allocations between parties, for instance, while awarding damages in contracts and tort cases or reorganizing a firm in Chapter 11. But in each case the dilemma of the judge is not identical since the judge requires different kinds of market data, which is available in varying degrees.

What we mean by market data is the availability of the costs and benefits for the individuals in question. Cost is the value attached to the satisfaction one must forgo (Mises 1998 [1949]: 97) or the opportunity sacrificed by the decision-maker to make the choice (Buchanan 1999 [1969]: 41). The difference between the value of the price paid, or the cost incurred, and the value of the goal attained is called benefit (Mises 1998 [1949]: 97). Cost and benefit is purely subjective, and can only be known to the decision-maker. Therefore the external observer cannot measure opportunity cost because there is no way by which this subjective experience can be directly observed (Buchanan 1999 [1969]: 41).

In some cases the judge has market data to make accurate valuations, but in the absence of such market data, the judge functions like a socialist central planner (See O'Driscoll (1980), Aranson (1992) and Stringham (2001)).[9]

In case of a well-defined contract where the market data exists on the current price of the goods of services in question, the problem of valuation is small. In many cases the judge must determine the rule, if it is one of *restitutio in integrum* (restitution to original position); or one, which only compensates the losses of the plaintiffs; or one, which awards the profits of the defendant. The valuation of the award is possible since usually, the valuation is made after the event, and data exists on the losses, suffered and profits made by the breach of contract.[10]

Tort cases often get more complicated, depending on the rule used by

---

[9]   Not specific to bankruptcy law, but common law in general; works by Rizzo (1980), Epstein (1980), O'Driscoll (1980), Aranson (1992) and Stringham (2001) discuss the problem of calculation to common law rules and cases.

[10]   This is not to say there is no subjectivity in values in contracts. In fact some rules like "remoteness of damage" may increase or decrease the subjectivity of the losses suffered or the profits made. However, I merely hold these valuations are already computed for the most part by the parties, and the judge often only adjudicates the rule.

the judge. If the rule of negligence is used, then the problem of valuation is clear because there is no unique objective measure of social cost (Rizzo 1980). The problem is exacerbated in determining the least cost avoider or the contribution of the plaintiff in the negligent act because data on the subjective costs of the participants is unavailable to the judge.

If there were a spectrum on the availability of market data for the judge, cases such as admiralty law, breach of contracts, etc. would be at one end of the spectrum where the judge has the relevant market data. On this spectrum tort cases would perhaps lie somewhere in the middle, where costs and benefits are more subjective and not revealed in judicial process. And, Chapter 11 reorganization is at the extreme end of the spectrum because the bankruptcy judge faces the valuation problem at two levels.

First, the judge needs to determine whether the firm is only financially distressed or also economically not viable i.e., the judge must determine if the firm should be (transferred to Chapter 7 and) liquidated or whether it should be preserved and reorganized under Chapter 11. Second, the judge needs to value the firm in order to pay the creditors in lieu of their debt. Essentially, both these problems are one of valuation: where the judge must predict values that have not been revealed due to the absence of a market exchange.

In the following sections, we detail the impossible task assigned to the judge in determining economically viable firms and rehabilitating them while simultaneously assigning shares of the firm to its creditors. This critique is divided in two parts. First, the judge does not have the relevant information required to determine if a firm should continue as an on-going concern or if the firm should be liquidated. Second, the judge does not have the relevant data to make an accurate valuation of the firm to make the hypothetical sale of the firm to its creditors.

3.1 Task before a Bankruptcy Judge

The procedure in the Code can be viewed in two categories. First, is the choice of Chapter 11 reorganization over the other remedies provided in the Code. And the second, is the actual procedure once a firm is placed within Chapter 11 reorganization.

There are primarily three ways by which a firm can end up in Chapter 11 reorganization. First, the debtors (usually the management) may file voluntarily.[11] Second, the creditors may file a case, also known as an

---

[11]   11 U.S.C 301 (2008).

involuntary filing.[12] Third, debtors may convert a case filed under Chapter 7 (liquidation) to Chapter 11.[13] Once filed, the judge must approve which Chapter the firm falls under, in other words determine if the firm must remain as a going concern or be sold in parts.

Once a firm is within the scope of Chapter 11 reorganization; the debtor (usually the management of the firm) is allowed to continue operating the corporation as debtor-in-possession[14] without any trustees. The firm is allowed to continue in business without any liquidation.[15] Once the petition is filed the debtors have 120 days to come up with a reorganization plan where usually the firm continues in operation; and the exclusive right to have that plan accepted by creditors for the first 180 days[16] also known as the "exclusivity period." Once this period is complete, any "party in interest" may file a plan.[17]

The reorganization plan proposed by the debtors-in-possession creates a different structure of ownership whereby the debt of the firm is converted into stock given as payment in lieu of debt to the creditors who then become the corporation's owners along with other stockholders.

United States Trustee[18] appoints a committee with the seven largest creditors.[19] Creditors are divided into class based on priority and the debtor then comes up with a reorganization plan and a disclosure statement on which the various classes of creditors vote. Ordinarily the vote of each class of creditors is required for a reorganization plan to be accepted. The court must then, satisfy itself that the requirements of the Code are fulfilled,[20] before approving the reorganization plan. There are two other important aspects the judge reviews before he approves the plan.

In case a creditor or a class of creditors dissents, there is a lengthening of the process and much litigation. However, even if one of the classes rejects the reorganization plan, the debtor may be able to confirm the plan under the *cramdown* process.[21] While consent is generally required from a group of creditors as a whole, in certain circumstances, even with

---

12   Ibid., 303.
13   Ibid., 706.
14   Ibid., 1101.
15   Ibid., 1108.
16   Ibid., 1121(b–d).
17   Ibid., 1121(c).
18   Ibid., 307, 321–22.
19   Ibid., 1102(a)(1).
20   This is essentially fulfilling 11 U.S.C 1129(a)(9)(A–C) requiring the payment of all administrative expenses, cash payment for pre-bankruptcy claims like employees and payment of taxes.
21   11 U.S.C 1129(a) (2008).

the dissent of a creditor or a class of creditors, the bankruptcy judge may proceed and *cramdown* the reorganization and change the structure of ownership of a firm. Another burden on the court before approving a plan is to ensure that it will not end up in reorganization again.[22] Also, known as the *feasibility test*, the judge must compare the new capital structure and the functioning of the reorganized firm to the other firms in the same industry before approving the plan.

Once the plan is approved the firm must discharge its debts, pay its taxes and fee to bankruptcy professionals. Once the debts are discharged, the old claims of the firm disappear and are replaced by the new obligations created by a new capital structure.

3.2 Reorganization v Liquidation

3.2.1 The filtering problem

According to the theory underlying Chapter 11, there are two types of firms in financial distress: firms that are economically viable and firms that are not economically viable. Ideally, firms that are economically viable, but in temporary financial distress should be preserved or reorganized and firms that are not economically viable should be liquidated. The first task of the bankruptcy judge is to determine if a case filed under Chapter 11 is economically viable or if the firms must be liquidated.

White (1994: 268) points out the filtering problem faced by a judge in determining whether a case that is filed under Chapter 11 should be reorganized or liquidated under Chapter 7. There are potentially two types of errors a judge can commit. If the judge keeps an inefficient firm under Chapter 11, then it is a Type I error. If on the other hand, an efficient though financially troubled firm, is liquidated under Chapter 7, then it is a Type II error (White, 1994: 273). White details how Chapter 11 fundamentally trades off towards Type II error for Type I error.

To eliminate both types of error and liquidating inefficient firms while preserving viable firms implies the judge should have a filtering process to differentiate the two. This is important since debtors (management) initiate most filings under Chapter 11[23] and they have an incentive to file under Chapter 11 and preserve the firm and save their jobs. The question is: does

---

[22]   Ibid., 1129(a)(11).
[23]   A review of Chapter 11 filings for big businesses during 1980–2010 showed that creditors filed only 41 cases, whereas debtors (or management) filed the remaining 839 cases. And only 15 cases out of 898 voluntarily converted to Chapter 7 liquidation – Lynn M. LoPucki's Bankruptcy Research Database available at http://lopucki.law.ucla.edu/index.htm.

the judge have the relevant information and incentives to separate the two types of firms and preserve viable firms while liquidating inefficient firms? There are two types of problems that a bankruptcy judge faces.

We believe that that judge does not have access to the relevant market data and faces two problems. First, is the problem of subjective costs and second, is the problem of decentralized information.[24]

Each party faces subjective costs and benefits known only to them at the time of decision-making (also known as choice influencing costs, Buchanan 1999 [1969]: 48). However, to the outside evaluator, only the objective value (or the choice-influenced costs) is apparent (Ibid.). There is no objective criterion to judge whether a firm should be held together as an on-going concern. It *only* depends on whether a buyer subjectively values the firm as a going concern and is willing to pay for it, or an owner values it as a going-concern in order to continue holding it.

Since value is subjective, the only way to determine the viability of an insolvent firm as an on-going concern is whether someone in the market is willing to buy it as such i.e., if a buyer in the market believes that the firm is worth more as a whole than in parts. If there is no such buyer, then the claim that the firm might be worth more as a going concern has no basis. The firm has such value *only* if someone is willing to pay for it.

Second, given the large number of creditors, and other potential buyers of the firms in the market, the judge must know which party values the firm the most. This information is decentralized and without a market process, or the process of bidding for the firm, this decentralized information is not revealed.

Therefore, the only way to determine the future profitability of an insolvent firm as a going concern is based on whether someone in the market is willing to buy it as such (or by outbidding other participants). If there is no such buyer, the assets must be sold off piecemeal in a liquidation process.

Given that the difference between an economically viable and a failed firm cannot be determined procedurally or judicially, but can only be determined in the market; Chapter 11 immediately becomes redundant. The very process of finding out whether firms should be reorganized must necessarily be outside of bankruptcy court. If the determination is made using the market, the necessity for Chapter 11 reorganization disappears.

If the judge determines which firms should be preserved or liquidated, he does so on a basis other than allocative efficiency, since he does not have

---

[24]   Also see Aranson (1992) for how the common law judge faces these two problems.

the relevant data. Typically the reason for keeping firms under Chapter 11 is to preserve and enhance the value and jobs that will be lost in liquidation.

3.2.2 Opportunity cost and the illusion of preserving and enhancing value

Bankruptcy policy assumes that failed firms are a problem for society and hence should be maintained as on-going concerns to preserve and enhance value. They commit the same fatal error that Bastiat pointed out by concentrating on the economic effect that can be seen as opposed to the effect that is unseen (Bastiat 1995 [1848]).

In bankruptcy, the dark side of failure is the misfortune encountered by failing firms and their workers and suppliers when such firms fall behind in the race to continue and improve performance. Individuals involved suffer losses, lose their jobs and suffer hard times. This highly visible and emphasized side of failure causes the belief that bankruptcy law must keep failing firms as going concerns, protect the jobs of employees and safeguard the interests of parties other than creditors such as suppliers, tort victims, etc. (Warren 1992).

While failed firms are a tragedy in the lives of the individuals involved in them, there is a brighter side of failure in the market process (Lee and McKenzie 1993: 22). This requires understanding that failed firms have an important role in the process of wealth creation.

Failures occur frequently in the market because successful ventures deny resources to the ventures that fail (Lee and McKenzie 1993:17). Failure is a matter of relative performance, of failing to do better than others. However, it is not just the failure that is relative but also the "better" which keeps changing. (ibid: 22) The bright side of resource scarcity is that some other product, satisfying some other desire is produced, perhaps more successfully (ibid: 18). Wants more urgently felt are being satisfied instead of those less urgently felt.

For instance, in 1997 Montgomery Ward filed for bankruptcy after having been routed by competition from department stores such as Target and Wal-Mart, big box specialty stores such as Home Depot, and a host of other rivals from on-line sellers to specialized boutiques. In fact, Montgomery Ward was just one of several old-line mid-sized department stores that expired during this time, including venerable chains such as Ames and numerous other national, regional, and local department stores that could no longer compete. Many other failing department stores were gobbled up by stronger rivals through mergers. Although many at the time predicted Montgomery Ward's eventual demise, they nonetheless launched an extended Chapter 11 reorganization, finally emerging in 1999 having closed many but not all of its outlets. The extended bankruptcy period did nothing to fundamentally rectify Ward's weak competitive position or draw consumers back into the store, and eventually Ward liquidated (Zywicki 2009:11).

When we view the other side of failure, it becomes clear that failure does not just imply that entrepreneurs are making errors. It implies that while some entrepreneurs are making errors, other entrepreneurs are making better plans and satisfying more urgent wants. The principle of scarcity dictates that the more successes there are, the more failures there are likely to be. If a resource has become relatively expensive, and a firm is unable to pay the factor payment to command that resource; it implies that other firms are outbidding the bidder to command the resource. While this seems like a failure, when the firm is successfully outbid, resources change hands and go to their highest valued use.

From this perspective, it is clear that resources are not destroyed in liquidation; only their ownership changes. And value must necessarily change with ownership. Whether the new owners will enhance value or reduce the overall value of the particular resource is unclear since there is no objective measure for the same. But in a process where all resources reach their highest valued use, social value increases.

Another aspect of preserving and enhancing value is the assumption that the bankruptcy judge can use a Kaldor-Hicks criterion and maximize the total welfare by determining if wealth is maximized in society by keeping a firm together or selling it in parts. Even in this decision of wealth maximization the bankruptcy judge runs into the same calculation and subjective costs valuation as discussed above (O'Driscoll 1980: 359). For a Kaldor-Hicks analysis is the ability to gather and sum up people's willingness to pay attached to different outcomes. Creating a forced exchange, where the creditors, even if unwillingly, must take a share in the reorganizer firm in lieu of their debt, creates an illusion of value and does not reveal the willingness to pay of the parties involved (Stringham, 2001: 42).

The existing firm has such value *only* if someone is willing to pay for it as a whole. The paradox is that if there were such a buyer, or indeed if the creditors could agree to reorganize the firm; the case would typically not even enter Chapter 11. In practice, almost all Chapter 11 cases involve situations where all creditors do not agree on the firm having value as a going concern.

3.3   Reorganization

In liquidation under Chapter 7, assets are sold to third parties. However, in reorganization under Chapter 11, the firm's assets are sold to creditors. Reorganization is therefore the sale of the firm as an on-going concern to the claimants. Since the sale is not made in the open market to third parties, but a hypothetical sale judicially allotted to the claimants, the question of valuation comes up. Chapter 11 policy makes the fatal error of assuming that the bankruptcy judge is in the position of an ideal observer or at least in a position to obtain information and observe matters that other market participants are unable to. In the following section we argue that the judge is not in the position of the ideal observer; but in fact in the position of a socialist central planner facing the problem of calculation.

Blum and Kaplan (1974: 656) explain many of the problems in valuation:

> The valuation procedure always produces a dollars and cents figure. Although that figure is mathematically exact it actually reflects in a single number a whole series of highly conjectural and even speculative judgments concerning long-range business expectations and hazards as well as social and general economic conditions. . . . The process is said to deceive by treating "soft" information as if it were "hard" and by cloaking predictions in the guise of mathematical certainty, under circumstances where consequences are drastic and final.

Judge Winner articulates the problems associated with finding with certainty the value of a firm in dollar and cents in *Consolidated Rock Products v. Dubois*:[25]

> With all of these things, to say that you can forecast—that you can appraise the values in the Canadian Arctic is to say that you can attend the County Fair with your crystal ball, because that is absolutely the only way you can come up with a result. . . . My final conclusion is that it is worth somewhere between $90 million and $100 million as a going concern, and to satisfy people who want precision on the value, I fix the exact value of the company at the average of those, $96,856,850, which of course is a total absurdity that anybody could fix a value with that degree of precision, but for the lawyers who want me to make that fool estimate, I have just made it.

While the problem has been articulated above as one of uncertainty of the future, this is exacerbated by the problems of decentralized information and lack of monetary prices. In the following section we explain these problems by comparing the role to the Soviet central planner.

3.3.1   Bankruptcy judge as a central planner

The problem of the central planner can be summarized as follows. Without the institution of private property in the means of production, there would be no market for means of production. Without the market for the means of production there would be no prices established for means of production. And without monetary prices reflecting the relative scarcity

---

[25]   312 U.S. 510 (1941).

of goods, the central planner cannot calculate the alternative use of capital goods (See Mises 1990 [1922]). We make the case that the same is true for a bankruptcy judge.

Within the Chapter 11 process, there is no requirement of consent over transfer of resources. The means of production are owned by nobody and the decision on how to use the means of production is proposed by the debtors in possession, voted on by creditors and approved by the judge, and consent is not essential for changes in ownership.

This implies that there is no competitive process for the bidding of the means of production used in reorganization. The real price or the scarcity of equity, debt, and all the assets of the firm are not known since there is no competitive bidding process to reveal that information. Since there is no bidding process, no exchange ratio or relative prices emerge for the means for production. Without the aid of such prices there is no means to calculate profit and losses in monetary terms since all values are subjective and unknown to anyone other than the individual. Therefore, the bankruptcy judge cannot value the firm and reorganize it in an accurate way that is possible with the aid of the market process.

(a) Consent   Private property in the market is the right associated with use, possession, alienation and sale. Therefore, there is an interest in the property to the exclusion of all other interests. Enforced property rights imply that the consent of the individual with the property right is required for use, possession, and alienation of the property. Therefore, private property brings with it two important concepts; of consent and interest. Consent protects the interest of a party, and at the same time also provides information of the subjective valuation the individual places on a particular property. Private property and the related concepts of consent and interest are critical to the market process.[26]

In Chapter 11 reorganization, creditors are divided into class based on priority and the debtor then comes up with a reorganization plan and a disclosure statement on which the various classes of creditors vote. Ordinarily the vote of each class of creditors is required for a reorganization plan to be accepted. In case a creditor or a class of creditors dissents, there is a lengthening of the process and much litigation, which can potentially be circumvented under the *cramdown* process. One of the mechanisms available to the bankruptcy judge in order to implement the reorganization is the *cramdown* process, wherein if a particular class of creditors does not

---

[26]   Cole (1999) argues how through the process of consent, important information regarding valuation is revealed.

agree to the proposed reorganization plan, acceptance may be forced on to them.[27]

The reorganization plan proposed by the debtors-in-possession creates a different structure of ownership whereby the debt of the firm is converted into stock given as payment in lieu of debt to the creditors who then become the corporation's owners along with other stockholders. But as owners, or as future owners, creditors have little say on the reorganization plan; since it may be forced on them if their consent is not readily available.

(b) Competitive process of bidding In Chapter 11 reorganization, due to the lack of necessity of consent, the competitive bidding for the control of a firm disappears. This is because there is no incentive to bid for the firms and it is better to use legal means to claim their share. In the reorganization process, plans are proposed, voted on and accepted or rejected for large groups. There is no individual competition for the resources in question. The debtors in possession propose some fixed combination of the means of production, and this plan must be accepted/rejected by creditors or decided by the judge. Not having a competitive bidding process for the use and control of resources results in a lack of exchange ratios, reflecting the relative scarcities of the assets in question, emerging from the process of judicial allotment.

Firms become insolvent due to errors by entrepreneurs which result in a combination of liabilities for which the owners are unable to pay (most typically borrowed capital on which they default on repayment). To eliminate this error and move towards economic efficiency,[28] where assets reach their highest valued use in the market, implies that those who want the asset most, will bid the most for it and acquire the asset for their proposed use among competing uses. However, if there is no bidding for the firm or the assets of the firm, judicial allocation cannot reveal the highest valued use of the firm and its assets.

(c) Prices and calculation Prices are formed through the actions of bidders competing for resources. These individuals ordinarily rank their choices and express them in monetary terms to trade in the market (Mises

---

[27] 11 U.S.C 1129(a) (2008).

[28] By economic efficiency; we mean allocative efficiency of the market process; i.e., where resources are channeled to their highest valued use. By allocative efficiency we mean that the means must be employed in such a way that no want more urgently felt should remain unsatisfied because the means were employed in the attainment of wants less urgent (Mises 1998 [1949]: 207). To conduct this analysis within the means ends framework; one needs to compare or ordinally rank the costs and benefits of the various means; which a bankruptcy judge cannot do.

1998 [1949]: 335). Therefore it must be remembered that monetary prices or the numerical meaning has no relevance when outside of bidding in the market process. It is merely a tool to value two or more choices.

Exchange ratios or their expression through monetary prices are important because only monetary prices can help calculate and solve the economic problem i.e., the problem of employing available means in such a way that wants more urgently felt do not remain unfulfilled while the means are wasted to satisfy a want less urgently felt (Mises 1998 [1949]: 207). The "economic" nature of the problem is one of measurement.

(d) The problem of calculation   The economic criterion implies that costs must be taken into account, which would be a simple arithmetic exercise if there were an objective cost and benefit for each resource. However, costs only mean opportunity costs i.e., market price of that resource, which reflects the subjective value of other market participants.

However, without exchange ratios emerging from bidding in a market process, the participants in the reorganization process have no means of evaluating the opportunity cost of keeping the firm as a going-concern.

To determine the opportunity cost of keeping the firm as going concern, the bankruptcy judge needs two types of information. First, the subjective values or costs of all the participants in the reorganization process, which are not reflected through prices; and second, the subjective values for the firm *outside the reorganization* in the regular market process for other resources, which are only reflected in the constellation of market prices. Without this knowledge, it is impossible to determine if the various resources in the firm are in their highest valued use and the bankruptcy judge has no way of accessing and assimilating that dispersed information.

Given the problem of rational economic calculation faced by the judge one may argue that there is no market for the means of production within the reorganization process; but there is a market outside the reorganization process. The judge may use such market prices. Alternately, the judge may use valuations based on past prices from the insolvent firm's balance sheet to ascertain the real value of the firm and how to reorganize it. The problem with this approach is that monetary prices or the numerical meaning have no relevance when outside of the market process (Mises 1949: 335). Neither past prices, nor the book value of the firm reflect how creditors value the firm individually or as a group because these values do not reflect the current subjective preferences of the creditors.[29]

---

[29]   Apart from the subjective cost faced by the decision-maker, there are two ways to view costs. First, direct outlay costs i.e., the expenditures a firm incurs

This information is dispersed in the market, without access to which there is no method for the judge to calculate costs and benefits that would enable him to channel the assets to their highest valued use. And the set of market prices is an "indispensible guide for the determination of the appropriate volume of production" (Hayek 1935).

Therefore the bankruptcy judge faces all the problems faced by a central planner. He simply does not have the relevant market data to determine the existence, value and future of a firm. If we juxtapose the judge with that faced by the Soviet planner, it becomes clear that the bankruptcy judge; though operating in a capitalist system; operates in an institutional vacuum because all the market process which enable economic calculation have been replaced with judicial processes.

4. INCENTIVES

There are two problems related with lack of incentives of the judge. The first and the obvious problem is simply that he is not personally vested in the success or the failure of an insolvent firm and therefore is less likely to take decisions like an entrepreneur. The second problem is that a judge does not face the real costs and benefits like an entrepreneur; he does not know the real costs and benefits in question.

Mises (2007 [1944]) points out the difference between a bureaucrat and an entrepreneur. A bureaucrat is bound by following rules and regulations that have been set by his superiors to control his arbitrariness. Therefore a bureaucrat or judge is rewarded based on his ability to follow the procedures and not on profits and losses or efficiency. There are many bureaucracies where the relative profits, losses and efficiencies cannot even be measured. On the other hand, an entrepreneur is bound by profits and losses that follow his decisions. When he runs a firm, since he is liable for the losses and is the residual claimant of the profits, he

---

in obtaining various factors of production. Second, the consumers' valuation of alternative products that other firms might have produced. These three notions of costs are not in contradiction in a perfectly competitive equilibrium (O'Driscoll and Rizzo 1996 [1985]: 48). In this kind of an equilibrium using the book valuation at that instant or the objective value of the firm will be akin to using the subjective value. This becomes a little more complicated when the behavior of a firm is in disequilibrium. In a world in constant flux, using expenditure outlays as costs is meaningless. This is the case bankruptcy judges are really faced with, and therefore using outlays (or choice influenced costs) as measures to value a firm does not reflect the true costs borne by the owners and creditors.

has the incentive to make the plans he thinks are best and his rewards are from the market.

The main point in the context of reorganizing a firm is to *know* the costs, one must *bear* the cost. And the entrepreneur bears the costs of his actions whereas the judge does not bear the cost of an unsuccessful reorganization or reap the benefit of a successful reorganization.

Like the bureaucrat, the judge's incentives are not aligned with that of an entrepreneur facing market forces. The judge bears no personal liability if a reorganized firm fails to make profits or repay creditors. Neither the judge's reputation nor his remuneration is impacted when his decisions regarding the insolvent firm are successful. A judge is only evaluated on the number of appeals his decisions are subject to and the number of decisions that are reversed by his superiors. It is unclear that an appellate judge who faces the same knowledge and calculation problems as the judge would do any better in his decision-making or find reasons to reverse the original orders.

Some argue that behavior of bankruptcy judges is a professional competition where the reward is to perform their service efficiently and effectively relative to their peers; and not the usual tangible rewards of salary and benefits (Cole 2002: 1890–91).

While the exact motivations of individual judges cannot be generalized or known with certainty, it is clear that judges are not evaluated based on the number of successful reorganizations they cause. By successful, we mean insolvent firms that go on to make a profit and prosper after Chapter 11 reorganization in the hands of the new owners. It is logical to extrapolate that judges are therefore not driven by a profit motive because the profits are not theirs to enjoy. This is the greatest difference between the incentives of an entrepreneur and a judge.

An entrepreneur may also be driven by job satisfaction, prestige, media exposure, peer pressure, etc.; but even where profits are not the motive, profits and losses act as a disciplining mechanism. In the context of bankruptcy reorganization; an entrepreneur who buys an insolvent or failed firm must turn it around into a profit-making firm or bear the losses himself, making the entrepreneur's incentives better aligned with the success or failure of the firm.

Given that the entrepreneur has the relevant incentives and information while the bankruptcy judge operates in a vacuum, the market allocation will eliminate the valuation problems faced in judicial allocation and ensure that resources flow to their highest valued use.

5. RENT-SEEKING: JUDICIAL AND POLITICAL ALLOCATION

The main consequence of the impossibility of the judge to make market allocations is that some other criterion of allocation must be used in order to revalue and allocate the firm. In this judicial allocation there is a role for negotiation by the stakeholders as well as discretion of the judge. Further, outside the bankruptcy court, there is room for political allocation at the legislative level. Various groups such as the bankruptcy lawyers, creditors, shareholders etc. have an incentive to lobby for such political allocation. In this section we describe the efficiency consequences of such allocation.

5.1 Judicial Allocation

In theory reorganization creates economic rents via the going-concern surplus. The problem is that to the extent that property rights in these rents are imperfectly allocated parties will invest real resources trying to divert some of those rents towards their claim.

This is similar to the problem under Soviet central planning where in the absence of property rights and market prices to allocate resources, political allocation incentivized individuals to capture the rents generated under the planning process (See Anderson and Boettke 1997).

Under Chapter 11 reorganization, the absolute priority rule prescribes a general principle to guide allocations. The rule is that before a class of investors can participate in Chapter 11 reorganization, all more senior classes must be compensated in full for their claims measured on the basis of their priority. In other words, senior creditors are paid before junior creditors and creditors are paid before shareholders.

The absolute priority rule prescribes the general principle under which allocations must be made; but it neither specifies actual allocations, nor is it inviolable. "Reorganizers have always understood, however, that this general formulation does not dictate a specific pattern of adjusting rights among investors. Reorganization plans are a result of a process in which representatives of the investors 'negotiate.'"(Blum and Kaplan 1974: 652–3).

Bankruptcy should protect property rights via the absolute priority rule. But the absolute priority rule is not always honored and there are exceptions to the rule wherein junior investors and shareholders also receive their claims. The "new value exception" originated in *Case v. Los Angeles Lumber Co.*,[30] is a court-made exception to the absolute priority rule. The

---

[30] 308 U.S. 106 (1939).

court permitted shareholders to retain an equity interest despite the unpaid claims of senior creditors if they contribute money or money's worth to the reorganized enterprise. This has created room for the shareholders to emerge as a formidable interest group in bankruptcy proceedings.

LoPucki and Whitford (1990: 190–94) show that there is a systematic deviation from the absolute priority rule in favor of junior interests. They find that shareholders of insolvent firms almost always received a share in the distribution under the plan. In case of insolvent firms the shareholders received a share out of fear that the shareholders as a group may create problems if their claims were not yielded to. In case of marginally solvent firms LoPucki and Whitford found that there are substantial deviations from the absolute priority rule giving the shareholders a larger share or "equitable sharing" between creditors and shareholders. Most importantly, they find, that this sharing was a product of difficulties with valuations and aggressive representation by shareholders yielded big rewards (ibid: 165–8). Their findings clearly confirm theory. The greater the rents generated, the greater the investment in seeking those rents.

5.2   Political Allocation

Given the rents generated in the bankruptcy process in general, there are various interest groups that form to capture the rents. While these take place outside of judicial allocation and operate to influence the legislative process of bankruptcy law and reforms; the efficiency losses of such allocation are equally important.

There are two notable groups in such political allocation. First, the creditors, who have not succeeded in forming a significant and well-organized group in bankruptcy law negotiations. Second, the bankruptcy lawyers and professions who have organized so successfully that they have skewed the bankruptcy law in their favor irrespective of the winners or losers.

Public choice analysis shows why bankruptcy lawyers have grouped so successfully. Bankruptcy lawyers have an interest in increasing the number of bankruptcies filed as well as the expense of each of those cases. Regardless of who files of bankruptcy the bankruptcy lawyers will benefit.

If we view the procedure of Chapter 11 and the amount of technical expertise required and the representation and negotiation involved, it is clear that it is impossible without the aid of bankruptcy lawyers. Bankruptcy lawyers have thus succeeded in capturing a large part of the rents generated from bankruptcy law in general (see Zywicki 2003).

Creditors on the other hand, have not been as successful as the bankruptcy lawyers. While it is in their interest to influence bankruptcy law and procedure, the creditors face a collective action problem. First, the interests of the creditors are not homogenous. The secured and unsecured creditors are locked in a zero sum game while distributing the assets of a firm since the debtor by definition cannot pay his debts. Finally, the risk involved in credit is reflected in the cost of credit. As the cost of unsecured credit increases there is a substitution effect towards secured credit. This however leads to diverging concerns between the types of creditors on the relevant issues to lobby.

Second, the creditors are difficult to organize because they are large in number and the benefit to each is relatively small while the costs of organizing are large (see Zywicki 2000, 2003).

6.   ALTERNATIVES TO CHAPTER 11

Therefore, the judicial process is no substitute for the market process which brings us to alternatives to Chapter 11 that do not create the same institutional, incentive and rent-seeking problems as Chapter 11 reorganization.

A bankruptcy judge is given the impossible task of allocating efficiently without access to the information and incentives afforded by the market process. The entrepreneur does not operate in this institutional vacuum and is therefore in a better position to value a firm. This brings us to alternatives to Chapter 11 reorganization.

The answer to the problem lies within the Bankruptcy Code in Chapter 7 that is usually used for liquidation. Many assume that a Chapter 11 process implies keeping the firm together and a Chapter 7 process implies selling off the firm in parts. This is not the real difference between the two. One can have Chapter 7 liquidation where the entire firm is sold as a going concern. The main difference is that under reorganization under Chapter 11, the firm's assets are *sold* to creditors. Under Chapter 7 liquidation, assets are sold to third parties. Reorganization is therefore the sale of the firm as an on-going concern *to existing claimants*.

As discussed, it is the internal sale of the firm to its creditors, without access to the information required for economic calculation, which makes accurate valuation by the judge impossible. However, if the goal is to keep the firm as an on-going concern; one can do the same by auctioning the firm as an on-going concern under Chapter 7 (Baird 1986: 136).

We second the suggestion by Baird that a going concern auction will fulfill the goal of bankruptcy law and at the same time escape the inefficiency of Chapter 11. There are two advantages to using liquidation or the market process relative to restructuring within bankruptcy courts: information and incentives.

First, in liquidation, the actors have access to dispersed information on the subjective values and tradeoffs faced by all other market participants. No individual is required to market decisions for the entire market; he must only make decisions for himself, given market ratios, which are inputs for his subjective value of the resource.

Second, the incentives of the creditors, debtors and owners of the firm are aligned with their interests. An entrepreneur is bound by profits and losses that follow his decisions. This implies that when he runs a firm, since he is liable for the losses and the residual claimant of the profits, he has the incentive to make the plans he thinks are best and his rewards are from the market.

The advantage of going concern auctions is that the problem of filtering the cases that must be reorganized and liquidated is sorted in the market place and the judge neither has to value the firm, nor filter firms that must be liquidated from those that must be preserved.

Repealing Chapter 11 reorganization and using Chapter 7 to liquidate or auction a firm as a going concern will direct the resources to their highest valued use, a task that is impossible for the judge.

Critics of this approach may point out the information problems faced by third-party entrepreneurs in Chapter 7 liquidation. Further they point out that the firm's insolvency is due to errors made by entrepreneurs, in the first place.

While entrepreneurs make errors just as judges make errors; we believe there are two reasons entrepreneurs will perform better than the judge when it comes to valuation.

First, the entrepreneur is not performing in the same institutional context as the judge and has access to relevant information. This does not mean that the entrepreneur has perfect or complete or costless information. It only implies that the entrepreneur operates in an institutional environment where the information enabling economic calculation is available. Second, the entrepreneur faces different incentives from the judge, which are more aligned with the success and the failure of the firm.

There is a difference between the judge and the entrepreneur, who are in the position of having to calculate value. The entrepreneur has an institutional framework of the market process that provides the exchange ratios he needs.

Therefore the entrepreneur has access to two strands of information the judge does not. First, he knows his own subjective valuations and can express it in monetary terms in the market. Second, the entrepreneur does not need to compute others' valuation in the market since the market price provides the knowledge of relative scarcity and within such relative scarcity the subjective valuations of other market participants.

7.   CONCLUSION

"The law cannot and should not aim toward the impossible" (Rizzo 1980: 291). Since the task before the bankruptcy judge is impossible to achieve, Chapter 11 reorganization is prone to other, less efficient forms of allocation such as rent seeking and lobbying. There is a better alternative to judicial allocation by using market allocation, we call for a repeal of Chapter 11 and suggest substituting it with going-concern auctions or liquidations under Chapter 7.

REFERENCES

Anderson, Gary M. and Peter J. Boettke. 1997. "Soviet Venality: A Rent-Seeking Model of the Communist State" *Public Choice*, 93(1–2): 37–53.

Adler, Barry E. 1992. "Bankruptcy and Risk Allocation" *Cornell Law Review* 77: 439–89.

Adler, Barry E. 1993. "Financial and Political Theories of American Corporate Bankruptcy" *Stanford Law Review* 45: 311–46.

Aranson, Peter H. 1992. "The Common Law as Central Economic Planning" *Constitution Political Economy* 3: 289–319.

Baird, Douglas G. 1986. "The Uneasy Case for Corporate Reorganization" *Journal of Legal Studies* 15: 127–47.

Baird, Douglas G. 1987a. "Loss Distribution, Forum Shopping, and Bankruptcy: A Reply to Warren" *University of Chicago Law Review* 54: 815–34.

Baird, Douglas G. 1987b. "A World Without Bankruptcy" *Law and Contemporary Problems*. 50: 173–93.

Baird, Douglas G. 1993. "Revisiting Auctions in Chapter 11" *Journal of Law and Economics* 36: 633–53.

Baird, Douglas G. 1998. "Bankruptcy's Uncontested Axioms" *The Yale Law Journal* 108(3): 573–99.

Baird, Douglas G. 2001 [1992]. *Elements of Bankruptcy.* New York: Foundation Press.

Baird, Douglas G., Thomas H. Jackson and Barry E. Adler. 2000. *Cases, Problems and Materials on Bankruptcy.* New York: Foundation Press.

Bastiat, Frédéric. 1995 [1848]. "What is Seen and What is Not Seen." In *Selected Essays on Political Economy,* translated by Seymour Cain and edited by George B. de Huszar. Irvington, NY: The Foundation for Economic Education, Inc.

Bebchuk, Lucian A. 1988. "A New Approach to Corporate Reorganizations" *Harvard Law Review* 101: 775–804.

Blum, Walter T. and Stanley A. Kaplan. 1974. "The Absolute Priority Doctrine in Corporate Reorganizations" *University of Chicago Law Review* 41(4): 651–84.

Bradley, Michael and Michael Rosenzweig. 1992. "The Untenable Case for Chapter 11" *Yale Law Journal* 101: 1043–95.

Buchanan, James M. 1999 [1969]. *Cost and Choice.* Indianapolis, IN: Liberty Fund.

Cole, G. Marcus. 1999. "A Calculus Without Consent: Mass Tort Bankruptcies, Future Claimants, and the Problem of Third Party Non-Debtor 'Discharge'" *Iowa Law Review* 84: 753–800.

Cole, Marcus. 2002. "'Delaware is Not a State': Are We Witnessing Jurisdictional Competition in Bankruptcy?" *Vanderbilt Law Review* 55: 1845–916.

Cole, G. Marcus, and Todd J. Zywicki. 2010. "Anna Nicole Smith Goes Forum Shopping: The New Forum Shopping Problem in Bankruptcy Law" *Utah Law Review* 3: 511–46.

Cooter, Robert. 2000. *The Strategic Constitution.* Princeton, NJ: Princeton University Press.

Craznetsky, John M. 1999. "Time, Uncertainty, and the Law of Corporate Reorganizations" *Fordham Law Review* 101: 2939–3004.

Epstein, Richard A. 1980. "The Static Conception of the Common Law" *Journal of Legal Studies* 9: 253–75.

Fisher, Timothy and Jocelyn Martel. 1999. "Should we abolish Chapter 11? Evidence from Canada" *Journal of Legal Studies* 28(1): 233–57.

Flynn, Ed. 1989. *Statistical Analysis of Chapter11*. Bankruptcy Division of the Administrative Office of the U.S. Court.

Fortgang, Chaim and Thomas Moers Mayer. 1985. "Valuation in Bankruptcy" *UCLA Law Review* 32: 1061–132.

Hayek, Friedrich A., ed., 1935. *Collectivist Economic Planning.* London: Routledge.

Hayek, Friedrich A. 1945. "The Use of Knowledge in Society" *American Economic Review* 35: 519–30.

Hotchkiss, Edith Shwalb. 1995. "Post Performance and Management Turnover" *The Journal of Finance* 50: 3–21.

Jackson, Thomas H. 1986. *The Logic and Limits of Bankruptcy Law.* Cambridge, MA: Harvard University Press.

Jenson-Conklin, Susan. 1992. "Do Confirmed Chapter 11 Plans Consummate? The Results of a Study and Analysis of the Law" *Commercial Law Journal* 97(3): 297–331.

Lee, Dwight R. and Richard B. McKenzie. 1993. *Failure and Progress: The Bright Side of the Dismal Science.* Washington DC: Cato Institute.

Levine, Michael E. "Why Bankruptcy is the Best Option for GM" *The Wall Street Journal*, November 17 2008. Accessed at http://online.wsj.com/article/SB122688631448632421.html.

LoPucki, Lynn M. 2006. *Courting Failure: How Competition for Big Cases is Corrupting the Bankruptcy Courts.* Ann Arbor, MI: The University of Michigan Press.

LoPucki, Lynn M. and Sara D. Kalin. 2001. "The Failure of Public Company Bankruptcies in Delaware and New York" *Vanderbilt Law Review* 54: 232–82.

LoPucki, Lynn M. and William C. Whitford. 1990. "Bargaining over Equity's Share in the Bankruptcy Reorganization of Large, Publicly Held Companies" *University of Pennsylvania Law Review* 139(1): 125–96.

LoPucki, Lynn M. and William C. Whitford. 1993. "Patterns in the Bankruptcy Reorganization of Large, Publicly Held Companies" *Cornell Law Review* 78: 597–618.

Mises, Ludwig von. 1990 [1922]. *Economic Calculation in the Socialist Commonwealth.* Auburn, AL: Ludwig von Mises Institute.

Mises, Ludwig Von. 1998 [1949]. *Human Action.* Irvington-on-Hudson: The Foundation for Economic Education, Inc.

Mises, Ludvig Von. 2007 [1944]. *Bureaucracy*. Indianapolis, IN: Liberty Fund.

O'Driscoll, Gerald P., Jr. 1980. "'Justice, Efficiency, and the Economic Analysis of Law: A Comment on Fried" *The Journal of Legal Studies* 9: 355–66.

O'Driscoll, Gerald P., Jr., and Mario J. Rizzo. 1996 [1985]. *The Economics of Time and Ignorance*. New York: Routledge.

Ostrom, Elinor. 1990. *Governing the Commons: The Evolution of Institutions for Collective Action.* New York, NY: Cambridge University Press.

Posner, Richard A. (1998). "Creating a Legal Framework for Economic Development" *The World Bank Research Observer* 13(1): 1–11.

Posner, Richard A. 2007 [1972] *Economic Analysis of Law.* New York, NY: Aspen Publishers.

Rasmussen, Robert K. 1991. "The Efficiency of Chapter 11" *Bankruptcy Developments Law Journal* 8: 319.

Rauh Joshua and Luigi Zingales. 2009. "Bankruptcy is Best to Save GM" *The Economists' Voice* February 2009.

Rizzo, Mario. J. 1980. "Law Amid Flux: The Economics of Negligence and Strict Liability in Tort" *Journal of Legal Studies* 9: 291–318.

Roe Mark J. 1983. "Bankruptcy and Debt: A New Model for Corporate Reorganization" *Columbia Law Review* 83: 527–602.

Schwartz Alan. 1993. "Bankruptcy Workouts and Debt Contracts." *Journal of Law and Economics* 36: 595–632.

Stringham, Edward. 2001. "Kaldor-Hicks Efficiency and the Problem of Central Planning" *Quarterly Journal of Austrian Economics* 4(2): 41–50.

Tabb, Charles. 2002. *Bankruptcy Anthology*. Anderson Publishing Co.

Warren, Elizabeth. 1987, "Bankruptcy Policy" *University of Chicago Law Review* 54: 775–814.

Warren, Elizabeth. 1992. "The Untenable Case for Repeal of Chapter 11" *Yale Law Journal* 102: 437–79.

Warren, Elizabeth. 1993. "Bankruptcy Policymaking in an Imperfect World" *Michigan Law Review* 92: 336–87.

White, Michelle. J. 1994. "Corporate Bankruptcy as a Filtering Device: Chapter 11 Reorganizations and Out-of-Court restructurings" *Journal of Law, Economics and Organization* 10(2): 268–95.

Zingales, Luigi. 2008. "Plan B" *The Economists Voice*. October 2008.

Zywicki, Todd. J. 2000. "Rescuing Business: The Making of Corporate Bankruptcy Law in England and the United States" *Bankr. Dev. J.* 16: 361.

Zywicki, Todd. J. 2003. "The Past, Present, and Future of Bankruptcy Law in America" *Michigan L. Rev.* 101: 2016

Zywicki, Todd. J. 2006. Is Forum Shopping Corrupting America's Bankruptcy Courts?" *Georgetown Law Journal* 94(4): 1141–95.

Zywicki, Todd. J. 2008. "Bankruptcy Is the Perfect Remedy for Detroit" *Wall Street Journal*, December 16, 2008.

Zywicki, Todd. J. 2009. "Circuit City Unplugged: Did Chapter 11 Fail to Save 34,000 Jobs?" Hearing before the United States House of Representatives Committee on the Judiciary – Subcommittee on Commercial and Administrative Law accessed at http://mercatus.org/sites/default/files/publication/Zywicki_Testimony_on_Circuit_City_-_March_11,_2009.pdf.

18. Family law, uncertainty, and the coordination of human capital

Steven Horwitz

INTRODUCTION

It has become commonplace in economics to analyze the family in many of the same ways we analyze the firm and to bring to the study of marriage the same sorts of strategic bargaining tools we use in other situations requiring mutual cooperation. When Austrian-influenced economists look at marriage and family, they can bring to bear the same tools that Austrians use to look at the firm and bargaining. Austrians explore these issues with some different tools than the mainstream, particularly the Austrian theory of capital, which can be applied to both physical and human capital. The Austrian understanding of capital differs in important ways from standard theory and is able to provide additional insights into how firms, and therefore families, are formed and sustain themselves.

Both marriage and the family can be understood as structures of human capital formed in the face of uncertainty and intended to create an ongoing enterprise of cooperation to achieve a set of goals at lower cost than feasible alternatives. Complicating this process is the dual nature of families, or households more generally, in which the members both produce for the market to earn income and engage in household production such as childcare, cleaning, and cooking. In addition, we can think of household production as including the production of the leisure activities that the married couple or full family enjoy, especially together. Assuming that not all of those household wants can be satisfied by market alternatives, married couples have to be concerned about two kinds of human capital: what we might term "market human capital" and "household human capital." Successful marriages and families are ones in which this dual human capital structure is sufficiently complementary to enable the members to satisfy both sets of wants and generate income and output (including the subjective emotional and psychological benefits of married and familial life) that are superior to alternatives.

A law and economics analysis of marriage and the family from a broadly Austrian perspective would explore the ways in which the law facilitates or complicates the coordination process by which couples form marriages and decide on questions of market and household production, including issues related to the number of children and their care. Because Austrian economics assumes a world of uncertainty and disequilibrium, it tends to conceptualize market processes, as well as non-market human action and social coordination, as ongoing processes of discovery in a world of fallible actors with limited knowledge. In such a world, the challenge for law and economics is taking seriously what Rizzo (1980) terms the role of "law amid flux." From this perspective, the relationship between the law and human action is less about generating *efficiency* than it is about facilitating *coordination*. Starting with Hayek (1937), Austrians have emphasized the ways in which markets are about the coordination of human plans and the role played by prices and other social institutions in facilitating that coordination process by enabling actors to overcome the limitations to their individual knowledge. Social institutions, including the law, are, in the words of Ludwig Lachmann (1971: 50), "nodal points of society, coordinating the actions of millions whom they relieve of the need to acquire and digest detailed knowledge about others and form detailed expectations about their future action." In what follows, I will explore the ways in which several specific laws affect the attempts of marital partners and families more generally to coordinate their behavior and form complementary structures of human capital to accomplish both market and household production.

CAPITAL, HUMAN CAPITAL, MARRIAGE, AND FAMILY[1]

As noted above, an Austrian view of marriage and family rests on its understanding of capital. In general, the resources that are inputs into a production process, and the intermediate goods that are produced prior to the final product, are what Austrians call capital. In the broadest terms, decision makers of any kind form capital combinations in pursuit of gain, whether it be utility or profit or something else. Human plans take time to unfold to their expected results, therefore any process that involves inputs at one time being transformed into outputs at another time is assumed to take place in a world of fragmentary knowledge and structural uncertainty. Actors combine the resources they believe, in the face of limited knowledge, will be most suitable for producing the results they desire. This emphasis on the beliefs of the actors involved is crucial for understanding

---

[1]   The following section borrows heavily from Horwitz and Lewin (2008).

the ways in which these plans can fail. Austrians see all human plans as being our "best guesses" about what we think will unfold in the future and that, given uncertainty, those plans have a significant likelihood of failing. The analysis to follow focuses on the role played by the law in helping to reduce some of that uncertainty by providing an institutional node of coordination around which marriage and family decisions can be oriented.

In the minds of the producers, the production process of the firm is seen as an integrated and complementary capital structure. Each of the capital items is believed by the producers to fit with the others in a structure that will produce the desired output. This complementarity at the outset of the production process is referred to as an "individual equilibrium" with respect to the capital structure the firm has created and the plan it hopes to execute. Note that the equilibrium here is not with respect to the objective conditions, but rather refers to the relationship between the capital structure and the goal of the producers' plan.

Another key to the Austrian approach is the heterogeneity of capital resources. Capital goods are seen as being specific to a range of uses, with the degree of specificity varying across the economy. Capital is not understood as an undifferentiated, homogenous lump of stuff that can be shaped in whatever way the producer deems necessary and used in any production plan. The very complementarity of a firm's production plan depends upon its ability to fit together heterogeneous capital inputs into an integrated structure (Lachmann 1978 [1956]). Rather than conceiving of capital as a lump of "K," as is often the case in neoclassical models, Austrians see it as a series of jig-saw puzzle pieces that need to be fitted together by producers who are attempting to turn them into meaningful patterns that will generate their desired output.

This conception of capital applies to both human and non-human resources. In understanding marriage and the family, almost all that is true of non-human capital is equally true of human capital. We can conceptualize actors as producers of a structure of human capital that includes all of the various skills, knowledge, education, experience and the like that each has acquired over a lifetime. Choices about the skills and knowledge people acquire will differ, and therefore any attempt at an integrated production plan that includes human actors will have to take account of the heterogeneity of human capital. This is true whether the production plan is created by a firm or by individuals forming a household. Like firms, individuals also have to consider the gains and losses of the particular human capital investments they make, and these will be *expected* gains and losses as individuals investing in human capital will face the same sort of uncertainty faced by market entrepreneurs investing in physical capital. The Austrian perspective on human capital allows us to view a marriage (and by implication, a family) as "an attempt to create an integrated structure of human capital within a household that is consistent with the plan the couple has to engage in the market and household production necessary to sustain the household" (Horwitz and Lewin 2008: 5). That household's plan can either succeed over time or fail, just as in a firm.

Because marriage and family involve both production for the market and the household, we can distinguish between two relevant types of human capital: (labor) *market-oriented* human capital and *household-oriented* human capital. Market-oriented human capital (MHC) refers to human capital whose value is realized in the labor market rather than the household. As with standard analyses, MHC can be either general or more firm-specific. Such human capital is directed toward earning income, so its relevance to household production is typically minimal. Household-oriented human capital (HHC), on the other hand, is primarily about direct household production. The most obvious and important type of HHC is the set of skills associated with childcare, but skills for house cleaning, gardening, laundry, car-pooling, cooking and the like are also relevant. HHC also contributes to the production of joint leisure activities. Given that any form of human capital accumulation takes time and effort, and therefore involves an opportunity cost, if one chooses to specialize in household production, one is necessarily specializing in the accumulation of specific kinds of human capital. Because the household as a production unit requires inputs in the form of both market-earned income and household human capital, most of human history has seen household members specialize in one or the other, with men in the labor market and women in the household as the historically most common combination in the industrial world.

The source of this specialization may follow actual or perceived comparative advantages. For example, if people believe that women have a comparative advantage in childcare, then perhaps biologically-endowed very small differences in comparative advantage may, through the accumulation of specific human capital, become magnified over time as human capital accumulation is subject to increasing returns via learning by doing (Becker 1981). Some HHC is also "marriage specific" in that it has more value inside a particular marriage than outside of it. That is, like MHC, HHC may be specialized to a particular household (i.e., it is *relationship or marriage-specific*) or it may be more generally applicable. (See Figure 18.1 below.)

One implication of this framework is that human capital investments by marital partners will depend on their expectations of the duration of the marriage. A marriage that ends unexpectedly, perhaps because of early death of either spouse or because of an increased likelihood of divorce

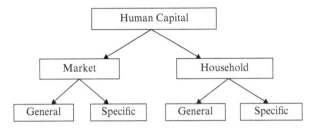

Figure 18.1   Types of human capital (Horwitz and Lewin 2008: 7)

as the marriage unfolds, will shorten the payoff period for human capital investments and increases the likelihood of a "capital loss" from the accumulation of HHC and especially marriage-specific human capital. Thus anything that engenders the expectation of a higher probability of marital dissolution is likely to reduce the accumulation of HHC. This process is enhanced by the falling gains from specialization in the household due to the increasing similarity of the human capital, both market and household, possessed by men and women.

At the core of the family is the marital dyad. One way of understanding a marriage is as a complementary human capital combination that enables the pair to accomplish both market and household production with a division of labor that each finds satisfactory. What sorts of combinations will be the most complementary will depend both on the human capital of the prospective marital partners and their preferences about market income and what they wish to produce in the household. For example, a marital dyad in which neither member wishes to have children will require a very different set of complementary human capital than one in which children are desired and the couple believes one parent should largely specialize in household production. As with a firm, the ideal complementary capital structure depends on what the production goal is.

Historically, the distinction between market and household production was much less stark than it has been in the last 200 years. Before the widespread use of wage labor, the household itself was the site of both household production and market production. The omnipresence of poverty also meant that income-producing concerns had to take precedence over all else, so most marriages had to pay more attention to income-producing human capital rather than more precise household-oriented human capital. In our own era, two things have changed. First, shrinking family size, better household technology, and more wealth to purchase market alternatives have led to a reduction in the gains from specialization in marriage. Although couples still must have complementarity, it is less often the case that pure specialization is the optimal pattern. Second, as households have changed from sites of market production to predominantly consumption and household production, the complementarity of the household human capital of married couples has become more about complementarities in their consumption activities. For example, do both have skills and preferences with respect to the same leisure activities? This is an outgrowth of the declining benefits of production-oriented specialization.[2]

Unlike the firm, the family does not have an unambiguous measure of success or failure such as profit and loss. At the most basic level, the continuation of a marriage indicates that it is being successful at some portion of its plan, even if it is staying together in the belief that doing so best serves the children. Their successful upbringing is often a central part of the plan. On the down side, divorce is clear evidence of plan failure. The failure reflects costs in excess of benefits, but can be due to either the couple exhausting the benefits of their relationship or some change that raises the costs, or both. In either case, on the assumption that the plan was understood as an indefinite one, divorce is a form of plan failure. Because plan failure is linked to the reliability of expectations, a complete Austrian understanding of marriage and family would have to explore the ways in which such expectations are formed and the role that particular institutions play in assisting that process. In examining the law and economics of the family, we can narrow that exploration to several legal rules that affect the family formation process and the ways in which human capital is accumulated and labor is divided within the family. Seen in this light, the law is crucial to the process by which families are formed and succeed as ongoing enterprises through the effect the law has on the accumulation of the various types of human capital and the formation of plans based on complementarities in the structure of the human capital of marital partners.

CUSTODY DECISIONS AND HUMAN CAPITAL ACCUMULATION

One way in which the law influences marriage and family decisions is through the preference for maternal custody of the children of divorce. Because women are more likely to end up with physical custody of the children if there is a divorce, they face stronger incentives to accumulate the kinds of human capital that will ensure they are able to cope with that

---

[2]   See the more extensive discussion of these issues in Horwitz (2015, Chs 4 and 5).

outcome.[3] There will be a strong incentive to accumulate more HHC on the margin as single parenthood will likely require more of their time in those activities. Even a single parent who can afford to pay for child care still must care for the children after the work day, and childcare is often quite "relationship specific." Spending the time to get to know one's children and how they behave and react is often the only way to do the job sufficiently well. The problem here is that the preference for maternal custody ends up weakening the bargaining positions of women facing divorce, which feeds back to make divorce more likely in the first place.

The majority of divorces happen within the first five to ten years of marriage, with the years after the kids leave the house being the second most common time. If one assumes that when men and women enter a marriage they consider what might happen if they get divorced, particularly if they have or plan to have children, we can see the effects of the preference for maternal custody on human capital. One result is that it strengthens the husband's bargaining power with respect to the division of labor within the household, which therefore affects each person's investment in HHC.

Consider the challenge that the possibility of divorce combined with single parenthood poses for women. On the one hand, women in marriages where the possibility of divorce is growing have an incentive to accumulate more MHC in order to ensure their ability to provide for the kids should divorce occur. On the other hand, having the majority of the physical custody of the kids would mean more time devoted to household production, creating an incentive to accumulate more HHC than they might have done in the absence of the rising risk of divorce. By implication, this also suggests that married men with children who see a divorce as increasingly likely have *less* incentive to engage in household production if they are assuming, as is likely to be the case, that the wife will get physical custody of the children. The dual pull of reasons to accumulate more of both types of human capital creates a significant time squeeze for women, as they do not wish to give up income but also see the relative burden of housework shifting in their direction at the same time. This process will take place in both individual marriages where the risk of divorce rises and across marriages in general as the overall divorce rate remains relatively high.

To the extent this is an accurate description of the process, two self-reinforcing results emerge as women end up with more HHC than they might ideally wish to have. First, it can exacerbate existing tensions in the

---

    [3]   Note that it is physical custody not legal custody that matters here. It is time spent with the children that matters for the human capital issues.

marriage, thereby further increasing the likelihood of divorce, which will thereby reinforce the rationale for acquiring more HHC. From an Austrian perspective, these endogenous processes can undermine the complementarity of the human capital combination on which the marriage was based. One small exogenous shift in the health of the relationship that increases the possibility of divorce can trigger an endogenous response that widens that crack to the point of undermining the complementarity of the whole joint structure of production that comprises the marriage. For example, as men, in response to some exogenous increase in marital tension, begin to shirk (perhaps rationally) household production and the burden shifts towards women, their shirking can be a source of discord independent of whatever exogenous factors raised the likelihood of divorce in the first place. As men shirk and women pick up more of the household production, and as this also puts an increasing strain on women's time as they do not wish to give up on market production, what once seemed a complementary structure of human capital now looks less so, as women become increasingly frustrated with the shift in the burden of housework.

If we imagine marriage as a plan based on expectations of future problems to be solved and an imagined structure of human capital to solve them, should the actual structure of human capital not turn out as expected and/or be unable to meet the needs of both partners and the family as a unit, we clearly have plan failure and the household equivalent of losses to a firm.

The second self-reinforcing piece of this process is the way in which the expectation of maternal custody after divorce leads women to accumulate more HHC than they might otherwise, which in turn makes them appear to be the better parent and reinforces the preference for maternal custody. Consider the couple going through difficulties and getting caught up in this process. The wife begins to take on more of the childcare and other household production, and the husband begins to shirk. When the court makes a decision on custody as part of the divorce, the wife will look like the better choice even though at an earlier time, the decision might have been more difficult. Thanks to the expectation of maternal custody, the incentive to accumulate HHC, especially the relationship-specific sort associated with childcare, leads to women appearing to be the better custody choice even though that may be largely a by-product of the expectation that they will get custody rather than longer-term human capital considerations. The result is that the expectation of maternal custody is self-reinforcing, which creates a challenge getting at whether or not it is a valid expectation. The expectation of maternal custody that has become part of the legal regime surrounding divorce can generate these self-reinforcing endogenous processes that erode the complementary human capital structures that are necessary for the coordination process that generates marital and familial success.

Is there a way out through side payments? One thought might be that larger child support payments by husbands, or better enforcement of existing arrangements, might mitigate matters. Such a strategy might reduce the incentive for women facing a potential divorce to accumulate MHC, but it would not address the dynamic through which household production shifts toward the woman. In fact, larger support payments could make that problem worse by encouraging women to accumulate even *more* HHC knowing that larger support payments would enable them to maintain their standard of living without accumulating as much new MHC as they would need without such payments. Despite the fact that an increase in the probability of divorce will lead women to increase their labor force participation rates or their work hours, their human capital structure will still tend to be less market-oriented than men's on average. To the degree that the cultural expectation is that household production is still more women's work than men's, and to the degree that the expectation of maternal custody after a divorce is still dominant, women's MHC will also likely be more general and less specific than that of their husbands. This is because a more specific structure would require more time to build up, the opportunity cost of which is the HHC that remains valuable thanks to the cultural expectations. The way the human capital structures that can emerge between the genders make the coordination of expectations more difficult, and thereby make divorce ("plan failure") more likely, is clearly affected by the interaction between these cultural expectations and the legal regime surrounding divorce and custody.

THE LAW AND ECONOMICS OF THE "SECOND SHIFT"

Looking at these issues through Austrian economics provides a different take on a problem that comes out of the sociology literature. The difference between men's and women's contributions to household production has narrowed in recent years, but not to the same degree as the way the gap between their work in the market has. Even as women have pulled much closer to equality with men in the market, there remains a larger gap between their contributions in the household. This is often termed the problem of the "second shift" (Hochschild 1989). Imagine a married couple with kids where both mom and dad work in the market. They come home after work and face the "second shift" of household production.

Dinner must get made, kids must be cared for, the house must be cleaned, lunches must be made for the next day, laundry may need to be done, and so forth. The data continue to indicate that the second shift is disproportionately born by women, even in dual-income marriages. Just as an example, married men in 1965 spent 4.5 hours per week on housework while their wives averaged 31.6. In 2004, those numbers were 10.9 and 19.0 hours (Jacobsen 2007: 111). The second shift has become more equal but the difference is still significantly wider than the gender earnings gap where women average close to 80 percent of male wages.

Although sociologists and gender theorists explain this phenomenon in terms of the stubbornness of gender norms and the lower status household production has in comparison to market production, economists might offer an additional explanation. The puzzle for economists is that theory explained men's historic lack of contribution to household production (and their corresponding lack of HHC) as the result of their opportunity costs in terms of market wages being significantly higher than that of their wives. Now that wages are far more equal, the opportunity costs would seem to be equal, yet we do not see the same equalization of contributions to household production.[4] The prior discussion of custody and human capital is a possible answer to that puzzle. If the legal regime surrounding divorce and custody does indeed combine with cultural expectations and a high divorce rate to produce both the expectation of maternal custody and the feedback effects on male and female contributions to household production as argued above, then it might explain the persistence of the inequality of the second shift. These factors would operate as countervailing force, in the aggregate, to the traditional opportunity cost argument's equalizing effect.

Consider the effects of the divorce/custody legal regime on the wife's labor market decisions if she senses a divorce is more likely in a marriage that involves children. She would, as argued earlier, have reason to increase her MHC, but not specific types of MHC that have a large opportunity cost in terms of household production, which is also more important than it used to be. She might opt for less time-intensive investments in general forms of MHC (e.g., clerical skills or finishing a college degree). This also makes sense because a single mother would be more likely to look for jobs that have flexible scheduling and other

---

[4]   In fact, over 40 years ago, McKenzie and Tullock (1975) flat-out predicted that the trend of more equal wages between men and women would, or at least should, lead to a leveling of the opportunity costs and more equal contributions to household production. So far anyway, that prediction has not come true.

compensating differentials that enable her to balance home and work. Such jobs are normally ones that require the more general kinds of market-oriented human capital.[5]

On the male side, the incentives are consistent with the previous story. Given the expectation of maternal custody, the husband's loss from a divorce is likely to be less than that of his wife.[6] If husbands are correct in assuming they will not have to engage in nearly as much child-related household production as their ex-wives will after a divorce, there is no reason to invest much in HHC as the marriage begins to deteriorate, if not before.[7] This process can be at work even in marriages that do not end in divorce.[8] The high rate of divorce and asymmetry in custody awards puts women in a weaker bargaining position when it comes to trying to enforce norms of equality in household production. If women are frustrated by the lack of household production by their husbands, it is not clear what leverage, other than moral suasion, they can use to change matters. If divorce is realistically on the table, men can hold out longer because the costs of plan failure are more likely to be less for them than for women due to the likelihood of maternal custody. If divorce is not on the table, the result can be women living with a higher burden of the household production than they expected or might have in a world with fewer divorces and/or a more even split in how custody is awarded. Her higher than expected contribution to the second shift happens even as her husband is likely to be working fewer hours in the labor market than his father was.[9] It is not just the actuality of divorce but its higher average probability combined with the expectation of maternal custody that generates the second shift imbalances that sociologists have pointed to.

---

[5]   Technological advances that make telecommuting for jobs with more specific MHC more feasible might change this argument.

[6]   Husbands who prefer custody, however, could experience substantial losses and might outweigh other cost savings. See Grossbard-Schechtman and Lemennicier (1999) for more on scenarios like this one.

[7]   Divorced men living alone might also not have to engage in other kinds of household production as well. The movie stereotype of the divorced father living alone in a messy apartment serving his kids takeouts during the times he has custody makes sense from this perspective.

[8]   See the "separate spheres" non-cooperative bargaining model of Lundberg and Pollak (1993).

[9]   Jacobsen (2007: 98–104) provides data on the decline in men's labor force participation at different age groups, and Cox and Alm (1999: 55) describe the decline in the average length of the work day, week, year, and lifetime.

NO-FAULT DIVORCE

One of the most discussed legal institutions with important economic effects on the family is no-fault divorce. Perhaps better called "divorce by unilateral demand," no-fault divorce statutes allow either party to a marriage to initiate divorce proceedings for whatever reason he or she wishes. Unlike years past, there is no need to argue that the other party is somehow at fault for causing problems that necessitate the divorce. Either party can exit the marriage contract simply because the relationship is no longer desired. No-fault divorce matters for the situation described in the previous section.

Is the lack of leverage women have somehow remediable? Could not husband and wife anticipate these inequities and contract around them? A premarital payment (a bride price) for example to the wife (or her family) might serve this purpose, or the marriage contract may incorporate the contingency of divorce and specify payments between the parties in proportion to their contribution to the human capital of the family as a unit *and according to who is judged to be at fault*, thus providing a disincentive for opportunism (see, for example, Rowthorn 1999: 670ff). To the extent that this is possible (and it may be only to a limited extent owing to the intrinsic incompleteness of contracts in a world of structural uncertainty), it will tend to encourage increased specialization in either household or market production, since it reduces the risk of divorce and the perils (to either spouse) of being locked into an unprofitable human capital structure. However, the advent of no-fault divorce has raised the risks of divorce and put a greater burden on prior contracts to safeguard the financial position of the abandoned spouse, thus explaining the rise in the use of pre-nuptial agreements in the no-fault era.

There is some disagreement on the effects of the introduction of no-fault divorce.[10] A complete contracting model would suggest that the parties would contract around any such effects in the long run through side payments. Thus a spouse contemplating abandoning the marriage may be deterred from doing so by a contract that divided the spoils according to the relative contributions to the net-worth of the marriage by either spouse.[11] The classic case is that of a husband whose wife's earnings has put him through medical school early in the marriage and who then

---

[10] See Parkman (2000) for a book-length economic critique of no-fault.

[11] As Grossbard-Schechtman and Lemennicier (1999) point out, the calculation of such 'net worth' is inherently problematic. Husband and wife will most likely have quite different estimates, as such estimates are based on different expectations and costs that are subjective in nature.

leaves her for another woman (Cohen 1987; Grossbard-Schechtman and Lemennicier 1999). Should the husband be liable to compensate the wife for her contribution to his human capital investment, including the long-term earnings she has forgone by not accumulating extra market-oriented human capital (as she was working and could not continue her education)? A suitable contract would negate the effects of a no-fault law by requiring a degree of compensation that would, in effect, transform it into a consensual divorce (as would be predicted by the Coase Theorem). Thus there would be no long-term effect on the incidence of divorce from the introduction of a no-fault divorce system and the abandonment of a consensual one. In the short-term one would expect a bump in the divorce rate as some spouses took advantage of the new law which had not been anticipated in the marriage contract. In a world of structural uncertainty, however, such complete contracts are difficult to imagine.

The evidence on the effects of no-fault on the divorce rate is mixed (see Peters 1992 and Allen 1998 for opposing views), but seems to support the case for a positive effect on the divorce rate (see the survey by Rowthorn 1999: 671–8, also Parkman 1998). This evidence suggests that such effects also cannot be contracted around because of transactions costs and an extreme reluctance or impossibility of taking fault into account in divorce settlements. The move to no-fault was a reaction to couples having to either fake "faults" to get a divorce, or engage in costly monitoring of each other's behavior to prove fault at the time of the divorce. No-fault was a clear transactions-cost reducer. However, rather than being an exogenous cause of a reduction in the permanence of marriages, it was more likely an endogenous result of changes in the institution. By the 1950s and 60s, Western marriage had completed its transformation from a primarily economic (and before that, political) institution, to one centered around human happiness and psychological/emotional goals (Coontz 2005). As a result, marital partners, especially women, wanted out for reasons beyond the canonical "abuse, adultery, and abandonment." They wanted to leave because they simply were not happy. No-fault was the endogenous response of legal institutions to this change in the institution of marriage as the prior regime made it more difficult for people to, in this case, act to get out of a failed marriage that reflected a failed marital human capital structure. The legal change has, however, opened the possibility of the sort of opportunistic behavior noted above, which in turn has reduced further the benefits of marriage.

If one thinks of marriage as, at least in part, a contractual obligation, it is perhaps surprising that no-fault divorce as a norm would gain wide acceptance. Contractual obligations in general are, after all, predicated on the ideas of performance and responsibility, with penalties for default.

This is an important basis for a free and stable society based on market transactions. It is not clear why one would think a marriage contract to be so different as not to fulfill a similar purpose. Without the expectation of performance and responsibility, as Rowthorn (1999: 663) has remarked, it becomes difficult for the parties to make credible commitments to each other, which discourages the type of investments that make marriage attractive and durable. If partners to a marriage cannot be assured that the other will live up to the terms of the contract, they are less likely to invest in the sorts of relationship-specific forms of human capital that are necessary to sustain the marriage and the larger family that might result. The analogies to the firm make some sense here: only where employees believe that their relationship with a firm will be ongoing will they be willing to invest in firm-specific forms of human capital.[12] Such investments must be undertaken in an environment that promises a continuing relationship because firm-specific human capital investments make employees less marketable outside the firm.

Yet even within the context of the firm, we generally do not restrict the right of employees to "unilaterally file for divorce for no reason" by quitting their jobs. Though less true of the ability of employers to fire employees, the right to break an employment contract without much of a reason remains largely the law of the land. The challenge for firms is how best to encourage employees to make the firm-specific investments necessary to be productive even as at-will employees know they can be fired at almost any time. Both sides of the labor market face uncertainties about the longevity of the relationship, so finding ways to signal longer-term commitment become crucial. Credibility of promises that both parties make will matter a great deal, but there are institutional solutions, such as a firm's willingness to pay for training or education. This signals to employees that the firm intends to reap the benefits of that investment by continuing the employment relationship on into the future.

In an environment where the probability of divorce is greater, marital partners have less incentive to do the very things necessary to sustain the marriage. Of course when divorce was costlier, the corresponding reduction in uncertainty about the future of the relationship meant that relationship-specific investments would have a more certain payoff, but in another sense were less necessary, especially for men who held more power in the relationship. With both parties being able to exit in a no-fault

---

[12] Such analogies can be pushed much further, for example, in fruitfully considering the relationship between spouses to be closely analogous to the relationship between employer and employee (Grossbard-Schechtman 1993).

regime, though with women still generally at a disadvantage, the question of how to make credible commitments in a world of uncertainty becomes a framework through which Austrians might choose to analyze the dynamics of modern marriage and their relationship to changes in the divorce rate.

With rising economic opportunities for women and increased market substitutes for household production reducing the net gains from marriage, perhaps the weakening of the ability of partners to make credible commitments to each other might not be quite so problematic as it would have been a couple of generations ago. One way in which the marital contract differs from others is that the parties to the contract may well have legal obligations to third parties that emerge from the contractual relationship (e.g., children). In the current environment, opting out of the marriage contract might be relatively costless for the contracting parties, but might have high costs for the children they are raising. No-fault divorce might well have been an understandable outcome of changes in the institution of marriage in terms of the preferences of husbands and wives, but the impact on children is not so clearly neutral.

The incentives created by no-fault do not necessarily apply only to the case of women afraid of being abandoned. Such a law may result in overly generous divorce settlements to the party who is primarily responsible for the break-up of the marriage. If there are children involved, and women are most likely to receive custody, the husband may find himself "deprived of his family home and paying a large part of his income to support a family from which he has been effectively expelled. . .[M]en will [thus plausibly] become increasingly mistrustful. . . . Any system which makes generous, unconditional awards following divorce is inviting abuse" (Rowthorn 1999: 671).

Rowthorn notes a legal initiative that attempts to give couples the choice to make marriage a more binding contract. In the late 1990s, the state of Louisiana introduced a twin-track system allowing couples to choose the kind of marriage they wanted. One type allows speedy, unilateral, no-fault divorce; the other is "covenant" marriage, which is harder to terminate and for which speedy divorce is only available in the case of fault at the request of the injured party. The definition of fault is narrowly drawn, and couples can convert from no-fault to covenant marriage, but the reverse is not allowed. This form of marriage is now an option in the states of Arizona, Arkansas, and Kansas as well. In Louisiana, the percentage of couples taking this option has been consistently around 1 percent, with the other states being even lower.[13] Given the prior discussion, it seems clear that

---

[13]   See the discussion and data here: http://marriage.about.com/cs/covenantmarri age/a/covenant_3.htm.

couples desire the flexibility of current no-fault divorce law, even though it might work to the pecuniary disadvantage of women and create problems for children. Again, there may well be strong nonpecuniary reasons that women wish to be able to leave marriages with the fewest transaction costs possible.

Finally, one might view no-fault as the solution to a different uncertainty problem. As I have argued, marriages are often best viewed as attempts to create complementary human capital inputs into the household and market production processes that comprise a family. Just as entrepreneurs who try to bring together physical and human capital face uncertainty over whether the combination of inputs they have chosen will be profitable, so do potential marriage partners face uncertainty about whether their human capital is as complementary as they believe, and *whether it will remain that way for the indefinite future*. One explanation for the increase in divorce rates that took place in the 1970s and 80s is that there were a number of marriages that were formed in the 1960s and 70s in which the partners faced increasing uncertainty about each other. The increased uncertainty led to incorrect expectations about the complementarity of their human capital and thereby created the plan failure we know as divorce.

Specifically, the change in gender roles starting in the 1960s had two implications. First, it was harder for men to know what to expect from prospective female partners with respect to their preferences about market and household production. Signals in the marriage market became very noisy and new ways of making clear what a prospective partner was "really like," or would be like in the future, had yet to really emerge. A consequence was that more marriages were likely to involve mismatched human capital thanks to the noisy signals. The second problem was that women *themselves* often guessed wrong about what they would be doing later in life. Survey data indicates that in the late 60s, only a minority of college-aged women expected to be in the labor force at age 35, but that a strong majority of those same women were, in fact, employed when they did reach 35. Their inaccurate expectations of their own future often led to underinvestments in human capital and partially explains the gender wage gap. These data also suggest that some marriages ended up with two working spouses despite the fact that neither one expected, or perhaps desired, that outcome. That mismatched structure of human capital might certainly threaten the sustainability of the marriage and be a contributor to rising divorce rates.

No-fault divorce can be seen as an effective institutional adaptation to this situation. With more bad matches happening thanks to the greater uncertainty, it would not be surprising to see a desire to reduce the cost of exiting failing marriages. No-fault has its drawbacks as I have noted, but the advantages of lower exit costs in a period of uncertainty would have been significant.

In the last decade or two, divorce rates have stabilized and there is evidence that among younger cohorts the rate is falling. The marriage rate has also fallen, suggesting that what we are getting these days are fewer, but better, marriages. As the revolution in gender roles has settled into more predictable patterns and younger people have figured out how to more clearly signal what they expect from a marriage, and women have formed more accurate expectations of their own future, the result may well be more sustainable combinations of human capital in the marriage market. This shift might also explain increased skepticism about no-fault. There have been some calls for moving away from unilateral divorce to a regime of mutual consent. Mutual consent would restore bargaining power to the weaker party even as it raised the costs of exit. With fewer but better marriages thanks to reduced uncertainty, a less open-ended divorce process might now be the more effective way for legal institutions to lead to more coordinated expectations.

MULTI-PARENT FAMILIES

One other issue facing the family that can be understood from a broadly Austrian perspective is how to deal with the large number of children who find themselves in families with more than two parents, thanks mostly to divorce and remarriage.[14] Until divorce became prevalent within the last 40 to 50 years, it made sense for the law and social institutions in general to map closely to the facts of biology and enshrine the idea of two parents as norm. The law, of course, has always recognized the possibility of single parenthood through death and has had ways of dealing with the remarriage of widows and widowers. However, even where children were present, this did not open up the possibility of more than two living persons with claims to functioning as a parent.[15] In a world of frequent divorce and remarriage, many children find themselves living in two different homes, each of which might have a married couple at the head of it, opening up

---

[14]   I leave out, for purposes of brevity, other types of families with more than two parents—such as adoptive parents, surrogate parents, and the biological parents of children of same-sex couples. I also ignore the possibility of plural marriage. Some or much of what I argue below might apply in those cases, but they raise other complications that are beyond the scope of this chapter.

[15]   On the relationship between the functions of the family and its form, see Horwitz (2005).

the possibility of as many as four people who are functioning as the child's parents.

The problem in these situations is that there can be adults engaged in the activities of parenting who the law does not recognize as having any sort of parental rights. The step-mother who disciplines a young child, or takes her to school or a doctor's appointment, is acting as a parent though she may have no legal rights with respect to her husband's child from his first marriage. Even something as simple as signing a permission slip for school can get very complicated if there are multiple households and more than two parents. One can also imagine the complications if a child gets sick with only the step-parent at home. In these kinds of situations, there are two related problems: 1) significant uncertainty about who is able to engage in what sorts of parental activities; and 2) higher transactions costs of dealing with problems as they arise (e.g., having to create medical care proxy or consent forms). The law as it stands in most states does not provide easy ways to solve these problems.[16]

Much recent Austrian research has focused on the endogeneity of legal and social norms.[17] Where earlier work looked at the way the spontaneous order of the market and other social processes depended crucially on the nature of the framing institutions such as the monetary system and the law, this more recent work is asking whether those framing institutions themselves are also the products of unplanned evolutionary processes and, if so, might we get better institutions than if we tried to design them.[18] If framing institutions work better when they are also the product of bottom-up evolutionary processes, it is because they are thereby able to evolve as the specific contexts for which they are problem-solvers change. Even as existing law might have been effective in a world where divorce and remarriage was rare, such law might need to change in response to changes in family structure.

A number of proposals for addressing things like the role of step-parents

---

[16]   Bailey (2015) reports on changes in the law in California in 2013 that recognized that there might be more than two people who meet the state's existing definition of a parent. It's important to note that this change did not include, for example, step-parents into the definition of a parent. Rather it simply allowed that there may be cases where more than two people meet the already existing definition. What I am suggesting in the text is the more radical idea that we should consider changing how we understand what a parent is by recognizing that de facto parenting behavior might be worth protecting with some types of parental rights. See the discussion to follow.

[17]   See, for example, Stringham and Zywicki (2011) and the references therein, as well as Boettke (2011).

[18]   See Horwitz (1998) on the relationship between "external" framing institutions and "internal" ones.

challenge the assumption that there must be no more than two parents. Most of these open the box of parental rights to more than two parents, often to parallel the way the law already recognizes the complexity of custody arrangements. The way these proposals do so is strikingly similar to the way in which Austrians and other economists have talked about property rights. Rather than view the right to a piece of property as a singular, undifferentiated "thing," the more recent perspective sees a property right as a bundle of different rights that get put together in different configurations under different circumstances. Some property rights include the ability to use the property in ways that others do not. Such limits might be negotiated by parties to a contract, but others might inhere in the specific piece of property, or the type of property, itself thanks to years of evolved case law. We can also note the way in which the work of Elinor Ostrom (1990) suggests that institutions that look like private property in a number of ways, but not all, can often be an effective means for dealing with common pool resources. "Property rights" may not entail the identical set of specific rights and obligations in all circumstances. We can separate, for example, certain kinds of use rights, some of which may not be part of any given bundle of property rights. Once the right of private property is understood as a set of specific rights bundled together, we can discover more effective ways the law might fine-tune those bundles to the particular problem the rights are attempting to solve.

The argument for opening up parental rights to more than two persons is analogous. Parental rights, like property rights, are best seen as a bundle of specific rights that parents have with respect to their minor children. In much of the law now, the assumption is that there are two parents both of whom have pretty much the same set of rights. However, one can imagine challenging both of those assumptions. With three or four adults all of whom have some responsibility for a child, why not extend some number of the rights bundled in what we now call parental rights to the non-biological or non-adoptive parents? If law helps reduce transaction costs of interaction, refusing to extend at least some parental rights beyond two parents makes for more complicated and costly interactions among those concerned with the welfare of the child. Such legal changes might also reduce the costs imposed on children in a regime of no-fault divorce. If law, like other institutions, evolves endogenously in response to changes in the external environment for which it serves as a coordination process, then as the problems change, so should the law. This is the sort of change in the law a small number of states have recently adopted.[19]

---

[19]   See the discussion in note 16.

A more radical, and perhaps more effective change, would be to not just expand the number of parents, but to unbundle the rights. There is no reason that a step-parent could not have the right to make decisions about health care or sign a school permission slip, without necessarily having other sorts of parental rights, or even the same financial obligations, as the biological parents. Courts already divide up custody agreements in all kinds of creative ways, so what is to stop the law from recognizing that some rights might best belong to more than two parents, but others not? The American Bar Association has drafted model legislation on how such arrangements might work, and similar schemes are already practice in places in Europe. Here too, if social institutions like the law are not just frameworks for the emergence of spontaneous order, but also themselves emergent phenomena that respond to changes in the way in which humans interact, it should not surprise us that the greater prevalence of multi-parent families might call forth the need for the law to evolve in response.

CONCLUSION

Looking at the law and economics of the family through the eyes of the Austrian school helps us to see two key points of analysis that other approaches might overlook. First, Austrians understand the role played by the law as a node of social coordination in a world of uncertainty. The law helps actors to formulate more accurate expectations of the actions of others and thereby promotes social cooperation and coordination. The law, therefore, needs to be a solution to, and not a cause of, uncertainty. This perspective illustrates how the challenges facing modern marriage and the family, especially those concerning divorce, are driven by the way the law frames people's ability to overcome uncertainty and achieve cooperation and coordination. In particular, a recent Austrian scholarship on the endogenous generation of rules, including the law, can help to see how the law can, and often must, change in response to new coordination problems.

Second, the Austrian understanding of capital, including human capital, sheds light on what makes for a sustainable marital partnership and provides a way of describing in more detail the nature of the coordination problem marriage involves. To the degree that the law facilitates rather than complicates the creation of complementary human capital structures between marital partners, it will contribute to better marriages and fewer divorces. Marriage and family, like business ventures, are voyages into the unknown that will work best when the surrounding institutions facilitate good signaling processes that help people coordinate in the face of that uncertainty. Looking the contemporary family through that lens sheds new light on both new and old problems.

REFERENCES

Allen, D.W. 1998. "No-fault Divorce in Canada: Its Cause and Effect," *Journal of Economic Behavior and Organizations* 37: 129–49.
Bailey. R. 2015. "A Baby with Five Parents? It's No Big Deal," *Hit and Run* weblog, August 5, available at http://reason.com/blog/2015/08/05/a-baby-with-five-parents-its-no-big-deal.
Becker, G.S. 1981. *A Treatise on the Family*, Cambridge, MA: Harvard University Press.
Boettke, P.J. 2011. "Anarchism and Austrian Economics." *New Perspectives on Political Economy* 7: 125–40.
Cohen, L. 1987. "Marriage, Divorce, and Quasi-Rents; or, 'I Gave Him the Best Years of My Life'," *Journal of Legal Studies* 16: 267–303.
Coontz, S. 2005. *Marriage, a History: From Obedience to Intimacy or How Love Conquered Marriage*, New York, NY: Viking.
Cox, W.M. and R. Alm. 1999. *Myths of Rich and Poor: Why We're Better Off Than We Think*, New York: Basic Books.
Grossbard-Schechtman, S.A. 1993. *On the Economics of Marriage: A Theory of Marriage, Labor, and Divorce*, Boulder, CO: Westview Press.
Grossbard-Schechtman, S.A. and B. Lemennicier. 1999. "Marriage Contracts and the Law-and-Economics of Marriage: an Austrian Perspective," *Journal of Socio-Economics* 28: 665–90.
Hayek, F.A. 1937. "Economics and Knowledge," reprinted in *Individualism and Economic Order*, Chicago: University of Chicago Press, 1948.
Hochschild, A.R. 1989. *The Second Shift*, New York, NY: Avon.
Horwitz, S. 1998. "Hierarchical Metaphors in Austrian Institutionalism: A Friendly Subjectivist Caveat," in *Methodological Issues in the Subjectivist Paradigm: Essays in Memory of Ludwig Lachmann*, Roger Koppl and Gary Mongiovi, eds, New York, NY: Routledge.
Horwitz, S. 2005. "The Functions of the Family in the Great Society," *Cambridge Journal of Economics* 29: 669–84.
Horwitz, S. 2015. *Hayek's Modern Family: Classical Liberalism and the Evolution of Social Institutions*, New York, NY: Palgrave Macmillan.
Horwitz, S. and P. Lewin. 2008. "Heterogeneous Human Capital, Uncertainty, and the Structure of Plans: A Market Process Approach to Marriage and Divorce," *Review of Austrian Economics* 21: 1–21.
Jacobsen, J.P. 2007. *The Economics of Gender*, 3rd ed., Malden, MA: Blackwell.
Lachmann, L.M. 1971. *The Legacy of Max Weber*, Berkeley, CA: The Glendessary Press.
Lachmann, L.M. 1978 [1956]. *Capital and Its Structure*, Kansas City, MO: Sheed Andrews and McMeel.
Lundberg, S. and R.A. Pollak. 1993. "Separate Spheres Bargaining and the Marriage Market," *Journal of Political Economy* 101: 988–1010.
McKenzie, R. and G. Tullock. 1975. *The New World of Economics*, Homewood, IL: Richard Irwin.
Ostrom, E. 1990. *Governing the Commons*, Cambridge: Cambridge University Press.
Parkman, A. 1998. "Unilateral Divorce and the Labor-Force Participation Rate of Married Women, Revisited," *American Economic Review* 88: 671–8.
Parkman, A. 2000. *Good Intentions Gone Awry*, Lanham, MD: Rowman and Littlefield.
Peters., E. 1992. "Marriage and Divorce: Reply," *American Economic Review* 82: 686–91.

Rizzo, M. 1980. "Law Amid Flux: The Economics of Negligence and Strict Liability in Tort," *The Journal of Legal Studies* 9: 291–318.

Rowthorn, R. 1999. "Marriage and Trust: Some Lessons from Economics," *Cambridge Journal of Economics* 23: 661–91.

Stringham, E. and T. Zywicki. 2011."Hayekian Anarchism," *Journal of Economic Behavior & Organization* 78: 290–301.

PART V

CONCLUSION

19. Conclusion: the future of "Austrian" law and economics

Peter J. Boettke and Todd J. Zywicki

The future of "Austrian" law and economics is informed and draws its inspirations from past methodological battles faced by the Austrian School in its development. The Austrian School of Economics was embroiled in several famous debates in the history of economic thought and methodology throughout the 19th and 20th century:

(1) The *methodenstreit* between Menger and the German Historical School. This would later be revisited in the contrast with American Institutionalism, and would eventually rear its head again in the debate over "scientism" as both Mises and Hayek would challenge both positivism and formalism.

(2) The *debate over macroeconomic volatility* with Keynes and Keynesianism, particularly over the use of aggregates in economic theory and the role of government in counter-cyclical policy.

(3) The *socialist calculation debate* directed first at the advocates of comprehensive central planning and later refined in the debate with advocates of market socialism.

What does not get as much attention in these discussions is the evolution of ideas that was spawned in these discussions. Take the socialist calculation debate—the challenge that Mises put forward in his 1920 article, "Economic Calculation in the Socialist Commonwealth," and then his 1922 book, *Socialism*, led to a variety of creative efforts to answer the challenge such as models of market socialism, linear programing and operations research, the New Welfare Economics, and mechanism design theory. On the other hand, these developments to prove the efficacy of socialist economic policy led to refinements of our understanding of the market process, one that addresses the "inefficiencies" of the market (i.e., externalities, monopoly power, underprovision of public goods, etc.) by elaborating on the evolution of entrepreneurial and institutional solutions to ameliorate such inefficiencies. These Austrian-inspired developments included transaction cost economics, property rights economics, public choice economics, and market process economics. Central to this interpretive slant in the narrative on the history of modern economic thought is law and economics.

The popular history of modern economic thought and policy tends to focus on the macroeconomics debate and thus in the post-WWII era Mises and Hayek fade into the background. Milton Friedman emerges as the leading representative of the classic *laissez-faire* position against government activism in economic policy. This is rightfully so, as Friedman both in the professional literature and in the popular imagination was the main defender of limited government in macroeconomic policy. But this narrative directs our attention away from the microeconomic debates that are at the core of economic theory—rational choice theory, market structure, price theory, and of course, the institutional infrastructure within which economic activity takes place.

The development of law and economics is intimately tied to the microeconomic debates in theory and policy, and in particular issues such as antitrust law and regulation. Major earlier figures in law and economics, such as Aaron Director, Henry Manne, Robert Bork, and Richard Posner, all wrote significant papers and books dealing with market theory and the price system, and the role that the institutional infrastructure played in shaping economic activity. This was, we argued in our introduction, a continuation of the research tradition of the Austrian School of Economics. And, we want to continue that discussion here.

We ended our introduction with a discussion of social cleavages and how an "Austrian" approach to law and economics might be well situated to provide guidance due to its long history tracing from Menger to Hayek on the examination of the endogenous formation of rules of just conduct and of the rule of law itself. As Menger (1883 [1985]: 147) argued, the most important questions of social theory were intimately connected to theoretically understanding the origin and change of the institutions that emerged spontaneously to govern human social interaction. Hayek would later pick up this intellectual challenge from Menger and examine the spontaneous order evident in the evolution of language, law, markets, mores, and civilization.

Our historical era has been defined by the collapse of communism, the continued frustration with efforts to orchestrate economic development through foreign aid programs, the mishaps with military-led exercises in nation building, and the reality of ethnic and religious strife in the failed and weak states throughout the globe. The research program in law and economics related to endogenous rule formation takes on, as we argued, a new urgency in a world where, analytically and empirically, we are effectively reasoning "out of anarchy." As students of human societies, we are constantly dealing with imperfect human beings interacting in a complex world with the aid of imperfect institutions and stumbling to find ways to live better together than we ever could in isolation of one another. We need rules that enable us to engage in productive specialization and peaceful cooperation with one another. We need rules that enable us to utilize our differences for mutual gain, rather than allow our differences to divide us. We as analysts cannot assume that conflicts will be resolved, and then proceed from there. Instead, we must examine how rules and their enforcement emerge that enable us to reach conflict resolution, and allow us to live with one another as neighbors rather than as enemies.

But the age-old puzzle and paradox of governance has been with us since Plato's Republic and the problem of guarding the guardians. The great economic historian, Douglass North, argued that the state was both the greatest source of economic development by clearly defining and enforcing property rights, and the greatest threat to development by predating and exploiting its citizens (North 1981: 20). How are states to be empowered, yet constrained? We may recognize as Adam Smith warned us, that commercial life will collapse to zero unless we are secure in our persons and property, and thus we require a civil magistrate to provide a watchful eye to protect against private predation. But once we create a state strong enough to protect us from private predation, we unfortunately create a public entity far stronger than any private party that can predate on us. Traditionally, social theory has tended to be pessimistic about the self-governing capacity of private individuals, and optimistic about the binding powers of constitutional rules and checks and balances to constrain the public predator. But there may be good reasons from the empirical record to reverse that presumption; we should be more optimistic about self-regulation because it works better than you think and more pessimistic about constitutional exercises at curbing the predatory capabilities of governments. Governments strong enough to establish binding institutions typically are strong enough to break those bonds any time they become inconvenient. When constitutions pinch, they become annoying to those in power, and so those in power tend to find ways around the constitutional constraints. But if constitutions are no longer binding, the constraining function of the constitution is lost. Rulers will not allow their hands to be tied.

As we pointed out, working through these age old puzzles in political theory and legal philosophy have taken on a new urgency in our age as we have seen the rise of illiberal democracies, the breakdown of civil society with failed and weak states, and even cracks in the core of the institutions of Western civilization throughout Europe and the United States over the past quarter century. Those deep social cleavages, and the impression that there are permanent winning political coalitions for the privileged, that

Buchanan and Tullock warned about in *The Calculus of Consent* are there to be seen. But, the social divisions are not exclusively due to ethnic and religious identities, as the unleashing of the interest group politics and the rent-seeking state witnessed throughout the West has created political coalitions that Milton Friedman once dubbed the "iron triangle" consisting of special-interest voters, vote-seeking politicians, and bureaucracy focused on agency survival (Friedman 1983).

Buchanan in his writings in public finance and public economics talked about wrestling with the "fiscal commons" and how treating the budget as a commons throughout the Western world has in fact weakened, if not destroyed, many of the democratic traditions that were in operation for a century or more that enabled the system to work. Our purpose is not to paint a dark picture of the future, but instead to simply raise the issue of what urgent topics are on the horizon for law and economics scholars that could draw inspiration from the Austrian school of economics. The public policy issues that must be addressed are not simply questions about the scale of government, but also must address the scope of government and the appropriate institutional infrastructure that will promote productive specialization and peaceful social cooperation.

Methodologically and analytically, this is best tackled by pursuing "invisible hand" theorizing. As has been argued, this style of reasoning is the hallmark of "mainline economics" from Adam Smith to Vernon Smith, and it consists of deriving the "invisible hand theorem" from the "rational choice postulate" via *institutional analysis*. Many critics of economic reasoning have misunderstood this "mainline economics" theorizing, and believe that the substantive propositions of economic theory rely on unrealistic and heroic assumptions concerning the behavioral capacities of individuals and a frictionless environment. But one would have to search in vain for such assumptions in Adam Smith, let alone F.A. Hayek, who instead were explicit in their rejection of hyper-rationality, full information, and perfectly competitive environments. Instead, their work would be better described as rational choice as if the choosers were human, and institutional analysis as if history matters.

Consistent with the themes we have stressed and the analytical tools of "invisible hand" style of reasoning, we can state the following as three questions that demand our attention in the field of law and economics:

(1) Why do most societies continue to use government to create law, rather than rely on the "market" for law?
(2) How do norms—perverse as well as benevolent—emerge in societies of rational actors, and how effective are the enforcement mechanisms that co-develop with the norms?

(3) How do norms that have evolved spontaneously ever change in a society of rational actors?

One of the real intellectual conundrums of the modern world is that if we recognize the role of spontaneously grown institutions, we must admit that actors within the society do not necessarily have to understand the function and purpose of those institutions to benefit from their operation. But, citizens may indeed have to understand and appreciate these spontaneously grown institutions in order for these institutions to be sustained and respected in our modern democratic societies.

The task of the scholar of law and economics is first and foremost a teaching and research one. We are to cultivate in our students an appreciation of spontaneous order so that they can be informed participants in the democratic process of collective decision making. But law and economics scholars are also citizens of the societies within which they live, and in that capacity, they can, based on the knowledge they have gained in their critical studies, engage in the reform effort of our institutions of law, and constitutional governance. In "Positive Economics, Welfare Economics, and Political Economy" (1959), Buchanan presents a solution to the balancing act between the necessity of positive analysis and desire for normative reform. In essence, positive political economy is comparative institutional analysis. The positive role that the economist can play in policy formation is one of "diagnosing social situations and presenting to the choosing individuals a set of possible changes" (1959: 127). The scope for those changes must be limited to "those social changes that may legitimately be classified as 'changes in law,' that is, changes in the structural rules under which individuals make choices" (1959: 131). The law and economics scholar cannot assume they are proffering advice as if to a benevolent despot, nor can they presume that they are in any privileged position over their fellow citizens. All they are legitimately permitted to do is to offer the proposed changes in the structural rules as hypothesis to be tested in the process of democratic deliberations over collective action.

This humility in the face of evolved rules applies with particular force to the evolved system of the common law and the efforts of many reformers to radically reform the common law along constructivist lines, including by many law and economics scholars. The assumption that the entirety of the effects of legal rules can be toted up in a cost-benefit analysis by the judge ignores the manner in which particular legal rules are embedded in a larger network of complementary rules and the various sets of implicit assumptions and institutions that have grown up around those particular rules. As a result, it is exceedingly difficult for a judge to understand the full ripple effects of changing one rule on the overall system of legal rules and other institutions (Zywicki and Sanders 2008).

It is our hope that this volume first provides an example of the breadth and depth of what the Austrian school approach to law and economics has to offer. We also hope that our volume can inspire a new generation of law and economics scholars to pick up the intellectual challenge and push the argument much further. And finally, we hope that some will see how, on the basis of positive science, law and economics can be an input into a more comprehensive and coherent re-examination of the legal, political, and social philosophical issues that confronts a society of free and responsible individuals, who want to live in caring communities and have the opportunity to prosper in a thriving market economy. Productive specialization and peaceful cooperation result when the institutional framework governing any society aligns incentives, mobilizes dispersed knowledge, and rewards those who discover and pursue the mutual gains from exchange and from innovation.

REFERENCES

Buchanan, James. 1959. "Positive Economics, Welfare Economics, and Political Economy," 2 *Journal of Law and Economics*, 124–38.
Buchanan, James and Gordon Tullock, 1962. *The Calculus of Consent, Vol. 3*. Ann Arbor, MI: University of Michigan Press.
Friedman, Milton, and Rose Friedman. 1983. *Tyranny of the Status Quo*. New York, NY: Harcourt Brace Javanovich.
Menger, Carl. 1883 [1985]. *Investigations into the Method of the Social Sciences*. New York, NY: New York University Press.
Mises, Ludwig von. 1920 [1990]. *Economic Calculation in the Socialist Commonwealth*. Translated by S. Alder. Auburn, AL: Ludwig von Mises Institute.
Mises, Ludwig von. 1922 [1981]. *Socialism: An Economic and Sociological Analysis*. Translated by J. Kahane. Auburn, AL: Ludwig von Mises Institute.
North, Douglass C. 1981. *Structure and Change in Economic History*. New York, NY: W.W. Norton & Company.
Zywicki, Todd J. and Anthony B. Sanders. 2008. "Posner, Hayek, and the Economic Analysis of Law," 93(2) *Iowa Law Review*, 559–603.

Index